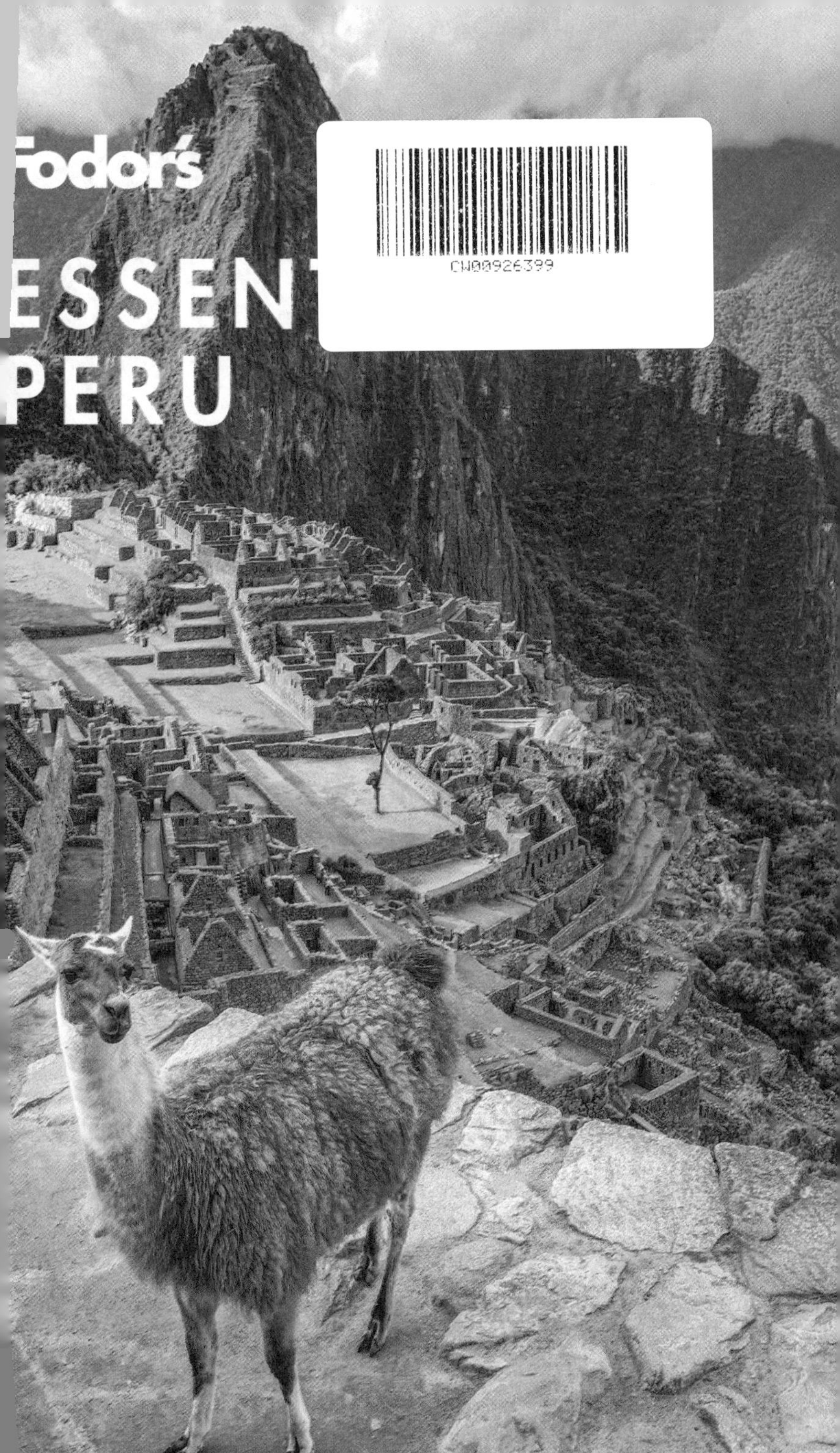
Fodor's
ESSENT
PERU
CW00926399

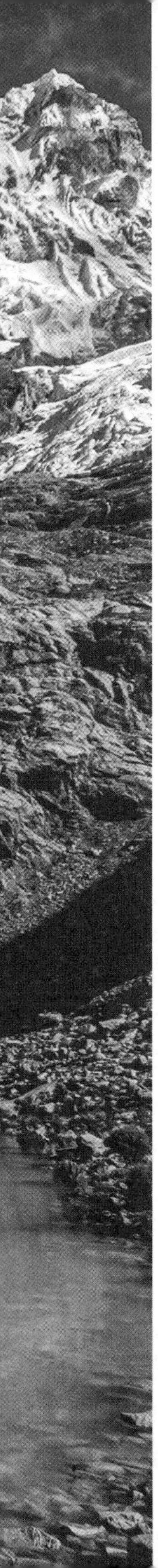

Welcome to Peru

Little did we realize that the emergence of a novel coronavirus in early 2020 would abruptly bring almost all travel to a halt. Although our Fodor's writers around the world have continued working to bring you the best of the destinations they cover, we still anticipate that more than the usual number of businesses will close permanently in the coming months, perhaps with little advance notice. We don't expect things to return to "normal" for some time. As you plan your upcoming travels to Peru, please confirm that places are still open and let us know when we need to make updates by writing to us at editors@fodors.com.

TOP REASONS TO GO

★ **Machu Picchu:** The famous Inca city is simply awe-inspiring—it lives up to the hype.

★ **Local Culture:** Festivals, open-air markets, and homestays reveal the real Peru.

★ **Inca Trails:** Ancient paths blazed by the Inca entice with ruins and fantastic views.

★ **Food:** In Lima and beyond, buzz-worthy chefs innovate with spectacular produce.

★ **Shopping:** Colorful hand-woven textiles, baby alpaca sweaters, and ceramics.

★ **Museums:** Past civilizations come alive through displays of gold, mummies, and more.

Contents

Fodor's Features

MAPS

Chapter 1

EXPERIENCE PERU

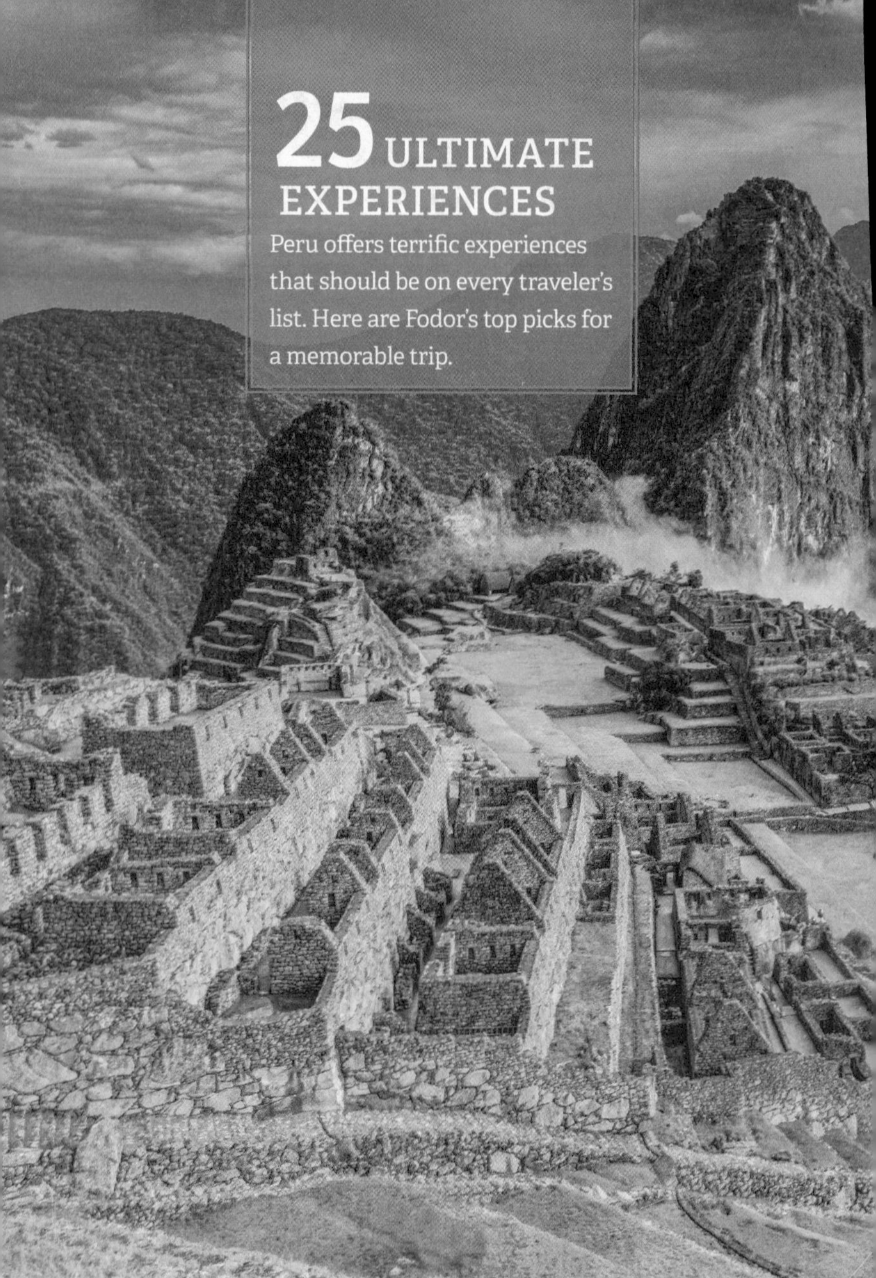

25 ULTIMATE EXPERIENCES
Peru offers terrific experiences that should be on every traveler's list. Here are Fodor's top picks for a memorable trip.

1 Machu Picchu

However many Instagram snapshots you've seen, they can't hold a candle to the mystical stonework and sublime geometry of the the Incas' most iconic ruin. (Ch.7)

2 Lake Titicaca

Take a day trip to the floating reed islands or plan a homestay with a family at this Andean lake, the birthplace of the sun god Inti. (Ch.5)

3 Cordillera Blanca

Towering over the town of Huaraz, this range draws trekkers with Peru's loftiest peaks, as well as pristine glacier lakes and highland valleys. (Ch.10)

4 Arequipa and Colca Canyon

Peru's fabled "white city" has convents and cathedrals made of pale volcanic stone, while nearby Colca Canyon is twice as deep as Arizona's big hole and has Andean condors to boot. (Ch.5)

5 Cebiche

Peru's national dish—raw fish "cooked" in lime juice with peppers and onions—has seemingly infinite permutations. Sample it at every opportunity in Lima's *cebicherías* and throughout Peru.

6 Train to Huancayo

This 14-hour trip from Lima to the central sierra will leave you breathless, as much from the heart-stopping Andean scenery and vertiginous bridges as from the altitude. (Ch.9)

7 Nazca Lines

These staggering geoglyphs on the coast south of Lima have baffled scientists for a century. Form your own theories as you soar over them in a private flight. (Ch.4)

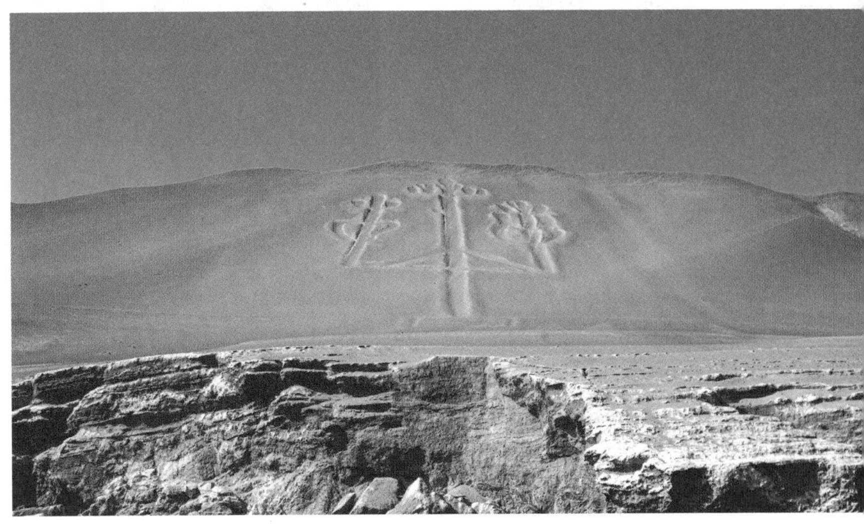

8 Cusco

This former Inca capital is one of South America's most magical places. Here, solar temples and Inca fortresses meld with Spanish cathedrals. (Ch.6)

9 Ollantaytambo

With its cobbled streets and rustic stone buildings, this living Inca village, continuously inhabited since the 13th century, looks substantially as it did in the 1400s. (Ch.6)

10 Tambopata National Reserve

Tambopata is one of Peru's remotest destinations, with jaguars, capybaras, marsh deer, and spider monkeys skittering through the brush. Local jungle lodges make for an ideal base camp. (Ch.8)

11 Máncora

Hang ten riding some of the best waves on the planet, then hang out poolside at a resort in this quintessential Peruvian beach town. (Ch.10)

12 Kuélap

This imposing citadel built by the warriors of Chachapoyas back in the 6th century AD is known as Machu Picchu 2.0. (Ch. 10)

13 Amazon River Cruise

No rusted-out tramp steamers here: Amazon riverboats are posh affairs, with chic cabins and multiple decks to allow you the best views of the jungle's wildlife. (Ch. 8)

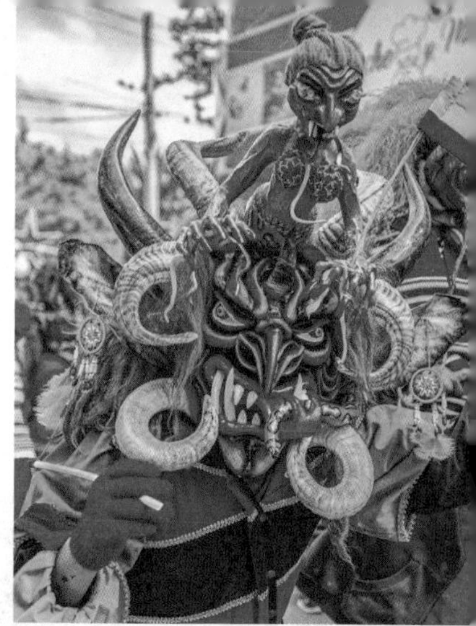

14 Traditional Festivals

From Cusco's Inca solar festival of Inti Raymi to Ayacucho's celebrations for Holy Week and Puno's Festival de la Virgen de la Candelaria, Peru's fiestas are some of the most joyous on the planet.

15 Lima's Museums

From ancient funerary bundles to erotic pre-Columbian pottery to contemporary fashion photography, Lima's must-see museums explore Peru's rich and complex history. (Ch. 3)

16 Pisco Tasting at Ica's Bodegas

Bodegas are traditional Peruvian wineries, and Ica, on Peru's south coast, is the place to visit them. (Ch. 4)

17 Caral

The oldest center of civilization in the Americas, this exceptionally well-preserved prehistoric site is impressive in terms of its design, complexity, and what it tells us about ourselves. (Ch. 3)

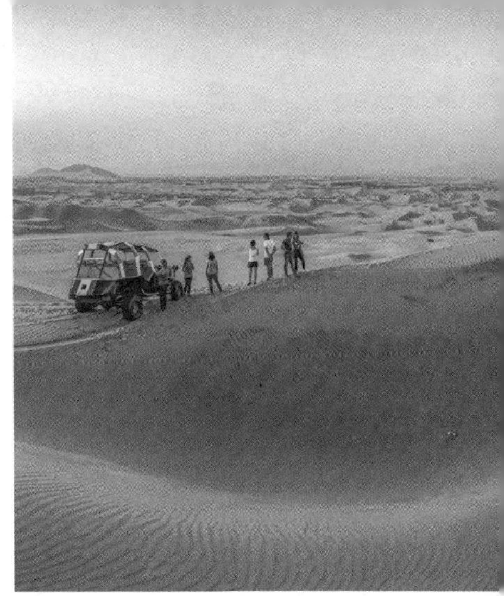

18 Huacachina

Dune buggies, sand boarding, and desert trekking will have you living out your wildest playground-sandbox fantasies in South America's only natural oasis. (Ch. 4)

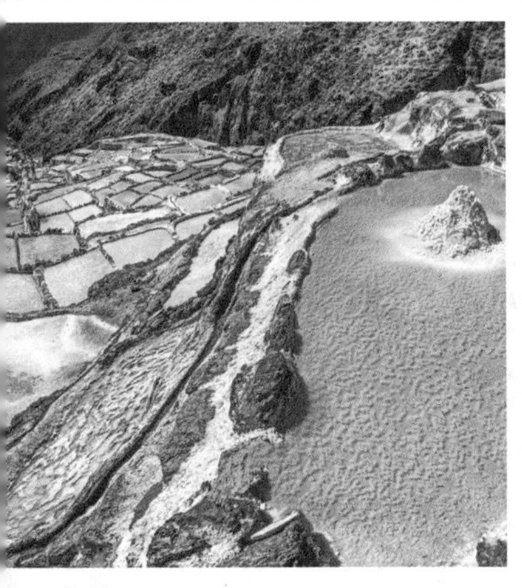

19 Salt Flats

The Maras salt flats offer incredible photo ops, an ancient engineering method to trap salt, and the country's finest salt. (Ch. 6)

20 Chan Chan

Peru's other lost city, Chan Chan is an immense maze of honeycombed walls and wavelike parapets on Peru's desert coast. (Ch. 10)

21 Lima's Top Restaurants

With two spots in the "World's Ten Best Restaurants" list, and 10 more in its "50 Best in Latin America," Peru's capital is a foodie mecca, drawing millions of hungry pilgrims to its exquisite eateries. (Ch. 3)

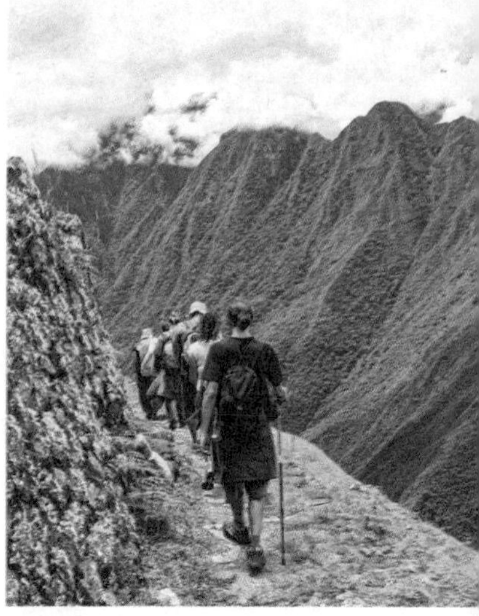

22 The Inca Trail

One of the most famous hikes on the planet, this four-day trek to Machu Picchu's Sun Gate is an unforgettable voyage through mountain defiles and Inca ruins. (Ch. 7)

23 Laguna 69

This electric-turquoise lake is one of the brightest jewels in the central Andes. The hike to it is one of Peru's most scenic, if you can handle the altitude. (Ch. 10)

24 Seven-Colored Mountain

Chasing rainbows definitely pays off at this kaleidoscopic crag east of Cusco, where the brilliant pinks, greens, and rusts emanate from the mineral-rich alluvial soil. (Ch. 6)

25 Islas Ballestas

Sea lions and Humboldt penguins, pelicans, and Peruvian boobies form the welcome committee at these guano-covered islands on Peru's south coast. (Ch.4)

WHAT'S WHERE

1 Lima. In Peru's cultural and political center, experience some of the best dining in the Americas, vibrant nightlife, and great museums and churches.

2 Nazca and the Southern Coast. The coastal stretch from Lima down to Chile looks to be nothing but lunar desert sands—but hidden among the dunes are Ica's wineries and the sand-boarding oasis of Huacachina. Wildlife-spotters will thrill to the sea lions and penguins at Paracas, while farther south, the Nazca Lines are like a question mark in the desert.

3 The Southern Andes and Lake Titicaca. Colca and Cotahuasi are the world's two deepest canyons. Peru's "second city," Arequipa, may also be its most attractive. Lake Titicaca is the world's highest navigable lake and home to the floating Uros Islands.

4 Cusco and the Sacred Valley. From sun temples to colonial convents, every stone here is magical. Outside the city, you can haggle for handicrafts at the Pisac market or stand in the shadow of colossal Inca forts at Sacsayhuaman and Ollantaytambo.

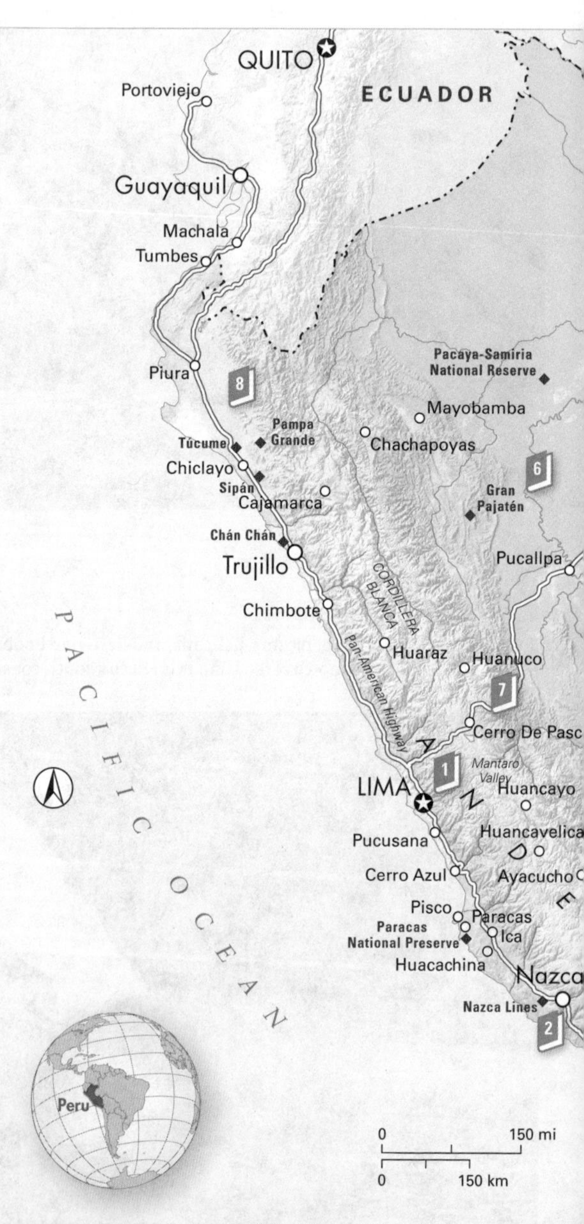

5 Machu Picchu and the Inca Trail. The great Machu Picchu, crowded or not crowded, misty rains or clear skies, never ceases to enthrall, and the Inca Trail is still the great hiking pilgrimage.

6 The Amazon Basin. Peru's vast tract of the Amazon may contain the world's greatest biodiversity. Fly into Iquitos or Puerto Maldonado for the wildlife preserves, jungle lodges, rain-forest hikes, and boat excursions.

7 The Central Highlands. Stretching from Huánuco south to Ayacucho, the central sierra contains some of Peru's most rugged—and sublime—landscapes. At Huancayo, the world's second-highest railroad passes through iron-red hills and blue mountain tarns. At Ayacucho, the Semana Santa festivities are some of the most raucous in all South America.

8 The North Coast and Northern Highlands. Go up the coast for beach life and inland to the Cordillera Blanca for some of the world's highest mountains. Many of Peru's greatest archaeological discoveries were made in the north.

Peru Today

POLITICS

Peru's politics tend to be fractious in the best of times, but for the past few years, the country has been roiled by a political uproar that's notable even by Peruvian standards. Corruption, parliamentary gridlock, an ex-president's suicide: since 2017, a chain reaction of scandals has plunged the government into ever-deepening turmoil. Whether that turmoil will end by allowing Peruvians to clean house and regain a modicum of faith in the political system remains to be seen.

The spark that lit the fuse came in 2016, when Pedro Pablo Kuczynski, an Oxford-trained economist and former minister of finance during the administration of Alejandro Toledo (2001–06), won the country's presidency by a scant 40,000 votes. Kuczynski faced an uphill battle from the get-go. Not only had his electoral opponent, Keiko Fujimori—daughter of disgraced former president Alberto Fujimori (1990–2000) and leader of the center-right Popular Force party—won a sizeable majority in Peru's Congress, but scarcely a year after the election, allegations surfaced that "PPK," as he was called, had had illicit dealings with the notorious Odebrecht construction firm while serving under Toledo. Odebrecht was, then as now, at the center of the so-called "Car Wash" scandal—a vast scheme of payoffs and system-rigging that began in Brazil and quickly engulfed leaders in at least 10 other Latin American countries. So when leaked company documents indicated the firm had paid Kuczynski for "consulting" work during the construction of the Interoceanic Highway between Peru and Brazil, Peruvians waited with bated breath to see what would happen.

Kuczynski was forced to resign in 2018 and arrested a year later. By July 2019, the scandal had swept up every Peruvian president in office since 2000. Alejandro Toledo, Kuczynski's former boss, fled to the United States, where he was arrested pending extradition in 2019, while Ollanta and Nadine Humala, the previous presidential couple (2011–16), face 20 years in prison. Most dramatically, ex-president Alan García (2006–11), whose appetite for kickbacks was famously Rabelaisian, shot himself to death rather than be detained by police on April 17, 2019.

After months of putting up obstructionist roadblocks to PPK's government, Keiko Fujimori, too, was arrested in October 2018, for accepting illegal campaign monies from Odebrecht. Meanwhile, a parallel scandal, that of the "Portside White Collars," disclosed connections between powerful Peruvian judges and drug traffickers in Lima's port of El Callao, prompting the shuttering of Peru's entire Board of Magistrates. President Martín Vizcarra governed on a platform of anti-corruption from 2018 until late 2020, when Peru's Congress abruptly ousted and replaced him. Violent protests erupted across Peru, resulting in the resignation of the interim president– Peru's third president in less than five years. All the while, the country grappled with a severe economic recession brought on by the coronavirus pandemic.

ARCHAEOLOGY

In Peru, millennial ruins are very much the trending topic. In late 2020, the figure of a huge 2,000-year-old cat carved into a hillside was discovered, thanks to drones and satellite imaging. In 2018, more than 50 new geoglyphs depicting human figures were discovered just northwest of Nazca City. Inca scholars, meanwhile, have been intrigued by two 2019 findings: Mata Indio, in the northern province of Lambayeque, is the site of a royal tomb containing idols and spondylus shells (highly prized by Inca culture), while some 1,100 km (700 miles) to the southwest, the settlement of Wat'a near Cusco towers 1,500 meters (5,000 feet) over Machu Picchu and may have been a kind of prototype for the famous citadel. The most striking discovery, though, comes from one of Peru's archaeological rock stars: in October 2019, Walter Alva, chief investigator at the tomb of El Señor de Sipán back in 1987, stumbled on a vast megalithic temple in his old stomping grounds near Chiclayo. Inside the sanctuary's 21 vaults, pre-Hispanic peoples appear to have performed fertility and water rituals that date back 3,000 years.

SPORTS

As is the case in most of South America, *fútbol* (i.e., soccer) evokes a quasi-religious fervor among Peruvians. This fanaticism reached fever pitch in 2018, when the perennial-underdog national team finally made it to the World Cup, sparking raucous street partying throughout the country before the club fell to France and Denmark in the final rounds. Losses aside, Peru's qualification gave hope to the team's ultra-loyal *hinchada* (fans), whose fierce nationalism is now invested in their team qualifying for FIFA World Cup 2022.

LITERATURE

The great colossus of Peruvian letters continues to be Mario Vargas Llosa, who was awarded the Nobel Prize for Literature in 2010 and is the last remaining figure of the so-called Boom that revolutionized the Latin American novel in the 1960s and '70s. Vargas Llosa still churns out fiction and criticism at an astonishing rate; many feel his latest novel, *Tiempos Recios* (*Fierce Times*), is his best in years. Meanwhile, other, younger voices have sought to narrate the realities of contemporary Peru. Standouts here include Santiago Roncagliolo (*Red April*), Alonso Cueto (*The Blue Hour*), Jeremías Gamboa (*Tell It All*), and Daniel Alarcón (*Lost City Radio*). The latter, especially, is accessible for non-Spanish speakers; his bilingual *Radio Ambulante* podcast for NPR is well worth checking out.

WOMEN

Before there was #MeToo, there was #NiUnaMenos. Born in Argentina in 2015, when a pregnant 14-year-old was found murdered by her boyfriend, the movement to combat violence against women (its name means "Not One More Lost") caught fire in Peru a year later, after a security-camera video showed a 25-year-old lawyer, Arlette Contreras, being viciously beaten and dragged by her ex through the lobby of an Ayacucho hotel. The incident set off the largest protest march in Peru's history: 500,000 people gathered in downtown Lima on August 13, 2016, to decry Peru's poisonous history of *machista* violence. Contreras went on to advocate for women's issues, being selected as one of *Time*'s 100 Most Influential People in 2017.

Women are increasingly taking the wheel in other areas of Peruvian life. In 2019, they made up 57 percent of university graduates, as well as 44 percent of Peru's work force. Their independence has fostered considerable entrepreneurship, too: 53 percent of the country's small and midsized businesses are now female-owned. To be sure, much remains to be done, and machismo continues to disfigure both work and family life. But if current trends are any indicator, Peru's women are more than up to the task.

Peru's Top Restaurants

MAIDO

Here, chef Mitsuharu Tsumura offers an exquisite introduction to Nikkei, the Japanese-Peruvian fusion cuisine, with dishes that run from sushi and sashimi to tiny pork-belly *chicharron* sandwiches.

ÁMAZ

In his eagerness to expose his guests to jungle foods they'd never heard of, chef Pedro Miguel Schiaffino forged ties with several Amazon tribes to source ingredients. The results are mouthwatering: paiche fish steamed with plantain in *bijao* leaves, shrimp cebiche with *cocona* (a jungle fruit) cooked in bamboo.

ASTRID Y GASTÓN

Challengers have tried to steal the crown from Gastón Acurio's trailblazing bistro novoandino, but none can equal its blend of innovation and flavor. À la carte selections include Peking *cuy* (guinea pig) and kid-goat risotto, or you can splurge on a 29-course, fixed-price tour of five different regions of Peru.

MALABAR

Upon entering, the understated décor and cozy bar make you feel you're in a private supper club—a sense heightened by chef Pedro Miguel Schiaffino's refined, unshowy virtuosity. Brazil-nut cheese, Andean potatoes in edible clay, cuy with yellow chile: here exotic ingredients fuse, like musical notes, to form delicate new harmonies. Added plus: the cocktails are the lightest and freshest in Lima.

MIL

Chef Virgilio Martínez's latest culinary concept is a total-immersion experience that includes a worshop at the Inca site of Moray, near Cusco, and culminates with an eight-course tasting menu.

HUANCAHUASI

From its beginnings in provincial Huancayo, this colorful eatery has gone on to open several wildly popular branches in Lima. No fusion food here: just authentic andino cuisine the way grandma would make it—if she were a master chef. Try the alpaca *saltado* (stir-fried.)

PICANTERÍA LA NUEVA PALOMINO

Picanterías are rustic dining halls from southern Peru, where farmworkers would sit in open-air sheds, devouring hearty local fare. To replicate the experience, this countrified joint in Arequipa's Yanahuara district features waitstaff in traditional costumes serving up exquisite local delicacies.

CENTRAL
This is the place that made Virgilio Martínez's reputation. And what a place it is: Amazon wood, open kitchen, garden labs, gray-stone tables. The new artsy Barranco locale lets Martínez and his wife, Pía León, experiment even more daringly with their eight- and 17-course tasting menus.

LA MAR CEBICHERÍA PERUANA
La Mar is Gastón Acurio's shrine to cebiche, the Peruvian national dish of raw fish "cooked" in lime juice and hot pepper. With an all-seafood menu that runs from soups to stews, pastas to maki rolls, it's an operation that takes full advantage of the owner's network of local fishermen to ensure quality and freshness.

CHEZ WONG
Javier Wong's renowned cebichería isn't chic: it's run out of his living room in a down-at-the heels Lima barrio. Neither is it wide-ranging: the menu consists of cebiche, simply prepared, plus a few other seafood dishes. It's just a culinary magician doing his thing.

RESTAURANT ROMANO RINCÓN CRIOLLO
In this lively Trujillo institution, the masses vote with their feet every day at lunchtime, when tables are mobbed with crowds ravenous for some of the best *comida norteña* (northern cooking) in the country. Cebiches, seafood, pastas, stewed goat and duck, *causas* (stuffed mashed potatoes): the 30-page menu staggers with its sheer variety.

TITI
In Lima, no one does *chifa*—Peru's version of Chinese food—better than Titi, whose unassuming digs on the ground floor of a San Isidro apartment building belie its culinary splendor. Order the lobster in house sauce.

What to Eat and Drink

PACHAMANCHA
Pacha means earth and *mancha* means oven in Quechua, and this quite literally describes the cooking method of this special-occasion meal of meat and vegetables cooked on hot stones and buried in the earth and best enjoyed in Peru's Sacred Valley.

CHICHA
Wondering why so many storefronts in Peru beckon visitors with red plastic bags tied to sticks? That's a sign that the establishment within serves *chicha*, Peru's version of beer, made from macerated and fermented corn. Chicha *morada* is the equally popular nonalcoholic version.

ALPACA
Alpaca is often served skewered or as a jerky; in fact, the word "jerky" comes from a Quechua word for an ancient Andean method of preserving alpaca meat.

LOMO SALTADO
This stir fry with chifa origins typically combines marinated strips of beef sirloin with soy sauce, a kick of ají chili, slices of juicy tomatoes, and French fries.

PISCO SOUR
The Gran Hotel Bolivar in Lima is *the* place to try Peru's favorite cocktail. The combination of pisco (a light but powerful grape-based brandy), lime juice, simple syrup, Angostura bitters, and fresh egg white makes the drink look like a cloud floating over tropical waters.

CUY
It is easy to visit Peru and eat well without trying guinea pig, but you should know that you will be missing out on a huge part of Peru's cultural heritage. Order cuy *al horno* for a full specimen atop a mass of noodles and potatoes or cuy confit at one of Lima's top restaurants.

CEBICHE
Perhaps the greatest gastronomic gift Peru has given the world is cebiche (ceviche): fish or shellfish cured in citric acid rather than cooked with heat. The traditional Peruvian presentation surrounds the seafood with *cancha* (large kernels of corn) and bite-sized, deep-fried nuggets of shrimp and other fish.

POTATOES
By some counts, a jaw-dropping 2,300 varieties of potatoes are still grown in Peru, and the local cuisine takes full advantage. The classic preparation, *papa* a la Huancaina, smothers boiled yellow potatoes in a creamy yellow chili pepper sauce. Also popular are causas, small rolls or mounds of mashed potato with a variety of toppings.

CHIFA CUISINE
The cooking of homesick Chinese immigrants has been embraced by diners in countries all over the world, but the gastronomic love affair between Peru and China is hot (thanks to the Peruvian *chile aji amarillo*) and heavy, to the point where dishes like *chaufa* (fried rice) are must-eats for the traveler aiming to explore the real Peru through food.

FRUIT SMOOTHIES
It's easy to find stores and stalls selling made-to-order fruity drinks, with flavors including *maracuya* (passion fruit), *aguaymanto* (goldenberry), carambola (star fruit), lucuma (fruit native to the highlands and coastal valleys), *chirimoya* (a tropical fruit), or pitaya (dragonfruit). Of these, the first three are more tart; lucuma and chirimoya more sweet, mellow, and custardy; and the pitaya is quite mild.

Top Day-Trips from Lima

CANTA AND OBRAJILLO, 105 MILES NORTHEAST OF LIMA

The twin towns of Canta and Obrajillo are a popular Lima escape with waterfalls, hiking trails, and horseback riding across the pristine valley.

PARACAS, 258 MILES SOUTH OF LIMA

The popular seaside town of Paracas, roughly three hours from Lima, is worth a full-day trip. The main attractions here are two nature reserves: the Islas Ballestas, famous for their colonies of sea lions and penguins and much more populous than Lima's Palomino Islands, and the Paracas Natural Reserve, with a coastal desert setting that offers breathtaking lookouts over the Pacific Ocean.

PALOMINO ISLANDS, 5 MILES WEST OF LIMA'S CITY CENTER

Lying right off the coast of Lima's main port of Callao, the Palomino Islands are home to herds of sea lions and various bird species, including the Humboldt penguin. The boat ride passes over a stretch of sea that's littered with shipwrecks, as this was once a passage for fearsome pirates and seafaring adventurers.

CARAL, 120 MILES NORTH OF LIMA

It's a little work to get here, but the ruins of Caral, a UNESCO World Heritage Site, are unmissable. Believed to be the most ancient city in the Americas, Caral was inhabited between the 26th and 20th centuries BCE. Scattered in the midst of the sandy desert backdrop of the Supe Valley, Caral Main Temple is 150 meters (492 feet) long and a sight to behold.

HUANCAYA, 206 MILES EAST OF LIMA

Not to be confused with Huancayo, the Huancaya Valley has turquoise lagoons, waterfalls, and shimmering natural pools—all part of the protected Nor Yauyos Cochas Landscape Reserve. Come for the stunning views and fishing.

LUNAHUANA, 115 MILES SOUTH OF LIMA

Plan to get here early in the morning, to allow plenty of time to try your hands at the local white-water rafting on the Cañete River. Once you are done with the rapids, the local bars are the perfect places to sample the region's piscos and wines, all produced in the surrounding hills.

PACHACAMAC, 25 MILES SOUTH OF LIMA

If ruins are your thing, don't forget to visit Pachacamac to enjoy three impressive pyramid-shaped temples set in the desert and facing the sea. The site has several areas, so taking a full day to explore with an English-speaking guide is highly recommended.

Chosica

CHOSICA, 12 MILES EAST OF LIMA

Don't just use this suburban town as a transport hub to hop on a bus to the Andes—make it a day (or half-day) trip from Lima's downtown. The draw is its permanent carnival plaza, filled with street vendors peddling their Peruvian foods and desserts, a fun spot if traveling with children in tow.

CHURIN, 126 MILES NORTHEAST OF LIMA

A sweet, lesser-known mountain getaway where visitors can soak in La Meseta, relaxing thermal baths set on the flanks of a forested mountain. The town also holds two interesting annual festivals, the Maca, which celebrates an aphrodisiac food, and another revolving around the cuy, the local guinea pig.

What to Buy

EKEKOS
Down on your luck? These little mustachioed dudes are just the ticket. Made from clay or ceramic and clad in chullos and ponchos, ekekos are good-luck amulets, tiny statues modeled after the Tiwanaku god of prosperity from Lake Titicaca.

ALPACA CLOTHING
Have you even been to Peru if you didn't buy something alpaca? Doubtful, given that the markets of cities like Cusco are piled high with everything from ponchos to pullovers, capes to cardigans, made from this Andean camelid's wool. Traditional weavers still ply their trade on backstrap looms, but *ojo*: genuine baby alpaca isn't cheap. Avoid the knockoffs by heading to trusted Cusco vendors like Lamaland in San Blas or by buying direct from the artisans in the village of Chinchero.

RETABLOS
In colonial times, they were folding altarpieces, toted around by itinerant friars to evangelize indigenous people in the sierra. Today, retablos are folk-art masterworks, portable dioramas depicting scenes from daily life in Peru's provinces, and a hallmark of Ayacucho in particular. Head to Quinua to see the maestros whittling away in their workshops, or take classes yourself at the Casa del Retablo in Huamanga. Fun fact: Many retablos portray the Yawar Fiesta, a bull-versus-condor ritual typical of the Andes.

PISCO
Peruvians are fanatics when it comes to their national firewater; after a dozen or so frothy-but-potent pisco sours in Lima's bars, you might be, too. Head straight to the source in Ica, where the bodegas' staff will regale you with house-made piscos from any number of varietals. Also, check out the Museos del Pisco in Lima or Cusco—or just visit an upscale supermarket like Wong or Vivanda.

CHULLOS
Ears aching from the Andean cold? This traditional headgear from the sierra will have you toasty in no time. A smash-up of Spanish and native sartorial traditions, the chullo was for centuries a garment of Peru's lower classes. Today, its colorful knits and distinctive earflaps grace the heads of everyone from presidents to runway models. Some of the prettiest designs can be found at the Pisac market or at Casa de la Mujer Artesana in Puno.

MATES BURILADOS
Fiestas, pre-Columbian gods, complete village histories: the miniature scenes depicted on these engraved gourds are mind-boggling. To make them, craftsmen etch the fruit's skin with tiny steel chisels (*buriles*) and then finish the whole with black and brown washes. The net effect is not unlike an Andean red-figure Greek vase. If you're in Huancayo, head to the suburbs of Cochas Chico and Cochas

Andean textiles

Grande for the best selection; otherwise, your best bets are Lima standbys like Dedalus in Barranco and the souvenir stalls on Avenida Petit Thouars.

GOLD AND SILVER

Peru's metalworking tradition dates from pre-Columbian times; by 400 AD or so, cultures like the Moche had very little to learn about the elaboration of gold and silver jewelry. That tradition still survives in towns like Catacaos in Piura, where craftsmen spin out tiny horseback figures from silver filigree, or San Pablo near Cusco, where you can find silver earrings studded with spondylus shells. In Lima, top-end Ilaria has stores in Larcomar and San Isidro.

MUSICAL INSTRUMENTS

The streets around Parque Kennedy in Lima's Miraflores district have traditional instruments at fair prices. Aymara Music sells *zampoñas* and *quenas* (Andean pan flutes), while the adjacent shops offer an assortment of guitars and *charangos* (tiny, 10-string Andean ukuleles).

***TORITOS* DE PUCARÁ**

Tradition holds these ceramic bulls have the power to confer everything from sexual potency to inner peace—not necessarily as the same time. Affix a pair of them over the door of your house, and *listo*: instant spiritual harmony. If you're in Puno, you can visit neighboring Pucará village to decorate your own torito in one of the artisan workshops. Or, in Cusco, steel yourself and descend into the mayhem of the Centro Artesanal Cusco on Avenida Tullumayo.

TEXTILES

Andean textile makers routinely draw on cultures such as the Paracas, Nazca, and Huari when spinning out their gorgeous technicolor creations. On Taquile near Puno, the *fajas* and *chumpis* (belts narrating the island's history) can fetch hundreds of dollars in the collectives, while in Ayacucho's Santa Ana neighborhood, weavers produce "3-D" designs, in which the pattern appears to leap off the garment's surface.

TOTORA-REED HANDICRAFTS

If the Uros people can weave whole islands out of totora, imagine what they can do with housewares. From baskets and fruit bowls to flower vases, these reed implements are supremely colorful and giftable. Best of all, they support Puno's indigenous communities. Artesanías Lupaca in the city has a good selection; you can also buy direct in Lake Titicaca.

What to Watch and Read

OPEN VEINS OF LATIN AMERICA BY EDUARDO GALEANO

Written in 1971, this much debated book remains a powerful cultural narrative and social treaty exposing five centuries of European and North American exploitation of South America's resources—including Peru's.

DEATH IN THE ANDES BY MARIO VARGAS LLOSA

One of the best novels by the prolific Peruvian writer is a gripping political thriller that harks back to the 1980s and the history of the Shining Path, Peru's cruel Maoist guerrilla group that ruled the sierra. This page-turner masterfully blends bits of Peru's tragic history, local folklore, and romantic depictions of the country's breathtaking landscapes.

TURN RIGHT AT MACHU PICCHU BY MARK ADAMS

Of all the books on Machu Picchu, Adams's is a popular, light, and yet informative read. Adams, a travel magazine editor who never went too far from his desk, decides to retrace the steps of Hiram Bingham III, Machu Picchu's "discoverer," together with an Australian survivalist and a group of Quechua-speaking porters. The result is a fun book on Peru's biggest attraction.

THE PERU READER: HISTORY, CULTURE, POLITICS BY ORIN STARN

Using a vast array of sources that range from essays, folklore, poetry, short stories, autobiographical material, and songs, this essential volume covers Peru's history from its pre-Columbian civilizations to contemporary struggles to achieve justice. *The Peru Reader* sheds light on how this multicultural nation allowed Andean, Amazonian, Asian, African, and European traditions to meet.

THE CONQUEST OF THE INCAS BY JOHN HEMMING

This is probably the best book ever written in English on the last days of the Inca. Hemming combines meticulous research with his elegant, eloquent writing style, making this book essential reading material for anyone who wants to better understand Peru's early civilization.

TRAIL OF FEATHERS: IN SEARCH OF THE BIRDMEN OF PERU BY TAHIR SHAH

One of the Brit-Afghan travel writer's best travelogues recounts his perilous jaunt through Peru's forests and mountains in search of a hidden truth about the Inca—were they really able to fly like birds? This book is full of insights on the Spanish treatment of the Inca, as well as on Peruvian folklore and magic and shamanic knowledge of plant-based hallucinogens; it also highlights encounters with local oddball characters.

MOTHER OF GOD BY PAUL ROSOLIE

The tale of this young naturalist turned explorer, who ventured deep into the Peruvian Amazon to get to the soul of the Madre de Dios wilderness, is really intoxicating. The author crosses some of the world's wildest terrain, battling life-threatening tropical diseases and his own mind as he struggles to keep sane in nature's ultimate playground.

BOLÍVAR: AMERICAN LIBERATOR BY MARIE ARANA

A brilliant biography of one of South America's most important historical figures, General Bolívar, who freed six countries from colonial rule. Arana's book relies on excellent scholarship but reads like a masterful novel giving due credit to an underappreciated Latin American hero.

THE CITY AND THE DOGS (LA CIUDAD Y LOS PERROS)

Inspired by one of Mario Vargas Llosa's novels, this not-so-stellar film production tells the story of four angry men who have formed an inner circle to fight off boredom while they negotiate the world of military academy. They face a chain of events that starts with theft and leads to murder.

GREGORIO

Directed by Grupo Chaski, this gritty urban tale is an important social drama focused on the life of a young Andean kid who moves with his family from the slow Peruvian sierra to the chaotic and violent streets of Lima. After his father falls ill and dies, adaptation and survival will change the ways the young man sees the world and his own mother.

JULIANA

Another Grupo Chaski gripping social drama, *Juliana* tells the story of a 13-year-old runaway, who fled home to escape her violent stepfather. In order to survive on the street, she'll cut her hair short to look like one of the baby gangsters that her brother has already become. This film won the UNICEF prize at the Berlin Film Festival and the audience's prize at Torino Film Festival in Italy

ALIAS 'LA GRINGA'

Alberto Durant directs the story of a likable criminal who can break out of any prison. When he escapes with the help of an intellectual inmate, La Gringa returns to pay back the favor—and instead finds himself in the midst of a prison riot.

RED INK (TINTA ROJA)

Directed by Francisco J. Lombardi, *Tinta Roja* is the story of Alfonso, a wannabe writer who decides to train his pen as a journalist. When Alfonso is assigned to the crime section of a local newspaper, he will experience firsthand the dirty world of Peruvian tabloids.

DAYS OF SANTIAGO (DIAS DE SANTIAGO)

Josué Méndez's film brings the sad story of retired Peruvian soldier Santiago to the silver screen. Santiago has trouble readjusting to society after having fought for his country, as he deals with post-traumatic stress disorder and family issues.

THE MILK OF SORROW (LA TETA ASUSTADA)

Claudia Llosa's drama tells the story of Fausta, a woman suffering from a rare disease called "Milk of Sorrow"—transmitted by the milk of pregnant women who were abused or raped during or soon after pregnancy. When Fausta's mother dies, she has to take drastic measures to not follow in her footsteps.

THE CLEANER (EL LIMPIADOR)

The award-winning debut of young director Adrián Saba is somewhat immature, but well depicts the relationship between a hardened forensic cleaner and a young, lovely boy, in a strange Lima ravaged by an imaginary pandemic.

ETERNITY (AYMARA: WIÑAYPACHA)

An old couple living in the Andes near Puno struggles for survival while waiting for their son's return from the city, where he went in search of better prospects. Directed by Óscar Catacora, *Eternity* is an important film shot completely in the Aymara language. It was long-listed in 2019 as Best Foreign Language Film at the 91st Academy Awards.

Touring Peru

WHY GO WITH AN OPERATOR?

At a time when it's easy to purchase many entrance tickets, train seats, and hotels rooms from your phone, the question of why you might need a tour operator in Peru is a reasonable one. The reality is, although the tourist infrastructure in Peru is constantly improving, it is still a destination that can be logistically challenging.

There are plenty of good reasons to entrust the details of your Peru travels to a tour company, and convenience and security are high among them. Transportation, on the ground in particular, is best left to the experts who will ensure that you and your belongings get safely to and from each point on your itinerary, as well as straightening things out if something goes wrong or finding last minute alternatives if there are cancellations or mishaps along the route. For many outdoor adventures, such as trekking or a trip into the Amazon rain forest, you will definitely want to be guided. In the case of the Inca Trail, it's required.

It's worth noting that licensed tour guides, such as are encountered in Cusco and Machu Picchu, have university degrees in tourism where they learn not just about Peruvian history, but also about the local flora and fauna. Another plus to having a local guide, especially if you do not speak Spanish and/or are on a quick trip, is he or she may be the only Peruvian you really get to talk to, therefore giving you some of the best insight into the modern-day culture of the country.

WHO'S WHO

Whether you purchase a packaged tour for your entire Peru trip or prefer to book shorter itineraries with local outfitters, the decision of which tour operator or operators to use will likely be the most important one you make for your vacation. We've compiled a short list of some of the best tour companies operating in Peru, from the big international outfitters to the best local companies, to provide a good range of specializations and budget options. Though you may be reluctant to buy a package directly from a Peruvian company, keep in mind that you may get the same tour you would buy from a U.S. company for considerably less money. If you want to stray from the beaten path, you may have no choice but to book directly with a Peruvian company.

TOP COMPANIES

Abercrombie & Kent This luxury travel company—with offices in the United Kingdom, United States, and Australia—organizes trips on seven continents, including Peru itineraries to that emblematic attraction of Machu Picchu, as well as has tours that combine the Wonder of the World with Ecuador's Galapagos Islands. Itineraries typically last anywhere from 8 to 12 days. Tailor-made itineraries are also available.

Popular package: Machu Picchu & the Sacred Valley, 8 days, from $6,295.

What they do best: Provide quality local guides, luxury accommodations, and private visits to spots few travelers get to.

Corporate responsibility: Support an organization in the Sacred Valley that provides meals, medical care, and education for children from poor families. ☎ *800/554–7016 in U.S., 01/421–7625 in Peru* 🌐 *www.abercrombiekent.com.*

Access Culinary Trips If your appetite for travel is matched by an appetite for incredible food, Access Culinary trips offers insider access to Peru's bucket-list-worthy culinary scene. Peek inside the kitchen of a top chifa restaurant before an exclusive dining experience;

sample pisco and cebiche in every variation, from classic to modern; learn to cook *lomo saltado* in a restaurant kitchen in Cusco; visit local markets and quinoa farms; and enjoy a traditional Pachamanca feast cooked in a ground oven of hot stones with a family in the Andes. And, when you are not eating, you are visiting the top sights and attractions of Peru with wonderful, knowledgeable guides.

Popular package: Lima, Cusco & Macha Picchu, 9 days, from $4,190.

What they do best: Immersive culinary travel; small groups experience authentic local food and connect with local chefs, makers, and producers.

Corporate responsibility: All trips are designed to be environmentally, socially, and culturally responsible. With no more than 12 guests on its culinary trips, the company is uniquely positioned to support small, locally owned businesses and eco-friendly lodging.

Aracari Travel Based in the capital city of Lima, Aracari is a Peruvian-owned travel agency that has been providing luxury travel tours for more than 20 years. It specializes in creating high-end responsible travel experiences that connect you with local cultures through firsthand expertise.

Popular package: Classic Luxury Trip Peru, 8 days, from $4,860.

Customized trips: Yes.

What they do best: Personalized travel itineraries based on local connections to offer unique experiences that are sustainable.

Corporate responsibility: In addition to supporting community projects with its tours, the company partners with La Otra Ruta, a group of videographers that works to showcase worthwhile nonprofit projects throughout Peru. ☎ *718/395–2406 in U.S., 1/651–2424 in Peru* ⊕ *www.aracari.com.*

Field Guides The international bird-watching specialist Field Guides runs half a dozen tours to different regions of Peru led by expert birding guides, who help their clients spot as many of the country's more than 1,800 bird species as possible.

Popular package: Machu Picchu and Abra Malaga, 10 days, starting at $4,550; travels from the highlands to the cloud forest of the Amazon Basin.

Customized trips: No.

What they do best: Getting bird-watchers to areas where they can see the greatest variety of species possible.

Corporate responsibility: The company makes regular contributions to conservation organizations. ☎ *800/728–4953 in U.S.* ⊕ *www.fieldguides.com.*

InkaNatura Travel One of the country's oldest ecotourism companies, InkaNatura Travel offers trips to its own nature lodges deep in the wilderness of the Manu Biosphere Reserve and Tambopata National Reserve in the Amazon Basin. These can be combined with visits to Cusco and Machu Picchu, and the company also has a selection of itineraries to the archaeological sites of northern Peru. They cater to bird-watchers, nature lovers, archaeology buffs, and travelers who want to experience a bit of everything.

Popular package: Sandoval Lake Lodge and Macaw Clay Lick, 6 days, from $1,493; this excellent tour offers the most affordable access to Amazon wildlife at an oxbow lake, macaw clay lick, and in the rainforest with overnights in the Sandoval Lake and Heath River Lodges.

Customized trips: Yes.

What they do best: Help travelers experience Peru's diversity of flora and fauna.

Corporate responsibility: Company practices sustainable tourism and donates a portion of profits to Peru Verde, a small environmental organization. ☎ *971/427–346 in Peru* 🌐 *www.inkanatura.com.*

Inkaterra This Peruvian company arranges customized luxury trips that combine access to the rainforest of Madre de Dios with the classic Cusco–Sacred Valley–Machu Picchu route with overnights at Inkaterra hotels, which are among the country's best.

Popular package: Inkaterra's most popular package runs seven days and starts at $3,850; combines the Amazon rainforest, Cusco, and Machu Picchu, with nights at Inkaterra properties.

Customized trips: Yes.

What they do best: Provide high-quality service and accommodations and exposure to some of the country's greatest attractions.

Corporate responsibility: The company conserves 42,000 acres of rainforest in Madre de Dios, supports scientific research, and has adopted sustainable tourism. Its tours are carbon neutral. ☎ *800/442–5042 in U.S. and Canada, 01/610–0400 in Peru* 🌐 *www.inkaterra.com.*

Kensington Tours One of the world's top-rated tour operators, Kensington Tours offers a dozen Peru itineraries with small groups and overnights in some of the country's best hotels. The company specializes in custom tours based on itineraries that range from a five-day Cusco and Machu Picchu trip to a two-week expedition that combines those highland treasures with a cruise on the Amazon River.

Popular package: Highlights of Peru, 8 days, from $3,384.

Customized trips: Yes.

What they do best: Organize custom luxury travel with top-rate local guides.

Corporate responsibility: The company's nonprofit, Kensington Cares, supports schools, clinics, and orphanages in East Africa. ☎ *866/904–3219 in U.S.* 🌐 *www.kensingtontours.com.*

Kuoda Travel Cusco-based Kuoda Travel specializes in personalized itineraries, particularly for families and couples. The Peruvian owner, Mery Calderon, manages the business, which has a series of suggested itineraries offered as starting points, but the company's true expertise is working with clients to design the perfect tailor-made trip. It also offers tours in Bolivia and to Ecuador's Galapagos Islands.

Popular package: The Jungle, Machu Picchu, and Lake Titicaca, 12 days, from $4,050; starts with three nights at the Reserva Amazonica in Madre de Dios, followed by Cusco, the Sacred Valley, and Machu Picchu and ending with a couple days at Lake Titicaca.

Customized trips: Yes.

What they do best: Cater to the interests and needs of individual clients.

Corporate responsibility: The company has a small foundation that runs development projects and after-school, computer literacy programs in half a dozen highland communities. ☎ *800/986–4150 toll-free in U.S. and Canada, 084/222–741 in Peru* 🌐 *www.kuodatravel.com.*

PERUVIAN HISTORY

by Paul Steele

About 15,000 years ago, the first people to inhabit what is now Peru filtered down from North and Central America. They were confronted by diverse and extreme environments at varying altitudes. An ocean rich in fish contrasts with sterile coastal valleys that are only habitable where rivers cut through the desert. To the east the valleys and high plateau of the Andes mountains slope down to the Amazon rainforest, home to exotic foods, animals, and medicinal plants.

Modern Peru incorporates all of these environmental zones. Long before the centralized state of the Inca empire, people recognized the need to secure access to varied resources and products. Images of animals and plants from coast and jungle are found on pottery and stone monuments in highland Chavin culture, c. 400 BC. Around AD 500 the Nazca Lines etched out in the desert also featured exotic jungle animals.

In the 15th century the Incas achieved unprecedented control over people, food crops, plants, and domesticated animals that incorporated coast, highlands, and the semitropical valleys. Attempts to control coca leaf production in the warmer valleys may explain Machu Picchu, which guards an important trading route.

When the Spaniards arrived in the 16th century, the search for El Dorado, the fabled city of gold, extended the Viceroyalty of Peru into the Amazon lowlands. Since independence in 1821, disputes, wars, and treaties over Amazon territory have been fueled increasingly by the knowledge of mineral oil and natural gas under the forest floor.

COTTON FIRST CULTIVATED IN PERU

Ceramics first used in Peru

3000 BC | 2500 BC | 2000 BC | 1500 BC

(far left) Moche ceramic, portrait of a priest; (above) Cerro Sechin ca. 1000 BC on Peru coast; (left) Mummified corpse skull.

2600–1000 BC BIG OLD BUILDINGS

Peru's first monumental structures were also the earliest throughout the Americas. Coastal sites like Aspero and Caral have platform mounds, circular sunken courtyards, and large plazas that allowed public civic-ceremonial participation. At Garagay and Cerro Sechin mud and adobe relief sculptures show images connected to death, human disfigurement, and human to animal transformation. A developing art style characterized by pronounced facial features like fanged teeth and pendant-iris eyes reached its height later in Chavin culture.

■ Visit: Kotosh, Sechín

900–200 BC CHAVIN CULTURE

Chavin de Huantar, a site not far from Huaraz, was famous for its shamans or religious leaders who predicted the future. A distinctive and complex imagery on carved stone monuments like the Lanzón and Tello Obelisk featured animals and plants from the coast, highlands, and especially the jungle. The decline of Chavin de Huantar coincided with the emergence of other oracle temples such as Pachacamac, south of modern Lima. The distinctive Chavin art style, however, continued to influence later cultures throughout Peru, including Paracas on the south coast.

■ Visit: Chavin de Huantar

600–50 BC ALL WRAPPED UP IN ICA

On the Paracas Peninsula, the desert holds the remains of an ancient burial practice. Corpses were wrapped in layers of textiles, placed in baskets, and buried in the sand. Many elaborately woven and embroidered garments that could be tens of meters long were only used to bury the dead and never worn in life. The mummy bundles of high status individuals were often accompanied by offerings of gold objects, exotic shells, and animal skins and feathers.

■ Visit: Museo Histórico Regional

Chavin culture begins | Paracas culture begins | Moche kingdom begins

1000 BC | 500 BC | 0 | 500 AD

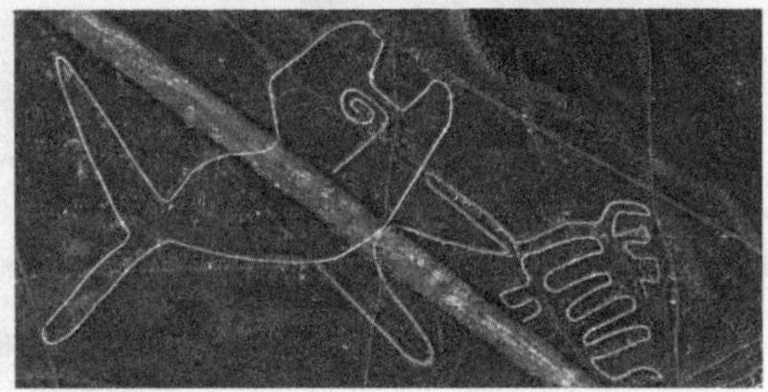

(above) Chavin de Huantar; (top right) Huaca de la Luna deity; (bottom right) Nazca ground picture of whale.

50 BC–AD 700

THE NASCANS

On Peru's south coast followed the Nasca, who are famous for the geoglyph desert markings known as the Nazca Lines. Thousands of long straight lines were constructed over many centuries, while around fifty animal outlines date to a more concise period of AD 400–600. An extensive system of underground aqueducts channeled water from distant mountains. In such a barren environment the Nazca Lines were probably linked closely to a cult primarily devoted to the mountain water source.

■ Visit: Cahuachi, Nazca Lines

AD 100–800

MOCHE KINGDOM

On Peru's north coast the Moche or Mochica controlled a number of coastal river valleys. Large scale irrigation projects extended cultivable land. The Temples of the Sun and Moon close to the modern city of Trujillo were constructed from millions of adobe or mud bricks and were some of the largest buildings anywhere in the ancient Americas. The high quality of Moche burial goods for individuals like the Lord of Sipan indicated a wide social gulf not previously seen in Peru. Full-time artisans produced metalwork and ceramics for Moche lords. The pottery in particular is famous for the realistic portrayal of individuals and for the naturalistic scenes of combat, capture, and sacrifice that could have been narrative stories from Moche mythology and history. Some themes like the sacrificing of war captives in the presence of the Lord of Sipan and the Owl Priest were probably reenacted in real life. A number of severe droughts and devastating el niño rains precipitated the decline of the Moche.

■ Visit: Pañamarca, Huaca de la Luna, Huaca del Sol

TIMELINE

(above) Wari face neck jar; (top right) Chan Chan, (bottom right) Kuélap.

550–950 WELCOME TO THE WARI EMPIRE

A new dominant highland group, the Wari, or Huari, originated close to the modern city of Ayacucho. Wari administrative centers, storage facilities, and an extensive road network were forerunners to the organizational systems of the Inca empire. The Wari were influenced by the iconographic tradition of a rival site, Tiahuanaco, in what is now Bolivia, which exerted control over the extreme south of Peru. After Wari control collapsed, regional kingdoms and localized warfare continued until the expansion of the Inca empire.

■ Visit: Pikillacta, Huari

900–1470 CHIMÚ KINGDOM

On the north coast the Chimú or Chimor succeeded the Moche controlling the coastal river valleys as far south as Lima. The capital Chan Chan was a bustling urban sprawl that surrounded at least 13 high-walled citadels of the Chimú lords. The city was built close to the ocean shore and continual coastal uplift meant that access to fresh water from deep wells was a constant problem. An extensive canal network to channel water from rivers never worked properly.

■ Visit: Chan Chan, Huaca Esmeralda

800–1480 THE FIGHTIN' CHACHAPOYAS

In the cloud forests of the eastern Andean slopes the Chachapoyas kingdom put up fierce resistance against the Incas. The Chachapoyas are famous for their mummified dead placed in cliff-top niches and for high quality circular stone buildings at sites like Kuélap, one of the largest citadels in the world. Kuélap may have been designed as a fortification against the Wari. Later the Incas imposed harsh penalties on the Chachapoyas who subsequently sided with the Spaniards.

■ Visit: Kuélap (Cuelap)

Arrival of the Spanish
Coastal cultures Ica and Chincha flourish
Height of Inca empire
1150 1350 1550

(left) Mama Occlo, wife and sister of Manco Capac, founder of the Inca dynasty, carrying the Moon; (above) Machu Picchu.

C. 1400 INCA ORIGINS

The Inca empire spanned a relatively short period in Peruvian history. The mythical origins of the first Inca Manco Capac, who emerged from a cave, is typical of Peruvian ancestor tradition. Spanish chroniclers recorded at least 10 subsequent Inca rulers although in reality the earlier kings were probably not real people. The famous Inca, Pachacuti, is credited with expansion from the capital Cusco. Inca iconographic tradition that followed geometric and abstract designs left no representational images of its rulers.

■ Visit: Isla del Sol

1450–1527 INCA EMPIRE

Within three generations the Incas had expanded far beyond the boundaries of modern Peru to central Chile in the south and past the equator to the north. The Amazon basin was an environment they did not successfully penetrate. Although the Incas fought battles, it was a two-way process of negotiation with *curacas*, the local chiefs that brought many ethnic groups under control. The empire was divided into four *suyu* or parts, centered on Cusco. At a lower level communities were organized into decimal units ranging from 10 households up to a province of 40,000 households. Individual work for the state was known as *mit'a*. Communities forcibly resettled to foreign lands were called *mitimaes*. The Incas kept a regular population census and record of all the sacred idols and shrines. The Incas spread the language Quechua that is still spoken throughout most of Peru and in neighboring countries.

■ Visit: Ollantaytambo, Machu Picchu, Pisac Ruins

EXTENSIVE DEPOPULATION THROUGHOUT PERU

1600 | 1650 | 1700

(above) The execution of Tupa Amaru; (left) Francisco Pizarro, Diego de Almagro, and Fernando de Luque planning the conquest of Peru.

1527–1542 ARRIVAL OF THE CONQUISTADORS

The Spanish conquistadors arrived on the coast of Ecuador and northern Peru bringing European diseases like smallpox that ravaged the indigenous population and killed the Inca king. They also introduced the name Peru. In 1532 a small band of conquistadors led by Francisco Pizarro first encountered the Inca ruler Atahualpa in Cajamarca. This famous confrontation of Old and New World cultures culminated with the capture of Atahualpa, who was later strangled. The Spaniards arrived in Cusco in 1533 and immediately took the city residences and country estates of the Inca elite for themselves. The resistance of Manco Inca could not drive the Spaniards out of Cusco, and by the end of the 1530s the Inca loyal supporters had retreated to Ollantaytambo, and then to the forested region of Vilcabamba that became the focus of Inca resistance for the next 30 years. In 1542 the Viceroyalty of Peru was created and a new capital city, Lima, became the political and economic center of Spain's possessions in South America.

■ Visit: Cajamarca, Ollantaytambo, Sacsayhuamán

1542–1572 END OF THE INCAS

A relatively small number of Spaniards overthrew the Incas because of support from many groups disaffected under Inca rule. Native Peruvians quickly realized, however, that these new lighter-skinned people were intent on dismantling their whole way of life. The 1560s nativist movement Taqui Onqoy, meaning dancing sickness, called on native gods to expel the Spaniards and their religion. In 1572 the Inca Tupa Amaru, mistakenly called Tupac Amaru, was captured and executed in public in Cusco.

■ Visit: Cusco

Large earthquake and tsunami devastates Lima

Peru declares independence
Battle of Ayacucho

1750 1800 1850

(above) Battle of Ayacucho, Bolivar's forces establish Peruvian independence from Spain 1824; (left) Simon Bolivar, aka "The Liberator."

SPANISH COLONIAL RULE

1572–1770

The Spanish crown increasingly sought more direct control over its American empire. A new viceroy, Toledo, stepped up the policy of *reducciones* in which formerly dispersed native communities were resettled into more easily controlled towns. This made it easier to baptize the native population into the Catholic church. The indigenous population was forced to work in mines such as Potosí, which became the biggest urban center in the Americas. Huge quantities of gold and silver were shipped to the Caribbean and then to Europe, and helped fund Spain's wars in Europe. Spanish hacienda estates introduced new food crops such as wheat, and new livestock like pigs and cows. The scale of native depopulation—more acute on the coast—is today reflected by the number of abandoned hillside terraces. The Inca elite and local chiefs started to adopt European dress; some found ways to prosper under new colonial regulations (like avoiding Spanish taxes if demonstrating Inca ancestry).

■ Visit: Colonial architecture of Arequipa, Ayacucho, Cusco, Lima, Trujillo

END OF COLONIAL RULE

1770–1824

The execution of the last Inca ruler in 1572 did not stop continued rebellions against Spanish colonial rule. In the eighteenth century an uprising led by the local chief José Gabriel Condorcanqui, who called himself Tupa Amaru II, foreshadowed the wars of independence that ended colonial rule in Peru and elsewhere in the Americas. Peru declared its independence in 1821 and again in 1824, when Símon Bólivar arrived from Colombia to defeat the remaining royalist forces at the battle of Ayacucho.

■ Visit: Pampas de Quinua

TIMELINE

Slavery abolished

Quechua language officially recognized

POPULATION MIGRATION TO BIG CITIES

Earthquake devastates South Peru

1900 | 1950 | 2000 | PRESENT

(above) Ollanta Humala; (right) Lima, Peru.

1824–1900 REPUBLICAN ERA

Despite an initial 20 years of chaos, when every year seemed to bring a new regime, the young republic was attractive to foreign business interests. Particularly lucrative for Peru were the export of cotton and guano—nitrate-rich bird droppings used for fertilizer. Peru benefited from foreign investment such as railroad building, but an increasing national foreign debt was unsustainable without significant industrial development. Disputes with neighboring countries, especially the War of the Pacific against Chile in which Lima was sacked, land to the south ceded, and the country bankrupted, deeply affected the nation.

1900–2000 20TH-CENTURY PERU

The twentieth century saw Peru's democracy repeatedly interrupted by military coups. The left-wing government of General Juan Velasco (1968–75) instituted agrarian reform and nationalized businesses. Democratically elected President Alan Garcia (1985–90) tried socialist policies that resulted in hyperinflation and capital flight. Economic insecurity combined with growing violence by the Shining Path guerrilla caused many Peruvians to emigrate and millions to move from the highlands to Lima. President Alberto Fujimori (1990–2000) reestablished economic stability and largely defeated the Shining Path, but authoritarianism and widespread corruption led to his downfall.

2000–PRESENT RECENTLY . . .

This century has brought Peru's longest stretch of democracy and economic growth, and a chain of scandals that have plunged the country into political turmoil. Fujimori's successor, Pedro Pablo Kuczynski, was elected in 2016, forced to resign in 2018, and arrested a year later, after getting caught up in a political scandal that eventually extended to include every Peruvian president in office since 2000. Former Minister of Transport and Communications, Martín Vizcarra, was sworn into office as president in 2018 with a promise to fight corruption. However, political dramas continue and threaten to deepen an economic crisis triggered by the coronavirus pandemic.

Chapter 2

TRAVEL SMART

Updated by
Marco Ferrarese

★ CAPITAL:
Lima

POPULATION:
32,971,854

LANGUAGE:
Spanish, Quechua, and Aymara

$ CURRENCY:
Peruvian sol

AREA CODE:
51

EMERGENCIES:
105

DRIVING:
On the right

ELECTRICITY:
220 volts/50 cycles; electrical plugs have two flat prongs (the same as in the United States)

TIME:
1 hour behind New York during daylight saving time; same time during the winter

WEB RESOURCES:
www.peru.travel
www.howtoperu.com
www.peruinformation.org

AIRPORT:
LIM

Know Before You Go

While Peru and its people are charmingly laid-back, some of Peru's top experiences require you to adopt a Type A travel personality and plan ahead. Unfortunately, you can't just show up and hike the Inca Trail or score a table at one of Latin America's top restaurants. And if you don't plan ahead for altitude sickness, it will ruin your trip.

YOU WILL GET HIGH
Even if you're very fit, if you climb to altitudes higher than 2,500 meters (8,200 feet), which includes areas such as Cusco, Machu Picchu, Puno and the Colca Canyon, and Lake Titicaca, you risk getting altitude sickness, which is life-threatening. If you plan to travel to areas at high altitude, see your doctor beforehand to discuss if a prescription of Diamox is advised. The best way to prevent altitude sickness is to ascend slowly, allowing your body to acclimatize. Allow time (a few days preferably) in your travel plans to adapt to a change in altitude, especially if you fly directly from Lima to Cusco.

JUST SAY YES TO COCA
Locals swear by *mate de coca*, an herbal tea brewed from coca leaves that helps with altitude acclimatization. Indigenous peoples have chewed the leaves of the coca plant for centuries to cope with Andean elevations. But the brewing of the leaves in an herbal tea is considered a more refined and completely legal way to ingest the substance, in Andean nations at least. Most restaurants and virtually all hotels have leaves and hot water available constantly. Leaves are also sold at most markets for a few soles, but you can't transport them outside of Peru. They are also illegal in most other Latin American countries, as well as in the United States. While the coca leaf in its natural form is a harmless and mild stimulant comparable to coffee, there is no doubt that cocaine can be extracted from the coca leaf (it takes over 800 pounds of coca leaves to make just 1 kg of cocaine) so if there's a possibility you might have a drug test when you return home, be careful with any form of coca consumption while in Peru.

DON'T DRINK THE WATER
Wherever you are in Peru, do not drink tap water. Buy bottled water or, at a minimum, boil your water or use a filter. You should also avoid ice.

PACK FOR THREE CLIMATES
Peru has three main climate zones: a desert coastal strip where winters are mild, cloudy, and foggy and summers are warm; the Andean highlands zone, which tends to be colder regardless of the season; and the Amazonian rainforest, which is hot and humid throughout the year. Pack layers. If you're trekking to Machu Picchu, bring comfortable clothes and shoes. While it can be hot, make sure you have a light jacket or sweater with you, as it can get chilly in the evenings. Cusco's rainy season falls between November and March, and while days may be warm, you will need a raincoat or waterproof jacket and waterproof shoes.

PLAN AHEAD FOR MACHU PICCHU
For many travelers, Machu Picchu is *the* reason to visit Peru and a once-in-a-lifetime experience. With this in mind, you'll want to plan ahead to avoid disappointment. Reserve train tickets for the trip to Aguas Calientes from Cusco or Ollantaytambo (do this first as train tickets sell out fast). Then you'll need tickets to Machu Picchu (sold in hourly entry slots) and a tour guide as you cannot enter the site without a guide. There are only 400 tickets available each day to visit the ruins *and* hike Huayna Picchu so you should purchase this type of ticket as far in advance as possible. Note: you must have your passport with you in order to enter Machu Picchu. There are no toilets inside the site, so pee before you enter!

PLAN AHEAD FOR THE INCA TRAIL

If you want to visit Machu Picchu via the Classic Inca Trail, you will need to plan for about four days of moderate to demanding trekking. To hike the trail, you'll need a government permit, which you can get through an official operator approved by La Dirección Desconcentrada de Cultura de Cusco government department. You can't do the trek on your own—you must do it on a guided tour. Only 500 people (300 guides and porters, 200 tourists) are allowed to start the Inca Trail per day, so you'll need to book a permit months in advance. You can check how many are left on a particular day by visiting the Ministry of Culture website.

FOODIES SHOULD MAKE RESERVATIONS

Home to some of the world's top restaurants, Lima is a foodie mecca so you will need to make your reservations in advance. If you have hotspots like Central, Maido, and Astrid y Gastón on your to-eat list, you will want to make reservations up to three months in advance.

LEARN SOME SPANISH

In Lima and other tourist centers, most Peruvians have an increasingly good command of English, but when you leave the cities, you'll find yourself in Spanish-speaking territory. On the remotest mountains, Quechua and Aymara may be the only languages spoken. It really pays off to learn even a few words of Spanish before you visit. Download Google Translate on your phone for more involved interactions outside Lima.

CASH IS KING

Credit cards are not widely accepted outside of main cities in Peru, so you will want to carry cash. U.S. dollars are accepted and are preferred for tipping tour guides and the like. Just note that if that if you buy something using USD, the cost may be more than if you pay in local currency. Also, your dollars will need to be in perfect condition, or they may be rejected. Another reason to carry cash: credit card transaction fees can add up to 15% to your bill. It's best to withdraw money as you go, rather than carrying a lot of cash at once.

LINGER IN LIMA

For many, Lima is just the entrance and departure point and a temporary stop on the way to ancient sites. The capital is not the prettiest, and it can take some time to get used to its hustle and traffic. That said, it's a mistake not to stay at least a couple of days to indulge in Lima's excellent dining scene or explore some of its secret sights.

TRY PISCO IN ICA

A pisco sour is a cultural tradition and a must-try while in Peru. Pisco is made in the bodegas near Ica (more precisely, between Ica and Pisco), and that's where you should go for a tasting. The name comes from the Pisco region, as opposed to the city, but today there aren't many well-known distilleries around Pisco itself. Drink responsibly, as it's strong stuff.

RESPECT THE CULTURE

Outside of Lima, Arequipa, and Cusco, most Peruvians live simple, rural existences bound by century-old traditions. In most villages, you'll see men and women still wearing traditional Andean attire. Most of these people are fervent Catholics who live morigerate existences of prayer. For this reason, be aware of local codes of conduct, values, and expectations: dress modestly, and avoid drinking excessively in public.

GET OFF THE TOURIST TRAIL

Few countries reward those who get off the beaten track more than Peru. For certain, you can breeze across the country in two weeks, visiting Cusco, Machu Picchu, and Lake Titicaca—but you'll do so with a number of other tourists. In Peru, taking time to explore off-the-grid villages, lesser trawled hiking trails, and forgotten forests grants a lifetime of incredible memories. Whether it is learning Spanish in a village along the coast, or choosing an offbeat location in the Andes or the jungle to slow down, Peru has always something to offer to those who dare go the extra mile and stay a while.

Getting Here and Around

Travel Times from Lima

To	By Air	By Car/Bus
Cusco	1 hour, 20 mins.	21½ hours
Puno	1 hour, 50 mins.	22 hours
Arequipa	1½ hours	15½ hours
Trujillo	1 hour, 15 mins.	9 hours

Because of the massive Andes Mountains that ripple through the country, most travelers choose to fly between the major cities of Peru. The good news is that domestic flights can be reasonable, sometimes less than US$100 per segment.

 Air

Almost all international flights into Peru touch down at Aeropuerto Internacional Jorge Chávez, on the northwestern fringe of Lima. Nonstop flying times to Lima are 5 hours, 35 minutes from Miami; 6 hours, 35 minutes from Houston; 7½ hours from New York; and 8 hours, 20 minutes from Los Angeles.

AIRPORTS

Peru's main international point of entry is Aeropuerto Internacional Jorge Chávez (LIM), 11 km (7 miles) from Lima's historic center and 17 km (10 miles) from Miraflores. It's a completely modern facility with plenty of shops, eateries, and flights that arrive and depart 24 hours a day. ATMs and currency exchange offices are in the arrivals area. ATMs can also be found in the departures area. You will get a better exchange rate from a bank-affiliated ATM or at a currency exchange on the street, so you may want to change or take out a small amount to pay any necessary taxis.

GROUND TRANSPORTATION

If your hotel doesn't offer to pick you up at the airport, you'll have to take a taxi. Arrange a ride with one of the official airport taxis whose companies have counters inside the arrivals area of the terminal or by using the ride-hailing service **Cabify** (🌐 *www.cabify.com*). A trip to most places in the city should cost no more than US$20–US$25. It's a 30-minute drive to El Centro and a 45-minute drive to Miraflores and San Isidro. During rush hour (8–10 am and 5–9 pm), driving times in Lima can double, so plan accordingly.

The Airport Express Lima is a very convenient and cheap bus service between Lima's airport and the hotels in Miraflores or San Isidro. Buses are equipped with on-board Wi-Fi, USB ports, and air-conditioning, and fares start at US$6 one way.

FLIGHTS

Dozens of international flights land daily at Lima's Aeropuerto Internacional Jorge Chávez; although most are from other Latin American cities, there are many from the United States as well. Delta flies from Atlanta, American flies from Miami and New York's JFK, United flies from Houston, and Spirit and JetBlue both fly from Fort Lauderdale. South American–based LATAM flies from Los Angeles and Miami and Air Canada flies from Toronto.

If you're arriving from other Latin American cities, you have a wide range of regional carriers at your disposal. LATAM has flights from most major airports in the region, as does Avianca, which now also flies direct between Bogotá, Colombia, and Cusco. Copa (affiliated with United) flies from its hub in Panama City, Aeroméxico flies from Mexico City, Aerolineas Argentinas flies from Buenos Aires, and Sky Airlines flies from Santiago, Chile.

DOMESTIC

With four mountain ranges and a large swath of the Amazon jungle running through Peru, flying is the best way to travel from Lima to most cities and towns. LATAM, the carrier that operates the majority of flights within the country, departs several times each day for Arequipa, Ayacucho, Cajamarca, Chiclayo, Cusco, Iquitos, Piura, Puerto Maldonado, Pucallpa, Tacna, Tarapoto, Trujillo, and Tumbes. Star Perú flies to Cusco, Huánuco, Iquitos, Pucallpa, Puerto Maldonado, and Tarapoto. Avianca flies to Arequipa, Cusco, Iquitos, Juliaca, Piura, Puerto Maldonado, and Trujillo. Viva Air Peru flies between Lima and Arequipa, Chiclayo, Cusco, Iquitos, Piura, and Tarapoto.

 Bus

The intercity bus system in Peru is extensive, and fares are quite reasonable. Remember, however, that mountain ranges often sit between cities, and trips can be daunting. It's best to use buses for shorter trips, such as between Lima and Ica or between Cusco and Puno. That way, you can begin and end your trip during daylight hours. If you stick with one of the recommended companies—such as Cruz del Sur, Ormeño, Inka Express, or CIVA—you can usually expect a comfortable journey.

Second-class buses (*servicio normal*) tend to be cramped and overcrowded, whereas the pricier first-class service (*primera clase*) is more relaxing and much more likely to arrive on schedule.

Bus fares are substantially cheaper in Peru than they are in North America or Europe. Timetables and tickets can be checked and bought in advance online at Redbus (🌐 *www.redbus.pe*) or Bus Tickets Peru (🌐 *www.busticketsperu.com*), but it's always cheaper to go to any bus terminal and ask around there. Competing companies serve all major and many minor routes, so it can pay to shop around if you're on an extremely tight budget, and there's always a bus going somewhere. Always speak to the counter clerk, as competition may mean fares are cheaper than the official price posted on the fare board.

For the 15-plus-hour journey between Lima and Arequipa, Cruz del Sur offers different price tiers, depending on how far the seat reclines, with first-floor seats being more comfortable. Inka Express, which promotes itself to tourists rather than the local market, uses large, comfortable coaches for the popular eight-hour journey between Cusco and Puno. Tickets are US$50, and the trip includes snacks, lunch, and guided visits at points of interest along the way; entrance fees for the sites are not included. For those who like flexibility and having everything organized, Peru Hop is another tourist-oriented bus company offering hop-on-hop-off bus trips between Lima and Cusco. You can choose how much time you want to stay at each stop. Buses have English-speaking guides and also stop at sights en route; they also connect to La Paz in Bolivia via Puno. Tickets start at US$129 for a three-day, four-stop itinerary between Lima and Cusco.

In general, tickets are sold at bus-company offices and at travel agencies. Be prepared to pay with cash, as credit cards aren't always accepted or incur higher charges, although you can typically order and pay by credit card on the Cruz del Sur website. Reservations aren't necessary except for trips to top destinations during high season. Summer weekends and major holidays are the busiest times. You should arrive at bus stations early for travel during peak seasons.

Getting Here and Around

 Car

In general, it's not a great idea to rent a car in Peru. Driving is a heart-stopping experience, as there seem to be unwritten traffic rules that you have to be from here to know. That said, there are a few places in Peru where having a car is a benefit, such as between Lima and points south on the Pan-American Highway. The highway follows the Pacific Ocean coastline before it cuts in through the desert, and stops can be made along the way for a picnic and a swim at the popular beaches around Asia at Kilometer 100. The highway is good, and although there isn't too much to see along the way, it's nice to have the freedom a car affords once you get to your destination.

If you do rent one, keep these tips in mind: outside cities, drive only during daylight hours, fill your gas tank whenever possible, make sure your spare tire is in good repair, and pay extra attention on mountain roads. In some areas, drivers caught using a cell phone receive a hefty fine.

Massive road-building programs have improved highways. Nevertheless, even in some parts of Lima, roads are littered with potholes. Beyond the urban centers, both street signs and lighting can be rare, and lanes may be unmarked. Roads are straight along the coast, but in the mountains, they snake around enough to make even the steadiest driver a little queasy. Fuel is pricey in Peru, with a gallon costing around US$3.85.

The major highways in Peru are the Pan-American Highway (*Panamericana* in Spanish), which runs down the entire coast; the Carretera Central, which runs from Lima to Huancayo; and the Interoceánica, which runs from Lima to Cerro de Pasco and on to Pucallpa before crossing through Brazil to the Atlantic Ocean. Most highways have no names or numbers; they're referred to by destination.

CAR RENTAL

The minimum age for renting a car in Peru is 25, although some agencies offer rentals to younger drivers for an additional fee, and a credit card is required. All major car-rental agencies have branches in downtown Lima as well as at Jorge Chávez International Airport that are open 24 hours. You can also rent vehicles in Arequipa, Chiclayo, Cusco, Piura, Puno, Tacna, and Trujillo.

The cost of rental cars varies widely but is generally between US$30 and US$60 for a compact, US$80 to US$100 for a full-size car or small SUV. A daily US$10 to US$20 collision damage waiver may be added to your bill.

DRIVING

Speed limits are 30 kph–60 kph (18.5 mph–37 mph) in residential areas, 80 kph–100 kph (50 mph–62 mph) on highways. Traffic tickets range from a minimum of US$12 to a maximum of US$120. The police and military routinely check drivers at roadblocks, so make sure your papers are easily accessible. Note that laws, especially outside big cities, can be left to the discretion of the officer, so be polite and respectful at all times. Peruvian law makes it a crime to drive while intoxicated, although many people ignore that prohibition (as everywhere).

ROADSIDE EMERGENCIES

The Touring y Automóvil Club del Perú will provide 24-hour emergency road service for members of the American Automobile Association (AAA) and affiliates upon presentation of their membership cards. (Towing is free within 30 km [18 miles] of several urban areas.) Members of AAA can purchase good maps there at low prices.

Ride-Sharing

Uber is available in Peru, but taxi-booking apps like Cabify (🌐 *www.cabify.com*) and Beat (🌐 *thebeat.co/pe*) are preferred. While Uber is fine for short drives around Lima and Cusco, Uber drivers are known to overcharge and "forget" to switch on the Uber app once they arrive to pick you up, and the company has a reputation for not following up with customer complaints in Peru. Local cars can be unreliable, too: they are generally old and without air-conditioning and, at times, even without seat belts. Cabify and Beat are safer, more reliable options. If you are looking to secure a ride from the airport into the city, you might want to instead avail of the convenient Airport Express Lima to reach Miraflores or San Isidro; rates start at US$6.

Train

Trains run along four different routes: between Cusco and Machu Picchu, between Cusco and Lake Titicaca, and between Lake Titicaca and Arequipa. The second highest train in the world runs between Lima and Huancayo, one or two times a month between May and November; tours last four days. Tickets can be purchased at train stations, through travel agencies, or online. During holidays or high season, it's best to get your tickets in advance.

Two companies offer train service to Machu Picchu. PeruRail, which has served the route since 1999, is operated by Belmond—the same company that runs one of the most luxurious and famous trains in the world, the Venice Simplon Orient Express between London and Venice. It travels to Machu Picchu from Cusco (technically from the nearby town of Poroy, about 20 minutes outside the city) and the Sacred Valley towns of Ollantaytambo and Urubamba. Inca Rail, which began service in 2010 and merged with Andean Railways in 2012, travels between Ollantaytambo and Machu Picchu. Foreigners are prohibited from riding the very inexpensive local trains that cover the route. The Machu Picchu station is not at the archaeological site itself, but in the nearby town of Aguas Calientes.

In May 2017, PeruRail completely revamped its Andean Explorer train service to points south of Cusco. It is now a sleeper train including a luxury dining car and a spa, and the company offers several different options, including single-day trips between Cusco and Lake Titicaca and three-day/two-night tours that take in Arequipa as well. Each departs on a different day of the week, depending on the trip chosen. The newly revamped Andean Explorer from Cusco to the lake is US$1,800 for two passengers, leaving at 11 in the morning from Cusco; culminating in a sunrise breakfast at Lake Titicaca; and including lunch, tour of Raqchi, tea time, predinner drinks, dinner, and, of course, your bed. Note that there are two different train stations in Cusco. Estación Poroy serves the Machu Picchu route, and Estación Wanchaq serves the Lake Titicaca route. Reserve and purchase your ticket as far ahead as possible, especially during holidays or high season. Reservations can be made directly with PeruRail through its website or through a travel agency or tour operator.

Essentials

Dining

Most smaller restaurants offer a lunchtime *menú* (also called *completo*), an incredibly good-value, prix-fixe meal (US$1.50–US$3) that consists of a soup, a main dish, sometimes a simple dessert, and a beverage. Peru is also full of cafés and bakeries, many with a selection of delicious pastries. Food at bars is usually limited to snacks and sandwiches. ■ **TIP→ Make reservations at least three months in advance for Lima's top restaurants.**

MEALS AND MEALTIMES

Food in Peru is hearty and wholesome. Thick soups are excellent, particularly *chupes* made of shrimp or fish with potatoes, corn, peas, onions, garlic, tomato sauce, eggs, cream cheese, milk, and whatever else happens to be in the kitchen. *Corvina* (a Pacific sea bass) is superb, as is paiche (a fish with a very large mouth that's found in jungle lakes and is now being farmed sustainably). Adventurous eaters can try piranha—it's delicious, but full of bones; *cebiche,* raw fish marinated in lime juice then mixed with onions and ajis (chili peppers), is another option. *Anticuchos* (marinated beef hearts grilled over charcoal) are a favorite street snack, and *pollo a la brasa* (rotisserie chicken) is so popular that the government includes it in its inflation figures. Peru's *choclo* (large-kernel corn) is very good, and it's claimed there are thousands of varieties of potatoes and other tubers, prepared in about as many ways.

Top-notch restaurants serve lunch and dinner, but most Peruvians think of lunch as the main meal, and many restaurants open only at midday. Served between 1 and 3 pm, lunch was once followed by a siesta, though the custom has largely died out. Dinner can be anything from a light snack to another full meal and Peruvians tend to eat it between 7 and 10 pm, although in Lima, this can extend later to 11.

Unless otherwise noted, the restaurants listed in this guide are open daily for lunch and dinner.

WINES, BEER, AND SPIRITS

Peru's national drink is the pisco sour, made with a type of pale grape brandy called pisco—close to 90 proof—derived from grapes grown in vineyards around Ica, south of Lima. Added to the pisco are lime juice, sugar, bitters, and egg white. It's a refreshing drink and one that nearly every bar in Peru claims to make best. Wines from Ica vineyards include such labels as Santiago Queirolo, Tacama, Taberno, and Ocucaje, but a relative newcomer, Intipalka, is probably the country's best. Ica's National Vintage Festival is in March.

Peruvian beer (*cerveza*) is also very good. In Lima try Pilsen Callao or sample the products from craft breweries like Candelaria, Sacred Valley Brewing Company, Nuevo Mundo, Cumbres, and Barbarian. In the south it's Arequipeña from Arequipa, Cusqueña from Cusco, and big bottles of San Juan from Iquitos, where the warm climate makes it taste twice as good. In Iquitos locals make Chuchuhuasi from the reddish-brown bark of the canopy tree that grows to 100 feet high in the Amazon rainforest. The bark is soaked for days in *aguardiente* (a very strong homemade liquor) and is claimed to be a cure-all. In Iquitos, however, it has been bottled and turned into a tasty drink for tourists. *Chicha,* a low-alcohol corn beer, is still made by hand throughout the highlands. An acquired taste, chicha can be found by walking through any doorway where a red flag is flying, though you may want to sample it at a restaurant to be safe.

What It Costs

$	$$	$$$	$$$$
AT DINNER			
under S/35	S/35–S/50	S/51–S/65	over S/65

Health and Safety

ALTITUDE SICKNESS

Altitude sickness, known locally as *soroche,* affects the majority of visitors to Cusco, Puno, and other high-altitude locales in the Andes. Headache, dizziness, nausea, and shortness of breath are common. When you visit areas over 3,000 meters (10,000 feet) above sea level, take it easy for the first few days. Avoiding alcohol will keep you from getting even more dehydrated. To fight soroche, Peruvians swear by mate de coca, a tea made from the leaves of the coca plant. (If you are subject to any type of random drug testing through your workplace, know that coca tea can result in a positive test for cocaine afterward.) Some travelers swear by the prescription drug acetazolamide (brand name, Diamox), which should be taken 48 hours before arriving at altitude. Whether that's an appropriate course is for you and your health-care professional to decide.

Spend a few nights at lower elevations before you head higher, especially if you are hiking or climbing in the mountains. If you must fly directly to higher altitudes, plan on doing next to nothing for the first day or two. Drinking plenty of water or coca tea and taking frequent naps may also help. If symptoms persist, return to lower elevations. If you have high blood pressure or a history of heart trouble or are pregnant, check with your doctor before traveling to high elevations.

COVID-19

A novel coronavirus brought all travel to a virtual standstill in early 2020. Although the illness is mild in most people, some experience severe and even life-threatening complications. Until a vaccine is widely available, travelers must be particularly careful about hygiene and to avoid any unnecessary travel, especially if they are sick.

Starting two weeks before a trip, anyone planning to travel should be on the lookout for some of the following symptoms: cough, fever, chills, trouble breathing, muscle pain, sore throat, new loss of smell or taste. If you experience any of these symptoms, you should not travel at all.

To protect yourself during travel, do your best to avoid contact with people showing symptoms. Wash your hands often with soap and water. Limit your time in public places, and, when you are out and about, wear a cloth face mask that covers your nose and mouth. You may wish to bring extra supplies, such as disinfecting wipes, hand sanitizer (12-ounce bottles were allowed in carry-on luggage at this writing), and a first-aid kit with a thermometer.

Given how abruptly travel was curtailed in March 2020, it is wise to consider protecting yourself by purchasing a travel insurance policy that will reimburse you for any costs related to COVID-19-related cancellations. Not all travel insurance policies protect against pandemic-related cancellations, so always read the fine print.

MOSQUITO-BORNE ILLNESSES

Mosquitoes and sand flies are a problem in tropical areas, especially at dusk; infectious diseases can be passed via mosquitoes. If you are traveling in an area where malaria is prevalent, use a repellent containing DEET, and take malaria-prevention medication before, during, and after your trip as directed by your physician. Note: you may have to start antimalarial medication weeks before your trip so ask about it early. You may not get through airport screening with an aerosol can of mosquito repellent, so opt for a spritz bottle or cream. Local brands of repellent are readily available in pharmacies. If you plan to spend time in the jungle, be sure to wear clothing that covers your arms and legs, sleep under a mosquito net, and spray bug repellent in living and sleeping areas.

Speak with your physician and/or check the Centers for Disease Control or World Health Organization websites for health alerts, particularly if you're pregnant, traveling with children, or have a chronic illness.

TRAVELER'S DIARRHEA

The most common illness is traveler's diarrhea, caused by viruses, bacteria, or parasites in contaminated food or water. In Lima and much of the center of Cusco, water supplies are chlorinated and should be safe to use for washing fruits and vegetables. Although many *limeños* drink the tap water, travelers should drink bottled, boiled, or purified water and drinks to avoid any issues, even when brushing your teeth. Many higher-quality hotels do purify their water, so inquire with the concierge. In the provinces, water may not be treated. Wash fruits and vegetables before eating, and avoid ice (order drinks *sin hielo*, or "without ice") or make sure the ice cubes are made with purified water. If you buy food from a street vendor, make sure it's cooked in front of you. Note that water boils at a lower temperature at high altitudes and may not be hot enough to rid it of the bacteria, so consider using purification tablets or a portable water filter. Local brands include Micropur. Mild cases of traveler's diarrhea may respond to Imodium, Pepto-Bismol, or Lomotil, all of which can be purchased in Peru without a prescription. You can also ask your doctor for a prescription for Cipro or other antibiotic commonly used to treat traveler's diarrhea before you travel. Drink plenty of purified water or tea—*manzanilla* (chamomile) is a popular folk remedy as is the *té anis,* which has a licorice taste.

IMMUNIZATIONS

No vaccinations are required to enter Peru, however, the Centers for Disease Control and Prevention (CDC) recommends hepatitis A and typhoid inoculations for all travelers to Peru. Hepatitis B, rabies, yellow fever, and malaria should be discussed with your medical professional, depending on where you will be traveling. It's a good idea to have up-to-date boosters for tetanus, diphtheria, and measles. In those areas where rabies is a concern, many hospitals have antirabies injections, but as these must be taken in a series, prevention is far easier. Children traveling to Peru should have their vaccinations for childhood diseases up to date.

Lodging

APARTMENT AND HOUSE RENTALS

Apartment rentals are not a viable option in most parts of Peru. They're becoming more common in Lima, however, and several other tourist centers. Aside from the convenience they offer, rentals can be cost-effective—you can often get a roomy two- or three-bedroom apartment for less than you'd pay for a shoe-box-size hotel room. One company that has proven reliable is Inn Peru, which rents apartments in Lima's Miraflores neighborhood. North American–based alternatives include HomeAway and Airbnb.

HOTELS

Peru's hotels range from bare-bones hostels to luxurious retreats tucked away in forgotten Andean valleys. In general, the highest-quality ones are in major urban centers (Lima, Arequipa, Cusco), but four- and five-star properties can still be found in smaller cities and rural areas that cater to high-end tourism or business. These will generally feature hot water, modern fixtures, and 24-hour concierge service. Midlevel hotels may lack some amenities but still offer a comfortable night's sleep for people who aren't looking for a flat-screen TV. There are many budget hotels that, although they have the word *hostel* in the name, are actually clean, comfortable, no-frills bed-and-breakfasts. Prices tend to reflect the property's age and amenities, but specialty lodges in the jungle or highlands may offer few comforts at any given price point. The name of a hotel does not necessarily have anything to do with its luxuriousness. A *posada,* for example, can be at the high, middle, or low end.

If you ask for a double room, you'll get a room for two people, but you're not guaranteed one large bed. If you'd like to avoid two twins, you'll have to ask for a *cama matrimonial* (literally a marriage bed), but don't worry, no wedding ring is required.

■ TIP→ Many older hotels in some of the small towns in Peru have rooms with lovely balconies or spacious terraces; ask if there's a room con balcón or con terraza when checking in.

WHAT IT COSTS

$	$$	$$$	$$$$
FOR TWO PEOPLE			
under S/250	S/250–S/500	S/501–S/800	over S/800

Money

Peru's national currency is the nuevo sol (S/). Bills are issued in denominations of 10, 20, 50, 100, and 200 soles. Coins are 1, 5, 10, 20, and 50 céntimos, and 1, 2, and 5 soles. (The 1- and 5-céntimo coins are rarely seen outside supermarkets in Lima.)

You'll want to break larger bills as soon as possible. Souvenir stands, crafts markets, taxi drivers, and other businesses often do not have change for anything larger than S/50. Be aware that many shops and establishments will not want to accept S/200 bills for fear of forgery, even though most ATMs dispense cash in such denominations. In that case, your best bet is breaking them at a bank or a moneychanger. Also be aware that U.S. dollars must be in pristine condition, as moneychangers and banks will not accept a bill with even the slightest tear. Likewise, counterfeiting is a big problem in Peru, and you should check all bills (both dollars and soles) immediately to confirm that they are real. The easiest method is to ensure that the color-changing ink does indeed change colors, from purple to black, and that flipping the bill under a direct source of light makes the small print to the left side of the bill shine. Do not feel uncomfortable scrutinizing bills; you can be sure that any cashier will scrutinize your bills twice as hard.

■ TIP→ If you're planning to exchange funds before leaving home, don't wait until the last minute. Banks never have every foreign currency on hand, and it may take as long as a week to order. For the best exchange rates, you're better off waiting until you get to Peru to change dollars into local currency.

Essentials

Packing

For sightseeing, casual clothing and good walking shoes are desirable and appropriate; most cities don't require formal clothes, even for evenings. If you're doing business in Peru, you'll need the same attire you would wear in U.S. and European cities: for men, suits and ties; for women, suits for day wear, and for evening, depending on the occasion—ask your host or hostess—a cocktail dress or just a nice suit with a dressy blouse.

Travel in rain-forest areas will require long-sleeve shirts, long pants, socks, sneakers, a hat, a light waterproof jacket, a bathing suit (if you want to swim), sunscreen, and insect repellent. You can never have too many large resealable plastic bags, which are ideal for protecting official documents from rain and damp and quarantining stinky socks.

If you're visiting the Andes, bring a jacket and sweater, or acquire one of the handknit sweaters or ponchos crowding the marketplaces. Evening temperatures in Cusco are rarely above 40°F. Layering is the key, and you may find you are constantly shedding and adding clothes throughout the day. For beach vacations, you'll need lightweight sportswear, a bathing suit, a sun hat, and lots of sunscreen. Peruvians are fairly conservative, so don't wear bathing suits or other revealing clothing away from the beach.

Other useful items include a travel flashlight and extra batteries, a pocketknife with a bottle opener (put it in your checked luggage), a medical kit, binoculars, and a calculator to help with currency conversions. A sarong or light cotton blanket can have many uses: beach towel, picnic blanket, and cushion for hard seats. Most important, always travel with tissues, baby wipes, or a roll of toilet paper, as restrooms are not always stocked with these necessities.

Passports and Visas

Visitors from the United States, Canada, the United Kingdom, Australia, and New Zealand require only a passport, valid for six months from date of travel, and a return ticket to be issued a visa on arrival for up to 183 days at their point of entry into Peru. Generally, your visa will be valid for a shorter period—one that coincides with your flight out of the country—unless you ask for more time. Even then, your visa's duration is at the discretion of the immigration officer.

If you are not happy with the duration of the tourist visa you've been given on arrival in Peru, you can always extend it online using the **Migraciones** website (🌐 *www.migraciones.gob.pe*). Most major cities have an Immigration department, but you don't have to visit: you can pay S/12 at any branch of Banco de la Nacion and collect a receipt from them. Once you have paid, log onto the Migraciones website and select *Prorroga de Permanencia en Linea*. Insert the required passport details and the number of extra days you want, being careful not to exceed 183 days in total from your first entry into Peru. On the next screen, you'll have to insert some of the numbers found at the bottom of your Banco de la Nacion payment slip. If all is correct, you'll receive your visa extension in your email a few minutes later. That's all you'll ever need to print and carry with you until you leave the country.

Tipping

Tipping Guides for Peru	
Bartender	S/1–S/5 per round of drinks, depending on the number of drinks
Bellhop	S/5–S/10 per bag, depending on the level of the hotel
Coat Check	S/3–S/5 per coat
Hotel Concierge	S/20 or more, depending on the service
Hotel Doorstaff	S/5–S/20 for help with bags or hailing a cab
Hotel Maid	S/10–S/20 a day (in cash, preferably daily since cleaning staff may be different each day you stay)
Hotel Room Service Waiter	S/5–S/10 per delivery, even if a service charge has been added
Porter at Airport or Train Station	S/3–S/5 per bag
Restroom Attendants	S/5 or small change
Skycap at Airport	S/3– S/10 per bag checked
Spa Personnel	15%–20% of the cost of your service
Taxi Driver	15%–20%
Tour Guide	10%–15% of the cost of the tour, per person
Valet Parking Attendant	S/10–S/20, each time your car is brought to you
Waiter	15%–20%, with 20% being the norm at high-end restaurants; nothing additional if a service charge is added to the bill

Taxes

An 18% *impuesto general a las ventas* (general sales tax) is levied on everything except goods bought from open-air markets and street vendors. It's usually included in the advertised price and should be included with food and drink. If a business offers you a discount for paying in cash, it probably means they aren't charging sales tax (and not reporting the transaction to the government).

By law, restaurants must publish their prices—including taxes and sometimes a 10% service charge—but they do not always do so. They're also prone to levy a cover charge for anything from live entertainment to serving you a roll with your meal. Hotel bills may also add taxes and a 10% service charge.

Departure taxes at Lima's Aeropuerto Internacional Jorge Chávez are US$29.74 for international flights and US$11.92 for domestic flights—all airlines now include the tax in their ticket prices.

On the Calendar

January

Festival de Marinera. The marinera is an elegant couple's dance using handkerchiefs as props and Trujillo is the capital of this dance. Festival de Marinera, as it's known in Spanish, features dance competitions, parades, and even exhibitions of the Peruvian Paso, a breed of horse recognized as part of the cultural patrimony of the Trujillo region. ✉ *Trujillo.*

February

Carnaval. Carnaval is celebrated in late February or early March with parades and folk dancing in most highland towns, though especially in Cajamarca, Ayacucho, Huaráz, and Puno.

Virgen de la Candelaria. Fireworks and colorful processions honor the Virgen de la Candelaria during the first half of February in Puno on Lake Titicaca. The faithful follow images of the Virgin Mary through the streets as troupes of dancers in elaborate costumes depict the struggle between good and evil. (The demons always lose.) ✉ *Puno.*

March

Semana Santa. Holy Week, or the week leading up to Easter (March or April), is celebrated with religious processions countrywide, though processions in Ayacucho and Arequipa are the most elaborate.

Festival Internacional de la Vendimia. The Festival Internacional de la Vendimia, or the International Harvest Festival, celebrates and promotes the wine region of southern Peru. Producers allow visitors to enter their vineyards and to learn about the making of pisco and wine, and a queen is famously chosen to ceremoniously stomp the first grapes of the season in the Ica Region. ✉ *Ica.*

May

Corpus Christi. Cusco's Corpus Christi festival in late May or early June begins with Mass in the Plaze de Armas surrounded by 15 statues of saints and representations of the Virgin Mary. The statues are carried from churches in nearby districts to be blessed. In late afternoon, the beaded, brocaded 15-foot statues are hoisted aloft and promenaded around the plaza, ending at the Cathedral. Reserve (as far in advance as possible) a table at a second-story restaurant or bar on the plaza for a good view.

June

Inti Raymi. Cusco's spectacular Inti Raymi (June 24) celebrates the winter solstice a few days late for historic reasons. The fortress ruins of Sacsayhuamán form the stage for a reenactment of an Inca ritual that beseeches the sun to return, with a proverbial cast of thousands.

Qoyllur Rit'i. Thousands of indigenous Peruvians flock to the Ausangate Glacier for Qoyllur Rit'i (June 9), a religious festival that mixes Inca and Christian rites in Sinakara, a Cusco department.

July

Fiestas Patrias. Peru's two-day Fiestas Patrias (July 28–29), which celebrate the country's independence from Spain in 1821, are marked by a military parade in Lima.

Virgen del Carmen. In mid-July, each end of the Colca Canyon has two days of celebrations to mark this festival, with singing, dancing, bullfights, food and drink, and parades in Chivay and Cabanaconde. After night falls, impressive fireworks light up in the sky. ✉ *Chivay.*

August

Corso de Amis. August 15 is the anniversary of Arequipa's founding and, each year, thousands take to the streets all day for the big parade, with music, dancing, traditional costumes, and decorated floats. ✉ *Arequipa* ☎ *054/223–265 iPeru tourist office.*

September

Mistura Culinary Festival. For 10 days in mid-September, visitors can try famous Peruvian potatoes and donuts (*picarones*) or simply enjoy local and international specialties served at numerous food stalls run by celebrity chefs, small vendors, and renowned restaurants.

October

El Señor de los Milagros. Of Peru's myriad Catholic celebrations, El Señor de los Milagros in Lima is the largest and perhaps the most important. The procession attracts hundreds of thousands of devotees and celebrants, who crowd through the streets of the city, singing and dancing, while vendors sell spiritual trinkets and medallions, together with a wide variety of typical dishes and sweets, including Turrón de Doña Pepa, a delicious soft and sweet paste made with eggs, butter, flour, anise, and fruit syrup.

December

La Virgen Inmaculada Concepción. Held in the first week of December, this big five-day event in Chivay and Yanque sees the performance of the local traditional Wititi dance and processions for the patron saint. ✉ *Chivay.*

Great Itineraries

If this will be your first trip to Peru, Cusco and Machu Picchu are practically obligatory. The question is "What else?" And the answer depends on how much time you have and what your interests are. You can combine Machu Picchu with a number of other Andean attractions, the Amazon rainforest, or pre-Inca archaeological sites on the coast. If this is not your first trip to Peru, the last itineraries in this section offer you something a little different.

ESSENTIAL PERU

The former Inca capital of Cusco and citadel of Machu Picchu are two of the most impressive places in South America and the reasons that most people visit Peru. If you only have a week, this is where you should go, but it is easy and highly recommended to combine a Machu Picchu pilgrimage with a visit to the rainforest in the nearby Madre de Dios Province.

DAY 1: LIMA

Lima has more to see than you could possibly pack into a day. You should definitely take a tour of Lima's historic Centro, or give yourself a few hours to explore it on your own, visiting **San Francisco** church and monastery and the **Museo de Arte de Lima (MALI).** In the afternoon, head to Pueblo Libre to visit the **Museo Nacional de Antropología y Arqueología** and the **Museo Rafael Larco Herrera,** or explore Miraflores and visit the **Parque de Amor.** In the evening, stroll around historic Barranco and have dinner there or at the **Huaca Pucllana,** in Miraflores, where you can explore a pre-Inca site before you eat.

DAY 2: CUSCO

From Lima, take an early-morning flight to the ancient Inca capital of **Cusco.** Try to get seats on the left side of the plane for an amazing view of snow-draped peaks toward the end of the flight. You'll want to take it easy upon arriving in Cusco, which is perched at almost 3,353 meters (11,000 feet) above sea level. Take a half-day tour, or visit a couple of sights such as the **Cusco Cathedral, Qorikancha,** the **Museo de Arte Precolombino,** or the **Museo Hilario Mendivil** on your own. Be sure to stop by the **Plaza de Armas** at night, before dining at one of the city's many excellent restaurants.

DAY 3: SACRED VALLEY

Dedicate this day to the sights of the surrounding highlands, starting with **Sacsayhuamán,** the Inca ruins above town. You could do a day trip to the **Sacred Valley,** or spend this night at one of the many hotels located there. The valley holds an array of interesting sites, such as the market town of **Pisac, Chinchero,** and the massive Inca fortress at **Ollantaytambo.** It is also lower, and thus warmer, than Cusco, and lies on the route to Machu Picchu, which means you can sleep a little later if you stay there.

DAYS 4 AND 5: MACHU PICCHU

Enjoy a local site in the morning, then take a Machu Picchu train, which winds its way past Inca ruins and luxuriant forest to the town of **Aguas Calientes.** Check into your hotel, then stroll down the road along the Urubamba River. On Day 5, get up early, and take the bus to **Machu Picchu,** the majestic citadel of the Inca. Head up the steep trail on the left shortly after entering the park, and climb to the upper part of the ruins for a panoramic view before you start exploring. If you're up for a tough hike up a steep, slightly treacherous trail, climb **Huayna Picchu,** the backdrop mountain, for vertiginous views of the ruins and surrounding jungle. **■ TIP→ Admission tickets to hike Huayna Picchu must be purchased months**

in advance for visits during the May–September high season. You may instead opt for the longer hike through the forest to the **Temple of the Moon.** After all the hiking, you should be ready for a late lunch in Aguas Calientes before taking the train and bus back to Cusco.

DAY 6: CUSCO TO LIMA

Take advantage of the morning to visit a site you missed on your first day in Cusco or to visit a few of the city's countless shops and markets. Fly to **Lima** (one hour) early enough to have lunch at one of the city's *cebicherías.* Use the afternoon to visit a museum or another attraction you missed on your first day there.

MADRE DE DIOS EXTENSION

The Essential Peru tour can easily be combined with a visit to the Amazon Basin by taking a short flight from Cusco to the adjacent Madre de Dios region on Day 6.

DAYS 6–8: TAMBOPATA NATIONAL RESERVE

Take an early-morning flight from Cusco to **Puerto Maldonado,** where someone from your nature lodge will meet you and take you to your lodging by boat. Your next three days will be filled with constant exposure to tropical nature on rainforest hikes and boat trips on oxbow lakes.

DAYS 9–10: LIMA

On Day 9, travel by boat to Puerto Maldonado and fly to Lima. You should arrive in time for a late lunch and some sightseeing. On Day 10, visit Lima attractions that you missed on Day 1.

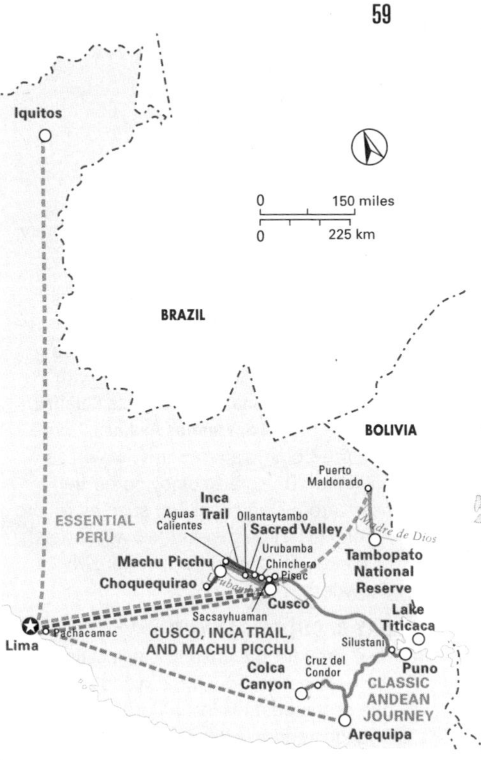

AMAZON RIVER EXTENSION

An alternative to the nature lodges of Madre de Dios is to visit the Amazon River proper, with a three-night river cruise or a stay at one of the nature lodges near Iquitos.

DAY 6: CUSCO TO IQUITOS

Fly to Lima in time for a connection to **Iquitos,** so that you can spend the night in that Amazon port city.

DAYS 7–9: AMAZON CRUISE OR LODGE

Board a riverboat for a three-day cruise up the **Amazon River,** or head to one of the area's nature lodges. You'll explore Amazon tributaries and lakes in small boats on daily excursions and perhaps visit an indigenous village.

DAY 10: IQUITOS TO LIMA

Disembark in Iquitos, and fly directly back to Lima.

Great Itineraries

CLASSIC ANDEAN JOURNEY

DAY 1: LIMA

Follow Day 1 of the Essential Peru itinerary.

DAY 2: AREQUIPA

From Lima, take an early-morning flight to **Arequipa,** a lovely colonial city with a backdrop of snowcapped volcanoes. Explore the city's historic center with its rambling **Monasterio de Santa Catalina** and the **Museo Santuarios Andinos,** home of a pre-Columbian mummy known as "Juanita." Be sure to enjoy some traditional arequipeña cooking, such as *rocoto relleno* (a hot pepper stuffed with beef) or *chupe de camarones* (river prawn chowder).

DAY 3: COLCA CANYON

Rise early for the drive to **Colca Canyon,** the deepest canyon in the world and one of the best places in Peru to spot an Andean condor. After lunch, take a hike, go horseback riding, or relax.

DAYS 4 AND 5: PUNO AND LAKE TITICACA

Rise early, and head to **Cruz del Condor,** the best place to spot those massive birds. Spend the rest of the day traveling overland through a series of Andean landscapes to **Puno,** on Lake Titicaca, the highest navigable lake in the world. Puno's 3,830-meter (12,500-foot) altitude can take your breath away, so have a light dinner, and rest for the day ahead.

Rise early on Day 5 and take a boat tour of **Lake Titicaca,** stopping at one of the **Uros Islands. Isla Taquile,** an island whose indigenous inhabitants are famous for their weaving skills, is also worth a visit. In the afternoon, visit the pre-Inca burial ground and stone *chullpas* at **Sillustani.**

DAY 6: PUNO TO CUSCO

Rise early for a full-day train or bus trip across more Andean landscapes to the ancient Inca capital of **Cusco,** a 330-meter (1,083-foot) drop in altitude. See Day 2 of the Essential Peru itinerary.

DAY 7: CUSCO

Follow Day 3 of the Essential Peru itinerary.

DAYS 8 AND 9: MACHU PICCHU

Follow Days 4 and 5 of the Essential Peru itinerary.

DAY 10: CUSCO TO LIMA

Follow Day 6 of the Essential Peru itinerary.

CUSCO, INCA TRAIL, AND MACHU PICCHU

Travelers in good physical condition can combine Peru's top cultural attractions with an unforgettable hike through phenomenal scenery.

DAY 1: LIMA

Follow Day 1 of the Essential Peru itinerary.

DAY 2: CUSCO

Follow Day 2 of the Essential Peru itinerary.

DAYS 3–6: INCA TRAIL AND MACHU PICCHU

Rise early this morning, and catch the train to Machu Picchu, but get off at Km 82, where the four-day trek on the **Inca Trail** begins. You'll start by following the Urubamba River to the ruins of **Llactapata,** from which you climb slowly to the first campsite, at 2,954 meters (9,691 feet). The next day is the toughest; you'll hike over **Warmiwanusca** pass at 4,198 meters (13,776 feet) and camp at 3,607 meters (11,833 feet). On Day 3 of the trek, you hike over two passes and visit several small Inca ruins. The last day is short, mostly downhill. You'll want to rise very early to reach Machu Picchu's **Inti Punku** (Sun Gate) by sunrise. Spend the morning exploring **Machu Picchu,** then bus down to Aguas Calientes, and check into your hotel.

DAY 7: SACRED VALLEY

On Day 7, sleep in, have a leisurely breakfast; and take an afternoon train to Ollantaytambo. If you spend the night there, explore the fortress above town in the late afternoon, when the crowd thins. But you may opt for spending this night at one of the lodges near Urubamba.

DAY 8: CUSCO TO LIMA

Bus to Cusco, and follow Day 6 of the Essential Peru itinerary.

CHOQUEQUIRAO EXTENSION

If you're up to a more challenging hike, less tourists, and more stunning Inca sites, you should travel from Cusco to Cachora and tackle a grueling two- to three-day trek to Choquequirao. It's a lesser-known lost Incan city similar to Machu Picchu, but without the tourists given its off-the-beaten-path location and level of difficulty. On the first day, you'll have to descend almost 3,200 meters (10,500 feet) to the Apurimac river at 1,200 meters (3,937 feet), and then start your ascent back up on the other side of the canyon. Basic accommodations are provided in the villages en route, with the best guesthouses being in Maranpata, set high at the top of the ridge. It's another three hours on foot to the sites from here, and at least another full day to hike back to Cachora. It's a four-hour taxi ride back to Cusco from there.

NORTH COAST AND MACHU PICCHU

This trip lets you trace the development of Lima's indigenous cultures by combining the pre-Inca archaeological sites of northern Peru with the classic Inca sites of southern Peru.

DAY 1: LIMA

Follow Day 1 of the Essential Peru itinerary.

DAYS 2 AND 3: CHICLAYO

Catch an early flight to the northern city of **Chiclayo,** which lies near some of the country's most important pre-Inca sites. A small, pleasant city near several excellent museums, Chiclayo is noticeably warmer than Lima. Spend two days visiting the nearby pyramids at **Túcume,** the **Museo Nacional Sicán, Museo Nacional Tumbas Reales de Sipán,** and the **Museo Arqueológico Nacional Brüning.**

DAYS 4 AND 5: TRUJILLO

Catch an early flight (40 minutes) to **Trujillo,** an attractive colonial city near the ancient structures of two other pre-Inca cultures. After checking into your hotel, explore the old city, which has some well-preserved colonial and 19th-century architecture. In the afternoon, head to the rambling ruins of **Chan Chan.** On Day 5, visit the archaeological sites of **Huaca de La Luna** and **Huaca del Sol,** as well as the beach and port of **Huanchaco,** where fishermen still use the tiny, pre-Columbian reed boats called *caballitos de totora.*

DAY 6: LIMA

Take a quick flight back to Lima, and visit some of the sights you didn't have time for on Day 1. Be sure to hit Barranco, a lovely area for an evening stroll and dinner.

DAY 7: CUSCO

Follow Day 2 of the Essential Peru itinerary.

DAY 8: SACRED VALLEY

Follow Day 3 of the Essential Peru itinerary.

DAYS 9 AND 10: MACHU PICCHU

Follow Days 4 and 5 of the Essential Peru itinerary.

DAY 11: CUSCO TO LIMA

Follow Day 6 of the Essential Peru itinerary.

Great Itineraries

SOUTHERN COAST AND CORDILLERA BLANCA

This tour combines cultural and natural wonders and takes you through an array of landscapes—from the desert to offshore islands to snowcapped mountains.

DAY 1: LIMA

Follow Day 1 of the Essential Peru itinerary.

DAYS 2 AND 3: ICA

Head south on the Pan-American Highway for four hours to **Ica.** After checking into your hotel, head for the **Huacachina** oasis for a dune-buggy ride or sand boarding, or arrange a tour of one of the nearby wineries.

DAY 4: NAZCA AND PARACAS

In the morning, do the flight over the enigmatic **Nazca Lines.** Then transfer to **Paracas** on the coast. In the afternoon, take a boat tour to the **Ballestas Islands,** where you'll see thousands of sea lions, birds, and tiny Humboldt penguins, as well as the massive candelabra etched on a hillside.

DAY 5: LIMA

The next day, return to **Lima.** If possible, stop at the pre-Inca site of **Pachacamac** on the way. Sightsee and shop in the afternoon, then enjoy a memorable meal at one of the city's great restaurants.

DAYS 6–10: HUARAZ

Travel overland to **Huaraz,** in the country's central Andes, where you'll want to take it easy while you acclimatize. If you're up for it, spend the next four days trekking on the Santa Cruz circuit, a gorgeous route into the heart of the **Cordillera Blanca** or take the Cordillera Huayhuash circuit, one of the world's most beautiful high-altitude hikes, whose full circuit takes up to nine days to complete. If you're not up for multiday treks, spend a couple of days doing less strenuous hikes to one of the Cordillera's turquoise lakes, and visit the ruins of **Chavín de Huantar.**

DAY 11: HUARAZ TO LIMA

Travel overland back to Lima. Follow Day 6 of the Essential Peru itinerary once you arrive.

NORTHERN ANDES AND CULTURES

The Northern Andes have some of Peru's most spectacular landscapes and the second most impressive Inca site after Machu Picchu: Kuélap. If you want to stray from the beaten path, explore this remote and fascinating region.

DAY 1: LIMA

Follow Day 1 of the Essential Peru itinerary.

DAY 2: JAEN AND CHACHAPOYAS

Catch the 90-minute flight to the northern city of **Jaen,** and take ground transportation (four hours) to **Chachapoyas.** Spend the afternoon exploring that attractive highland town.

DAY 3: CHACHAPOYAS AND GOCHTA

Rise early, and take a tour to **Gochta,** one of the world's highest waterfalls, which involves several hours of hiking. If you're not up for the hike, take a tour to see the burial monuments of the pre-Inca Chachapoyas culture.

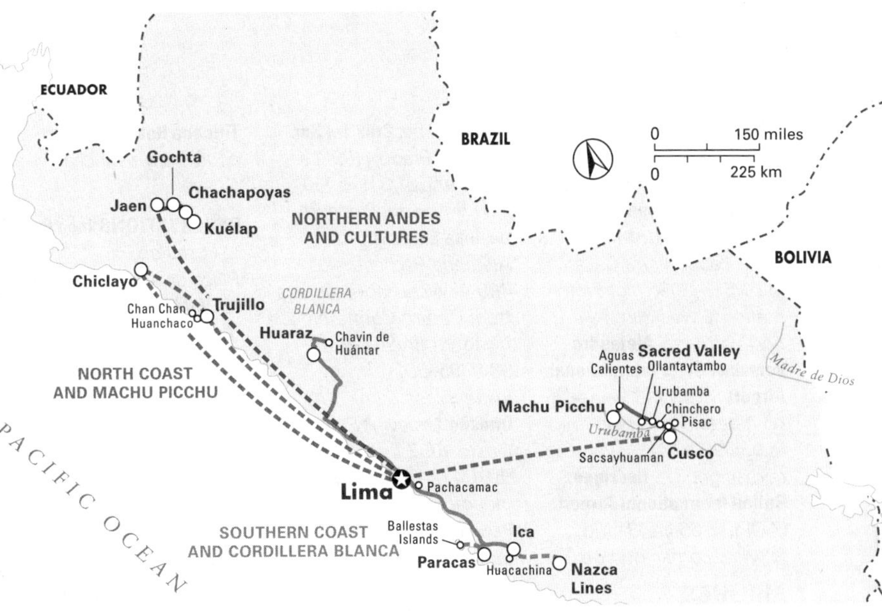

DAY 4: KUÉLAP

Rise early for the four-hour drive up the Utcubamba Valley to the massive pre-Inca fortress of **Kuélap.** Spend several hours exploring that impressive site, which contains more than 400 structures, before returning to Chachapoyas.

DAY 5: CHACHAPOYAS TO LIMA

Rise early for the four-hour drive to Jaen and the flight to Lima. Spend the afternoon visiting sights you missed on Day 1. A longer, archaeology-intensive alternative is to continue by land to Chiclayo, and spend Days 6–9 following the itinerary for Days 2–5 of the North Coast and Machu Picchu tour.

DAY 6 OR 10: LIMA

Fly to Lima, and follow Day 6 of the Essential Peru itinerary.

KUÉLAP TIPS:

- Kuélap is located in a cloud forest, so wear a light waterproof jacket and bring a sweater.

- The trip to Kuélap includes a scenic-but-scary cable-car ride (20 soles) as well as a 10-minute hike. You will need to climb jagged stone steps sometimes covered in moss, so wear sturdy hiking boots.

- To visit Kuélap responsibly, visit outside peak season, if possible. Also, consider taking the old route rather than the cable car to support the small communities that are now bypassed.

Contacts

 Air

AIRPORTS

Aeropuerto Internacional Jorge Chávez. (*LIM*). ⊠ *Av. Faucett s/n, Callao* ☎ *01/511–6055 flight information* ⊕ *www.lima-airport.com/eng.* **Alejandro Velasco Astete International Airport .** (*CUZ*). ⊠ *Velasco Astete s/n, Cusco* ☎ *084/222–611* ⊕ *www.corpac.gob.pe.* **Rodríguez Ballón International Airport.** (*AQP*). ☎ *054/443–460* ⊕ *www.corpac.gob.pe.*

AIRLINES

LATAM. ⊠ *José Pardo 513, 1st fl., Miraflores* ☎ *866/435–9526 in North America, 01/213–8200 in Lima* ⊕ *www.latam.com.* **Star Perú.** ⊠ *José Pardo 485, Miraflores* ☎ *1–757/550–1526 in North America, 01/705–9000 in Lima* ⊕ *www.starperu.com.* **Viva Air Perú.** ☎ *08/005–5786 from Peru, 844/569–7126 from U.S.* ⊕ *www.vivaair.com.*

GROUND TRANSPORTATION

Airport Express Lima. ⊠ *Av. Jose Larco 812 (with San Martin), Miraflores* ☎ *+51/1446-5539* ⊕ *www.airportexpresslima.com.*

 Bus

CIVA. ⊠ *Javier Prado Este 1155, La Victoria* ☎ *01/418–1111* ⊕ *www.civa.com.pe.* **Cruz del Sur.** ⊠ *Javier Prado 1109, La Victoria* ☎ *01/311–5050* ⊕ *www.cruzdelsur.com.pe.* **Inka Express.** ⊠ *Av. Alameda Pachacutek 499-A, Wanchaq* ✣ *Across from Centro Confraternidad* ☎ *084/247–887, 984/705–301* ⊕ *www.inkaexpress.com.* **Ormeño.** ⊠ *Javier Prado Oeste 1057, La Victoria* ☎ *01/472–5000* ⊕ *www.grupo-ormeno.com.pe.* **Peru Hop.** ⊠ *812 Avenida Larco, Miraflores* ☎ *51/124–221–40* ⊕ *www.peruhop.com.*

Car

EMERGENCY SERVICES

Touring Club del Perú. ⊠ *Trinidad Morán 698, Lince* ☎ *01/611–9999 emergencies, 01/611–9999 information* ⊕ *www.touring.pe.*

Ride-Sharing

Beat. ⊕ *www.thebeat.co.en.* **Cabify.** ⊕ *cabify.com/en/peru/lima.*

 Train

TRAIN STATIONS

Estación Poroy—PeruRail (Cusco–Machu Picchu Route). ⊠ *Calle Roldan s/n, Poroy, Cusco.* **Estación Wanchaq—PeruRail (Cusco–Lake Titicaca Route).** ⊠ *Pachacutec s/n, Wanchaq, Cusco.*

RESERVATIONS

Inca Rail. ⊠ *Portal de Panes 105, Plaza de Armas, Cusco* ☎ *084/581–860 sales and reservations* ⊕ *www.incarail.com.* **PeruRail.** ⊠ *Portal de Carnes 214, Plaza de Armas, Cusco* ☎ *084/581–414 call center* ⊕ *www.perurail.com.*

Health

HEALTH WARNINGS

Centers for Disease Control and Prevention. (*CDC*). ☎ *800/232–4636 international travelers' health line* ⊕ *www.cdc.gov/travel.* **World Health Organization.** (*WHO*). ⊕ *www.who.int.*

Lodging

APARTMENT RENTALS

Airbnb.com. ⊕ *www.airbnb.com.* **HomeAway.** ☎ *877/228–3145* ⊕ *www.homeaway.com.* **Inn Peru.** ☎ *01/998–578–350 in Peru* ⊕ *www.innperu.com.*

U.S. Embassy

United States. ⊠ *Av. La Encalada, Cuadra 17, Surco* ☎ *01/618–2000* ⊕ *pe.usembassy.gov.*

Chapter 3

LIMA

Updated by
Mike Gasparovic

 Sights	 Restaurants	 Hotels	 Shopping	 Nightlife
★★★★☆	★★★★★	★★★★★	★★★★☆	★★★★★

WELCOME TO LIMA

TOP REASONS TO GO

★ **South America's Best Food:** From *cebiche* (raw fish marinated in lime juice) to Japanese-Peruvian fusion, Lima's foodie scene is red-hot, drawing a million gastro-tourists a year with the best bites on the continent.

★ **Lima Baroque:** In the city's historic Centro, churches such as the Iglesia de San Francisco have elaborate facades and mind-blowing ornamentation.

★ **Cool Digs:** More than 30 archaeological sites dot Lima's neighborhoods, including the pre-Inca Huaca Pucllana in Miraflores and the Huaca Huallamarca temple in San Isidro.

★ **Handicrafts:** Avenidas La Paz and Petit Thouars in Miraflores are shop-till-you-drop destinations for crafty types. Come energized: these stalls sell everything from alpaca textiles to silver-filigree jewelry.

★ **Ocean Views:** Like to listen to the waves? Lima's *malecones* (seaside promenades) in neighborhoods like Miraflores and Barranco look out over stunning Pacific vistas.

Most of Lima's colonial-era churches and mansions are in El Centro, along the streets surrounding the Plaza de Armas. From there, an expressway called Paseo de la República (aka Vía Expresa) or a traffic-clogged thoroughfare called Avenida Arequipa takes you south to San Isidro and Miraflores, two upscale neighborhoods where you'll find the bulk of the city's dining and lodging options. Southeast of Miraflores is Barranco, where the colonial architecture is complemented by art galleries, ocean views, and bohemian charm.

1 **El Centro.** The Plaza Mayor (the city's main square) and nearby Plaza San Martín are two of the grandest public spaces in South America. Nearly every block has something to catch your eye, whether it's the soaring *churrigueresco* portal of a 17th-century church or the enclosed wooden balconies on a posh colonial palace. Unfortunately, some parts of the neighborhood need a face-lift.

2 **San Isidro.** The city's nicest residential neighborhood surrounds Parque El Olivar, a grove of olive trees, where half-timbered homes are set among the gnarled, 400-year-old trunks. Nearby are a pre-Columbian pyramid and the city's oldest golf course, but the main attraction for travelers is the district's selection of restaurants and hotels.

3 **Miraflores.** Part tony suburb, part tourist mecca, Miraflores has the city's best selection of hotels, restaurants, bars, and boutiques, which draw locals from all over the city. Visit El Parque del Amor and the string of other green spaces along the malecón: the view from the coastal cliffs is unforgettable.

4 **Barranco.** The city's most bohemian and also most charming neighborhood, Barranco combines historic architecture, nightlife, a vibrant art scene, and gorgeous Pacific vistas. Bars and eateries surround the Parque Municipal and the nearby Bajada de los Baños, a cobblestone path leading down to the beach. In the evening, this area fills with young people looking to party.

5 **Pueblo Libre.** Home to Lima's best museum, the Museo Arqueológico Rafael Larco Herrera, this neighborhood retains its village feel from the days before it was swallowed by the all-devouring Lima sprawl.

EL CENTRO
1
PLAZA BOLÍVAR
EL AGUSTINO
BREÑA
SAN COSME
SANTA BEATRIZ
LA VICTORIA
PUEBLO LIBRE
5
JESÚS MARÍA
VISCAS
SAN LUIS
LINCE
MAGDALENA
SAN ISIDRO
2
NUEVA FLORIDA
SAN BORJA
PLAZA MARQUINA
SURQUILLO
3
MIRAFLORES
SURCO
4
BARRANCO
SAN ROQUE
Pacific Ocean
Avenida Argentina
Avenida Colonial
Avenida Alfonso Ugarte
Avenida Abancay
Av. República de Venezuela
Avenida Arica
Av. Almirante Miguel Grau
Av. Nicolás de Ayllón
Avenida Brasil
Vía Expresa Paseo de la República
Avenida Manco Cápac
Av. Mariano Cornejo
Av. Simon Bolívar
Av. Universitaria
Avenida Nicolás Arriola
Av. Petit Thouars
Av. Arequipa
Av. Álvarez de Arenales
Avenida La Marina
Av. Faustino Sánchez Carrión
Avenida Javier Prado Este
Avenida Javier Prado Oeste
Circuito de Playas
Av. Augusto Pérez Aranibar
Avenida Angamos Este
Av. Angamos Oeste
Avenida República de Panamá
Avenida de Tomás Marsano
Av. Alfredo Benavides
0
1 mi
0
1 km

For almost 300 years, Lima stood as the seat of Spanish power in South America, the stronghold from which a king's decrees ruled an entire continent. Flash-forward to the new millennium. Today, Peru's capital is a vibrant, manic, dirty, traffic-choked, crazily beautiful, endlessly fascinating megalopolis of 10 million people, with an indomitable fighter's spirit and an against-all-odds hope for the future.

It's easy to dis Lima. Homicidal drivers and blaring car horns, pesky vendors, and sooty fumes: the city does its best to make a bad impression. Its own writers have fulminated against it, dubbing it "*Lima la horrible*." And yet, stand before the jalousied *casonas* (big houses) of the Plaza de Armas at nightfall, or the cliffs of Barranco with the waves lapping in the distance, and you'll feel something stir. Lima, like no other city, gets under your skin.

The city's history has been as seismic as the earthquakes that periodically shake it. Founded by Francisco Pizarro as La Ciudad de Los Reyes—The City of Kings—in 1535, it was for centuries the capital of the Viceroyalty of Peru, which stretched from present-day Colombia to Argentina, and whose silver and gold, flowing into Lima's coffers from the mines at Potosí, made it one of the richest cities in the world. After being liberated from Spain by José de San Martín in 1821, the town was visited by an odd assortment of notables, from Charles Darwin to Herman Melville, who called its mist-shrouded streets "the strangest, saddest thou can'st see."

Then came expansion. The walls that had surrounded the downtown were demolished in 1870, making way for a burgeoning population. A former hacienda yielded to the opulent residences of San Isidro; the construction of tree-lined Avenida Arequipa brought beachgoers to Miraflores and Barranco. Suddenly, following World War II, everything exploded. Migrations from the Andes spiked. Terrorist convulsions in the 1980s caused whole districts to spring up, sometimes literally overnight. By 1990, Lima's population had surged to over 6 million. Crime intensified; traffic slowed to a crawl.

Fast-forward three decades. Today, the once-dystopic capital is a bustling urban hive, with all the excitement—and problems—of modern megacities. Lack of planning and faulty infrastructure still cause headaches, and too many *limeños* live in impoverished *pueblos jóvenes* (improvised shantytowns on the city's hillsides). But Lima makes up for its chaos with its buoyant energy and never-throw-in-the-towel spirit.

Since 2000, Peru's stability and economic resurgence have injected new life into its capital. Gastronomy, mining, and textiles are booming, flooding the city with cash. Residents who used to steer clear of the historic *centro* now happily stroll its streets. Who knows? Perhaps Peru's City of Kings is on its way to becoming regal once more.

Planning

When to Go

The weather in Lima is a mirror inverse of North America's. Summer, from December to April, is largely sunny, with daytime temperatures well above 80°F and pleasant, if humid, nights and mornings. From May to November, by contrast, the city turns cloudy and gray, with morning fog and nighttime temperatures that occasionally dip down around 50°F. The coastal region gets little precipitation, so you'll rarely find your plans ruined by rain, but there are winter days when you'll have to endure a miserable foggy drizzle locals call *la garúa*.

Getting Here and Around

AIR

If you're flying to Peru, you'll touch down at Aeropuerto Internacional Jorge Chávez, in the port district of El Callao. Once you're in the main terminal, the crowds can be overwhelming, so do yourself a favor, and arrange for a transfer through your hotel. You can also hire a cab from one of the companies stationed in the corridor outside of customs, or take an Airport Express Lima bus, which drops passengers off at seven major hotels in the city.

Various airlines handle domestic flights, so getting to and from major tourist destinations is easy. LATAM is the carrier with the most national flights, with a dozen per day to Cusco and several daily departures to Arequipa, Cajamarca, Chiclayo, Iquitos, Juliaca (Puno), Piura, Puerto Maldonado, Trujillo, and Tumbes. Star Perú is relatively inexpensive and flies to Cajamarca, Chiclayo, Cusco, Huánuco, Iquitos, Pucallpa, Puerto Maldonado, and Tarapoto. Viva Air Perú, an even more affordable discount airline, flies to Arequipa, Cajamarca, Chiclayo, Cusco, Iquitos, Piura, Tacna, and Tarapoto.

AIRPORT Aeropuerto Internacional Jorge Chávez. ✉ *Av. Faucett s/n, Callao* ☎ *01/517–3100* 🌐 *www.lima-airport.com.*

CARRIERS LATAM. ✉ *Av. Santa Cruz 771, inside Wong supermarket, Miraflores* ☎ *01/213–8200* 🌐 *www.latam.com.* **Star Perú.** ✉ *Av. José Pardo 495, Miraflores* ☎ *01/705–9090* 🌐 *www.starperu.com.* **Viva Air Perú.** ✉ *Av. Faucett s/n, Callao* ☎ *01/705–0107* 🌐 *www.vivaair.com.*

AIRPORT TAXIS Airport Express Lima. ✉ *Av. Faucett s/n, Callao* ☎ *01/446–5539* 🌐 *www.airportexpresslima.com.* **CMV Taxi.** ✉ *Av. Paz Soldán 170, Of. 701, San Isidro* ☎ *01/219–0266* 🌐 *www.cmvtaxi.pe.* **Taxi Green.** ☎ *998/267–148* 🌐 *www.taxigreen.com.pe.*

BUS

Lima's bus system is notorious. Full of rattletrap vehicles and insane drivers, it's also extremely confusing for non-locals who don't know the city's street names. True, fares are cheap—usually S/1–S/2 for a ride—but don't expect much in the way of comfort. You also need to watch your belongings, as pickpockets and bag-slashers can be a problem. A better way to travel between Barranco, Miraflores, and El Centro is the Metropolitano, a modern, high-speed bus line that runs down the middle of the Paseo de la

República to the underground Estación Central in front of the Sheraton Lima Hotel. Service is from 6 am to 10 pm, and each trip costs S/2.50. Be warned, however: the buses turn into sardine cans during rush hour. The system uses rechargeable electronic cards you can buy from a vending machine for S/5. Stations on Avenida Bolognesi in Barranco and Avenida Benavides in Miraflores are walking distance from hotels, but the route is far from most lodgings in San Isidro.

CONTACTS Metropolitano. ☎ *01/428–3333* 🌐 *www.metropolitano.com.pe.*

CAR

Before renting a car in Lima, stop and reconsider. Aside from the demented drivers and horrendous traffic, parking can be a hassle, and you can get anywhere you need to go with other modes of transport. If you do decide to brave it, remember that most rental agencies also offer the services of a driver. Avis, Budget, and Hertz have branches at Jorge Chávez Airport that are open 24 hours, as well as additional offices in Miraflores.

CONTACTS Avis. ✉ *Av. Faucett s/n, Callao* ☎ *01/207–6000* 🌐 *www.avis.com.* **Budget.** ✉ *Av. José Larco 998, Miraflores* ☎ *01/447–4229* 🌐 *www.budgetperu.com.* **Hertz.** ✉ *Pje. Tello 215, Miraflores* ☎ *01/445–5716* 🌐 *www.hertzperu.com.pe.*

TAXI

For most visitors, taxis are the best way to get around Lima. A caveat, however: in Peru the vehicles are unmetered, meaning you have to negotiate the fare with the driver before getting in (a good rule of thumb is to offer 75 percent of the initial price quoted). This problem can be obviated by using an app like Uber or EasyTaxi or by taking one of the black taxis that service the tourist hotels (the concierge will be glad to call one for you). A journey between two adjacent neighborhoods should cost between S/8 and S/12; longer trips run between S/20 and S/50. When calculating travel times, be sure to factor in Lima's morning (7–9:30 am) and evening (4–8 pm) rush hours, which are horrendous.

CONTACTS Taxi Peru Remisse. ☎ *01/480–0500* 🌐 *www.taxiperuremisse.com.* **Taxi Seguro.** ☎ *01/492–6283* 🌐 *www.taxiseguro.online.*

Emergencies

Several clinics have English-speaking staff, including the Clínica Anglo-Americana in San Isidro. There is a pharmacy on every other (or every third) block of Lima's main streets.

HOSPITALS Clínica Anglo Americana. ✉ *Cl. Alfredo Salazar 350, San Isidro* ☎ *01/616–8900* 🌐 *www.clinicaangloamericana.pe.*

PHARMACIES Inkafarma. ✉ *Av. José Larco 495B, Miraflores* ☎ *987/392–690* 🌐 *www.inkafarma.pe.* **Mifarma.** ✉ *Av. José Larco 401, Miraflores* ☎ *01/612–5000* 🌐 *www.mifarma.com.pe.*

Health and Safety

Peru's tap water is iffy, so drink only bottled water, and avoid unwashed lettuce and other raw vegetables. When eating cebiche and *tiradito* (thinly sliced, marinated fish), both made with raw seafood, the citric acid in the lime-juice marinade is efficient at killing bacteria, but because these dishes are often prepared to order, it's best to let yours stew in the juice a bit before eating.

As for Lima's streets, take locals' reports of ubiquitous *rateros* (thieves) with a grain of salt. Yes, opportunity theft can be a problem, but assault and other violent crimes are rare, at least in the areas tourists would have reason to visit. Remember you're in a developing Latin American country, and take the appropriate precautions. El Centro is generally safe during the day, but can be dicey at night, so stick to the two main plazas and Jirón de la Unión (the pedestrian thoroughfare that connects them). Residential neighborhoods such as Miraflores, San Isidro, and Barranco are very secure due to a strong police presence, but be on guard when away from the main streets. The biggest problem you're likely to encounter is pickpockets in crowded markets and on public transportation; keep your wallets and purses in front of you at all times.

In case of trouble, contact the Tourist Police (☎ *0800–22221*). English-speaking officers will help you report a crime. For more serious emergencies, call the police (☎ *105*) or fire department (☎ *116*).

Hotels

There's no shortage of lodging in Lima. Across the city, flags wave above the doorways to hotels, indicating that international travelers are welcome. If you have some money to spend, the capital has some astonishing accommodations. For something special, bypass the towers of glass and steel, and opt instead for such charmers as the Country Club Lima Hotel, Hotel B, or Second Home Peru. *Hotel reviews have been shortened. For full information, visit Fodors.com.*

WHAT IT COSTS in Nuevo Soles

$	$$	$$$	$$$$
HOTELS			
under S/250	S/250–S/500	S/501–S/800	over S/800

Restaurants

Lima has long been a popular destination among foodies, but its dining scene is now hotter than ever. Two of the city's eateries were listed in San Pellegrino's World's 50 Best Restaurants list for 2019; ten figure in the 50 Best Restaurants in Latin America (including the number-one and-two slots); and the World Travel Awards has named Peru the World's Leading Culinary Destination for seven years running. Nor is the country's culinary bounty just for the expense-account set. Midrange and even budget options here are frequently better than top-shelf eateries in many North American towns. In Lima, as elsewhere, folks vote with their feet, so if you're wandering around and see a place that seems busy, go ahead and get a table: it's probably good.

WHAT IT COSTS in Nuevo Soles

$	$$	$$$	$$$$
RESTAURANTS			
under S/35	S/35–S/50	S/51–S/65	over S/65

Tours

Bike Tours of Lima
BICYCLE TOURS | If you prefer to pedal, this company offers half-day bike tours of Miraflores and San Isidro or Barranco, as well as a full-day tour that includes the historic El Centro. ✉ *Cl. Las Camelias, Parque Combate de Abtao, San Isidro* ☎ *935/679–594* 🌐 *biketoursoflima.com* 🎫 *From $30.*

Ecocruceros
BOAT TOURS | Wildlife enthusiasts will enjoy the half-day boat tour to the Islas Palomino, off the coast of El Callao and home to more than 4,000 sea lions and abundant bird life. This is a chilly trip from June to December, but you can

swim with the sea lions from January to May. ✉ *Jr. Manco Capac 133, Callao* ☎ *01/226–8530* 🌐 *www.ecocruceros.com* 🎫 *From $59.*

LimaVision

GUIDED TOURS | LimaVision offers the best selection of city tours, by day or night, including a full-day excursion that combines a city tour with a visit to the ruins of Pachacamac. The company also offers a Peruvian *caballos de paso* horse show, a gastronomic tour, and a full-day tour to the ruins of Caral—the oldest urban center in the Americas. ✉ *Cl. Chiclayo 444, Miraflores* ☎ *01/447–7710* 🌐 *www.limavision.com* 🎫 *From $35.*

Mirabus

BUS TOURS | This company offers a variety of tours on open-top double-decker buses, from the classic city tour to a selection of night tours, including one that hits all the highlights downtown. Mirabus also runs tours to the pre-Columbian ruins of Pachacamac or to the Palomino Islands near Callao. Most tours depart from Calle Mártir José Olaya, near La Lucha Sanguchería in Miraflores's Parque Kennedy. ✉ *Cl. Mártir José Olaya 190, Parque Kennedy, Miraflores* ☎ *01/242–6699* 🌐 *www.mirabusperu.com* 🎫 *From $15.*

Visitor Information

Travelers can find information about Lima and the rest of Peru at iPerú, which has English- and Spanish-language materials. The city runs the Oficina de Información Turística, or Tourist Information Office, in the rear of the Municipalidad de Lima.

INFORMATION iPerú. ✉ *Av. Jorge Basadre 610, San Isidro* ☎ *01/421–1627* 🌐 *www.peru.travel* ✉ *Larcomar, Malecón de la Reserva and Av. José Larco, Level 2, Stand 225, Miraflores* ☎ *01/234–0340* 🌐 *www.peru.travel.* **Oficina de Información Turística - Bienvenido a Lima.** ✉ *Pje. Nicolás de Ribera 145, El Centro* ☎ *01/632–1542* 🌐 *www.visitalima.pe.*

El Centro

In colonial times, Lima was the seat of power for the Viceroyalty of Peru, which ruled over territory extending from Panama to Chile. With power came money, as is evident from the grand scale on which everything was built. The finely carved doorways of some Lima mansions stand two stories high. At least half a dozen churches would be classified as cathedrals in any other city. And the Plaza de Armas, the sprawling main square, is spectacular.

History, however, has not always been kind to the neighborhood known as El Centro. Earthquakes struck in 1687 and 1746, leveling many of the buildings surrounding the Plaza de Armas. Other landmarks, such as the Iglesia de San Augustín, were nearly destroyed by artillery fire in skirmishes that have plagued the capital. But many buildings are simply the victims of neglect. It's heartbreaking to see the wall on a colonial mansion crumbling or an intricately carved balcony splintered beyond repair. But the city government has recently made an effort to restore its historic center. After years of decline, things are steadily improving.

An unhurried visit to the historic district's main attractions takes a full day, with at least an hour devoted to the Museo de Arte de Lima. ■ **TIP→ Make sure to take the guided tour of the Convento de San Francisco, and don't miss the Plaza San Martín.**

GETTING AROUND

If you're in Lima for any length of time, chances are you're staying in Miraflores, Barranco, or San Isidro—all a quick taxi ride from El Centro. As taxis usually take the expressway, you'll be downtown in 20–30 minutes. (You can also take the Metropolitano, which is slightly faster.) The best way to get around El Centro once you're there is on foot; the historic area is quite compact.

Sights

Barrio Chino

NEIGHBORHOOD | A ceremonial arch at the corner of Jirones Ucayali and Andahuaylas marks the entrance to Lima's compact Chinatown, which consists of ten square blocks of markets and *chifas* (Peruvian-Chinese restaurants). Of the latter, the best are Chifa San Joy Lao, which dates from 1927, and Salón Capón and Wa Lok on Jirón Paruro. ✉ *Jr. Ucayali and Jr. Andahuaylas, El Centro.*

★ Casa de Aliaga

HOUSE | From the outside, you'd never guess this was one of Lima's most opulent addresses. Commonly known as Casa de Aliaga, this stunning example of Spanish-colonial architecture a block from the Plaza de Armas was built in 1535 by Jerónimo de Aliaga, one of Pizarro's officers, and has been continuously inhabited by his descendants ever since. Each room boasts a different period décor, from colonial to republican, and Jerónimo's German-made sword is still on display in one of the salons. To visit, you must hire an officially approved guide or go as part of a city tour. ✉ *Jr. de la Unión 224, El Centro* ☎ *01/427–7736* 🌐 *www.casadealiaga.com* 🎫 *S/50.*

Casa de Correos y Telégrafos

GOVERNMENT BUILDING | Inaugurated in 1897, this regal structure looks more like a palace than a post office. You can buy a postcard or send a package, but most people come to admire the exuberance of an era when no one thought twice about placing bronze angels atop a civic building. At one time, locals deposited letters in the mouth of the bronze lion by the front doors. About half of the building is given over to the Casa de la Gastronomía Peruana, dedicated to the country's culinary traditions, which charges admission. The museum entrance is on Jirón Conde Superunda, whereas the post office entrance is on Jirón Camaná. ✉ *Jr. Camaná 157, El Centro* ☎ *01/426–7624* 🎫 *S/3.*

Casa Riva-Agüero

HOUSE | A pair of balconies with *celosías*—intricate wood screens through which ladies could watch passersby unobserved—grace the facade of this rambling mansion from 1760. Step inside, and the downtown traffic fades away as you stroll across the stone courtyard and admire the ancient galleries and woodwork. Peru's Catholic University, which administers the landmark, uses it for changing folk-art exhibitions, but the real reason to come is for a glimpse into a colonial-era home. **■ TIP→ The house still retains many of its original neoclassical and Second Empire furnishings.** ✉ *Jr. Camaná 459, El Centro* ☎ *01/626–6600* 🌐 *ira.pucp.edu.pe/el-instituto/casa-riva-aguero/sobre-la-casa-de-riva-aguero* 🎫 *S/2* ⏲ *Closed weekends.*

★ Casa Torre Tagle

HOUSE | This mansion sums up the graceful style of the early 18th century. Flanked by a pair of elegant balconies, the stone entrance is as expertly carved as that of any of the city's churches. The patio is a jewel of the Andalusian baroque, with slender columns supporting delicate Moorish arabesques. The Casa Torre Tagle currently holds offices of the Foreign Ministry and is open to the public only on weekends, when you can check out the tiled ceilings of the ground floor and see the house's 18th-century carriage. Across the street is Casa Goyeneche, which was built some 40 years later in 1771, and was clearly influenced by the rococo movement. ✉ *Jr. Ucayali 363, El Centro* ☎ *01/204–2400* 🌐 *www.rree.gob.pe/torretagle360/SitePages/index.html* 🎫 *Free* ⏲ *Closed weekdays.*

Catedral

RELIGIOUS SITE | In its nearly 500-year history, Lima's cathedral has been torn down, built back up, razed by earthquakes, shot at, hollowed out, and remodeled too many times to count. Miraculously, however, it's still here, and today shines more resplendently than

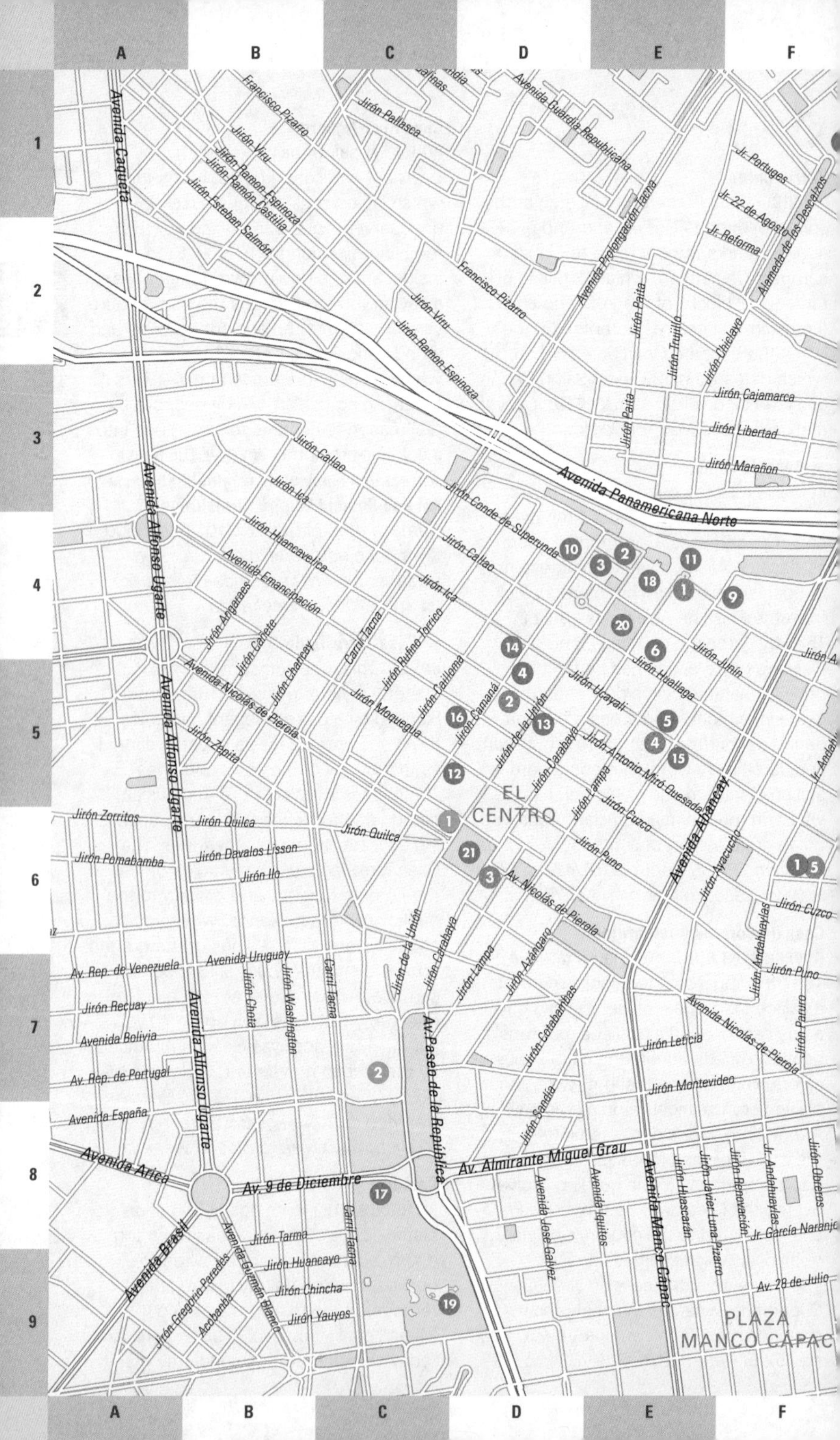

A
B
C
D
E
F
1
2
3
4
5
6
7
8
9
EL CENTRO
PLAZA MANCO CÁPAC
Avenida Caquetá
Francisco Pizarro
Jirón Pallasca
Avenida Guardia Republicana
Jirón Viru
Jirón Ramon Espinoza
Jirón Ramón Castilla
Jirón Esteban Salmón
Avenida Prolongación Tacna
Jr. Portuges
Jr. 22 de Agosto
Jr. Reforma
Alameda de los Descalzos
Jirón Paita
Jirón Trujillo
Jirón Chiclayo
Jirón Cajamarca
Jirón Libertad
Jirón Marañon
Avenida Panamericana Norte
Jirón Callao
Jirón Ica
Jirón Huancavelica
Avenida Emancipación
Jirón Conde de Superunda
Avenida Alfonso Ugarte
Jirón Angaraes
Jirón Cañete
Jirón Chancay
Carril Tacna
Jirón Rufino Torrico
Jirón Cailloma
Jirón Camaná
Jirón de la Unión
Jirón Carabaya
Jirón Lampa
Jirón Moquegua
Avenida Nicolás de Pierola
Jirón Zepita
Jirón Ucayali
Jirón Junín
Jirón Huallaga
Jirón Antonio Miró Quesada
Avenida Abancay
Jirón Cuzco
Jirón Puno
Jirón Ayacucho
Jirón Zorritos
Jirón Quilca
Jirón Pomabamba
Jirón Davalos Lisson
Jirón Ilo
Av. Nicolás de Pierola
Jirón Andahuaylas
Jirón Cuzco
Jirón Puno
Av. Rep. de Venezuela
Avenida Uruguay
Jirón Chota
Jirón Washington
Jirón Recuay
Avenida Bolivia
Av. Rep. de Portugal
Avenida España
Av. Paseo de la República
Jirón Azángaro
Jirón Cotabambas
Jirón Sandia
Jirón Leticia
Jirón Montevideo
Avenida Nicolás de Pierola
Jirón Paruro
Avenida Arica
Av. 9 de Diciembre
Av. Almirante Miguel Grau
Avenida Manco Cápac
Avenida Jose Galvez
Avenida Iquitos
Jirón Huascarán
Jirón Javier Luna Pizarro
Jirón Renovación
Jr. Andahuaylas
Jirón Obreros
Jr. García Naranjo
Av. 28 de Julio
Avenida Brasil
Jirón Gregorio Paredes
Acobamba
Avenida Guzmán Blanco
Jirón Tarma
Jirón Huancayo
Jirón Chincha
Jirón Yauyos

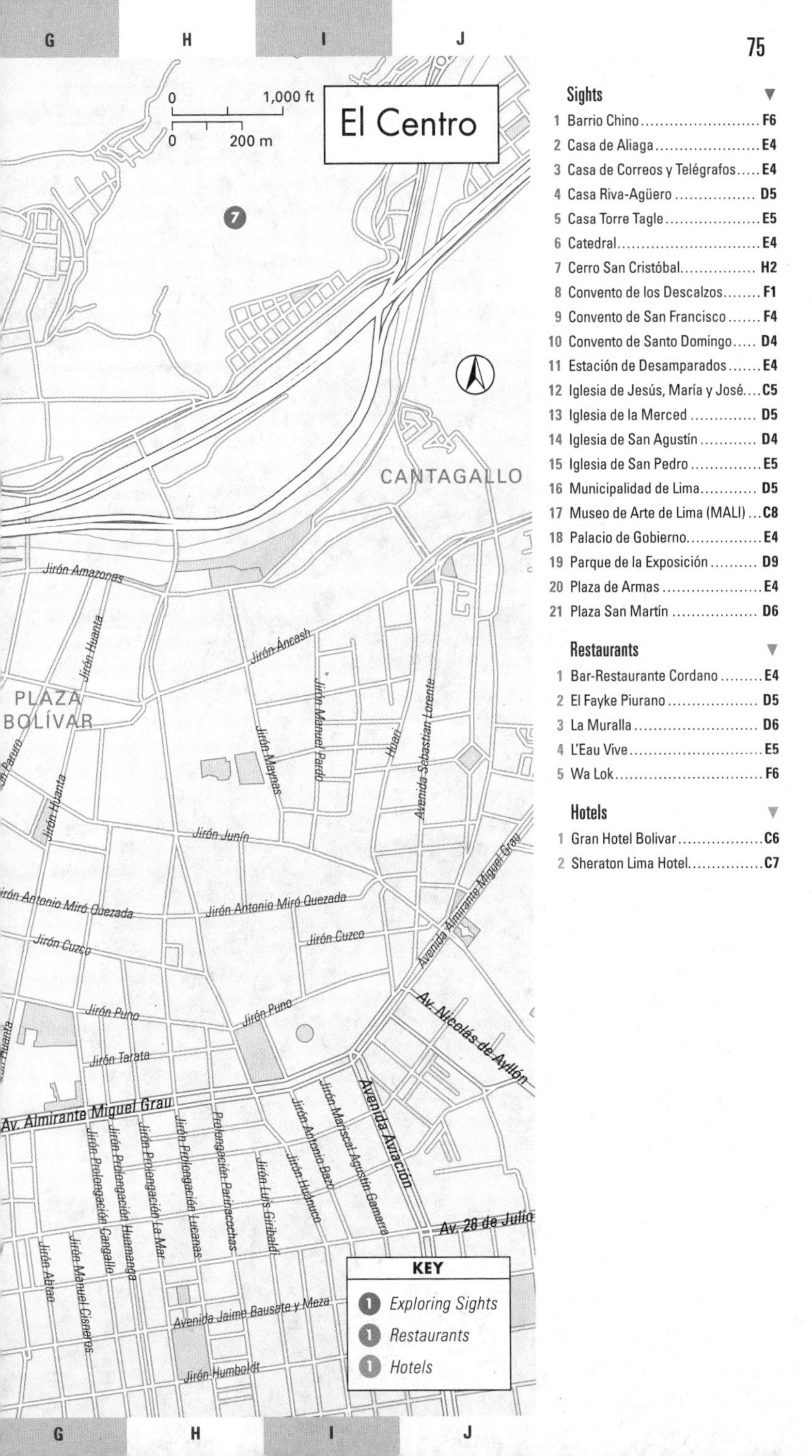

Sights

1 Barrio Chino F6
2 Casa de Aliaga E4
3 Casa de Correos y Telégrafos E4
4 Casa Riva-Agüero D5
5 Casa Torre Tagle E5
6 Catedral E4
7 Cerro San Cristóbal H2
8 Convento de los Descalzos F1
9 Convento de San Francisco F4
10 Convento de Santo Domingo D4
11 Estación de Desamparados E4
12 Iglesia de Jesús, María y José C5
13 Iglesia de la Merced D5
14 Iglesia de San Agustín D4
15 Iglesia de San Pedro E5
16 Municipalidad de Lima D5
17 Museo de Arte de Lima (MALI) C8
18 Palacio de Gobierno E4
19 Parque de la Exposición D9
20 Plaza de Armas E4
21 Plaza San Martín D6

Restaurants

1 Bar-Restaurante Cordano E4
2 El Fayke Piurano D5
3 La Muralla D6
4 L'Eau Vive E5
5 Wa Lok F6

Hotels

1 Gran Hotel Bolivar C6
2 Sheraton Lima Hotel C7

Did You Know?

For more than 400 years, Lima's cathedral has undergone numerous reconstructions and face-lifts thanks to earthquakes.

ever, despite its hodgepodge of artistic styles and endless, meddling restorations. The church visitors see today is actually the basilica's fourth incarnation, reconstructed after the earthquakes of 1687 and 1746. The facade impresses with its stately Renaissance portal and neoclassical bell towers, but the interior is where the real action's at. Here, under arched ceiling vaults traced with fretwork and delicately carved choir stalls, you'll find crypts for Lima luminaries and recently excavated mass tombs for commoners. Crowning it all is the mausoleum of Francisco Pizarro himself, complete with the lead box that once held his skull. Recorded tours in English are available. ✉ *Jr. Carabaya s/n, El Centro* ✥ *East side of Plaza de Armas* ☎ *01/427–9647* 🎫 *S/10* ⏲ *Closed Sat. after 1 and Sun. before 1.*

Cerro San Cristóbal

VIEWPOINT | Rising over the northeastern edge of the city is this massive hill, recognizable from the cross at its peak—a replica of the one once placed there by Pizarro. On a clear day, more common during the southern summer, the views of the city below are lovely. **■ TIP→ The neighborhood at the base of the hill is sketchy, so hire a taxi or take a tour to the summit and back. Tour buses leave continuously from the Plaza de Armas until 5 or 6 pm.** ✉ *El Centro.*

Convento de los Descalzos

RELIGIOUS SITE | Founded in 1592 as a retreat for Franciscans who wanted to escape the bustle of worldly Lima, this functioning monastery offers an intriguing glimpse into a colonial convent. Walled up in its self-sufficient cloisters, the good friars did more than just pray: they also ran an infirmary, a pharmacy with Amazonian plants, even a distillery for making pisco. The temple's ornamentation can be stunning—the chapel is inlaid with Nicaraguan cedar and mother-of-pearl—but what truly captivates here are the silences. The tolling bells still summon the faithful to prayer. ✉ *Cl. Manco Capac 202A, Alameda de los Descalzos, El Centro* ☎ *01/481–0441* 🌐 *www.facebook.com/museodelosdescalzospaginaoficial* 🎫 *S/10* ⏲ *Closed Mon.*

★ Convento de San Francisco

RELIGIOUS SITE | With its ornate facade and bell towers, ancient library, and catacombs full of human skulls, the Convento de San Francisco is one of Lima's most impressive sites. The catacombs hold the remains of some 75,000 people, some of whose bones have been arranged in eerie geometric patterns (warning: the narrow, dusty tunnels aren't for the claustrophobic). Meanwhile, the convent's massive church, the Iglesia de San Francisco, is the quintessential example of Lima baroque. Its handsome, carved portal is like an oversized *retablo*, projecting the church's sacred space out onto the busy street, while the central nave is known for its beautiful ceilings carved in a style called Mudejar (a blend of Moorish and Spanish designs). The 50-minute tour includes the church, the library, ample colonial art, and the catacombs. ✉ *Jr. Ancash 471, El Centro* ☎ *01/426–7377* 🌐 *www.museocatacumbas.com* 🎫 *S/15.*

★ Convento de Santo Domingo

RELIGIOUS SITE | If the Iglesia de San Francisco is Lima Gothic—all skulls and penitential gloom—Santo Domingo represents the city's sunny side. From pink facade to rococo tower, every detail here glows with charm. The main cloister is especially enticing: long arcades with Sevillian tiles, gardens redolent of jasmine, coffered ceilings carved from Panamanian oak. But don't overlook the chapter room, which housed Peru's University of San Marcos when it was founded in 1551, or the tombs of Santa Rosa de Lima and San Martín Porres, the first two saints in the New World. In a city given over to the here and now, this temple offers a glimpse into another world. ✉ *Jr. Conde de Superunda and Jr. Camaná, El Centro* ☎ *01/426–5786* 🌐 *www.conventosantodomingo.pe* 🎫 *S/10.*

Retablos Explained

You can tell a lot about colonial-era churches by their *retablos*, altarpieces that are almost always massive in scale and over-the-top in ornamentation. Most are made of elaborately carved wood and coated with layer upon layer of gold leaf. Indigenous peoples frequently did the carving, so look for unusual elements such as symbols of the sun and moon that figure prominently in pre-Columbian religion. You may be surprised that Jesus is a minor player on many retablos, and on others he doesn't appear at all. That's because these retablos often depict the life of the saint for which the church is named. Many churches retain their original baroque altarpieces, but others saw theirs replaced by much simpler neoclassical ones with sober columns and spare design. If you wander around the church, you may find the original relegated to one of the side chapels.

Estación de Desamparados

BUILDING | Inaugurated in 1912, Desamparados Station was the centerpiece for the continent's first railway, which stretched from the port of Callao to the Andean city of Huancayo. The station was named for a Jesuit church and monastery that stood next door at the time of its construction but that have since been demolished. It now holds the Casa de la Literatura Peruana (House of Peruvian Literature), with exhibits on national writers and a reading library. It's well worth stepping inside to admire the building's elegant art nouveau interior, especially the stained-glass skylight. ✉ *Jr. Ancash 207, El Centro* ☎ *01/426–2573* 🌐 *www.casadelaliteratura.gob.pe* 🎟 *Free* ⏲ *Closed Mon.*

Iglesia de Jesús, María y José

RELIGIOUS SITE | The 1713 Church of Jesus, Mary, and Joseph may be smaller than some of El Centro's other sanctuaries, but inside is a feast for the eyes. Retablos representing various saints rise from the main altar and line both walls. This is the only church in Lima to retain its original baroque ornamentation, untouched by earthquakes or changing artistic fads. ✉ *Jr. Camaná 765, El Centro* ☎ *01/427–6809* 🎟 *Free* ⏲ *Closed noon–3 daily and all day Sun.*

Iglesia de la Merced

RELIGIOUS SITE | Nothing about this colonial-era church could be called restrained. Take the pink-and-gray stone facade, for instance: done in an over-the-top style known as churrigueresco, it piles on twisty Solomonic columns, geometric cornices, a scalloped entryway, and an arms-outstretched statue of the Virgin that gestures down at worshippers below. The interior is no different. The main altar has a stunning monstrance and a silverwork medallion from the 16th century, while the intricately carved choir stalls, dating from the 1700s, have images of cherubic singers. You could lose yourself for hours contemplating the layer upon layer of detail in this stunning temple. **■ TIP→ Don't miss the grave of Fr. Urraca, a Lima saint said to have been tempted by the devil within these very walls.** ✉ *Jr. de la Unión at Jr. Miro Quesada, El Centro* ☎ *01/427–8199* 🎟 *Free* ⏲ *Closed 1–3:30.*

Iglesia de San Agustín

RELIGIOUS SITE | Disfigured by the violence of Peru's history—earthquakes and war—this church, or more specifically, its magnificent facade, remains one of the summits of religious art in the New World. Carved in stone in 1710 in the churrigueresco style (a Spanish variant of the baroque), it's crowded with images alluding to the life of St. Augustine, who is depicted stamping out heresy on the cornice above the main door. Inside, look for the macabre masterpiece *La Muerte* (*Death*), by the great 18th-century indigenous sculptor Baltasar Gavilán. ✉ *Jr. Ica 251, El Centro* 🎫 *Free.*

Iglesia de San Pedro

RELIGIOUS SITE | The Jesuits built three churches in rapid succession on this corner, inaugurating the current temple in 1638. It remains one of the finest examples of early-colonial religious architecture in Peru. The facade is remarkably restrained, but the interior shows all the extravagance of the era, including a series of baroque retablos thought to be the best in the city. The one dedicated to St. Francis Xavier soars to an apocalyptic culmination, with carved saints and angels towering over the viewer. Also notable are the canvases by Bernardo Bitti, who arrived on these shores from Italy in 1575 and influenced an entire generation of painters with his style. In the sacristy is *The Coronation of the Virgin*, one of his most famous works. **■ TIP→ Don't miss the side aisle, where gilded arches lead to chapels decorated with beautiful hand-painted tiles.** ✉ *Jr. Azángaro 451, El Centro* ☎ *01/428–3010* 🌐 *www.sanpedrodelima.org* 🎫 *Free* ⏲ *Closed 1–5.*

Municipalidad de Lima

GOVERNMENT BUILDING | Although it resembles the colonial-era buildings that abound in the area, City Hall was constructed in 1944. Step into the foyer to see the stained-glass windows above the marble staircase. To the south of the building is a popular pedestrian walkway called the Portal de los Escribanos, or Passage of the Scribes, lined with restaurants. On the right, you'll find the entrance to a small gallery run by City Hall that hosts exhibitions by Peruvian artists. ✉ *Jr. de la Unión 300, El Centro* ☎ *01/632–1300* 🌐 *www.munlima.gob.pe.*

★ **Museo de Arte de Lima (MALI)**

MUSEUM | Built in 1871 as the Palacio de la Exposición, this mammoth neoclassical structure was designed by the Italian architect Antonio Leonardi, with metal columns from the workshop of Gustav Eiffel (who later built the famous Parisian tower). The ground floor hosts temporary exhibitions by national and international artists, while the second level houses a permanent exhibition that spans Peru's past, with everything from pre-Columbian artifacts and colonial-era art to republican-era paintings and drawings that provide a glimpse into 19th- and 20th-century Peruvian life. One of the museum's treasures is the collection of *quipus*, or "talking knots"—webs of strings that were the closest thing the Incas had to writing. **■ TIP→ Leave time to sip an espresso in the café near the entrance.** ✉ *Paseo Colón 125, El Centro* ☎ *01/204–0000* 🌐 *www.mali.pe* 🎫 *S/30* ⏲ *Closed Mon.*

Palacio de Gobierno

CASTLE/PALACE | This neobaroque palace north of the Plaza de Armas is the official residence of Peru's president. It was built on the site where Francisco Pizarro was murdered in 1541 and has undergone several reconstructions, the most recent of which was completed in 1938. The best time to visit is at noon, when you can watch soldiers in red-and-blue uniforms conduct an elaborate changing of the guard, all to the tune of "El Condor Pasa." It's not quite Buckingham Palace, but it is impressive. Tours are offered on Saturday from 9 to 10:30 am, but reservations must be made at least a few days ahead of time. ✉ *Jr. de la Unión s/n, El Centro* ☎ *01/311–3900* 🌐 *www.presidencia.gob.pe* 🎫 *Free.*

Parque de la Exposición

CITY PARK | Eager to prove it was a world-class capital, Lima hosted an international exposition in 1872. Several of the buildings constructed for the event still stand, including the neoclassical Palacio

History Walk

Almost all of Lima's most interesting historical sites are within walking distance of the **Plaza de Armas.** The fountain in the center can be used as a slightly off-center compass. The bronze angel's trumpet points due north, where you'll see the **Palacio de Gobierno.** To the west is the neocolonial **Municipalidad de Lima,** and to the east are the **Catedral** and the adjoining **Palacio Arzobispal.** Peek inside the cathedral, one of the most striking in South America. From there, head north on Jirón Carabaya, the street running along the east side of the Palacio de Gobierno, until you reach the butter-yellow **Estación de Desamparados,** the former train station. Follow the street as it curves to the east, and in a block you'll reach the **Convento de San Francisco,** which has one of the city's most spectacular colonial-era churches, complete with eerie catacombs.

de la Exposición, which now serves as the Museo de Arte de Lima. Meanwhile, the park itself has become a busy meetup spot. Stroll through the grounds, and you'll find the eye-popping Pabellón Morisco, or Moorish Pavillion. Painstakingly restored, this Gothic-style structure has spiral staircases leading to a stained-glass salon on the second floor. The nearby Pabellón Bizantino, or Byzantine Pavilion, most closely resembles a turret from a Victorian-era mansion. ✉ *Paseo Colón and Av. Wilson, El Centro* 🎫 *Free.*

★ Plaza de Armas

PLAZA | This massive square has been the center of the city since 1535. Over the years it has served many functions, from open-air theater for melodramas to impromptu ring for bullfights. Huge fires once burned in the center for people sentenced to death by the Spanish Inquisition. Much has changed over the years, but one thing remaining is the bronze fountain unveiled in 1651. It was here that José de San Martín declared the country's independence from Spain in 1821. ✉ *Jr. Junín and Jr. Carabaya, El Centro.*

Plaza San Martín

PLAZA | This spectacular plaza is unlike any other in the city. It's surrounded on three sides by neocolonial buildings dating from the 1920s, the pale facades of which are lit at night, when the plaza is most impressive. Presiding over the western edge is the Gran Hotel Bolívar, a pleasant spot for a pisco sour. Even if you're not thirsty, you should step inside for a look at its elegant lobby. At the plaza's center is a massive statue of José de San Martín, the Argentine general who brought about the independence of Argentina, Chile, and Peru from Spain. ✉ *Between Jr. de la Unión and Jr. Carabaya, El Centro.*

Restaurants

El Centro abounds in both high-quality cuisine and cheap, filling food. A highlight is the Barrio Chino, packed with dozens of Chinese-Peruvian restaurants called chifas, but the run-down neighborhood that surrounds it makes it inadvisable to head there after dark. Restaurants on the main plazas are better dinner options.

Bar-Restaurante Cordano

$ | **PERUVIAN** | Dating from 1905, this venerable Lima institution has served up ham sandwiches and pisco sours to Peru's presidents for over a century. Every inch of the décor—the worn wooden bar, the old black-and-white photos, the well-stocked saloon shelves and cabinets—oozes history. **Known for:** butifarra sandwiches; solid criollo cooking; who's-who clientele. *Average main: S/25 Jr. Ancash 202, El Centro 01/427–0181 www.facebook.com/RestauranteBarCordano.*

El Fayke Piurano

$$ | **PERUVIAN** | This bustling two-story eatery specializes in *comida norteña*—northern cooking from the city of Piura. That means delicious grouper cebiche, *seco de cabrito* (goat stew), and green tamales—all in gut-busting portions. **Known for:** excellent northern cuisine; huge portions; local hole-in-the-wall. *Average main: S/35 Jr. Huancavelica 165, El Centro 01/428–6697 www.facebook.com/elfaykepiurano.*

La Muralla

$$ | **PERUVIAN** | Hungry office workers crowd this excellent criollo restaurant every day at lunchtime for heaping plates of fettucinne a la *huancaína* (pasta in cheese sauce) and *pescado a lo macho* (fish topped with spicy seafood). The setting, looking out over Lima's old fortified walls, is one of the greenest you'll find downtown. **Known for:** lomo saltado; lush setting with the Cerro San Cristóbal in the background; good pastas. *Average main: S/36 Parque La Muralla, El Centro 01/713-4982 www.facebook.com/lamurallarestaurante.*

L'Eau Vive

$$ | **FRENCH FUSION** | Run by nuns who serve satisfying (though not extraordinary) French food and sing the "Ave Maria" nightly at 9, L'Eau Vive sits in a restored mansion across the street from Palacio Torre Tagle. Trout baked in cognac and duck in orange sauce are two dishes that bring the locals back time and again. **Known for:** singing nuns; inexpensive three-course lunches; solid French cooking. *Average main: S/40 Jr. Ucayali 370, El Centro 01/427–5612 Closed 3:30–7:30 and Sun.*

Wa Lok

$$ | **CHINESE** | The best chifa in Chinatown, Wa Lok is known for such memorable dishes as *calamares rellenos* (shrimp-stuffed squid tempura), *taipá* (wok-fried chicken, pork, shrimp, and vegetables), and *pato pekinés* (Peking duck). It's best to go with a group and share, or ask for half orders. **Known for:** traditional Chinese cuisine; excellent Peking duck; good seafood. *Average main: S/44 Jr. Paruro 878, El Centro 01/427–2750 www.walok.com.pe.*

Hotels

Gran Hotel Bolívar

$$ | **HOTEL** | Although this grande dame hotel retains the splendor of the days when its guests included Ernest Hemingway and Mick Jagger, it lacks some of the conveniences offered by newer lodgings. **Pros:** historic atmosphere; convenient location; good value. **Cons:** rooms are a bit worn; spotty Wi-Fi coverage; no air conditioning or heat. *Rooms from: S/350 Plaza San Martín, Jr. de la Unión 958, El Centro 01/761–9869 www.granhotelbolivar.com.pe 99 rooms Free breakfast.*

Sheraton Lima Hotel

$$ | **HOTEL** | This concrete monolith may be removed from the city's best dining and nightlife options, but it offers easy access to the historic district and is just a short Metropolitano ride from San Isidro, Miraflores, or Barranco. **Pros:** plenty of amenities; close to downtown; easy access to Metropolitano buses. **Cons:** massive; a bit far from the city's best eateries; lacks personality. *Rooms from: S/370 Paseo de la República 170, El Centro*

☎ *01/315–5000* 🌐 *www.marriott.com/hotels/travel/limsi-sheraton-lima-hotel-and-convention-center* 🛏 *430 rooms* 🍽 *Free breakfast.*

Nightlife

BARS

Bar Hotel Maury

BARS/PUBS | This handsomely wood-paneled hotel bar is where the pisco sour took on its definitive final form. The man responsible, Don Eloy Cuadros, has learned his trade well: after 60 years on the job, he still whips up refreshing cocktails that are a perfect break from sightseeing in El Centro. ✉ *Jr. Ucayali 201, El Centro* ☎ *01/428–8188* 🌐 *maury-hotel-lima.hotel-ds.com.*

El Bolivarcito

BARS/PUBS | This popular bar just to the right of the Hotel Bolívar's entrance overlooks the Plaza San Martín and makes a wicked pisco sour. Or step inside to the main bar and restaurant, which offer tables on an elevated terrace and a more subdued setting. ✉ *Gran Hotel Bolívar, Jr. de la Unión 958, El Centro* ☎ *01/427–2788.*

Museo del Pisco

BARS/PUBS | Artisanal cocktails are what's on tap at this atmospheric saloon patterned after an Ica *bodega* (winery).The classic pisco sours are formidable, but even better are the ginger-ale-based *chilcanos* and the citrus-and-berry-laced *frutales*. The expert mixologists are happy to make recommendations. ✉ *Plaza de Armas, Jr. Carabaya 193, El Centro* ☎ *993/500–013* 🌐 *www.museodelpisco.org.*

Performing Arts

Brisas del Titicaca

THEMED ENTERTAINMENT | Run by a nonprofit cultural association, this supper-club theater showcases Peru's colorful *danzas folklóricas*, especially those from Puno, near Lake Titicaca. The music, costumes, and virtuosic footwork evoke the joyous frenzy of the region's Virgen de la Candelaria festival. Take a cab when you go; the theater is a bit hard to find. ✉ *Jr. Héroes de Tarapacá 168, El Centro* ☎ *01/715–6960* 🌐 *www.brisasdeltiticaca.com.*

Shopping

MARKETS

Mercado Central

OUTDOOR/FLEA/GREEN MARKETS | Its official name is El Mercado Municipal Gran Mariscal Ramón Castilla, but limeños refer to this sprawling market as simply "El Mercado Central." Here hundreds of vendors display the ingredients of the city's varied cuisine, from hooks hung with slabs of meat to trays piled high with seafood. There are also wheels of cheese stacked above tubs of olives, open sacks full of dried potato chunks or *ají* peppers, and bundles of spices that double as natural remedies. If you want the see the real Peru, this is it. ✉ *Jr. Ucayali at Jr. Ayacucho, El Centro.*

San Isidro

San Isidro is Lima's money district, in more than one sense. Not only is it an enclave for Peru's vestigial aristocracy, but the area around Canaval y Moreyra contains the city's financial heart, with headquarters for several large banks and international corporations. This is where you'll find some of Lima's swankiest real estate: the houses can be positively palatial, with Lexuses and BMWs in the driveways and 24-hour armed guards patrolling outside.

San Isidro's residential nature means it's short on tourist attractions (though the 400-year-old olive groves of El Olivar are a lovely spot for strolling). Instead, the main reason most travelers come here is to shop or dine out. If you're into designer threads or jewelry, the parallel boulevards of Camino Real and

Conquistadores are filled with chi-chi boutiques, and some of the city's best eats can be had near the *óvalo* (traffic circle) at Avenida Paz Soldán. The area also boasts a few glitzy resto-bars for late-night drinks, but more folks come here to sleep in the neighborhood's hotels than to party outside them.

GETTING AROUND

The easiest way to visit the widely dispersed attractions in San Isidro is by taxi, but you could also explore the neighborhood on foot in two or three hours.

Sights

Huaca Huallamarca

ARCHAEOLOGICAL SITE | FAMILY | This mud-brick pyramid, thought to be a place of worship, predates the Incas. Painstakingly restored on the front side, it seems out of place among the neighborhood's upscale homes and apartment buildings. Here you'll find a small museum with displays of objects found at the site, including several mummies. From the upper platform you can take in views of San Isidro. *Av. Nicolás de Rivera and Av. El Rosario, San Isidro 01/222–4124 S/5 Closed Mon.*

Parque El Olivar

CITY PARK | FAMILY | For years, this rambling olive grove was slowly being eroded, as homes for wealthy limeños were built in and around its perimeter. The process was halted in the 1960s, in time to save more than 1,500 gnarled olive trees. Some of the trees are four centuries old and still bear fruit. A network of sidewalks, flower beds, fountains, and playgrounds makes this 20-hectare (50-acre) park a popular spot on weekend afternoons. *Av. Los Incas, between Av. Paz Soldán and Cl. Carolina Vargas de Vargas, San Isidro msi.gob.pe/portal/nuestro-distrito/turismo-distrital/bosque-el-olivar Free.*

Restaurants

Most of San Isidro's restaurants are on or near Avenida Conquistadores, the neighborhood's main shopping street. Avenida Dos de Mayo, north of Avenida Javier Prado, also has eateries worth visiting.

★ Astrid y Gastón Casa Moreyra

$$$$ | PERUVIAN | The flagship restaurant of Peru's most celebrated chefs, spouses Gastón Acurio and Astrid Gutsche, occupies a meticulously restored colonial mansion named Casa Moreyra. Dishes are available à la carte, but the big event here is the 16-course, prix-fixe tasting menu, which takes you on a journey through Peru's culinary regions in the span of two hours. **Known for:** exquisite tasting menu; inventive use of humble Peruvian ingredients; gorgeous setting. *Average main: S/500 Av. Paz Soldán 290, San Isidro 01/442–2777 www.astridygaston.com.*

Como Agua Para Chocolate

$ | MEXICAN | One of Lima's few Mexican restaurants, this colorful spot near Parque El Olivar serves some innovative dishes as well as the usual tacos and enchiladas. The house specialties are *barbacoa de cordero* (lamb grilled in avocado leaves), *pescado a la veracruzana* (fish in a slightly spicy tomato sauce), and *albóndigas al chipotle* (spicy meatballs served with yellow rice), but you can also get fajitas and good quesadillas. **Known for:** great margaritas; traditional Mexican fare; super-friendly owners. *Average main: S/34 Cl. Pancho Fierro 108, San Isidro 01/222–0174 Closed Sun.*

Lima 27

$$$ | PERUVIAN | This dark-gray mansion with a bright red foyer looks like Dracula's love shack at night, but inside you'll find a chic lounge and two elegant dining rooms. Local epicureans gather here to savor a creative fusion of Peruvian and continental cuisine, from *cabrito loche* (roast kid with squash ravioli) to *atún costra* (tuna in a sesame-pepper crust)

A
B
C
D
E
F
1
2
3
4
5
6
7
8
9
LINCE
SAN ISIDRO
Av. San Felipe
C. Luis M. Sanchez Cerro
Jirón Inca Ripac
Jirón Belisario Flores
Jirón Manuel Candamo
Avenida José Pardo de Zela
Jirón José Bernardo Alcedo
Jirón Leon Velarde
Avenida General César Canevaro
Avenida José Leal
Jirón Sinchi Roca
Mama Ocllo
Av. Julio Cesar Tello
Jirón Cápac Yupanqui
Jirón Garcillaso de la Vega
Jirón Francisco de Zela
Jirón Almirante Martin Guisse
Jirón General José María Córdova
Jirón Mariscal William Miller
Jirón Carlos Alayzay Roel
Avenida Álvarez de Arenales
Avenida Arequipa
Jirón Risso
Jirón Mariscal Gregorio Las Hera
Jirón Tomás Guido
Av. Militar
Francisco Lazo
Jirón Pedro Conde
Jirón José de la Torre Ugarte
Jirón Domingo Casanova
Jirón Soledad
Avenida Cesar Vallejo
Calle Roma
Juan Bielovicic
Calle Carlos Porras Osores
Calle Guillermo Marconi
Avenida Guillermo Prescott
Alberto Alexander
Calle Manco Segundo
Jirón José de la Torre Ugarte
Luis Pasteur
Avenida Dos de Mayo
C. Cápac Yupanqui
Jirón Garcillaso de la Vega
Francisco de Zela
Jirón Almirante Martin Guisse
General Córdova
Jirón Mariscal William Miller
Jirón Carlos Alayzay Roel
Av. Álvarez de Arenales
Av. Javier Prado Este
Avenida Javier Prado Oeste
Av. Paseo Parodi
C. Manuel Bañón
Av. Jorge Basadre
Avenida Jorge Basadre
Av. Victor Andrés Belaunde
Avenida Nicolas de Rivera
Av. Daniel Hernandez
Avenida Arequipa
C. Sebastian Telleria
Calle Manuel Fuentes
Calle Federico Villarreal
Avenida Petit Thouars
Calle José Choquehuanca
C. Lizardo Alzamora Oeste
Avenida Aurelio Miró Quesada
C. Ernesto Plascencia
0
1,000 ft
0
200 m
Avenida Camino Real
C. Los Libertadores
Av. Los Conquistadores
Calle La República
Pasaje Padre Constancio Bollar
Av. Los Incas
C. Antero Aspillaga
Calle Prolongación Arenales
Av. General Juan Antonio Pezet
Avenida General Juan Antonio Pezet
Avenida Miguel Cervantes
Bulevard Roosevelt
Avenida Álvarez Calderón
C. Gervasio Santillana
C. Rio de Janeiro
C. Teniente José Romanet
Calle Alferez Alfredo Salazar
Calle Santa Margarita
Calle Independencia
Avenida Arequipa
Avenida Petit Thouars
Av. Los Conquistadores
Avenida Santa Cruz
Avenida Francisco Tudela y Varela
Calle Almirante Lord Cochrane
C. José del Llano Zapata
Calle Almirante Lord Nelson
Avenida Santa Cruz
Av. Comandante Espinar
C. Carlos A. Salaverry
C. Mariano Melgar
Calle General Córdova
Av. Hipólito Unanue
Av. Federico Villarreal
C. 8 de Octubre
C. Ignacio Merino
Av. Augusto Perez Aranibar
Av. Angamos Oeste
C. Independencia
Calle Coronel Inclán

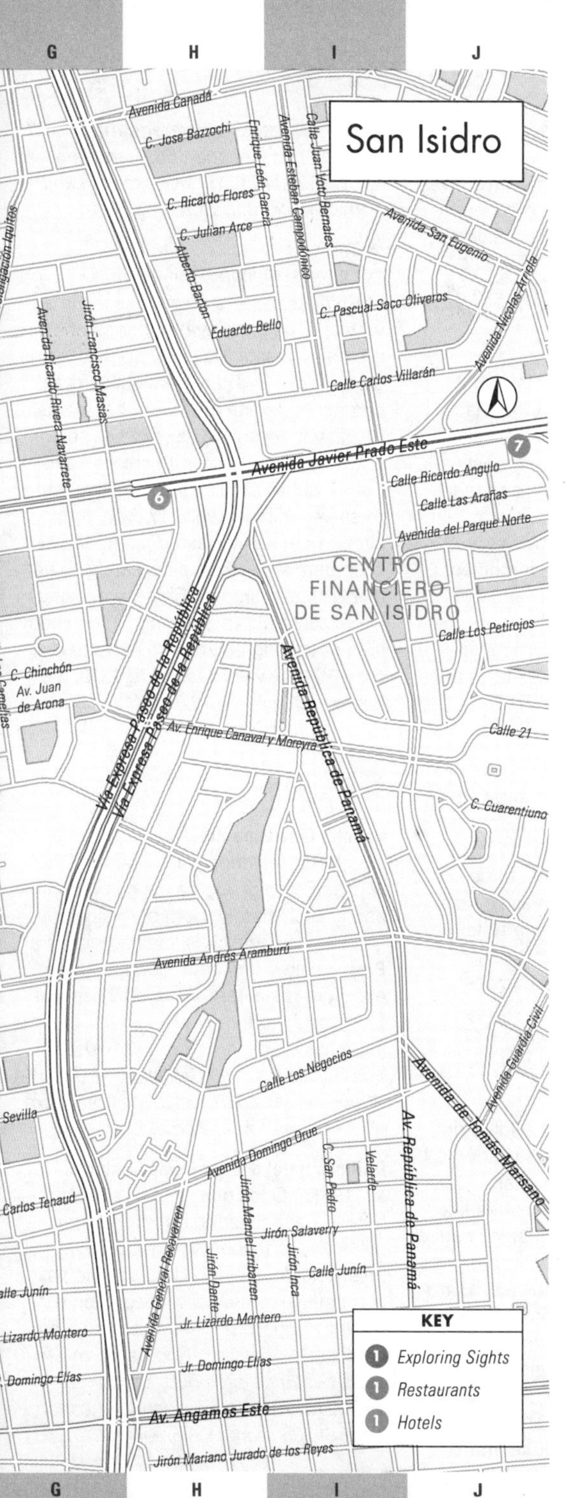

Sights

1 Huaca Huallamarca C5
2 Parque El Olivar E6

Restaurants

1 Astrid y Gastón Casa Moreyra E5
2 Como Agua Para Chocolate E5
3 Lima 27 .... E5
4 Malabar E4
5 Nanka E4
6 Osaka D7
7 Titi J3

Hotels

1 Country Club Lima Hotel A5
2 Delfines Hotel & Convention Center A5
3 Pullman Lima San Isidro D4
4 Sonesta Hotel El Olivar E5
5 Swissôtel Lima D5
6 The Westin Lima Hotel and Convention Center H3

to *gnocchis crocantes* (crispy gnocchi smothered in a mushroom-and-artichoke-heart ragout). **Known for:** inventive fusion dishes; popular terrace bar on weekends; imaginative presentations. *Average main: S/63 Cl. Santa Luisa 295, San Isidro 994/204–416 www.lima27.com No dinner Sun.*

★ Malabar

$$$$ | **PERUVIAN** | Chef-owner Pedro Miguel Schiaffino travels the Peruvian Andes and Amazon in search of weird and unfamiliar ingredients that most cooks—and locals—overlook, and then incorporates them into the menu at Malabar. His list of dishes changes several times a year to ensure fresh ingredients, but most of them are organic and free-range. **Known for:** true foodie experience; exotic ingredients; jungle-themed cuisine. *Average main: S/66 Av. Camino Real 101, San Isidro 01/440–5200 malabar.com.pe Closed Sun.*

Nanka

$$ | **PERUVIAN** | At this bistro run by an Australian-Peruvian couple, the emphasis is on sustainable, locally sourced, organic ingredients. Lofty sentiments, to be sure—but it also helps that this pair can really cook. **Known for:** environmentally conscious cooking; good duck dishes; lots of vegetarian and vegan choices. *Average main: S/50 Cl. Manuel Bañón 260, San Isidro 01/467–8417 www.nanka.pe No dinner.*

Osaka

$$$$ | **JAPANESE FUSION** | This wildly popular Japanese-fusion eatery is renowned for its sushi bar, but its Peruvian tiraditos and Chinese seafood dishes like broiled scallops braised in a spicy sauce are equally masterful. Settle into one of the low tables, and sink your teeth into *quinua maguro* (seared tuna medallions served with mashed lucuma fruit and crunchy quinoa), or grilled sirloin and sautéed mushrooms atop miso mashed potatoes. **Known for:** sushi and sashimi; scrumptious cebiche; Chinese and Nikkei favorites. *Average main: S/70 Av. Pardo y Aliaga 660, San Isidro 01/222–0405 www.osakanikkei.com No dinner Sun.*

★ Titi

$$ | **CHINESE FUSION** | Chifa, Peru's version of Chinese food, is ubiquitous in Lima, with cheapo order-by-number establishments on practically every corner. In this glutted market, Titi towers above the competition, with a kitchen that works magic with even the simplest ingredients. *Tallarín saltado* with chicken and pork is subtly smoky and crackling with fresh vegetables, while *kru yoc*, the kitchen's most requested plate, dresses crisp pork slices with a delicately sweet glaze. **Known for:** best Chinese cooking in Lima; scrumptious suckling pig on Friday; super-fresh ingredients. *Average main: S/50 Av. Javier Prado Este 1212, San Isidro 01/224–8189 chifatiti.com No dinner Sun.*

Hotels

Country Club Lima Hotel

$$$ | **HOTEL** | Historic paintings from the Museo Pedro de Osma hang in the lobby and in each stately room of this colonial-style hotel, which is itself a work of art. **Pros:** architectural gem; doting service; excellent restaurant. **Cons:** a bit removed from the action; new wing is less charming; pricey. *Rooms from: S/650 Cl. Los Eucaliptos 590, San Isidro 01/611–9000 www.countryclublimahotel.com 82 rooms Free breakfast.*

Delfines Hotel & Convention Center

$$ | **HOTEL** | Once one of Lima's best, this hotel's star has faded slightly, but it's still a pleasant spot with good views. **Pros:** quiet location; golf course views; competitive rates. **Cons:** décor a bit dated; removed from most restaurants and bars; pool is small. *Rooms from: S/420 Cl. Los Eucaliptos 555, San Isidro 01/215–7000 www.losdelfineshotel.com 205 rooms Breakfast.*

Pullman Lima San Isidro

$$ | **HOTEL** | This plain cement building with square windows doesn't look like much from the street, but step into its sleek lobby, or browse the menu at its chic Peruvian fusion restaurant Chabuca, and you'll see why this is one of Lima's more popular hotels. **Pros:** friendly staff; convenient location; heated lap pool. **Cons:** nothing Peruvian about the décor; undistinguished aesthetics; occasional misunderstandings with the front desk. *Rooms from: S/450 ✉ Av. Jorge Basadre 595, San Isidro ☎ 01/208–1200 🌐 all.accor.com 252 rooms Free Breakfast.*

Sonesta Hotel El Olivar

$$ | **HOTEL** | Standing at the edge of an old olive grove, this dark-green hotel enjoys one of the most relaxing settings in San Isidro, especially when you experience it from the sun deck and pool on the top floor. **Pros:** convenient location; view of the park at on-site restaurant; relaxing setting. **Cons:** small standard rooms; interior rooms are dimly lit; pool is a bit small. *Rooms from: S/330 ✉ Cl. Pancho Fierro 194, San Isidro ☎ 01/712–6000 🌐 www.sonestaelolivar.com 144 rooms Free breakfast.*

Swissôtel Lima

$$$ | **HOTEL** | A popular hotel with business travelers, the Swissôtel has well-appointed rooms, excellent in-house dining, and a convenient location in an office complex a few blocks from many shops and restaurants. **Pros:** plush rooms; first-rate service; four excellent on-site dining options. **Cons:** slightly isolated location; expensive; situated in a concrete jungle. *Rooms from: S/600 ✉ Centro Empresarial Real, Av. Santo Toribio 173, San Isidro ☎ 01/421–4400 🌐 www.swissotel.com/hotels/lima 345 rooms No meals.*

The Westin Lima Hotel and Convention Center

$$$$ | **HOTEL** | This 30-story glass tower offers an airy lobby and guest rooms, which have walk-in closets, marble baths with tubs and showers, and floor-to-ceiling windows through which you can admire the urban panorama. **Pros:** close to shopping and Metropolitano bus lines; incredible views from rooms; great exercise facilities. **Cons:** far from tourist sights; pricey; attracts conference crowds. *Rooms from: S/900 ✉ Cl. Las Begonias 450, at Av. Javier Prado, San Isidro ☎ 01/201–5000 🌐 www.marriott.com/hotels 301 rooms Breakfast.*

Nightlife

BARS

Bitter Cocktail Club

BARS/PUBS | The bartenders at this hipster grotto have really nailed the speakeasy vibe: you need to request a password through the bar's website to be allowed to enter. What awaits you inside are some of the most delicious drinks in Lima, as well as red curtains, leather sofas, and a generally cool vibe. *✉ Av. Conquistadores 556, San Isidro ☎ 967/121–217 🌐 bittercc.com.*

Carnaval

BARS/PUBS | This posh cocktail emporium is the brainchild of Aaron Díaz, former beverage director at Astrid y Gastón and expert mixologist at high-end bars throughout Latin America. Using ingredients such as green Chartreuse, elderberry juice, and mescal, he whips up drinks that have Lima's smart set raving. The snacks are outstanding, too. *✉ Av. Pardo y Aliaga 662, inside an office building, San Isidro ☎ 986/787–755 🌐 carnavalbar.com.*

Shopping

BOOKS

Librería Communitas

BOOKS/STATIONERY | Not a few limeños consider this the city's best bookstore. The labyrinthine shelves contain tens of thousands of titles—many of them in English. *✉ Av. Dos de Mayo 1684, San Isidro ☎ 01/222–2794 🌐 communitas.pe.*

Peña Party

A great way to experience Peruvian folk music and dance is to visit a *peña*, a kind of smash-up between a dance hall and a supper club that offers *música criolla*, rhythmic waltzes performed with guitars and *cajones* (wooden boxes used for percussion). Some peñas also feature *huaynos* (a musical genre typical of the sierra) or folk dances from the country's coastal and Andean regions.

La Candelaria Drawing a mix of locals and foreigners, La Candelaria is located in an attractive art deco building a couple blocks east of Barranco's Parque Municipal. The restaurant, where food and drink are à la carte, opens at 9 pm, and shows (there's a cover charge) combining the folklores of the coast, mountains, and jungle start at 10:30 on Thursday, Friday, and Saturday. ✉ *Av. Bolognesi 292, Barranco* ☎ *01/247–1314* 🌐 *www.lacandelariaperu.com* ☞ *Closed evenings Mon.–Wed. and Sun. all day.*

La Dama Juana The most tourist-friendly peña, La Dama Juana offers 90-minute shows in an atmospheric Spanish-colonial-style building in Barranco. Performances start at 8:30 pm, and a traditional Peruvian buffet is served from 7:30 to 10 pm. There's also a Sunday show that starts at 2:30 pm; the buffet opens at 12:20. ✉ *Av. República de Panamá 240, Barranco* ☎ *01/248–7547* 🌐 *ladamajuana.com.pe.*

La Oficina This lively peña is one of the most famous in the city. Weekend shows of Afro-Peruvian music from the country's south coast culminate with a *brindis* (toast) around 2 am, when hundreds of pisco-sour glasses are raised. ✉ *Cl. Enrique Barrón 441, Barranco* ☎ *01/247–6544* ☞ *Closed evenings Mon.–Wed. and Sun. all day.*

Sachún With more than three decades in business, Sachún's mix of Andean folk dancing and música criolla draws a predominantly older crowd. The food here is a cut above that at other peñas. ✉ *Av. del Ejército 657, Miraflores* ☎ *01/441–4465* 🌐 *www.facebook.com/SachunPeru* ☞ *Closed Sun.–Wed.*

CLOTHING

Kuna

CLOTHING | Kuna offers an array of quality alpaca-wool clothing, from ponchos to coats, with bright colors and some of the nicest designs in the country. ✉ *Av. Jorge Basadre 380, San Isidro* ☎ *01/440–2320* 🌐 *kunastores.com.*

HANDICRAFTS

Indigo

CRAFTS | On a quiet street in San Isidro, Indigo invites you to wander through at least half a dozen different rooms filled with unique items. There's a selection of whimsical ceramics inspired by traditional designs, as well as modern pieces. In the center of it all is an open-air café. ✉ *Av. El Bosque 260, San Isidro* ☎ *01/440–3099* 🌐 *www.galeriaindigo.com.pe.*

Miraflores

With its flower-filled parks and wide swaths of green overlooking the ocean, this seaside suburb is the alpha and omega for most visitors to Lima. Not only does it have the city's best selection of hotels and restaurants, but its boutiques, cafés, bars, and dance clubs are second to none. Some travelers who find themselves in Lima for a short time manage never to leave this tiny haven.

Miraflores's centerpiece is Parque Kennedy, a lively gathering spot between Avenida José Larco and Avenida Diagonal. Here, locals as well as tourists come to peruse local handicrafts, listen to concerts, or people-watch at one of the sidewalk restaurants. There's a cute, dinosaur-filled playground for kids, and the park is home to a throng of well-fed resident cats, who live off the beneficence of the local matrons.

Miraflores is also where the commercial sirens of Lima sing loudest. Larcomar, a tony cliffside mall with views of the Pacific, has rows of frou-frou shops that woudn't be out of place on Rodeo Drive, while the handicrafts markets along Avenida Petit Thouars vanquish even the hardiest retail warriors with their onslaught of ponchos, silver jewelry, and Andean flutes. If you're interested in Lima's food scene, don't neglect the district's markets and *bioferias* (organic-food fairs). Many chefs buy their ingredients at the Mercado No. 1 in Surquillo, right across the bridge near the Metropolitano bus station on Avenida Ricardo Palma, while on Saturday mornings, the Bioferia Miraflores offers locally grown foods at the Parque Reducto on Avenida Benavides.

GETTING AROUND

A popular walk in Miraflores is the 20-minute stroll south from Parque Kennedy down busy Avenida José Larco to Larcomar. The mall's gorgeous views and ocean breezes are a perfect setting for its glitzy shops and restaurants. From there you can walk either east or west: the top of the coastal cliff is lined in both directions with a string of green spaces and an ocean-view promenade called the malecón. Miraflores is about 10 minutes from San Isidro or Barranco and 30 minutes from El Centro by taxi or the Metropolitano bus.

Sights

El Faro la Marina

LIGHTHOUSE | FAMILY | Constructed in 1900, this little lighthouse at the north end of Parque Antonio Raimondi, a short walk north from the Parque del Amor, has guided ships for more than a century. On sunny weekends, the large park that surrounds it is one of the most popular spots in Miraflores, with paragliders floating overhead and bicyclists and skateboarders rolling along the ocean-view malecón. Children of all ages play on the lawns and playground. ✉ *Malecón Cisneros at Cl. Madrid, Miraflores.*

★ **Huaca Pucllana**

ARCHAEOLOGICAL SITE | FAMILY | Rising out of a nondescript residential neighborhood is Lima's most-visited *huaca*, or pre-Columbian temple—a huge, mud-brick platform pyramid that covers several city blocks. The site, which dates from at least the 5th century, has ongoing excavations, and new discoveries are announced every so often. A tiny museum highlights a few of those finds. Knowledgeable, English-speaking guides will lead you through reconstructed sections to the pyramid's top platform and, from there, to an area that is being excavated. ■ **TIP→ This site is most beautiful at night, when parts of it are illuminated. Thirty-minute partial tours are available during this time.** ✉ *Cl. General Borgoño cuadra 8 s/n, Miraflores* ☎ *01/617–7148* 🌐 *huacapucllanamiraflores.pe* 🎫 *S/15 during the day, S/17 at night* ⏲ *Closed 5–7 pm daily and at night Mon. and Tues.*

Lugar de la Memoria

MUSEUM | From 1980 to 2000, two terrorist groups waged a fierce war against the Peruvian state: Sendero Luminoso and the Movimiento Revolucionario Tupac Amaru. Their assaults and the brutal reaction of the Peruvian military left some 70,000 citizens dead—mostly poor *campesinos* (country folk) from the sierra . This somber museum commemorates that dark period, with historical exhibits

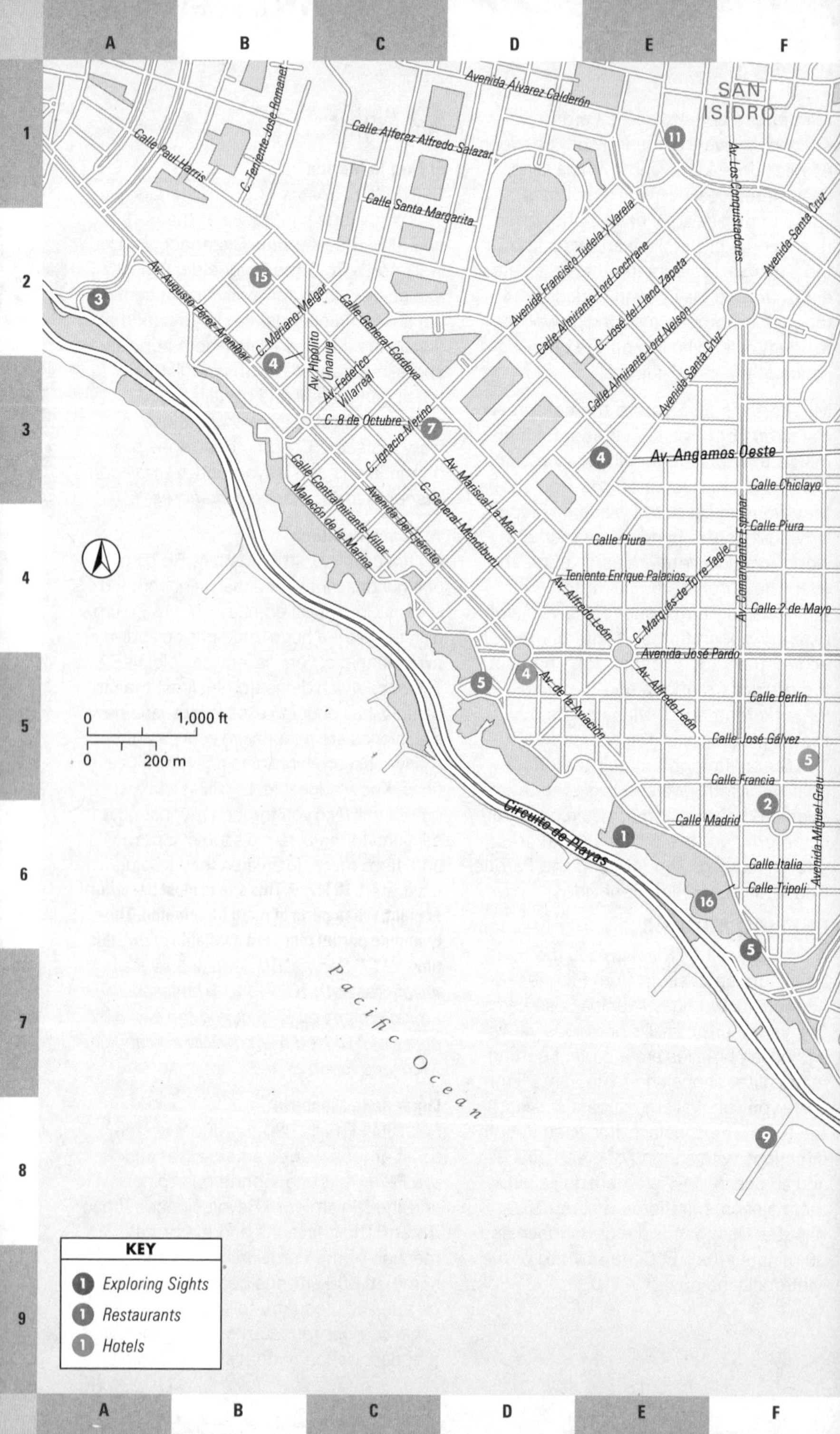

A
B
C
D
E
F
1
2
3
4
5
6
7
8
9
SAN ISIDRO
Avenida Álvarez Calderón
Calle Alferez Alfredo Salazar
Calle Santa Margarita
Calle Paul Harris
C. Teniente Jose Romanet
Av. Augusto Pérez Aranibar
C. Mariano Melgar
Av. Hipólito Unanue
Av. Federico Villarreal
Calle General Córdova
C. 8 de Octubre
C. Ignacio Merino
Av. Mariscal La Mar
C. General Mendiburu
Avenida Del Ejército
Calle Contralmirante Villar
Malecón de la Marina
Avenida Francisco Tudela y Varela
Calle Almirante Lord Cochrane
C. José del Llano Zapata
Calle Almirante Lord Nelson
Avenida Santa Cruz
Av. Los Conquistadores
Avenida Santa Cruz
Av. Angamos Oeste
Calle Chiclayo
Calle Piura
Calle Piura
Av. Comandante Espinar
Teniente Enrique Palacios
C. Marqués de Torre Tagle
Av. Alfredo León
Calle 2 de Mayo
Avenida José Pardo
Av. de la Aviación
Av. Alfredo León
Calle Berlín
Calle José Gálvez
Calle Francia
Calle Madrid
Avenida Miguel Grau
Calle Italia
Calle Tripoli
Circuito de Playas
Pacific Ocean
0
1,000 ft
0
200 m
KEY
Exploring Sights
Restaurants
Hotels

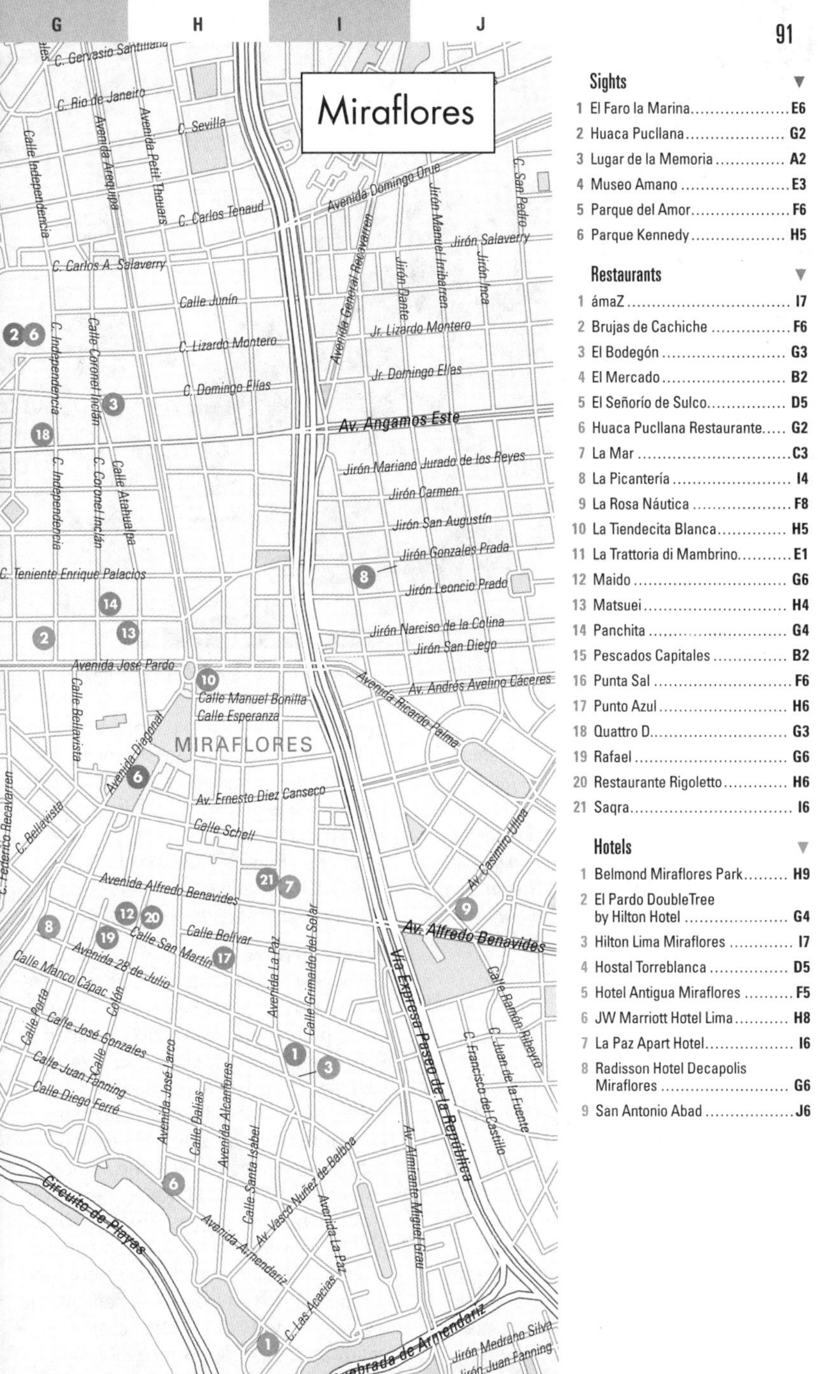

Sights

1 El Faro la Marina E6
2 Huaca Pucllana G2
3 Lugar de la Memoria A2
4 Museo Amano E3
5 Parque del Amor F6
6 Parque Kennedy H5

Restaurants

1 ámaZ I7
2 Brujas de Cachiche F6
3 El Bodegón G3
4 El Mercado B2
5 El Señorío de Sulco D5
6 Huaca Pucllana Restaurante G2
7 La Mar C3
8 La Picantería I4
9 La Rosa Náutica F8
10 La Tiendecita Blanca H5
11 La Trattoria di Mambrino E1
12 Maido G6
13 Matsuei H4
14 Panchita G4
15 Pescados Capitales B2
16 Punta Sal F6
17 Punto Azul H6
18 Quattro D G3
19 Rafael G6
20 Restaurante Rigoletto H6
21 Saqra I6

Hotels

1 Belmond Miraflores Park H9
2 El Pardo DoubleTree by Hilton Hotel G4
3 Hilton Lima Miraflores I7
4 Hostal Torreblanca D5
5 Hotel Antigua Miraflores F5
6 JW Marriott Hotel Lima H8
7 La Paz Apart Hotel I6
8 Radisson Hotel Decapolis Miraflores G6
9 San Antonio Abad J6

The tile mosaics of Parque del Amor in Miraflores take their inspiration from Barcelona's Park Güell.

and video testimony from many of the victims. The displays are all in Spanish, but even if you don't know the language, this place makes an impression. ■ **TIP→ An even more powerful exhibit on Sendero Luminoso is available on the sixth floor of the Museo de la Nación, in the district of San Borja.** ✉ *Bajada San Martín 151, Miraflores* ☎ *01/618–9393* 🌐 *lum.cultura.pe* 🎫 *Free* 🕑 *Closed Mon.*

Museo Amano

MUSEUM | Although relatively small, this private museum of pre-Columbian artifacts holds some of the city's best textiles, in addition to well-preserved ceramics and other handiwork. The museum was founded by Japanese businessman and collector Yoshitaro Amano in 1964 and expanded and remodeled by his offspring in 2015. The chronological exhibition charts Peru's artistic development from 800 BC to the 15th century across four halls packed with well-preserved artifacts from pre-Inca cultures, including the Paracas, Nazca, Moche, and Chancay. The impressive collection of weavings contains some that are almost 2,000 years old; miraculously, many have retained their vivid colors and (sometimes comic) imagery. Displays are in English and Spanish; you can also call ahead to reserve an English-speaking guide. ✉ *Cl. Retiro 160, Miraflores* ☎ *01/441–2909* 🌐 *www.museoamano.org* 🎫 *S/30.*

Parque del Amor

CITY PARK | **FAMILY** | You could be forgiven for thinking you're in Barcelona when you stroll through this lovely park designed by Peruvian artist Victor Delfín. As in Antoni Gaudí's Park Güell, which provided inspiration, the benches here are encrusted with broken pieces of tile. In keeping with the romantic theme—the name translates as "Park of Love"—the mosaic includes sayings such as *Amor es como luz* ("Love is like light"). The centerpiece is a massive statue of two lovers locked in a passionate embrace. The park affords a sweeping view of the Pacific, and on windy days, paragliders take off from an adjacent green. ■ **TIP→ Across the bridge from the park, you can see the Intihuatana by**

Fernando de Szyszlo, a huge concrete sculpture inspired by an Inca astronomical clock. ✉ *Malecón Cisneros, Miraflores* 🎫 *Free.*

Parque Kennedy

CITY PARK | **FAMILY** | What locals call Parque Kennedy is, strictly speaking, two parks. A smaller section, near the óvalo, or roundabout, is Parque 7 de Junio, whereas the rest of it is Parque Kennedy proper. On the park's east side stands Miraflores's stately Parroquia La Virgen Milagrosa (Church of the Miraculous Virgin), built in the 1930s on the site of a colonial church. The equally young colonial-style building behind it is the Municipalidad de Miraflores (district town hall). Several open-air cafés along the park's eastern edge serve decent food and drink. At night, a round cement structure in front of those cafés called La Rotonda fills up with handicraft vendors, and the park becomes especially lively. Street vendors also sell popcorn and traditional Peruvian desserts such as *picarones* (fried donuts bathed in molasses), *mazamorra morada* (a pudding made with blue-corn juice and fruit), and *arroz con leche* (rice pudding). This park is the most popular meetup spot for the entire district. ✉ *Between Av. José Larco and Av. Diagonal, Miraflores* 🎫 *Free.*

Restaurants

Miraflores is home to the biggest concentration of good restaurants in Lima. Although a few of them are clustered around Parque Kennedy, many are scattered farther afield and are best reached by taxi.

★ ámaZ

$$$ | **PERUVIAN** | Chef Pedro Miguel Schiaffino (of Malabar fame) spent years exploring the Peruvian Amazon and experimenting with its ingredients before opening this low-key Miraflores bistro. The result is a world-class eatery that lets you experience the flavors of the rainforest without leaving the urban jungle. **Known for:** inventive Amazonian dishes; nine-dish "abruta fiesta" menu; upscale, eclectic environment. $ *Average main: S/62* ✉ *Av. La Paz 1079, Miraflores* ☎ *01/221–9393* 🌐 *amaz.com.pe* ⏲ *No dinner Sun.*

Where to Paraglide

PerúFly If you visit any of the parks in Miraflores with ocean views on a windy day, you'll likely see brilliantly colored paragliders in the sky above the cliffs. PerúFly offers 10-minute tandem flights that take off from a spot just north of Parque del Amor and cost S/272, which includes a video. Call ahead to make sure there is enough wind to fly. ✉ *Parque Raimondi, Malecón Cisneros, Miraflores* ☎ *970/547–238* 🌐 *www.perufly.com.*

Brujas de Cachiche

$$$ | **PERUVIAN** | Though its name evokes folklore, "Witches of Cachiche" is an elegant, modern spot that offers variations on traditional Peruvian cuisine. Delicacies include as *corvina en salsa de camarones* (sea bass in a roasted-crayfish sauce) or *cabrito a la norteña* (stewed kid). **Known for:** elegant atmosphere; extensive wine list; classy bar/lounge. $ *Average main: S/64* ✉ *Cl. Bolognesi 472, Miraflores* ☎ *01/447–1133* 🌐 *www.brujasdecachiche.com.pe* ⏲ *Closed Sun. night.*

★ El Bodegón

$$ | **PERUVIAN** | Just when you thought Gastón Acurio couldn't possibly do anything more for his country's gastronomy, he opens this nostalgic *homenaje* to Peru's home cooking of yesteryear. In a corner tavern filled with dark wood and old photos, he polls his customers on their favorite dishes from their childhoods, and then makes them new. **Known for:** homey ambience; ridiculously good crab causas (potato salads); classic Peruvian cooking, done to perfection.

$ *Average main: S/35* ✉ *Av. Tarapacá 197, Miraflores* ☎ *01/301–1552* 🌐 *www.elbodegon.com.pe.*

El Mercado

$$$ | **SEAFOOD** | Cebiches and tiraditos made with sustainably sourced fish are the focus at this hot new seafood emporium from Rafael Osterling (of Rafael fame). The open kitchen and interior-patio design complement the lightness of the recipes, which frequently incorporate Asian accents. **Known for:** melt-in-your-mouth causas; inventive cebiches; sushi and sashimi. $ *Average main: S/60* ✉ *Av. Hipólito Unanue 203, Miraflores* ☎ *01/221–1322* 🌐 *www.rafaelosterling.pe/es/el-mercado.html* ⏲ *No dinner. Closed Mon.*

El Señorío de Sulco

$$$ | **PERUVIAN** | Owner Isabel Álvarez has authored several cookbooks on traditional Peruvian cuisine, which is the specialty here. Start with one of various cebiches or *chupe de camarones* (a creamy river-prawn soup) if in season, then move on to *arroz con pato* (rice and duck with a splash of dark beer) or *huatia sulcana* (a traditional beef stew). **Known for:** cebiche; traditional food; good service. $ *Average main: S/54* ✉ *Malecón Cisneros 1470, Miraflores* ☎ *01/441–0389* 🌐 *www.senoriodesulco.com* ⏲ *No dinner Sun.*

Huaca Pucllana Restaurante

$$$ | **PERUVIAN** | The view of the adjacent, 1,500-year-old, pre-Inca ruins is reason enough to dine at Huaca Pucllana, but the sumptuous Peruvian and international cuisine is a close second. The best tables are outside, with a view of the ruins, which are spectacularly floodlit at night. The Peruvian-fusion menu includes treats such as grilled alpaca in a mustard sauce with corn soufflé and paiche (an Amazon fish) with Brazil-nut flakes and a spicy cocona (jungle fruit) sauce. **Known for:** priceless view of pre-Inca ruins; quality Peruvian cuisine; yummy desserts. $ *Average main: S/56* ✉ *Huaca Pucllana, Cl. General Borgoño at Cl. Ayacucho, Miraflores* ☎ *01/445–4042* 🌐 *www.resthuacapucllana.com* ⏲ *Closed 4–7 pm.*

★ **La Mar**

$$$ | **SEAFOOD** | Chef Gastón Acurio's reinvention of the traditional *cebichería* is one of Lima's most popular lunch spots. The décor is minimal, but the menu offers a kaleidoscopic selection of delectable seafood dishes. **Known for:** amazing seafood; bustling atmosphere; large shareable portions. $ *Average main: S/56* ✉ *Av. La Mar 770, Miraflores* ☎ *01/421–3365* 🌐 *www.lamarcebicheria.com* ⏲ *No dinner.*

La Picantería

$$$ | **PERUVIAN** | Located just steps outside Miraflores near the Mercado No. 1 in Surquillo, this rustic tavern harkens back to Peru's *picanterías* (country restaurants) of old. The drill is simple: you sit down on one of the wooden benches, you choose your fish (or shellfish), and you tell the waiter how you want it prepared. **Known for:** fresh-off-the-dock seafood; traditional country hospitality; great beef ribs. $ *Average main: S/55* ✉ *Cl. Francisco Moreno 388, Miraflores* ☎ *01/241–6676* 🌐 *www.picanteriasdelperu.com* ⏲ *No dinner. Closed Sun.*

La Rosa Náutica

$$$$ | **SEAFOOD** | This rambling, Victorian-style complex perched over the Pacific at the end of a breakwater serves up quality seafood with spectacular views, complete with surfers riding the waves as the sun goes down. Signature dishes include a mixed fish, scallops, and octopus cebiche, and grilled *corvina* (sea bass) with a leek fondue sauce. **Known for:** great ocean views; various cebiche options; elegant service. $ *Average main: S/72* ✉ *Espigón 4, Circuito de Playas, Miraflores* ☎ *01/445–0149* 🌐 *www.larosanautica.com.*

La Tiendecita Blanca

$$$ | **SWISS** | This old-fashioned Swiss eatery first flung open its doors in 1936, and little has changed since. It still serves a selection of quality European and Peruvian cuisine in a refined atmosphere,

with ornately painted wooden details on the doors and along the ceiling that evoke the Old Country. *Rösti* (grated potatoes with bacon and cheese) and three kinds of fondue are among the traditional Swiss options. **Known for:** three kinds of fondue; excellent three-course lunches; decadent desserts. *Average main: S/60 Av. José Larco 111, Miraflores 01/241–1124 www.latiendecitablanca.com.pe.*

La Trattoria di Mambrino

$$ | **ITALIAN** | After a quarter-century in business, this remains one of Lima's best Italian restaurants. The proof is on the plate: dishes such as artichoke ravioli and fettuccine *magnífico* (with a prosciutto, Parmesan, and white-truffle sauce) are perennial favorites. **Known for:** homemade pastas; world-class desserts; unhurried customer service. *Average main: S/49 Larcomar, Malecón de la Reserva 610, Miraflores 01/447–5941 www.latrattoriadimambrino.com.*

★ Maido

$$$$ | **PERUVIAN** | Mitsuharu Tsumura is one of Lima's most innovative chefs, and his exquisite Nikkei (Japanese-Peruvian) creations have garnered for Maido the top slot on San Pellegrino's Best Latin American Restaurants list for three years running (be sure to reserve at least three months in advance). Tsumura changes things up frequently, but his menus always include cebiches and *nigiris* (sushi with Peruvian flavors), plus cooked dishes such as *asado de tira mitsuke* (braised short ribs with pickled ginger and fried rice), cod *misayaki* (marinated in miso with sweet potato and Brazil nuts), and *sanguichitas* (a plate of unique sandwiches). **Known for:** Nikkei cuisine; 13-course tasting menu; superb sushi and sashimi. *Average main: S/75 Cl. San Martín 399, Miraflores 01/313–5100 www.maido.pe No dinner Sun.*

Matsuei

$$$ | **JAPANESE** | The sushi chefs shout out a greeting as you enter the teak-floored dining room of this Miraflores standout, which dates back over 50 years. The kitchen specializes in sushi and sashimi, but if raw is not your thing, there's also plenty of hot food such as tempuras, teriyakis, and *kushiyaki*, a broiled chicken fillet with ginger sauce. **Known for:** ancestral Japanese cooking; super-fresh seafood; scrumptious stir-fried rice. *Average main: S/54 Cl. Atahuapa 195, Miraflores 981/310–180 matsueiperu.com.pe No dinner Sun.*

Panchita

$$ | **PERUVIAN** | Situated on a quiet Miraflores side street, and featuring a wood-burning oven and a cozy lounge where locals linger over cocktails late into the evening, this understated eatery serves up comfort food, Gastón Acurio–style. Nearly everything on the menu is good, but standouts include the *anticuchos* (kebab-like skewers, usually of beef hearts, but here also with more imaginative options such as swordfish) and *cochinilla de 21 días*, a whole suckling pig with meat so juicy you won't need the accompanying *zarza criolla* (pickled onions) Go late at night, when the mood is mellow and romantic. **Known for:** classic criollo cooking; excellent tacu-tacus; multidish samplers. *Average main: S/50 Av. Dos de Mayo 298, Miraflores 01/242–5957 panchita.pe No dinner Sun.*

Pescados Capitales

$$ | **SEAFOOD** | This vast, whitewashed restaurant with a laid-back vibe is popular with limeños, who flock here for its inventive recipes and fresh seafood. The name is a play on the Spanish term for the seven deadly sins, and *gula* (gluttony)—think fettuccine with a mix of scallops, shrimp, and squid in a spicy cream sauce—is one of many sins worth committing here. **Known for:** inventive seafood dishes; busy lunchtime vibe; good jungle-accented selections. *Average main: S/50 Av. Mariscal La Mar 1337, Miraflores 01/706–0610 www.pescadoscapitales.com No dinner Sun.*

Punta Sal

$$ | **SEAFOOD** | On a sunny afternoon, the view of the malecón and its graceful paragliders from the upper floors of this restaurant is as good as the food—which is excellent. Dishes include classic cebichería fare such as *tiradito criollo* (thin slices of marinated fish covered in a yellow-pepper sauce), *conchitas a la parmesana* (scallops on the half-shell smothered in garlic and toasted cheese), or *pescado a la chorrillana* (fish fillet in a tomato, onion, and chili sauce). *Piqueos,* platters of appetizers, are fun to share. **Known for:** classic limeño seafood; great view; packed on weekends. *Average main: S/42 Malecón Cisneros at Av. Tripoli, Miraflores 01/242–4524 www.puntasal.com No dinner.*

Punto Azul

$$ | **SEAFOOD** | Generous portions of quality seafood at reasonable prices are the reason there's usually a line at this Miraflores standby. Classic Peruvian dishes such as cebiche, *arroz con mariscos* (rice with seafood), and *parihuela* (a seafood soup) keep the locals coming back. **Known for:** traditional seafood dishes; affordable prices; good rep among locals. *Average main: S/38 Cl. San Martín 595, Miraflores 01/445–8078 puntoazulrestaurante.com No dinner Sun. No lunch Mon.*

Quattro D

$ | **CAFÉ** | **FAMILY** | The green-and-white striped awning ensures that you won't miss this café, which is a favorite among young couples and harried parents with children in tow. Although it's menu includes pastas, sandwiches, and economical lunch specials, most people come here for one thing: ice cream. *Average main: S/15 Av. Angamos Oeste 408, Miraflores 981/475–385 4d.pe.*

Rafael

$$$ | **PERUVIAN** | This small corner house seems inconspicuous, but at mealtimes it's invariably packed with foodies feasting on Rafael Osterling's culinary creations. One of Lima's best chefs, Osterling mixes Peruvian, Mediterranean, and Asian influences in a menu brimming with innovation. **Known for:** pastas with seafood; Mediterranean flavors; delicious duck dishes. *Average main: S/64 Cl. San Martín 300, Miraflores 01/242–4149 www.rafaelosterling.pe.*

Restaurante Rigoletto

$$ | **ITALIAN** | On a quiet street a block and a half from the busy intersection of Larco and Benavides, this small restaurant in a renovated house is known for its southern-Italian cuisine. The Peruvian owner worked at one of Miami's best Italian eateries before setting up shop in Miraflores. **Known for:** great pastas; reasonable prices; traditional osso buco. *Average main: S/40 Cl. Colón 161, Miraflores 01/444–3046 www.restauranterigoletto.com Closed Sun.*

Saqra

$$ | **PERUVIAN** | The name of this attractive eatery is Quechua for "little devil," which captures well the kitchen's playful take on Peruvian cuisine. Here you'll enjoy smash-up dishes such as gnocchi a la huancaína and panko-crusted prawns with a passion-fruit ginger-pisco sauce. **Known for:** creative recipes; funky but romantic setting; pleasant terrace. *Average main: S/45 Pje. El Suche, Av. La Paz 646, Miraflores 01/650–8884 www.saqra.pe Closed Sun.*

Hotels

Belmond Miraflores Park

$$$$ | **HOTEL** | The spacious ocean-view rooms here overlook the city's coastline and the sea beyond, affording one of Lima's best panoramas. **Pros:** ocean-view rooms worth the extra cost; executive-lounge access means free food and drinks; luxurious bedding. **Cons:** very pricey; city-view rooms disappointing; service can occasionally be slow.

Continued on page 102

FOOD IN PERU

by Mark Sullivan

When Peruvians talk about *comida criolla*, or typical food, they aren't talking about just one thing. This is a vast country, and dishes on the table in coastal Trujillo might be nowhere in mountainous Cusco. And all bets are off once you reach places like Iquitos, where the surrounding jungle yields exotic flavors.

REGIONAL CUISINE

A woman preparing *anticuchos.*

Cebiche

THE CAPITAL

Lima cooks up the widest variety of Peruvian and international foods. One of the most influential immigrant communities is the Chinese, who serve traditional dishes in restaurants called *chifas*. One favorite, *lomo saltado*, strips of beef sautéed with onions, tomatoes, and friend potatoes, is now considered a local dish.

THE COAST

When you talk about the cuisine of the country's vast coastal region, you are talking about seafood. Peruvians are very particular about their fish, insisting that it should be pulled from the sea that morning. The most common dish is *cebiche*, raw fish "cooked" in lime juice. It comes in endless variations—all delicious.

THE ALTIPLANO

Hearty fare awaits in the altiplano. Because it keeps so well over the winter, the potato is the staple of many dishes, including the ubiquitous *cau cau*, or tripe simmered with potatoes and peppers. A special treat is pachamanca, a Peruvian-style barbecue where meat and potatoes are cooked in a hole in the ground lined with hot rocks. In Huancayo, the local specialty is *papa a la huancaina*, boiled potato covered in yellow chili-cheese sauce.

THE AMAZON

Fish is a staple in the Amazon, and you'll know why once you taste paiche and other species unknown outside this area. One of the best ways to try local fish is *patarashca*, or fish wrapped in bijao leaves and cooked over an open fire. Restaurants here are very simple, often just a few tables around an outdoor grill.

IT'S ALL ABOUT THE FISH

Peru's high-altitude lakes, including Lake Titicaca, and rivers spawn some very tastey *trucha* (trout).

In Peru, restaurants known as *cebicherías* serve more than the marinated fish called cebiche. The menu may intimidate those who can't tell *lenguado* (sole) from *langosta* (lobster). Don't worry—just order a series of dishes to share. Local families pass around huge platters of pescado until they are picked clean, then gesture to the server for the next course.

The fragrant *parihuela* is soup overflowing with fish, shrimp, and chorros (mussels) still in their shells. *Tiradito* is similar to cebiche but leaves off the onions and adds a spicy yellow-pepper sauce. A platter of *chicharrones de calamar*, little ringlets of deep-fried squid, should be given a squeeze of lime. For a nice filet or whole fish, many restaurants suggest a dozen or more preparations.

ON THE SIDE

CHOCLO
A pile of large-kernel corn.

Camote
Boiled sweet potatoes. The sweetness is a wonderful contrast to the citrus marinade.

Cancha
A basket full of fried corn that's usually roasted on the premises. Highly addictive.

Chifles
A northern coast specialty of thin slices of fried banana.

Zarandajas
A bean dish served in the northern coast.

Papas
Potatoes, boiled, fritas (fried), or *puré* (mashed).

SPUD COUNTRY

POTATO ON THE PLATE

The potato, or its cousin the yucca, is rarely absent from a Peruvian table. Any restaurant offering *comida criolla*, or traditional cuisine, will doubtless serve *cau cau* (tripe simmered with potatoes and peppers), *papa a la huancaina* (potatoes in a spicy cheese sauce), or ocopa (boiled potatoes in peanut sauce). Just about everywhere you can find a version of *lomo saltado*, made from strips of beef sautéed with tomatoes, onions, and fried potatoes. Some 600,000 Peruvian farmers, most with small lots in the highlands, grow more than 3,250,000 tons of potatoes a year.

POTATO HISTORY

The potato comes from the Andes of Peru and Chile (not Idaho or Ireland), where it has been grown on the mountain terraces for thousands of years. There are endless varieties of this durable tuber: more than 7,000 of them, some of which are hardy enough to be cultivated at 15,000 feet. The Spanish introduced potatoes to Europe in the late 1500s.

(above) Preparing *pachamanca*; (left) Discovering the potato.

GET YOUR PURPLE POTATOES HERE!

Peru's potatoes appear in all colors of the spectrum, including purple, red, pink, and blue. They also come in many strange shapes.

SCIENCE POTATO

The International Potato Center (Centro Internacional de la Papa), outside of Lima, conducts spud research to help farmers and open markets, particularly for the great variety of Andean potatoes. Its genebank preserves seeds and *in vitro* plantlets of more than 10,500 potato varieties and 8,500 sweet potato varieties, in order to conserve that diversity and share it with crop breeding programs around the world.

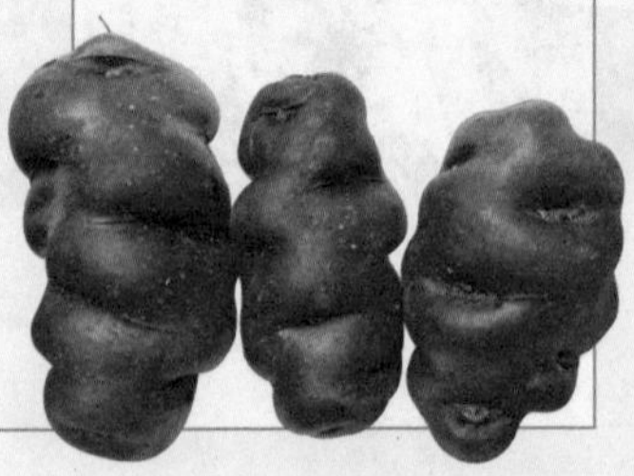

OTHER STAPLES

CORN: Almost as important as potatoes is corn. You might be surprised to find that the kernels are more than twice as large as their North American friends. Most corn dishes are very simple, such as the tamale-like *humitas*, but some are more complex, like the stew called *pepián de choclo*. A favorite in the humid lowlands is *inchi capi*, a chicken dish served with peanuts and toasted corn. A sweet purple corn is the basis for chicha morada, a thick beverage, and *mazamorra*, an even thicker jelly used in desserts. Even ancient Peruvians loved popcorn, kernels were found in tombs 1000 years old in eastern Peru. Also discovered were ceramic popcorn poppers from 3000 AD.

Hot pepper tip: Never rub your eyes after handling a hot pepper, and avoid contact with your skin.

PEPPERS: Few Peruvian dishes don't include *ají*, the potent hot peppers grown all over the country. You'll find several everywhere—*amarillo* (yellow pepper), rocoto (a reddish variety), and *panca* (a lovely chocolate brown variety), but there are hundreds of regional favorites. Some, like ají *norteño*, are named for the region of origin, others, like the cherry-sized ají *cereza*, are named for what they resemble. Such is the case with the ají *pinguita de mono*, which, roughly translated, means "small monkey penis." It is one of the hottest that you'll find.

FOR ADVENTUROUS EATERS

CUY: What was served at the Last Supper? According to a baroque painting hanging in the Iglesia de San Francisco in Lima, it was guinea pig. The painting shows a platter in the middle of the table with a whole roasted guinea pig, including the head and feet.

This dish, called *cuy chactado* or simply cuy, has long been a staple of the altiplano. Cuy is a bit hard to swallow, mostly because it is served whole. The flavor is like pork, and can be sweet and tender if carefully cooked.

(Top, right) *humita*; (bottom) Peruvian eating guinea pig.

ANTICUCHOS: When a street vendor fires up his grill, the savory scent of *anticuchos* will catch your attention. Beef hearts in the Andes are a delicacy. Marinated in herbs and spices, these strips of meat are incredibly tender. They have become popular in urban areas, and you're likely to run across restaurants called *anticucherías* in Lima and other cities.

ALPACA: Nearly every visitor to Cusco and the surrounding region will be offered a steak made of alpaca. It's not an especially tasty piece of meat, which may be why locals don't eat it very often. But go ahead—you can impress the folks back home.

$ *Rooms from: S/1600* ✉ *Malecón de la Reserva 1035, Miraflores* ☎ *01/610–4000* 🌐 *www.belmond.com* 🛏 *81 rooms* 🍽 *Free breakfast.*

El Pardo DoubleTree by Hilton Hotel
$$ | **HOTEL** | The comfortable rooms, rooftop pool, and large health club make this hotel a good option for travelers. **Pros:** well-stocked business center; rooftop pool; central location. **Cons:** impersonal feel; views are unimpressive; room décor is bland. $ *Rooms from: S/400* ✉ *Cl. Independencia 141, Miraflores* ☎ *01/617–1000* 🌐 *hilton.com* 🛏 *241 rooms* 🍽 *Breakfast.*

Hilton Lima Miraflores
$$$ | **HOTEL** | Located on a quiet residential street a short walk from both Larcomar and Parque Kennedy, this sleek hotel offers chic rooms with urban views and the service and amenities you'd expect from a Hilton. **Pros:** attractive rooms with spacious baths; rooftop deck with pool and Jacuzzis; charming on-site restaurant. **Cons:** mediocre views; some rooms are a little dark; service can be a bit slow. $ *Rooms from: S/780* ✉ *Av. La Paz 1099, Miraflores* ☎ *01/200–8000* 🌐 *www.hilton.com* 🛏 *207 rooms* 🍽 *No meals.*

Hostal Torreblanca
$$ | **HOTEL** | Although this eclectic older building is a little far from the center of Miraflores, it's just a block from a park overlooking the ocean and is a good option for travelers with a limited budget. **Pros:** strong local character; near oceanfront park; attractive décor. **Cons:** smallish rooms; on a busy traffic circle; a bit of a walk to many bars and restaurants. $ *Rooms from: S/290* ✉ *Av. José Pardo 1453, Miraflores* ☎ *01/242–1876* 🌐 *www.torreblancaperu.com* 🛏 *24 rooms* 🍽 *Free breakfast.*

★ **Hotel Antigua Miraflores**
$$ | **B&B/INN** | Black-and-white marble floors and crystal chandeliers greet you as you stroll through the antiques-filled lobby of this salmon-colored mansion, where boutique hotel–style accommodations are surprisingly affordable. **Pros:** beautiful setting; spacious rooms; hospitable staff. **Cons:** additional charge for certain breakfast items; some suites are a bit small; hot-water pressure is occasionally weak. $ *Rooms from: S/300* ✉ *Av. Grau 350, Miraflores* ☎ *01/201–2060* 🌐 *www.antiguamiraflores.com* 🛏 *81 rooms* 🍽 *Free breakfast.*

★ **JW Marriott Hotel Lima**
$$$ | **HOTEL** | In addition to being at the heart of the action, across the street from the Larcomar shopping mall, rooms in this gleaming glass tower have impressive ocean views. **Pros:** stunning ocean views; attractive, airy lobby lounge; indoor pool. **Cons:** corner deluxe rooms lack ocean view; traffic outside can be noisy on weekends; a bit of a walk to Parque Kennedy. $ *Rooms from: S/600* ✉ *Malecón de la Reserva at Av. José Larco, Miraflores* ☎ *01/217–7000* 🌐 *www.marriott.com* 🛏 *300 rooms* 🍽 *No meals.*

La Paz Apart Hotel
$$ | **HOTEL** | Most rooms here are small apartments with a dining/living room, making the hotel popular for lengthier stays. **Pros:** excellent location; decent-sized apartments; good value. **Cons:** lots of street noise; Wi-Fi can be weak; showers in need of an upgrade. $ *Rooms from: S/275* ✉ *Av. La Paz 679, Miraflores* ☎ *01/242–9350* 🌐 *www.lapazaparthotel.com* 🛏 *27 rooms* 🍽 *Free breakfast.*

Radisson Hotel Decapolis Miraflores
$$$ | **HOTEL** | Bright, comfortable rooms, a convenient location, and competitive rates make this hotel a good option for travelers who like high-end amenities but don't want to pay a fortune for them. **Pros:** some rooms come with ocean views; competitive rates; good on-site fusion restaurant. **Cons:** not quite up to luxury-hotel standards; service could be better; décor is a bit dull. $ *Rooms from: S/526* ✉ *Av. 28 de Julio 151, Miraflores*

Changing of the guard, Peru-style, in front of the Palacio de Gobierno (Government Palace) in El Centro.

01/625–1200 www.radissonhotels.com 105 rooms Free breakfast.

San Antonio Abad

$ | B&B/INN | This mansion in a residential neighborhood offers atmosphere, tranquility, and very reasonable rates; the rambling old building has common areas with colonial-style furnishings overlooking a small courtyard. **Pros:** short walk to the center of Miraflores; cozy furnishings; good breakfast. **Cons:** some dated décor; beds could be improved; no air-conditioning. *Rooms from: S/225 Cl. Ramón Ribeyro 301, Miraflores 01/447–6766 26 rooms Free breakfast.*

Nightlife

BARS

Huaringas

BARS/PUBS | Occupying several floors of a lovely old house next to the restaurant Brujas de Cachiche, Huaringas is a pleasant place for a drink, though it can get packed on weekends. *Cl. Bolognesi 460, Miraflores 01/243–8151.*

La Cuina de Bonilla

TAPAS BARS | One of a dozen bars on Calle Manuel Bonilla, La Cuina is known for its ample selection of tapas—from mushrooms sautéed with garlic to *tortilla española* (Spanish omelet)—and good lineup of microbrewery beers. The tables out front are a nice spot for a drink. *Cl. Manuel Bonilla 124, Miraflores 01/241–2189 www.lacuina.pe.*

Nuevo Mundo Draft Bar

BARS/PUBS | This laid-back pub in the heart of Miraflores sells draft and bottled beers from several microbreweries. The food is also unusually good. *Cl. Manuel Bonilla 103, Miraflores 946/323–351 www.facebook.com/NuevoMundoBarLima.*

Sukha Buda Lounge

BARS/PUBS | The giant Buddha statue that presides over this vast, airy club may seem a bit over the top, but the place is quite popular, in part because it doesn't charge a cover. There's often a good DJ, and though there's no dance floor, customers get up and groove wherever there's room as the night progresses. ✉ *Cl. Dos de Mayo 694, Miraflores* ☎ *956/553–912* 🌐 *www.sukha.pe* ☞ *Closed Sun.–Tues.*

DANCE CLUBS

Lima Bar

DANCE CLUBS | Down several flights of stairs from the lower level of the Larcomar shopping center is this cavernous dance club, a see-and-be-seen destination for Lima's beautiful people. The club and the shopping center are built into a cliff, so if you need a break, step out back for a sweeping view of the Lima coast. The bar is open Friday and Saturday from 9 pm to 6 am. ✉ *Larcomar, Malecón de la Reserva 610, next to Pardos, Miraflores* ☎ 🌐 *www.facebook.com/LimaBarLarcomar* ☞ *Closed Sun.–Thurs.*

Son de Cuba

DANCE CLUBS | There are plenty of places to dance in Miraflores, but this Cuban-owned bar on the Calle de las Pizzas is among the most entertaining. On weekends, it offers salsa classes from 7 to 9, and a live band plays Cuban beats from 11:30 pm to 2:30 am. A DJ spins Latin dance music the rest of the time. ✉ *Cl. San Ramón 277, Miraflores* ☎ *941/494–941* 🌐 *www.facebook.com/salsotecasondecuba.*

LGBTQ

Legendaris

DANCE CLUBS | With its big dance floor and convenient location a few blocks west of Parque Miraflores's southern end, Legendaris is a popular weekend spot, drawing a young, mostly gay and lesbian crowd. ✉ *Cl. Berlin 363, Miraflores* ☎ *01/446–3435* 🌐 *www.facebook.com/discotecalegendarismiraflores* ☞ *Closed Mon.–Wed.*

ValeTodo Downtown

DANCE CLUBS | After midnight, head to one of Lima's most popular dance clubs, ValeTodo Downtown, which draws a young, largely LGBT crowd. A balcony filled with comfy couches overlooks the cavernous dance floor, where revelers move and mingle. Not only does the club open early (9 pm), but it closes late, with drag queens performing around 3 am on weekends. ✉ *Pje. Los Pinos 160, Miraflores* ☎ *01/446–8222* 🌐 *www.mundovaletodo.com.*

LIVE MUSIC

Cocodrilo Verde

MUSIC CLUBS | Two blocks west of Parque Kennedy, Cocodrilo Verde features some of Peru's best musicians, plus visiting acts that play everything from jazz to salsa and bossa nova. Shows start anytime between 9 and 11 pm, depending on the night. ✉ *Cl. Francisco de Paula Camino 226, Miraflores* ☎ *01/444–2381* 🌐 *www.cocodriloverde.com.*

El Tayta

MUSIC CLUBS | On the second floor of an old building across from Parque Kennedy, El Tayta has live guitar music (mostly Latin pop) performed by duos or trios. ✉ *Av. José Larco 437, Miraflores* ☎ *01/444–3317* 🌐 *www.facebook.com/eltaytaperu* ☞ *Closed Sun.*

Jazz Zone

MUSIC CLUBS | It's easy to miss the Jazz Zone, hidden in a colonial-style shopping complex called El Suche. Head up a bright-red stairway to the dimly lit second-story lounge for performances of everything from Latin jazz to blues and flamenco, with salsa or other dance music on weekends. Shows start at 10:30. ✉ *Pje. El Suche, Av. La Paz 656, Miraflores* ☎ *994/273–659* 🌐 *www.jazzzoneperu.com* ☞ *Closed Sun.*

Performing Arts

Centro Cultural Ricardo Palma

CULTURAL FESTIVALS | There is always something going on at the Centro Cultural Ricardo Palma, a municipal cultural center three blocks south of Parque Kennedy. It hosts nightly concerts, dance performances, and plays at affordable prices. ✉ *Av. José Larco 770, Miraflores* ☎ *01/617–7265* 🌐 *www.facebook.com/culturamiraflores.*

Shopping

ANTIQUES

Avenida La Paz is the best street for rare-antiques finds in Miraflores. The street changes name on the north side of Avenida Ricardo Palma, becoming Calle Alfonso Ugarte, but you'll find some antiques shops and fairs there as well.

El Frailero

ANTIQUES/COLLECTIBLES | Brooding saints dominate the walls of this small shop, which also has some interesting ceramic and silver figures. It's open only for a few hours in the afternoon and evening, but the owners live nearby and are happy to open the store at other times if you give them a call. ✉ *Av. La Paz 551, Miraflores* ☎ *01/447–2823* 🌐 *www.facebook.com/elfrailero.*

El Nazareno

ANTIQUES/COLLECTIBLES | One of several small antiques shops in the Pasaje El Suche (a small, colonial-style complex), El Nazareno has an eclectic selection of antique statues and religious art, as well as handicrafts such as woven rugs. ✉ *Pje. El Suche, Av. La Paz 646, No. 5, Miraflores* ☎ *01/447–8344.*

La Linea del Tiempo

ANTIQUES/COLLECTIBLES | This store offers a mix of old and new, including antique paintings, ceramics, jewelry, and other collectables. ✉ *Av. La Paz 640, Miraflores* ☎ *993/032–248* 🌐 *www.facebook.com/Lalineadeltiempo.*

BOOKS

El Virrey

BOOKS/STATIONERY | This huge bookstore has countless volumes on Peruvian art, cooking, history, and other subjects. There's also a pleasant café, and the owners host frequent nighttime events. ✉ *Cl. Bolognesi 510, Miraflores* ☎ *01/444–4141* 🌐 *elvirrey.com.*

CLOTHING

All Alpaca

CLOTHING | One of several shops in Miraflores specializing in alpaca clothing, All Alpaca sells sophisticated sweaters, ponchos, coats, and more. There's a second shop at Avenida José Larco 1005. ✉ *Cl. Schell 377, Miraflores* ☎ *01/242–8051* 🌐 *allalpacaweb.com.*

Kuna

CLOTHING | Lots of stores stock clothing made of alpaca, but Kuna is one of the few to also offer articles made from vicuña, a cousin of the llama that produces the world's finest and most expensive wool. The shop offers an excellent selection of scarves, sweaters, shawls, and coats in an array of colors and styles. Kuna has a second branch in the Larcomar shopping center. ✉ *Av. Larco 671, Miraflores* ☎ *01/447–1623* 🌐 *www.kunastores.com.*

Sol Alpaca

CLOTHING | Conveniently located on busy Avenida José Larco, this popular shop offers a colorful mix of alpaca clothing with lovely designs. The selection includes sweaters, shawls, coats, hats, and scarves. It also has shops in the Larcomar shopping center and in the Amano Museum. ✉ *Av. José Larco 847, Miraflores* ☎ *01/651–7453* 🌐 *www.solalpaca.com.*

HANDICRAFTS

Agua y Tierra

CRAFTS | Ceramics, hand-painted or embroidered fabrics, and other handicrafts of the country´s Amazonian tribes decorate the windows of this small shop two blocks east of Parque Miraflores, but it also has some Andean statues and retablos. ✉ *Av. Ernesto Diez Canseco 298, Miraflores* ☎ *01/444–6980* 🌐 *aguaytierra.negocio.site* 🕒 *Closed Sat. and Sun.*

Andean Treasures

CRAFTS | Two blocks north of Larcomar on Avenida José Larco is this modern shop, with a selection of quality alpaca clothing and handicrafts that include jewelry, mini retablos from Ayacucho, and *toritos de Pucará* (ceramic bulls from the Puno region). ✉ *Av. José Larco 1219, Miraflores* ☎ *01/243–2627.*

★ La Floristeria

CRAFTS | The tiny but charming La Floristeria, in front of the Pasaje El Suche complex, is filled with quality handicrafts from a select group of artisans: hand-painted trays, ceramic-figure-packed *retablos ayacuchanos* (decorative, portable altar boxes that depict religious events), jewelry, weavings, candles, and other colorful collectables. ✉ *Av. La Paz 644, Miraflores* ☎ *01/444–2288.*

JEWELRY

H. Stern

JEWELRY/ACCESSORIES | It's unlikely you'll find gold jewelry elsewhere as distinctive as the pieces at H. Stern. The well-regarded South American chain specializes in designs influenced by pre-Columbian art. There are also branches in the Miraflores Park Hotel and at the airport. ✉ *JW Marriott Hotel Lima, Malecón de la Reserva at Av. José Larco, ground fl., Miraflores* ☎ *01/242–3610* 🌐 *www.hstern.net.*

MALLS

Larcomar

SHOPPING CENTERS/MALLS | This open-air shopping center is one of Miraflores's big crowd-pleasers. It's built into the cliff at the end of Avenida José Larco, so it's almost invisible from the street. The dozens of shops, bars, and restaurants are terraced, and some of them have impressive views of the coast and ocean below. ✉ *Malecón de la Reserva and Av. José Larco, Miraflores* ☎ *01/625–4343* 🌐 *www.larcomar.com.*

MARKETS

Just north of Avenida Ricardo Palma in Miraflores, Avenida Petit Thouars has half a dozen souvenir markets crammed with vendors, all of whom expect you to bargain. There are also countless smaller shops tucked into the same neighborhood between Avenida Arequipa and the Vía Expresa, so allow time to wander.

La Portada del Sol

GIFTS/SOUVENIRS | Excellent-quality goods can be found at La Portada del Sol. In this miniature mall, the vendors show off their wares in glass cases lighted with halogen lamps. Some accept credit cards. ✉ *Av. Petit Thouars 5411, Miraflores.*

Mercado Indio

GIFTS/SOUVENIRS | Ask a local about the best place for handicrafts in Lima, and you'll probably be told to go to Mercado Indio. The selection ranges from mass-produced souvenirs to one-of-a-kind pieces, and since most vendors will bargain, you can often get very good deals. ✉ *Av. Petit Thouars 5245, Miraflores.*

Barranco

Tiny Barranco is big on charm. In the 19th century, middle- and upper-class limeños would come to this seaside resort to splash around along the cliffs of the Costa Verde, while the poets and artists who congregated in its cafés added a bohemian, fin de siècle vibe. Today, these establishments have given way to bars, discos, and high-rises looking out over the beach, but locals have managed to preserve the area's traditional, vaguely hipster-ish character.

Barranco is ground zero for Lima's burgeoning arts scene. At its north end, the Museo de Arte Contemporáneo hosts exhibitions and wine-and-cheese events for the smart set, while farther south, photographer Mario Testino's gallery is a mecca for aspiring shutterbugs. Nor are the performing arts lacking: a night out here can include a show of Afro-Peruvian *música negra* at one of the many peñas or a tour through the country's danzas folklóricas in a cultural center like La Candelaria. And don't ignore the street-art scene: right now, this 'hood is one of the continent's hot spots.

Chabuca Granda, a criollo singer dear to the heart of nearly all Peruvians, once crooned her nostalgia for a lost Barranco, "hidden among leafy trees and longings." One stroll through this lovely enclave, and you'll see what she meant.

GETTING AROUND

To get your bearings in Barranco, head to the Parque Municipal, one of the nicest of the city's plazas. To the south, the pinkish building with the clock tower is the Biblioteca Municipal, or Municipal Library, while to the north is the parish church of La Santísima Cruz. From the square, steps lead down to Lima's romantic Bridge of Sighs, or Puente de los Suspiros. Passing below the bridge, in the shade of ancient trees, is the Bajada de los Baños, lined with wonderful old houses and colorful bougainvillea, and at whose terminus you'll find the waves of Playa Barranquito. On the beach, a string of bars and restaurants comprises one of Lima's most popular meeting spots at night.

Sights

Bajada de los Baños

PROMENADE | FAMILY | This cobbled walkway leading down to the "baths"—Barranco's beaches—is shaded by leafy trees and lined with historic architecture. Once the route local fishermen took to reach their boats, it's now a popular promenade at night, when boleros and ballads can be heard from the adjoining restaurants. At the bottom of the hill, a covered wooden bridge takes you across a busy road, the Circuito de Playas, to a promenade containing beaches and restaurants. A short walk to the north is Playa Barranquito; Playa Agua Dulce is half a mile south. ✉ *Barranco* ✢ *One block west of Parque Municipal.*

El Mirador

VIEWPOINT | FAMILY | Head down the path to the left of La Ermita church and you'll come upon El Mirador, a scenic lookout with a splendid view of Lima's coastline all the way out to the port of El Callao. It's especially attractive at night, when you can see an illuminated cross and Christ statue on the promontory in Chorrillos to the south. There are also several good bars here, plus local criollo musicians who'll sing you "*La flor de la canela*" for a small tip. ✉ *Barranco* ✢ *North of Puente de los Suspiros, next to Iglesia la Ermita.*

Galleria Lucía de la Puente

MUSEUM | Lucía de la Puente represents some of the best artists in Peru, as well as other South American nations, at Lima's premier gallery, which occupies a historic house on Barranco's most charming street. Some of de la Puente's private collection is on display next door, in the public areas of Hotel B. ✉ *Jr. Sáenz Peña 206, Barranco* ☎ *01/477–0237* 🎟 *Free* ⏲ *Closed Sun.*

Museo de Arte Contemporáneo—Lima (MAC)

MUSEUM | Lima's newest art museum is run by a privately funded institute on land donated by the Municipality of Barranco. Its minimalistic, rectangular exhibition spaces house a permanent collection by Latin American and European artists that dates from the past 60 years, as well as temporary shows that change every few months. The main hall overlooks a metal sculpture by Veronica Wiesse perched over a reflection pond; beyond it lies a small park that's used for fairs and other events. ✉ *Av. Grau 1511, Barranco* ☎ *01/514–6800* 🌐 *www.maclima.pe* 🎟 *S/10* ⏲ *Closed Mon.*

Museo Mario Testino (MATE)

MUSEUM | Occupying a refurbished, turn-of-the-century house near the Museo Pedro de Osma, this small museum exhibits photos by renowned Peruvian fashion photographer Mario Testino. It has rooms dedicated to the likes of Kate Moss, Gisele Bündchen, and Madonna, as well as a few photos of indigenous Peruvians in traditional Andean dress. A separate building holds a sampling from the last photo shoot of Princess Diana before her untimely death. The gift shop has some great postcards, and the museum's café is a pleasant spot for a light meal or drink. ✉ *Av. Pedro de Osma 409, Barranco* ☎ *01/200–5400* 🌐 *www.mate.pe* 🎫 *S/10* 🕒 *Closed Mon.*

★ Museo Pedro de Osma

MUSEUM | Even if it contained no art, this century-old Beaux-Arts mansion would be worth the trip for its design elements alone. The mansard-roofed structure—with inlaid wood floors, delicately painted ceilings, and stained-glass windows in every room—was the home of a wealthy collector of religious artifacts. The best of his collection is permanently on display. The finest of the paintings, the 18th-century *Virgen de Pomata,* combines Marian iconography with indigenous symbols in the Holy Mother's mountain-shaped robes festooned with garlands of corn. Other halls contain canvases of archangels, fine silverwork, and sculptures of Huamanga alabaster. Make sure to visit the manicured grounds. ✉ *Av. Pedro de Osma 423, Barranco* ☎ *01/467–0063* 🌐 *www.museopedrodeosma.org* 🎫 *S/30* 🕒 *Closed Mon.*

Parque Municipal

CITY PARK | Elegant royal palms, swirls of purple-and-yellow bougainvillea, and the surrounding colonial architecture make this park a Lima standout. Its southern end is lined with historic buildings, the most prominent of which is the library, with its pink clock tower. To the west stands Barranco's Iglesia La Hermita, a lovely neo-Gothic structure unfortunately closed to the public since its roof caved in during a 1940 earthquake. A nearby staircase leads down to the Puente de los Suspiros and Bajada de los Baños. ✉ *Barranco* ✣ *Between Av. Pedro de Osma and Av. Grau* 🎫 *Free.*

Puente de los Suspiros

BRIDGE/TUNNEL | This romantic wooden walkway over the tree-shaded Bajada de los Baños has been the site of countless lovers' trysts. The name translates as "Bridge of Sighs," and it's inspired a host of criollo songs, most famously Chabuca Granda's legendary hit of the same title from 1960. ✉ *Bajada de los Baños, Barranco.*

Restaurants

In keeping with its bohemian reputation, Barranco has a slew of bars and cozy cafés, but its dining options tend to be traditional taverns for home cooking rather than chic foodie galleries. Most are just a short walk from the neighborhood's hotels.

★ Amoramar

$$$ | **PERUVIAN** | Amoramar doesn't look like much from the street, but step through the door, and you'll discover an oasis of poinciana trees in a restored adobe house. Seafood dominates the menu, with a selection ranging from the traditional pulpo a la parrilla to creative recipes such as *atún saltado* (tuna strips sautéed with onions and aji peppers), *chaufa de quinua* (vegetarian stir-fry with quinoa), and *canilla de cordero* (roast lamb in a mild chili sauce). **Known for:** excellent seafood; eclectic dining setting; scrumptious pastel de choclo con mariscos (corn pudding with seafood). 💲 *Average main: S/58* ✉ *Jr. García y García 175, Barranco* ✣ *Near corner of Miraflores and Bolognesi* ☎ *01/619–9595* 🌐 *www.amoramar.com* 🕒 *Closed 4–8 pm. No dinner Sun.*

Sights

1 Bajada de los Baños C5
2 El Mirador C5
3 Galleria Lucia de la Puente C3
4 Museo de Arte Contemporáneo—Lima (MAC)............... C2
5 Museo Mario Testino (MATE) C6
6 Museo Pedro de Osma C6
7 Parque Municipal....... D5
8 Puente de los Suspiros C5

Restaurants

1 Amoramar E4
2 Antica Pizzería C4
3 Cala........................ C4
4 Central C6
5 Chifa Chung Yion........ D4
6 Isolina Taberna Peruana.................... C5
7 Restaurante Arlotia..... D5
8 Songoro Cosongo....... D5

Quick Bites

1 La Bodega Verde C5

Hotels

1 3B Barranco's Bed & Breakfast......... C3
2 Hotel B C3
3 Second Home Peru...... C5
4 Villa Barranco............ C4

Antica Pizzeria

$$ | **ITALIAN** | This Italian eatery is the place to head on a cool night, offering a rustic but warm ambience and great food. The extensive menu includes a wide array of salads and fresh pastas served with your choice of a dozen sauces, but Antica is best known for its pizza: more than 50 different kinds baked in a wood-fired oven. **Known for:** super-thin-crust pizza; rustic ambience; excellent salsa arrabiata. *Average main: S/40 ✉ Av. Prolongación San Martín 201, Barranco ☎ 01/247–3443 🌐 www.anticapizzeria.com.pe.*

Cala

$$$ | **SEAFOOD** | One of Lima's surprisingly few waterfront dining options, Cala has an impressive selection of dishes to complement its ocean vistas. The Peruvian-fusion cuisine ranges from crab ravioli in seafood soup to quinoa-crusted salmon and tenderloin with mushrooms, quinoa, and spinach. **Known for:** great seafood and sushi bar; ocean vistas; well-stocked bar. *Average main: S/52 ✉ Playa Barranquita, Circuito de las Playas, Barranco ☎ 01/477–2020 🌐 www.calarestaurante.com ⏲ No dinner Sun.*

★ Central

$$$$ | **PERUVIAN** | After years working in some of the best kitchens of Europe and Asia, superstar cuisinier Virgilio Martínez returned to Lima to launch this chic, airy venue for his culinary talents—and quickly garnered a reputation as one of Latin America's best chefs. He and his wife, María Pía Leon, change their menu every six months, but each iteration celebrates the country's edible biodiversity with fresh and often organic ingredients. **Known for:** exquisite gastronomic experimentation with multicourse menus; coastal, Andean, and Amazonian cuisine; one of Lima's hottest restaurants (reserve at least a month ahead). *Average main: S/400 ✉ Av. Pedro de Osma 301, Barranco ☎ 01/242–8515 🌐 www.centralrestaurante.com.pe ⏲ Closed Sun. No lunch Sat.*

Chifa Chung Yion

$$ | **CHINESE FUSION** | Don't let the unremarkable facade fool you: the food at this historic chifa can hold its own with the best in Lima's Barrio Chino . Soups are a standout, as are delicacies such as *chancho asado* (roast pork) and *pato al ajo* (garlic duck). **Known for:** delicious soups; hearty portions; slow service. *Average main: S/36 ✉ Jr. Unión 126, Barranco ☎ 01/477–0550 🌐 www.facebook.com/ChifaChungYionPaginaOficial.*

Isolina Taberna Peruana

$$$ | **PERUVIAN** | Meat lovers wait in line here for a chance to savor chef José del Castillo's slow-cooked osso buco, *seco de asado de tira* (short-rib stew), or *costillar de cerdo a la chorrillana* (crispy pork ribs with tomatoes and onions). It's the kind of food Peruvians have eaten for centuries, impeccably prepared and served in a tavern setting. **Known for:** traditional meat dishes; big portions; great lomo saltado. *Average main: S/51 ✉ Av. San Martín 101, Barranco ☎ 01/247–5075 🌐 isolina.pe ⏲ No dinner Sun.*

Restaurante Arlotia

$$ | **BASQUE** | Basque food in Lima? *Claro que sí*—and it's one of the freshest, most welcome additions to Barranco's dining scene in recent years, with quinoa salads, ham-and-cheese empanadas, croquettes, quiches, and a range of tapas that is surprising for such a small kitchen. For something more substantial, try one of the Basque main courses like *rabo de toro* (oxtail) or *bacalao al pil-pil* (salt cod in garlic). **Known for:** great tapas; Spanish wine list; authentic Basque cuisine. *Average main: S/36 ✉ Av. Grau 340, Barranco ☎ 01/256–2269 🌐 www.facebook.com/restaurante.arlotia ⏲ Closed Mon.*

Songoro Cosongo

$ | **PERUVIAN** | This family-run restaurant serves the kind of traditional dishes limeños have eaten for generations, such as anticuchos and sudado. Owner Hernán Vega doesn't strive to please the gourmets; he focuses on authentic cuisine. **Known for:** home-style Peruvian cooking; excellent pisco sours; owner performs music at night. *Average main: S/34 Jr. Ayacucho 281, Barranco 01/247–4730 www.songoro-cosongo.com.*

Coffee and Quick Bites

La Bodega Verde

$ | **CAFÉ** | With its flagstone path and leafy lucuma tree dappling a quiet patio with shade, this green café is an oasis. The gourmet teas and coffees, artisanal sandwiches, and fruity milk shakes rejuvenate even the most worn-out traveler. **Known for:** proximity to Parque Municipal; great patio; quality coffee and tea. *Average main: S/15 Jr. Sucre 335-A, Barranco 981/112–096 www.facebook.com/labodegaverde No dinner.*

Hotels

Hotel B

$$$$ | **B&B/INN** | Also known as Arts Boutique Hotel B, this lodging-cum-art gallery in a refurbished, turn-of-the-century mansion is a feast for the senses, with its impressive collection of works by up-and-coming Latin American artists, 1920s charm, rooftop deck, and impeccable service. **Pros:** contemporary art collection; excellent service; complimentary breakfast and afternoon tea. **Cons:** pricey; noisy; some rooms are better than others. *Rooms from: S/1334 Av. San Martín 301, Barranco 01/206–0800 hotelb.pe 17 rooms Breakfast.*

★ Second Home Peru

$$ | **B&B/INN** | This 100-year-old Tudor-style house on a cliff overlooking the sea and surrounded by a sculpture garden is one of Lima's loveliest lodging options. **Pros:** gorgeous setting; home of sculptor Victor Delfín; oceanfront rooms with jaw-dropping views. **Cons:** limited guest services; no restaurant; no air-conditioning. *Rooms from: S/300 Cl. Domeyer 366, Barranco 01/247–5522 www.secondhomeperu.com 8 rooms Free breakfast.*

3B Barranco's Bed &Free breakfast

$$ | **B&B/INN** | Budget-conscious travelers appreciate this modern B&B's sleek accommodations, convenient location, and reasonable rates. **Pros:** quiet rooms; reasonable rates; useful amenities. **Cons:** short on personality; décor is dull; place fills up fast. *Rooms from: S/285 Jr. Centenario 130, Barranco 01/247–6915 www.3bhostal.com 16 rooms Free breakfast.*

★ Villa Barranco

$$$ | **B&B/INN** | Staying in this meticulously restored 1920s mansion on a quiet street near Barranco's malecón is a bit like staying with friends, thanks to the laid-back atmosphere and helpful staff. **Pros:** gorgeous historic home; ocean views; friendly, helpful staff. **Cons:** some rooms have small bathrooms; breakfast is a bit skimpy; some areas not well ventilated. *Rooms from: S/700 Cl. Carlos Zegarra 274, Barranco 01/396–5418 ananayhotels.com/villa-barranco 9 rooms Breakfast.*

Nightlife

BARS

Ayahuasca

BARS/PUBS | The refurbished 19th-century mansion that houses Ayahuasca would be worth visiting even if it wasn't Barranco's chicest bar. The wild decor—it's named for a hallucinogen used by Amazonian tribes—and light menu only add to the allure. *Av. Prolongación San Martín 130, Barranco 981/044–745 www.ayahuascarestobar.com.*

Barra 55

BARS/PUBS | This stylish lounge has quickly become Lima's hippest night spot. The décor is Nordic; the drink of choice, gin and tonic; the cuisine, tapas. There's no sign outside, but the super-cool welcome from the bartenders makes it clear you're in the right place. ✉ *Av. 28 de Julio 206D, Barranco* ☎ *986/634–193* 🌐 *www.facebook.com/barr55.*

Barranco Beer Company

BREWPUBS/BEER GARDENS | Bored with Peru's beer selection? This microbrewery a block north of Barranco's Parque Municipal not only offers several house brews, but also has sandwiches on home-baked bread, empanadas, and blue-corn pizza. ✉ *Av. Grau 308, Barranco* ☎ *01/247–6211* 🌐 *barrancobeercompany.pe.*

Juanito

BARS/PUBS | Facing Barranco's main square is one of the neighborhood's most venerable establishments, though the premises definitely veer toward the bare-bones and bohemian. Built by Italian immigrants in 1905, the former pharmacy is packed nightly with limeños drawn by the cheap drinks, historic setting, and ham sandwiches. ✉ *Av. Grau 270, Barranco* ☎ *941/536–016* 🌐 *www.facebook.com/eljuanitodebarranco.*

La Posada del Mirador

BARS/PUBS | When you're in Barranco, a pleasant place to start off the evening is La Posada del Mirador, at the end of the path behind La Ermita church. The bar has a second-story balcony that looks out to sea, making this a great place to watch the sunset or enjoy a nightcap. ✉ *Cl. Ermita 104, Barranco* ☎ *01/256–1796* 🌐 *laposadadelmirador.com.*

Piselli

BARS/PUBS | This lovely little bar in an adobe building one block south of Barranco's main square is a memorable spot for a drink, with its high beamed ceilings and glass cabinets filled with liquor bottles. Weekend nights draw a substantial crowd. ✉ *Av. 28 de Julio 297, Barranco* ☎ *01/252–6750* 🌐 *www.facebook.com/PiselliBarranco* ☞ *Closed Sun.*

Santos Comedor y Cantina

BARS/PUBS | Popular with the young crowd, Santos occupies one floor of a historic building up the steps from the Puente de los Suspiros. Its long balcony overlooking the Bajada de los Baños affords one of the best views in Barranco. ✉ *Jr. Zepita 203, Barranco* ☎ *054/1469–6147* 🌐 *www.facebook.com/Santos.Barranco.pe.*

DANCE CLUBS

Picas

DANCE CLUBS | In a remodeled old building under the Puente de los Suspiros, Picas is the hippest spot on the Bajada de los Baños. There are usually DJs on weekends, when it gets so crowded you'll feel like you're dancing in an elevator. It also has a decent kitchen, perfect for a late-night snack. ✉ *Bajada de los Baños 340, Barranco* ☎ *994/081–078* 🌐 *www.picas.com.pe.*

Rústica

DANCE CLUBS | In the back of this restaurant on the Parque Municipal is an airy bar with a big dance floor that gets packed on weekend nights, when DJs spin Latin and international hits. ✉ *Parque Municipal 105, Barranco* ☎ *01/680–7070* 🌐 *rustica.com.pe.*

LIVE MUSIC

La Noche

MUSIC CLUBS | La Noche is in a funky old house at the far end of the pedestrian street lined with bars known as El Bulevar de Barranco. The building includes a concert hall with a separate entrance (and admission fee) where local rock, Latin pop, and jazz bands perform. It's a great place for a drink even if you don't see the show. ✉ *Pje. Sanchez Carrión 199A, at Av. Bolognesi, Barranco* ☎ *981/128–198* 🌐 *www.lanoche.com.pe.*

La Posada del Ángel

MUSIC CLUBS | La Posada del Ángel is decorated with a wild collection of antiques and art, including statues of angels. It's one of the few bars in Barranco suited to conversation, and guitarists perform Latin American classics from 10 pm to 2 am. The bar has two more locations just down the street at Prolongación San

Martín 157 and Avenida Pedro de Osma 222. ✉ *Av. Pedro de Osma 164, Barranco* ☎ *943/554–488.*

Shopping

HANDICRAFTS

Artesanías Las Pallas

CRAFTS | On a quiet street one block east of busy Avenida Grau, this shop is in the home of Mari Solari, who has been selling handcrafted goods and folk art for decades. She works with some of the best artisans in the Andes and Amazon basin. Ring the doorbell and someone will let you in. ✉ *Cl. Cajamarca 212, Barranco* ☎ *01/477–4629.*

★ Dédalo

CRAFTS | Housed in a restored mansion on Barranco's stately Avenida Sáenz Peña, this Aladdin's cave–like *tienda* specializes in contemporary work, as opposed to the traditional handicrafts sold by most shops. It's packed with the colorful creations of dozens of independent artists and artisans, including an impressive selection of jewelry. The little café in the back garden is a pleasant spot to take a breather while traipsing around Barranco. ✉ *Av. Sáenz Peña 295, Barranco* ☎ *01/652–5400* 🌐 *dedalo.pe* ⏲ *Closed Sun. in Feb.*

Activities

Playa Barranquito

BEACHES | A short walk north of the pedestrian bridge at the bottom of Barranco's Bajada de los Baños, this narrow beach is one of Lima's most popular. The sand is dark gray, and when the sea is rough it is unsafe for swimming. But that doesn't stop Playa Barranquito from getting packed from December to April, when vendors stroll through the crowd selling snacks (which inevitably generates litter on the beach). It's a quiet spot the rest of the year except for the cries of seagulls and the rumble of cars passing on the Circuito de Playas. **Amenities:** food and drink, parking (fee); toilets. **Best for:** sunset; walking. ✉ *Circuito de Playas, ½ km (¼ mile) north of Bajada de los Baños, Barranco.*

Pueblo Libre

Limeños often speak of their city's "*barrios tradicionales,*" and none is more *tradicional* than Pueblo Libre. Here, the sense of heritage is evident on every corner: in the old-timers talking politics in its quiet parks, in its tiny peñas tucked into side alleys, in the late-night gatherings in its century-old watering holes. So steeped is the district in its criollo past, it often seems a throwback to an older Lima—a place of leisurely Sunday lunches and exaggerated courtesy, arm-in-arm walks with grandparents and evening visits to the parish church.

Pueblo Libre's rootedness has a long history. During Peru's wars for independence, Simón de Bolívar and José de San Martín, South America's two great liberators, both lived here (though not simultaneously) in a mansion formerly owned by the Spanish viceroy. Later, it was the seat of the country's provisional government when Lima was occupied by Chile in the War of the Pacific. Nowadays, the district's main draws for travelers are its two great museums, the Museo Nacional de Antropología, Arqueología e Historia and the Museo Larco. In their different ways, both tell the same story: the millennial epic of Peru's evolution since it became one of civilization's birthplaces 5,000 years ago.

GETTING AROUND

The most convenient way to reach Pueblo Libre is a taxi ride, which takes 20–30 minutes from Miraflores or Barranco.

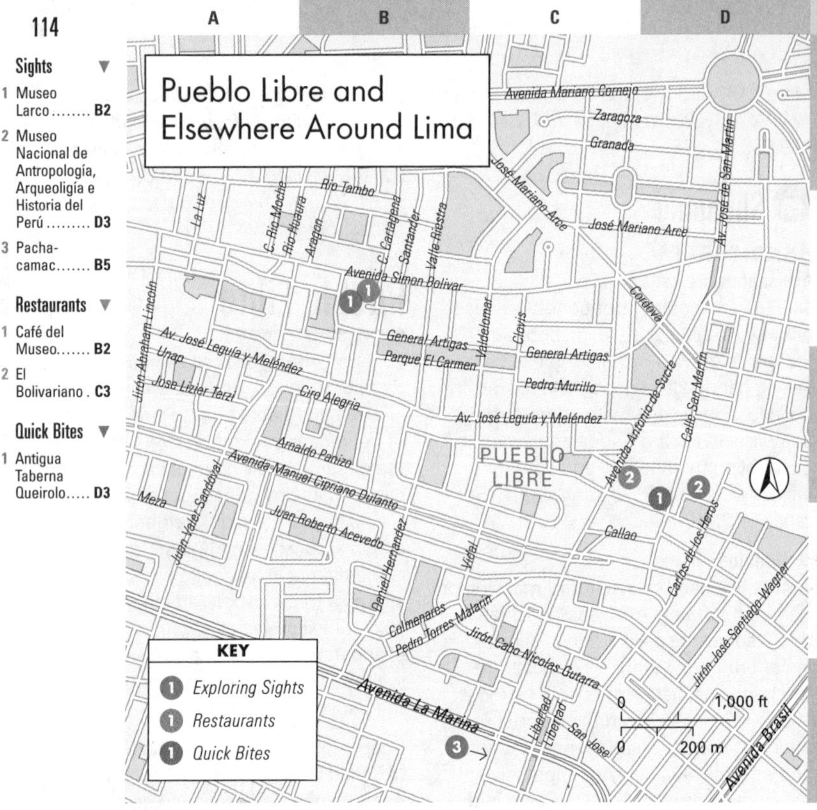

Sights

★ Museo Larco

MUSEUM | Hot-pink bougainvillea spills over the white walls of this lovely colonial mansion, which is built atop a pre-Columbian temple. What those walls house is the city's most exquisite collection of ancient art, with works from all of Peru's major pre-Hispanic cultures spanning several thousand years. Highlights include a Moche stirrup vessel detailing grisly human sacrifices, a selection of Inca quipus, and thousands of ceramic "portrait heads" that give astonishingly realistic insights into their subjects' personalities. The *sala erótica* reveals that Peru's ancient artisans were an uninhibited lot, creating clay pottery adorned with explicit sexual images. Guides are a good idea, and the cost is just S/35 per group. The café overlooking the museum's garden is an excellent option for lunch or dinner. ✉ *Av. Bolívar 1515, Pueblo Libre* ☎ *01/461–1312* 🌐 *www.museolarco.org* 🎫 *S/30.*

Museo Nacional de Antropología, Arqueología e Historia del Perú

MUSEUM | **FAMILY** | The country's most extensive collection of pre-Columbian artifacts can be found at this sprawling museum. Beginning with 8,000-year-old stone tools, Peru's history is narrated through the sleek granite obelisks of the Chavín culture, the intricate weavings of the Paracas, and the colorful ceramics of the Moche, Chimú, and Incas. A fascinating pair of mummies from the Nazca region is thought to be more than 2,500 years old. They are so well preserved that you can still see the grim expressions

Side Trip: Caral

Predating the pyramids at Giza by some 400 years, Caral is the oldest city in the Western Hemisphere. Archaeologists say it has revolutionized their ideas about the very nature of *Homo sapiens*. Yet this vast pyramid complex in Peru's Supe valley remains virtually unknown, to tourists and locals alike. Discovered by archaeologist Ruth Shady Solis in 1994, Caral is one of the most astonishing sites in the Americas, since it marks one of only six spots on earth where humans crossed what scholars call "the great divide"—i.e., where civilization itself began. When you go, you'll find excellent signage in Spanish and English, as well as informed docents to guide you through this UNESCO World Heritage Site. Walking amid its crumbling pyramids and sunken plazas, it's impossible not to imagine a priest in his headdress and tunic, arms hieratically outstretched over the fire pit before him. ■ TIP→ **The site is some 220 km (120 miles) north of Lima and not easy to find, so your best bet for visiting is to take an all-day tour.** Admission is S/11. ☎ *01/205–2500* 🌐 *www.zonacaral.gob.pe*

on their faces. The exhibits occupy two colonial houses, in one of which the Venezuelan general Simón de Bolívar, who led South America's wars of independence, lived while helping to organize a newly freed Peru. ■ TIP→ **Much of the museum is currently closed for remodeling, but the exhibits are slated to reopen before Peru's bicentennial in July of 2021. Meanwhile, the areas having to do with the country's post-independence history can still be visited.** ✉ *Plaza Bolívar, Pueblo Libre* ☎ *01/321–5630* 🌐 *mnaahp.cultura.pe* 🎫 *S/10* ⏲ *Closed Mon.*

Restaurants

Café del Museo

$$ | **PERUVIAN** | Sequestered inside the walls of the colonial palace that houses the Museo Larco, this is one of the most charming places in Lima to enjoy a meal. The Peruvian-fusion menu offers everything from empanadas to ravioli stuffed with squash to *seco de cordero* (stewed lamb) served with rice and beans. **Known for:** gorgeous setting; Peruvian-fusion cuisine; good desserts. 💲 *Average main: S/45* ✉ *Museo Larco, Av. Bolívar 1515, Pueblo Libre* ☎ *01/461–1312* 🌐 *cafe.museolarco.org.*

★ **El Bolivariano**

$$ | **PERUVIAN** | Set in a colonial *finca* (farm house) that dates from 1780, this Lima institution offers some of the heartiest down-home cooking in the entire capital. Criollo classics such as seco de cabrito and *costillas de cerdo con tacu-tacu* (ribs with pan-fried rice and beans) are especially well done, but you'd be hard-pressed to find a weak spot anywhere on the extensive menu. **Known for:** pescado a lo macho; good pisco sours and chilcanos; lively crowd with dancing after 11 pm on weekends. 💲 *Average main: S/40* ✉ *Cl. Rosa Toledo 289, Pueblo Libre* ☎ *01/463–0434* 🌐 *www.elbolivariano.com* ⏲ *No dinner Sun.*

Coffee and Quick Bites

Antigua Taberna Queirolo

$ | **PERUVIAN** | Chalkboard menus, shelves piled to the ceiling with locally made wines and piscos, a worn wooden bar, and even a hand-cranked telephone give this venerable institution—a Lima mainstay since 1880—its nostalgic charm. The place serves delicious ham sandwiches smothered in zarza criolla and chilcanos made with pisco bottled in the factory next door. **Known for:** old-timey atmosphere; excellent homemade piscos; ham sandwiches and other criollo classics. [$] *Average main: S/15* ✉ *Jr. San Martín 1090, Pueblo Libre* ☎ *01/460–0441* 🌐 *antiguatabernaqueirolo.com* 🕒 *No dinner Sun.*

Elsewhere Around Lima

A few of Lima's most interesting sights are in outlying neighborhoods such as Monterrico and Pachacamac. The most convenient way to reach them is a quick taxi ride.

Sights

Pachacamac

ARCHAEOLOGICAL SITE | Sacred to the god of earthquakes, this sprawling adobe temple was for 1,300 years the chief pilgrimage destination on Peru's Pacific coast. What those votaries came to see was Pachacamac—"he who moves the earth"—a scowling lord carved into a wooden staff wielded by the sanctuary's fearsome priests (elsewhere, he appears on ceramic vessels as a strange, griffin-like creature, with a bird's beak and feline claws). Pachacamac's cult began with the Lima culture around 200 AD, but it grew when the Huari took over the complex some four centuries later. It exploded when the Incas came in 1470, elevating the earth-shaker to the rank of their own creator-god and erecting a sun temple in his honor on the bluff's apex. Today, visitors can meander through the pre-Inca Painted Temple, with its traces of red brick, as well as the hilltop Temple of the Sun that looks out on the Pacific. An on-site museum offers informative displays. ■ **TIP→ The best way to visit Pachacamac is by taking a half-day guided tour with an agency like Mirabus, since the site is 32 km (20 miles) south of downtown, and getting a taxi back can be tricky.** ✉ *Km 31.5, Panamericana Sur* ☎ *01/321–5606* 🌐 *pachacamac.cultura.pe* 🎟 *S/15* 🕒 *Closed Mon.*

BEACHES

Playa Agua Dulce

BEACHES | The nicest of Lima's public beaches, Playa Agua Dulce is a wide swath of gray sand that slopes into calm water. It gets packed from December to April, when vendors wander through the crowd and families enjoy picnic lunches. **Amenities:** parking, toilets. **Best for:** sunset; walking. ✉ *Circuito de Playas, 1 km (½ mile) south of Bajada de los Baños, Chorrillos.*

Punta Hermosa

BEACHES | **FAMILY** | Getting to this beach south of Lima on the Pan-American Highway might not be the most scenic drive in the world, but it's worth the headaches. When the waves are big, surfers ride the breaks on the beach's northern end. If this section of the beach is packed, as it's wont to be on summer weekends, head to the southern end for a more tranquil setting. There's a small selection of restaurants that offer fresh seafood with an ocean view. ⚠ **The rip currents can be dangerous, especially when the waves are bigger.** **Amenities:** food and drink. **Best for:** surfing; swimming; walking. ✉ *Km 40, Panamericana Sur, Punta Hermosa.*

Chapter 4

NAZCA AND THE SOUTHERN COAST

Updated by
Michael Gasparovic

Sights	Restaurants	Hotels	Shopping	Nightlife
★★★★★	★★★☆☆	★★★★☆	★★☆☆☆	★★☆☆☆

WELCOME TO NAZCA AND THE SOUTHERN COAST

TOP REASONS TO GO

★ **Mysteries in the Desert:** Marvel at the mysterious Nazca Lines, giant shapes and figures etched into the desert floor by an enigmatic ancient civilization. These colossal artworks continue to baffle archaeologists and are only fully visible from the sky.

★ **Island Life:** Boats cruise the Islas Ballestas for glimpses of sea lions, condors, flamingos, and millions of guano-producing seabirds in the Paracas National Reserve.

★ **Wine and Pisco Tasting:** Go wine tasting in the grape-growing valleys near Lunahuaná, Chincha, and Ica, sampling Peru's most famous drink, pisco, in the stunning local *bodegas* (traditional wineries).

★ **Seaside Luxury:** Sprawling luxury coastal resorts have sprung up in Paracas. Kick back and enjoy these posh palaces as bases for exploring area attractions.

★ **Sandboarding:** Test your nerve and skill by sandboarding down the giant dunes at the oasis town of Huacachina, then nurse your injuries in the lagoon's magical healing waters.

Southern Peru is connected to Lima by the Panamericana (Pan-American Highway), which runs down the coast to Pisco and the Paracas Peninsula before cutting inland to Ica and Nazca. Between Lima and Pisco are a variety of small coastal towns, all just off the Panamericana. Towns are laid out in the usual Spanish-colonial fashion around a central Plaza de Armas. This is usually a good place to look for services such as banks, lodgings, and transportation.

1 Cerro Azul. The Beach Boys' "Surfin' Safari" made this beach village famous, but for locals, it's as much about Jet Skiing, 4x4 riding, and enjoying fresh seafood as about riding the waves.

2 Asia. Popular and oh-so-exclusive, this beach resort is where Lima's beautiful people go to party in the summer.

3 Lunahuaná. Looking for adrenaline *and* relaxation on a day trip from the capital? This picturesque pueblo has white-water rapids and one of Peru's best wine festivals.

4 Tambo Colorado. Inca ruins close to Lima? *¡Claro!* This adobe outpost is constructed on the same grand scale as the citadels of the Sacred Valley.

5 Pisco. This quiet town is a good place to rest and refuel before heading out to the local wineries. Nearby is the city of Chincha, the hub of Afro-Peruvian culture.

6 Paracas. Wildlife lovers will thrill to these islands, affectionately dubbed "the poor man's Galapagos." Sea lions, Humboldt penguins, and dolphins are just some of the new friends you'll meet among the wave-lashed rocks.

7 Ica. The big draw at this dusty southern city are the bodegas, elegant wineries that produce pisco, Peru's potent national liquor. Local tours stimulate your intellect as well as your palate—plus, they include fantastic lunches.

8 Huacachina. Sandboarding and buggy-riding are just some of the activities at this lovely desert oasis.

9 Nazca. In this desert town, the pre-Columbian geoglyphs are so spectacularly otherworldly, they became Peru's official trademark.

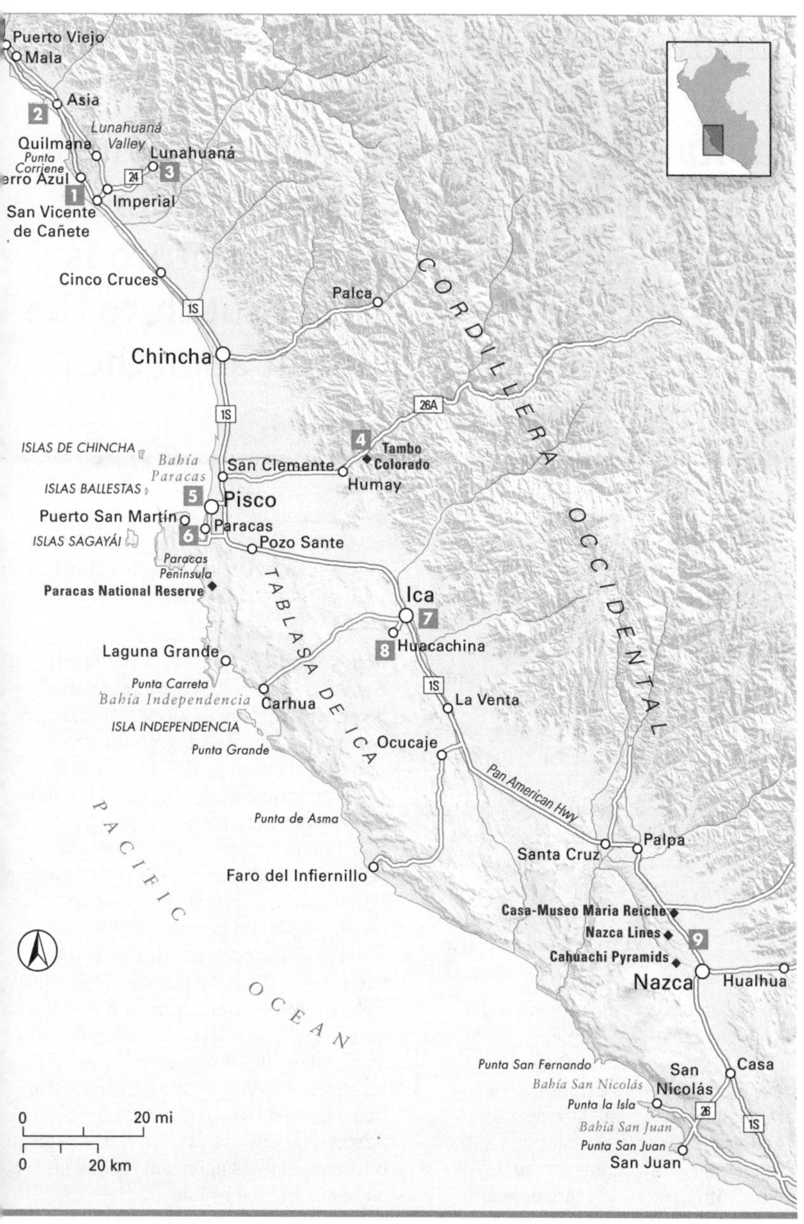

Puerto Viejo
Mala
Asia
Lunahuaná Valley
Quilmana
Punta Corriene
Cerro Azul
Lunahuaná
24
Imperial
San Vicente de Cañete
Cinco Cruces
1S
Palca
CORDILLERA OCCIDENTAL
Chincha
26A
ISLAS DE CHINCHA
Bahía Paracas
Tambo Colorado
San Clemente
Humay
ISLAS BALLESTAS
Pisco
Puerto San Martín
Paracas
ISLAS SAGAYÁI
Pozo Sante
Paracas Peninsula
Paracas National Reserve
TABLASA DE ICA
Ica
Huacachina
Laguna Grande
Punta Carreta
Bahía Independencia
Carhua
La Venta
ISLA INDEPENDENCIA
Punta Grande
Ocucaje
Pan American Hwy
PACIFIC OCEAN
Punta de Asma
Santa Cruz
Palpa
Faro del Infiernillo
Casa-Museo Maria Reiche
Nazca Lines
Cahuachi Pyramids
Nazca
Hualhua
Punta San Fernando
Bahía San Nicolás
San Nicolás
Casa
Punta la Isla
26
Bahía San Juan
Punta San Juan
San Juan
0 20 mi
0 20 km

From vineyards to sand dunes, rocky beaches to islands teeming with wildlife, the area south of Lima is wild and enthralling. Day-trippers and weekend warriors typically hew close to the capital, where hypnotic waves provide a soundtrack for some of Peru's toniest resorts. Meanwhile, more adventurous souls find their way farther south, to the uncanny marvels that await amid the desert.

Long before its advent as a tourist mecca, Peru's Southern Coast was home to a bevy of pre-Columbian civilizations. The undisputed stars were the Nazca, creators of one of South America's most mind-blowing attractions, the enigmatic Nazca Lines. Numbering in the hundreds, and comprising animals, humans, and perfectly drawn geometric shapes, these giant diagrams are etched into the desert floor over areas so vast they can be seen properly only from the air. How, why, and for whom they were created remains a mystery, though theories range from irrigation systems to launch pads for alien spacecraft. You can make your own conjectures as you soar over them in a privately chartered craft.

The Nazca weren't the region's only advanced civilization. The Paracas culture arrived as early as 900 BC and over the next thousand years established a line of coastal towns that still exists today. The Paracas people are long gone, and the Inca Empire conquered the region in the 15th century, yet these desert dwellers left behind some of Peru's most advanced weavings, ceramics, effigy vessels, and metal jewelry, along with a network of eerie cemeteries beneath the sands.

Peru's Southern Coast isn't all Ancient Civ. With a sunny climate, great wines, and charming fishing villages, this region has been a favorite vacation destination for generations of *limeños* eager to escape the big city. It's also been a commercial hub. For years during the mid-19th century, the region was the center of Peru's riches, which took the rather odorous form of guano—bird droppings, found in vast quantities on islands off the coast of Paracas and a rich source of natural fertilizer. Shipped to North America and Europe from the deepwater port of Pisco, guano proved so lucrative, there was even a war over it—the Guano War of 1864–66, in which Spain battled Peru for possession of the nearby Chincha Islands. Today, the region enchants with its abundant marine life and stark natural beauty.

MAJOR REGIONS

North of Pisco. Quiet coastal hamlets, opportunities for white-water rafting, and even some significant Inca ruins are the top draws along this easily accessible section of the Peruvian coast. This area is the favored weekend getaway for many limeños, some of whom have grand summer residences in exclusive resorts like Asia, far from the homes of local fishermen and farmers. Follow their lead, and head south to enjoy the sun, smog-free air, and overflowing plates of hearty criollo cooking. Or, if you're an adrenaline junkie, get your fix at Lunahuaná, where the rafting runs from chill to super-gnarly, depending on the season.

Pisco and the Paracas Peninsula. On August 15, 2007, just before midnight, an earthquake measuring 8.0 on the Richter scale struck the Southern Coast of Peru. In the process, it decimated the city of Pisco, long a favorite spot for vacationers and wine connoisseurs from the capital. Pisco is still struggling to rebuild—indeed, to this day, there are whole city blocks that lie in rubble—but the good news is that its neighbor to the south, Paracas, stepped up to fill the gap.

And step up it has. With its rugged beaches and islands swarming with wildlife, this coastal hamlet has become the top choice for day-trippers from Lima, a place to take in the sea breezes and head out in a launch to see the flamingos, penguins and other guano-producing seabirds that throng the arch-shaped rocks offshore. Paracas's tourist options have proliferated. Cruise ships now dot the horizon at nearby Puerto San Martín, and a wave of chic resorts has reenergized (and commercialized) the town's economy. Yet Paracas somehow manages to conserve its air of quiet isolation, especially for those venturing among the crags of its stark cliffside reserve.

Ica and Nazca. South of Pisco, the thin black highway cuts through desert vast and pale as cracked parchment, with nothing but sand and sky on the ash-colored horizon. As you gaze out at the endless miles of desert, you'd be forgiven for thinking there's little to hold your attention in this part of Peru.

Yet you couldn't be more wrong. With good wines, year-round sunshine, strange lunar landscapes, and giant drawings left by one of the world's most enigmatic ancient cultures, the far Southern Coast is one of Peru's highlights. The surprises start in Ica, a scrubby, dusty traffic jam of a town that conceals a secret: the green vines and clay-colored *tinajas* (ceramic jars) of its bodegas—wineries where pisco, the national firewater, is distilled. Visiting these historic institutions for a wine-tasting over lunch, you'll be beguiled by Peruvian hospitality at its most charming. Afterwards, head to Huacachina, where, in an oasis just outside the city limits, adrenaline junkies on sandboards take kamikaze dives down 200-foot dunes, and buggies buck like broncos as they lurch across the sands.

Last stop on the way south is Nazca, home of an ancient culture that scratched an advanced civilization out of the barrenness. The Nazca left behind their irrigation systems and some masterful ceramics, but their trademark is the huge geoglyphs etched into the Martian topsoil of the region. Pilgrimage site or solar calendar? Map of the constellations or supplication to the gods of water? No one knows for sure. Scholars can debate the Nazca lines' riddle, and new shapes continue to be discovered. But amid the frenzied speculation, these colossal artworks only preserve their inscrutable silence.

Planning

When to Go

Although the weather in southern Peru is consistently arid throughout the year, the best time to visit is in summer and autumn (November through April), when the rivers are ripe for rafting and kayaking and harvest festivals spice up the small towns. During holidays—Christmas, Carnaval, the grape harvest, Easter, the mid-June religious festivals, and Peru's independence day in July—hotels are often booked to capacity.

FESTIVALS

Ica is a good place to experience local culture in a celebratory mood, with several festivals during the year, including Carnaval in February, Ica Week in mid-June, and the Ica Tourist Festival in late September. The Fiesta de la Vendimia (Harvest Festival), at the start of the grape-pressing season, is a highlight.

El Señor de Luren
On the third Monday in October and again at Easter, Ica's streets are lined with carpets of flowers for an overnight pilgrimage, in which thousands of the faithful move in procession with a highly illuminated image of "El Señor" (Christ), said to have come ashore here after a shipwreck in the mid-16th century. ✉ *Ica*.

Fiesta de la Vendimia
In early March, the grape harvest heralds this week-long celebration of the local wine industry, with winery visits, grape-stomping contests, an agricultural fair, a beauty pageant, a parade, and fireworks. ✉ *Ica* 🌐 *www.facebook.com/vendimiadeica.pe*.

Fiesta de Verano Negro
Afro-Peruvian culture is the focus of this celebration in Chincha in late February and early March, with music, dance, food, and other events. Look for El Alcatraz dance, in which a male dancer tries to set his partner's cloth tail on fire with a candle. ✉ *Chincha*.

Getting Here and Around

With the Panamericana following the coastline all the way to Chile, southern Peru is prime territory to explore by road. Bus travel is easy and inexpensive. Larger companies such as Cruz del Sur, Peru Bus, and Oltursa serve all major towns. Minivans, called *combis,* and share taxis shuttle between smaller towns and usually depart from the Plaza de Armas.

AIR

Pisco's military airport has finally opened its doors to commercial traffic, but as of now, the only flights are seasonal ones to Cusco. This means that for the moment, the nearest airport to the region is in Lima, where ground transportation can be arranged via bus or tour operator. The landing strips in Paracas and Nazca are closed to commercial air traffic.

BUS

Numerous companies work the route from Lima to Arequipa. Always take the best service you can afford: in addition to being less comfortable, cheaper carriers have less stringent safety standards, and the section of highway between Nazca and Cusco is notorious for robbery, especially on overnight services. Cruz del Sur, Oltursa, Peru Bus, and Ormeño provide the most reliable service and have the most departures from Ica, whereas the quality of vehicles and on-board service is notoriously patchy with other operators. An upstart young company, Peru Hop, offers flexible, hop-on, hop-off service all along the Southern Coast and will pick you up at your hotel.

CAR

The Pan-American Highway runs the length of southern Peru, some of it along the coast, some through desert, some over plateaus and mountains. It's paved and in good condition, but be sure to have fully equipped first-aid and repair kits. Besides breakdowns, hazards include potholes, rock slides, sandstorms, and heat. You'll find many service stations along this route, most of which have clean bathrooms and convenience stores. Off the highway, conditions are less predictable. Roads may be poor in the eastern highlands and around the Paracas Reserve. Four-wheel-drive vehicles are recommended for all driving except on the main highway and within major cities.

Your only real options to rent a car are in Lima or Arequipa.

Restaurants

Casual dress is the order of the day. Reservations are seldom necessary. If you're on a budget, look for the excellent-value set menus at lunchtime, where a three-course meal can be as little as S/10. Throughout the south, seafood is king, and you will never be far from a plate of *cebiche* (fresh raw fish cured in fresh citrus juices) or *camarones* (shrimp). In Chincha and rural villages closer to Lima, there's Afro-Peruvian fare like *tacu tacu,* a mass of seasoned, pan-fried rice and beans. In Ica, try *tejas,* candies made of *manjar blanco,* a sweet, pudding-like milk spread. A treat available only during harvest festivals is *cachina,* a partially fermented wine.

Hotels

Accommodations in southern Peru range from luxury resorts to spartan *hostales* that run less than S/30 per night. Top-rated hotels usually have more than standard amenities, which might include such on-site extras as a spa, sports facilities, and business and travel services, and such room amenities as minibars, safes, faxes, or data ports. Midrange hotels might have only some of the extras. There are also more basic accommodations, which may have shared baths or be outside the central tourist area. If you're arriving without a reservation, most towns have places to stay around the Plaza de Armas or bus and train stations. *Hotel reviews have been shortened. For full information, visit Fodors.com.*

WHAT IT COSTS in Nuevo Soles

$	$$	$$$	$$$$
RESTAURANTS			
under S/35	S/35–S/50	S/51–S/65	over S/65
HOTELS			
under S/250	S/250–S/500	S/501–S/800	over S/800

Cerro Azul

143 km (89 miles) south of Lima; 15 km (9 miles) north of Cañete.

"*Aquí está tranquilo,*" say the locals, and tranquil it certainly is in this small fishing town, made famous by the Beach Boys' song "Surfin' Safari," between Cañete and Pucusana. The hustle and bustle of the old days, when the town made its living as a port for the exportation of guano and pisco, is long gone, and now the only industry you'll see is the fishermen repairing their nets down by the waterfront.

Limeños trickle in on the weekends, arriving as much for the town's charmingly off-beat character as for the peace and quiet. On the weekend the local brass band parades through the streets before and after the church services. The local church, instead of ringing its bell, sets off fireworks in the Plaza de Armas as an unconventional call to prayer.

GETTING HERE AND AROUND

Any bus heading south from Lima will pass by Cerro Azul (S/10–S/15 depending on the bus) on the Pan-American Highway, from where you can catch a combi for S/1 or mototaxi for S/6 to the center.

Sights

Huarco

ARCHAEOLOGICAL SITE | The ruins of this pre-Hispanic fort are minimal, but they conceal a tragic history. The Huarco were a tiny seaside kingdom that resisted the incursions of the Inca Empire in the 15th century. After the Inca surrounded them, they walled themselves up in this fort and threw themselves into the sea rather than surrender. All that remains are crumbling walls overlooking a precipitous cliff. ✉ *Cerro Azul* 🎫 *Free.*

Hotels

Cerro Azul Hostal

$ | **HOTEL** | In a town short on accommodation, this little hostel is one of the most reliable options and fills up quickly on weekends and holidays. **Pros:** close to the beach; good lodgings for groups; nice terraces in some rooms. **Cons:** small rooms; no restaurant during the off-season; service can be chaotic. 💲 *Rooms from: S/120* ✉ *Cl. Los Eucaliptos 106* ☎ *01/284–6052* 🌐 *www.cerroazulhostal.com* 🛏 *16 units* 🍽 *No meals.*

Asia

145 km (90 miles) south of Lima; 125 km (78 miles) north of Pisco.

This is Peru's version of the Hamptons. During the summer months, from about the end of December to March, much of middle- and upper-class Lima flees the capital on weekends to a stretch of beach communities that is anchored in Asia (pronounced *ah*-see-ah). Here, at the Boulevard de Asia, a temporary satellite city is set up, complete with a go-kart track and concert venues. Many of Peru's familiar chains—such as Pardo's, Wong, Ripley, and Illaria—populate a lively commercial zone that mostly shutters when the summer ends. Most visitors here stay in private residential developments that flank the boulevard for about 20 to 30 km (12 to 20 miles) in either direction. In most cases, if you don't know someone in these communities, your only option is the public beaches. Traditionally, this area has been targeted primarily at residents of Lima and hasn't seen many tourists, but that's starting to change. A few hotels have sprung up, including lively properties near the boulevard, and resort-style places farther away. You'll find better beaches elsewhere in Peru, but if hanging with the country's elite is what you're after, then this is the place.

GETTING HERE AND AROUND

To reach Asia, take a bus to Km 97.5 on the Pan-American Highway.

Hotels

Aquavit Hotel

$$ | **HOTEL** | In the midst of the action on the Asia boulevard, this is a clublike party hotel, with rooms overlooking a central pool area with palm trees and white daybeds that look straight out of South Beach. **Pros:** convenient; in the middle of everything; good vibe for young travelers. **Cons:** can get loud; events take over the pool area some weekends; 20-minute walk to the beach. 💲 *Rooms from: S/250* ✉ *Km 97.5, Blvd. de Asia (Panamericana Sur)* ☎ *01/530–7801* 🌐 *www.aquavithotel.com* 🛏 *38 rooms* 🍽 *No meals.*

Estelar Vista Pacifico Resort

$$ | **RESORT** | This resort-style condo hotel was the first major international property to open on one of Asia's beaches, and thus far, it's the most complete. **Pros:** some rooms have sea views; decent restaurant; great pool and beach area. **Cons:** 10 km (6 miles) from Boulevard de Asia; some service issues; a bit pricey relative to hotel quality. 💲 *Rooms from: S/500* ✉ *Km 109, Panamerica Sur, Sarapampa* ☎ *01/630–7777* 🌐 *estelarvistapacifico.com* 🛏 *116 rooms* 🍽 *Free breakfast.*

Lunahuaná

14 km (9 miles) east of Cerro Azul; 150 km (93 miles) south of Lima; 85 km (53 miles) north of Pisco.

Flanked by arid mountains, the beautiful valley of the Río Cañete cuts a swath of green inland from Cañete to reach the tiny but charming town of Lunahuaná, the center for some of Peru's best white-water rafting. The season is from December to March, when the water is at its highest, creating rapids that can reach up to Class IV. Most of the year, however, the river is suitable for beginners. Rafting companies offering trips line Calle Grau in town.

If you're more interested in whetting your palate than wetting your backside, Lunahuaná is a great spot to enjoy the products of the region: wines and piscos from the surrounding wineries and distilleries and freshwater prawns straight from the river. ■ TIP→ **In March you can celebrate the opening of the grape-pressing season at the Fiesta de la Vendimia.** The rest of the year, join the locals and while away the afternoon trying the variety of cocktails from the pisco stands dotted around the flower-filled main plaza; the *maracuya* (passion fruit) sour in particular is a winner. If the cocktails, sun, and lazy atmosphere don't get the better of you, just down the road from Lunahuaná lie the **Incahuasi** ruins, an Inca site said to have been the military headquarters of Túpac Yupanqui. There's not a great deal to see, although Inca enthusiasts may find it interesting.

GETTING HERE AND AROUND

To reach Lunahuaná, take a bus to Km 143 on the Pan-American Highway to the turnoff to San Vicente de Cañete and Imperial. There you can catch a combi for the hour-long ride to Lunahuaná for S/7.50.

Hotels

Los Palomos de Lunahuaná
$$ | **HOTEL** | Set on a curve of the Río Cañete, this whitewashed, contemporary hotel is a laid-back, rambling property surrounded by nature. **Pros:** nice pub; great regional food in the restaurant; beautiful pool area. **Cons:** doesn't feel like Lunahuaná; service is a bit slow; a bit pricey. *Rooms from: S/500* *Km 35, Langla* *998/889–645* *hotellospalomos.com* *17 rooms* *Free breakfast.*

Refugio Viñak
$$$ | **B&B/INN** | In a breathtaking setting high in the Andean foothills, this cozy lodge affords access to more than 80 km (50 miles) of hiking trails that offer a glimpse of Andean life few tourists will ever see. **Pros:** stunning setting; family-size rooms; all-inclusive. **Cons:** extremely remote, 110 km (68 miles) northeast of Lunahuaná; expensive; not much to do in poor weather. *Rooms from: S/612* *Santiago de Viñak Village, Viñak* *01/221–1313* *www.refugiovinak.com* *11 rooms* *All-inclusive.*

Río Alto Hotel
$ | **HOTEL** | **FAMILY** | The sounds of the river lull you into relaxation at this hacienda-style hotel just outside Lunahuaná, and its family vibe has made it popular with visitors from Lima. **Pros:** riverside location; large pool; flower-filled terrace to kick back on. **Cons:** small rooms; a bit far from center of Lunahuaná; no travel services. *Rooms from: S/177* *Km 39.5, Cañete–Lunahuaná Hwy.* *01/284–1125* *www.rioaltohotel.com* *25 rooms* *All-inclusive.*

Villasol Hotel
$$ | **HOTEL** | Listen to the sounds of the Río Cañete from your room or enjoy the river views while floating lazily in the pool at this large hotel that makes the most of its spectacular riverside location. **Pros:** riverside location; spectacular pool area; river views from some rooms. **Cons:** some rooms only have views of the lawn;

unimaginative room furnishings; parking on the front lawns. [$] *Rooms from: S/260* ✉ *Km 37.5, Cañete–Lunahuaná Hwy.* ☎ *01/284–1127* 🌐 *luzdelosandes.com/villa* *55 rooms* *Free breakfast.*

Tambo Colorado

132 km (82 miles) southeast of Lunahuaná; 45 km (28 miles) east of Pisco.

The ruins of this administrative center and burial site make up one of the best-preserved Inca sites on the Southern Coast. Although the ruins are somewhat off the beaten track down poor roads, this archaeological complex rarely fails to impress.

GETTING HERE AND AROUND

There is no public transportation to Tambo Colorado. Many hotels and travel agencies in Ica and Paracas offer four-hour tours of the archaeological site for around S/80.

Afro-Peruvian Beat

A sprawling town midway between Cañete and Pisco, Chincha is famous for its riotous Afro-Peruvian music. If you're in the area during late February, stop by to celebrate the Fiesta de Verano Negro, when Chincha's neighborhood of El Carmen shakes its booty day and night. A highlight is El Alcatraz, a dance in which a hip-swiveling male dancer tries to set his partner's cloth tail on fire with a candle. Outside of festival time, there are several good pisco bodegas to tour, plus a couple of excellent criollo restaurants.

Sights

Iglesia de San Juan Bautista de Huaytará
RELIGIOUS SITE | Catch your breath and drive up to this beautifully restored colonial church, built on the foundation of an Inca temple 2,800 meters (9,200 feet) above sea level. ✉ *Pisco* ✣ *Off Libertadores Wari, 69 km (43 miles) east of Tambo Colorado* *Free.*

★ Tambo Colorado
ARCHAEOLOGICAL SITE | The great Inca Pachacutec himself probably stayed at this, one of Peru's most underrated archaeological sites. The labyrinthine alleyways and trapezoidal plaza of this huge adobe settlement were devised as an outpost for soldiers and visiting dignitaries of the far-flung Andean empire, making it the most important Inca site on the Peruvian coast. Today, Tambo Colorado is incredibly well preserved, owing to its bone-dry setting. When you go, you'll feel some of the same grandeur found in the stones of the Sacred Valley around Cuzco.

Tambo Colorado, or Pucahuasi ("red resting place") in Quechua, derives its name from the bright bands of imperial red, yellow, and white with which it was once blazoned. The site comprises several sections laid out around a large central plaza, and you can see the quarters where the great Inca received his guests. **■ TIP→ Notice that the plaza's distinctive trapezoid shape is reflected throughout the site—look for trapezoid windows and other openings—and thought to have been an earthquake-proofing measure, necessary in this extremely volatile region.** Be sure to visit the museum on the premises, which houses many finds by the great archaeologist Julio C. Tello, the site's discoverer. ✉ *Via Libertadores, 40 km east of Pisco, Pisco* *S/7.50.*

Surfing

South of Lima, you'll find a string of sandy beaches, most of them backed by massive sand dunes. The water is cold and rough, the waves are big, and lifeguards are nonexistent.

Sound appealing? Then pick up your board, and head south to see why Peru is becoming one of South America's hottest surfing destinations.

For a sure bet, head to **Punta Hermosa**, a town near Km 44 on the Pan-American Highway (about an hour's drive south of Lima), which, with its numerous reefs and coves, has the highest concentration of high-quality surf spots and breaks all year round.

Fancy yourself a pro? The largest waves in South America, some 7 meters (23 feet) high, roll into nearby **Pico Alto**, with nearly 20 good breaks around the Pico Alto Surf Camp. Paddle out from Punta Hermosa via Playa Norte to reach the reef, although be warned—these waves are for the very experienced and crazy only!

Excellent surfing is also much closer to shore at the town of **Cerro Azul**, at Km 132 of the Panamericana. Long tubular waves break right in front of the town, so be prepared for an audience. A pleasant fishing village, Cerro Azul is a popular weekend and holiday destination, and the beach gets crowded during peak times. Go midweek if you want the place to yourself.

Peru doesn't have a huge surfing tradition, but to see where a small slice of local history was made, head to **Punta Rocas**, 42 km (26 miles) south of Lima, where, in 1965, Peruvian surfer Felipe Pomar became something of a national hero when he won the World Surfing Championships. The reef break here provides a classic wave for beginners and advanced surfers alike.

There's even some decent surfing in the middle of Lima. Just off the coast of Miraflores, on the **Costa Verde** beach road, you can find four surfable beaches, all within a 15-minute walk of one another. Right near the Rosa Náutica restaurant, Redondo, Makaha, La Pampilla, and Waikiki are breaks for beginners, but their proximity to the city means the water can be more than a little polluted. Think you've just paddled past a jellyfish? It's more likely a plastic bag.

Surfing in Peru is best from March to December, with May probably being ideal. Although the climate is dry year-round, in winter the Pacific Ocean can get very chilly (although it's never particularly warm, and wet suits are advisable year-round). The coastal fog, known as *la garúa*, can also leave you with little to look at.

Pisco

30 km (19 miles) south of Chincha.

Lending its name to the clear brandy that is Peru's favorite tipple and a source of fierce national pride, the coastal town of Pisco and its surroundings hold a special place in the country's psyche. It's the point where the Argentine hero José de San Martín landed with his troops to fight for Peru's freedom from Spanish rule. It's the city from which pisco was first exported. And it's an important seaport that had its heyday during the 1920s, when guano (bird droppings used as fertilizer) from the nearby Islas Ballestas was worth nearly as much as gold.

Modern-day Pisco shows little evidence of its celebrated past. Instead, what you'll find is a city still struggling to get fully back on its feet after the disaster of August 2007, when a magnitude-8 earthquake shook the town for three minutes.The use of adobe (mud brick) as the main building material had left a vast number of Pisco's buildings unable to withstand the quake, and hundreds of lives were lost as homes, churches, and hospitals collapsed during the tremor. Most travelers now base themselves in Paracas, just a few kilometers down the coast. As for its celebrated namesake drink? There aren't many well-known distilleries around Pisco itself. There are a couple of good restaurants where you can try different brands, but really, you can do that in pretty much any quality eatery in Peru. Generally speaking, pisco is made in the bodegas near Ica (more precisely, between Ica and Pisco), and that's where you should go for tastings.

GETTING HERE AND AROUND

If you arrive by bus, you may find yourself dropped off at the Pisco turnoff on the Panamericana rather than in the town itself, so ask for a direct service. If you do end up disembarking on the highway, there are taxis waiting that make the run into town for around S/5. Drivers who work this route have a bad reputation for taking travelers only to hotels from which they receive a commission. Always insist on being taken to the destination of your choice, and ignore anyone who tells you that the hotel has closed, moved, or changed its name. Transportation within Pisco is generally not necessary: the central area is easily covered on foot, although those venturing out at night should take a taxi.

BUS CONTACTS Oltursa. ✉ *Carretera Paracas, Paracas* ☎ *511/708–5000* 🌐 *www.oltursa.pe.* **Peru Bus.** ✉ *Villa los Angeles Mz. A lt. 11* ☎ *056/531–014* 🌐 *www.perubus.com.pe.*

Restaurants

As de Oros

$$ | SEAFOOD | This 40-year-old Pisco institution hosts pool parties and dancing on weekends, but it's the seafood specialties like whole fried *chita* (rockfish) and *sudado de choros* (shellfish stew) that keep the crowds coming. Roast goat, grilled meats, and *sopa seca* (noodles in basil sauce) round out the extensive menu. **Known for:** fresh seafood; great regional cooking; dancing on weekends. Ⓢ *Average main: S/35* ✉ *Av. San Martín 472* ☎ *056/532–010* 🌐 *www.asdeoros.com.pe* ⊗ *Closed Mon.*

La Viña de Huber

$$ | PERUVIAN | Locals recommend this restaurant on the outskirts of town as the best around; judging from the lunchtime crowds, they can't be too far wrong. The three brothers who run the kitchen cook up modern regional Peruvian cuisine such as sole fillets rolled with bacon and served with passion-fruit dipping sauce or fish stuffed with spinach and sautéed in a pisco-and-pecan broth. **Known for:** huge portions; northern specialties; spicy grilled pork. Ⓢ *Average main: S/35* ✉ *Prolongación Cerro Azul 601* ☎ *056/536–456* 🌐 *www.lavinadehuber.com.*

Hotels

The 2007 earthquake destroyed many accommodations in Pisco, and a good number have closed up shop or moved to nearby Paracas, which has become the base for most travelers. It's recommended that you look for lodging in Paracas, but if you must stay in Pisco, the Hostal San Isidro is structurally sound and has been repaired since the quake. If you decide to stay elsewhere, avoid the hotels housed in precarious-looking, multistory, adobe constructions.

Pisco Country

¡El pisco es peruano! And don't try to tell the locals any different. This clear brandy that takes its name from the Pisco region is Peru's national drink and a source of unrelenting patriotic pride. It would take a very brave, very foolish person to suggest that pisco was invented in Spain, or worse still, in neighboring Chile. Yes, when in Peru, the only thing you need to know is that *el pisco es 100% peruano.*

Fiery and potent, pisco is hands-down the most popular liquor in Peru and is drunk on just about every social occasion. Invited to someone's house for dinner? Chances are you'll be welcomed with a pisco sour, a tart cocktail made from pisco, lime juice, egg white, sugar, and bitters. Heading to a party? You're sure to see at least a couple of people drinking *Peru libres*—a Peruvian take on the classic Cuba libre, using pisco instead of rum and mixing it with Coca-Cola. Of course, the real way to drink pisco is *a lo macho*—strong and straight up. It will certainly put hair on your chest.

Pisco is derived from grapes, like wine, but is technically an aguardiente, or brandy. Through a special distillation process involving a serpentine copper pipe, the fermented grapes are vaporized and then chilled to produce a clear liquor. In Peru, there are multiple variations of pisco: the single-grape pisco *puro*; a blend of grapes, such as Quebranta mixed with Torontel and Muscatel, called pisco *acholado*; pisco *aromatico*, made from straight aromatic grapes; and pisco *mosto verde*, in which the green musts are distilled during the fermentation process.

Legend has it that pisco got its name from sailors who tired of asking for "aguardiente de Pisco" and shortened the term to "pisco." (The name meant "little bird" in the language of the indigenous people, and it still refers to the port city as well as a nearby river.)

Today, Peru produces more than 7.5 million liters annually, 40% of which is exported to the United States. In 1988, the liquor was designated part of the country's national patrimony, and, each year, Peruvians celebrate the Pisco Festival in March as well as the National Day of the Pisco Sour on the first Saturday of every February.

Hostal San Isidro
$ | **B&B/INN** | A relaxing oasis away from the dust of the Pisco streets, this friendly, family-run guesthouse is a top place to drop your bags and rest your weary bones. **Pros:** very welcoming hosts; great pool; free laundry service. **Cons:** near the cemetery; expensive dorm rooms; high walls are somewhat fortresslike. *Rooms from: S/140* *Cl. San Clemente 103* *056/536–471* *18 rooms* *No meals.*

Paracas

15 km (10 miles) south of Pisco.

After the 2007 quake, Paracas quickly leapfrogged Pisco as the most important tourist hub on the Southern Coast. Several major coastal resorts from big-name chains like Doubletree and Libertador (now part of Starwood) have since opened, and others quickly followed. The small-town feel and cluster of petite inns and restaurants around a central fishing pier are still there, though for the passing

Take a boat trip out to Islas Ballestas to observe the marine birds and sea lions.

tourist the exploring options have quadrupled. Apart from being the launching point for trips in the Paracas National Reserve and Islas Ballestas, this is a good base for pisco-tasting adventures, dune-buggy riding near Ica, and trips to the Nazca Lines.

GETTING HERE AND AROUND

A taxi from Pisco to Paracas runs about S/20, or you can take a half-hour Chaco–Paracas–Museo combi to El Chaco for S/3. From Paracas, you can catch a fast motorboat to the reserve and islands.

To visit the Islas Ballestas, you must be on a registered tour, which generally involves an hour or two cruising around the islands among sea lions and birds. Motorboat tours usually leave from El Chaco jetty at 8 and 10 am. For the calmest seas, take the early tour. ■ **TIP→ You'll be in the open wind, sun, and waves during boat trips, so dress appropriately, and prepare your camera for the mists in July and August.** It takes about an hour to reach the park from the jetty; you're close when you can see the Candelabra etched in the coastal hills. A two-hour tour costs around S/40. Some tours continue on to visit the Paracas Peninsula during the afternoon for around S/40 extra.

TOURS

Guided tours of Paracas National Reserve and the Ballestas Islands are offered by Zarcillo Connections in Paracas. Ballestas Travel represents several agencies that sell park packages. Just about every hotel in Pisco and Paracas will assist in booking tours, and most include transportation to and from the dock at Paracas. Make sure your boat has life jackets.

Ballestas Travel

BOAT TOURS | Half-day boat tours of the Islas Ballestas and/or the Paracas National Reserve are the primary service provided by this agency. ✉ *Av. Paracas, Playa El Chaco, Pisco* ☎ *01/257–1146* 🌐 *ballestastravel.com* 💳 *From S/40.*

Peru Kite
SPECIAL-INTEREST | This company offers kitesurfing and windsurfing in Paracas Bay, including lessons and equipment rentals. ✉ *Av. Los Libertadores L-36* ☎ *929/485–667* 🌐 *www.perukite.com* 🎫 *From S/200 for 1-hr lesson.*

Venturia
BOAT TOURS | The luxury tours operated out of the Libertador Paracas hotel include exclusive lunches in vineyards or at desert tent camps, as well as straightforward boat tours of the Islas Ballestas. ✉ *Av. Paracas 173* ☎ *01/712–7000* 🌐 *www.venturia.com.pe* 🎫 *From S/100.*

Zarcillo Connections
BOAT TOURS | Based out of the Zarcillo Paradise hotel in Paracas, this is one of the largest tour operators in the region, with a full range of options from boat tours of the Islas Ballestas to visits to Inca sites such as Tambo Colorado. ✉ *Av. Principal de Ingreso al Chaco 101* ☎ *056/536–636* 🌐 *www.zarcilloconnections.com* 🎫 *From S/40.*

Sights

★ Islas Ballestas
NATURE PRESERVE | Spectacular rocks pummeled by waves and wind into *ballestas* (arched bows) along the cliffs are what characterize this haven of jagged outcrops and rugged beaches, which serve as home to thousands of marine birds and sea lions. You're not allowed to walk onshore, but you wouldn't want to—the land is calf-deep in guano. **■ TIP→ Bring a hat, as tourists are moving targets for multitudes of guano-dropping seabirds. Also, be prepared for the smell—between the sea lions and the birds, the odor can be overpowering.** A boat provides the best views of the abundant wildlife: sea lions laze on the rocks, surrounded by Humboldt penguins, pelicans, seals, boobies, cormorants, and even condors, which make celebrity appearances for the appreciative crowds in February and March. On route to the islands is Punta Pejerrey, the northernmost point of the isthmus and the best spot for viewing the enormous, cactus-shape **Candelabra** carved in the cliffs. It's variously said to be a religious symbol from the Chavín culture, a Masonic emblem left by the liberator José de San Martín, or a staff of the Inca creator-god Viracocha. ✉ *Paracas.*

★ Reserva Nacional de Paracas
NATURE PRESERVE | If a two-hour jaunt around the Islas Ballestas doesn't satisfy your thirst for guano, sea lions, and seabirds, then a land trip to this 280,000-hectare (700,000-plus-acre) park just might. The stunning coastal reserve, on a peninsula south of Pisco, teems with wildlife. Pelicans, condors, and red-and-white flamingos congregate and breed here; the latter are said to have inspired the red-and-white flag General San Martín designed when he liberated Peru. Onshore you can't miss the sound (or the smell) of the hundreds of sea lions, while on the water you might spot penguins, sea turtles, dolphins, manta rays, and even hammerhead sharks.

Named for the blustering *paracas* (sandstorms) that buffet the coast each winter, the Reserva Nacional de Paracas (Paracas National Reserve) is Peru's first park for marine conservation. Organized tours take you along the thin dirt tracks that crisscross the peninsula, past sheltered lagoons, rugged cliffs full of caves, and small fishing villages. This is prime walking territory, as you can stroll from the bay to the **Julio Tello Museum,** and on to the fishing village of **Lagunilla** 5 km (3 miles) farther across the neck of the peninsula. Adjacent to the museum are colonies of flamingos, best seen June through July (and absent January through March, when they fly to the sierra). Hike another 6 km (4 miles) to reach **Mirador de Lobos** (Sea-Lion Lookout) at Punta El Arquillo. Carved into the highest point in the cliffs above Paracas Bay, 14 km (9 miles) from the museum, is the **Candelabra.** Note that you must hire a guide to

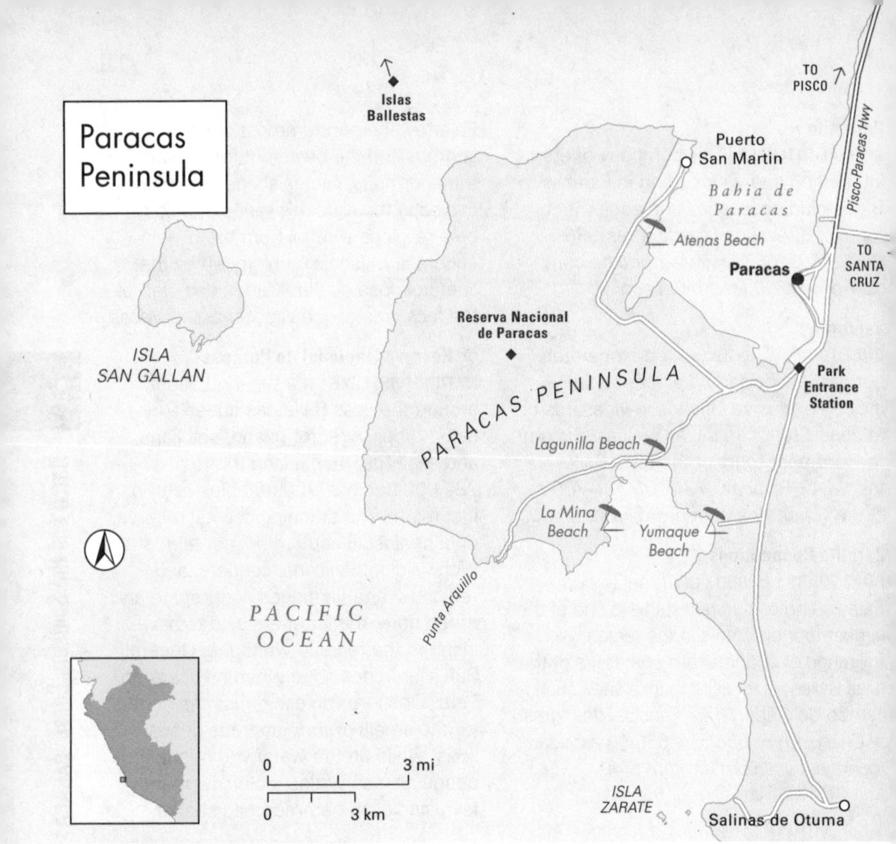

Paracas Peninsula

Islas Ballestas
TO PISCO
Puerto San Martin
Bahia de Paracas
Pisco-Paracas Hwy
Atenas Beach
TO SANTA CRUZ
Paracas
ISLA SAN GALLAN
Reserva Nacional de Paracas
PARACAS PENINSULA
Park Entrance Station
Lagunilla Beach
La Mina Beach
Yumaque Beach
Punta Arquillo
PACIFIC OCEAN
0 3 mi
0 3 km
ISLA ZARATE
Salinas de Otuma

explore the land trails. Minibus tours of the entire park can be arranged through local hotels and travel agencies for about S/40 for four hours. ✉ *Paracas* 🌐 *www.sernanp.gob.pe/de-paracas* 🎫 *S/5.*

Restaurants

Pukasoncco Arte y Restaurante
$$ | **PERUVIAN** | This funky-cozy eatery is a smash-up between an art studio and a kitchen; owner Sansón Velásquez is equally adept with paintbrush and whisk. He'll whip up any dish that suits your fancy, from Ica-style beef stew to river-shrimp soup, discoursing all the while on the abstract and indigenous elements in his colorful canvases. **Known for:** cool art-studio vibe; mega-fresh ingredients; chef's recommendations when choosing dishes. 💲 *Average main: S/35* ✉ *Alameda Alan García Pérez Mz. B lt. 9, El Chaco* ☎ *926/208–021* 🌐 *pukasoncco.jimdofree.com* 🕑 *Closed Mon.*

3 Keros by the Sea
$$$ | **SEAFOOD** | This seafood restaurant in Paracas's Peruvian Yacht Club sets the standard for dining in Paracas. Chef Ricardo Behar makes a point of talking to his guests and tailoring his cooking to individual preferences. **Known for:** interactive consultations with the owner; inventive seafood preparations; quiet setting. 💲 *Average main: S/60* ✉ *Alameda Alan García Pérez, Yacht Club Peruano* ☎ *955/749–828* 🕑 *Closed Mon. and Tues.*

Hotels

Sleepy Paracas really comes alive only during the Peruvian summer (December to March), when city dwellers arrive to set up residence in their shore-front vacation homes. If you're visiting out of season, be warned—many hotels close during the low season or scale back their service and concentrate on repairs.

Aranwa Paracas

$$$$ | RESORT | FAMILY | Part of the growing Peruvian Aranwa chain, this sprawling upscale resort has a lot going on, making it good for families, active types, spa-seekers, and conference delegates alike. **Pros:** lots of space; beautiful pools; very kid friendly. **Cons:** overpriced; can be noisy; restaurant not on the level of the hotel itself. *Rooms from: S/1200 ✉ El Chaco, La Puntilla Lote C ☎ 056/580–600 🌐 www.aranwahotels.com 134 rooms Free breakfast.*

Doubletree Hotel Paracas

$$$$ | RESORT | FAMILY | The first major resort hotel to hit the Paracas coast, this all-suite, family-friendly retreat opened in 2009 and sits just a few steps down the beach from the more luxurious Libertador. **Pros:** Club de Paco kids' club; variety of dining options; huge pool. **Cons:** pools can become overcrowded on summer weekends; adults without kids might be turned off; pricey. *Rooms from: S/900 ✉ Lote 30–34, Urb. Santo Domingo ☎ 056/581–919 🌐 hilton.com 124 rooms No meals.*

★ Hotel Paracas Libertador

$$$ | RESORT | A member of Starwood's swanky Luxury Collection, the ultra-chic Libertador was created from the rubble of the once-famous Hotel Paracas, destroyed in the 2007 earthquake. **Pros:** beachfront location; great prices for basic rooms; all rooms have terraces. **Cons:** wind can pick up at times near the pool; daybed rentals are pricey; beach is not as beautiful as other stretches on Peru's coast. *Rooms from: S/650 ✉ Av. Paracas 173 ☎ 056/581–333 🌐 www.libertador.com.pe 120 rooms No meals.*

La Hacienda Bahia Paracas

$$$ | RESORT | FAMILY | Opened in 2009, this hotel may not be as flashy as the nearby Libertador or Doubletree, but it's nearly as nice, and the daily supervised activities for kids are a hit with families. **Pros:** package deals; amazing pool; outstanding staff. **Cons:** slow during the week; only one restaurant; somewhat overpriced. *Rooms from: S/750 ✉ Santo Domingo Lote 25 ☎ 01/213–1010 🌐 www.hoteleslahacienda.com 68 rooms Free breakfast.*

Refugio del Pirata

$ | B&B/INN | Friendly and in a terrific location for those heading out on early-morning boat excursions, this ramshackle guesthouse is popular with backpackers and tour groups alike. **Pros:** central location in town; lovely terrace with port views; easy to organize tours via the affiliated travel agency on the ground floor. **Cons:** no restaurant; frequently noisy; interior rooms small and dark. *Rooms from: S/170 ✉ Av. Paracas Lote 6 ☎ 056/545–054 🌐 refugiodelpirata.com 14 rooms No meals.*

San Agustín Paracas

$$ | RESORT | This straightforward Paracas resort, one of the more affordable options on the strip, is also one of the most grown-up, with fewer kids running around and, overall, fewer bells and whistles. **Pros:** nice pool area; not as many families; all rooms have sea views. **Cons:** pricey; fewer amenities than neighboring properties; some problems with front-desk service. *Rooms from: S/330 ✉ Chaco de la Puntilla ☎ 056/580–420 🌐 hotelessanagustin.com.pe/en/ 123 rooms Free breakfast.*

Ica

72 km (45 miles) southeast of Paracas.

A bustling commercial city with chaotic traffic and horn-happy drivers, Ica challenges you to find its attractive side. Step outside the city center, however, and you'll see why this spot attracted the Spanish way back in the 16th century—and also why those conquistadors couldn't have picked a better place to build their coastal plantations. With their verdant fields and snow-covered mountains, the surrounding environs are relaxing and cheerful, with helpful residents, likely due as much to the nearly never-ending sunshine as to the high-quality wines and piscos produced by the local bodegas and distilleries. This is a town of laughter and festivals, especially during the culmination of the growing season, which occupies most of March and April.

The city center's colonial look comes from its European heritage. Ica was founded by the Spanish in 1563, making it one of the oldest towns in southern Peru. It later became an important regional center and was invaded by Chile during the War of the Pacific (1879–84). Ica suffered badly in the 2007 earthquake, when many of the colonial-era buildings, including most of the famous churches, were damaged, but today it has in great measure recovered. Aside from its vineyards, it's also famous for its pecans and high-stepping horses, called *caballos de paso*.

Ica's vineyards and haciendas are a source of national pride, and its fine bodegas are a major attraction. Most are open year-round, but the best time to visit is February to April, during the grape harvest. The Tacama and Ocucaje bodegas are generally considered to have some of the best-quality wines, and the Quebranta and Italia grape varietals are well regarded for pisco. ■ **TIP→ The Peruvian autumn is the season for Ica's Fiesta de la Vendimia, where you can enjoy parades, sports competitions, local music and dancing, and even catch beauty queens stomping grapes.** It's also a great time to be introduced to the vast selection of local wines and piscos, as well as an opportunity to try homemade concoctions not yet on the market.

The city's excitement also heightens for such festivals as February's Carnaval, Semana Santa in March or April, and the all-night pilgrimages of El Señor de Luren in March and October. Other fun times to visit are during Ica Week, around June 17, which celebrates the city's founding, and the annual Ica Tourist Festival in late September.

GETTING HERE AND AROUND

Tourism in Ica is all about wineries. Most are close to the city and easily accessed by road. ■ **TIP→ If you don't have your own car (or don't want to be the designated driver on a winery trip), pick the wineries you'd like to see, and ask a taxi driver to quote you a price. For some bodegas, there are colectivos (shared taxis) that depart from near the main square for S/2.** You can also hop on one of the prearranged tours offered by most hotels. The going rate for a four-hour taxi ride taking in three wineries close to the city is around S/50; if you go on a formal tour, you'll pay up to S/40 per person.

Taxis in Ica include the noisy but distinctive three-wheeled mototaxis. A taxi ride between Ica and Huacachina costs S/8.

The bus companies Cruz del Sur and Peru Bus have the most departures from Ica, though dozens of other companies also make trips north or south along the Panamericana. Buses usually depart from the station on Avenida José Matias Manzanilla and go to Lima (5 hours, S/30), Pisco (1 hour, S/10), and Nazca (3 hours, S/15). Taxi colectivos to Lima (3½ hours, S/40) and Nazca (2 hours, S/25) leave from in front of the bus station when full.

BUS CONTACTS Cruz del Sur. ✉ *Cl. Fray Ramón Rojas 189* ☎ *056/480–100* 🌐 *www.cruzdelsur.com.pe.* **Peru Bus.** ✉ *Av. Matias Manzanilla 130* ☎ *01/205–2370* 🌐 *www.perubus.com.pe.*

TOURS

Most hotels can arrange tours of the Nazca Lines, but several travel companies also specialize in local explorations. Book ahead, because flights over the lines are often sold out. Make sure the guide or agency is licensed and experienced. Professional guides must be approved

Sights

1 Iglesia San Francisco ... **B2**
2 Museo Científico Javier Cabrera **C2**
3 Museo Histórico Regional **A5**

Restaurants

1 El Cordón y La Rosa **C2**
2 El Otro Peñoncito... **A4**

Hotels

1 Casa Sur **A1**
2 El Carmelo Hotel & Hacienda ... **A1**
3 Hotel Las Dunas **A1**
4 Hotel Viñas Queirolo..... **D1**
5 Villa Jazmin **A1**

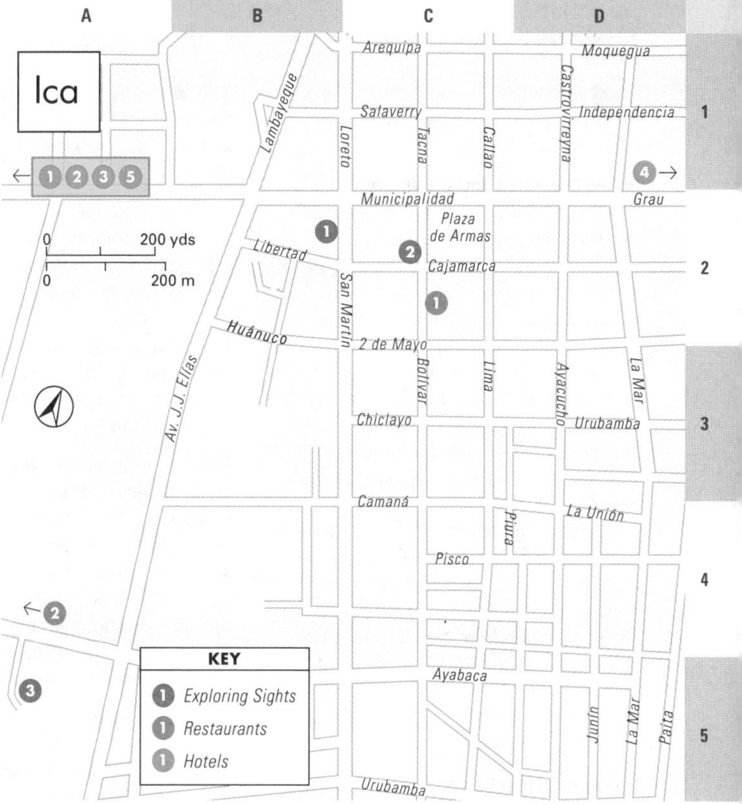

Ica

KEY

Exploring Sights
Restaurants
Hotels

by the Ministry of Tourism, so ask for identification before you hire.

Desert Adventure

ADVENTURE TOURS | This tour operator will arrange dune buggy and sandboarding around the Huacachina oasis and throughout the Ica desert. It also offers camping excursions for individuals or groups. ✉ *Desert Nights Hostel, Balneario de Huacachina s/n* ☎ *056/228–458* 🌐 *desertadventure.net* 🎫 *From S/150.*

Ica Desert Trip Peru (Roberto Penny Cabrera)

EXCURSIONS | One fellow you can't miss in Ica is Roberto Penny Cabrera, who is a direct descendant of Ica's founding family and who lives right on the Plaza de Armas. After a long career in mining, Roberto started this company and began offering tours of the nearby desert in his fully equipped, four-wheel-drive jeep. He's fascinated with the fossils of gigantic sharks and whales he's come across and has a collection of huge incisors. ✉ *Cl. Bolivar 178* ☎ *056/237–373* 🌐 *www.facebook.com/robertopennycabrera* 🎫 *From S/420 per day.*

Sights

Iglesia San Francisco

RELIGIOUS SITE | Soaring ceilings, ornate stained-glass windows, and the fact that it's the only one of Ica's colonial-era churches left standing after the 2007 earthquake make this the city's grandest religious building. Yet even this colossal monument didn't escape the quake unscathed. **■ TIP→ If you look on the floor toward the front of the church you can see the gouges left in the marble blocks by falling pieces of the church altar.** It's said that the statues of the saints stood serenely throughout the quake and didn't move an inch. ✉ *Avs. Municipalidad y San Martín* 🎫 *Free.*

Museo Científico Javier Cabrera

MUSEUM | Curious to find the *real* meaning of the Nazca Lines? Head to this small building on the Plaza de Armas, which contains a collection of more than 11,000 intricately carved stones and boulders depicting varied pre-Columbian themes, ranging from ancient surgical techniques to dinosaurs. The charismatic and eccentric founder, Dr. Javier Cabrera, studied the stones for many years, and the staffers are more than happy to explain to you how they prove the existence of an advanced pre-Columbian society that created the Nazca Lines as a magnetic landing strip for their spacecraft (they even have the diagram to prove it!). It's a good idea to make a reservation before you go, as hours are irregular. ✉ *Cl. Bolívar 170* ☎ *056/227–676* 🌐 *www.museocientificojaviercabrera.com* 🎫 *S/35 with guided tour.*

Museo Histórico Regional

MUSEUM | It may be a little out of the way, but don't let that stop you from visiting this compact museum with a vast and well-preserved collection on regional history—particularly from the Inca, Nazca, and Paracas cultures. Note the *quipus*, mysterious knotted, colored threads thought to have been used by the Incas to count commodities and quantities of food. ■ **TIP→ Fans of the macabre will love the mummy display, where you can see everything from embalmed humans to a mummified bird.** The squeamish can head out back to view a scale model of the Nazca Lines from an observation tower. You can also buy maps (S/1) and paintings of Nazca motifs (S/5). The museum is about 1½ km (1 mile) from the main square. It's not advisable to walk, so take the opportunity to jump into one of the distinctive, three-wheeled mototaxis that will make the trip for around S/5. ✉ *Av. Ayabaca 895* ☎ *056/234–383* 🌐 *museos.cultura.pe/museos/museo-regional-de-ica-adolfo-bermúdez-jenkins* 🎫 *S/7.50.*

WINERIES

If you can't imagine anything better than sampling different varieties of wine and pisco at nine in the morning, then these Ica region wineries are most definitely for you. Most make their living from tourism and, as a way of boosting sales, devote a good portion of any tour to the tasting room. Tours are free, although the guides do appreciate tips.

■ **TIP→ Peruvians like their wines sweet and their pisco strong.** If you're unused to drinking spirits straight up, follow this tried-and-true Peruvian technique for a smoother drop: after swirling the pisco around the glass, inhale the vapors. Before exhaling, take the pisco into your mouth and taste the flavor for four seconds. As you swallow, exhale!

Bodega El Catador

WINERY/DISTILLERY | A favorite stop on the tour circuit, this family-run bodega produces wines and some of the region's finest pisco. Tour guides are happy to show you a 300-year-old section of the distillery that's still in operation. If you're here in March, try to catch the annual Fiesta de Uva, when the year's festival queen tours the vineyard and gets her feet wet in the opening of the grape-pressing season. The excellent Taberna restaurant and bar is open for lunch after a hard morning's wine tasting. If you don't want to drive, take a colectivo taxi from near the Plaza de Armas (S/2). ✉ *Km 294, Panamericana Sur, Fondo Tres Equinas 104* ☎ *056/403–516* 🌐 *www.elcatador.pe.*

Bodega Lazo

WINERY/DISTILLERY | One of the more enjoyable alcohol-making operations to visit is owned by Elar Bolívar, who claims to be a direct descendent of the liberator Simón de Bolívar himself (some locals shrug their shoulders at this). Regardless, Elar's small, artisanal operation includes

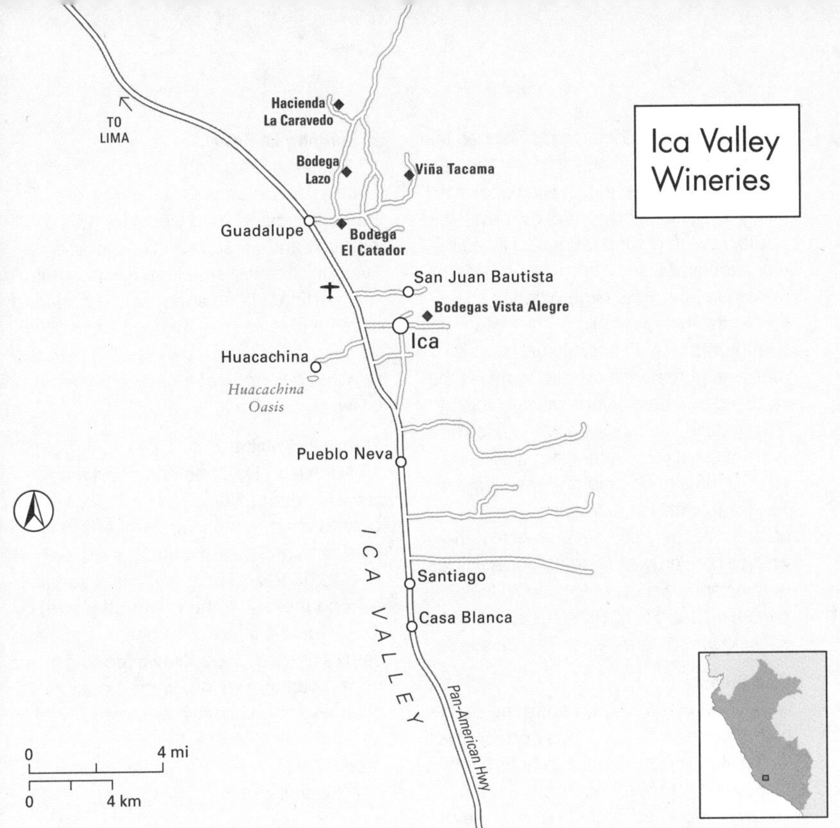

a creepy collection of shrunken heads (Dutch tourists, he says, who didn't pay their drink tab), ancient cash registers, fencing equipment, and copies of some of the paintings in Ica's regional museum. The question is, who really has the originals: Elar or the museum? As part of your visit, you can taste the bodega's recently made pisco, straight from the clay vessel. The pisco is so-so, but the atmosphere is priceless. Some organized tours include this bodega as part of their itinerary. It's not a safe walk from town, so take a cab if you come on your own. ✉ *Camino de Reyes s/n, San Juan Bautista* ☎ *981/264–883* 🌐 *www.facebook.com/bodegalazo1809*.

Bodegas Vista Alegre

WINERY/DISTILLERY | A sunny brick archway welcomes you to this large, pleasant winery, which has been producing fine wines, pisco, and sangria since it was founded by the Picasso brothers in 1857. A former monastery and now the largest winery in the valley, it's a popular tour-bus stop, so come early to avoid the groups. Tours in English or Spanish take you through the vast pisco- and wine-making facilities at the industrial-sized production center before depositing you in the tasting room. ⚠ **It's not safe to walk here from downtown Ica, so if you don't have your own vehicle, take a taxi.** ✉ *Km 2.5, Camina a la Tinguiña* ☎ *01/248–6757* 🌐 *www.vistaalegre.com.pe*.

Hacienda La Caravedo

WINERY/DISTILLERY | Dating from 1684, this is one of the oldest working distilleries in the Americas. For the past few years, the historic hacienda has been continually upgraded, now that it is the home of internationally famous brand Pisco Portón. Master distiller and pisco celebrity Johnny

Schuler designed the new distillery so that it would move liquid only through the natural forces of gravity, which allows for small-batch distillation and control over every bottle. On the guided tours, you'll see several traditional pisco-making methods on the estate, from the large wooden press to the gravity-fed channels. Then you'll see the modern additions, such as the roof garden that was planted to offset the carbon dioxide emissions created during fermentation, as well as a water-treatment system to recycle water from distillation into a source of irrigation for the vineyards. Tours end with, of course, a tasting. With prior notice, they can set up lunch in the vineyard or Peruvian Paso horseback rides. Reservations are essential. ✉ *Km 291, Panamericana Sur* ☎ *01/711–7800* 🌐 *www.caravedopisco.com/hacienda-la-caravedo.*

Viña Tacama

WINERY/DISTILLERY | After suffering earthquake damage in 2007, this 16th-century hacienda took the opportunity to overhaul its now very modern operation. Internationally renowned, it produces some of Peru's best labels, particularly the Blanco de Blancos and Don Manuel Tannat wines and the Demonio de los Andes line of piscos. Stroll through the rolling vineyards—still watered by the Achirana irrigation canal built by the Incas—before sampling the end result. **■ TIP→ The on-site restaurant is one of the best in Ica.** The estate is about 11 km (7 miles) north of town. ✉ *Camina a la Tinguiña s/n* ☎ *056/581–030* 🌐 *www.tacama.com.*

Restaurants

Ica boasts several good eateries inside the city limits. However, if you're headed out to tour the bodegas in the morning, know that some of the region's best restaurants are to be found at the wineries themselves. Indeed, Viña Tacama and Bodega El Catador are both worth visiting for the food alone. But nearly any on-site bodega restaurant is going to be decent.

El Cordón y La Rosa

$ | **PERUVIAN** | This bright little spot bills itself as a *criollazo*, a total onslaught of Peruvian coastal cooking. With its big portions and broad menu, it definitely lives up to that claim. **Known for:** generous portions; large appetizers for sharing; attractive setting. 💲 *Average main: S/20* ✉ *Av. Los Maestros D-14* ☎ *056/218–012* 🌐 *www.facebook.com/elcordonylarosa* ⏲ *No dinner Sun.*

El Otro Peñoncito

$ | **PERUVIAN** | Don't be surprised if chef Hary Hernandez (aka "Sir Hary") comes over to chat during your meal at this half-century-old Ica institution: his passion for food and hospitality is legendary. Among the dishes he might offer are *pollo a la iqueña* (chicken in pecan-and-pisco sauce) or fried trout. **Known for:** traditional coastal cooking; warm hospitality; changing menu. 💲 *Average main: S/30* ✉ *Cl. Bolívar 255* ☎ *999/910–210* 🌐 *www.facebook.com/RestElOtroPenoncito* 💳 *No credit cards.*

Hotels

Casa Sur

$ | **HOTEL** | This is one of Ica's hidden gems, with amenities you'd expect to find only in a much larger hotel. **Pros:** quiet; superb attention to detail; good food and great value. **Cons:** high walls make it seem cut off from the city; service can be slow; pool is often closed. 💲 *Rooms from: S/180* ✉ *Av. La Angostura 367* ☎ *056/256–101* 🛏 *16 rooms* 🍽 *No meals.*

El Carmelo Hotel & Hacienda

$ | **HOTEL** | **FAMILY** | With rooms built around a central courtyard complete with an ancient grape press and a working pisco distillery, it's hard to tell whether this quirky property on the road between Ica and Huacachina is a hotel or a bodega-style theme park. **Pros:** wicker-filled, open-air sitting room; chance to see the pisco-making process up close; zoo and playground to entertain the kids. **Cons:**

out-of-town location; rooms are on the small side; Wi-Fi is weak in many rooms. $ *Rooms from: S/220* ✉ *Km 301.2, Pan-American Hwy.* ☎ *056/232–191* 🌐 *www.elcarmelohotelhacienda.com* *58 rooms* *Breakfast.*

Hotel Las Dunas

$$ | **RESORT** | **FAMILY** | For a taste of the good life, Peruvian style, head to this top-end resort between Ica and Huacachina, a favorite getaway for Peruvian families. **Pros:** beautiful grounds; activities for children; decent restaurant. **Cons:** out of town; resort aesthetic; schedules for activities can be inconvenient. $ *Rooms from: S/350* ✉ *Av. La Angostura 400* ☎ *056/256–224* 🌐 *www.lasdunashotel.com* *133 rooms* *No meals.*

★ **Hotel Viñas Queirolo**

$$ | **HOTEL** | There's no better property in the country for experiencing Peru's wine and pisco industry than this charming bodega-based hacienda surrounded by 400 hectares (988 acres) of Santiago Queirolo's verdant vineyards. **Pros:** atmospheric and authentic; unique in the region; great on-site restaurant. **Cons:** a bit out of the way, making local public transportation impractical; occasional problems with the reservation process; some staff members don't speak English. $ *Rooms from: S/450* ✉ *Carretera a San José de los Molinos* ☎ *965/397–086* 🌐 *www.hotelvinasqueirolo.com* *20 rooms* *Breakfast.*

Villa Jazmin

$ | **HOTEL** | This intimate inn garners rave reviews, and the charming dune setting and small but inviting pool make it a good place to chill for a few days while exploring the area. **Pros:** good in-house restaurant; eco-friendly; less crowded than other Ica resorts. **Cons:** rooms can be dark; the pool is more for lounging than swimming; far from downtown. $ *Rooms from: S/180* ✉ *Los Girasoles MZ C-1, Lote 7, La Angostura* ☎ *056/258–179* 🌐 *www.villajazmin.net* *20 rooms* *No meals.*

Shopping

Ica is an excellent place to pick up Peruvian handicrafts with regional styles and motifs. Tapestries and textiles woven in naturally colored llama and alpaca wool often have images of the Nazca Lines and historical figures. In particular, look for *alfombras* (rugs), *colchas* (blankets), and *tapices* (hangings).

Huacachina

5 km (3 miles) southwest of Ica.

Drive 10 minutes through the pale, mountainous sand dunes southwest of Ica, and you'll suddenly see a gathering of attractive, pastel-colored buildings surrounding a patch of green. It's not an oasis on the horizon, but rather the lakeside resort of Huacachina, a palm-fringed lagoon of jade-tinged waters whose sulfurous properties are reputed to have healing powers. The view is breathtaking: a collection of attractive, colonial-style hotels in front of a golden beach, with a backdrop of snow-covered peaks against the distant sky. In the 1920s, Peru's elite traveled here on holiday, and today the spacious resorts still beckon. The lake is a pilgrimage site for those with skin and other health problems, sandboarders who want to tackle the 100-meter (325-foot) dunes, and budget travelers who pitch tents in the sand or sleep under the stars.

GETTING HERE AND AROUND

Huacachina sits on the opposite side of the highway from the center of Ica. Take any bus to Ica, and hire a mototaxi to the oasis for about S/5.

Restaurants

La Casa de Bamboo

$ | **CAFÉ** | This pleasant garden café beside Hostería Suiza has a vegetarian-friendly vibe, with lots of quinoa and salads on offer. Dishes on the eclectic menu are all made from scratch by the British owner, and range from Thai curries and falafel to pastas and crepes. **Known for:** vegetarian dishes; desserts; beachy vibe. *Average main: S/15 Av. Perotti s/n 944/255–871 www.facebook.com/La-Casa-de-Bamboo-123418741040046.*

Oasis de América

$ | **PERUVIAN** | In a resort where mediocre tourist fare is the norm, this Peruvian eatery stands out. Here, after a long day on the dunes, you can replenish your system with a host of seafood options, as well as *chicharrones* (fried chicken or fish) and a few local specialties like *carapulcra con sopa seca. Average main: S/30 Huacachina Laguna Zona Reservada 056/632–451 www.oasisdeamerica.com.*

Hotels

★ El Huacachinero

$$ | **B&B/INN** | Hands-down Huacachina's best budget lodging, this is a beautiful bargain in the oasis of Peru—clean, safe, and with its own little bar featuring a mural of Ica's now-disappeared camel herd. **Pros:** fantastic pool area with hammocks; dune-buggy service and sandboard rental; some rooms have A/C. **Cons:** often full; noisy parrots; three of the rooms don't have en suite bathroom. *Rooms from: S/270 Av. Perotti, Balnearia de Huacachina 056/217–435 www.elhuacachinero.com 24 rooms Free breakfast.*

Hostería Suiza

$ | **B&B/INN** | It may not be the most jumping joint in town, but this laid-back guesthouse is a good spot for enjoying the beauty of the desert landscape without having to deal with the constant party that you'll find in some other hotels. **Pros:** peaceful atmosphere; friendly staff; great pool. **Cons:** restaurant only serves breakfast; furnishings are a little old-fashioned; no A/C. *Rooms from: S/180 Balneario de Huacachina 264 056/238–762 www.hosteriasuiza.com.pe 35 rooms Free breakfast.*

Hotel Mossone

$ | **HOTEL** | Here you can imagine life as it was in Huacachina's heyday, thanks to a picture-postcard location fronting the lagoon and gorgeous Spanish colonial–style architecture. **Pros:** fantastic lagoonside location; great pool; lounge bar is the best spot in town for watching the sun set over the dunes. **Cons:** often full with tour groups; can be noisy; some rooms need refurbishing. *Rooms from: S/220 Balneario de Huacachina s/n 056/213–630, 01/261–9605 in Lima www.facebook.com/Hotel.Mossone 32 rooms No meals.*

Activities

SANDBOARDING

Ever fancied having a go at snowboarding, but chickened out at the thought of all those painful next-day bruises? Welcome to the new adventure sport of sandboarding, a kinder, gentler way to hit the slopes. Surrounded by dunes, Huacachina is the sandboarding capital of the world: every year, European sports fans arrive here in droves to practice for the international sandsurfing competitions on Cerro Blanco, the massive dune 14 km (8 miles) north of Nazca.

With no rope tows or chairlifts to get you up the hills, the easiest way to get started is to go on a dune-buggy tour (equipment included), offered by just about every hotel in town. In these converted vehicles, you'll be driven (quickly) to the top of the dunes, upon which you can board, slide, or slither down to be picked up again at the bottom. Drivers push their vehicles hard, so be prepared for some heart-stopping moments. It's best to go in the morning or late afternoon, when the sand is not as hot and doesn't melt the wax off your board. Be sure to wear a long-sleeved shirt and long pants!

Nazca

136 km (85 miles) southeast of Ica.

What do a giant hummingbird, a monkey, and an astronaut have in common? Well, apart from the fact that they're all etched into the floor of the desert near Nazca, no one really seems to know. Welcome to one of the world's great mysteries—the Nazca Lines, hallmark of one of Peru's most enigmatic ancient civilizations.

A mirage of green in the desert, lined with cotton fields and orchards and bordered by crisp mountain peaks, Nazca was a quiet colonial town unnoticed by the rest of the world until 1901, when Peruvian archaeologist Max Uhle excavated sites around it and discovered the remains of a unique pre-Columbian culture. Set 598 meters (1,961 feet) above sea level, the town has a dry climate—scorching by day, nippy by night—that was instrumental in preserving centuries-old relics from Inca and pre-Columbian tribes. ■ **TIP→ The area has more than 100 cemeteries, where the humidity-free climate has helped preserve priceless jewelry, textiles, pottery, and mummies.** Overlooking the parched scene is the 2,078-meter (6,815-foot) Cerro Blanco, the highest sand dune in the world.

GETTING HERE AND AROUND

Be prepared: Nazca is all about tours, and it may seem like everyone in town is trying to sell you one at once. The minute you poke your nose outside the bus door, you'll be swamped with offers for flights over the lines, hotels, and trips to the Chauchilla Cemetery. Use common sense about any offers made to you by touts at the bus station: if it's cheap, there's probably a good reason why. That said, a tour with a reputable agency is a great way to catch all of Nazca's major sites. Recommended firms include Alegría Tours in Nazca and Zarcillo Connections in Paracas.

All buses arrive and depart from the *óvalo* (roundabout), where Avenida Callao meets the Panamericana Sur. To see the lines from ground level, taxis will make the 30-minute run out to the mirador for around S/50, or you can do it the local way and catch any northbound bus along the Panamericana for just S/3. ■ **TIP→ Flights over the lines are best in the early morning, before the sun gets too high and winds make flying uncomfortable.** Standard flights last around 30 minutes and cost between US$60 and US$140, depending on the season. You'll also have to pay an airport tax of S/30. There are similar lines at nearby Palpa; some tour operators offer flyovers of both sites. Flight tickets are available from travel agencies and many hotels in town or directly from the airline offices near the airport. Buying tickets in advance will save you time. You can also pay on the spot at the airport, but because planes won't take off until all seats are filled, you may spend most of your morning hanging around the dusty Panamerica Sur watching while others take off and land.

BUS CONTACTS Cruz del Sur. ✉ *Cl. Lima and Cl. San Martín* ☎ *01/311–5050* 🌐 *www.cruzdelsur.com.pe.*

TOURS

Aero Nasca and upstarts Aero Paracas and Alas Peruanas all offer services. The latter are small operations with varying office hours, so check at the airport for schedules. Most sightseeing flights depart from Nazca, although Aero Paracas also originates in Lima and Pisco. Note that these flights are often overbooked year-round; arrive early to check in for your flight, as there's a chance you'll get bumped if you're late.

Safety records for many of the companies are spotty at best. In 2010, seven tourists were killed when their Nazca Airlines flight crashed in the desert. Airlines change owners and names frequently, so it's hard to know exactly who you are flying with.

Aero Nasca

AIR EXCURSIONS | Thirty-minute flights over the Nazca Lines, 60-minute flights over the Nazca and Palpa Lines together, or a full-day tour from Lima include a transfer from your hotel to the airport and a video introduction about the lines. ✉ *Aeropuerto Maria Reich, Km 447, Panamericana Sur* ☎ *01/768–5326* 🌐 *www.aeronasca.com* 🎫 *From S/250.*

Aero Paracas

AIR EXCURSIONS | This airline offers mostly 30-minute flights over the Nazca and Palpa Lines. In some cases, it will fly from Paracas or Lima. ✉ *Av. Javier Prado Oeste 870, Lima* ☎ *01/641–7000* 🌐 *www.aeroparacas.com* 🎫 *From S/250.*

Alas Peruanas

ADVENTURE TOURS | A variety of flights over the Nazca Lines and other area sites are available. Their longer Discovery tours include flights over the Palpa Lines and Cahuachi ruins. They can also arrange transportation from Ica, Paracas, and Pisco. ✉ *Cl. Lima 168* ☎ *056/522–497* 🌐 *www.alasperuanas.com* 🎫 *From S/250.*

Alegría Tours

ADVENTURE TOURS | Tours of lesser-known desert sites are the specialty here, including four-hour trips to the Cahuachi cemeteries and the Cantalloc Aqueducts. They can also add a sandboarding excursion on Nazca's Usaka dunes. ✉ *Hotel Alegría, Cl. Lima 168* ☎ *056/522–497* 🌐 *www.alegriatoursperu.com* 🎫 *From S/100.*

Sights

Cahuachi Pyramids

ARCHAEOLOGICAL SITE | Within a walled, 3,400-square-meter (4,050-square-yard) courtyard west of the Nazca Lines is an ancient ceremonial and pilgrimage site. Six adobe pyramids, the highest of which is about 21 meters (69 feet), stand above a network of 40 mounds with rooms and connecting corridors. Grain and water silos are also visible inside, and several large cemeteries lie outside the walls. Used by the early Nazca culture, the site is estimated to have existed for about three or four centuries before being abandoned around AD 500. Cahuachi takes its name from the word *qahuachi* (meddlesome). La Estaquería, with its mummification pillars, is nearby. Tours from Nazca, 34 km (21 miles) to the east, visit both sites for around S/40 with a group and take three hours. ✉ *Nazca.*

Casa-Museo Maria Reiche

MUSEUM | To see where a lifelong obsession with the Nazca Lines can lead you, head to the former home of the German anthropologist who devoted her existence to studying them. There's little explanatory material here among the pottery, textiles, mummies, and skeletons from the Paracas, Nazca, Wari, Chincha, and Inca cultures, so don't expect any grand archaeological revelations. What you'll see instead is the environment in which Maria Reiche lived and worked. A scale model of the lines is behind the house; her grave lies not far away. Take a bus from the Ormeño terminal to the Km 416 marker to reach the museum, which is 1 km (½ mile) from town. ✉ *Km 416, Panamericana Sur, San Pablo* ☎ *056/521–372* 🌐 *www.facebook.com/MausoleoMariaReicheParaLasLineasDeNasca* 🎫 *S/5.*

Cementerio de Chauchilla

CEMETERY | In the midst of the pale, scorched desert, 30 km (19 miles) south of Nazca, lies this ancient cemetery, whose precincts are littered with sun-bleached skulls and shards of pottery. *Huaqueros* (grave robbers) have ransacked the site over the years, and, until a couple of years ago, the mummies unearthed by their looting sprouted from the earth in a jumble of bones and threadbare weavings. Now, however, they are housed neatly inside a dozen or so covered tombs. It's an eerie sight, since the mummies still have hair attached, as well as mottled, brown-rose

Continued on page 148

by Ruth Anne Phillips

NAZCA LINES

On the surface of the southern Peruvian coastal desert or "Pampa" between the Nazca and Ingenio River valleys are the Nazca Lines. The Nazca Lines are enormous figures, geometric designs and straight lines etched into the desert's surface called geoglyphs. There are more than 1,000 enormous figures, geometric shapes and straight lines, some arranged as ray centers. While the most famous of the lines appear on the Pampa de San José near Nazca as well as on the hillsides of the valleys of the Río Grande de Nazca, the geoglyphs are throughout a larger area that comprises 400 square miles.

*Nazca images shown in relation to each other; not at true scale.
Panamericana Hwy.
INGENIO VALLEY
Hevon
Parrot
Aligator
Spiral
Lizard
Watch Tower
Spider
Parrot
Rose
Tree
Hands
See Plant
Hummingbird
One of the hummingbirds is five times the length of a large airplane.
Condor
Cat
Monkey
Dog
Discovered in 2020, this gigantic cat geoglyph dates to the late Paracas period, more than 2,000 years ago, making it the oldest geoglyph unearthed at Nazca to date.
How big is the Nazca line?
120 m (394 ft)
109.7 m (360 ft)
84 m (275.5 ft)
84.5 m (277 ft)
90 m (295 ft)
48.8 m (160 ft)
88.4 m (290 ft)
The Monkey
American football field
World largest airplane
(An-225 Mriya)
FIFA official soccer field

THINGS TO LOOK FOR

The biomorphic designs include monkeys, birds, a spider, plants, and a number of fantastical combinations and somewhat abstracted humanoid creatures. One of the monkeys is 180 feet long while a hummingbird is five times the length of a large airplane. At least 227 spirals, zigzags, triangles, quadrangles, and trapezoids make up the geometric designs, with one trapezoid measuring over 2,700 feet

A trapezoid.

by 300 feet. The straight lines represent the greatest proportion of the geoglyphs: 800 single or parallel lines stretch on for miles, ranging in width from less than two feet to hundreds of feet.

Many of the lines haphazardly overlap each other, which indicates that as a group they were not pre-planned.

CONSTRUCTION

Modern archaeologists have recreated surprisingly simple construction methods for the geoglyphs using basic surveying techniques. Sight poles guided the construction of straight lines and strings tied to posts helped create circular designs. Wooden posts that may have been used as guides or end markers and an abundance of fancy potsherds, possibly used in rituals, have been found along many of the lines.

AGE

The extremely dry climatic conditions of the Pampa have helped preserve the lines; most date from c. 500 AD, during the florescence of the Nazca culture (c. 1–700 AD). A small number, however, may date to after the Nazca period to as late as 1000 AD.

Shell

See Birds

Panamericana Hwy.
(18 miles from Nazca to Ingenio Valley)

TO NAZCA

Astronaut

Whale

HISTORY AND MYSTERY

An archaeologist examines the lines.

Though the Nazca Lines are difficult to see from the ground due to their enormous size, some can be seen from nearby hillsides. It's widely believed that the lines were first properly seen from an airplane, but they were "discovered" by archaeologists working near Cahuachi in the mid-1920s. American archaeologist, Alfred L. Kroeber was the first to describe them in 1926, but it was Peruvian archaeologist Toribio Mejía Xesspe who conducted the first extensive studies of the Nazca Lines around the same time.

By the late 1920s, commercial planes began flying over the Pampa and many reported seeing the Nazca Lines from the air. It was not until American geographer and historian, Paul Kosok and his second wife Rose, flew over the Nazca drainage area in 1941, however, that the Nazca Lines became a widely known phenomenon in the United States and Europe.

THE CREATIVE PROCESS

The dry desert plain acts as a giant scratchpad as the darker oxidized surface can be swept away to reveal the lighter, pale pink subsurface. Many of the shapes are made with one continuous line that has piles of dark rocks lining the edges creating a dark border.

Stylistic comparisons between the figural Nazca Lines and images that appear on Nazca ceramics have helped establish their age.

THEORIES ABOUND

The Nazca Lines have incited various scholarly and popular theories for their construction and significance. Kroeber and Xesspe, observing the lines from the ground, believed that they served as sacred pathways. Kosok, seeing the lines from the air, observed the sun setting over the end of one line on the day of the winter solstice and thought they must have marked important astronomical events. German mathematician Maria Reiche, who studied the lines and lived near them for decades, expanded upon Kosok's astronomical theories. Modern scholars, however, have demonstrated that the lines' alignment to celestial events occurred at a frequency no greater than chance. Other theories posit that they were made for earth, mountain, or sky deities. After Cahuachi was determined in the 1980s to have been a large pilgrimage center, the idea that the lines acted as a sacred pathway has gained new momentum. Another plausible theory suggests that the Nazca Lines marked underground water sources.

Spaceman figure, San Jose Pampa

IT'S THE ALIENS, OF COURSE

Popular theories have promoted the "mystery" of the Nazca Lines. One influential author, Erich von Däniken, suggested in his 1968 best-selling book *Chariots of the Gods* (reprinted several times and made into a film) that these giant geoglyphs were created as landing markers for extraterrestrials. Archaeologists and other scientists have dismissed these theories. The aliens deny them as well.

VISITING THE NAZCA LINES

The "Candelabra of the Andes" or the "Paracas Candelabra" on the Peninsula de Paracas.

The best way to view the Nazca Lines is by air in small, low-flying aircraft. Local companies offer flights usually in the early morning, when viewing conditions are best. You can fly over several birds, a few fish, a monkey, a spider, a flower, a condor, and/or several unidentified figures. While seeing the amazing Nazca Lines is a great experience, the sometimes questionable-looking airplanes with their strong fumes and pilots who seem to enjoy making nausea-inducing turns and twists can be worrisome. Because of poor safety records, planes are often grounded. Check with your tour operator before booking a trip with any local airline.

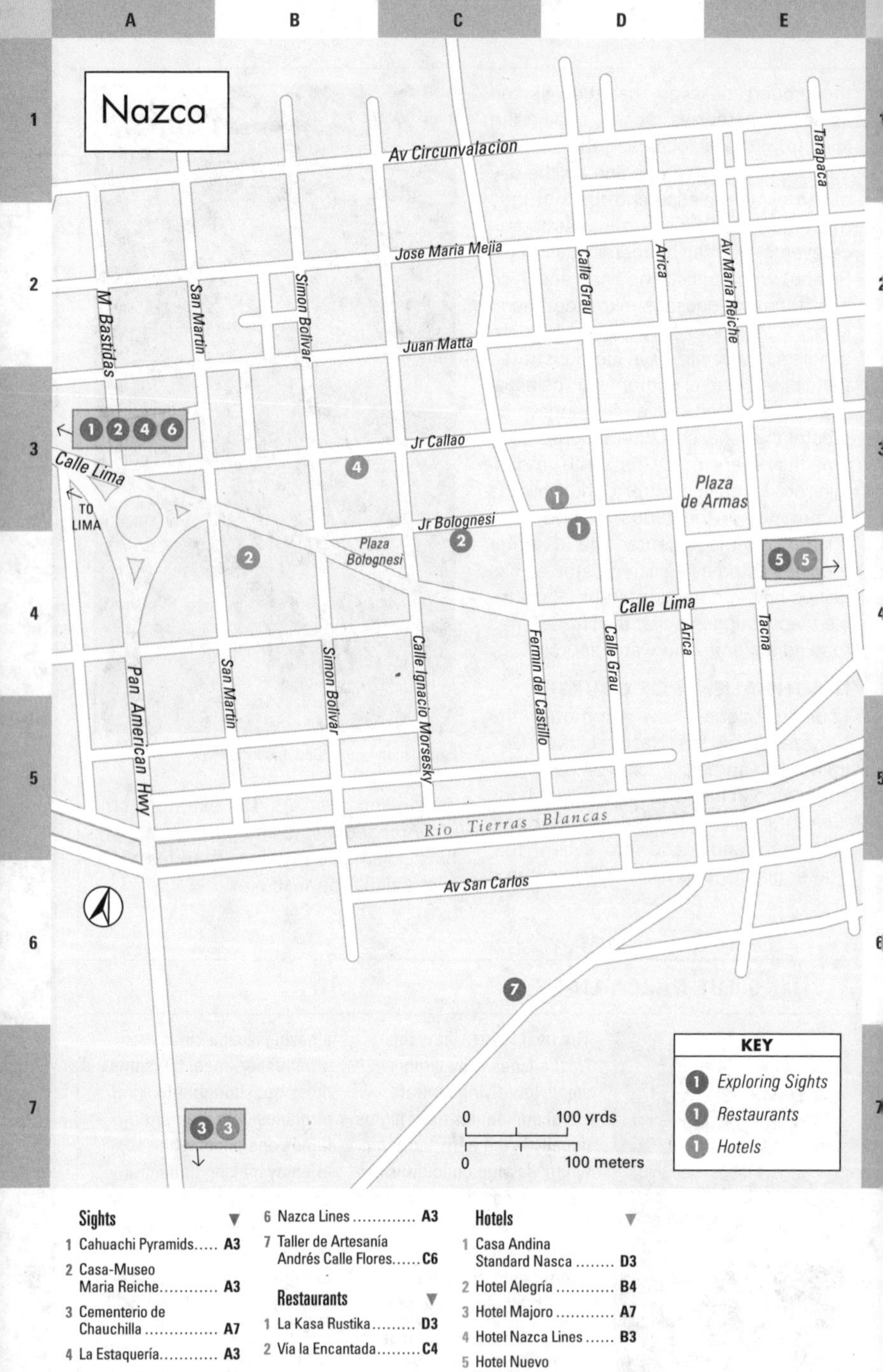

Sights

1 Cahuachi Pyramids..... **A3**
2 Casa-Museo Maria Reiche............ **A3**
3 Cementerio de Chauchilla **A7**
4 La Estaquería............ **A3**
5 Museo Antonini.......... **E4**
6 Nazca Lines **A3**
7 Taller de Artesanía Andrés Calle Flores...... **C6**

Restaurants

1 La Kasa Rustika......... **D3**
2 Vía la Encantada......... **C4**

Hotels

1 Casa Andina Standard Nasca **D3**
2 Hotel Alegría **B4**
3 Hotel Majoro **A7**
4 Hotel Nazca Lines **B3**
5 Hotel Nuevo Cantalloc................. **E4**

skin stretched around empty eye sockets and gaping mouths with missing teeth. Some are wrapped in tattered burial sacks, though the jewelry and ceramics with which they were laid to rest are long gone. Tours from town take about three hours and cost around S/50. Visits to the cemetery are also packaged with Nazca Lines flights. ✉ *Carretera a Chauchilla* 🎟 *S/8.*

La Estaquería

ARCHAEOLOGICAL SITE | These wooden pillars, 34 km (21 miles) west of Nazca, carved of *huarango* wood and placed on mud-brick platforms, were once thought to have been an astronomical observatory. More recent theories, however, lean toward their use in mummification rituals, perhaps to dry bodies of deceased tribal members. They are usually visited on a tour of Cahuachi. ✉ *Nazca* 🎟 *Free.*

Museo Antonini

MUSEUM | For an overview of the Nazca culture and the various archaeological sites in the region, this Italian-run museum is the best in town. The exhibits, made up of materials excavated from the surrounding digs, are heavy on scientific information and light on entertainment, although the display of Nazca trophy skulls will appeal to the morbid, and textiles fans will appreciate the display of painted fabrics from the ancient adobe city of Cahuachi. All the signage is in Spanish, so ask for the translation book at the front desk. Don't miss the still-functional Nazca aqueduct in the back garden. ✉ *Av. de la Cultura 600* ☎ *056/523–444* 🎟 *S/15, S/20 with a camera.*

★ Nazca Lines

ARCHAEOLOGICAL SITE | No less astonishing than Machu Picchu or other Peruvian wonders, this UNESCO World Heritage Site was discovered (or rediscovered) in 1926 by Peruvian archaeologist Toribio Mejía Xesspe, who stumbled upon them on a walk amid the foothills. Almost invisible from ground level, the lines were made by removing the surface stones and piling them beside the lighter soil underneath. More than 300 geometrical and biomorphic figures, some measuring up to 300 meters (1,000 feet) across, are etched into the desert floor, including a hummingbird, a monkey, a spider, a pelican, a condor, a whale, and an "astronaut," so named because of his goldfish-bowl-shaped head. In 2020, a research team came across a faded feline outline on a hillside. The catlike geoglyph stretches for 37 meters (120 feet) and has been dated to between 200-100 BCE, meaning it's part of the Late Paracas period and older than any of the other geoglyphs found in the area. Theories abound as to the purpose of these symbols, from landing strip for aliens to astronomical rituals or travel markers. Since 2000, investigators have discovered hundreds of additional figures, leading many to speculate that science hasn't begun to fathom this most puzzling of Peru's ancient mysteries. ✉ *Pampas de San José* ✣ *20 km (12 miles) northwest of Nazca town.*

Taller de Artesanía Andrés Calle Flores

MUSEUM | Everyone comes to town for the Nazca Lines, but a more contemporary spot that's also worth visiting is the studio of Tobi Flores. His father, Andrés Calle Flores, years ago discovered Nazca pottery remnants in local museums and started making new vase forms based on their pre-Columbian designs. Today, the younger Flores hosts a funny and informative talk in his ceramics workshop, and afterward you can purchase some beautiful pottery for reasonable prices. It's a quick walk across the bridge from downtown Nazca; at night, take a cab. ✉ *Pje. Torrico 240, off Av. San Carlos* ☎ *056/522–319* 🎟 *Free.*

Restaurants

La Kasa Rustika

$ | **PERUVIAN** | All the classics of Peruvian cooking are on offer at this well-loved local hangout. The *corvina a lo macho* (sea bass in shellfish sauce) and the pepper steak are both scrumptious. **Known for:** classic Peruvian cooking; good vegetarian options; communicative staff. $ *Average main: S/30* ✉ *Av. Bolognesi 372* ☎ *056/324–463* 🌐 *www.facebook.com/Lakasarustika.*

★ Vía La Encantada

$ | **PERUVIAN** | With food that is as modern as the stylish interior, this is the best spot in town to try Peruvian-fusion cuisine. The *pollo a lo oporto* (chicken in a port wine sauce) is a standout, as is the cocktail list, including the tricolor Machu Picchu pisco cocktail. **Known for:** criollo and international cuisine; friendly atmosphere; long menu. $ *Average main: S/30* ✉ *Av. Bolognesi 282* ☎ *056/524–216* 🌐 *www.facebook.com/Vía-La-Encantada-Restaurant-200966340281249.*

Hotels

★ Casa Andina Standard Nasca

$ | **HOTEL** | Part of a national chain, this hotel offers the best value for the money of any of Nazca's top-end lodgings. **Pros:** welcoming service; good value; Wi-Fi and business center. **Cons:** pool is on the small side; no elevator; some rooms are smaller than others. $ *Rooms from: S/215* ✉ *Av. Bolognesi 367* ☎ *056/523–563, 01/319–6500 in Lima* 🌐 *www.casa-andina.com* *60 rooms* *Free breakfast.*

Hotel Alegría

$ | **HOTEL** | Long a favorite with travelers, this classic Nazca hotel is set around a sunny courtyard with swimming pool—a perfect spot to relax after a dusty morning flight over the Nazca Lines. **Pros:** friendly staff; good pool; book exchange. **Cons:** smallish rooms; often full; can be noisy when groups arrive. $ *Rooms from: S/200* ✉ *Cl. Lima 166* ☎ *056/522–702* 🌐 *www.hotelalegria.net* *45 rooms* *Free breakfast.*

Hotel Majoro

$ | **HOTEL** | Set amid 60 acres of fragrant gardens and surrounded by cotton fields, this quiet, 80-year-old hacienda and former Augustine convent, situated 1½ km (1 mile) from the airport, offers a taste of life on a farm. **Pros:** peaceful atmosphere; lovely gardens with alpacas and vicuñas on the grounds; good travel services. **Cons:** out of town; popular with tour groups; some airplane noise. $ *Rooms from: S/230* ✉ *Km 453, Panamericana Sur* ☎ *056/522–481* 🌐 *www.hotelmajoro.com* *62 rooms* *Free breakfast.*

★ Hotel Nazca Lines

$ | **HOTEL** | Mixing colonial elegance with all the mod-cons, this historic hacienda is a Nazca landmark. **Pros:** magnificent pool; nightly lectures; colonial charm. **Cons:** busy staff; tour groups; dull decor. $ *Rooms from: S/225* ✉ *Av. Bolognesi 147* ☎ *941/254–279* 🌐 *www.facebook.com/Hotel-Nazca-Lines-273252063116966* *78 rooms* *Free breakfast.*

Hotel Nuevo Cantalloc

$$ | **RESORT** | At this sprawling, hacienda-style resort a 10-minute drive from the center of Nazca, the owners have created an eclectic look that adds modern touches to the farmhouse setting. **Pros:** two pools; spa; beautiful surrounding landscape. **Cons:** far from town; often empty; amenities could be more luxurious given the price. $ *Rooms from: S/430* ✉ *Desvío Puquio Km 3–4, Pan-American Hwy. S* ☎ *056/522–264* 🌐 *www.facebook.com/hotelnuevocantalloc/?rf=346925028723654* *40 rooms* *Free breakfast.*

Chapter 5

THE SOUTHERN ANDES AND LAKE TITICACA

Updated by
Marco Ferrarese

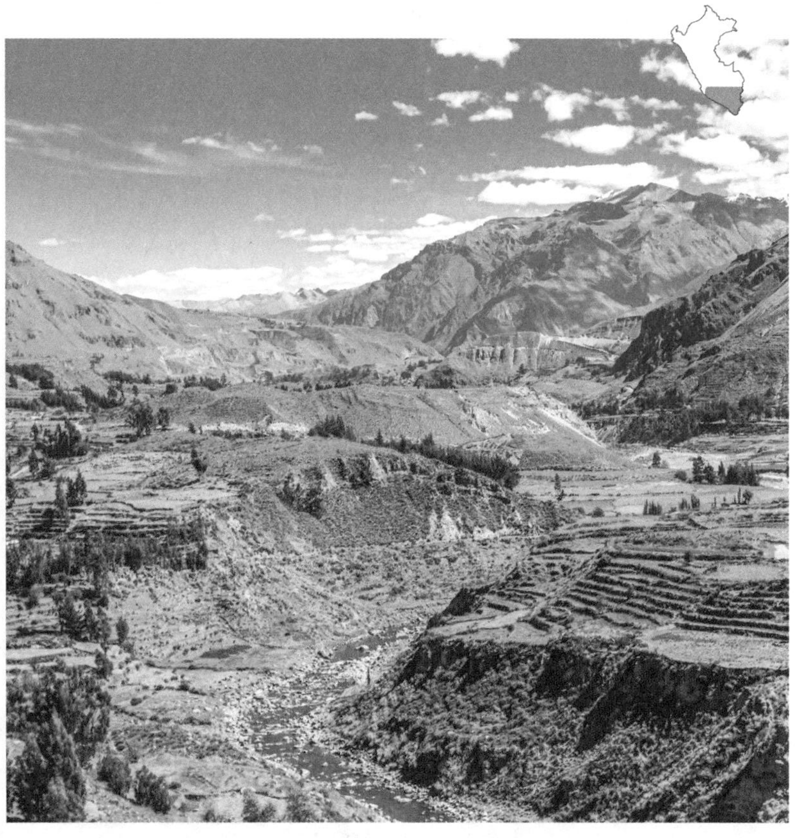

Sights ★★★★★

Restaurants ★★★★☆

Hotels ★★★★★

Shopping ★★★★★

Nightlife ★★☆☆☆

WELCOME TO THE SOUTHERN ANDES AND LAKE TITICACA

TOP REASONS TO GO

★ **Wild Rivers:** Fantastic rapids and gorges make Colca Canyon and Cotahuasi Canyon the region's best-known kayaking, rafting, and hiking spots.

★ **Folk Fiestas:** Whether it's the Virgen de la Candelaria Festival in Puno, Arequipa's annual anniversary, or Semana Santa in Chivay, Peru's culture is celebrated with more than 300 festive folkloric dances featuring brightly colored costumes.

★ **Wildlife:** Llamas, vicuñas, and alpacas roam the Reserva Nacional Salinas y Aguada Blanca, giant Andean condors soar above Colca Canyon, and rare bird species nest at Lake Titicaca and in other highland lakes.

★ **Shopping:** Along with Arequipa's alpaca stores, this region is also a mine of yarn, leather products, guitars, and antiques.

★ **Lake Titicaca:** The birthplace of the sun is a magical sight, as are the floating Uros Islands made of totora reeds.

The southernmost corner of Peru is a rugged and enchanting land of deep canyons, captivating heritage cities, and high plateaus lapped by the shimmering waters of Lake Titicaca—the world's highest navigable body of water. A perfect gateway to western Bolivia (which shares the eastern coast of Titicaca with Peru), the Southern Andes pack a smorgasbord of colors that deserve to be savored slowly—from the weaving and traditional woolen attire of tribes on Taquile and the floating Uros Islands to the llama-strewn ravines of the Colca and Cotahuasi Canyons and the whitewashed facades of churches in Arequipa and Puno.

1 Arequipa. It's an ancient colonial town that mixes old and new, pulsating with exciting nightlife and top-of-the-range dining.

2 Cotahuasi Village and Vicinity. Go wild in one of the world's deepest canyons, a part of Peru that's still pretty much off the beaten track.

3 Chivay. Stroll the charming old plaza, and take a dip in the thermal hot springs as you gear up for an encounter with the elusive Andean condor.

4 Puno. A stunning cathedral dominates the plaza of this vibrant and cultural city that sits right on the shore of Titicaca.

5 Lake Titicaca. Whether you take a day-trip to the floating Uros Islands or stay here for a bunch of days, the birthplace of the Incas offers infinite charm.

6 Sillustani. Soaring like ancient towers, the tombs of the Qulla people make

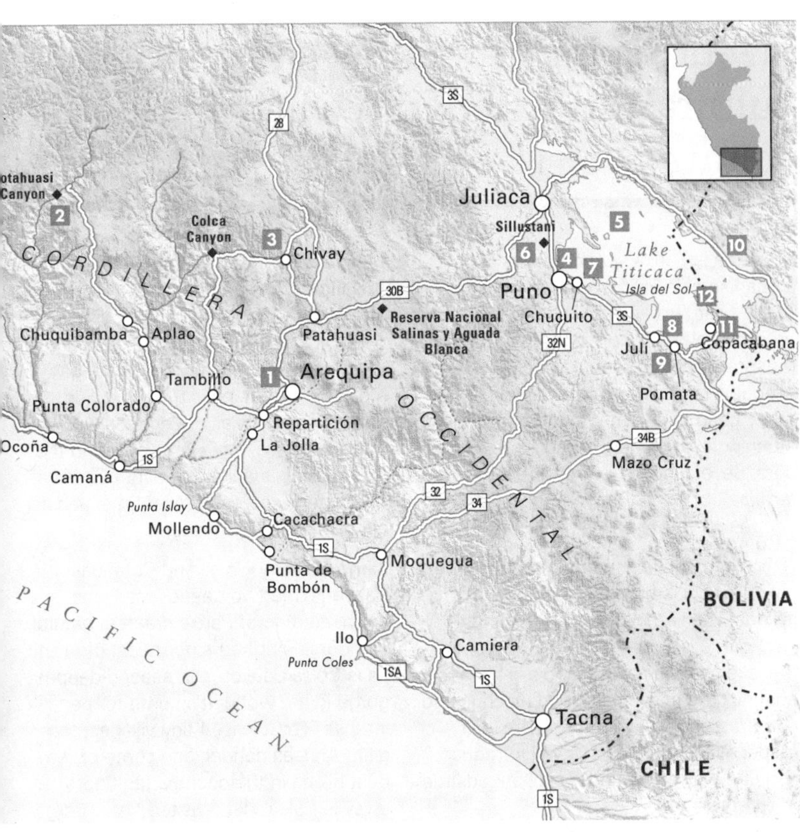

for a haunting day-trip from Puno.

7 Chucuito. To experience quaint Peruvian life without the crowds, head up 3,875 meters (12,713 feet) to this village on Titicaca's western shore.

8 Juli. Peru's "*pequeña Roma*" (little Rome) has four 16th- and 17th-century churches and a laid-back vibe.

9 Pomata. The magnificent Templo de Pomata Santiago Apóstolo, founded in 1700, proudly dominates this small lakeside town.

10 The Bolivian Side of Lake Titicaca. Pastoral landscapes and small villages dot this idyllic corner of southwestern Bolivia, which shares part of Lake Titicaca with Peru.

11 Copacabana, Bolivia. The jumping-off point to Titicaca's most beautiful offshore islands.

12 Isla del Sol and Isla de la Luna, Bolivia. Glide on a boat to these car-free, sacred Inca islands dotted with ruins and see how time has stood still for centuries.

Though often overshadowed by Cusco and the Sacred Valley, the south of Peru has some of the most dynamic, jaw-dropping geography and exciting cultural attractions anywhere in the country.

Arequipa is Peru's second-largest city, a Spanish-colonial maze, with volcanic white sillar (volcanic rock) buildings, well-groomed plazas, and wonderful food, museums, and designer alpaca products. Arequipa is close to Colca Canyon, where many head to see the famed gorge for its stunning beauty, depth, and Andean condors. Several hours farther out is the very remote Cotahuasi Canyon, the world's deepest gorge.

A rival in magnificence to Machu Picchu, Lake Titicaca is home to the floating islands. The Uros Islands are around 40 man-made islands—constructed from the lake's totora reeds—and are literally floating. The natives are the Quechua and Aymara peoples, who still speak their respective languages and will introduce you to a way of life that has changed little in centuries.

Puno, an agricultural city on the shores of Titicaca, is the jumping-off point for exploring the lake and is Peru's folkloric capital. A dusty-brown city most of the time, Puno is a colorful whirlwind during festivals. The region's many fiestas feature elaborate costumes, storytelling dances, music, and lots of merrymaking. Each November and February Puno, puts on two spectacular shows for local holidays.

MAJOR REGIONS

Arequipa. Known as La Cuidad Blanca, or The White City, for its dazzling sillar—a white volcanic rock from which nearly all the Spanish-colonial buildings are constructed—Arequipa is the most European-looking city in all of Peru. It's also the most romantic one. Here you'll find the ice mummy Juanita, the Santa Catalina Monastery, scores of museums, and a sophisticated dining scene.

Canyon Country. Colca and Cotahuasi Canyons, the two deepest canyons on earth, are two of Peru's greatest natural wonders. Four hours northeast of Arequipa is Colca Canyon, the second-deepest gorge in the world. It's home to the intense Río Colca, 14 tiny villages, the giant Andean condor, and some of the best hiking in the country. Ten hours away is Colca's less-visited sister gorge, the world's deepest canyon, Cotahuasi Canyon, now a tourist destination in its own right. Colca is the far more visited, more accessible of the two, and recently has a seen a boom in five-star resorts and laid-back family inns. Cotahuasi, a little more than 150 meters (nearly 500 feet) deeper than Colca, is much more remote and reached only by the most rugged adventurers, though if you can withstand long, bumpy hours in a car or bus, you'll find an unspoiled terrain rarely visited by outsiders.

Puno and Lake Titicaca. Lake Titicaca is one of the most breathtaking parts of Peru, though in literal terms that may have something to do with the altitude. The azure-blue waters of the lake paired with an even bluer sky are a sight to behold, indeed. The region is one of the most culturally significant places in the entire Andes. Not only are more festivals held here than anywhere else, but the Quechua and Aymara peoples who inhabit isolated islands like Taquile and Amantani have preserved their customs over centuries with little change. The Islas de Uros, floating islands that were man-made using totora reeds, are a magical display of color and originality. This is where the Incas were born, and ancient ruins, such as those at Sullustani, are scattered all over the area. For many travelers, a visit to Lake Titicaca is the highlight of their trip.

The Bolivian Side of Lake Titicaca. Most visitors to Puno continue their Lake Titicaca exploration across the border in Bolivia—easy to do, as border-hopping doesn't require a visa for most nationalities. Copacabana is a friendly tourist town and the home of the Virgin of the Candelaria, whose original statue rests inside the stunning cathedral dominating the main plaza. The town is also the jumping-off point for explorations of the Isla del Sol and Isla de la Luna, two pristine islets with neither roads nor cars and believed to be the birthplace of the sun and the Inca dynasty. The three villages of Yumani, Challa, and Challapampa are connected by hiking trails that pass by enticing ancient Inca ruins. Day tours make a whistle-stop of all the major historical sights, but taking your time and staying at least for one night to soak up the timeless atmosphere is a much better idea.

Planning

When to Go

In the mountains and high plains, the blistering sun keeps you warm from May through early November, but nights get cold. Rainy season is from mid-November until April, when it's cooler and cloudy, but rain isn't a guarantee. Use sunscreen, even if it's cloudy.

Planning Your Time

Arequipa, Colca Canyon, Puno, and Lake Titicaca are often add-ons to a trip to Machu Picchu. They are all part of what is often referred to as the "Southern Circuit," as they are located south of both Lima and Cusco. Rather than just linking the journey between those two cities, however, they make good destinations on their own and offer a different and larger perspective of the country than simply the "Lost City of the Incas."

Arequipa is a good jumping-off point to the Southern Andes and Lake Titicaca. Acclimatize while taking in the sights, then head to the Colca Canyon. The four-hour drive travels over Patapampa Pass, with views of the Valley of the Volcanoes, and through the Reserva Nacional Salinas y Aguada Blanca, where herds of wild vicuñas, llamas, and alpacas graze. At the canyon, you can go on a multiday hike or relax at a country lodge, but nearly everyone comes to spy condors at Cruz del Condor viewpoint. Afterward, either continue by car to Puno or head back to Arequipa and on to Puno and Lake Titicaca by bus or plane. There, you can book an overnight island homestay, visit the floating islands, and/or see the Sillustanti ruins. From Puno, some head to Bolivia while others move on to Cusco by bus or plane. Similarly, you can travel to Puno from Cusco and begin your exploration in the opposite direction.

Festivals

Some of Peru's festivals and events provide a good reason to choose a particular time of year to travel, notably Carnaval in February and town anniversary celebrations in June (Chivay) and August (Arequipa). Make your reservations far in advance if you plan to travel at these times.

Corso de Amis

CULTURAL FESTIVALS | August 15 is the anniversary of Arequipa's founding and, each year, thousands take to the streets all day for the big parade, with music, dancing, traditional costumes, and decorated floats. ✉ *Arequipa* ☎ *054/223–265 iPeru tourist office.*

La Virgen Inmaculada Concepción

CULTURAL FESTIVALS | Held in the first week of December, this big five-day event in Chivay and Yanque sees the performance of the local traditional Wititi dance and processions for the patron saint. ✉ *Chivay.*

Virgen de la Candelaria

Vast numbers of singers, dancers, and marching bands parade through the streets, accompanying the statue of the Virgin in early February each year in one of Peru's biggest celebrations, designated in 2014 as a UNESCO Intangible Cultural Heritage. You'll also see a huge range of traditional dances, performed in colorful costumes. It's also celebrated with much fanfare in Chivay. ✉ *Puno* 🌐 *www.virgencandelaria.com.*

Virgen del Carmen

CULTURAL FESTIVALS | In mid-July, each end of the Colca Canyon has two days of celebrations to mark this festival, with singing, dancing, bullfights, food and drink, and parades in Chivay and Cabanaconde. After night falls, impressive fireworks light up in the sky. ✉ *Chivay.*

Getting Here And Around

AIR

Flights to anywhere in southern Peru take between 30 minutes and an hour, and a one-way ticket costs US$90 to US$190. LATAM (🌐 *www.latam.com*) has daily flights between Lima and Rodríguez Ballón International Airport, 7 km (4½ miles) from Arequipa. Peruvian Airlines (🌐 *www.peruvianairlines.com.pe*) and Avianca (🌐 *www.avianca.com*) also have daily flights. LATAM and Avianca offer daily flights to Aeropuerto Manco Cápac in Juliaca, the closest airport to Puno and Lake Titicaca. It takes 45 minutes to drive from Juliaca to downtown Puno.

BUS

Traveling by road between Arequipa and Puno takes about six hours. Service is also good between Puno and Cusco and so is the road between Puno and Copacabana in Bolivia. Cruz del Sur (🌐 *www.cruzdelsur.com.pe*), CIVA (🌐 *www.civa.com.pe*), Inka Express (🌐 *www.inkaexpress.com*), and Flores (🌐 *floreshnos.pe*) have offices in Puno and Arequipa, and each runs daily buses between the two cities. For your comfort and safety, take the best service you can afford. There is also the potential for pickpockets on night buses; choosing a reputable company can help avoid this. Several bus companies sell tickets that go direct, so buy one of those, or be prepared for a long slog, during which drivers stop for every passerby. Bus stations in Peru are known for crime, mostly theft of your belongings, so always hold on to your bags.

CAR

Car rental services are in Arequipa's center and at the airport. Keep your car travel to daylight hours: night driving poses a number of risks—blockades, crime on tourists, and steep roads. A 4x4 is needed for the canyons. Although the road from Arequipa to Chivay is perfectly paved, the last hour of the journey is windy and has steep cliffs. Use even more caution if traveling into Cotahuasi Canyon: only half of the 10-hour drive is paved, and even the paved areas develop potholes.

TAXI

Ask any *arequipeño*, and they'll tell you Arequipa has three major concerns: earthquakes, the looming threat of volcanoes, and taxis. The city has the most taxis per capita of any city in Peru. Pint-size yellow cars, namely miniature Daewoo Ticos, clog the streets. Pollution is high, there are accidents aplenty, and rush-hour traffic rivals that of Los Angeles. Taxis are also readily available in Puno although, as a smaller city, the numbers are not as vast as in Arequipa.

TRAIN

Train travel on PeruRail (🌐 *www.perurail.com*) is slow but scenic and more relaxing than a bus blasting reggaeton. A Pullman train ticket means more comfort, not to mention a meal and increased security. The train goes only between Cusco and Puno. It's a popular way to take in the dramatic change of scenery as you ride over La Raya Pass at 4,315 meters (14,157 feet). The trip takes about nine hours and includes a stop at the highest point. The route runs only a few days per week, depending on the season. For a full listing of PeruRail trips, check out the website. It's now possible to book online. PeruRail also runs a luxury train service with en-suite doubles and a luxe restaurant car, the Andean Explorer (🌐 *www.perurail.com/trains/belmond-andean-explorer)*, in collaboration with Belmond. The 2N/3D trip shuttles between Cusco and Arequipa, with an overnight stop in Puno and a half-day exploration of the Uros and Taquile Islands. All transfers and meals are included.

Health and Safety

Visiting mountain towns and Lake Titicaca can bring on *soroche* (altitude sickness). Nonprescription remedies include *mate de coca* (coca tea) and *pastillas de sorojchi* (over-the-counter pills). As these latter contain only caffeine, aspirin, and an aspirin substitute, your own preferred headache remedy is just as good. Drink lots of bottled water and forego alcohol, coffee, and heavy meals at first. Be aware that prescription altitude medication is typically sulfa-based, a substance many people have allergies to. **■ TIP→ There is no substitute for proper acclimatization.**

Colca Canyon is generally safe, as are Arequipa and Puno. Nevertheless, don't walk alone at night, know where your money is, and educate yourself on the good and bad parts of town. Police presence has increased in Arequipa. Use only recommended taxi companies, or have someone call one for you. But walking around the plaza, even at night, is safe in Arequipa. Hiking El Misti alone is not recommended. Puno is generally safe in the tourist areas, but at night, the port and the hills should be avoided.

Restaurants

You can find everything from *cuy* (guinea pig) to wood-fired pizza at the many excellent restaurants in Arequipa and Puno, where dining possibilities range from traditional fare to sophisticated Novo Andino cuisine and international dishes. Food in Arequipa is known for strong, fresh flavors, from herbs and spices to vegetables served with native Andean foods like alpaca meat and *olluco,* a colorful Andean tuber. In the mountains, the cool, thin Andean air calls for hearty, savory soups and heaps and heaps of carbs in the form of the potato. Whether they're fried, boiled, baked, with cheese, in soup, or alone, you will be eating potatoes. In Puno, fresh trout or kingfish from the lake is served in almost every restaurant. Puno also has a special affection for adobe-oven, wood-fired pizza.

Hotels

Arequipa and Puno are overloaded with hotels. Although a growing number of resorts and chain hotels are set along the lakeside, most of the properties within the city of Puno are small boutique hotels with local owners pining to get in on the tourist boom in this otherwise agricultural town. As a commercial business center, Arequipa has more high-end hotels that cater to business travelers, and given its fame for being the romance city, it also has lots of small inns. *Hotel reviews have been shortened. For full information, visit Fodors.com.*

WHAT IT COSTS in Nuevo Soles			
$	**$$**	**$$$**	**$$$$**
RESTAURANTS			
under S/35	S/35–S/50	S/51–S/65	over S/65
HOTELS			
under S/250	S/250–S/500	S/501–S/800	over S/800

Arequipa

150 km (93 miles) south of Colca Canyon; 200 km (124 miles) south of Cotahuasi Canyon.

Cradled by three steep, gargantuan, snow-covered volcanoes, the jaw-dropping, white-stoned Arequipa, one of the most visually stunning cities in Peru, shines under the striking sun at 2,350 meters (7,710 feet). This settlement of nearly 1 million residents grew from a collection of Spanish-colonial churches and homes constructed from white sillar (volcanic stone) gathered from the surrounding terrain. The result is nothing less than a work of art—short, gleaming-white buildings contrast with the charcoal-color mountain backdrop of El Misti, a perfectly shaped cone volcano.

The town was a gathering of Aymara Indians and Incas when Garí Manuel de Carbajal and nearly 100 more Spaniards founded the city on August 15, 1540. After the Spanish arrived, the town grew into the region's most profitable center for farming and cattle raising—businesses still important to Arequipa's economy. The settlement was also on the silver route linking the coast to the Bolivian mines. By the 1800s, Arequipa had more Spanish settlers than any town in the south.

Arequipeños call their home La Ciudad Blanca, "The White City," and the "Independent Republic of Arequipa"—they have made several attempts to secede from Peru and even designed the city's own passport and flag. Today, the town is abuzz with adventure outfitters leading tours into the surrounding canyons, locals and visitors mingling at bars and cafés in 500-year-old sillar buildings, and shoppers seeking the finest alpaca threads anywhere in the country. **■ TIP→ On August 15, parades, fireworks, bullfights, and dancing celebrate the city's founding.**

Arequipa enjoys fresh, crisp air, and warm days averaging 23°C (73°F) and comfortable nights at 14°C (57°F). To make up for the lack of rain, the Río Chili waters the surrounding foothills, which were once farmed by the Inca and now stretch into rows of alfalfa and onions.

GETTING HERE AND AROUND

Arequipa's airport is on the outskirts of the city, and there are plenty of taxis waiting to take you into the center. Many hotels also offer pickup and drop-off. The cost is about S/40.

Walking is the best option around the city center. Most sights, shops, and restaurants are near the Plaza de Armas. For a quick, cheap tour, spend S/5 and catch a Vallecito bus for a 1½-hour circuit around calles Jerusalén and San Juan de Díos. Taxis are everywhere and cost about S/5–S/10 to get around the center or to Vallecito.

Arequipa has two bus terminals side by side on Avenida Ibañez and Avenida Andrés Avelino Cáceres. Most people leave out of the older Terminal Terreste, where most bus companies have offices, whereas the newer terminal Terrapuerto sees less traffic. In day time, local buses connect both bus terminals to the city center and Yanahuara for a mere S/1.50.

TAXI Cabify. 🌐 *www.cabify.com.* **Taxi Turismo Arequipa.** ☎ *054/458–888,* 🌐 *www.facebook.com/TaxiTurismoArequipa.*

TIMING

Most sites are open morning and afternoon but close for a couple of hours at midday. Churches usually open 7 to 9 am and 6 to 8 pm, before and after services.

HEALTH AND SAFETY

Wear comfortable walking shoes, and bring a hat, sunscreen, a Spanish dictionary or phrase book, some small change, and a good map of town. At 2,350 meters (7,510 feet), Arequipa is quite high. If you're coming directly from Lima or from the coast, carve out a day or two for acclimatization.

MEDICAL Clínica Arequipa SA. ✉ *Puente Grau and Av. Bolognesi* ☎ *054/599–000* 🌐 *www.clinicarequipa.com.pe.* **Hospital III Regional Honorio Delgado.** ✉ *Av. Daniel Alcides Carrión 505, La Pampilla* ☎ *054/231–818, 054/219–702,* 🌐 *www.hrhdaqp.gob.pe.* **Hospital Goyeneche.** ✉ *Av. Goyeneche s/n, Cercado* ☎ *054/231–313.*

POLICE Policía de Turismo. ✉ *Cl. Jerusalén 315* ☎ *054/282–613.*

VISITOR INFORMATION

Centro de Información de Turismo de Arequipa. ✉ *108 Plaza de Armas* ☎ *54/234–074* 🌐 *www.facebook.com/turismompa.*
Iperu Oficina de Información Turística. ✉ *Portal de la Municipalidad 110, Plaza de Armas* ☎ *054/223–265* 🌐 *www.peru.travel/en/useful-data/iperu* ✉ *Aeropuerto Rodríguez Ballón, Arrivals* ☎ *054/299–191* 🌐 *www.peru.travel/en/useful-data/iperu.*

TOURS

For the standard one- or two-day tours to Colca Canyon, most agencies pool their customers, so quality varies little. The following two options offer more personalized service and tend to be more attentive to their clients.

Giardino

HIKING/WALKING | Since 1995, Giardino Tours has been running tours all over the region, building up a reliable infrastructure and keeping current on any new developments in the area. They have received various awards for providing quality service. ✉ *Cl. Jerusalén 604-A* ☎ *054/200–100* 🌐 *www.giardinotours.com* 🎫 *From S/90.*

Peru Mistika Travel

GUIDED TOURS | The team here has years of experience in tourism in the region and offers a variety of great tours, including off-the-beaten-path adventures and small-size, tailored expeditions. They bring a fresh outlook and energy to the Arequipa tour agency scene, offering their clients personalized care and service. ✉ *Cl. Santa Marta 304, Of. 208* ☎ *051/962–910–999 for calls and WhatsApp reservations* 🌐 *www.perumistikatravel.com* 🎫 *From S/59.*

Sights

Casa del Moral

HOUSE | One of the oldest architectural landmarks from the Arequipa baroque period was named for the ancient *mora* (mulberry) tree growing in the center of the main patio. One of the town's most unusual buildings, it now houses the Banco

Sur, but it's open to the public. Over the front door, carved into a white sillar portal, is the Spanish coat of arms as well as a baroque-Mestizo design that combines puma heads with snakes darting from their mouths—motifs found on Nazca textiles and pottery. The interior of the house is like a small museum, with alpaca rugs, soaring ceilings, polished period furniture, and a gallery of colonial-period Escuela Cusqueña (Cusco School) paintings. Originally a lovely old colonial home, it was bought in the 1940s by the British consul and fully restored in the early 1990s. ✉ *Cl. Moral 318 at Cl. Bolívar* ☎ *054/285–371* 🎫 *S/5* 🕓 *Closed Sun.*

Casa Goyeneche

HOUSE | This attractive Spanish-colonial home was built in 1888. Ask the guard for a tour, and you'll enter through a pretty courtyard and an ornate set of wooden doors to view rooms furnished with period antiques and Escuela Cusqueña (Cusco School) paintings. ✉ *Cl. La Merced 201 at Palacio Viejo* 🎫 *Free, but if you get a tour, a small donation is expected* 🕓 *Closed weekends.*

Casa Tristan del Pozo

HOUSE | This small museum and art gallery, sometimes called Casa Ricketts, was built in 1738 and is now the Banco Continental. Look for the elaborate puma heads spouting water. Inside you'll find colonial paintings, ornate Peruvian costumes, and furniture. ✉ *Cl. San Francisco 115* 🌐 *fundacionbbva.pe/casonas/casa-tristan-del-pozo* 🎫 *Free* 🕓 *Closed Sun.*

Casona Iriberry

HOUSE | Unlike the other mansions, Casona Iriberry has religious overtones. Small scriptures are etched into its structure, exemplifying Arequipa's Catholic roots. The back of the house is now the Centro Cultural Cháves la Rosa, which hosts some of the city's most important contemporary arts events, including photography exhibits, concerts, and films. The front of the compound is filled with colonial-period furniture and paintings. ✉ *Plaza de Armas, San Augustin and Cl. Santa Catalina* ☎ *054/204–482* 🎫 *Free to look around, charge for certain events* 🕓 *Closed weekends.*

Tipping the Guard

In colonial mansions, museums, or landmarks that are free, guards are happy to show you around, but they typically work for tips. Anything from S/5 to S/10 is appropriate.

★ Catedral

RELIGIOUS SITE | You can't miss the imposing twin bell towers of this 1612 cathedral, with a facade guarding the entire eastern flank of the Plaza de Armas. **■ TIP→ As the sun sets the imperial reflection gives the cathedral an amber hue.** The interior has high-vaulted ceilings above a beautiful Belgian organ. The ornate wooden pulpit, carved by French artist Buisine-Rigot in 1879, was transported here in the early 1900s. In the back, look for the *Virgin of the Sighs* statue in her white wedding dress and the figure of Beata Sor Ana de Los Ángeles, a nun from the Santa Catalina Monastery who was beatified by Pope John Paul II when he stayed in Arequipa in 1990. A fire in 1844 destroyed much of the cathedral, as did an 1868 earthquake, so parts have a neoclassical look. In 2001, another earthquake damaged one of the bell towers, which was repaired to match its sister tower. ✉ *Plaza de Armas, between Cl. Santa Catalina and Cl. San Francisco* ☎ *054/213–149* 🌐 *www.museocatedralarequipa.org.pe* 🎫 *S/10* 🕓 *Closed Sun.*

Chaqchao Chocolates

TOUR—SIGHT | **FAMILY** | Educate your passion for chocolate at this store and workshop, where you learn how it gets from bean to bar by making tasty treats from fair-trade, Peruvian-sourced cacao.

If you don't have time for the workshop, you can shop the store for delicious souvenirs. ✉ *Cl. Santa Catalina 204* ☎ *054/234–572* 🌐 *www.chaqchao-chocolates.com* 🎫 *USD$25 for workshop.*

Convento de la Recoleta

RELIGIOUS SITE | One of Peru's most extensive and valuable libraries is in this 1648 Franciscan monastery. With several cloisters and museums, it's a wonderful place to research regional history and culture. Start in the massive, wood-paneled, wood-floored library, where monks in brown robes quietly browse 20,000 ancient books and maps, the most valuable of which were printed before 1500 and are kept in glass cases. Pre-Columbian artifacts and objects collected by missionaries to the Amazon are on display, as is a selection of elegant colonial and religious artwork. Guides are available (remember to tip). To reach the monastery, cross the Río Chili by Puente Grau. It's a 10- to 15-minute walk from the Plaza de Armas, but it's best to take a taxi. ✉ *Recoleta 117* ☎ *054/270–966* 🎫 *S/10.*

Iglesia de la Compañía

RELIGIOUS SITE | Representative of 17th-century religious architecture, this complex was built by the Jesuits in 1573, and its bone-white buildings incorporate many decorative styles and touches—the detail carved into the sillar arcades is spectacular. The side portal, built in 1654, and main facade, built in 1698, show examples of Andean Mestizo style, with carved flowers, spirals, birds—and angels with Indian faces—along gently curving archways and spiral pillars. Inside, **Capilla St. Ignatius** (St. Ignatius Chapel) has a polychrome cupola and 66 canvases from the Cusco School, including original 17th-century oil paintings by Bernardo Bitti. Hike up to the steeple at sunset for sweeping views of Arequipa. The former monastery houses some of the most upscale stores in the city and contains two cloisters, which can be entered from General Morán or Palacio Viejo. The main building is on the southeast corner of the Plaza de Armas. ✉ *General Morán at Álvarez Tomás* ☎ *054/212–141* 🎫 *Chapel S/5.*

Iglesia de San Francisco

RELIGIOUS SITE | This 16th-century church has survived numerous natural disasters, including several earthquakes that cracked its cupola. Inside, near the polished silver altar, is the little chapel of the Sorrowful Virgin, where the all-important Virgin Mary statue is stored. **■ TIP→ On December 8, during Arequipa's Feast of the Immaculate Conception, the Virgin is paraded around the city all night atop an ornate carriage and surrounded by images of saints and angels. A throng of pilgrims carry flowers and candles.** Visit the adjoining convent (S/10) to see Arequipa's largest painting and a museum of 17th-century religious furniture and paintings. ✉ *Zela 103* ☎ *054/384–103* 🎫 *Free* ⏲ *Convent closed Sun.*

Iglesia y Convento de Santo Domingo

RELIGIOUS SITE | With hints of the Islamic style in its elegant brick arches and stone domes, this cathedral carries an aura of elegance. Step inside to view simple furnishings and sunlight streaming through stained-glass windows as small silver candles flicker along the back wall near the altar. A working Dominican monastery is in back. ✉ *Cl. Santo Domingo and Piérola* ☎ *054/213–511* 🎫 *Free.*

La Mansión del Fundador

HOUSE | First owned by the founder of Arequipa, Don Garcí Manuel de Carbajal, La Mansión del Fundador, about 6.5 km (4 miles) outside Arequipa—about a 20-minute journey—is a restored colonial home and church. Alongside the Río Sabandía, the sillar-made home perches over a cliff and is said to have been built for Carbajal's son. It became a Jesuit retreat in the 16th century, and, in the 1800s, was remodeled by Juan Crisostomo de Goyeneche y Aguerrevere. While intimate, the chapel is small and simple, but the home is noted for its vaulted-arch ceilings and spacious patio. There's also a

A
B
C
D
E
F
1
2
3
4
5
6
7
8
9
Tronchadero
Francisco Mostajo
Arica
Jerusalén
Avenida Lima
Paz Soldán
Alfonso Ugarte
Cuesta del Angel
Jirón Urubamba
Las Beatas
Calle Misti
Avenida Francisco Bolognesi
Río Chili
Quinta Vivanco
Pasaje Ripacha
Avenida Ejercito
La Recoleta
Avenida La Marina
C. Ugarte
Calle Moral
Villalba
Calle Simón Bolívar
Santa Catalina
Jerusalén
Carlos Llosa
Ayacucho
Mariano Melgar
Santa Marta
Calle San Francisco
Calle San José
Mercaderes
Plaza de Armas
Calle Santo Domingo
Nicolás de Piérola
Dean Valdivia
San Camilo
Alto de la Luna
Calle Perú
Francisco Pizarro
2 de Mayo
Zamacola
Avenida Emmel
Beaterio
Garaicochea
Avenida José Abelardo Quiñones
San Agustín
Francisco Bolognesi
Villalba
Calle Sucre
Calle La Merced
Belló Horizonte
Ernesto Loreto
Avenida La Marina
Lima
Avenida San Martín
Álvarez Thomas
San Juan de Dios
Toribio Pacheco
Gómez Sánchez
Avenida Lima
Luna Pizarro
Alameda Mario Vargas Llosa
Salaverry
Tacna y Arica
Quinta Romaña
Leticia
Jorge Chávez
García de Carbajal
7 de Junio
15 de Agosto
3 de Diciembre
0
500 ft
0
500 m

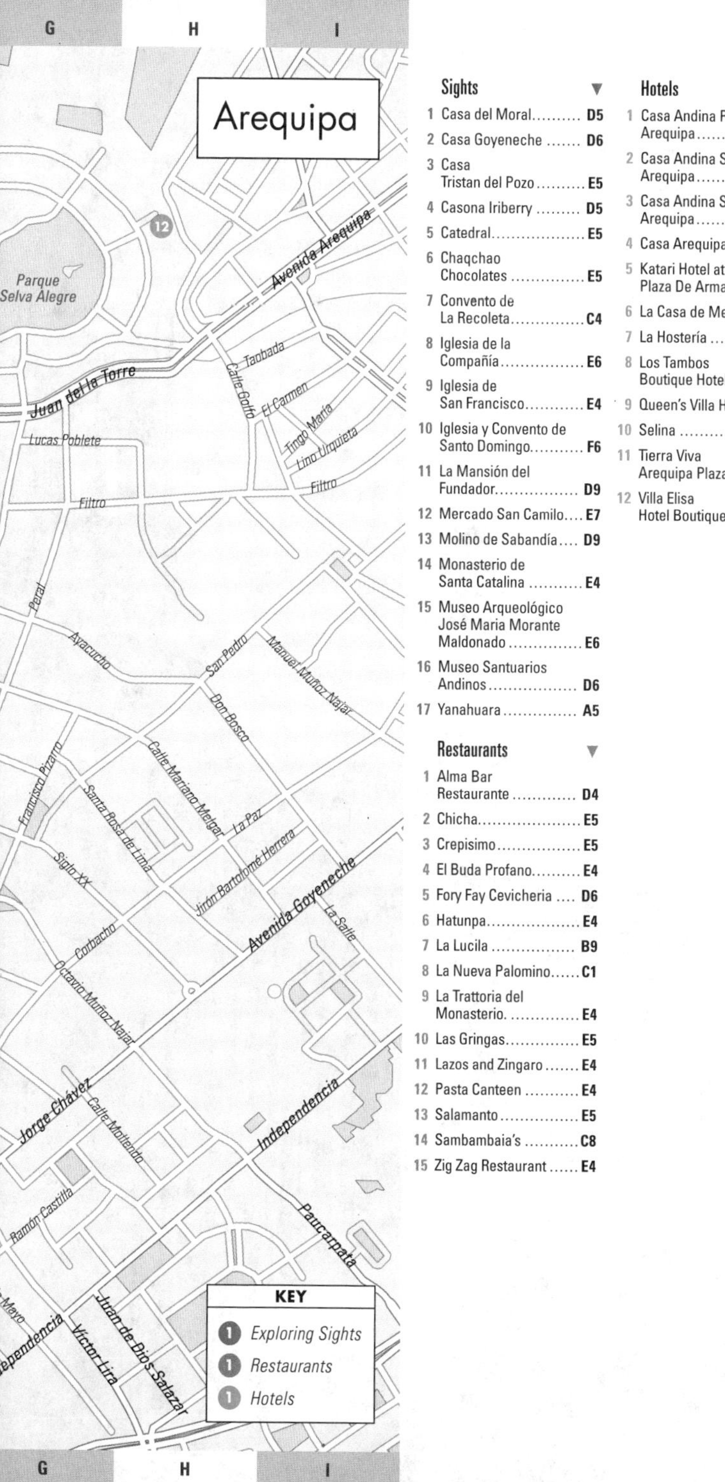

Sights

1 Casa del Moral.......... **D5**
2 Casa Goyeneche **D6**
3 Casa Tristan del Pozo.......... **E5**
4 Casona Iriberry **D5**
5 Catedral.................. **E5**
6 Chaqchao Chocolates **E5**
7 Convento de La Recoleta............... **C4**
8 Iglesia de la Compañía................. **E6**
9 Iglesia de San Francisco............ **E4**
10 Iglesia y Convento de Santo Domingo........... **F6**
11 La Mansión del Fundador................. **D9**
12 Mercado San Camilo.... **E7**
13 Molino de Sabandía.... **D9**
14 Monasterio de Santa Catalina **E4**
15 Museo Arqueológico José Maria Morante Maldonado **E6**
16 Museo Santuarios Andinos **D6**
17 Yanahuara **A5**

Restaurants

1 Alma Bar Restaurante **D4**
2 Chicha..................... **E5**
3 Crepisimo................. **E5**
4 El Buda Profano.......... **E4**
5 Fory Fay Cevicheria **D6**
6 Hatunpa................... **E4**
7 La Lucila **B9**
8 La Nueva Palomino...... **C1**
9 La Trattoria del Monasterio. **E4**
10 Las Gringas............... **E5**
11 Lazos and Zingaro **E4**
12 Pasta Canteen **E4**
13 Salamanto................ **E5**
14 Sambambaia's **C8**
15 Zig Zag Restaurant **E4**

Hotels

1 Casa Andina Premium Arequipa................. **D4**
2 Casa Andina Select Arequipa.................. **E6**
3 Casa Andina Standard Arequipa.................. **F3**
4 Casa Arequipa **B8**
5 Katari Hotel at Plaza De Armas......... **D6**
6 La Casa de Melgar **F4**
7 La Hostería **D4**
8 Los Tambos Boutique Hotel.......... **D5**
9 Queen's Villa Hotel...... **B9**
10 Selina **F3**
11 Tierra Viva Arequipa Plaza........... **F5**
12 Villa Elisa Hotel Boutique.......... **H2**

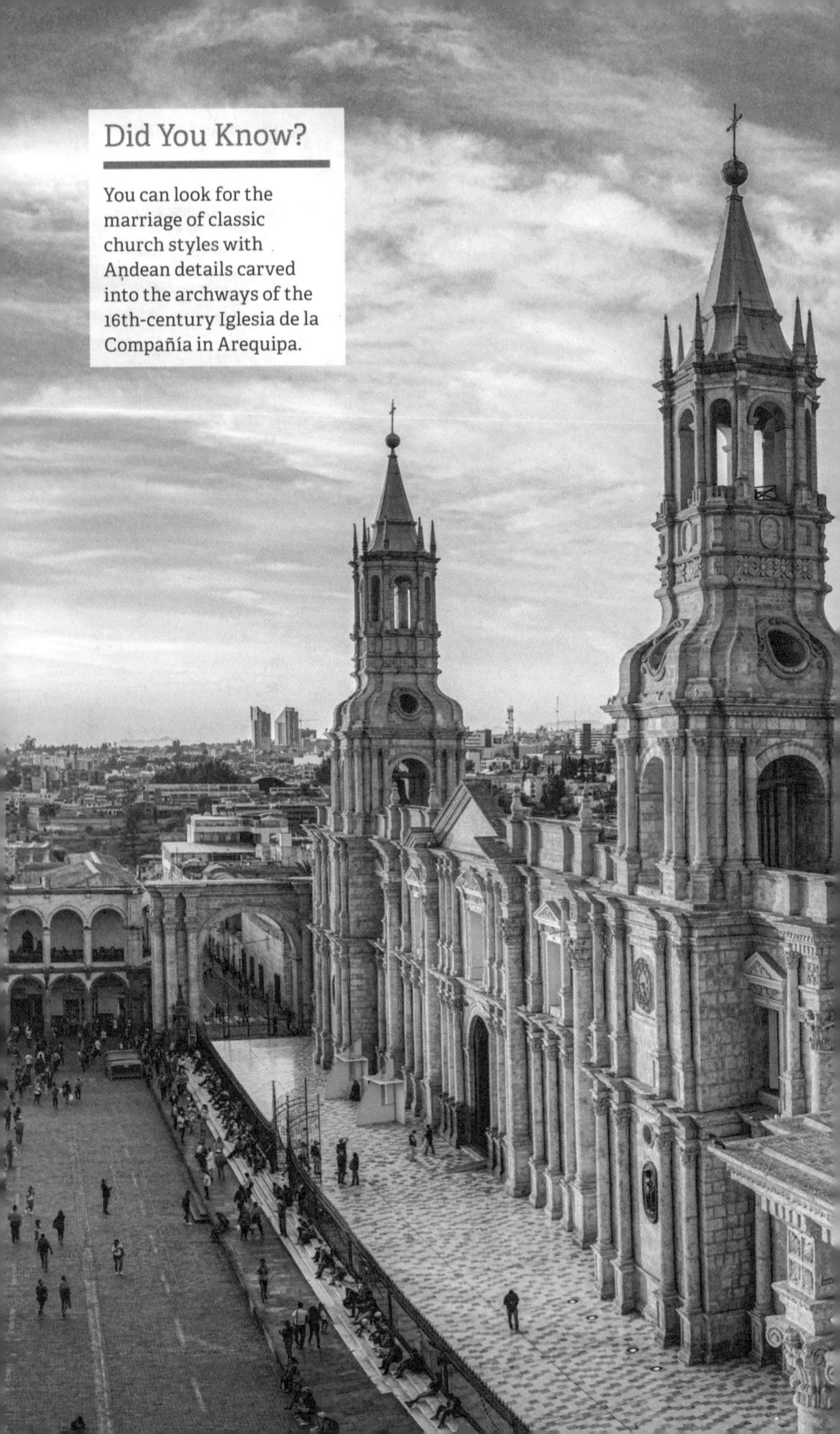

Did You Know?

You can look for the marriage of classic church styles with Andean details carved into the archways of the 16th-century Iglesia de la Compañía in Arequipa.

cafeteria with a bar on-site. To reach the home, go past Tingo along Avenida Huasacache. ✉ *Av. Paisajesta s/n, Socabaya* ☎ *054/982–311–988* 🌐 *www.lamansiondelfundador.com* 🎫 *S/13.*

Mercado San Camilo

MARKET | This jam-packed collection of shops sells everything from snacks and local produce to clothing and household goods. It's an excellent place geared more to locals than tourists so you can spot rare types of potatoes, sample *queso helado* (ice cream), or eat *chicharrones* (deep-fried pork). It's on Calle San Camilo, between Avenidas Peru and Piérola. ✉ *Cl. San Camilo 352* 🎫 *Free.*

Molino de Sabandía

BUILDING | There's a colorful story behind the area's first stone *molino* (mill), 7 km (4 miles) southeast of Arequipa. Built in 1621 in the gorgeous Paucarpata countryside, the mill fell into ruin over the next century. Famous architect Luis Felipe Calle was restoring the Arequipa mansion that now houses the Central Reserve Bank in 1966 when he was asked to work on the mill project. By 1973, the restoration of the volcanic-stone structure was complete, and Calle liked the new version so much that he bought it, got it working again, and opened it for tours. Bring your swimsuit and walking shoes in good weather—there's a pool and trails amid the lovely countryside. Adjoining the site is the traditional village of Yumina, which has numerous Inca agricultural terraces. If you're not driving, flag a taxi for S/25–S/30 or take a *colectivo* (shared taxi) from Socabaya in Arequipa to about 2 km (1 mile) past Paucarpata. ✉ *Cl. Molino, Sabandia* ☎ *51/959–839–545* 🌐 *en.elmolinodesabandia.com* 🎫 *S/10.*

★ Monasterio de Santa Catalina

HISTORIC SITE | A city unto itself, this 5-acre complex of mud-brick, Iberian-style buildings—a working convent and one of Peru's most famed cultural treasures—is surrounded by vibrant fortresslike walls and separated by neat, open plazas and colorful gardens. Founded in 1579 and closed to the public for the first 400 years, Santa Catalina was an exclusive retreat for the daughters of Arequipa's wealthiest colonial patrons. Now visitors can catch a peek at life in this historic monastery. Narrow streets run past the Courtyard of Silence, where teenage nuns lived during their first year, and the Cloister of Oranges, where nuns decorated their rooms with lace sheets, silk curtains, and antique furnishings. Though it once housed about 400 nuns, fewer than 30 call it home today. Admission includes a one-hour guided tour (tip S/15–S/20) in English. Afterward, head to the cafeteria for the nuns' famous *torta de naranja* (orange cake), pastries, and tea. Besides Tuesday and Wednesday, when it closes at 8, opening hours are from 9 to 5. There are also night tours on Tuesday and Thursday, but times can vary, so check before you go. ✉ *Cl. Santa Catalina 301* ☎ *054/221–213* 🌐 *www.santacatalina.org.pe* 🎫 *S/40.*

Museo Arqueológico José Maria Morante Maldonado

MUSEUM | With a solid collection of indigenous pottery and textiles, human-sacrificed bones, and gold and silver offerings from Inca times, this archaeology museum at the Universidad Nacional de San Agustín provides insight into local archaeology and ruins. ✉ *Cl. Alvarez Thomas 200* ☎ *054/288–881* 🌐 *www.unsa.edu.pe/eventos/museo-arqueologico-jose-maria-morante* 🎫 *S/5* ⏲ *Closed weekends.*

★ Museo Santuarios Andinos

MUSEUM | Referred to as the Juanita Museum, this fascinating little museum at the Universidad Católica Santa Maria holds the frozen bodies of four young girls who were apparently sacrificed more than 500 years ago by the Inca to appease the gods. The "Juanita" mummy, said to be frozen around the age of 13, was the first one to be found in 1995

Courtyard in the Monasterio de Santa Catalina, Arequipa

near the summit of Mt. Ampato by local climber Miguel Zárate and anthropologist Johan Reinhard. When neighboring Volcán Sabancaya erupted, the ice that held Juanita in her sacrificial tomb melted, and she rolled partway down the mountain and into a crater. English-speaking guides will show you around the museum, and you can watch a video detailing the expedition. ✉ *Cl. La Merced 110* ☎ *054/286–613* 🌐 *www.ucsm.edu.pe/museo-santuarios-andinos* 🎫 *S/20.*

Yanahuara

NEIGHBORHOOD | The eclectic little suburb of Yanahuara, northwest of the city, is the perfect spot for lunch or a late-afternoon stroll. The neighborhood has amazing views over Arequipa at a lookout constructed of sillar stone arches, complete with a Pisco Museum and a little park for soaking in glorious sunsets. On a clear day, the volcanoes El Misti, Chachani, and Picchu can be seen. Stop in at the 1783 Iglesia Yanahuara. The interior has wrought-iron chandeliers and gilt sanctuaries surrounding the nave. Ask to see the glass coffin that holds a statue of Christ used in parades on holy days. To reach Yanahuara, head across the Avenida Grau bridge, then continue on Avenida Ejército to Avenida Lima, and from there, it's five blocks to the plaza. It's a 15-minute walk or an 8-minute cab ride from the city center. ✉ *Arequipa.*

SIDE TRIPS

Reserva Nacional Salinas y Aguada Blanca

NATURE PRESERVE | Several types of South American camelids thrive at this vast nature reserve of desert, grass, and flamingo-filled lakes. Indeed, you might see herds of beige-and-white vicuñas, llamas, and alpacas all grazing together on the sparse plant life of its open fields. Wear good walking shoes for the uneven terrain, and bring binoculars. Also bring a hat, sunscreen, and a warm jacket, as the park sits at a crisp 3,900 meters (12,795 feet). The reserve is 35 km (22 miles) north of Arequipa, just beyond volcano El Misti. If you're headed to Colca Canyon or Puno from Arequipa, you have to pass through the reserve to get there, but tours really just rush through the area, stopping only at the Laguna de Pampa Blanca for a glimpse of wild vicuñas. If you hire private transport, you can visit the cave paintings at Sumbay and spend some time to properly hike across this barren expanse. The Toccra interpretation center, with detailed information in English and Spanish on the area's flora and fauna, is located 2½ hours from Arequipa and is open to the public from 9 to 4. ✉ *Between Arequipa and Colca Canyon* ☎ *054/257–461.*

Toro Muerto

ARCHAEOLOGICAL SITE | Toro Muerto is the world's largest petroglyph field, where hundreds of volcanic rocks are thought to have been painted more than 1,000 years ago by the Huari (or Wari) culture. There are sketches of pumas, llamas, guanacos, and condors, as well as warriors and dancers. Head higher for expansive views of the desert. It's hot and windy, so bring water, a hat, and sunglasses. Toro Muerto is 164 km (102 mi) northwest of Arequipa, and, unless you are driving, guided tours are the most effective way to visit in a day. ✉ *Arequipa.*

Yura

TOWN | About a half-hour drive from Arequipa, this serene little town is settled in the western foothills of the Volcán Chachani. Take the road 27 km (17 miles) farther to reach rustic thermal baths, where you can take a dip in naturally heated water that ranges from 70°F to 82°F. You can soak in any weather and enjoy a picnic along the river in summertime. Admission to the hot springs is S/5, and they're open daily from 8 to 3. From the old Arequipa train station, there's bus service to Yura, which takes close to an hour and costs S/5. ✉ *Arequipa.*

Restaurants

Comida arequipeña (Arequipan cuisine) is a special version of *comida criolla.* Perhaps the most famous dish is *rocoto relleno,* a large, spicy red pepper stuffed with meat, onions, and cheese. Other specialties to try are *cuy chactado* (deep-fried guinea pig), and *adobo* (pork stew), a local cure for hangovers. *Picanterías* are where locals head for good, basic Peruvian meals and cold Arequipeña beer served with *cancha* (fried, salted corn kernels).

The west side of the Plaza de Armas has dozens of restaurants along the balcony above the Portal de San Agustín. The first blocks of Calle San Francisco and Calle Santa Catalina north of the Plaza de Armas are lined with cafés, restaurants, and bars.

Alma Bar Restaurante

$$ | **INTERNATIONAL** | With its placement in the gorgeous Casa Andina Premium hotel, a historic monument, this gourmet restaurant is worth a visit for the setting alone. The menu is quite varied, using local ingredients to create international dishes as well as give a new flair to traditional Peruvian ones, like *rocoto relleno con pastel de papa* (stuffed red peppers) or carpaccio *de lomo* (beef carpaccio). **Known for:** historic setting; nice atmosphere; inventive cuisine. $ *Average main: S/48* ✉ *Casa Andina Premium Arequipa, Calle Ugarte 403* ☎ *054/226–907* 🌐 *www.casa-andina.com/en/restaurants.*

★ Chicha

$$$ | **PERUVIAN** | With a covered courtyard that evokes images of a traditional yet upscale outdoor picantería, the offerings at celeb-chef Gastón Acurio's stylish bistro provide delicious gourmet twists on typical regional fare. Unlike many restaurants offering fusion menus, the plate sizes here are ample. **Known for:** regionally inspired gourmet dishes; traditional yet upscale feel; decent portions. $ *Average main: S/53* ✉ *Santa Catalina 210* ☎ *054/287–360* 🌐 *www.chicha.com.pe.*

Crepisimo

$ | **FRENCH** | With an extensive variety of sweet and savory crepes, as well as quality espresso, pisco sours, and craft beers, you could easily spend the day in this artistic, Euro-styled restaurant, little sister to the Zig Zag restaurant on Calle Zela. Check out the terrace for great views of the Monasterio de Santa Catalina and volcanoes. **Known for:** variety of crepes; great service; lively atmosphere. *Average main: S/20 Santa Catalina 208 054/206–020 www.crepisimo.com.*

El Buda Profano

$ | **JAPANESE** | It may look like a hole-in-the-wall, but this small, Canadian-owned restaurant rolls up excellent vegan sushi—the perfect break from all of Arequipa's Novo Andino food. The sample menu for two, which includes 20 pieces of sushi, miso soup, and gyoza, lets you nibble on a wide variety of rolls for one reasonable price. **Known for:** vegan food; international clientele; sample menu for two. *Average main: S/10 Cl. Bolívar 425 51/ 977–228–590 www.elbudaprofano.com No credit cards.*

★ Fory Fay Cevicheria

$ | **SEAFOOD** | Ask any arequipeño to name their favorite fish joint, and Fory Fay tops the list. For more than two decades, the laid-back, rustic lunch spot has served some of the freshest *cebiche* (fresh raw fish cured in fresh citrus juices) around, including of *erizo* (sea urchin). **Known for:** well-established local favorite; fresh, carefully selected seafood; eclectic decor. *Average main: S/20 Alvarez Thomas 221 054/242–400 No dinner.*

Hatunpa

$ | **PERUVIAN** | **FAMILY** | Facing each other on Calle Ugarte, Hatunpa's two colorful, attractive locations are very popular for their tasty *papas andinas*. You can choose from set options (such as *lomo de res* with peppers, mushrooms, pickles, and béchamel sauce) or decide which local ingredients tickle your fancy to create a customized topping for your crunchy, oven-roasted potatoes. **Known for:** local food with a twist; friendly atmosphere; customized choice of toppings. *Average main: S/20 Cl. Ugarte 208 054/419–317 www.facebook.com/Hatunpa.*

La Lucila

$ | **PERUVIAN** | Rivaling La Nueva Palomino for Arequipa's favorite picantería, La Lucila has been in operation for more than 70 years. Although its beloved namesake owner passed away in 2012, her recipes—iconic regional dishes that have been passed down through generations—live on, as does the simple, rustic atmosphere. **Known for:** traditional regional food; historic location; chupe de camarones (spicy shrimp chowder). *Average main: S/30 Cl. Grau 147, Sachaca 054/205–348, 054/232–380 www.facebook.com/LaLucilaPicanteria No dinner.*

★ La Nueva Palomino

$$ | **PERUVIAN** | Chef Mònica Huertas is one of the great promoters of arequipeña cuisine, and, to many, this is the most authentic restaurant in town. She uses many of the same classic recipes—some more than a century old—that her mother and grandmother used, and her preparations of regional standards such as rocoto relleno, adobo, *lechón al horno* (oven-roasted pork), chupe de camarones, and *queso helado* (ice cream) have become the definitive recipes. **Known for:** legendary recipes; authentic local dishes; sprawling grounds and gardens. *Average main: S/45 Pje. Leoncio Prado 122, Yanahuara 054/252–393 www.facebook.com/pg/LaNuevaPalomino Closed Tues. No dinner.*

Las Gringas

$ | **PIZZA** | With interesting and fresh organic ingredients topping its delicious pizzas and focaccias, this courtyard restaurant is a fun and relaxing place to have dinner or just get an espresso and a quick bite to eat. It also offers gluten-free and vegan options, as well as a wide variety of craft beers. **Known for:** great pizza with unusual toppings; vegan and gluten-free options; craft beers. $ *Average main: S/34* ✉ *Cl. Santa Catalina 204* ☎ *054/399–895* 🌐 *www.facebook.com/LasGringasPizza.*

La Trattoria del Monasterio

$$ | **ITALIAN** | This intimate restaurant serves some of the best Italian food in southern Peru, and if you're not sure you want Italian food in Peru, its special location in the Monasterio de Santa Catalina (the entrance is outside the compound, though windows look in) is enough to merit a visit and a meal. A fusion menu featuring homemade pastas (try the delicious cannelloni with *lomo saltado*), gnocchi, and risottos—paired with seafood, meats, and creative, savory sauces—is offered, and although there are Novo Andino options, you can find them elsewhere, so stick with the excellent Italian fare here. **Known for:** excellent Italian food; homemade pasta; extensive wine menu. $ *Average main: S/48* ✉ *Cl. Santa Catalina 309* ☎ *054/204–062* 🌐 *www.latrattoriadelmonasterio.com* ⏲ *No dinner Sun.*

Lazos and Zingaro

$$ | **STEAKHOUSE** | Rubbing walls with each other, these two restaurants are part of the same franchise and are a good choice for a fine *parrilla* (Lazos) or fusion Peruvian-European dishes and wines (Zingaro). Lazos is one of Arequipa's best steak houses, so meat is what you come for—and there is plenty of it, including delicious cuts of beef, alpaca, and sausage; Zingaro, on the other hand, adds a local twist to international plates like pastas and has an extensive fish menu. **Known for:** grilled meats; extensive wine list; expensive-feeling setting. $ *Average main: S/45* ✉ *San Francisco 309 & 313* ☎ *054/399–895* ⏲ *No dinner Sun.*

Pasta Canteen

$ | **ITALIAN** | Craving hand-pulled pasta in the southern Andes? Fight for a spot at one of the two rustic wooden tables, and belly-up for authentic Italian cuisine. **Known for:** homemade food; do-it-yourself menu; rustic-Italian trattoria feel. $ *Average main: S/29* ✉ *Cl. Puente Grau 300* ☎ *952/167–232* 🌐 *www.facebook.com/pastacanteen.*

★ **Salamanto**

$$$$ | **PERUVIAN** | Reconstructing rich ancestral dishes in a modern way, Salamanto prepares locally sourced meats and fish, together with native corn, papas andinas, and algae and mushrooms from El Valle Sagrado, with centuries-old methods and modern spices and sauces. Try a seven- or ten-course tasting menu, accompanied by carefully selected local wines. **Known for:** ancient-made-contemporary Peruvian; immersive experience; curated, local wine list. $ *Average main: S/87* ✉ *Cl. San Francisco 211* ☎ *054/577–061* 🌐 *salamanto.com.*

Sambambaia's

$ | **PERUVIAN** | Specializing in both classic Andean meat and fish dishes, as well as international fare, this restaurant is in the quiet residential neighborhood of Vallecito, a 10-minute walk from the Plaza de Armas. Try the chef's favorite, a tender, juicy *lomo al vino tinto* (beef tenderloin in red wine), but if you're craving something more familiar, wood-oven pizza is another specialty of the house. **Known for:** variety of dishes; lomo al vino tinto; excellent service. $ *Average main: S/32* ✉ *Luna Pizarro 304, Vallecito* ☎ *054/223–657* 🌐 *www.sambambaias.com.pe.*

★ **Zig Zag Restaurant**

$$ | **FRENCH** | Everything here—from its grand iron spiral staircase and sillar stone walls to its Novo Andino cuisine, extensive wine list, and decadent desserts—is done with exquisite detail and attention. The menu, using a fusion of gourmet techniques from the Alps and Andes, is a harmonious mix of fresh local foods. **Known for:** delicious fusion cuisine; elegant architecture; fabulous service. $ *Average main: S/50* ✉ *Zela 210* ☎ *054/206–020* 🌐 *www.zigzagrestaurant.com.*

Arequipa has one of the highest-quality collections of inns and hotels anywhere in Peru. Although the larger resorts and chain hotels tend to cater to tour groups and business travelers, there are dozens of charming, small, independently run bed-and-breakfasts within a few blocks of the Plaza de Armas.

★ Casa Andina Premium Arequipa
$$ | **HOTEL** | Set in the city's former coin mint, a national historical monument, this midsize hotel features massive colonial-era common rooms with arched stone walls, oil paintings, and period furnishings. **Pros:** historic building; modern comforts; excellent amenities. **Cons:** modern rooms do not have the charm of the colonial ones; not all rooms have views; some rooms are dark. *Rooms from: S/465 Ugarte 403 51/959–173–189 www.casa-andina.com 40 rooms Free breakfast.*

Casa Andina Select Arequipa
$$ | **HOTEL** | You don't get any more central than this mid-level hotel with modern rooms, excellent service, and a superb location right on Plaza de Armas. **Pros:** central location; rooftop pool; great service. **Cons:** somewhat bland decor; interior rooms lack view; central location comes with noise. *Rooms from: S/360 Plaza de Armas, Portal de Flores 116 054/412–930 www.casa-andina.com 58 rooms Breakfast.*

Casa Andina Standard Arequipa
$$ | **HOTEL** | As with Casa Andina properties elsewhere in Peru, the Arequipa branch offers comfortable but basic rooms, nicely decorated with Andean textiles. **Pros:** good location; good breakfast; comfortable but basic rooms. **Cons:** tour-group heavy; no frills; noise travels from surrounding rooms. *Rooms from: S/375 Cl. Jerusalén 603 051/213–739 www.casa-andina.com 103 rooms Free breakfast.*

★ Casa Arequipa
$$ | **B&B/INN** | The individually designed rooms at this neoclassical boutique hotel are all decked out in luxuriously high-quality motifs and bedding—every last detail has been considered, and it's all so personalized that a stay here is almost like a stay with your best friends. **Pros:** impeccable service; comfortable bedding; quiet, upscale residential neighborhood. **Cons:** books up fast; not near any stores; a 10- to 15-minute walk from the center of town (you need a taxi at night). *Rooms from: S/250 Av. Lima 409, Vallecito 054/284–219 www.arequipacasa.com 13 rooms Free breakfast.*

★ Katari Hotel at Plaza de Armas
$ | **HOTEL** | Sitting right on the Plaza de Armas and facing the cathedral, this central boutique hotel offers traditional Arequipan heritage with opulent rooms and contemporary amenities. **Pros:** beautiful terrace with views of the Plaza de Armas and volcanoes; buffet breakfast served on the terrace; authentic decor and feel. **Cons:** not all rooms have views of the Plaza de Armas; suites are not much larger than standard rooms; courtyard-facing rooms can be noisy. *Rooms from: S/105 Portal de la Municipalidad 128 054/213–141 www.hotelkatari.com 15 rooms Free breakfast.*

La Casa de Melgar
$ | **B&B/INN** | In a beautiful tiled courtyard surrounded by fragrant blossoms and dotted with trees, this 18th-century home is believed to have been a onetime temporary residence of Mariano Melgar, Peru's most romantic 19th-century poet. **Pros:** high on the charm scale; garden is great for relaxing; close to shops and restaurants. **Cons:** rooms can get cold in rainy season; some rooms are small or have thin walls; front desk staff can be curt. *Rooms from: S/210 Melgar 108 054/222–459 www.lacasademelgar.com 31 rooms Free breakfast.*

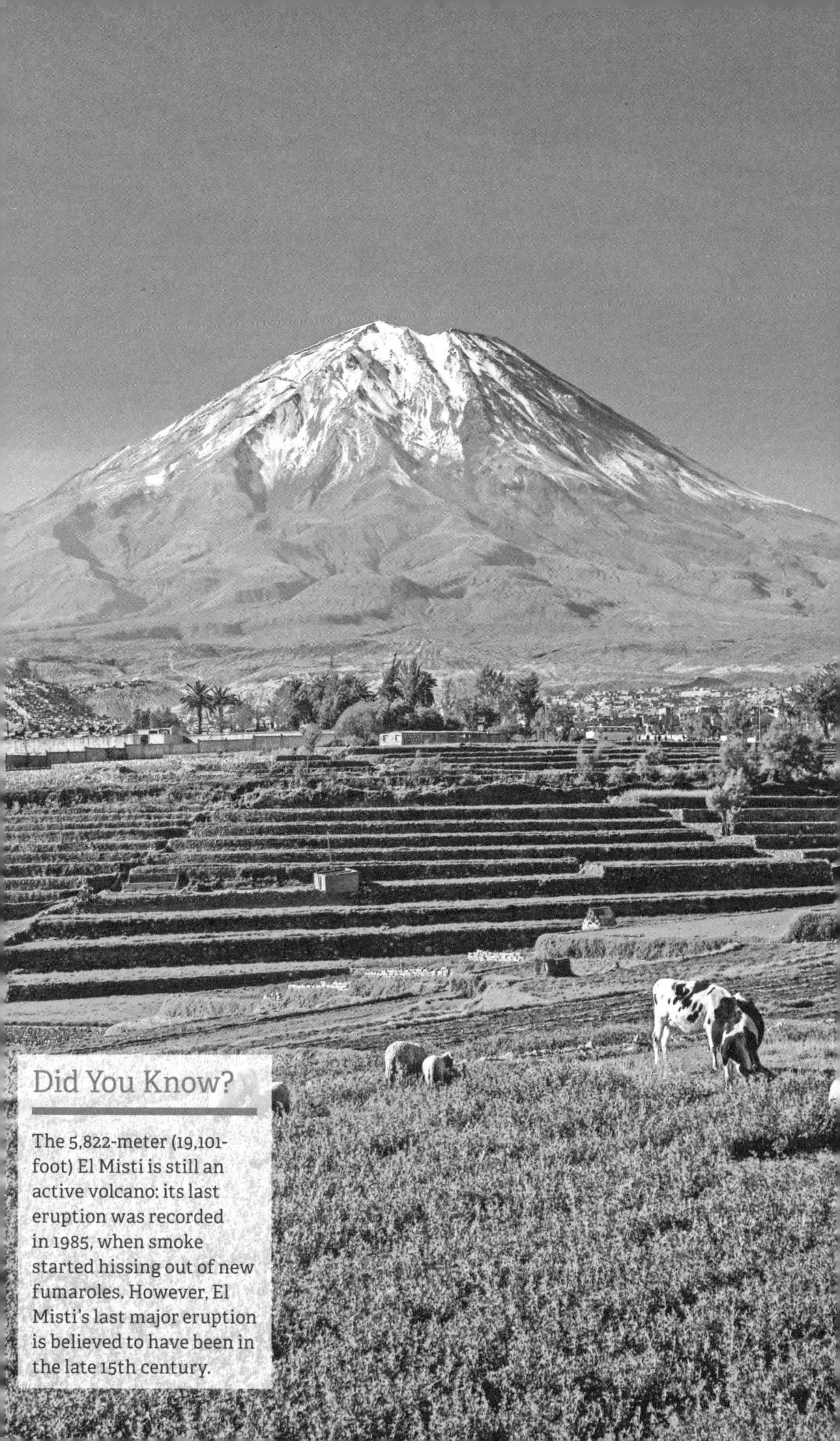

Did You Know?

The 5,822-meter (19,101-foot) El Misti is still an active volcano: its last eruption was recorded in 1985, when smoke started hissing out of new fumaroles. However, El Misti's last major eruption is believed to have been in the late 15th century.

La Hosteria

$$ | **B&B/INN** | For a quiet hotel with old Spanish-colonial charm and modern amenities, opt for a superior room with a view at this traditional hacienda. **Pros:** central location; colonial charm; somewhat faded but good-value Roman baths. **Cons:** front rooms have street noise; breakfast is basic; spa and baths need some repairs. *Rooms from: S/255 Bolivar 405 054/289–269, 054/281–779 www.lahosteriaqp.com.pe 20 rooms Free breakfast.*

Los Tambos Boutique Hotel

$$ | **HOTEL** | Located half a block from the Plaza de Armas, this stylish boutique hotel offers practical, comfortable rooms with a very homey atmosphere. **Pros:** great value; homey atmosphere with fireplace in the lobby; modern, large bathrooms. **Cons:** some rooms have no views; corridors are narrow and a bit claustrophobic; no restaurant (but plenty nearby). *Rooms from: S/255 Puente Bolognesi 129 993/741–243 lostambos.com.pe 16 rooms Free Breakfast.*

Queen's Villa Hotel

$$ | **HOTEL** | In the up-and-coming Vallecito neighborhood, a short walk from the center (and removed from its noise), this boutique hotel has a resort-like pool area, leafy gardens, and a terrace with views over the city to the mountains. **Pros:** quiet neighborhood; great pool; attentive service. **Cons:** uninspiring interior design; away from the plaza; room styles vary so you may want to ask for a more modern option. *Rooms from: S/286 Luna Pizarro 512, Vallecito 054/283–060 www.queensvillahotel.com 25 rooms Free breakfast.*

Selina

$ | **B&B/INN** | Part of a trendy hostelling and co-working space franchise, Arequipa's branch of Selina earns points for its stunning location set around a well-manicured garden filled with birds and artsy installations. **Pros:** vibrant artsy atmosphere; variety of room options; outdoor swimming pool. **Cons:** rooms are basic; pool area can be noisy; service can be inconsistent. *Rooms from: S/200 Cl. Jerusalén 606 51/915–070–792 www.selina.com 20 Free breakfast.*

★ Tierra Viva Arequipa Plaza

$ | **HOTEL** | The Peruvian Tierra Viva chain is known for offering a great balance of price and quality, and its Arequipa property is no exception. **Pros:** great quality for reasonable cost; ample buffet breakfast; central location. **Cons:** rooms are a little basic; some rooms face street (and noise). *Rooms from: S/210 Cl. Jerusalén 202 054/234–161 www.tierravivahoteles.com 21 rooms Free breakfast.*

★ Villa Elisa Hotel Boutique

$ | **B&B/INN** | This family-owned boutique hotel truly makes you feel welcome, with charming rooms, comfortable beds, pretty gardens, a friendly staff, and delicious breakfasts. **Pros:** tranquil and welcoming; beautiful grounds; good location. **Cons:** first-floor room windows are right on garden; not for those who want a more anonymous hotel experience; hotel restaurant has limited menu. *Rooms from: S/240 Manuel Ugarteche 401 054/221–891 www.villaelisahb.com 20 rooms Free breakfast.*

Nightlife

Most of the after-dark entertainment revolves around a number of cafés and bars near the city center along Calle San Francisco, Calle Zela, and Calle Santa Catalina. Many of these bars and cafés offer creative cocktails and character; some nights there's live music, typically of the rock variety. If you're dining around the plaza, there are usually groups of musicians playing traditional music and hawking their CDs.

BARS

Ad Libitum

BARS/PUBS | Head to this relaxed artistic heaven, popular with thirsty locals, for cheap cocktails and fun music. There's also a light menu. ✉ *San Francisco 233* ☎ *054/384–184* 🌐 *www.facebook.com/adlibitum.cafebar.*

Arequipa Beer Club

BARS/PUBS | If you are a connoisseur of beers, the sheer number of Peruvian craft brews sold at this popular bar may make you a repeat customer. Tucked up a wooden stairway, Arequipa Beer Club also shares a courtyard with Las Gringas so you can order one of their delicious pizzas as you imbibe. ✉ *Santa Catalina 204* ☎ *054/234–572* 🌐 *www.facebook.com/ArequipaBeerClub.*

Casona Forum

BARS/PUBS | Enter this large sillar building, open since the late 1980s, and you'll find a choice of several bars. The bar Retro stages live concerts and dancing to hits from the '70s to '80s. At Forum you can dine among tropical furnishings or dance the night away. Terrasse offers great views while dining and a chance to hone your karaoke skills. At Zero, you can belly up to the pub-style bar, grab a beer, and shoot some pool, or you can just hang out at the Chill Out sofa bar. ✉ *San Francisco 317* ☎ *054/204–294* 🌐 *www.casonaforum.com.*

Museo Del Pisco

WINE BARS—NIGHTLIFE | For an education in booze-onomics, come to this upscale pub and bistro that doubles as a pisco museum, and stay to have a couple of their strong sours and *chilcanos* (Peruvian brandy cocktails) while you enjoy burgers and well-executed Peruvian staples. ✉ *Santa Catalina Ancha 398* ☎ *51/542-815–83* 🌐 *www.museodelpisco.org.*

★ Nowhere Cerveza Artesanal

BREWPUBS/BEER GARDENS | Tucked up a side alley in a quiet part of town, this Canadian-Peruvian-owned brewery and beer garden is a popular hangout. To make things more interesting, the beer selection changes each fortnight, offering up all the shades of ale—from cream to red and sour. The industrial-chic bar has tall, comfy tables and chairs where you can feast on proper American-styled hamburgers (S/18) and staple bar food, and the open, well-tended garden welcomes smokers. It shuts by 11 pm (come early to enjoy the happy hours), and it's closed on Sunday and Monday for brewing more beers. ✉ *Combate Naval* ✥ *No street number but in front of house 104* ☎ *51/920–123–135* 🌐 *www.facebook.com/nowhereaqp.*

LGBTQ

Although not as gay friendly as Lima, Arequipa does have a small, progressive gay and lesbian scene.

Imperio

DANCE CLUBS | Located right in the center of town, making it easy and safe to reach, this LGBT club, which is straight friendly as well, is the place to go for a dance-filled evening. The club's cover is lower before midnight, and it offers a variety of themed events on Saturday. ✉ *Cl. Jerúsalen 201-I* ☎ *972/419–693.*

LIVE MUSIC

Casona 7

MUSIC CLUBS | **FAMILY** | Housed in a beautiful colonial mansion, this cultural center has a family-friendly restaurant and hosts Arequipa's most colorful show of Peruvian folk music and dancing. It's open every day but Sunday from 7 pm to 9 pm. ✉ *Palacio Viejo 325* ☎ *51/941–083–932* 🌐 *casona7.com.*

Centro Cultural Peruano Norteamericano

ART GALLERIES—ARTS | It's worth swinging by this venue, not just for announcements of evening concerts of traditional and classical music, but also for art and photography exhibits and other cultural offerings. ✉ *Melgar 109* ☎ *054/391–020* 🌐 *www.cultural.edu.pe/arequipa.*

Shopping

Arequipa has the widest selection of Peruvian crafts in the south. Alpaca and llama wool is woven into brightly patterned sweaters, ponchos, hats, scarves, and gloves, as well as wall hangings, blankets, and carpets. Look for *chullos* (woolen knitted caps with earflaps and ties), transported from the Lake Titicaca region. Ceramic *toros* (bulls), also from the Titicaca area, are a local favorite to hold flowers or money, and you can even see them sitting in the rafters of homes to bring good luck.

At the Plaza San Francisco, the cathedral steps are the site of a daily flea market that has delicate handmade jewelry. Across the street at the Fundo el Fierro, crafts vendors tout bargains on clothing, ceramics, jewelry, and knickknacks in a cobblestone courtyard; deals can be had until about 8 pm. Arequipa is also an excellent place to purchase inexpensive but well-constructed handmade guitars. Avenida Bolognesi has lines of such workshops. Behind the cathedral on the narrow Pasaje Catedral, boutiques sell jewelry and knickknacks made of Arequipa agate, and there are many clothing stores along Santa Catalina where you can find goods made from sheep's wool, alpaca, and vicuña.

In recent years several upscale shopping centers have popped up.

DESIGNER ALPACA CLOTHING

Arequipa is churning out scores of fashionistas who are responsible for creating some of the country's most sophisticated alpaca knits. Since many couturiers make their home in Arequipa, a few have alpaca clothing outlets, such as Jenny Duarte.

Jenny Duarte

CLOTHING | Come here for fine dresses from a French-trained local designer who doesn't shy away from using alpaca and other regional fibers. Her designs are now being sold in Lima, Paris, and Monaco. ✉ *Cuesta del Ángel 305, Yanahuara* ☎ *054/275–444* 🌐 *www.jennyduarteperu.com/en* ⏲ *Closed Sun.*

Kuna

CLOTHING | With shops in Lima, Arequipa, Puno, and Cusco, this is one of the go-to destinations in Peru for alpaca scarves, gloves, socks, sweaters, and jackets. ✉ *Santa Catalina 210* ☎ *054/282–485* 🌐 *www.kuna.com.pe.*

Mallkini Alpaca Sanctuary

CLOTHING | Mallkini has a mission: to sell fine alpaca products and give 5% of each purchase to the Mirasol boarding school for disadvantaged Andean children. ✉ *Santa Catalina 118* ☎ *054/202–525* 🌐 *www.mallkini.com.*

Mundo Alpaca

CRAFTS | The Michell Group, the umbrella company of Sol Alpaca, also owns this tourist-friendly upscale boutique. In addition to an inventory of high-quality fabrics and clothes, there's a petting zoo with alpacas and llamas, an art gallery, and a textile museum. ✉ *Alameda San Lázaro 101* ☎ *054/202–525* 🌐 *mundoalpaca.com.pe.*

Sol Alpaca

CLOTHING | The Michell Group's Sol Alpaca has gone haute couture, constructing fine-quality knits and helping Peru make its mark on the international fashion scene. ✉ *Santa Catalina 120 A* ☎ *054/221–454* 🌐 *www.solalpaca.com.*

MALLS

Claustros de la Compañia

SHOPPING CENTERS/MALLS | One of the best things about shopping in colonial cities is you get to do it in beautiful historic buildings. As you wander through the connected courtyards of the Claustros de la Compañia, you'll find a variety of small shops with unique wares. Some of these also have larger outlets a little outside of the center, so be sure to ask if you find pieces that you really like. ✉ *General Morán 118.*

Patio del Ekeko

SHOPPING CENTERS/MALLS | If you're looking for good-quality gifts and souvenirs, head to this shopping complex, which has a branch of alpaca store Kuna, Illaria silver, an artisanal foodstuff shop, and more. ✉ *Mercaderes 141* ☎ *054/215–861* 🌐 *www.elekeko.pe.*

Cotahuasi Village and Vicinity

379 km (235 miles) north of Arequipa.

Cotahuasi is the largest settlement in canyon country and the first you'll stumble upon. In the hills at 2,680 meters (8,793 feet), whitewashed colonial-style homes line slim, straight lanes before a backdrop of Cerro Hiunao. Most visitors kick off their stay in this Quechua-speaking community of 3,500 residents, where there are a few basic hostels, restaurants, a small grocery store, a 17th-century church with a bell tower, and the Plaza de Armas. Most hiking trails begin or end here. Many families rent burros to tourists to help carry their load, especially kayakers who walk eight hours down to the gorge with their kayaks.

Driving northwest from Cotahuasi Village for two hours will lead you to Pampamarca, a town known for exquisite woven rugs; it's three hours from here to the hot springs and waterfalls of Josla and Uskune. On the other side of the valley, a demanding trek leads adventurers past Huari ruins to the rock formations of the Bosque de Rocas de Wito, where you can take in the peaks of extinct volcanos Solimana and Firura.

Advance Prep

Cotahuasi is not so traveler savvy yet, so don't expect to just show up in a town, buy a map, hire a guide, and get on your way. At the very least, you should purchase a canyon map at the South American Explorers clubhouse in Lima or visit the Colca Trek office in Arequipa. That said, to minimize hiccups, it's best to plan your visit with a tour operator in Arequipa.

GETTING HERE AND AROUND

Cotahuasi Canyon is a travel destination in the making, and, outside of expert extreme-sports enthusiasts, few people venture here. If you're not taking a bus or coming with a tour operator, driving anything but a 4x4 is asking for trouble. The jagged, rocky dirt roads are full of cliffs and narrow corners. Dry for most of the year, the roads get muddy from December to April (rainy season), a time when you're also likely to encounter random streams flowing across the road.

Hire a guide regardless of season and not just for safety: because this region is so remote, you're likely to see much more with a guide. Purek Cotahuasi Tours (🌐 *www.facebook.com/Cotahuasitourss*, ☎ *51/958–046–982*) are established and recommended, and their owner Mirko is a fountain of local information. All buses travel through the night. Bus companies Transportes Cromotex (☎ *054/ 426-836*) and Transportes Reyna (☎ *054/430–612*) go from Arequipa to Cotahuasi daily at 7 am, 6 pm, or 7 pm, arriving in Cotahuasi Village after a 10–12-hour trip, in time for sunrise.

Every hour from 6 am to 6 pm, minivan services shuttle between Cotahuasi's main road and the village of Alca (one hour). From there, vans go to Puyca at 5 am and 3 pm. A useful daily *combi* (minivan) leaves Cotahuasi for Quechualla (two hours) at 6 am, passing the Catarata de Sipia and the cactus forest on the way and returning the next day at 8:30 am from Quechualla. A daily run to Pampamarca (two hours) leaves from the bus station at 4 pm, returning at 7 am the next day.

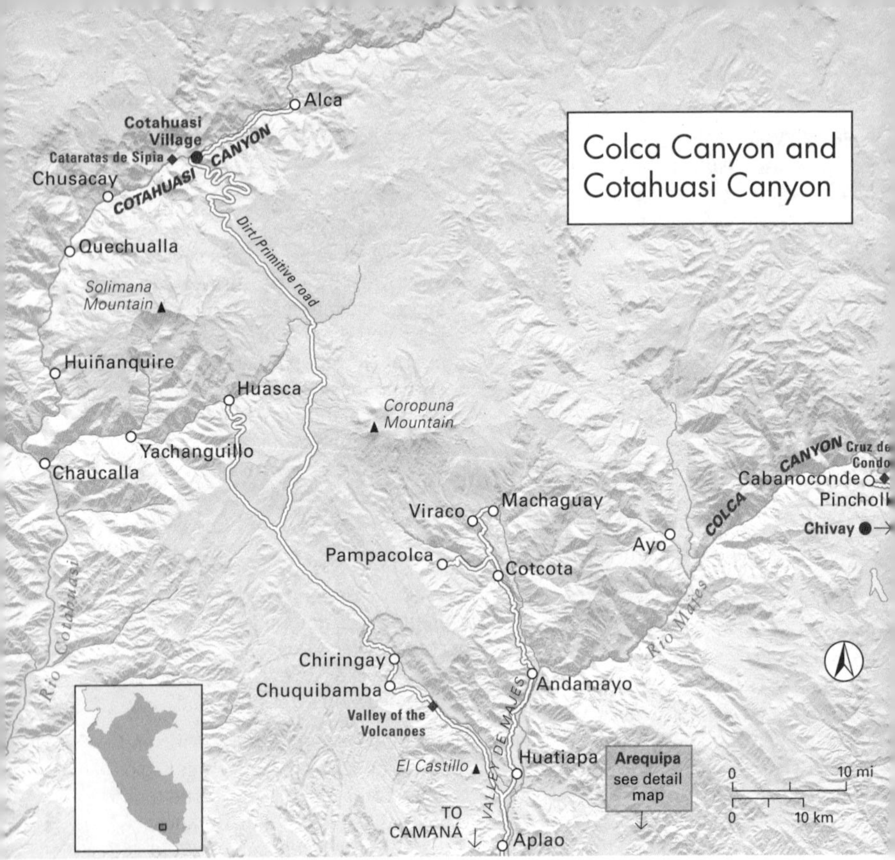

Colca Canyon and Cotahuasi Canyon

Alca
Cotahuasi Village
Cataratas de Sipia
COTAHUASI CANYON
Chusacay
Quechualla
Dirt/Primitive road
Solimana Mountain
Huiñanquire
Huasca
Coropuna Mountain
Yachanguillo
Chaucalla
Río Cotahuasi
COLCA CANYON
Cruz de Condo
Cabanoconde
Pinchollo
Chivay
Machaguay
Viraco
Ayo
Pampacolca
Cotcota
Río Majes
Chiringay
Chuquibamba
Andamayo
Valley of the Volcanoes
VALLEY DE MAJES
El Castillo
Huatiapa
Arequipa see detail map
TO CAMANÁ
Aplao
0 10 mi
0 10 km

■ **TIP→ If you're driving, know that gas stations are few on the long stretch between Corire (near Toro Muerto) and the village of Cotahuasi.**

Sights

Cataratas de Sipia

CANYON | Below the village of Cotahuasi is the valley of Piro, the gateway to the canyon, which is close to this 150-meter-high (492-foot), three-tiered, 10-meter-wide (33-foot) waterfall. ■ **TIP→ Sipia Falls is the most-visited attraction in the entire canyon.** ✉ *Arequipa* 🎫 *Free.*

★ **Cotahuasi Canyon**

CANYON | Colca Canyon may be the region's most famous natural attraction, but at 3,354 meters (11,001 feet), Cotahuasi is the world's deepest gorge, beating Colca Canyon by 163 meters (534 feet). It's nearly twice as deep as the Grand Canyon. The canyon has been carved by the Río Cotahuasi, which becomes the Río Ocuña before connecting to the Pacific. Its deepest point is at Ninochaco, below the quaint administrative capital of Quechualla and accessible only by kayak. Kayak explorations first documented the area and measured its depth in the mid-1990s. Since then, paddling the Cotahuasi River's Class V rapids is to kayakers what scaling Mount Everest is to mountaineers.

The road from Arequipa to the Cotahuasi Canyon ranks with the great scenic routes of the world. As you pass Corire and Toro Muerto, the road rides the western side of snowcapped Nevado Coropuno (6,424 meters, 21,076 feet), Peru's third-highest mountain, offering spectacular views as you descend into the valley

Crossing into Chile

The border with Chile, about 40 km (25 miles) from Tacna or 440 km (273 miles) from Arequipa, is open daily and very easy to cross. All you need is your passport with a minimum validity of six months. From Tacna, scores of colectivos will give you a ride to the other side for about S/40, or you can take a bus headed to Arica from Tacna, departing hourly.

Typically, drivers will help with border formalities, even the colectivo drivers. The road journey takes about an hour. Any train aficionado would enjoy the slow, somewhat bumpy but beautiful train ride from Tacna to Arica, which takes more than an hour, leaves twice a day (8:30 am and 5:30 pm; 9 am and 7 pm from Arica to Tacna), and costs S/15.

of Cotahuasi. ■ **TIP→ Logistically speaking, it's a bumpy 11- to 13-hour bus ride or 10 hours by four-wheel drive from Arequipa.** The pavement ends in Chuquibamba after about five hours of driving, and then resumes for the last hour of the drive, at the Mirador of Cotahuasi and for the descent into the canyon. There is no fee to enter. ✉ *Arequipa* 🎫 *Free.*

Hotels

Cotahuasi doesn't offer the wealth of accommodation choices of the Colca Canyon, but there are a few basic lodges that will do just fine when you are exploring the area.

★ Hotel Hatun Huasi

$ | **HOTEL** | This simple hotel, the friendliest in Cotahuasi, has two stories of basic yet clean and well-maintained en-suite rooms set around the pleasant garden of a local household. **Pros:** warm and considered hospitality; in the center of the village; hot water and Wi-Fi (not a given elsewhere). **Cons:** no-frills rooms; common spaces are shared with the owners; internet can be spotty in bad weather. 💲 *Rooms from: S/130* ✉ *Cl. Centenario 307, Chivay* ☎ *054/581–054* 🌐 *hatunhuasi.com* 🛏 *12 rooms* 🍽 *Free breakfast.*

Hotel Valle Hermoso

$ | **HOTEL** | What it lacks in refinement or luxury, this simple, rustic property, hemmed by green mountains, more than makes up for with its stunning location. **Pros:** idyllic yet central location; lovely garden setting for dining; good value. **Cons:** a little basic; rustic feel not for everyone; you pay extra for eggs at breakfast. 💲 *Rooms from: S/160 0* ✉ *Cl. Tacna 106, Chivay* ☎ *054/581–057* 🌐 *www.hotelvallehermoso.com* 🛏 *20 rooms* 🍽 *Free breakfast.*

Activities

Many operators in Arequipa and Cusco offer multiday excursions. Three- to five-day tours are the most common, although some may last up to 10 days or more. A few local hikers provide custom tours for visitors as well.

HIKING

Cotahuasi Canyon is an awesome place to explore by foot. The backdrop of snow-capped Volcán Coropuna and Solimana is fantastic, the high desert plains offer a rest from the steep upward rocky canyon terrain, and the untouched villages provide a cultural aspect. Hikes can go between 1,830 meters (6,000 feet) and 6,400 meters (21,000 feet) in height, so prepare for the altitude. Temperatures remain about 65°F–70°F during the day, dipping below 45°F on any given night. Ancient Inca paths wind throughout the canyon and its terraces. ■ **TIP→ Beware: many of these ancient trails are narrow, rocky, and hang over the side of the canyon.** Newer trails parallel some of the ancient ones and are generally safer.

Sipia Falls is a solid three- to four-hour trek from Cotahuasi Village, and it's a hard-on-your-knees hike down that includes two bridge crossings, but the first taste of being in the canyon is a surreal experience. It's also possible to reach the falls by hailing a colectivo or driving your own 4x4 from the Cotahuasi road to the Sipia Bridge, where the road ends. From here it's a 45-minute hike to the falls.

If you're going on a multiday excursion, continue on the trail from Cotahuasi to Sipia to the Chaupo Valley and the citrus-tree village of Velinga, a good place to camp. From Velinga it's on to Quechualla, where you'll pass through the 1,000-year-old Wari ruins, rock forests, and cactus forests. One of the last major points along this route is Huachuy, where you can again camp. Beyond this point things get trickier, as you'll have to cross the Río Cotahuasi. Many guides use a cable system to reach Yachau Oasis, Chaucalla Valley, and eventually Iquipi Valley.

HIKING DOWNRIVER

Three hours farther south from Cotahuasi along a thin track against the canyon wall—which climbs to 400 meters (1,312 feet) above the river—is Chaupo, a settlement surrounded by groves of fruit trees, where it's also possible to camp. The area's main attraction is the nearby Catarata de Sipia, a thunderous waterfall plunging 150 meters (490 feet) into an endless gorge. A few kilometers farther along the trail through Velinga is the impressive Bosque de Cactus de Judio Pampa, a forest strewn with giant cactus, some of which reach up to 15 meters (49 feet) in height. Hike past ruins at Huña before reaching Quechualla, where the ancient farming terraces of Maucullachta, an old Wari city, are visible across the gorge. If you continue walking for a few more hours beyond Quechualla, you can end your adventure at the tiny settlement of Ushua, which overlooks dramatically one of the canyon's deepest points.

HIKING UPRIVER

In Cotahuasi Village, the route forks, leading northeast along the Río Cotahuasi or due north. Either way is possible by 4x4 and colectivo or on foot. Heading northeast, about 10 km (6 miles) out of town is the village of Tomepampa. After that is the small town of Alca, near the hot springs of Luicho, the most developed in the area. Even farther east is 3,700-meter-high (12,139-foot-high) Puica, from where it's a 2-km (1.2-mile) uphill hike to the pre-Huari ruins of Maukallacta. The mirador and waterfalls of Alljoyaku nearby offer chances to see condors bathing during the rainy season (Dec.–March). Continuing to the northwest following the Huarcaya River valley you'll reach the beautiful Lauripampa Plateau, set in the shadow of 5,455-meter-high (17,897-foot-high) Nevado Huanzo and peppered by sublime woods of *Puya raimondii*— the world's largest bromeliad.

WHITE-WATER RAFTING

White-water rafters can challenge the rapids anywhere from the upper Cotahuasi, near the village, almost to the Pacific. The river is divided into four sections: the Headwaters, beginning upstream from Cotahuasi Village; Aimaña Gorge; Flatwater Canyon; and the Lower Canyon.

The Lower Canyon is a mix of Class III and V rapids, without much portage. Most rafting operators put in at the village of Velinga and use this part of the river for tours.

Cotahuasi rafting trips are offered infrequently, maybe only once or twice a year, and should be booked well in advance. Due to the extreme nature and logistical complications of running these extremely challenging trips, there are only a couple of Peruvian and international operators offering them, and they do so between May and June only. You want to book such tours with serious professionals only to avoid cutting corners on safety.

Chivay

136 km (85 miles) north of Arequipa.

The largest town in the Colca Canyon region is Chivay, a small, battered-looking village with a population of about 5,000. Most tourist facilities are here, which are not many, but include restaurants, hotels, a medical clinic, a tourist information center, and the canyon's only ATMs. Make sure to withdraw enough cash for your stay. As you approach Chivay, you'll pass through a stone archway signifying the town entrance, where AUTOCOLCA, the government authority over Colca Canyon, stops cars to ask if they are headed to see the condors. If you're headed to Cruz del Condor or any of the churches in the 14 villages, you must purchase the S/70 Boleto Turistico, which will be asked for again at the entrance of the Mirador and will also get you into specific attractions like La Calera Hot Springs and the church at Cabanaconde. Most agency tours do not include this entry fee in their prices.

■ **TIP→ Please note that the popular 2D/1N Colca Canyon tours leaving from Arequipa are very rushed and barely scratch the area's surface.** They tick off must-see sights such as the Cruz del Condor viewpoint and La Calera Hot Springs, but offer very poor insight in the area's local life and traditions and don't even enter the canyon proper at Cabanaconde. We recommend taking a longer tour which includes some hiking, or visiting the area by yourself—these days, roads and transportation options from and to Arequipa, Puno, and Cusco are excellent and easy to organize.

Setting Up Camp

With no official campgrounds, setting up a tent most anywhere is customary. You'll likely encounter very few people, if any, on your trek.

Chivay marks the eastern end of the canyon's rim; the other end is marked by Cabanaconde, a small village hemmed by green mountains where most multiday hikes into the canyon begin and end. As you come into Chivay, the road splits off into two: one, less traveled because of its rocky rutted surface, goes along the canyon's northern edge to the villages of Coporaque, Ichupampa, and Lari; the other is perfectly paved and follows the southern rim, leading to Cruz del Condor and the small towns of Yanque, Maca, and Cabanaconde.

GETTING HERE AND AROUND

You can explore the area by hiring a private guide, renting a four-wheel-drive vehicle, joining a tour from Arequipa, or going by bus. A standard two-wheel-drive car won't do. Arequipa is the jumping-off point for nearly everyone headed to Colca Canyon, and most will either come on a tour or take a bus that stops at either Chivay, the first town you come to, which takes about five hours to reach from Arequipa, or Cabanaconde, about another hour farther. Sporadic combi service links each town in the middle.

Chivay is a four-hour drive from Arequipa. The road takes you through the Reserva Nacional Salinas y Aguada Blanca and over the Patapampa Pass, where, at 4,910 meters (16,109 feet), you can view nearly the entire Valley of Volcanoes. The road is paved all the way from Arequipa to Cabanaconde. Most who visit Colca Canyon experience altitude sickness along the way, so bring plenty of water.

Some of the nicer hotels will have oxygen tanks.

Taxis are a good way to go from town to town if long hikes or mountain biking aren't your thing. Taxis and inexpensive shared minivans (S/1.5–S/5) shuttle between the different villages and line up around the Plaza de Armas in Chivay. Most taxi rides will cost S/30–S/65.

4M Express (*busperu4m.com*) and Inka Express (*www.inkaexpress.com*) run direct luxury tourist bus services equipped with guides. These buses leave from Chivay's Plaza de Armas and make several sightseeing stops along the way. Buses to Puno (S/170) leave daily at 8 am and 1 pm. For Cusco (S/220), 4M Express buses leave on Monday, Wednesday, and Friday at 7 am, while Inka Express departs on Tuesday, Thursday, and Saturday at 12:30 pm. If you come to Chivay without a tour, Inka Express also has daily 6:30 am departures to Cruz del Condor from Chivay's Plaza de Armas. Regular buses also depart from Chivay Bus Station to Arequipa (S/17) several times daily, as well as to Cabanaconde (S/5) via Cruz del Condor at 4 am, 7 am, 2:30 pm, and 5:30 pm.

VISITOR INFORMATION Autocolca. *Republica de Chile 228, Arequipa* *054/531–143* *www.colcaperu.gob.pe.* **Yanque Tourist Information Office.** *Plaza Principal de Yanque, Arequipa* *+51/949–745–250* *www.facebook.com/turismoyanquecolca.*

Sights

Church of the Inmaculada Concepción
RELIGIOUS SITE | Built in Mestizo-baroque style, this important 17th-century church, with its Latin cross and detached chapels, dominates one side of Yanque's Plaza de Armas. Its facade, which has been undergoing restoration, is one of the best in the Colca Valley, featuring Ashlar stone that is richly decorated in high relief. *Plaza de Armas, Yanque* *054/ 203–010.*

Valley of the Volcanoes

This spectacular, 65-km (40-mile) crevasse north of Colca Canyon includes a line of 80 extinct craters and cinder cones. Looming over the scene is active Volcán Coropuna, the third-highest peak in Peru. Andagua, at the head of the valley, has the best tourist facilities in the area. The valley is about five hours by a rocky, half-paved, half-dirt road from Colca Canyon. There are several multiday hikes from Colca Canyon that must be arranged in Arequipa or Cabanaconde—ask for help at Pachamama.

★ Colca Canyon
CANYON | Flying overhead, you can't miss the green, fertile trough as it cuts through the barren terrain, but it's all an illusion; only scrub brush and cactus cling to the canyon's sheer basalt sides and miles of ancient terraces. **■ TIP→ The canyon is named for the stone warehouses (colcas) used to store grain by an ancient culture that lived along the walls of the gorge.**

Carved into the foothills of the snow-covered Andes and sliced by the silvery Río Colca, Colca Canyon is 3,182 meters (10,440 feet) deep. The more adventurous can embark on a hike into the canyon—typically a two-, three-, or five-day excursion. Bird lovers (and anyone with a penchant for amazement) can visit the Cruz del Condor, currently home to 38-odd animals. Culture seekers can spend a night with a native family. Light hikers and archaeology aficionados can observe points along the rim, and those seeking pure relaxation can hit one of the all-inclusive lodges that offer horseback riding and thermal baths. *Chivay* *S/70.*

Arrange a tour in Arequipa to hike and explore the Colca Canyon and Valley, one of Peru's most dramatic and spectacular landscapes.

★ Cruz del Condor

CANYON | Cruz del Condor is a haunt for the giant birds, particularly at dawn, when they soar on the thermal currents rising from the deep valley. At 1,200 meters (3,937 feet), the "condor cross" precipice, between the villages of Pinchollo and Cabanaconde, is the best place to spot them. **■ TIP→ From June to August, you're likely to see close to 20 or more condors during a morning visit.** By October and November, many of the female birds are nesting, so your chances of eyeing flocks are slim, though you'll likely spot a few birds. It is possible to take a taxi or bus to the Cruz del Condor from Chivay, but if you take a tour from there, your guide will likely only speak Spanish. If you want a guided tour in English, you will need to set this up with a tour operator ahead of time in Arequipa or Cusco. If you overnight in Cabanaconde or Chivay, you can also visit the Mirador before the sun sets. It's when the condors return to their nests, and you'll have the place all to yourself. ⊠ *Chivay.*

La Calera Hot Springs

HOT SPRINGS | Often included in tours leaving from Arequipa, a visit to Chivay's hot springs is perfect to enjoy the canyon's narrow slopes alfresco while soaking in naturally heated pools. The setting is relaxing, and locks are provided to secure your gear and bags. It's a 3-km (1.86-mile) walk from Plaza de Armas or a quick colectivo ride (S/1) from the square. ⊠ *Chivay* 🎫 *S/15.*

Uyo Uyo Ruins

ARCHAEOLOGICAL SITE | Whether on foot or on horseback, a visit to the ruins of this pre-Columbian stone village makes for a perfect half-day trip from Yanque. Uyo Uyo, which sits on a hillside overlooking the canyon valley and a crown of snowcapped mountains, was a pre-Inca village attributed to the Collagua people of the region. It was later occupied by the Incas and destroyed by Spanish conquistadores to force the natives to move to Yanque. The ruins are within walking distance of the Colca Lodge, only 800 meters (2,625 feet) from the

Canyon Life

Quechua farmers once irrigated narrow, stacked terraces of volcanic earth along the canyon rim to make this a productive farming area. These ancient fields are still used for quinoa and *kiwicha* (amaranth) grains, and barley grown here is used to brew Arequipeña beer.

Most of those who live along the rim today are Collagua Indians, whose settlements date back more than 2,000 years. Their traditions persevered through the centuries. In these unspoiled Andean villages you'll still see Collaguas and Cabana people wearing traditional clothing and embroidered hats. Spanish influence is evident in Achoma, Maca, Pinchollo, and Yanque, with their gleaming white sillar (volcanic-stone) churches.

The area is steeped in colorful folklore tradition, and locals like a good fiesta. Some of the larger festivals include La Virgen de la Candelaria, a two-day fiesta in Chivay on February 2 and 3. Later in the month, Carnaval is celebrated throughout the valley. Semana Santa (Holy Week) in April is heavily observed, but for a more colorful party, don't miss Chivay's annual anniversary fiesta on June 21. From July 14 to 17, the Virgen del Carmen, one of the larger celebrations, kicks off with parades on both ends of the canyon: Cabanaconde and Chivay. All Saints' Day is well honored on November 1 and 2, as is La Virgen Imaculada on December 8, the best time to see traditional Watiti dance performances.

main road up a winding footpath; they can also be reached directly from Yanque in two or three hours following a well-marked trail via Sifon Bridge. Uphill from the ruins is a waterfall that stems from the glaciers of Nevado Misti. The visitor center next to the beginning of the 15-minute trek to the ruins collects a S/5 entry fee. ✉ *Yanque.*

Restaurants

Restaurants in Chivay are not so plentiful and not varied, especially when it comes to the ubiquitous tourist-oriented buffets. You'll come into town on 22 de Agosto, which leads to the Plaza de Armas, where you'll find most options. There are also a few basic restaurants in Cabanaconde and Yangde, including the excellent and mostly organic La Granja del Colca in a rural area on the highway.

Incafe Restaurant

$ | **PIZZA** | Expect a good mix of inexpensive Peruvian and North American staple dishes, including thin-crust pizzas, at this restaurant-bar on the main square. It makes a stop in Yanque all the more pleasant. **Known for:** coffee and pizzas; bright and friendly atmosphere; central location. [$] *Average main: S/20* ✉ *Main Plaza, Yanque* ☎ *51/996–472–853* 🌐 *www.facebook.com/RestaurantIncafe.*

InnKas Resto Bar

$ | **PERUVIAN** | This long-standing Peruvian restaurant, tucked on a corner of Chivay's Plaza de Armas, serves reliable and tasty alpaca, chicken, and beef mains that include lomo saltado and *pollo chimichurri* (grilled chicken with piquant sauce), as well as a choice of pastas to quell comfort-food cravings. Excellent and inexpensive espressos pair up with crepes and a variety of cakes. **Known for:** lively yet intimate setting; delicious cakes; excellent coffee. *$ Average main: S/30 ✉ Plaza de Armas 705 ☎ 51/952–354–443.*

★ La Granja del Colca

$$ | PERUVIAN | Set along the highway to Cabanaconde near Cruz del Condor and surrounded by ample fields, the hotel Kunturwassi is best known for its excellent organic restauran. All the food, including meats, is sourced or raised locally. **Known for:** organic foods; farm-to-plate philosophy; surrounded by nature. *$ Average main: S/40 ✉ Km. 9.5, Carretera Cruz del Condor ☎ 54/233–120 ⊕ www.restaurantcolca.com.*

McElroy's Pub

$ | PERUVIAN | Owned by a true Irishman, this pub dishes up good pizzas, burgers, and sandwiches alongside the usual Peruvian dishes. It has a pool table and packs in most of the gringos in town. **Known for:** burgers and pizzas; gringo clientele; sociable atmosphere. *$ Average main: S/30 ✉ Plaza de Armas 200 ☎ 51/943–333–184 ⊕ www.facebook.com/McElroysIrish.*

Hotels

Chivay is tiny, but it has plenty of hotels, from budget to moderate, and even a few luxury options. If you're planning on staying one night in Colca Canyon, it makes sense to stay in Chivay. If you'll be in the area for longer, consider one of the lodges in the valley, which are more inclusive, with offerings such as dining, hiking, biking, and horseback riding. Cabanaconde is the best option if you want to explore the canyon on foot.

★ Aranwa Pueblito Encantado del Colca

$$$ | RESORT | FAMILY | Although the exterior of this upscale resort and spa along the Colca River feels more condo than boutique, the rooms are modern and airy, the amenities are superb, it houses one of the better restaurants and bars in the area, offers a stunning get-away-from-it-all location, and authentic Peruvian hospitality and culture. **Pros:** full-service spa; secluded location with stunning views; modern and spacious rooms. **Cons:** inelegant exterior; a taxi ride away from anything else; bumpy ride to this escape. *$ Rooms from: S/700 ✉ Cusipampa 1 s/n, Salihua, Coporaque ☎ 511/207–0440, 855/384–6625, 054/383–850 ⊕ www.aranwahotels.com ⇆ 41 rooms 🍴 Free breakfast.*

High Sun

Don't forget sunblock! At high altitudes the rays can be fierce, even with clouds. Often the brisk mountain temperatures trick you into thinking it's too cool for a burn.

★ Belmond Las Casitas

$$$$ | RESORT | At the most luxurious property in the Colca area, with service and amenities to match, each thatched bungalow has its own outdoor terrace with a private heated pool, heated smooth-stone floors, and deep bathtubs beneath skylights for after-dark soaking and stargazing (though you can get an even better view from the outdoor showers). **Pros:** beautiful rooms; gorgeous grounds and setting; private hot springs and full-service spa. **Cons:** pricey; remote location; some rooms are a bit of a walk from reception. *$ Rooms from: S/1680 ✉ Fundo La Curiña s/n, Yanque ☎ 996/998–355 ⊕ www.belmond.com ⇆ 20 bungalows 🍴 Free breakfast.*

Casa Andina Standard Colca

$ | B&B/INN | Part of the national Casa Andina chain, this hotel is much quainter than the company's typical urban properties, with stand-alone bungalow-style cabins built of locally quarried rock, thatched roofs, and wood flooring. **Pros:** planetarium (with shows in English) and observatory; good breakfast; cozy lounge and fireplace. **Cons:** disconnected from nature; small bathrooms; rooms can get cool (but electric blankets are available). *Rooms from: S/238* *Cl. Huayna Capac s/n* *051/213–9739* *www.casa-andina.com* *51 rooms* *Free breakfast.*

Colca Lodge

$$$ | RESORT | FAMILY | One of the most complete resorts in Colca, with its own hot springs and solar heating, this hotel is at the same time relaxing and family friendly. **Pros:** lots of activities; hot springs and full-service spa; solar heating. **Cons:** hot springs closed February and March; too remote to avoid using the on-site facilities; walk up and down to pools is a little steep. *Rooms from: S/534* *Fundo Puye s/n, Caylloma, Yanque* *054/531–056* *www.colca-lodge.com* *45 rooms* *Free breakfast.*

Colca Trek Lodge

$$ | B&B/INN | Situated in Pinchollo, a small town just 15 minutes from the Cruz del Condor viewing point, this tranquil lodge is surrounded by gorgeous scenery and in the perfect location for trekking and mountain-climbing excursions. **Pros:** gorgeous location; great food; access to trekking. **Cons:** not much to do for nonhikers; rustic so no Wi-Fi or TVs in rooms; some noise from neighboring rooms. *Rooms from: S/270* *Cl. San Sebastian I–5, Pinchollo* *054/206–217* *www.colcatreklodge.com* *12 rooms* *Free breakfast.*

El Refugio

$$ | RESORT | Located about five minutes from Chivay and set in a stunning landscape hugged by mountains and lush greenery alongside a rushing river—the sound will lull you to sleep at night—this peaceful hotel allows you to take refuge from the world without compromising comfort. **Pros:** private natural hot springs; beautiful location; peaceful escape. **Cons:** a distance from town; many steps to get down to the lodge; rooms can be cooler in the evening so pack accordingly. *Rooms from: S/360* *Fundo Putuco (carretera rural a Cabanaconde)* *054/959–603–753, 054/257–901* *www.refugiohotelcolca.com* *33 rooms* *Free breakfast.*

★ Killawasi Lodge

$$ | B&B/INN | A boutique lodge with rustic-chic decor, Killawasi's location, in the countryside but close to the small town of Yanque, provides the perfect balance of escape to nature and access to local culture. **Pros:** beautiful, tranquil setting; perfect location for exploring; excellent service and tours. **Cons:** nearby town is charming but tiny; not much else nearby; you may need to stay longer than a night to merit the trip. *Rooms from: S/315* *Cl. Caraveli 408, Yanque* *51/982–526–277* *www.killawasilodge.com* *14 rooms* *Free breakfast.*

La Casa de Mama Yacchi

$ | B&B/INN | If you're passing through and want to save on your lodging budget, this quiet hotel in the countryside offers great value for basic rustic-chic rooms, many of which have gorgeous views. **Pros:** great value; tranquil location; beautiful views from many rooms. **Cons:** basic rooms; gets cold; taxi needed to get anywhere. *Rooms from: S/210* *Caylloma s/n, Coporaque* *054/241–206* *www.lacasademamayacchi.com* *No credit cards* *28 rooms* *Free breakfast.*

Pachamama

$ | B&B/INN | The best guesthouse in Cabanaconde has a homey and warm feel—probably thanks to its wood-fire oven, which constantly churns out the finest pizzas in the region. **Pros:** lively bar; several language spoken; excellent pizzas. **Cons:** few rooms available; backpacker atmosphere; rooms and facilities are basic but clean. *Rooms from: S/120* *San Pedro, Cabanaconde, Coporaque* *51/959–316–322* *pachamamahome.com* *7* *Free breakfast.*

Shopping

Galeria artes del Colca

GIFTS/SOUVENIRS | This colorful shop sells a wide range of cool local souvenirs—including postcards, wood engravings, handmade books, fabrics, and jewelry—all produced by many talented local artists. ✉ *Salaverry 129* ☎ *51/959–224–570* 🌐 *www.artesdelcolca.com.*

Activities

Most organized adventure-sports activities should be arranged from Arequipa or Cusco, especially rafting and multiday treks into the canyon. Many upper-tier hotels and resorts in the canyon offer packages, have their own tour guides, and have activities like horseback riding and mountain-bike rentals. If you wait until you get to the canyon, you may have trouble finding an English-speaking guide. Therefore, tours are best booked through an agency ahead of time. While in Chivay, don't miss the chance to try one of the exciting zipline courses available to get a bird's-eye view of the canyon.

HIKING

Hiking is the only way to really experience the Colca Canyon. Bring lots of water (the valley has water, but it's more expensive, as it's "imported" from Arequipa), sunscreen, a hat, good hiking shoes, high-energy snacks, and sugar or coca leaves to alleviate altitude sickness. And layer your clothes—one minute the wind may be fierce and the next you may be sweltering in the strong sun.

■ TIP→ Pick up a copy of Pachamama's excellent free Trekking Map of the Colca Canyon before striking off from Cabanaconde. The map has in-depth itineraries for both single and multiday hikes.

Along the canyon: Along the south side of the canyon, it's possible to do an easy hike from the observation points between Cruz del Condor, the other viewpoint Cruz del Cura, and Pinchollo. Paths are along the canyon rim most of the way; however, in some places you have to walk along the road. The closer to Cruz del Condor you are, the better the paths and lookouts get.

Another short hike, but more uphill, is on the north rim starting in Coporaque. At the Plaza de Armas, in the corner to the left of the church, you'll see an archway. Go through the archway, take a right uphill, and you'll be on the trail, which goes from wide to narrow but is defined. **■ TIP→ Following the trail up for about an hour, you'll come to ancient burial tombs (look down) with actual skeletons.** The trail climbs up a cliff, which overlooks the valley. It's about a two-hour hike to the top, and, in some spots, it is very steep, and the rocks are crumbly. After the tombs, the path becomes confusing and splits in many directions.

Into the canyon: Trails into the canyon are many but rough. You don't necessarily need a guide, but if you prefer one, several adventure-tour operators provide government-certified hiking guides. Local guides are also easily found but may not speak much English. Packages range from two- to eight-day treks. The Cabanaconde area is the entry point for most of these.

The most popular multiday hike is the three-day/two-night trek. Starting at Pampa San Miguel, about 20 minutes (on foot) east of Cabanaconde, the trail to San Juan Chuccho (one of the larger villages along the river) begins. The steep slope has loose gravel, passes 3,400-meter-high (11,155-foot-high) Mirador de San Miguel, and takes about four hours. In San Juan Chuccho, sleeping options are family-run hostels or a campground. Day two consists of hiking on fairly even terrain through the small villages of Tapay, Coshnirwa, and Malata before crossing the river and into the lush green village of Sangalle, or as locals call it, the "oasis", a mini paradise along the Río Colca, with hot springs and waterfalls. On day three, you'll hike four to five hours uphill to the rim and arrive in Cabanaconde by lunch. Otherwise, you can divert west via the Mirador de Apacheta to Belen, and from there either proceed south via Pacila to the hot springs at Llahuar (from where a path returns directly to Cabanaconde, taking about five hours one way), or stick to the western trail and walk for roughly seven hours up to Fure. One hour farther west is the beautiful Huaruro Waterfall and the end of the trail. It takes roughly eight hours to return to Cabanaconde via Sangalle from here.

■ TIP→ It's not recommended to hike alone here. So many paths are in this area that it can be overwhelming to even the most experienced trekkers.

Carlos Zárate Adventures
HIKING/WALKING | You can hire Carlos Zárate and his hiking and mountain guides for all types of treks, including the more difficult ones, in the region. Guides speak Spanish, English, and French. ✉ *Cl. Jerusalén 505A, Arequipa* ☎ *054/202–461* 🌐 *www.zarateadventures.com* *From S/180.*

Colca Trek
HIKING/WALKING | With more than 30 years of experience in adventure tours in the area, Vlado Soto is a pioneer of Colca Canyon trekking. Passionate about outdoor excursions, Vlado is constantly out there himself, checking the routes and investigating new trails. Colca Trek specializes in longer trekking tours, as well as day-trips, city tours, rafting excursions, and mountain biking. You can also get topographical maps of the entire region in the company's office. ✉ *Cl. Jerusalén 401-B, Arequipa* ☎ *054/206–217* 🌐 *www.colcatrek.com.pe* *From S/285.*

Colca Zip Lining
ZIP LINING | This established operator offers three different Colca Valley courses, ranging in length from the 610-meter (2,000-foot) "scenic" run to the 1,981-meter (6,500-foot) "extreme" run. Though not essential, reservations are appreciated. ✉ *Chivay* ☎ *51/958–989–931* 🌐 *www.colcaziplining.com.*

Bring cash!

There are ATMs in Chivay but nowhere else in the Colca Canyon or valley area. Soles and U.S. dollars (no bills larger than US$20) are accepted.

WHITE-WATER RAFTING

The Río Colca is finicky. Highly skilled paddlers long to run this Class IV–V river. Depending upon the season, the water level, and the seismic activity of the local volcanoes, the rapids change frequently. In some areas, they're above Class V; in others, they're slow enough to be considered Class II–III. Below Colca Canyon, conditions on the Río Majes (the large downstream section of the Río Colca) are reliable, with superb white-water rafting. Skilled rafters start in Huambo by renting mules for S/20–S/30, and, for the next eight hours, descend to the river. The waters at this point are Class III, but when the Río Mamacocha dumps in, it's Class IV and V rapids.

Paddlers who have tried to run the entire river through the canyon have failed more often than succeeded. There are a few well-known operators to consider, which is important, given the river's intensity.

The following operators specialize in adventure tours in the Colca and Cotahuasi Canyons. For the standard one- or two-day tours of Colca Canyon, see tour operators listed under Arequipa.

Amazonas Explorer
WHITE-WATER RAFTING | Based in Cusco and one of the most reputable adventure companies in the country, Amazonas Explorer is one of the few that offer rafting trips in Cotahuasi. Owner Paul

Cripps, an inveterate rafter himself, keeps abreast of current conditions and ensures that the best equipment and highest degree of safety practices are employed. ✉ *Av. Collasuyo 910, Cusco* ☎ *844/380–7378 from U.S., 958/729–904 office in Peru* 🌐 *amazonas-explorer.com* 🎫 *From USD$3161.*

Bio Bio Expeditions

TOUR—SPORTS | One of the leaders in kayaking and rafting operators around the world, Bio Bio Expeditions offers 11-day, all-inclusive runs down the Cotahuasi rivers. All guides are trained in first aid and swift-water rescue. ☎ *800/246–7238* 🌐 *www.bbxrafting.com* 🎫 *From USD$3700.*

Peru North

WHITE-WATER RAFTING | This British-run travel company organizes adventurous, multiday rafting and hiking expeditions in both the Colca and Cotahuasi Canyons. Prices start at USD$3,500. ☎ *203/286–1581* 🌐 *www.perunorth.com.*

Puno

975 km (606 miles) southeast of Lima.

Puno doesn't win any beauty pageants—brown, unfinished, concrete homes, old paved roads, and dusty barren hills have dominated the landscape for years. It's a sharp contrast to Puno's immediate neighbor, Lake Titicaca. Some people arrive in town and scram to find a trip on the lake, but don't let the dreary look of Puno stop you from exploring its shores; it's considered Peru's folklore capital.

Puno retains traits of the Aymara, Quechua, and Spanish cultures that settled on the northwestern shores of the lake. Their influence is evident in the art, music, dance, and dress of today's inhabitants, who call themselves Children of the Sacred Lake. Much of the city's character comes from the continuation of ancient traditions—at least once a month, a parade or a festival celebrates some recent or historic event.

A huge contrast to the constant barrage of people trying to sell you things in Cusco's Plaza de Armas, the city and main plaza of Puno exist for the local residents. Although the number of hotels and restaurants that really cater to the tastes of foreign travelers is growing, it is doing so quite slowly. If you are in the city, stick to the Plaza de Armas and the pedestrian-only streets such as Avenida Lima, avoid the lakeshore, and take taxis after dark.

GETTING HERE AND AROUND

Although Puno does not have an airport, you can fly into Juliaca's Aeropuerto Manco Capac, about 45 minutes away. The airport is served by LATAM airlines (🌐 *www.latam.com*) for flights between Juliaca, Cusco, and Lima, sometimes with a stop along the way. Avianca (🌐 *www.avianca.com*) also operates between Juliaca and Lima. Most hotels in Puno will pick you up on arrival; otherwise, you can take one of the waiting tourist buses (S/5) or organize a private taxi for about S/60–S/80.

The Terrestre bus terminal is at Primero de Mayo 703 and Bolívar, and many companies also have offices here. Puno is a connection point for trips between Arequipa, Cusco, and La Paz, Bolivia, so there are frequent buses throughout the day for each destination. Reputable companies include Civa, Ormeño, and Tour Peru. Cruz del Sur is probably the best of the bunch and also leaves from the main terminal. Inka Express and Turismo Mer specialize in buses that run between Puno and Cusco, stopping at various tourist sites along the way to break up the trip.

The train station for PeruRail and the Belmond Andean Explorer for trips to and from Cusco, Estación Huanchaq (☎ *084/581–414*), is at the end of Avenida Sol on Avenida La Torre just outside the center of town. Service between the

Festival Time!

Although any time of year is suitable for traveling to Puno and Lake Titicaca, visiting during a festival of dance, song, and parades is ideal. The streets are flooded with people; the folklore experience is passionate and a lot of fun. Preserving the choreography of more than 140 typical dances, Puno's most memorable celebration is the Festival of the Virgen de la Candelaria, held on February 2 and during Carnaval. A cast of several hundred elaborately costumed Andean singers, dancers, and bands from neighboring communities parades through the streets carrying the rosy-white-complexioned statue of the Virgin. During the rest of the year, the statue rests on the altar of the San Juan Bautista Church. Puno Week, as it's informally known, occurs the first week of November and is equally fun. When Puno isn't having a celebration, it reverts to its true character, that of a small, poor, Andean agricultural town. On the lake, Isla Taquile celebrates a vivid festival the last week of July.

towns runs three or four times a week, depending on the season.

Restaurants, shops, Internet services, banks, and drugstores line the four-block pedestrian-only street Jirón Lima, between Pino Park (sometimes called Parque San Juan after the San Juan Bautista Church nearby) and the Plaza de Armas.

Puno has tricycle taxis—which resemble Asian tuk-tuks and are driven by bicycle pedalers—with a carriage and cost only S/3–S/4 to go nearly anywhere in the city. But if you're heading to a mirador high up on the hill and you don't want the pedaler to keel over, take an auto taxi, which costs S/3–S/7. There are also mototaxis, which cost around S/4, and inexpensive public buses (S/1.5) shuttling between the center, the lake, and the Terrestre bus station.

BUS Cruz del Sur. ✉ *Terminal Terrestre C-10* ☎ *051/368–524* 🌐 *www.cruzdelsur.com.pe.* **Inka Express.** ✉ *Jr. Tacna 346* ☎ *051/365–654* 🌐 *www.inkaexpress.com.* **Turismo Mer.** ✉ *Jr. Tacna 336* ☎ *051/367–223 office, 051/365–617 bus station* 🌐 *www.turismomer.com.*

TRAINS PeruRail. ✉ *Estacion Puno, La Torre 224* ☎ *084/581–414* 🌐 *www.perurail.com.*

TAXIS Radio Taxi Milenium. ☎ *051/353–134.*

HEALTH AND SAFETY

At 3,827 meters (12,556 feet) above sea level, Puno challenges your system, so eat lightly, skip the alcohol (trust us!), forego your morning jog, and take it easy your first two or three days.

■ TIP→ **Walking around the port after dark is not smart.** When the sun goes down, the port gets desolate, so if you're at the handicrafts market or are returning from an outing on the lake and suddenly it's dusk, catch a cab.

MEDICAL Manuel Nuñez Butron National Hospital. ✉ *Jr. Ricardo Palma 120* ☎ *051/367–128, 051/368–862 emergencies* 🌐 *www.hrmnb.gob.pe.* **Medicentro Tourist's Health.** ✉ *Jr. Moquegua 193* ☎ *051/365–909, 951/620–937.*

POLICE Police. ✉ *Jr. Deustua 530* ☎ *051/366–271, 051/353–988.* **Policía de Turismo.** ✉ *Jr. Deustua 538* ☎ *051/354–764.*

VISITOR INFORMATION

iPeru Oficina Información Turística. ✉ *Plaza de Armas, corner Jr. Deustua and Jr. Lima* ☎ *051/365–088* 🌐 *www.peru.travel.* **Migraciones.** ✉ *Ayacucho 270-280* ☎ *051/357–103* 🌐 *www.migraciones.gob.pe.*

Sights

Catedral

RELIGIOUS SITE | Etchings of flowers, fruits, and mermaids playing an Andean guitar called the *charango* grace the entrance of this 17th-century, Spanish baroque church. Sculpted by Peruvian architect Simon de Asto, the stone facade is one of the most eclectic of any church in the area. Decorations in the comparatively plain interior mainly consist of a silver-plated altar and paintings from the Cusco School. ✉ *Plaza de Armas* *Free* *Closed Sun.*

Cerrito de Huajsapata

MEMORIAL | A statue honoring Manco Cápac, the first governor and founder of the Inca Empire, sits on this hill overlooking Puno. Legend has it that there are caves and subterranean paths in the monument, which connect Puno with the Koricancha Temple in Cusco. It's technically a 10-minute walk from town, four blocks southwest of Plaza de Armas, but it's all uphill and a bit off the beaten path. **■TIP→ A few robberies have been reported, so stick with a group or take a taxi.** ✉ *Off Cl. Choquehanca.*

Conde de Lemos Balcony

HISTORIC SITE | An intricately carved wooden balcony marks the home where Viceroy Conde de Lemos stayed when he arrived in Puno to counter rebellion around 1668. Behind the cathedral, it is today home to the National Culture Institute of the Department of Puno. ✉ *Corner of Cls. Deustua and Conde de Lemos* *Free.*

El Yavari

MUSEUM | The restored Victorian iron ship was built in Birmingham, England, in 1861. It was subcontracted by the Peruvian Navy to patrol the waters of Titicaca, so it was dismantled and its 2,766 pieces and two crankshafts were loaded onto a freighter and shipped to the Pacific coast port of Arica, which was then in Peru but which today belongs to Chile. Mules and porters carried the pieces 467 km (290 miles) through the Andes Mountains to Puno. The journey took six years, and it was Christmas Day 1870 before it was reassembled and launched on Lake Titicaca. Now a museum, it's docked at the end of a pier by the Sonesta Posada del Inca Hotel. After remaining idle for 40 years, the vessel took a trial run in 1999 after volunteers rebuilt its engine. ✉ *Av. Sesquicentenario 610, Sector Huaje* ☎ *051/369–329* 🌐 *www.yavari.org* *Donation.*

Iglesia San Juan Bautista

RELIGIOUS SITE | This 18th-century church has been entrusted with the care of the Virgin of Candlemas, the focus of Puno's most important yearly celebration in February, the Festival de la Virgen de la Candelaria. The statue rests on the main altar. It's worth passing by at night to see the neon exterior lighting. ✉ *Jr. Lima and Parque Pino.*

La Casa del Corregidor

HOUSE | Reconstructed more than five times, this 17th-century colonial building, once a chaplaincy, now houses a fair-trade café, a library, and a few upscale handicraft stores. It was originally home to Silvestre de Valdés, a Catholic priest who served as a *corregidor* (a Spanish official who acts as governor, judge, and tax collector) and who oversaw construction of the nearby cathedral. The house had a long history of changing owners until its present owner, Ana Maria Piño Jordán, bought it at public auction. ✉ *Deustua 576* ☎ *051/351–921* 🌐 *www.casadelcorregidor.pe* *Closed Sun.*

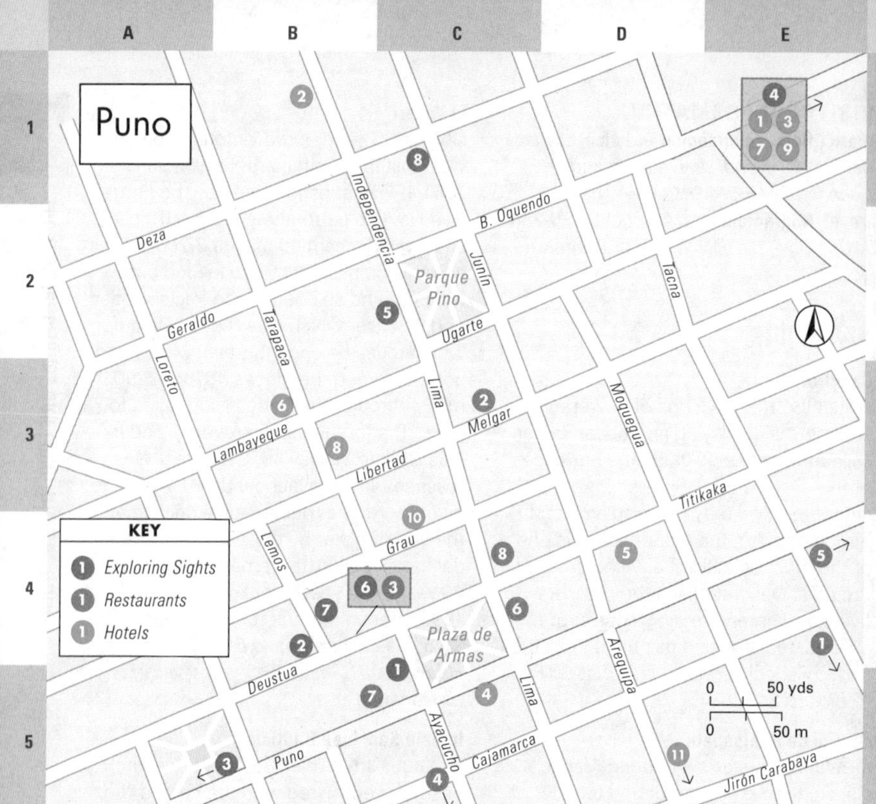

Sights

1 Catedral C5
2 Cerrito de Huajsapata B4
3 Conde de Lemos Balcony B5
4 El Yavari E1
5 Iglesia San Juan Bautista C2
6 La Casa del Corregidor B4
7 Museo Carlos Dreyer B4
8 Museo de la Coca y Costumbres C1

Restaurants

1 Alma Cocina Viva E4
2 Balcones de Puno C3
3 Café Bar B4
4 La Table Del' Inca C5
5 Loving Hut Titicaca Vegan E4
6 Mojsa C4
7 Pacha Restaurant & Draft Bar B5
8 Restaurant Museo la Casona C4

Hotels

1 Casa Andina Premium Puno E1
2 Casa Andina Standard Puno B1
3 GHL Hotel Lago Titicaca Puno E1
4 Hotel Hacienda Plaza de Armas C5
5 Hotel Hacienda Puno D4
6 Intiqa Hotel B3
7 Isla Suasi E1
8 Qelqatani B3
9 Sonesta Posadas del Inca E1
10 Tierra Viva Puno Plaza C4
11 Titilaka D5

Museo Carlos Dreyer

MUSEUM | An exhibit of 501 gold pieces called the "Great Treasure of Sillustani" has helped to make this one of the most important regional archaeological museums in southern Peru. The intimate museum is named for famed Puno painter and antiques collector Carlos Dreyer Spohr, whose oil-on-canvas works you can view here, in addition to exploring exhibits of pre-Hispanic and colonial art, weavings, silver, copper works, delicate Aymara pottery, pre-Inca stone sculptures, and historical Spanish documents on the founding of Puno. Plan to spend about an hour here. ✉ *Conde de Lemos 289* 🎫 *S/15* ⏲ *Closed Sun.*

Museo de la Coca y Costumbres

MUSEUM | A hidden gem, this museum pays tribute to the infamous coca leaf and Peruvian folklore. The quaint museum includes a folklore exhibit as well as everything you'd ever want to know about the coca leaf. Presented in English and Spanish, displays are well constructed with educational videos and photographs. The mission is not to promote coca but merely to share the plant's history and culture. The folklore exhibit displays elaborately constructed costumes worn during festivals and shares the history behind the dances. Visit the store and purchase some coca-based products or have your future read in the leaves. ✉ *Jr. Ilave 581* ☎ *951/927–826* 🌐 *www.museodelacoca.com* 🎫 *S/10.*

Restaurants

Many small restaurants line Jirón Lima, including those that serve Novo Andino and classic regional foods. On the menu you'll find fresh fish from the lake—particularly good are *trucha* (trout) and *pejerrey* (kingfish mackerel)—and an abundance of quinoa and other typical Peruvian dishes like *lechón al horno o cancacho* (highly spiced baked suckling pig); *pesque o queso de quinua* (fish fillet prepared with quinoa, cheese, and tomato sauce); and *chairo* (lamb and tripe broth cooked with vegetables and freeze-dried potatoes known as *chuño*).

Alma Cocina Viva

$$ | **INTERNATIONAL** | Inside the Casa Andina Premium Puno hotel, this contemporary eatery with cozy fireplaces is one of the few upscale options in the city. The lake views alone are worth the visit, and prices are similar to those at the town's lesser alternatives. **Known for:** views; modern takes on regional ingredients; international food. 💲 *Average main: S/45* ✉ *Av. Sesquicentenario 1970–72* ☎ *051/363–992* 🌐 *www.casa-andina.com/private-collection-puno.*

Balcones de Puno

$$ | **PERUVIAN** | Come to this upscale tavern, tucked on the first floor of a heritage building hemmed with wooden balconies, to try a range of alpaca- and quinoa-based dishes, all served with zest and creativity. The wood-fired pizzas are also recommended. **Known for:** inventive alpaca-based options; good wood-fired pizza; traditional dance and music shows. 💲 *Average main: S/40* ✉ *Libertad 354* ☎ *051/365–300* 🌐 *www.balconesdepuno.com.*

★ Café Bar

$ | **CAFÉ** | This laid-back café-bar is the only thing keeping La Casa del Corregidor alive these days. It offers some of the best international food and bar snacks you can find in Puno, as well as a wide variety of craft beers and great coffee drinks. **Known for:** chill ambience; snacks; garden seating. 💲 *Average main: S/24* ✉ *La Casa del Corregidor, Deustua 576* ☎ *051/351–921* 🌐 *www.cafebar.casadel-corregidor.pe.*

★ La Table Del'Inca

$$ | **FRENCH** | This chic, French-Peruvian restaurant, one of the best bets in town for a nice meal, is set in a beautifully renovated colonial building, where the walls are adorned with paintings by a local surrealist. Although you can order dishes à la carte, it's better to opt for the

prix-fixe menu, which will allow you to try more dishes for a lower price. **Known for:** delicious fusion food; reasonable prix-fixe menu; great atmosphere. *Average main: S/40 Jr. Ancash 239 994/659–357 Closed Sun.*

Loving Hut Titicaca Vegan

$ | **VEGETARIAN** | This no-frills vegan restaurant, one of the few such options in Puno, is actually decent, and the inexpensive set-lunch menu is a great value. The options are many and varied, with dishes like soups, quinoa, and falafel. **Known for:** vegan set menu; large portions; reasonable prices. *Average main: S/12 Jr. Jose Domingo Choquehuanca 188 51/353–523 www.lovinghut.com/pe No credit cards Closed Sun. and after 7 pm.*

★ Mojsa

$$ | **PERUVIAN** | Located in a beautiful colonial building, there are a couple of intimate tables on the balcony overlooking the Plaza de Armas, while the more lively interior rooms make it seem like a popular place to eat for both Peruvians and travelers. Mojsa, which means "delicious" in the Aymara language, serves reasonably priced Novo Andino cuisine, fused with fresh traditional and criollo flavors in an elegant space with wood floors and a long bar. **Known for:** beautiful building; reasonable prices; attentive service. *Average main: S/37 Plaza de Armas, Lima 635 051/363–182 mojsarestaurant.com.*

Pacha Restaurant & Draft Bar

$ | **PERUVIAN** | Right next to Puno's Catedral, this Novo Andino restaurant pairs good food and a social atmosphere with a selection of Peruvian craft and imported Belgian beers, some of the strongest in the world. The cuy, trucha, alpaca, and cebiche dishes are all tasty and well-presented; there's a good-value tourist menu; and the local, award-winning *tunki* coffee, bittersweet and strong, is the cherry on top. **Known for:** craft beers; social atmosphere; locally roasted tunki coffee. *Average main: S/30 Puno 521 51/941–447–264 www.facebook.com/PachitaGourmet.*

Restaurant Museo La Casona

$ | **PERUVIAN** | An upscale modern restaurant but with colonial-era artwork and antiques throughout, this two-decades-old local institution is filled with savory aromas of flavorful soups and grilled meats and fish. Try local fare, such as the *lomo de alpaca* (alpaca steak) or their take on quinoa soup, a must-try dish wherever you go in Peru. **Known for:** tasty local fare; ample portions; reasonable prices. *Average main: S/30 Av. Lima 423 051/351–108 www.lacasona-restaurant.com.*

Hotels

Puno can be cold at night, so bring warm clothes. The fanciest hotels have central heating systems, but most others have portable electric heaters in the rooms. Air-conditioning is unheard of here outside of the five-star lodgings, but you probably won't want it anyway. Always check heating options when you book, and make sure there are extra blankets on hand when you check in. As Puno has few notable attractions, there is less of a need to stay in town as in other Peruvian cities. The best upscale hotels are outside town on the lakeshore—a peaceful setting that affords lovely water views. Bear in mind, the only convenient restaurants will be those located in the hotels, with the city a taxi ride away.

Casa Andina Premium Puno

$$ | **HOTEL** | Out of the two Casa Andina properties in Puno (the other is a less expensive Casa Andina Standard property), this pricier lakeside hotel is the best, offering comfortable rooms with great natural light and all the modern amenities you need. **Pros:** lakeside views; good restaurant; private dock is convenient for Lake Titicaca tours. **Cons:** decor is minimalist; rooms are small; a distance

from town. $ *Rooms from: S/457* ✉ *Av. Sesquicentenario 1970–72, Sector Huaje* ☎ *051/363–992* 🌐 *www.casa-andina.com* 🛏 *45 rooms* 🍴 *Free breakfast.*

Casa Andina Standard Puno

$ | **HOTEL** | With basic but comfortable rooms and the great service associated with the Casa Andina chain, this standard-level hotel is also centrally located, making it easy to head out for a tour by day or for dinner in the evening. **Pros:** centrally located; clean and comfortable rooms; reliable chain service. **Cons:** lacks atmosphere; basic; no elevator. $ *Rooms from: S/248* ✉ *Jr. Independencia 143* ☎ *051/367–803* 🌐 *www.casa-andina.com* 🛏 *50 rooms* 🍴 *Free breakfast.*

GHL Hotel Lago Titicaca Puno

$$ | **RESORT** | Although it may look a little institutional from the outside, inside this low-rise hotel, which functions more like a resort, is the most luxurious stay close to the city—just 5 km (3 miles) away on Isla Esteves, an island in Lake Titicaca that's connected to the mainland by a causeway. **Pros:** lakeside views; most comfortable rooms in the Puno area; upscale restaurant and oxygen room on-site. **Cons:** 10 minutes from town; some windows don't open; some bathroom are small. $ *Rooms from: S/409* ✉ *Isla Esteves* ☎ *051/367–780, 051/367–780* 🌐 *www.ghllagotiticaca.com/en* 🛏 *123 rooms* 🍴 *Free breakfast.*

Hotel Hacienda Plaza de Armas

$ | **HOTEL** | At the most centrally located of all Puno hotels, right in the Plaza de Armas, all the rooms are comfortable and have modern bathrooms with tubs; some rooms also have balconies and Jacuzzis. **Pros:** central location; colonial features; modern and comfortable rooms. **Cons:** not all rooms have a view; central location brings noise; some rooms could do with updates. $ *Rooms from: S/208* ✉ *Plaza de Armas, Jr. Puno 419* ☎ *051/367–340* 🌐 *www.hhp.com.pe* 🛏 *30 rooms* 🍴 *Free breakfast.*

Hotel Hacienda Puno

$ | **HOTEL** | Panoramic views of Lake Titicaca and its surroundings can be viewed from the endless windows that line the restaurant atop this Spanish-colonial hotel with an old-world feel, and some of the rooms share the view. **Pros:** two blocks from Plaza de Armas; colonial common areas; great views. **Cons:** simple design; soom rooms do not have views; no frills. $ *Rooms from: S/199* ✉ *Deustua 297* ☎ *051/365–134* 🌐 *www.hhp.com.pe* 🛏 *64 rooms* 🍴 *Free breakfast.*

Intiqa Hotel

$ | **HOTEL** | The comfortable rooms here are modern, but the hotel is also full of local flavor, thanks to plenty of indigenous art and artifacts. **Pros:** modern rooms and bathrooms; historic touches; central location. **Cons:** some rooms can be noisy; water pressure and temperature can be inconsistent; compact public spaces. $ *Rooms from: S/203* ✉ *Tarapacá 272* ☎ *051/366–900* 🌐 *www.intiqa-hotel.com* 🛏 *24 rooms* 🍴 *Breakfast.*

★ Isla Suasi

$$$ | **RESORT** | **FAMILY** | An ecological paradise for those who can afford it, this exclusive hotel is on Isla Suasi, on a remote end of Lake Titicaca (a 5½-hour boat ride from Puno, including a stop at Uruos). **Pros:** gorgeous and tranquil setting; lots of activities; private cottage with butler who lights inroom stove every night. **Cons:** remote so you will want to stay at least two nights; no TVs in rooms may bother some; no outlets in rooms. $ *Rooms from: S/770* ✉ *Isla Suasi* ☎ *051/351–102* 🌐 *www.islasuasi.pe* 🛏 *23 rooms* 🍴 *All-inclusive.*

Qelqatani

$ | **HOTEL** | On a quiet street about a five-minute walk from Jirón Lima, this is an affordable, cozy place to lay your head after a day on the lake, with basic but clean and comfortable rooms. **Pros:** great value for your money; centrally located; great staff. **Cons:** interior is dark at night; older building; no frills. $ *Rooms from:*

S/177 ✉ *Tarapacá 355* ☎ *051/351–470* 🌐 *www.qelqatani.com* 🛏 *42 rooms* 🍽 *Free breakfast.*

Sonesta Posadas del Inca

$$ | **HOTEL** | Weavings, polished wood, and indigenous art lend character to this thoroughly modern hotel, one of Puno's original upscale options, on the shores of Lake Titicaca. **Pros:** on the lake with outdoor seating; good heating; comfortable beds. **Cons:** five minutes from town; breakfast timing not great for tours; area is really busy. 💲 *Rooms from: S/406* ✉ *Sesquicentenario 610, Sector Huaje* ☎ *051/364–111* 🌐 *www.sonesta.com/sonestaposadas* 🛏 *70 rooms* 🍽 *Free breakfast.*

Tierra Viva Puno Plaza

$ | **HOTEL** | A great base for tours, this modern hotel has comfortable rooms with orthopedic beds, heating, and indigenous weavings that inject color and local flair. **Pros:** centrally located; comfortable beds; local crafts. **Cons:** fairly simple design; close to plaza so can be noisy; breakfast buffet is unexceptional. 💲 *Rooms from: S/199* ✉ *Cl. Grau 270* ☎ *051/368–005* 🌐 *tierravivahoteles.com/peru/puno* 🛏 *30 rooms* 🍽 *Free breakfast.*

★ Titilaka

$$$$ | **RESORT** | **FAMILY** | Part of the luxe Relais & Châteaux brand, this is the best hotel on the lake, period—a stylish all-inclusive ecotourism resort with contemporary flair and an off-the-beaten-path location. **Pros:** all-inclusive with gourmet restaurant; luxurious rooms with heated floors; lake views. **Cons:** may be too secluded for some; excursions are all shared with other guests unless you pick a private program; menu lacks variety for longer stays. 💲 *Rooms from: S/3006* ✉ *Huenccalla, Peninsula Titilaka* ☎ *017/005–100, 051/17–005–111* 🌐 *www.titilaka.com* 🛏 *18 rooms* 🍽 *All-inclusive.*

Nightlife

Dozens of small bars and lounges are packed in on Jirón Lima, often one flight up from the street. That said, many establishments are dated in style and music, so you're better off enjoying an evening drink at your hotel or a craft beer at the café-bar in the Casa del Corregidor.

Pacha Mixology

BARS/PUBS | The only molecular bar in Puno is a central spot for a mean cocktail. The pisco sours are recommended. What you can't miss, however, happens on the third floor, where sister bar Mixology of Pisco has a pool table, rock music, and tall stools around a circular bar. That's where the house mixologists shuffle spirits in test tubes and alembics, preparing your drinks with a unique kind of magic. ✉ *Lima 370* ☎ *051/363–630* 🌐 *www.facebook.com/pachitamolecular.*

Pub Ekeko's

BARS/PUBS | This lively pub-cum-discotheque may not be stellar in terms of either music or presentation, but it's a popular place for locals to have a drink and strut their stuff. It's also the go-to spot in town for televised soccer. When there are no games on, there's music and dancing. The quiet downstairs venue serves wood-fired pizza and other hearty fare. ✉ *Lima 365* ☎ *051/365–986.*

Shopping

La Casona Parodi

CLOTHING | In this colonial building, a few small, high-end shops sell alpaca sweaters, jewelry, and handicrafts. ✉ *Jr. Lima 394.*

Mercado Artesanal

CRAFTS | Model reed boats, small stone carvings, and alpaca-wool articles are among the local crafts sold near the Port at Puno's Mercado Artesanal. If you find you aren't equipped for Puno's chilly evenings, it's the place to buy inexpensive woolen goods, though the cheaper they are, the more likely they are a synthetic blend (which will still keep you warm). Make sure you know where your wallet or purse is while you're snapping a photo of this colorful market, which is open 8–6. ✉ *Av. Simon Bolivar and Jr. El Puerto.*

Mercado Central

OUTDOOR/FLEA/GREEN MARKETS | If you're looking for some fresh produce, Andean cheeses, flowers, or bulk food, stroll through the Mercado Central. Keep a close guard on your belongings. ✉ *Jr. Tacna between Jr. F. Arbulu and Jr. Oquendo.*

Lake Titicaca

Forms Puno's eastern shoreline.

Stunning, unpredictable, and enormous, Lake Titicaca is a world of unique flora, fauna, cultures, and geology. Lago Titicaca, which means "lake of the gray (*titi*) puma (*caca*)" in Quechua, borders Peru and Bolivia, with Peru's largest portion to the northwest. Although Peru boasts the largest port in Puno (57% of the lake is in Peru), Bolivia's side has Isla del Sol and Isla de la Luna, two beautiful islands with great views and Inca ruins. The lake itself is larger than Puerto Rico, with an average depth of 7.5 meters (25 feet) and a minimum temperature of 38°F. Lake Titicaca gains 1.5 meters (5 feet) of water in summer (rainy season) and loses it again in winter (dry season).

The Bahía de Puno, separated from the lake proper by the two jutting peninsulas of Capaschica and Chucuito, is home to the descendants of the Uro people, who are now mixed with the Aymara and Quechua. The lakeshores are lush with totora reeds—valuable as building material, cattle fodder, and, in times of famine, food for humans.

Although it's generally cold, the beaming sun keeps you warm and, if you don't slather on sunscreen, burned.

GETTING HERE AND AROUND

A boat is necessary for traveling the lake. Most people go to the islands with a tour, but colectivo boats in Puno Bay (and Copacabana on the Bolivian side) will transport you for S/30–S/45. Most boats are super slow and super old, and they won't leave port unless at least 10 people are smooshed aboard. A four-hour trip will take only an hour in one of the newer speedboats that the higher-end tour companies now use.

ESSENTIALS

TOURS OF LAKE TITICACA

Excursions to any of the islands on Lake Titicaca, including the floating islands of the Uros, can be arranged through tour agencies in Puno. Most tours depart between 7:30 and 9 am, as the lake can become choppy in the afternoon. For Amantani and Taquile, you also can take the shared local boat at the Puno dock. Two daily departures go to Taquile at 7:30 am (S/25 round trip) and to Amanatani at 8:20 am (S/30 round trip), while boats for the Uros Islands leave from 6 am to 4:30 pm (S/10 round trip) as soon as they fill up with at least ten passengers. Since tours cost about S/30–45 per person and include English-speaking guides, taking these slow boats is only useful if you want to spend more time on any of the islands.

All Ways Travel

GUIDED TOURS | In addition to kayaking trips and standard tours to the floating islands and Sillustani, All Ways Travel offers specialty cultural trips to rural communities on the lake and elsewhere in the Puno region. It's a true, socially responsible operator that also invests in ways to help improve the lives of the people in these communities, such as creating libraries. ✉ *Casa del Corregidor, Jr. Deustua 576, 2nd fl., Puno* ☎ *051/775–328* 🌐 *www.titicacaperu.com* 🎫 *From S/170.*

Edgar Adventures

GUIDED TOURS | Since 1996, Edgar Adventures has specialized in upscale and adventure trips around the region include standard tours to the Uros, Taquile and Amantani Islands, and multiday kayaking trips on Lake Titicaca. ✉ *Jr. Lima 328, Puno* ☎ *051/353–444* 🌐 *www.edgaradventures.com* 🎫 *From S/90.*

Row Peru

ADVENTURE TOURS | Row Peru features a unique way to enjoy the beauty of Lake Titicaca—by paddling outrigger canoes. Rowing allows you to enjoy your surroundings while having a low impact on the environment. You can choose from such options as sunrise paddles, nature paddles, afternoon visits to the floating islands of Uros, or multiday tours. No prior experience is necessary. ✉ *Hotel Libertador Jetty, Esteves Island, Puno* ☎ *992/755–067* 🌐 *www.rowperu.com* 🎫 *From S/117.*

Sights

★ Amantani Island

ISLAND | This island has a small set of pre-Inca ruins that are a highlight of a visit here, along with the experience of the traditional life of its mainly agrarian society. Although it's dusty and brown and not as pretty as Taquile, Amantani is renowned for its homestay programs that bring in boatloads of visitors each day, giving some, albeit touristic, insight into the life of the people here. Facilities and food are basic but cozy. Every tour operator in Puno runs overnight trips here, usually combined with a stop on the Uros Islands and Taquile. Most of the younger generations here speak Spanish and even a smidgen of English, but the older generation speaks only Aymara. Amantani has a population of about 4,500. Sacred fertility rituals are held in its two pre-Inca temples, one of which is dedicated to masculine energy and the other to the feminine. The island is 45 km (28 miles) from Puno and almost three hours away by boat from Taquile.

Anapia and Yuspique Island

ISLAND | In the Winaymarka section of Lake Titicaca, near the Bolivian border, are the Aymara-language islands of Anapia and Yuspique. This off-the-beaten-path, two-day trip can be done with a tour operator or on your own, but, due to logistics, using an operator is probably best. There islands are home to 280 families, very few of whom speak English or even Spanish.

The trip usually begins in Puno, where you board a bus for two hours to the village of Yunguyo, near Punta Hermosa, and then catch a sailboat for a 1½-hour ride to the flat but fertile Anapia. On arrival, hosts meet visitors and guide them back to their family's home for an overnight stay. The day is then spent farming, tending to the animals, or playing with the children. It also includes a hiking trip to the nearby and less populated Yuspique Island, which is home to 100 wild vicuñas. Here, the women cook lunch on the beach, typically, fresh fish with *huatia* (potatoes cooked in a natural clay oven and buried in hot soil with lots of herbs).

After returning to Anapia, you'll experience traditional family life with evening activities such as music or dance. All Ways Travel runs tours, with the proceeds going to the families. You can do this trip on your own for about S/350 by following the itinerary and taking a water colectivo from Punta Hermosa to Anapia. Public transportation to the islands only runs on Thursday and Sunday.

★ Islas Los Uros

ISLAND | Known as the floating islands, Islas los Uros are man-made islands woven together with totora reeds that grow in the lake shallows. Replenished often with layers because the underbelly reeds rot, these tiny islands resemble floating bales of hay and average 3 meters (10 feet) thick. They were

Continued on page 203

THE ISLANDS of Lake Titicaca

According to legend, under orders from their father, the Sun God, the first Inca—Manco Cápac—and his sister—Mama Ocllo rose from the deep blue waters of Lake Titicaca and founded the Inca empire. Watching the mysterious play of light on the water and the shadows on the mountains, you may become a believer of the Inca myth.

Reed Boat Head, Uros

This is the altiplano—the high plains of Peru, where the earth has been raised so close to the sky that the area takes on a luminous quality. Lake Titicaca's sharp, sparkling blue waters may make you think of some place far from the altiplano, perhaps someplace warm. Then its chill will slap you back to reality and you realize that you're at the world's highest navigable lake, 12,500 feet above sea level. The lake's surface covers 8,562 sq km (3340 sq miles) and drops down 282 meters (925 ft) at its deepest.

Most of Lake Titicaca is a National Reserve dedicated to conserving the region's plant and animal life while promoting sustainable use of its resources. The reserve extends from the Bay of Puno to the peninsula of Capachica. It's divided into two sectors: one surrounds the Bay of Puno and protects the resources of the Uros-Chuluni communities; the other, in the Huancané area, preserves the totora-reed water fields and protects the nesting area of more than 60 bird species, including the Titicaca grebe.

DID YOU KNOW?

The floating islands likely date from before the Inca empire. But since the reeds are constantly replenished, they've found a way to remain forever young.

THE FLOATING ISLANDS

Uru woman and totora reeds boat.

ISLAS LOS UROS

Islas Los Uros, known as the Floating Islands, are man-made islands woven together with tótora reeds that grow in the lake shallows. Replenished often with layers because the underbelly reeds rot, these tiny islands resemble floating bails of hay. Walking on them feels like walking on a big waterlogged sponge, but they are sturdy.

VISITING

Trips to the Los Uros typically take 30 minutes. While some travelers marvel at these 62-plus islands, some call them floating souvenir stands. Yes, locals sell trinkets, but visiting the floating islands is a glimpse into one of the region's oldest cultures, the Uros. Now mixed with Aymara culture it's a form of human habitation that evolved over centuries. The closest group of "floating museums" is 7 km (4.35 miles) from Puno.

ISLAND LIFE

The islanders make their living by fishing, trapping birds, and selling visitors well-made miniature reed boats, weavings, and collages depicting island life. You can hire an islander to take you for a ride in a reed boat. Although there's no running water, progress has come to some of the islands in the form of solar-powered energy and telephone stations. Seventh Day Adventists converted the inhabitants of one island and built a church and school.

HOMESTAY TIP

It's tradition for most families not to have visitors help in the kitchen, and on several islands families will not eat with visitors. It's also customary to bring a gift—usually essentials like fruit, dried grains, matches, and candles.

TAQUILE & AMANTANI ISLANDS

Folk dances on Taquile island.

TAQUILE ISLAND

35 km (22 miles) east of Puno in the high altitude sunshine, Taquile's brown dusty landscape contrasts with green terraces, bright flowers, and the surrounding blue waters. Snow-capped Bolivian mountains loom in the distance.

Taquile folk are known for weaving some of Peru's loveliest textiles, and men create textiles as much as the women. Islanders still wear traditional dress and have successfully maintained the cooperative lifestyle of their ancestors. The annual Taquile festival the third week of July is a great time to visit.

Taquile is on a steep hill with curvy long trails, which lead to the main square. There are many ways to reach the top of Taquile where there are Inca and Tiahuanaco ruins—you can climb up the 533 stone steps, or take a longer path.

AMANTANI ISLAND

The island of Amantani is 45 km (28 miles) from Puno and almost three hours away by boat from Taquile. Amantani has pre-Inca ruins, and a larger, mainly agrarian society, whose traditional way of life has been less exposed to the outside world until recently. Not as pretty as Taquile, Amantani is dusty and brown.

Locals were losing population to the mainland before a community-based project helped them dive into the tourist industry and organize homestays. Although the project has been a success, make sure you will be your host's only guests for a more intimate experience.

Most of the younger generations speak Spanish and even a smidgen of English, but the older generation speaks only Aymara. Amantani has a population of about 4,500 Quechua. Sacred fertility rituals are held in its two pre-Inca temples, one of which is dedicated to masculine energy and the other to the feminine.

Amantani woman spinning yarn from wool.

ISLA DEL SOL, BOLIVIA

Adventurous travelers, with a couple days to spare, will want to journey on to Bolivia. After crossing the border, and getting to the pleasant lakeside town of Copacabana (visit the striking Moorish-style cathedral), go on by boat to the Isla del Sol, Lake Titicaca's largest island, where there are tremendous views, Inca ruins, and hotels.

Isla del Sol is the best place to visit and to stay on the lake and is the mythological birthplace of the pre-Inca and Inca. The views of the Cordillera Real mountains are amazing, especially at dawn and dusk, and the island has beautiful white sandy beaches and an extraordinary terraced landscape. Ruins include the Inca palace of Pilkokaina and a strange rock formation said to be the birthplace of the sun and moon, and an excellent Inca trail across the island. Alternatively, you can just laze around and soak up the cosmic energy.

En route to Isla del Sol, boats sometimes stop at **Isla de la Luna**, where the ruins of Iñacuy date back to the Inca conquest. You'll find an ancient convent called Ajlla Wasi (House of the Chosen Women). Stone steps lead up to the unrestored ruins of the convent.

The legends that rise out of Lake Titicaca are no more mysterious than discoveries made in its depths. In 2000 an international diving expedition bumped into what is believed to be a 1,000-year-old pre-Inca temple. The stone structure is 660 feet long and 160 feet wide, with a wall 2,699 feet long. The discovery was made between Copacabana and the Sun and Moon islands.

(pictured top and bottom) Isla del Sol, the Island of the Sun, on Lake Titicaca, Bolivia.

originally created so communities could escape attacks from stronger, more aggressive neighbors. Today they stay in one place. While some travelers marvel at these 40-plus islands, some call them floating souvenir stands. Yes, locals try to sell trinkets insistently, but a visit to the floating islands affords a glimpse at a form of human habitation that has evolved over centuries. It also offers insight into one of the region's oldest cultures, the Uros, which is now mixed with Aymara culture. The closest group of "floating museums" is 7 km (4.35 miles) from Puno.

The islanders make their living by fishing, hunting, cutting reeds, collecting eggs, trapping birds, and selling visitors well-made miniature reed boats and other handicrafts. Virtually every operator offers a stop to the more touristed of these islands as part of their standard lake tour but you can also find trips (or ask your tour operator specifically) to islands less visited where you can get a more intimate look at the culture.

Llachon Peninsula

TRAIL | One of the peninsulas that form the bay of Puno, Llachon juts out on the lake near Amantani and Taquile. **■ TIP→ The land is dry and barren with rows of pre-Inca terraces, and original ancient paths and trails, which are great for exploring.** Locals are more than willing to guide visitors on a light trek to Cerro Auki Carus. Here a circular temple remains the sacred place for villagers to honor the Pachamama (Mother Earth). As the highest point on the peninsula, Cerro Auki Carus serves as an excellent viewpoint to admire the splendor of Lake Titicaca. You can venture out yourself from the port in Puno via water colectivo and then arrange a homestay once in Llachon, or for slightly more money, you can have a tour operator arrange the accommodations for you. By land back from Puno it's about two to three hours. Llachon is also a great place to kayak. Cusco-based Explorandes as well as Edgar Adventures offer kayak excursions around here.

★ Taquile Island

ISLAND | East of Puno in the high-altitude sunshine, Taquile's brown, dusty landscape contrasts with green terraces, bright flowers, and the surrounding blue waters. Snowcapped Bolivian mountains loom in the distance.

Taquile folk, both men and women, are known for weaving some of Peru's loveliest textiles, a UNESCO Intangible Heritage. Islanders still wear traditional dress and have successfully maintained the cooperative lifestyle of their ancestors. The most important piece in Taquile's obligatory knitted "uniform" is the chullo. This large, floppy hat is worn high on the head and indicates a man's social status: if it's red-and-white, he is single; if it's red/pink, he's married. Here, weaving is also often the basis of social relations. For example, if a man wants to marry, he most show that he can make his own chullo.

Taquile's steep hill has long, curvy trails leading to the main square, where islanders often perform local dances for tourists. There are many ways to reach the top of Taquile, where there are Inca and Tiahuanaco ruins. The most popular way is to climb the 533 stone steps, though if you want to avoid an arduous walk, some tours will take you to the other side, thus avoiding the steps. The island is 35 km (22 miles) from Puno, and the trip takes about four hours in a slow boat and two hours on a speedboat each way with no transportation on land once you arrive. There are a few shops and small restaurants, as well as an excellent textile store. Overnight stays are primarily based in local homes, and most tours include lunch with a local family. Note that the annual Taquile festival the third week of July is a great time to visit.

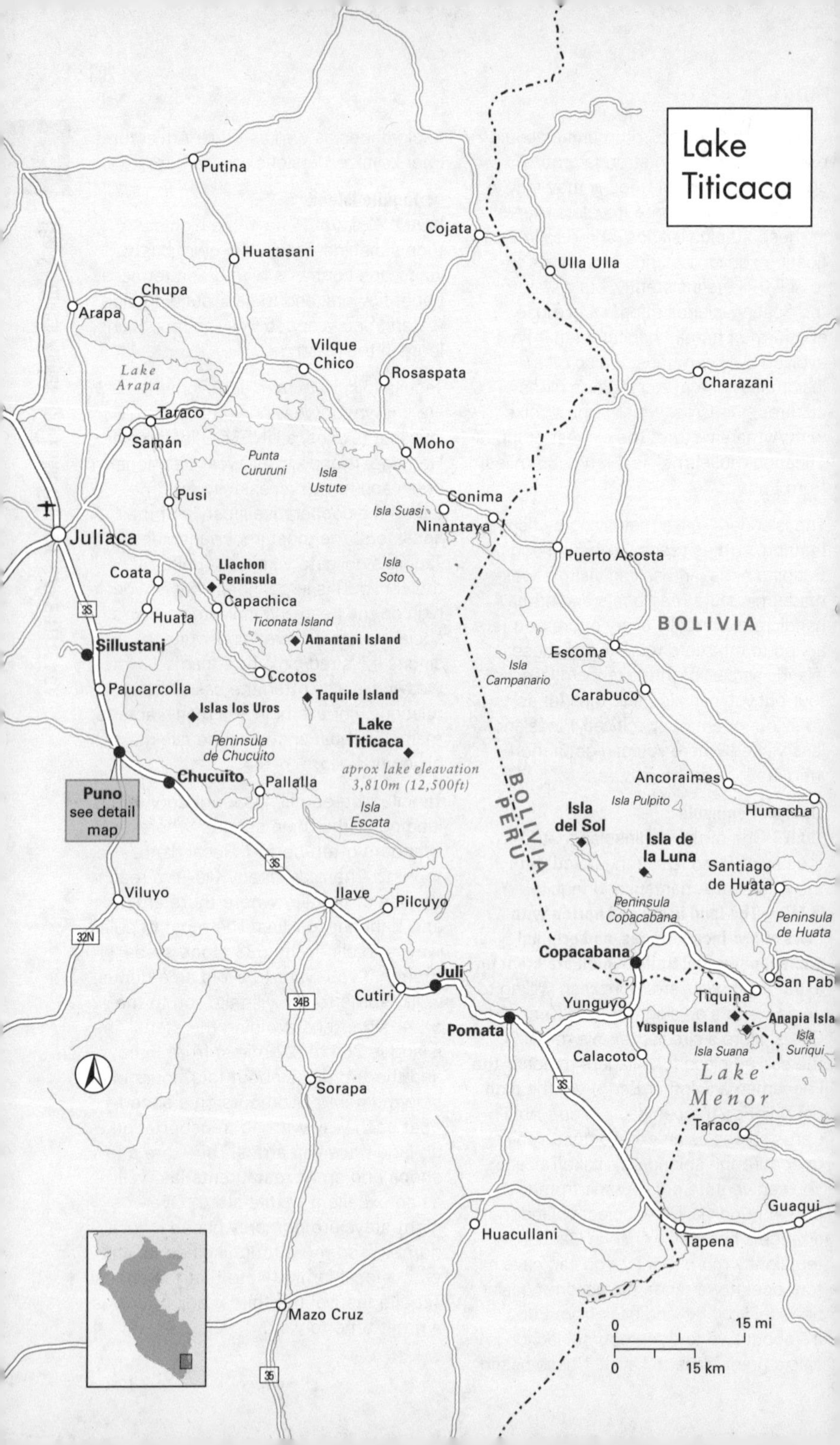

Lake Titicaca
Putina
Cojata
Huatasani
Ulla Ulla
Chupa
Arapa
Lake Arapa
Vilque Chico
Rosaspata
Charazani
Taraco
Samán
Moho
Punta Cururuni
Isla Ustute
Pusi
Conima
Isla Suasi
Ninantaya
Juliaca
Puerto Acosta
Coata
Llachon Peninsula
Isla Soto
Capachica
Huata
Ticonata Island
BOLIVIA
Amantani Island
Sillustani
Escoma
Isla Campanario
Ccotos
Paucarcolla
Carabuco
Taquile Island
Islas los Uros
Lake Titicaca
Peninsula de Chucuito
aprox lake eleavation 3,810m (12,500ft)
Chucuito
Pallalla
Ancoraimes
Isla Pulpito
Humacha
Puno see detail map
BOLIVIA
PERU
Isla Escata
Isla del Sol
Isla de la Luna
Santiago de Huata
Viluyo
Ilave
Pilcuyo
Peninsula Copacabana
Peninsula de Huata
Copacabana
Juli
San Pab
Cutiri
Tiquina
Yunguyo
Pomata
Yuspique Island
Anapia Isla
Isla Suana
Isla Suriqui
Calacoto
Lake Menor
Sorapa
Taraco
Guaqui
Huacullani
Tapena
Mazo Cruz
0
15 mi
0
15 km
3S
32N
34B
35

Sillustani

30 km (19 miles) northwest of Puno.

Looking out over Lake Umayo, a small body of water just off the main lake northwest of Puno on the way to Juliaca, these magnificent stone burial towers are one of the main attractions on Lake Titicaca. The oldest date back more than 1,100 years, well before the Incas. Restaurants, locals selling textiles and souvenirs, a museum, and bathrooms are located near the site.

GETTING HERE AND AROUND

There is little to no public transportation to the archaeological site, so unless you have your own vehicle, opt for a half-day trip here, offered by every tour operator in Puno for about S/50–S/60.

Sights

Sillustani

ARCHAEOLOGICAL SITE | High on a hauntingly beautiful peninsula in Lake Umayo is the necropolis of Sillustani, where 28 stone burial towers represent a city of the dead that both predated and coincided with the Inca empire. The proper name for a tower is *ayawasi* (home of the dead), but they're generally referred to as *chullpas*, which are actually the shrouds used to cover the mummies inside. This was the land of the Aymara-speaking Colla people, and the precision of their masonry rivals that of the Inca. Sillustani's mystique is heightened by the view it provides over Lake Umayo and its mesa-shaped island, El Sombrero, as well as by the utter silence that prevails, broken only by the wind over the water and the cries of lake birds.

Most of the chullpas date from the 14th and 15th centuries, but some were erected as early as AD 900. The tallest, known as the Lizard because of a carving on one of its massive stones, has a circumference of 8.5 meters (28 feet). An unusual architectural aspect of the chullpas is that the circumference is smaller at the bottom than the top. To fully appreciate Sillustani, it's necessary to make the long climb to the top; fortunately, the steps are wide, and it's an easy climb. Some schoolchildren will put on dances. If you take photos of mothers and children and pet alpacas, a donation of a few soles will be appreciated.

Totora Reeds

The totora reeds of Islas los Uros are 70% chloride and 30% iodine and calcium. Once the reed is pulled from its root, the white base known as *chullo* is often eaten for its iodine or wrapped around wounds to relieve pain. It can also serve as a natural "cooling pack" by splitting it open and placing it on the forehead. Uros commonly use it to brew reed-flower tea, and in desperate times it can be eaten as food. It's also used to cure hangovers.

Chucuito

20 km (12 miles) southeast of Puno.

Chucuito (in Aymara: *Choque-Huito,* Mountain of Gold) is the first of several small towns that dot the lake as you travel from Puno into Bolivia. If you aren't interested in architecture and colonial churches, or don't care to see another undeveloped Peruvian town, then chances are you won't enjoy these communities. Having said that, Chucuito, surrounded by hillsides crisscrossed with agricultural terraces, has one novelty you won't find elsewhere—its Temple of Fertility, or Templo de Inca Uyu.

Indeed, the temple is the most interesting thing to see in Chucuito, which is almost a ghost town. The main plaza has a large stone Inca sundial as its centerpiece, and there are two Renaissance-style 16th-century churches, **La Asunción** alongside the plaza and **Santo Domingo** on the east side of town. Neither one has been maintained, but both are open for services.

GETTING HERE AND AROUND

You'll need your own vehicle to get here, but once here, your feet are all you'll need. For a more enjoyable way of taking in the sights, there are afternoon horseback-riding tours offered by the **Posada de Santa Barbera** (*www.facebook.com/hotelposadasantabarbara*) where you can also spend the night.

Sights

Templo de Inca Uyu

RELIGIOUS SITE | Better known as the Temple of Fertility or Temple of the Phallus, this structure doesn't quite meet the dictionary's description of a temple as a stately edifice. Rather, it's an outdoor area surrounded by a pre-Inca and Inca-made stone walls that block the view of a "garden" of anatomically correct phallic stone sculptures. Each 1-meter (3-foot) penis statue points toward the sky at the Inca sun god or toward the ground at Pachamama (Mother Earth). From ancient times through today, this site has been visited by women who sit for hours on the little statues believing that doing so will increase their fertility. Hours are sporadic, so you may need to ask around for the caretaker to get in. *Chucuito* *S/5.*

Hotels

Taypikala Hotel & Spa

$ | **HOTEL** | This hotel, which is surprisingly modern given the remote location, has rooms that are as comfortable and up-to-date as you can find in the city. **Pros:** views of the lake; modern rooms; indoor pool and sauna. **Cons:** remote location; far from the harbor where tour boats are located; not all rooms have spa baths. *Rooms from: S/231* *Cl. Sandia* *051/792-252* *www.taypikala.com* *77 rooms* *Free breakfast.*

Juli

On Lake Titicaca, 84 km (52 miles) southeast of Puno.

At one time, this village may have been an important Aymara religious center, and it has served as a Jesuit training center for missionaries from Paraguay and Bolivia. Juli has been called "Little Roma" because of its disproportionate number of churches. Four interesting churches in various stages of restoration are San Pedro Mártir, Santa Cruz de Jerusalén, Asunción, and San Juan de Letrán. The latter has 80 paintings from the Cusco School and huge windows worked in stone. Juli has a Saturday-morning market in the main square. It's not a handicrafts market, but rather a produce and animal market where the barter system is in full effect, and the trade of animals is interesting to watch. It starts at 9 am and is over by noon.

GETTING HERE AND AROUND

You'll need your own vehicle to get here, and the drive from Puno to Juli takes about 1½ hours.

Pomata

108 km (67 miles) southeast of Puno.

This small village on the lake on the way to Copacabana and the Bolivian border is worth a quick stop to visit the spectacular church on the main plaza and enjoy the beautiful views.

GETTING HERE AND AROUND

You will need your own transportation to get here.

A boat sails across Lake Titicaca, on the border between Bolivia and Peru.

Sights

Santiago Apóstol de Nuestra Señora del Rosario

RELIGIOUS SITE | The main attraction in the small lakeside town of Pomata is this church, built of pink granite in the 18th century and containing paintings from the Cusco School and the Flemish School. Its Mestizo-baroque carvings and translucent alabaster windows are spectacular, and the altars are covered in gold leaf. Pomata is also famous for fine pottery, especially for its *toritos de Pucará* (bull figures). ✉ *Pomata*.

The Bolivian Side of Lake Titicaca

You'll hear much talk about crossing Lake Titicaca from Peru to Bolivia via hydrofoil or catamaran. At this time, however, you cannot go completely across without stopping at the border and walking from Peru into Bolivia or vice versa. **■ TIP→ You can still use hydrofoils (only through Crillón Tours) and catamarans in your journey to Bolivia's side of the lake from Copacabana on the Bolivian side, then on to the Sun and Moon Islands for an overnight or two on Sun Island.**

CROSSING THE BORDER

Since December 2019, U.S. citizens and most other nationalities do not need to obtain a visa to travel to Bolivia, and hopping across to the other side of Lake Titicaca has become easier than ever. A yellow fever vaccination certificate (approximately USD$150 in the United States, valid for 10 years) is sometimes required to show upon entry, though proof is not always requested unless you intend traveling to the Bolivian side of the Amazon. The vaccine must be taken at least 10 days before exposure.

If you're taking a bus from Puno, two hours into the ride the bus will stop just after Yunguyo for border-crossing procedures. Most higher-end bus services hand you immigration forms on the bus. As you leave Peru, you'll get off to get an exit stamp from Peruvian immigration, and then walk through to the small Bolivian immigration building, where you get an entrance stamp for a maximum stay of 90 days. From there, you catch up with your bus, which will be waiting for you. Keep all immigration documents and your passport safe; you may need these when leaving Bolivia. The border closes at 6 pm daily.

Those entering from Peru generally overnight in Copacabana, which provides easy access to the lake and the surrounding countryside. Buses from Puno to Copacabana are available through any operator or by going directly to the Puno Bus Terminal where there are several companies offering this route. Buses cost around S/30 and depart from the Puno Bus Terminal at 7 and 7:30 am and 2 pm daily. Many buses continue on to La Paz and don't include the 15-minute boat crossing (S/2) over the scenic Tiquina Strait, where you'll have to alight from the bus. Don't forget to carry your luggage with you. Your bus will be waiting for you on the other shore.

GETTING AROUND

The border-crossing tours have packages from USD$150 to USD$400. Reputable agencies include Crillón Tours and Transturin Ltd. Based in Bolivia, tours go from Puno to La Paz and vice versa. Both include pickup from your hotel in Puno and transfer by first-class bus to the border in Yunguyo (a three-hour drive). After crossing the border, you take a bus to Copacabana, a funky beach town (30 minutes). The most expensive and comfortable way to get to Isla del Sol and Isla de la Luna is by Crillón Tours hydrofoil from the Inca Utama Hotel, but cheaper boats leave from Copacabana at 8:30 and 1:30 daily. The journey takes about two hours and costs (B)25. Once you are on the island, it's walking all the way, unless a mule has been organized through your hotel ahead of time. The tourist office, on the northern side of Isla del Sol, offers private guides for (B)100 or (B)10 per person when booking groups of 10 or more.

TOUR OPERATORS

Crillón Tours

GUIDED TOURS | The largest and most respected tour operator on the Bolivian side of Lake Titicaca, Crillón Tours offers every sort of trip imaginable between La Paz and Copacabana and can work with most budgets. They operate hydrofoil and boat transfers between Puno in Peru and the islands and own the best hotel on the Isla del Sol, which you can only stay at through their packages. So if you want to stay on the island, it's a good idea to get a quote from Crillón. ✉ *Av. Camacho 1223, La Paz* ☎ *122/337–533 in Bolivia* 🌐 *crillontours.travel.*

Transturin

GUIDED TOURS | Titicaca catamaran trips, with stops at the Isla del Sol and other attractions, are the main offering of Transturin. ✉ *Achumani Cl. 6, No. 100, La Paz* ☎ *122/422–222 in Bolivia, 786/735–5833 from U.S.* 🌐 *www.transturin.com* 🎫 *From (Bs)700.*

Hotels

Inca Utama Hotel & Spa

$$$ | **HOTEL** | The location may be too remote for those not traveling on Crillón Tours' hydrofoils, which make their harbor here, but this hotel offers a place to lodge that's more tranquil than many of the properties right in Copacabana. **Pros:** lakeside location; observatory with powerful telescope; hydrofoil transportation. **Cons:** remote location; rooms can be cold, even with heaters; spa is basic. $ *Rooms from: (B)410* ✉ *86 Carretera Asfaltada, Huatajata* ✥ *Km 80, off hwy. from La Paz to Copacabana* ☎ *122/337–533* 🌐 *crillontours.com/index.php/en/our-infrastructure-2/inca-utama-hotel-spa* *67 rooms* 🍽 *Free breakfast.*

Copacabana, Bolivia

79 km (49 miles) from Huatajata.

A pleasant, if touristy, town, Copacabana provides easy access to the lake, the islands, and the surrounding countryside. It is also a major pilgrimage destination for devout Bolivians at Easter—and lost South American hippies all year. A highlight is watching the sunset over the water from the Stations of the Cross, the highest point of Copacabana.

GETTING HERE AND AROUND

Several companies have buses departing from the main terminal in Puno around 7 am and 2 pm for around S/30; the ride takes about 3½ to 4 hours. Buses returning to Puno (Bs 30) leave Copacabana around 7:30 am and 1:30 pm, as well as later in the afternoon at 5 pm, and take three hours. It's theoretically possible to drive a rental car from Puno to Copacabana, but passing through Bolivian customs, even if you have all of your paperwork in order, can be a time-consuming hassle. It's easier just to go with public transportation, as a car isn't really needed once you reach Copacabana. In the town's main plaza, the tourist booth is the place to find information about the area.

ESSENTIALS

Virtually everything you need to find in Copacabana, be it a bank, an Internet café, or a restaurant, you will likely find either on the Plaza 2 de Febrero or on the main street that heads down to the pier, Avenida 6 de Agosto. The town is so small and the street numbers so problematic, you'll save time walking around those two areas, rather than trying to wander and find something.

POLICE Police. ✉ *Av. Nossa Sra* ☎ *02/222–5016,.*

POST OFFICE Copacabana Post Office. ✉ *206 Del Monte Place.*

VISITOR INFORMATION Centro de Informacion Turistica. ✉ *Av. 16 de Julio.*

Sights

Cerro Calvario

MEMORIAL | Marking the highest point of Copacabana are the Stations of the Cross, built in the 1950s for the thousands of pilgrims who summit the hill for prayer and penance on Good Friday. For many tourists, these stone monuments serve as the ideal spot to admire the city and watch the sunset. ✉ *Cl. Destacamento 211.*

Copacabana Cathedral

RELIGIOUS SITE | The town's breathtaking Moorish-style cathedral, built between 1610 and 1619 and formerly known as the Basilica of Our Lady of Copacabana, is where you'll find the striking sculpture of the Virgin of Copacabana. There was no choice but to build the church, because the statue, carved by Francisco Yupanqui in 1592, was already drawing pilgrims in search of miracles. If you see decorated cars lined up in front of the cathedral, the owners are waiting to have them blessed for safe travel. Walk around to a side door on the left and light a candle for those you wish to remember, then admire the gaudy glitter and wealth of the church interior itself. Throngs of young Paceños do the three-day walk to Copacabana from La Paz to pay homage to the statue with a candlelight procession on Good Friday. You can combine your visit with the semiscramble up past Cerro Calvario (Calvary Hill) on the point above the town. If the climb doesn't knock you out, the view will. ✉ *Copacabana.*

Horca del Inca

RELIGIOUS SITE | Dating from the 14th century BC, this structure in the southeast part of the city was originally built by the pre-Inca Chiripa culture as an astronomical observatory. Four of the seven horizontal rock slabs were later destroyed by the Spanish who believed gold was hidden inside. The remains of the ruins show signs of vandalism, yet still warrant a visit for those wanting to blend culture and exercise. The slope is steep and rather challenging, but the view of Lake Titicaca will help alleviate the pain. ✉ *Copacabana* ✣ *End of Cl. Murillo* 🎫 *(Bs)15.*

Restaurants

Copacabana has a wide array of hotels, hostels, international cafés, and bars and pizza joints, which reflects its popularity as a weekend destination from La Paz and as the crossing point for travelers from Peru. There's a lot of competition, but most places offer the same dishes, none of which are prepared in a particularly memorable—or recommendable—way. The best thing to do for lunch or dinner is wander along Avenida 6 de Agosto and window-shop first. The market has tasty, inexpensive coffee, fruit juices, and sandwiches for breakfast, and different choices of *completo* (a super-cheap, S/5, set menu that includes soup, a main dish, and a drink) until 6 pm. You can find the famous trout dishes everywhere.

Gourmet ALI

$$ | **PERUVIAN** | Set inside the inner courtyard of Hostal Sofía, this Peruvian fusion restaurant, with tables that spill out onto the marbled tiles up front, has somewhat of a comforting Middle Eastern feel. Not luxurious by any means, it's still one of the town's best midrange options—one where you can escape the backpacker hordes for a quiet meal. **Known for:** trout lasagna; more relaxing ambience than most; varied menu. $ *Average main: (B)60* ✉ *6 de Agosto* ✣ *Inside Hostal Sofia's main hall* ☎ *591/730–007–4.*

La Orilla

$$ | **CONTEMPORARY** | Touted by many as the best in town, this maritime-themed restaurant with a terrace puts a creative spin on trout dishes, including spinach-and-bacon or Tex-Mex versions. Although it makes those ubiquitous pizzas, you can take a break from the usual fare with Andean falafel dishes, curries, or crepes. **Known for:** vegetarian-friendly menu; Tex-Mex choices; falafel. $ *Average main: (B)60* ✉ *6 de Agosto* ☎ *591/2–862–226–7.*

Pan America

$$ | **PIZZA** | It may look like the typical cookie-cutter traveler bistro from the outside, but don't dismiss Pan America, which offers thin-crust pizzas, European-style coffee, and delicious quinoa tiramisu. The homey interiors are decorated with vintage furniture and memorabilia, but it's best to sit at one of the few tables out on the cobbled main square, so you can dine while looking up at the cathedral. **Known for:** thin-crust pizzas; coffee and cakes; all profits fund sustainable projects for the local indigenous peoples. $ *Average main: (B)35* ✉ *Plaza 2 de Febrero* ☎ *591/737–285–86* 🌐 *www.facebook.com/PanAmericaCopacabana.*

Pit Stop

$ | **PIZZA** | Renovated in 2020, this hip vegan bakery packs in travelers who come for the pizzas, focaccias, gluten-free tortillas, empanadas, proper espressos, and filling breakfast platters. Next door, their side business, Baguette About It , prepares yummy sandwiches that mix South American and international flavors—think avocados, mango chutney, and spices—and has a good selection of cocktails and beers. **Known for:** vegan options; traveler friendly; neighboring sister establishment with a good selection of cocktails and beers. $ *Average main: (B)15* ✉ *16 de Julio* ☎ *591/737–417–49.*

★ Trattoria Sapori d'Italia

$$ | **ITALIAN** | Experience real Italian food in a quiet backstreet off Copacabana's main tourist drag. With a very limited menu of pizza, gnocchi, polenta, and tagliatelle and only five rustic wooden tables, Sapori d'Italia attracts with its homey and simple taverna-style setup, warmly furnished to resemble the dining hall of an Italian countryside home. **Known for:** delicious pizzas; intimate and

exclusive setting; homey Italian food. [$] *Average main: (B)50* ✉ *Jaregui 4* ✣ *Next to the main entrance of Hostal Las Olas* ☎ *591/795-416-14* ⊙ *No lunch.*

Hotels

Hostal Las Olas
$$ | **HOTEL** | **FAMILY** | This lovely and eclectic boutique property on a hill with a stunning view of Lake Titicaca's azure-blue waters is one of the best options in town. **Pros:** magical views; unique, spacious rooms; eco-friendly. **Cons:** up a hill; the beds could be more comfortable; breakfast not included. [$] *Rooms from: (B)400* ✉ *Cl. Michel Pérez* ☎ *02/862-2112* 🌐 *www.hostallasolas.com* *8 rooms* *No meals.*

★ **Hotel La Cupula**
$$ | **B&B/INN** | It's worth staying on in Copacabana just to enjoy this hotel's gorgeous views out over the bay and the delicious on-site restaurant (closed for lunch on Tuesdays). **Pros:** excellent value; extra heaters in rooms; beautiful gardens with alpacas. **Cons:** breakfast not included; some rooms lack private bathrooms; not all rooms have views. [$] *Rooms from: (B)297* ✉ *Cl. Michel Pérez 1-3* ☎ *02/862-2029* 🌐 *www.hotelcupula.com* *16 rooms* *No meals.*

Hotel Lago Azul
$$ | **HOTEL** | A surprisingly good value for the prime lakefront location right on the beach and under the Cerro Calvario, this blue-hued hotel may look a bit lackluster from the outside, but it has well-appointed rooms with plush beds and romantic blue-velvet curtains. **Pros:** smack on the lakefront; unobstructed views; great value. **Cons:** the lakefront location can get noisy in the mornings; a bit characterless; bathrooms are on the small side. [$] *Rooms from: (B)300* ✉ *Costanera 13* ☎ *591/286-225-81* 🌐 *www.facebook.com/HotelLagoAzulCopacabana* *20 rooms* *Free breakfast.*

★ **Hotel Rosario Del Lago Titicaca**
$$$ | **HOTEL** | One of the nicest accommodations in Copacabana, this colonial-style hotel is a few blocks from the main plaza. **Pros:** great views of the lake; modern rooms; full amenities. **Cons:** suites can fill up fast; no elevators; limited breakfast options. [$] *Rooms from: (B)415* ✉ *Cl. Rigoberto Paredes and Av. Costanera* ☎ *02/862-2141, 02/245-1341 in La Paz* 🌐 *www.hotelrosario.com* *25 rooms* *Free breakfast.*

Isla del Sol and Isla de la Luna, Bolivia

12 km (7½ miles) north of Copacabana.

One of the most popular trips on Lake Titicaca is to these two mountainous islands a short boat ride from Copacabana. Although most visitors come on a day-trip, others stick around to take advantage of the small, family-run hostels on Isla del Sol and to soak in the timeless atmosphere of the alleged birthplace of the Incas. Considered sacred islands, in local mythology, this is where the god Viracocha emerged from the lake and created the sun and the moon. There are no cars on either island, only steep trails between the ports and villages.

GETTING HERE AND AROUND

The most comfortable—and expensive—way to get here is by hydrofoil from the Inca Utama Hotel in Huatajata (🌐 *incautamahotelhuatajata.com-hotel.com*), but cheaper boats leave from Copacabana at 8:30 am and 1:30 pm and return from Isla del Sol's south port at Yumani at 8:30 am, 1:30 pm, and 4 pm. Most people join the half-day tours (Bs30 round trip) that every tout will offer along the main road to Copacabana's port. These are not bad value as they are cheaper than the local boats and, if catching the 8:30 am departure, allow about five or six hours to explore the island. You can explore on your own or by joining one of the guided tours of the Inca sites (Bs20 extra, payable on the boat).

■ **TIP→ Don't start your day trip to Isla del Sol at 1:30 pm because by the time you'll have reached Yumani, you'll only have one hour left to see a couple of nearby sights.** The journey from Copacabana takes about 90 minutes. Once you are on the island, there is a (Bs)10 entry fee collected by locals, and it's walking all the way, unless a mule has been organized through your hotel ahead of time. The tourist office, on the northern side of Isla del Sol, offers private guides for (Bs)100 or (Bs)10 per person when booking groups of 10 or more.

On Wednesday, Saturday, and Sunday, one daily boat leaves Copacabana at 1:30 pm (Bs35) for the only north port, called Challa Pampa, which sees fewer visitors. Alighting at Challa Pampa and walking to Yumani on the ancient Inca trail that crisscrosses the island was the most popular trip on Isla del Sol. Sadly, due to tribal conflicts related to the uneven distribution of the tourist dollar among the island's ancestral Aymara communities, at the time of research it was still not possible to hike across the island. Check the situation on arrival at Copacabana before deciding to set off. ■ **TIP→ Locals suggest visiting either one of the villages for the time being, even though some travelers have reported making it across without issues.**

TOUR OPERATORS Andes Amazonia. ✉ *Av. 20 de Octubre 2396, Copacabana* ☎ *591/2242–1258* 🌐 *www.andes-amazonia.com.*

VISITOR INFORMATION Red de Turismo Comunitario del Lago Titicaca. ✉ *Av. 6 de Agosto and Av. 16 de Julio, Copacabana* ✣ *Plaza Sucre* ☎ *077/729–9088,* 🌐 *www.titicacaturismo.com.*

Sights

★ Isla del Sol

ARCHAEOLOGICAL SITE | The largest of Lake Titicaca's islands, Isla del Sol is the best place to visit and stay on the lake. The views of the Cordillera Real mountains are amazing, especially at dawn and dusk, and the island has beautiful white sandy beaches and an extraordinary terraced landscape. Ruins include the Inca palace of Pilkokaina and a strange rock formation said to be the birthplace of the sun and moon. Before you set off, check on the situation involving the excellent Inca trail across the island—disagreements between the island's northern and central communities has blocked free crossing as of late. In the past, some travelers would take a boat to the northern community of Challa Pampa and then hike three to four hours to the southern community of Yumani, where most accommodations (and the main "village") can be found. Although rewarding, the island trail lacks shade and few spots sell water along the way. If your goal is to just laze around and soak up the cosmic energy, then be sure to disembark at the southern boat port of Yumani or at Pilkokaina, where most boats make a pit stop on the way, unless you are staying at one of the few hotels on the north side. One of the best beaches on Isla del Sol is located on the north end, directly behind the museum. Regardless of your destination, plan on hiking at least 30 minutes uphill from the boat port. Nearly every property is staggered high on the slope, which means that both altitude and fitness should be taken into consideration. If you stay at Crillón Tours' Posada, they will take you to the pier where the walk is a bit longer but avoids the challenging, steep steps up from the Yumani harbor. ✉ *Copacabana.*

Isla de la Luna
ARCHAEOLOGICAL SITE | En route to Isla del Sol, boats sometimes stop at Isla de la Luna, where the ruins of Iñacuy date back to the Inca conquest. You'll find an ancient convent called Ajlla Wasi (House of the Chosen Women). Stone steps lead up to the unrestored ruins of the convent. ✉ *Copacabana.*

Restaurants

Like it or not, there's more pizza than trout on Isla del Sol. Most resorts have their own restaurants, often with very good views and some international chefs and variety. In Yumani, dining options are simple and always run by local families, but they often have the best views over the ridge, and they dish up pretty decent food. Beyond pizza, almost identical set lunches and dinners cost between (Bs)20 and (Bs)35.

Las Velas
$ | **PIZZA** | Fancy organic vegetarian pizza at 4,010 meters (13,156 feet) up—why not? This candle-lit local home, furnished with just a handful of tables and full of authentic family atmosphere, stands proud and popular on a forested clearing near the top of Cerro Quñuani. **Known for:** long-ish waits for made-from-scratch dishes; Bolivian staples like trout and kingfish; beautiful sunsets. [$] *Average main: (B)50* ✉ *Yumani Village, Isla del Sol* ☎ *591/712–356–16.*

Restaurant Pachamama
$ | **PERUVIAN** | Overlooking a crest on the western side of the lake, this adobe-and-corrugated-iron restaurant has wooden tables facing what is possibly the most beautiful view in Yumani. The usual menu of pizzas, completos, and trout mix well with the scenery and the more-than-adequate cocktails. **Known for:** lake views; hearty set menus; serves breakfast. [$] *Average main: (B)35* ✉ *Yumani Village, Isla del Sol* ☎ *591/7123–9679* 💳 *No credit cards.*

Hotels

You will be amply rewarded for your climb up the steps from the port—the higher you go, the cheaper the hostels, or *posadas.* They are almost all quite basic so, in most cases, you will be trading the bells and whistles of upper-quality hotels for a peaceful retreat with gorgeous views. If you go without a reservation, you'll likely find women or children waiting at Yumani's port to invite you to stay. The north side of the island is more barren but also has attractive options, including a place on the beach itself.

Hostal Jallala
$$ | **B&B/INN** | A bargain price and a location high up on the island's central crest, with a view that encompasses both sides of the coast, make this a very appealing property. **Pros:** unparalleled views; comfortable and spacious rooms for families; great value. **Cons:** high up the central crest of the island; owners live on the premises; no frills. [$] *Rooms from: (B)300* ✉ *Yumani Village, Isla del Sol* ☎ *591/681–654–04* 🌐 *n/a* 🛏 *8 rooms* 🍽 *Free breakfast* 💳 *No credit cards.*

Hostal Phaxsi
$$ | **B&B/INN** | If you don't relish the idea of hauling your luggage up to the village, consider this option in Yumani Port, where several large rooms—housed behind adobe walls and small verandas facing the lake—have pastel color schemes, plush beds, spacious en-suite baths, and air-conditioning. **Pros:** unobstructed lake views; good value; a bit more character than other properties in town. **Cons:** boat and tourist traffic gets noisy in the mid-afternoon; solar-powered showers, so warmer as day goes on. [$] *Rooms from: (B)300* ✉ *Yumani Port, Isla del Sol* ☎ *591/719–580–15* 🌐 *n/a* 🛏 *4 rooms* 🍽 *Free breakfast* 💳 *No credit cards.*

★ La Estancia Ecolodge
$$$ | **B&B/INN** | Staggered on a hillside, each of this property's bungalows is named for a type of flora and has an unobstructed view of Lake Titicaca, making this the perfect place to watch the sunrise. **Pros:** excellent views; great showers; dinners integrate local flavors. **Cons:** expensive for location; meals are at a set time; Wi-Fi is not great. *Rooms from: (B)443 South end, Isla del Sol 591/2244–0989 www.ecolodge-laketiticaca.com 15 rooms Some meals.*

Palla Khasa
$$$ | **HOTEL** | Just steps from Yumani, this well-manicured top property has 14 circular stone bungalows with gas heaters that look like Inca turrets from afar. **Pros:** scenic; within walking distance of other food options; fireplace in the dining hall. **Cons:** an hour uphill from the port; service can be hit or miss; can be cold at night but extra blankets available. *Rooms from: (B)570 Yumani Village, Isla del Sol 591/732–115–85 pallakhasa-lodgeandtours.com 14 bungalows Free breakfast.*

★ Posada del Inca Eco Lodge
$$$$ | **B&B/INN** | Your stay at this lovely posada, what is surely the best lodging on the island, begins with a 30-minute mule ride from the boat dock to the garden-lobby, where fruit trees shade handmade reed couches, and the hillside location offers sweeping lake views. **Pros:** high standard of service; good food; most comfortable rooms on the island. **Cons:** must be booked with more expensive hydrofoil tour; you may have to walk uphill and steps from the port; rooms can be cool but electric blankets are available. *Rooms from: (B)1000 Isla del Sol South end 591/2233–7533 www.facebook.com/posadadelinca 20 rooms Some meals.*

Chapter 6

CUSCO AND THE SACRED VALLEY

Updated by
Maureen Santucci

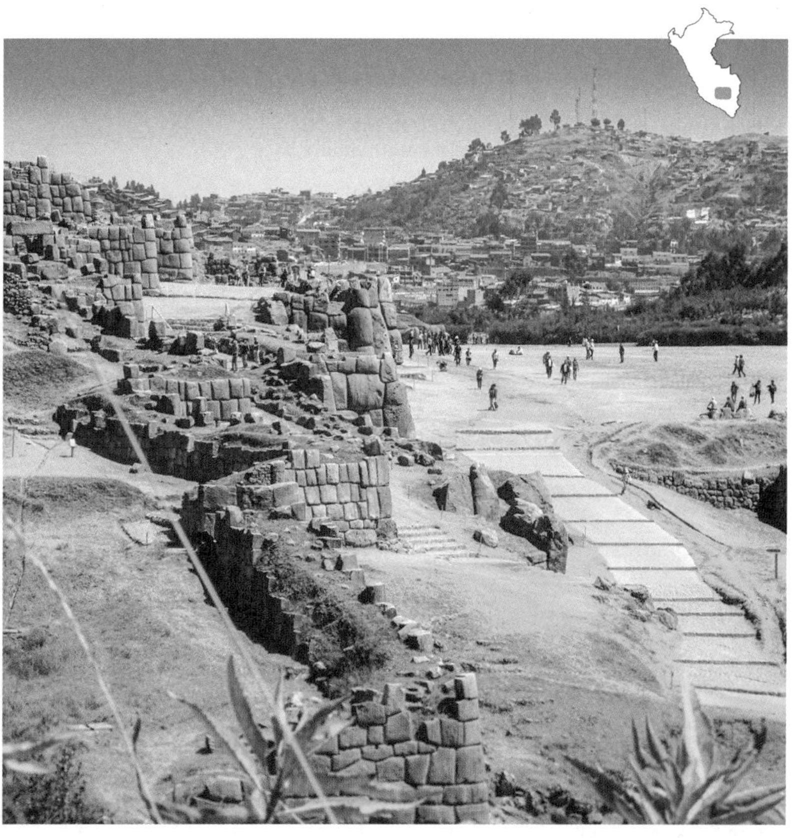

Sights	Restaurants	Hotels	Shopping	Nightlife
★★★★★	★★★★☆	★★★★★	★★★★★	★★★☆☆

WELCOME TO CUSCO AND THE SACRED VALLEY

TOP REASONS TO GO

★ **Alpaca Clothing:** Nothing says "Cusco" quite like a sweater, shawl, poncho, or scarf woven from the hair of the alpaca.

★ **Andean Cuisine:** Where else in the world will you find roasted *cuy* (guinea pig) and alpaca steaks rubbing shoulders on fine-dining menus?

★ **Inca Architecture:** Wonder at the ability of the Inca to construct stone walls so precisely, using 15th-century technology, and to position a temple so it would be illuminated best at the exact moment of the solstice.

★ **Layered Religion:** Take a closer look at the walls—every Catholic church was built on the site, and often the foundation, of an Inca *huaca*, or sacred place.

★ **Hotels with History:** Many Cusco hotels are former convents, monasteries, dwellings of sacred women, or palaces of Spanish conquerors.

★ **Sacred Playground:** The Sacred Valley is an adventurer's playground for hiking, biking, rafting, and even stand-up paddleboarding.

1 **Cusco.** Once capital of the Inca Empire, and one of the most popular destinations in Peru, this historical city is known for its archaeological remains, Spanish colonial architecture, and cobblestone streets.

2 **Sacsayhuamán.** This fortress-temple complex lies at the northern edge of Cusco.

3 **Qenko.** Named for the crooked canal cut out of its rock and probably used for ancient death rituals.

4 **Puka Pukara.** A pink-stone complex guarding the road to the Sacred Valley may have served as a fort, hunting lodge, or storage site and definitely offers great views.

5 **Tambomachay.** These three stepped terraces of Inca stonework were built over a natural spring and likely served as a ceremonial site.

6 **Valle del Sur.** The region that runs along the highway southeast of Cusco to Sicuani offers charming untouristed towns and the sites of Tipón and Pikillacta.

7 **Rainbow Mountain.** This breathtaking painted mountain is one of Peru's top attractions/photo ops.

8 **Taray.** A great stop for high-quality textiles before the market in Pisac.

9 **Pisac.** This village in the Sacred Valley of the Incas is most known for its Incan ruins and large market.

10 **Huaran.** A scenic stop on your way from Pisac to Urubamba.

11 Huayllabamba. Rest and rejuvenate a night or two here at either the Inkaterra Hacienda or the Aranwa Sacred Valley.

12 Yucay. A charming, less-touristed spot just outside Urubamba.

13 Urubamba. The surrounding countryside offers gorgeous scenery and good hotels, but it's most often visited for its Machu Picchu rail service.

14 Chinchero. Try to visit this on a Sunday for its colorful artisan market on the central plaza.

15 Moray and Salineras. Typically combined on a day-trip from Cusco, the grass-covered, terraced agricultural rings of Moray and the Salineras geometric salt pools offer some of the most breathtaking scenery in the Sacred Valley.

16 Ollantaytambo. Located in the far western reaches of the Sacred Valley, around a 1½–hour drive from Cusco, Ollantaytambo is home to the a fortress and other important Inca sites.

"Bienvenidos a la ciudad imperial del Cusco," announces the flight attendant when your plane touches down at a lofty 3,300 meters (10,825 feet) above sea level. "Welcome to the imperial city of Cusco." This greeting hints at what you're in for in Cusco, one of the world's great travel destinations.

The juxtaposition of cultures—Inca and Spanish colonial, but also modern—makes this city fascinating. This is a rare place where, if you take the time to sit and observe, you will see a culture that is going through a transformation in front of your very eyes. Where else can you see a child in traditional dress leading a llama on colonial streets while talking on a smartphone?

The area's rich history springs forth from the Inca tale that describes how Manco Cápac and his sister-consort Mama Ocllo were sent by the Sun God, their father, to enlighten the people of Peru. Setting off from Lake Titicaca sometime in the 12th century with the directive to settle only where their golden staff could be plunged fully into the soil, they traveled far across the *altiplano* (high plains) until reaching the fertile soils surrounding present-day Cusco. They envisioned Qosqo (Cusco) in the shape of a puma, the animal representation of the Earth in the indigenous cosmos, which you can still see today on city maps. But not all was Inca in southern Peru. Not far from Cusco sits Pikillacta, a pre-Inca city constructed by the Wari culture that thrived between AD 600 and 1000. It's an indication that this territory, like most of Peru, was the site of sophisticated civilizations long before the Inca appeared.

By the time Francisco Pizarro and the Spanish conquistadors arrived in 1532, the Inca Empire had spread from modern-day Ecuador in the north down through Peru and Bolivia to Chile. Sadly, the city's grandeur could do little to save an empire weakened by internal strife and civil war. Stocked with guns and horses, which the Inca had never seen, and carrying new diseases, against which they had no immunity, the Spanish arrived with the upper hand, despite smaller numbers. In 1532, the Spanish seized Atahualpa, the recently instated Inca ruler, while he was in Cajamarca to subdue rebellious forces. The Inca's crumbling house of cards came tumbling down, though pockets of resistance remained for years in places such as Ollantaytambo.

After sacking the Inca Empire, Spanish colonists instituted new political and religious systems, superimposing their beliefs onto the old society and its structures. They looted gold, silver, and stone and built their own churches, monasteries, convents, and palaces directly onto the foundations of the Inca sites. This is one of the most striking aspects of the city today. The Santo Domingo church was built on top of Qorikancha, the Temple of the Sun. And it's downright ironic to think of the cloistered convent of Santa Catalina occupying the same site as the equally cloistered Acllawasi, the home of the Inca chosen women, who were selected to serve the Sun in the Qorikancha temple. The cultural combination appears in countless other ways: witness the pumas carved into the cathedral doors. The city also gave its name to the Escuela Cusqueña (Cusco School) of art, in which new-world artists combined Andean motifs with European-style painting, usually on religious themes. You'll chance on paintings that could be by Anthony Van Dyck but for the Inca robes on New Testament figures, and Last Supper diners digging into an Andean feast of *vizcacha* (a type of chinchilla) and fermented corn.

The Río Urubamba flows, at its closest, about 30 km (18 miles) north of Cusco and passes through a valley about 300 meters (980 feet) lower in elevation than Cusco. The northwestern part of this river basin, romantically labeled the Sacred Valley of the Inca, contains some of the region's most appealing towns and fascinating pre-Columbian ruins. A growing number of visitors are heading here directly upon arrival in Cusco to acclimatize. The valley's altitude is slightly lower and its temperatures are slightly higher, making for a physically easier introduction to this part of Peru.

MAJOR REGIONS

Cusco. Whether you go before or after your visit to the Sacred Valley and Machu Picchu, you'll be missing out if you don't spend some time in Cusco. This city is a mix of new and old: ancient Inca walls holding up baroque colonial buildings, inside of which lie some of the city's most contemporary restaurants and shops. Colonial churches and cultural museums dot the plaza, and funky modern cafés sit side by side with traditional galleries of Cusqueñan art in San Blas. Inca gems are everywhere, even along the traffic-heavy business district of Avenida El Sol, home of Cusco's star attraction, the Qorikancha Sun Temple.

Side Trips from Cusco. Just outside the city lies one of Peru's most spectacular and serene regions, filled with Andean mountains, tiny hamlets, and ancient Inca ruins. In a half-day trip you can visit some of Peru's greatest historical areas and monuments, just beyond Cusco's city limits, such as Sacsayhuamán, perched high on a hill overlooking the city, or the spectacular sights of Qenko, Puka Pukara, and Tambomachay.

The Urubamba Valley, northwest of Cusco and functioning as the gateway to the Sacred Valley of the Inca, which extends farther northwest, attracts the puma's share of visitors going to Machu Picchu, especially those looking to catch their breath—and some R and R—in the region's idyllic setting. Additionally, the Valle del Sur, a stretch of highway running southeast of Cusco to Sicuani, boasts lesser-known, but equally impressive, Inca and pre-Inca sites. Vinicunca, or Rainbow Mountain, will require a full day to visit (best visited on a tour), but have you even been to Peru if you don't post that rainbow backdrop to your social media accounts?

Sacred Valley of the Inca. A pleasant climate, fertile soil, and proximity to Cusco made the Urubamba River valley a favorite with Inca nobles, many of whom are believed to have had private country homes here. Inca remains and agricultural terraces lie throughout the length of this so-called Sacred Valley of the Inca. Cusco is hardly the proverbial urban jungle, but in comparison, the Sacred Valley is positively captivating, with its lower elevation, fresher air, warmer temperatures, and rural charm. You may find yourself joining the growing ranks of visitors who base themselves here and make Cusco their day trip, rather than the other way around.

Planning

When to Go

Cusco's high season is June through early September (winter in the southern hemisphere) and the days around the Christmas and Easter holidays. Winter means drier weather and easier traveling but higher lodging prices and larger crowds. Prices and visitor numbers drop dramatically during the November-through-March summer rainy season, except around the holidays.

The Sacred Valley has increasingly taken on a dual personality, depending on the time of day, day of the week, and month of the year. Blame it on Pisac and its famous market. Every Cusco travel agency offers a day tour of the Sacred Valley, with emphasis on Tuesday, Thursday, and Sunday to coincide with the town's larger market days, and they all seem to follow the same schedule: morning shopping in Pisac, buffet lunch in Urubamba, afternoon browsing in Ollantaytambo. You can almost always sign up for one of these tours at the last minute—even early on the morning of the tour—especially if you're here in the September-to-May off-season. Note that the best guides are used for private tours and often get booked up far in advance. On nonmarket days and during the off-season, however, Pisac and the rest of the Sacred Valley are quieter. In any case, the valley deserves more than a rushed day tour if you have the time.

Planning Your Time

The typical tour of the Cusco region combines the city with the Sacred Valley and Machu Picchu in three whirlwind days. We recommend devoting at least five days to get the most out of your visit—including one day to get acclimated to the high altitude.

Getting Here And Around

AIR

LATAM (🌐 *www.latam.com*) connects Cusco with Lima, Arequipa, Juliaca, and Puerto Maldonado. Avianca (🌐 *www.avianca.com*) and VivaAir (🌐 *www.vivaair.com.pe*) offer direct flights between Lima and Cusco, while Amaszonas (🌐 *www.flyamas.com*) flies direct between Cusco and Santa Cruz and La Paz, Bolivia. While LATAM is by far the most expensive for foreign travelers, it also has the most reliable service by far and the most options in travel times. You can find offices for airlines along the Avenida El Sol, but be sure you are dealing with the real thing, as many small agencies post large signs with the airline logos.

■ TIP→ Avianca is the next most reliable and VivaAir, while the cheapest option, should be avoided.

BUS

Cusco's main bus terminal is at the Terminal Terrestre in Santiago, not far from the airport. The best company running from Cusco is Cruz del Sur (🌐 *www.cruzdelsur.com.pe*), which has its own terminal on Avenida Industrial in Bancopata. Bus and van travel between Cusco and the Sacred Valley is cheap, frequent . . . and sometimes accident-prone; taxis (shared or private) are by far the better option.

CAR

For exploring the Sacred Valley, a car is nice to be able to get around, but driving anywhere in Peru seems to have its own unwritten rules, so hiring a car and driver or going by taxi is usually the safest option. **Armando Agüero** (☎ *974/213–172 armandoah@gmail.com*) is one such driver. He speaks Spanish, English, French, and Portuguese, and he can connect with other drivers as needed.

The vehicular tourist route ends at Ollantaytambo. Cusco is the only place to rent a vehicle. Nevertheless, you won't need or want to drive inside the city;

heavy traffic, lack of parking, and narrow streets, many of them pedestrian-only, make a car a burden.

Highways are good, and traffic is relatively light in the Sacred Valley, but any trip entails a series of twisting, turning roads as you head out of the mountains near Cusco and descend into the valley. Most people get here by way of an organized tour, but you can hire a taxi to take you around. Alternatively, you can take a *colectivo* taxi or van from Cusco (US$2–US$3.50). They depart daily from Pavitos, close to the intersection with Avenida Grau. This is the best place to hire a private taxi to the valley on the street. **TIP→ Watch for the rooftop bulls as you pass through the valley.** The road to Machu Picchu ends in Ollantaytambo; beyond that point it's rail only.

TAXI

Cusco's licensed taxis have a small official taxi sticker on the windshield, but these are difficult to see. Choose ones that have the name and number of a company on the top. Fares are S/3–S/5 for any trip within the central city and S/4–S/6 after 10 pm. Have your hotel or restaurant call a taxi for you at night.

Mototaxis—three-wheeled motorized vehicles with room for two passengers—ply the streets of Sacred Valley towns.

Touring the Sacred Valley from Cusco with one of the city's taxis costs about US$80–US$90, but the exact price depends largely on your negotiating skills.

TRAIN

PeruRail (🌐 *www.perurail.com*) is the most established operator in Peru. The route between Cusco and Puno is only offered as sleeper-car service and it departs Cusco on Tuesday and returns from Puno on Wednesday. Another package has you departing on Thursday morning, visiting Lake Titicaca, and continuing on to Arequipa. Three classes of daily service to Machu Picchu depart from Cusco's Poroy station, about 20 minutes from the Plaza de Armas. Trains depart early in the morning—with the luxury *Hiram Bingham* service departing from Poroy at 9:05 am. Trains depart throughout the day from the Ollantaytambo station. Those departing from the San Pedro station located right in Cusco should be avoided due to the lengthy switchback to get out of the city. Purchase tickets in advance from the PeruRail sales office in the Plaza de Armas, online, or from a travel agency. Inca Rail (🌐 *www.incarail.com*) also has trains from Cusco, Poroy, and Ollantaytambo to Machu Picchu.

Discounts and Deals

Offering access to 14 of Cusco's best-known tourist attractions, the **Boleto Turístico** (tourist ticket) is the all-in-one answer to your tourism needs. There are four different passes you can purchase. For S/130 you can get a 10-day pass that lets you visit all 14 sites in the city and around the Sacred Valley. Alternatively, you can opt for one of three amended circuits outlined in the Boleto Parcial (partial ticket), each S/70. Although always subject to change, the participating sites have remained the same for some time. Certain big-name attractions (such as Cusco Cathedral and other religious sites) have their own entrance fees, with some offering grouped passes. Regardless, if you want to see sites such as Sacsayhuamán and Pisac, you have to buy the ticket, which can be purchased at the first site you visit or, ahead of time, at the **Comite de Servicios Integrados Turisticos Culturales del Cusco** (COSITUC) (✉ *Av. El Sol 103* ☎ *084/261–465* 🌐 *www.cosituc.gob.pe*), open daily 8–6.

Health and Safety

ALTITUDE SICKNESS

You'll likely encounter altitude sickness, known as *soroche,* at Cusco's 3,300-meter (10,825-foot) elevation. Drink lots of fluids, but eliminate or reduce alcohol consumption, and eat lightly as much as possible for the first day or two. Many hotels have an oxygen supply for their guests' use that can minimize the effects. The prescription drug acetazolamide can help. Check with your physician about it (allergies to the drug are not uncommon) and about traveling here if you have a heart condition or high blood pressure or are pregnant.

■ TIP→ Warning: Sorojchi pills are a Bolivian-made altitude-sickness remedy whose advertising pictures a tourist vomiting at Machu Picchu. Its safety has not been documented, and it contains only pain relievers and caffeine, so it's best avoided.

SAFETY

Cusco is a fairly safe city, especially for its size, with a huge police presence on the streets, especially around tourist centers such as the Plaza de Armas, where you will see some specifically indicated as tourist police. Nonetheless, petty crime, such as pickpocketing, is not uncommon: use extra vigilance in crowded markets or when getting on and off buses and trains, and be sure to keep track of bags when stopping to eat.

WATER

Tap water is not safe to drink here. Stick with the bottled variety, *con gas* (carbonated) or *sin gas* (plain).

Restaurants

Although many of the restaurants in Cusco and the Sacred Valley have stuck to the same old menus—variations on traditional Peruvian cuisine or often poorly executed standards such as pizza and burritos—this has been continually changing. The valley is still lagging behind in this area, but both have been adding more and more first-rate fusion as well as international restaurants to their mix. You may not find either place to be as before, but what you will pay for a gourmet meal at a place like MAP Café is far less than you would pay at its equivalent in New York or Los Angeles, and the food will be just as good. *Prices in the reviews are the average cost of a main course at dinner or, if dinner is not served, at lunch.*

Hotels

Hotels run the gamut in Cusco and the Sacred Valley, from low-end backpacker dorms to splurgey five-star hotels. (Note that what are referred to as hostels, or *hostales,* here are often lovely low-cost bed-and-breakfasts.) If you like to travel in style, you've got plenty of choices, and virtually all of them in Cusco are in historical buildings, many with Incan foundations. Lodgings in Cusco have shockingly early checkout times: expect to have to vacate your room by 9 or 10 am. All lodgings will hold your luggage if you're not leaving town until later in the day, as well as while you are off on a trek or on a side trip. *Hotel reviews have been shortened. For full information, visit Fodors.com.*

WHAT IT COSTS in Nuevo Soles

	$	$$	$$$	$$$$
RESTAURANTS				
	under S/35	S/35–S/50	S/51–S/65	over S/65
HOTELS				
	under S/250	S/250–S/500	S/501–S/800	over S/800

Tours

The biggest two concerns most people have when considering using an agency are price and being restricted to a specific itinerary. If you choose a moderately priced Peruvian agency (these are typically ones that will charge about US$750 for a Classic Inca Trail), the percentage that they will mark up a personalized itinerary usually isn't that much beyond what you would pay doing it yourself. As for restrictions, be sure to make it clear to them what your priorities are, and if you want some downtime in places, let them know.

Another question when booking tours is whether to go for a group tour or book a private one. Prices can vary from place to place, but if you are working with an agency, be sure to ask what the difference in price is. For example, a tour to the Sacred Valley with a group is about US$25, not including lunch or admissions. Group size can be up to 30 people and, when it is not high season, you may end up in a bilingual group where more explanation is often given in whichever language the bulk of the group speaks. You can get the same private tour for up to six people for around US$260. Whether it is worth it to you or not will depend on your interests. You'll be able to hear your guide better, explanations can be geared toward your particular obsessions (history, culture, architecture, or plants, for example), you can decide which sites you want to see, and you can stay as long as you like rather than being herded back onto the bus before you're ready. Making your own decisions is key. If you get tired of seeing "rocks," however impressively they have been assembled, you can get your guide to take you to a site that's off the beaten path, on a walk through the country, or to the best *chicheria* (corn-beer vendor).

■ TIP→ If you need to pay in dollars, as agencies sometimes request, they cannot be even the slightest bit torn. When it comes to soles, many shops do not have change, so it's best to use the larger bills at higher-end shops and restaurants so that you will have small coins and bills for the smaller ones.

The sites immediately north of Cusco (Sacsayhuamán, Qenko, Puka Pukara, and Tambomachay) are best and most easily taken in via an organized tour. Although both the Urubamba Valley and Valle del Sur are readily accessible by public transportation, most travelers prefer the convenience of a tour to bouncing between buses—the entire sightseeing circuit is about 170 km (105 miles). Tours are easily organized from one of the many kiosks in Cusco (US$15–US$30), or if you prefer a more intimate, less tourist-driven trip, you can hire a taxi (US$80–US$90) and a guide (US$80-$100).

If you want to spend time in Lima, plan to do so at the end of your trip. That way, if you run into transportation problems, you will be less likely to miss your flight home.

SELECTING A TOUR OPERATOR

"¿Holaaaa—trip to Machu Picchu?" With so many touts in Cusco's streets hawking tours to Peru's most famous sight, it's tempting to just buy one to make them stop asking. Anyone who offers an Inca Trail trek departing tomorrow should be taken with less than a grain of salt—Inca Trail hikes need to be booked months in advance. Don't make arrangements or give money to someone claiming to be a travel agent if they approach you on the street or at the airport in Cusco or Lima. It's best to have a recommendation or select one that is listed here or on 🌐 *www.peru.info*.

TOUR OPERATORS

Amazonas Explorer

ADVENTURE TOURS | For more than 30 years, this company has specialized in top-quality adventure and cultural tours. From gentle half days to two-week adventures, it offers an alternative to rote bus tours and crowds of other tourists. Known for using high-quality equipment and the best guides around, tours include hiking, biking, rafting, and even stand-up paddleboarding. The company is the first Peruvian member of 1% for the Planet, which helps fund sustainable tourism and native tree planting. ✉ *Av. Collasuyo 910, Cusco* ☎ *084/252–846, 844/380–7378* 🌐 *amazonas-explorer.com* 🎫 *From USD$150.*

Andina Travel

EXCURSIONS | Specializing in trekking and alternatives to the Inca Trail, Andina Travel also offers standard Sacred Valley and Machu Picchu tours as well as biking and rafting excursions. ✉ *Plazoleta Santa Catalina 219, Cusco* ☎ *084/251–892* 🌐 *www.andinatravel.com* 🎫 *From USD$90.*

Apumayo Expediciones

ADVENTURE TOURS | This operator offers a full gamut of nonconventional treks and adventure tours, including those focused on rafting and biking. It also specializes in trips geared toward people with disabilities. ✉ *Jr. Ricardo Palma N-11, Urb. Santa Monica* ☎ *084/246–018* 🌐 *www.apumayo.com* 🎫 *From USD$144.*

Aspiring Adventures

ADVENTURE TOURS | Started by two longtime professionals in adventure travel, this agency specializes in tours that go off the beaten path. In addition to visiting the must-see sights, you will have the opportunity to engage with Peruvian culture in a more intimate way than with more typical tours. This boutique company excels in personal service, ensuring that the trip you get exceeds even the highest of expectations. ☎ *877/438–1354 U.S. and Canada, 643/489–7474 worldwide* 🌐 *www.aspiringadventures.com* 🎫 *From USD$95.*

Cusco Top Travel & Treks

SPECIAL-INTEREST | Run by the wildly talented and witty David Choque, this company specializes in a range of packaged and comfort-class, custom-built tours. ✉ *Urbanización Cerveceros 3-A, Wanchaq* ☎ *084/234–130, 994/703–027* 🌐 *www.cuscotoptravelperu.com* 🎫 *From USD$125.*

El Chalan

SPECIAL-INTEREST | This operator organizes single- and multiday horseback-riding tours for all levels (beginner to professional) throughout the Sacred Valley. The ranch uses only the elegant Peruvian Paso horse, a breed known for its smooth, dancing gait that does not bounce the rider up and down like a typical trot. Riders and horses alike are carefully tended to and looked after. ✉ *Km 75, Autopista Urubamba–Ollantaytambo, Urubamba* ☎ *984/737–897, 084/201–541* 🌐 *www.haciendadelchalan.com* 🎫 *From USD$95.*

Enigma

ADVENTURE TOURS | Small, customized adventure trips let you enjoy trekking, rafting, mountain climbing, mountain biking, or horseback riding led by professional guides. ✉ *Calle Fortunato L. Herrera 214, Magisterio* ☎ *084/222–155* 🌐 *www.enigmaperu.com* 🎫 *From USD$158.*

Explorandes

ADVENTURE TOURS | Established in 1975, this is one of the longest-running tour agencies in Peru. It specializes in adventure tours, including rafting and trekking trips in the area around Cusco, and organizing customized, guided expeditions throughout the Andes in Peru and Ecuador. It also offers special opportunities to visit indigenous communities. ✉ *Paseo Zarzuela Q-2, Huancaro* ☎ *084/238–380* 🌐 *www.explorandes.com* 🎫 *From USD$75.*

Gravity Peru

ADVENTURE TOURS | Want to do your touring from the back of a mountain bike? The Gravity Peru people live to ride and are ready and waiting to introduce you to the best trail for your interest and skill level. Single- and multiday rides are available, and they include a full-suspension MTB bike (value of USD$3,000), all equipment, a guide, and more. ✉ *Av. Centenario 707, Cusco* ☎ *984/501–311* 🌐 *www.gravityperu.com* 🎫 *From USD$180 for a full-day mountain-bike tour.*

Llama Pack Project

ECOTOURISM | This nonprofit organization enables impoverished highland communities to regain economic viability in a way that also sustains their culture: by helping to reintroduce purebred llamas, which are a more valuable resource than the mixed-breed ones commonly found today. What does this mean for you? The opportunity to go on a half-, full-, or multiday trek with these picturesque beasts of burden. You'll have a chance to learn more about the llamas and visit communities or archaeological sites depending on which trek you choose, all while enjoying gorgeous Andean landscapes and contributing to the survival of local villages and their way of life. ✉ *Km 70.5, Carretera Urubamba-Ollantaytambo s/n, Sector Huincho, Urubamba* ☎ *998/003–114* 🌐 *www.llamapackproject.com* 🎫 *From USD$75.*

Pachamama Explorers

SPECIAL-INTEREST | This company has more than two decades of experience with a specialty in trekking the Inca Trail and alternative routes, as well as in creating customized itineraries. It promoted porter welfare before regulations were set in place. ✉ *Cusco* ☎ *989/551-082* 🌐 *www.pmexplorers.com* 🎫 *From USD$140.*

Piuray Outdoor Center

ADVENTURE TOURS | As an alternative to trekking and sightseeing, Piuray Outdoor Center offers kayaking and stand-up paddleboarding (suitable for almost everyone) trips with and without yoga on beautiful Piuray Lake in the middle of the Andes, 35 minutes from Cusco en route to the Sacred Valley. Other atypical offerings include bird-watching and cooking classes. Transportation from Cusco and snacks are included. ✉ *Piuray Outdoor Center, Pongobamba, Chinchero* ☎ *992/755–067* 🌐 *piuray.pe* 🎫 *From USD$55.*

River Explorers

ADVENTURE TOURS | As the name indicates, this company specializes in rafting and kayaking excursions (of from one to six days) on the Urubamba and Apurimac rivers. It also offers standard trekking tours. ✉ *Urb. Kennedy A, Brillantes B-36, Cusco* ☎ *084/431–116* 🌐 *riverexplorers.com* 🎫 *From USD$130.*

SAS Travel

ADVENTURE TOURS | With more than 25 years in business, Cusco-based SAS Travel is one of the longer-running companies in the area and well known especially for its treks. Although the company does offer private treks, it is the one to call if you prefer hiking with a larger group. ✉ *Calle Garcilaso 270, Cusco* ☎ *084/249–194* 🌐 *www.sastravelperu.com* 🎫 *From USD$85.*

TopTurPeru

SPECIAL-INTEREST | This internationally recognized, local company is run by Raul Castelo and family. An archaeoastronomy expert, Raul has been sought out by *National Geographic* and other documentary-filmmaking entities worldwide. That experience stands him and his team in good stead as they design customized travel itineraries and private tours for their clients. ✉ *Calle Saphi 877 B-6, Cusco* ☎ *084/243–234, 974/215–160* 🌐 *www.topturperu.com* 🎫 *From USD$125.*

Unique Peru Tours

SPECIAL-INTEREST | This agency delivers exactly what the name promises: tours that offer something different, such as hikes with llamas, trips to rarely visited communities, and the inclusion of ancient ceremonies with offerings to Mother Earth. Whether you prefer an itinerary oriented toward adventure excursions, cultural tours, or spiritual experiences, or a combination of all three, this company's highly personalized tours promise to intimately connect you with Peruvian life, past and present, in a trip that matches your specific interests. ✉ *Wanchaq* ☎ *974/213–172* 🌐 *www.uniqueperutours.com* 🎫 *From USD$235.*

United Mice

ADVENTURE TOURS | One of the more popular Inca Trail operators, United Mice has been guiding adventurers on multiday hikes since 1987. It also offers a variety of alternative treks throughout the Cusco region. ✉ *Av. Pachacutec 424 A-5, Cusco* ☎ *084/221–139* 🌐 *www.unitedmice.com* 🎫 *From USD$85.*

Wayki Trek

ADVENTURE TOURS | This unique, indigenously managed operator specializes in Inca Trail and alternative trekking. It's known for its great guides and excellent customer service. ✉ *Calle Quera 239, Cusco* ☎ *084/224–092 bookings* 🌐 *www.waykitrek.net* 🎫 *From USD$92.*

Cusco

Cusco is a fascinating blend of old and new. It was once the capital of the Inca Empire, and colonial buildings now top Inca foundations flanked on all sides by the throngs of locals in colorful dress, visitors headed to Machu Picchu, and locals shopping in the daily markets.

If you arrive in Cusco with the intention of hopping on the train to Machu Picchu the next morning, you'll probably have time only to take a stroll through the Plaza de Armas and visit Qorikancha (the Temple of the Sun) and the Catedral. The city merits more exploration, however, at either the start or the end of your trip. Consider spending at least two days in Cusco, giving you time to acclimate to the altitude and to get to know this city of terracotta roofs and cobblestone streets. Note that churches and some restaurants close for a few hours in the middle of the day. Also, although some of the city's museums close on Sunday (such as the Qoricancha temple), most are open, albeit with shorter hours.

Cusco takes its newest role as tourist favorite in stride, and absorbs thousands of travelers with an ample supply of lodgings, restaurants, and services. That a polished infrastructure exists in such a remote, high-elevation locale is a pleasant surprise.

GETTING AROUND

Cusco's Aeropuerto Internacional Teniente Alejandro Velasco Astete (CUZ) is about 15 minutes from the center of town. An army of taxis waits at the exit from baggage claim, and they charge wildly varying rates to take you to the city center. Compare some rates, have your hotel pick you up, or carry your bags out to the street, where the standard price to the center is S/8–S/10.

Cusco's center is most enjoyably explored on foot. Many of the streets open to vehicular traffic are so narrow that it's simply faster to walk. ■ **TIP→ Cusco streets have a habit of changing names every few blocks or even every block.** Many streets bear a common Spanish name that everyone uses but have newly designated street signs with an old Quechua name to highlight the city's Inca heritage: the Plaza de Armas is Haukaypata, the Plaza Regocijo is Kusipata, Triunfo is Sunturwasi, Loreto is Intikijlli, Arequipa is Q'aphchijk'ijllu, and intermittent blocks of Avenida El Sol are labeled Mut'uchaka, and so on.

Report any problems with tour companies, hotels, restaurants, and the like to INDECOPI, a tourist-focused government agency.

Cusco has kept steady with the times so that the simplest way to order a taxi is to download the Easy Taxi app on your smartphone; it will find you a taxi close to your location and, with your GPS enabled, help the app to find you as well. If you are not in an area with taxis roaming outside, ask your hotel or restaurant to order you one. If you do pick up a taxi on the street, make sure that it is one that works with a company, recognizable by the name it will typically be touting on the top.

Acclimatizing with Coca Tea

Take it easy! Cusco is a breathless 3,300 meters (10,825 feet) above sea level, with 30% less oxygen in the atmosphere—a fact you'll very soon appreciate as you huff and puff your way up its steep cobbled streets. The best way to avoid altitude sickness is to take it easy on your first few days. There's no point in dashing off on that Inca hike if you're not acclimatized—altitude sickness is uncomfortable at best and can be very dangerous.

Locals swear by *mate de coca*, an herbal tea brewed from coca leaves that helps with altitude acclimatization. Indigenous peoples have chewed the leaves of the coca plant for centuries to cope with Andean elevations. But the brewing of the leaves in an herbal tea is considered a more refined and completely legal way to ingest the substance, in Andean nations at least. Most restaurants and virtually all hotels have leaves and hot water available constantly.

AIRPORT Aeropuerto Internacional Teniente Alejandro Velasco Astete. (*CUZ*) ✉ *Av. Velasco Astete s/n* ☎ *084/222–611.*

BUS Cruz del Sur. ✉ *Av. Industrial 121, Bancopata* ☎ *084/243–261* 🌐 *www.cruzdelsur.com.pe.* **Ormeño.** ✉ *Terminal Terrestre de Cusco* ☎ *084/261–704* 🌐 *www.grupo-ormeno.com.pe.*

RENTAL CAR Hertz. ✉ *Av. El Sol 803* ☎ *084/248–800* 🌐 *www.gygrentacar.com.* **Manu Rent A Car.** ✉ *Urb. Quispicanchis, Calle Venezuela K-15* ☎ *084/233–382, 984/110-308 Mobile* 🌐 *www.manurentacar.com.*

TRAIN Inca Rail. ✉ *Portal de Panes 105, Plaza de Armas* ☎ *084/581–860* 🌐 *www.incarail.com.* **PeruRail.** ✉ *Portal de Carnes 214, Plaza de Armas* ☎ *084/581–414* 🌐 *www.perurail.com.*

HEALTH AND SAFETY

MEDICAL Clínica Pardo. ✉ *Av. de la Cultura 710, Plaza Tupac Amaru* ☎ *084/231–718, 989/431–050 24 hrs* 🌐 *www.clinicapardo.com.pe.* **Dr. Eduardo Luna.** ☎ *984/761–277.* **Hospital Regional.** ✉ *Av. de la Cultura s/n, Wanchaq* ☎ *084/231–131, 084/223–691 Emergencies 24 hr* 🌐 *hrcusco.gob.pe.*

POLICE INDECOPI. ✉ *Urb. Constancia Mz A-11-12, Wanchaq* ☎ *012/252–987* 🌐 *www.indecopi.gob.pe.* **Policia Nacional.** ✉ *Plaza Tupac Amaru* ☎ *084/249–654.* **Tourism Police.** (*POLTUR*) ✉ *Plaza Tupac Amaru* ☎ *084/235–123.*

VISITOR INFORMATION

DIRCETUR. (*Dirección Regional de Comercio Exterior y Turismo*) ✉ *Plaza Tupac Amaru, Mz. Lote 2, Wanchaq* ☎ *084/233–761* 🌐 *www.dirceturcusco.gob.pe.* **iPerú.** ✉ *Portal de Harinas 177* ☎ *084/596–159* ✍ *iperucusco@promperu.gob.pe* 🌐 *www.peru.travel/en.*

Plaza de Armas and Around

For thousands of years, the heart of Cusco, formerly called Haukaypata and now known as the Plaza de Armas, has served as the pulse of the city. Yet where you once would have found Inca ceremonies and parades in front of the many palaces that stood here, today you'll find a more modern procession of postcard sellers, shoe-shiners, and artists angling for your attention. It's no surprise that they congregate here—with the stupendous Catedral dominating the northeastern side of the plaza, the ornate Templo de la Compañía sitting to the

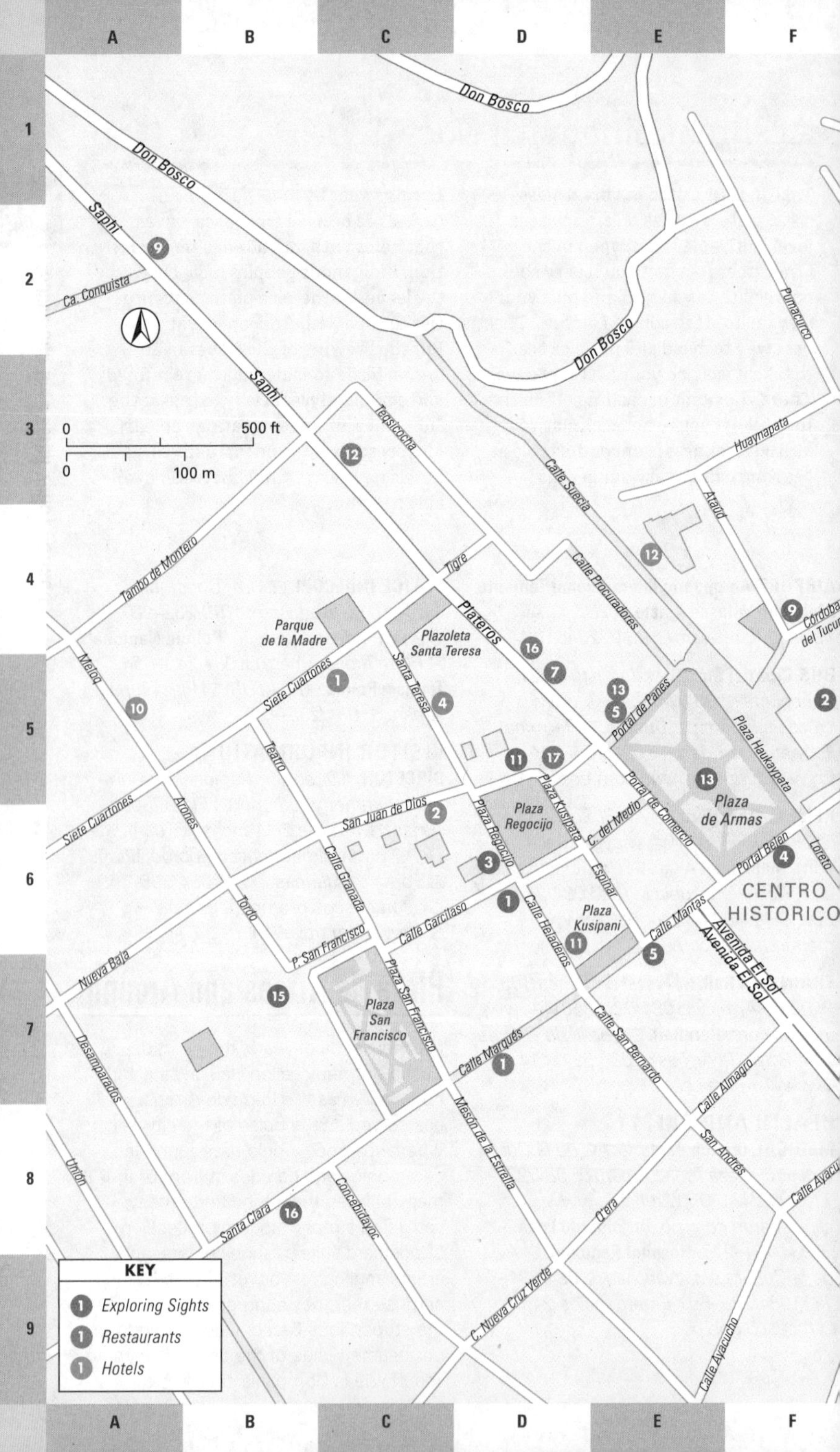
A B C D E F
1 2 3 4 5 6 7 8 9
Don Bosco
Saphi
Ca. Conquista
0 500 ft
0 100 m
Tecsecocha
Huaynapata
Pumacurco
Calle Suecia
Ataud
Tambo de Montero
Tigre
Calle Procuradores
Córdoba del Tucuman
Plateros
Parque de la Madre
Plazoleta Santa Teresa
Meloq
Siete Cuartones
Santa Teresa
Portal de Panes
Plaza Haukaypata
Teatro
Plaza Kusipata
Plaza Regocijo
Plaza de Armas
Siete Cuartones
Arones
San Juan de Dios
Plaza Regocijo
C. del Medio
Portal de Comercio
Loreto
Calle Granada
Espinar
Portal Belen
CENTRO HISTORICO
Tordo
Calle Garcilaso
Plaza Kusipani
Calle Heladeros
Calle Mantas
P. San Francisco
Avenida El Sol
Nueva Baja
Plaza San Francisco
Calle San Bernardo
Desamparados
Calle Marques
Calle Almagro
Mesón de la Estrella
San Andrés
Unión
Concebidayoc
Santa Clara
Calle Ayacu
Q'era
C. Nueva Cruz Verde
Calle Ayacucho
KEY
Exploring Sights
Restaurants
Hotels

Sights

1 Casa de Garcilaso D6
2 Catedral F5
3 ChocoMuseo D6
4 Iglesia de La Compañía de Jesús F6
5 La Merced E6
6 Monastério de Santa Catalina de Siena G6
7 Museo de Arte Precolombino G4
8 Museo de Arte Religioso del Arzobispado H5
9 Museo Inka F4
10 Museo Machu Picchu Casa Concha G6
11 Museo Municipal de Arte Contemporáneo ... D5
12 Palacio de Inca Roca H5
13 Plaza de Armas E5
14 Qorikancha I9
15 Templo de San Francisco B7
16 Templo Santa Clara B8

Restaurants

1 Café Dos X 3 .... D7
2 Cicciolina G5
3 Greens Organic G5
4 Incanto G5
5 Inka Grill E5
6 Justina G5
7 Kintaro D5
8 Kion G5
9 Korma Sutra A2
10 La Bodega 138 .... H5
11 La Bondiet D6
12 La Cantina C3
13 La Feria E5
14 MAP Café G4
15 Marcelo Batata G5
16 Morena Peruvian Kitchen D5
17 Museo del Café D5
18 Papachos G5
19 Uchu G4

Hotels

1 Andean Wings C5
2 Aranwa Cusco Boutique Hotel C6
3 Casa Cartagena G3
4 Costa Del Sol Ramada Cusco C5
5 Fallen Angel Guest House G4
6 Hotel Libertador Palacio del Inka I8
7 Hotel Monasterio G4
8 JW Marriott Cusco H6
9 La Casona G4
10 Niños Hotel A5
11 Palacio Nazarenas G4
12 Tierra Viva Cusco Plaza E4

southeast, and gorgeous Spanish-colonial arcades forming the other two sides, the plaza is one of the most spectacular areas of Cusco.

Directly north of the Plaza de Armas, behind the Catedral and to the east and west for about three blocks, is a section of the city that boasts scores of upscale shops, fine restaurants, and the city's best cultural museum, the Museo de Arte Precolombino. Walk 15 minutes northwest to reach Colcampata, said to be the palace of the first Inca ruler, Manco Cápac. The charming Plazoleta Nazarenas is the perfect place for a stroll and is far quieter than the bustling Plaza de Armas. Many travelers often mistake this section for the artists' neighborhood of San Blas, but San Blas requires a bit more of a hike, about two steep blocks farther uphill.

After the colonial charm of central Cusco and San Blas, head south of the plaza for a timely reminder that you're still in Peru. Traffic, smog, and horn-happy drivers welcome you to the noisy and unattractive Avenida El Sol, where the colonial charm of the city is hidden but for one glaring exception: Cusco's if-you-have-time-for-only-one-thing tourist attraction, the Qorikancha, or Temple of the Sun. Don't miss it. **■ TIP→ Plaza Regocijo, although southwest of the Plaza de Armas, has re-created itself in the last five years from a once low-level tourist area to a clean, upscale area (catering to cusqueños and travelers alike) with gourmet restaurants and high-end shopping.**

One of the prettiest of Cusco's plazas with its center fountain, the Plaza Regocijo, lies just to the west of the Plaza de Armas. It's worth a short jaunt over there for a more relaxing bench to rest and people-watch, as well as because two of the museums included on the Boleto Turístico are located on the plaza. This is also where you'll find one of Cusco's favorite attractions for kids of all ages, the ChocoMuseo.

Rainbow Flags 

All the rainbow flags on the Plaza de Armas and elsewhere may make Cusco seem really LGBTQ friendly. But those flags are actually the flag of Cusco, based on the banner of the Inca Empire.

 Sights

Casa de Garcilaso
(Museum of Regional History)
HOUSE | You'll find a bit of everything in this spot, which may leave you feeling like you've seen it all before. Colonial building? Check. Escuela Cusqueña paintings? Check. Ancient pottery? Check. Inca mummy? Check. This is the colonial childhood home of Inca Garcilaso de la Vega, the famous chronicler of the Spanish conquest and illegitimate son of one of Pizarro's captains and an Inca princess. Inside the mansion, with its cobblestone courtyard, is the Museo de Historia Regional, with Cusco School paintings, pre-Inca mummies—one from Nazca has a 1½-meter (5-foot) braid—ceramics, metal objects, and other artifacts. ✉ *Heladeros at Garcilaso* ☎ *084/223–245* 🎫 *Boleto Turístico.*

ChocoMuseo
MUSEUM | **FAMILY** | This museum provides a delicious introduction to the history and process of chocolate making, from cacao bean to bar. Workshops allow you to make your own sweets; they are offered three times a day for a minimum of three people at an additional cost of S/75, and advance reservations are required. There is an additional museum location in Ollantaytambo near the archaeological site and in Pisac near the main square. An on-site shop is a great place for gift shopping, if you want to give the museum a pass. ✉ *Calle Garcilaso 210, 2nd fl., Plaza Regocijo* ☎ *084/244–765* 🌐 *www.chocomuseo.com* 🎫 *Workshops from S/75.*

Iglesia de La Compañía de Jesús
HISTORIC SITE | With its ornately carved facade, this Jesuit church on the Plaza de Armas gives the Catedral a run for its money in the beauty stakes. The Compañía, constructed by the Jesuits in the 17th century, was intended to be the most splendid church in Cusco, which didn't sit too well with the archbishop. The beauty contest between the churches grew so heated that the pope was forced to intervene. He ruled in favor of the Catedral, but, by that time, the *iglesia* was nearly finished, complete with a baroque facade to rival the Catedral's grandeur. The interior is not nearly so splendid, however, although it's worth seeing the paintings on either side of the entrance depicting the intercultural marriage between a Spanish conquistador and an Inca princess. Tourists are admitted to Masses under the condition that they participate in them; start wandering around and taking photos, and you'll be shown the door. ✉ *Plaza de Armas* 🎫 *S/10.*

★ **La Catedral** (*The Cathedral Basilica of the Assumption of the Virgin*)
RELIGIOUS SITE | Dominating the Plaza de Armas, the monumental Cathedral Basilica of the Assumption of the Virgin (or Cusco Cathedral) is one of Cusco's grandest buildings. Built in 1550 on the site of the palace of the Inca Wiracocha and using stones looted from the nearby Inca fortress of Sacsayhuamán, the cathedral is a perfect example of the imposition of the Catholic faith on the indigenous population. The grander the building, went the theory, the more impressive (and seductive) the faith. With soaring ceilings, baroque carvings, enormous oil paintings, and glittering gold-and-silver altars, the cathedral certainly seemed to achieve its aim.

Today, Cusco's Catedral is one of the town's star attractions, noted mainly for its amazing collection of colonial art that mixes Christian and non-Christian imagery. Entering the Catedral from the Sagrada Familia chapel, head to your right to the first nave, where you'll find the famous oil painting (reputed to be the oldest in Cusco) depicting the earthquake that rocked the town in 1650. Among the depictions of burning houses and people fleeing, you'll see a procession in the plaza. Legend has it that during the earthquake, the citizens removed a statue of Jesus on the cross from the Catedral and paraded it around the plaza—halting the quake in its tracks. This statue, now known as the Señor de los Temblores, or Lord of the Earthquakes, is Cusco's patron, and you'll find him depicted in many Cusqueñan paintings.

To see the famous statue, head across the Catedral to the other side, where in the nave and to the right of the passage connecting the Catedral to the adjoining Iglesia del Triumfo, you'll find El Señor himself. The dark color of his skin is often claimed to be a representation of the indigenous people of Cusco; actually, it's the effect of years of candle smoke on the native materials used in its fabrication.

Una foto amigo?

Cusco is one of the most colorful cities in the world, and you can't be here for more than five minutes without noticing all the women and young children walking the streets in full traditional costume, most towing a llama or endearingly cuddling a lamb or puppy. They are more than happy to pose for photos. In fact, that's how they make their money, so make sure to pay up when asked. The going rate for a photo is S/1–S/2.

Did You Know?

Since the late 1500s, a procession has carried statues of saints from area churches to the Catedral for Cusco's Corpus Christi celebration (60 days after Easter).

Those interested in the crossover between indigenous and Catholic iconography will find lots to look at. Figures of pumas, the Inca representation of the Earth, are carved on the enormous main doors, and in the adjoining Iglesia del Triumfo you'll see an Andean Christ in one of the altars flanking the exit. ■ TIP→ **No one should miss the spectacular painting of the Last Supper, by the indigenous artist Marcos Zapata, where you'll see the diners tucking into a delicious feast of viscacha (wild chinchilla) and chicha (a corn beverage)!**

The cathedral's centerpieces are its massive, solid-silver altar, and the enormous 1659 María Angola bell, the largest in South America, which hangs in one of the towers and can be heard from miles away. Behind the main altar is the original wooden *altar primitivo* dedicated to St. Paul. The 64-seat cedar choir has rows of carved saints, popes, and bishops, all in stunning detail down to their delicately articulated hands. ■ TIP→ **If you're interested in a more in-depth look, enlist the services of a guide—you'll find them right outside the Catedral. Agree on a price before you start; it will cost a minimum of S/30 per group.** Alternatively, there is a free audio guide. ✉ *Plaza de Armas* ☎ *084/254–285* 🎫 *S/25; combined admission with Templo de San Blas and Museo de Arte Religioso S/30.*

La Merced

RELIGIOUS SITE | The church may be overshadowed by the more famous Catedral and Iglesia de la Compañía, but La Merced contains one of the city's most priceless treasures—the Custodia, a solid gold container for Communion wafers more than a meter high and encrusted with thousands of precious stones. Rebuilt in the 17th century, this monastery, with two stories of portals and a colonial fountain, gardens, and benches, has a spectacular series of murals that depict the life of the founder of the Mercedarian order, St. Peter of Nolasco.

No Photos!

To protect historical artifacts from light, guards in Cusco's museums and churches are notoriously watchful about prohibiting all types of photography, flash or not, still or video, within their confines. The exception is the Qorikancha, which allows limited photography, but not of the fragile Escuela Cusqueña (Cusco School) paintings on its walls.

A small museum is found to the side of the church. ✉ *Mantas 121* 🎫 *Church free, museum S/10* ⏲ *Closed Sun.*

Monasterio de Santa Catalina de Siena

RELIGIOUS SITE | An extensive collection of Cusqueñan religious art is the draw at this still-working Dominican convent, which incorporates a 1610 church with high and low choirs and baroque friezes. Although there's not much to show of it these days, the convent represents another example of the pasting of Catholic religion over indigenous faiths—it was built on the site of the Acllawasi, the house of some 3,000 Inca chosen women dedicated to teaching, weaving Inca ceremonial robes, and worship of Inti, the Inca sun god. The entire complex was given a face-lift in 2010. ✉ *Santa Catalina Angosta 401* 🎫 *S/8.*

★ Museo de Arte Precolombino

MUSEUM | For a different perspective on pre-Columbian ceramics, head to this spectacular museum, known as MAP, where art and pre-Columbian culture merge seamlessly. Twelve rooms in the 1580 Casa Cabrera, which was used as the convent of Santa Clara until the 17th century, showcase an astounding collection of pre-Columbian art from the 13th to 16th centuries, mostly in the form of carvings, ceramics, and jewelry. The art and artifacts were made by the Huari and Nazca, as well as the Inca, cultures. The stylish displays have excellent labels in Spanish and English that place the artifacts in their artistic and historical context. On the walls is commentary from European artists on South American art. Swiss artist Paul Klee wrote: "I wish I was newly born, and totally ignorant of Europe, innocent of facts and fashions, to be almost primitive." Most Cusco museums close at dark, but MAP remains open every evening. For a break after a walk around, find your way to the on-site café, one of Cusco's best restaurants (reservations are required for dinner). ✉ *Plaza de la Nazarenas 231* ☎ *084/595–092* 🌐 *mapcusco.pe* 🎫 *S/20.*

Museo de Arte Religioso del Arzobispado
MUSEUM | The building may be on the dark and musty side, but this San Blas museum has a remarkable collection of religious art. Originally the site of the Inca Roca's Hatun Rumiyoq palace, then the juxtaposed Moorish-style palace of the Marqués de Buenavista, the building reverted to the Archdiocese of Cusco and served as the archbishop's residence. In this primary repository of religious art in the city many of the paintings in the collection are anonymous, but you'll notice some by the renowned indigenous artist Marcos Zapata. A highlight is a series of 17th-century paintings that depict the city's Corpus Christi procession. Free audio guides are available. ✉ *Hatun Rumiyoq and Herejes, San Blas* ☎ *084/231–615* 🎫 *S/15; S/30 combined admission with Catedral and Templo de San Blas.*

Museo Inka
MUSEUM | Everyone comes to "ooh" and "eeww" over this archaeological museum's collection of Inca mummies, but the entire facility serves as a comprehensive introduction to pre-Columbian Andean culture. Packed with textiles, ceramics, and dioramas, there's a lot to see here, and displays bear labels in Spanish and English. One room is dedicated to the story of Mamakuka ("Mother Coca"), and documents indigenous people's use of the coca leaf for religious and medicinal purposes. The building was once the palace of Admiral Francisco Aldrete Maldonado, the reason for its common designation as the Palacio del Almirante (Admiral's Palace). ✉ *Ataúd at Córdoba del Tucumán* ☎ *084/237–380* 🌐 *museoinka.unsaac.edu.pe* 🎫 *S/10* 🕒 *Closed Sun.*

Museo Machu Picchu Casa Concha
MUSEUM | Artifacts that Hiram Bingham unearthed during his 1911 "discovery" of Machu Picchu and brought back to Yale University resided with the university for a century. After a hotly contested custody battle, an agreement was reached between Peru and Yale, and the artifacts began to be returned to Peru in 2011. Some can now be seen on display at this small but fascinating museum housed in a colonial mansion built atop the palace of Tupac Yupanqui. While the artifacts are interesting, the real reason to go is for the video, which presents research findings on these pieces. If you have time, visit the museum before your trip to Machu Picchu for a deeper understanding of what is currently known, and still unknown, about this world wonder. ✉ *Calle Santa Catalina Ancha 320* ☎ *084/255–535* 🌐 *www.museomachupicchu.com* 🎫 *S/20* 🕒 *Closed Sun.*

Museo Municipal de Arte Contemporáneo
MUSEUM | Take a refreshing turn back toward the present in this city of history. As is typically the case in Cusco, the museum is housed in a colonial mansion. But the art exhibits, which rotate constantly, display some of the best work that contemporary Peruvian artists have to offer. ✉ *Portal Espinar 270, Plaza Regocijo* ☎ *084/240–006* 🎫 *Boleto Turístico* 🕒 *Closed Sun.*

Palacio de Inca Roca
CASTLE/PALACE | Inca Roca lived in the 13th or 14th century. Halfway along his palace's side wall, nestled amid other stones, is a famous 12-angled stone, an example of masterly Inca masonry.

There's nothing sacred about the 12 angles: Inca masons were famous for incorporating stones with many more sides than 12 into their buildings. If you can't spot the famous stone from the crowds taking photos, ask one of the shopkeepers or the elaborately dressed Inca figures hanging out along the street to point it out. Around the corner is a series of stones on the wall that form the shapes of a puma and a serpent. Kids often hang out there and trace the forms for a small tip. ✉ *Hatun Rumiyoc and Palacio.*

Plaza de Armas (*Haukaypata*)
HISTORIC SITE | With park benches, green lawns, and splendid views of the Catedral, Cusco's gorgeous colonial Plaza de Armas invites you to stay awhile. Take a seat on one of those park benches, and the world will come to you—without moving an inch, you'll be able to purchase postcards, paintings, and snacks, organize a trip to Machu Picchu, get your photograph taken, and get those dirty boots polished. **■ TIP→ What you see today is a direct descendant of imperial Cusco's central square, which the Inca called the Haukaypata (the only name indicated on today's street signs) and which extended as far as the Plaza del Regocijo.** According to belief, this was the exact center of the Inca Empire, Tawantinsuyo, the Four Corners of the Earth. Today, continuing the tradition, it's the tourism epicenter. From the plaza you'll see the Catedral and Iglesia de la Compañía de Jesús on two sides and the graceful archways of the colonial *portales,* or covered arcades, lining the other sides. Soft lighting bathes the plaza each evening and creates one of Cusco's iconic views. Many of the city's frequent parades (and some protests) pass through the plaza, especially on Sundays. Enjoy the views of colonial Cusco, but note that any attempt to sit on one of those inviting green lawns will prompt furious whistle-blowing from the police. ✉ *Plaza de Armas.*

★ **Qorikancha**
ARCHAEOLOGICAL SITE | Built to honor the sun god, the Empire's most important deity, Qorikancha translates as "Court of Gold." Walls and altars were once plated with gold, and in the center of the complex sat a giant gold disc, positioned to reflect the sun and bathe the temple in light, while terraces were once filled with life-size gold-and-silver statues of plants and animals. Much of the wealth was removed to ransom the captive Inca ruler Atahualpa during the Spanish conquest. Eventually, the structure was passed on to the Dominicans, who constructed the church of Santo Domingo using stones from the temple and creating a jarring imperial–colonial architectural juxtaposition. An ingenious restoration lets you see how the church was built on and around the temple. In the Inca parts of the structure left exposed, estimated to be about 40% of the original temple, you can admire the mortarless masonry, earthquake-proof trapezoidal doorways, curved retaining wall, and exquisite carvings that exemplify the artistic and engineering skills of the Inca. The S/15 entrance allows you to visit the Monasterio de Santa Catalina and Qorikancha's ruins and church; a free pre-recorded tour is available, but hire a guide to get the most out of the site. ✉ *Pampa del Castillo at Plazoleta Santo Domingo* 🎫 *Ruins and church S/15; museum entrance via Boleto Turístico.*

Templo de San Francisco
RELIGIOUS SITE | Close to the Plaza de Armas, the Plaza de San Francisco is a local hangout. There's not a lot to see in the plaza itself, but if you've wandered this way, the Templo de San Francisco church is interesting for its macabre sepulchers with arrangements of bones and skulls, some pinned to the wall to spell out morbid sayings. A small museum of religious art with paintings by Escuela Cusqueña artists Marcos Zapata and Diego Quispe Tito is in the church sacristy. ✉ *Plaza de San Francisco* ✣ *3 blocks south of Plaza de Armas* ☎ *084/221–361* 🎫 *S/10.*

Corpus Christi Festival

Cusco's Corpus Christi festival in late May or June is a deeply religious affair with Mass in the Plaza de Armas surrounded by 15 statues of saints and representations of the Virgin Mary. The statues are brought from churches in nearby districts and come to Cusco to be blessed. In the early afternoon, the beaded, brocaded, 15-foot statues are hoisted onto the shoulders of teams of men and promenaded around the plaza, with the men genuflecting at various altars and ending at the Catedral. It's a daylong party, and the whole city crams into the Plaza de Armas to watch the parade, eat, drink, and make merry. ■ TIP→ **Cusco's Plaza de Armas has many second-story restaurants and bars with a view of the action if you want to stay above the fray. Go early for the best views.**

Templo Santa Clara

RELIGIOUS SITE | Austere from the outside, this incredible 1588 church takes the prize for most eccentric interior decoration. Thousands of mirrors cover the interior, competing with the gold-laminated altar for glittery prominence. Legend has it that the mirrors were placed inside in order to tempt locals into church. Built in old Inca style, using stone looted from Inca ruins, this is a great example of the lengths that the Spanish went to in order to attract indigenous converts to the Catholic faith. ✉ *Santa Clara s/n* 🎫 *Free.*

Restaurants

Cafe Dos X 3

$ | **CAFÉ** | Pouring some of the best coffee in the city from a special house blend, this café is a Cusco icon; Martin Chambi photos help anchor it in Peru, but the jazz and bohemian atmosphere make it feel more cosmopolitan. It's great for a quick bite, as well as for picking up fliers on current cultural offerings. **Known for:** great coffee; cool atmosphere; tasty, low-priced desserts. $ *Average main: S/6* ✉ *Calle Marqués 271* ☎ *084/232–661* 💳 *No credit cards* ⏲ *No dinner. Closed Sun.*

★ Cicciolina

$$$ | **MEDITERRANEAN** | Everyone seems to know everyone at this second-floor eatery, part lively tapas bar, part sit-down, candlelit restaurant. The tapas are delicious and varied, while the main dishes offer fabulous Mediterranean cuisine with twists from the Andes. **Known for:** soul-satisfying dishes; wine list; best place for romantic dinner. $ *Average main: S/52* ✉ *Sunturwasi 393, 2nd fl., Triunfo* ☎ *084/239–510* 🌐 *www.cicciolinacuzco.com.*

Greens Organic

$$ | **PERUVIAN** | Serving delicious dishes that you can feel good about eating, too, this restaurant's use of top-quality, locally produced, and organic ingredients makes it the go-to place in town. Whether you are a carnivore or a vegetarian, you'll find options to make your mouth water and ensure you leave satisfied. **Known for:** fresh organic ingredients; healthy options; friendly service. $ *Average main: S/45* ✉ *Santa Catalina Angosta 135, 2nd fl., Plaza de Armas* ☎ *084/243–379* 🌐 *www.cuscorestaurants.com.*

Incanto

$$ | **MEDITERRANEAN** | Stylish contemporary design in an Andean setting has made this large, upscale restaurant near the Plaza de Armas a hit with those looking for a classy night out. It dishes

up Mediterranean-Andean fusion cuisine, meaning that traditional Italian favorites are given a twist thanks to the use of Peruvian ingredients and flavors. **Known for:** Italian food with a Peruvian flair; upscale atmosphere; tasty cocktails. *Average main: S/47 Santa Catalina Angosta 135, Plaza de Armas 084/254–753 www.cuscorestaurants.com.*

Inka Grill

$$ | PERUVIAN | FAMILY | Featuring soups, salads, a plethora of tasty appetizers, sandwiches, and hearty main dishes, as well as delicious desserts, this popular restaurant located in the Plaza de Armas offers both comfort and gourmet choices, all with a Peruvian flair. It's a great place to go when you are with a group that has varying tastes—even the pickiest of palates should find something to suit them—and it also features live Peruvian music. **Known for:** variety of options; fine cuts of meat; excellent service. *Average main: S/39 Portal de Panes 115, Plaza de Armas 084/262–992 www.cuscorestaurants.com.*

Justina

$ | PIZZA | Pizza is the only thing on the menu here, and drinks are limited, but if it's pizza and wine you're craving, this is one of the best places to get them. The atmosphere is relaxed—starting from the moment you enter the courtyard—but the colonial building is cozy, with only a few tables, so get here early. **Known for:** great pizza; reasonably priced wine; cool atmosphere. *Average main: S/32 Calle Palacio 110 084/255–475 Closed Sun. No lunch.*

Kintaro

$$ | JAPANESE | If you're craving Japanese food, you can get the real deal at Kintaro. Amid a quietly elegant atmosphere, you can order miso soup, udon, teriyaki dishes, tempura, a wide variety of fresh and authentic sushi, and hot or cold sake. **Known for:** authentic Japanese; fresh sushi; salad-plus-main combos. *Average main: S/42 Calle Plateros 334, 2nd fl., Plaza de Armas 084/260–638 www.kintarocuzco.com Closed Sun.*

Kion

$$ | CHINESE FUSION | There are plenty of *chifa*—Peruvian–Cantonese cuisine—restaurants to be found along the side streets of town, but the best by far is Kion, with its modern decor and attentive service. Although the menu has many familiar Chinese offerings, like wontons and fried rice, the Peruvian influences and preparations make it a nice change from your neighborhood wok and, indeed, from straight-up Peruvian eateries. **Known for:** best fusion Chinese; modern Asian decor; Peking duck in three stages. *Average main: S/40 Calle Triunfo 370, 2nd fl., Triunfo 084/431–862 www.cuscorestaurants.com.*

Korma Sutra

$ | INDIAN | Given the popularity of curries in England, it should come as no surprise that the best Indian food in town is served by a native Brit. You'll find a good assortment of spiciness here, from mild to mouth-on-fire; you'll also find vegetarian options. **Known for:** best Indian food in town; reasonable prices; good portion sizes. *Average main: S/22 Calle Saphi 726, Interior 9, San Blas 984/132–032 Closed Sun.*

La Bodega 138

$$ | PIZZA | The wide selection of pizzas, pastas, soups, and salads here, as well as a few great desserts, ensure that you will leave feeling satisfied. In particular, the unique blue cheese, bacon, and *sauco* (elderberry) pizza can't be beat. **Known for:** pizza and pasta dishes; craft beers; great salads. *Average main: S/35 Herrajes 138 084/260–272 No credit cards.*

La Bondiet

$ | CAFÉ | This is a great spot to regroup, caffeinate, and make use of the Wi-Fi after a hard morning's sightseeing. The coffee is quality, there's a huge range of mouth-watering cakes, and you can also grab breakfast, sandwiches, and slices. **Known**

Did You Know?

On Cusco's Plaza de Armas, the Catedral was constructed atop the foundations of an Inca palace.

for: good coffee; ice cream; excellent pastries. 💲 *Average main: S/16* ✉ *Heladeros 118* ☎ *084/246–823* ⏲ *No dinner.*

★ La Cantina

$$ | **WINE BAR** | More a wine bar than a restaurant, La Cantina has walls lined with Italian vintages that are poured by a friendly and attentive staff, creating a setting that invites both sampling and lingering. For your meal, there are delicious pizzas with wafer-thin crusts and high-quality ingredients, plus meats and cheeses from the Old Country and a killer tiramisu for dessert. **Known for:** excellent Italian wines; delicious wafer-thin pizza; imported meats and cheeses. 💲 *Average main: S/35* ✉ *Saphy 554, Plaza de Armas* ☎ *084/242–075.*

La Feria

$$ | **PERUVIAN** | Traditional Peruvian cuisine, rather than the stuff of gourmands, is a food of the people, served on the street or in family-style restaurants called *picanterías*. At La Feria, you can enjoy good country eating Andean style, with generous portions of such typical fare as slow-cooked pork, beef ribs, *anticuchos* (kebabs), and much more. **Known for:** traditional Peruvian food and atmosphere; varieties of homemade chicha; overlooking the Plaza de Armas. 💲 *Average main: S/48* ✉ *Portal de Panes 123, 2nd fl., Plaza de Armas* ☎ *084/286–198* 🌐 *www.cuscodining.com.*

MAP Café

$$$$ | **PERUVIAN** | Museum eateries don't routinely warrant a mention, but this small, glass-enclosed, elegant café inside the courtyard of the Museo de Arte Precolombino is actually one of the city's top restaurants. It has top prices to boot, but it's still a bargain compared with what this quality meal would cost in New York or Los Angeles. **Known for:** first-class dining and presentation; prix-fixe dinner menu; cool atmosphere in courtyard of museum. 💲 *Average main: S/66* ✉ *Plazoleta Nazarenas 231* ☎ *084/242–476* 🌐 *www.cuscorestaurants.com.*

★ Marcelo Batata

$$ | **PERUVIAN** | Start with a drink made from one of the many house-made pisco infusions, and then move on to the Peruvian fusion that is Batata's specialty, in particular, mouthwatering alpaca steaks. With a rooftop terrace and a cozy interior dining room, the vibe here is in the sweet spot between upscale-but-friendly and romantic. **Known for:** Novo Andino cuisine; pisco infusions; cooking classes. 💲 *Average main: S/50* ✉ *Calle Palacio 121, 2nd fl.* ☎ *084/776-148* 🌐 *www.cuzcodining.com.*

Morena Peruvian Kitchen

$$ | **PERUVIAN** | Bright, cheerful, and just off the Plaza de Armas, the Australian-Peruvian owned Morena serves its own delicious takes on Peruvian standards, with a variety of traditional appetizers and mains that are perfect for mixing and matching to make your own tasting menu. The soups, sandwiches, smoothies, and other light fare are ideal for when you're adjusting to altitude; tea, coffee, juices, heavenly desserts, craft beers, and creative cocktails round out the offerings. **Known for:** tasty takes on Peruvian classics; pisco drinks; great service. 💲 *Average main: S/42* ✉ *Calle Plateros 348-B* ☎ *084/437–832* 🌐 *www.morenaperuviankitchen.com.*

Museo del Café

$ | **CAFÉ** | Café, restaurant, bar, museum, and shop—this is somewhat of a one-size-fits-all, housed in the second-oldest colonial mansion in Cusco with a comfortable and welcoming decor. On the menu are excellent coffee drinks that can be made with a variety of processes your barista will be happy to explain, as well as tasty food, great cocktails, and more. **Known for:** great coffee drinks; tasty food; comfortable, chill atmosphere. 💲 *Average main: S/32* ✉ *Calle Espaderos 136, Plaza de Armas* ☎ *084/263–264* 🌐 *www.museodelcafecusco.com.*

Papachos
$$ | **BURGER** | The brainchild of Gastón Acurio, Peru's most famous chef, Papachos is the place to go for a fresh take on the burger. With a sports bar atmosphere, the restaurant has a huge menu with plenty of other choices, but it's the burgers you come here for. **Known for:** great burgers; unique toppings; delicious desserts. *Average main: S/36 Portal de Belen 115, 2nd fl., Plaza de Armas 084/228–205 www.papachos.com.*

Uchu
$$$ | **PERUVIAN** | You could easily just feast on tasty appetizers at this upscale, minimalist-design spot, but you'd be missing out on the real highlight—an entrée cooked at your table on a heated volcanic stone. Choice, fresh selections of beef, alpaca, fish, chicken, and shrimp, are brought to your table seared on the outside, allowing you to complete cooking them to your personal preference. **Known for:** table-side cooking on lava stone; highest quality meats and fish; ample portions. *Average main: S/55 Calle Palacio 135 084/246–598 www.cuzcodining.com.*

Hotels

Andean Wings
$$ | **HOTEL** | Housed in a 16th-century colonial mansion, this boutique hotel does an outstanding job of complementing its historical backdrop with artistic design—though all rooms have first-class amenities, each room is uniquely decorated with original artwork and features such as chandeliers, canopy beds, or Jacuzzi tubs. **Pros:** luxurious rooms; excellent bar and restaurant; design is a visual feast. **Cons:** some rooms are smaller with less light; not all designs may be to your taste; on the less favored side of the main plaza. *Rooms from: S/298 Siete Cuartones 225 084/243–166 www.andeanwings.com 17 rooms Breakfast.*

Corn 1,000 ways

Corn is a staple of the Peruvian diet—wander the streets of Cusco long enough, and you'll soon see it being popped, steamed, and roasted into a healthful carbo-snack. *Chicha*, a corn beer drunk at room temperature and sold from rural homes that display a red flag (and in many restaurants), is a surprisingly tasty take on the old corncob, though it can have adverse effects on the foreign tummy. You may want to stick to the nonalcoholic chicha *morada*, made from purple corn.

Aranwa Cusco Boutique Hotel
$$$ | **HOTEL** | Everywhere you look, there are original pieces of art juxtaposed with modern furnishings at this luxurious boutique hotel housed in a 16th-century colonial mansion. **Pros:** luxury service; historic setting; intimate feel. **Cons:** some rooms have better views than others; not on the popular side of the Plaza de Armas; corridors can be noisy. *Rooms from: S/627 San Juan de Dios 255 084/604–444 www.aranwahotels.com 43 rooms Free breakfast.*

★ **Casa Cartagena**
$$$$ | **HOTEL** | Set in a restored, 17th-century property—on a cobblestone street just a few blocks north of the Plaza de Armas—this elegant boutique hotel has whitewashed walls, exposed wood beams, and colorful Peruvian embroidered pillows (also available for sale in the gift shop) juxtaposed with trendy lamps and contemporary Italian furniture. **Pros:** in the historic center of Cusco; elegant mix of old and new; excellent breakfast and service. **Cons:** thin walls; pricey; requires walking uphill or a roundabout taxi ride. *Rooms from:*

S/1575 ✉ Pumacurco 336 ☎ 084/224–356 🌐 www.casacartagena.com ⛿ 16 rooms 🍽 Free breakfast.

Costa del Sol Ramada Cusco

$$ | HOTEL | This upscale option, where rates are a fraction of those at other Cusco lodgings, has two wings: the front half, which drips with colonial charm—with accommodations set around the attractive, arcaded courtyard of a 17th-century building (once the home of the Marquis of Picoaga)—and the new wing, which features modern rooms and minimalist design but is still big on comfort. **Pros:** excellent value for top-end lodging; mix of modern and colonial room options; family suite options. **Cons:** rooms on the modern side are a bit lacking in charm; restaurant not on the same scale as some other luxury hotels; heavy doors sometimes cause noise in hallways. *$ Rooms from: S/393 ✉ Calle Santa Teresa 344 ☎ 084/252–330 🌐 www.costadelsolperu.com ⛿ 90 rooms 🍽 Free breakfast.*

Fallen Angel Guest House

$$$ | HOTEL | This luxury boutique hotel features four of the most unusually designed suites you will find anywhere—picture a lofted bedroom with blue-and-brown floral wallpaper, a claw-foot tub with a red canopy curtain, chandeliers, and modern art everywhere. **Pros:** unique style; excellent service; fantastic breakfast included. **Cons:** may be noisy, as it is above the Fallen Angel restaurant, which stays open until 11; room designs might not be to everyone's taste; only one room has a balcony. *$ Rooms from: S/600 ✉ Plazoleta Nazarenas 221, San Blas ☎ 084/258–184 🌐 www.fallenangelincusco.com ⛿ 4 rooms 🍽 Free breakfast.*

Hotel Libertador Palacio del Inka

$$$$ | HOTEL | Close enough to but still removed from the hubbub of the Plaza de Armas, this hotel has made the most of its gorgeous colonial past—it was the last home of Francisco Pizarro, the first governor of Peru—while upgrading its room design. **Pros:** luxurious spa; some rooms have views of the Sun Temple; part of the Marriott group of hotels. **Cons:** there are other colonial-era hotels with a lower price tag; no air-conditioning; some rooms can be on the dark side. *$ Rooms from: S/1077 ✉ Plazoleta Santo Domingo 259 ☎ 084/231–961 🌐 www.marriott.com ⛿ 203 rooms 🍽 Free breakfast.*

Hotel Monasterio

$$$$ | HOTEL | Restoration of the landmark 1592 Monastery of San Antonio Abad—where the chapel has an ornate gold altar and Cusqueña art, and the serene cloister will take your breath away—allowed one of Cusco's top hotels to retain an austere beauty, from the elegant lounge bar to the compact rooms that blend colonial furnishings with remote-control window blinds, TVs that pop up from cabinets, and other mod-cons. **Pros:** stylish rooms with all the conveniences; stunning public spaces; beautiful building and location. **Cons:** rooms are on the smaller side; expensive (everything including Wi-Fi is charged); very busy lobby. *$ Rooms from: S/1188 ✉ Palacio 140, Plazoleta Nazarenas ☎ 084/604–000 🌐 www.belmond.com/hotel-monasterio-cusco ⛿ 122 rooms 🍽 Free breakfast.*

JW Marriott Cusco

$$$$ | HOTEL | Step through the enormous original 16th-century doorway and into the plush lobby for a feel of this property, a beautiful and comfortable blend of old and new, featuring large rooms with amenities such as oxygen pumped in on request (at an extra charge), in-room thermostats, down comforters, and king-size beds. **Pros:** large comfortable rooms; close to the Plaza de Armas; local weaver with llama in the courtyard daily. **Cons:** not everyone will appreciate the blending of past and present; some fees are charged upon arrival, not at time of booking; some rooms have no windows to the outside. *$ Rooms from: S/850 ✉ Calle Ruinas 432, at San Agustín ☎ 084/582–200 🌐 www.marriott.com ⛿ 153 rooms 🍽 Free breakfast.*

★ La Casona

$$$$ | **HOTEL** | Colonial with more than a touch of class, this exclusive, 11-suite boutique *casa* comes complete with a manicured interior courtyard; stately sitting and dining areas; and rooms with heated floors, antique-looking but modern bathtubs, and marbled showers. **Pros:** serenely situated and spoil-yourself stylish; colonial palace setting; personalized service. **Cons:** books up fast in high season; one of the most expensive hotels in town; up a steep hill from the plaza. *Rooms from: S/1862* ✉ *Plaza Nazarenas 113* ☎ *084/245–314, 866/242–2889 reservations from U.S., 855/409–1456 reservations from Canada* 🌐 *www.inkaterra.com* *11 suites* *Free breakfast.*

Niños Hotel

$ | **HOTEL** | For lodging with a social conscience, this is a great budget option: proceeds from your stay at the "Children's Hotel" provide medical and dental care, food, and recreation for disadvantaged cusqueño children who attend day care on premises and cheerfully greet you as you enter the courtyard. **Pros:** wonderfully welcoming staff; charming colonial building; proceeds benefit a good cause. **Cons:** slightly out of the way; some rooms are small and very basic; not all rooms have private bathrooms. *Rooms from: S/180* ✉ *Meloq 442* ☎ *084/231–424* 🌐 *www.ninoshotel.com* *No credit cards* *20 rooms* *No meals.*

★ Palacio Nazarenas

$$$$ | **HOTEL** | A former palace and convent dating from the 18th century, Palacio Nazarenas, located just off the Plaza de Armas, is one of Cusco's most glamorous hotels, featuring spacious, locally inspired suites surrounding seven cloistered terraces. **Pros:** excellent and friendly staff; historic setting in a central location; top-notch spa. **Cons:** not all rooms have balconies; swimming pool is outdoors; more luxurious suites have a price to match. *Rooms from: S/1770* ✉ *Plaza Nazarenas 144* ☎ *84/582–222* 🌐 *www.belmond.com/palacio-nazarenas-cusco* *55 suites* *Breakfast.*

Tierra Viva Cusco Plaza

$$ | **HOTEL** | Part of the reliable, Peru-based, Tierra Viva chain, this branch is set in a historic building and makes a comfortable base, with beautiful colonial common areas and rooms that have orthopedic mattresses and details like artisanal weavings and wooden floors. **Pros:** central location; historic building; some rooms have gorgeous city views. **Cons:** simple decor; lacks the charm of boutique hotels; can have noise issues due to location. *Rooms from: S/306* ✉ *Suecia 345, Plaza de Armas* ☎ *084/245–858* 🌐 *www.tierravivahoteles.com* *20 rooms* *Breakfast.*

Nightlife

BARS AND PUBS

Museo del Pisco

BARS/PUBS | If you only have time for one bar while you're in Cusco, make it this atmospheric spot. Not only does it serve great pisco drinks (you can even get a pisco tasting on the fly), but it also offers tapas if you want to nosh as you drink. There's often live music as well. ✉ *Santa Catalina Ancha 398* ☎ *084/262–709* 🌐 *www.museodelpisco.org.*

Norton Rat's Tavern

BARS/PUBS | The second-floor tavern has a great outdoor balcony overlooking the Plaza de Armas, perfect for enjoying a beer (especially if you want an import) and watching the people go by. ✉ *Santa Catalina Angosta N 116, Plaza de Armas.*

Paddy's Irish Pub

BARS/PUBS | The dark-wood, second-floor Paddy's serves pints of Guinness and old-fashioned Irish pub grub such as Philly cheesesteaks, pita sandwiches, and chicken baguettes. ✉ *Triunfo 124, Plaza de Armas* ☎ *084/225–361* 🌐 *www.paddysirishbarcusco.com.*

Inti Raymi

Inti is the Quechua name for the sun, which the Inca worshipped. Inca rulers were considered to be descended from Inti, thus legitimizing their authority over the people. The most important festival was Inti Raymi, held on June 24, marking the winter solstice and the beginning of the new year. Each June, Cusco is once again home to the Inti Raymi celebration, which begins at the Qorikancha with dances and processions, making its way to Sacsayhuamán, where a variety of ceremonies are performed. There is a cost to attend the festivities at Sacsayhuamán, but those held in the center of Cusco are free. ■ **TIP→ If you plan to travel to Peru at this time, reservations should be made well ahead of time because of the influx of visitors.**

DANCE CLUBS

Ukukus

DANCE CLUBS | Dance the night away at Ukukus, a hugely popular pub and disco that hops with a young crowd, often until 5 am. This is one of the best (and only) places in town to hear live music from local talent, often featuring traditional Peruvian tunes with a modern twist. ✉ *Plateros 316, 2nd fl.* ☎ *084/254–911*.

Performing Arts

THEATER

ICPNA Cusco

ART GALLERIES—ARTS | Created to promote understanding between Peru and the United States through educational and cultural programs, this center puts on some of the most varied cultural offerings in the city. It also has a small art gallery with new shows every month. ✉ *Av. Tulumayo 125* ☎ *084/224–112* 🌐 *www.icpnacusco.org*.

Shopping

ART AND REPLICAS

★ **Ilaria**

ART GALLERIES | This is Cusco's finest silver store, with an ample selection of replicas of colonial-era pieces, as well as some really creative and elegant originals. The internationally recognized shop is based in Lima, though there are multiple locations in Cusco, including ones in the Monasterio, Casa Andina Private Collection, and JW Marriott hotels. ✉ *Portal de Carrizos 258, Plaza de Armas* ☎ *084/246–253* 🌐 *www.ilaria.pe*.

CERAMICS

★ **Seminario**

CERAMICS/GLASSWARE | The Cusco shop of famed ceramics maker Pablo Seminario is now housed in the MAP museum building. Known around the world, it is an ideal place to get a locally made gift that is truly special. Prices are lower at the source, in the Sacred Valley town of Urubamba. ✉ *Plaza Nazarenas 231* ☎ *084/246–093* 🌐 *www.ceramicaseminario.com*.

CRAFTS AND GIFTS

Andean Treasures

CRAFTS | This reasonably priced crafts shop has many original pieces including tapestries, ceramics, and alpaca clothing. ✉ *Calle Mantas 118* ☎ *084/228–931*.

Arte y Canela

CRAFTS | If you're looking for modern twists on folkloric crafts, check out Arte y Canela, which sells a variety of high-end silver jewelry and household goods, all with a regional artistic flair. ✉ *Portal de Panes 143, Plaza de Armas* ☎ *084/221–519* 🌐 *www.arteycanela.com*.

SPORTING GOODS

The North Face

CLOTHING | There are three locations for this well-known supplier of outdoor wear. In the center, there is one right on the Plaza de Armas and another at Plazoleta Espinar 188; the third store is in the Real Plaza, Cusco's mall. It's best to buy directly from the company, as there have been problems with inferior knockoffs of North Face products being sold in Peru. ✉ *Portal de Comercio 195, Plaza de Armas* ☎ *084/227–789* 🌐 *www.thenorthface.com.pe.*

RKF

SPORTING GOODS | Forget to pack your winter jacket for the Inca Trail? No problem: check out RKF, where you'll find a variety of quality (mostly imported) outdoor goods from the top brands like Mountain Hard Wear and Columbia. ✉ *Portal Carrizos 252, Plaza de Armas* ☎ *084/254–895* 🌐 *www.rockford.pe.*

Speedy Gonzales

SPORTING GOODS | Although the shop sells camping equipment, it's also the first place to check if you get to town and want to rent something for your trek. They also do repairs. ✉ *Procuradores 393, Plaza de Armas* ☎ *992/725–430.*

TEXTILES

Alpaca's Best

TEXTILES/SEWING | With several stores in Cusco, Alpaca's Best sells quality knits but also has a good selection of jewelry. ✉ *Portal Confiturias 221, Plaza de Armas* ☎ *084/249–406* 🌐 *alpacas-best.com.*

★ Arte Antropología

TEXTILES/SEWING | If you're looking for something truly unique, you must make your way here. Part museum, mostly a store, this has been a labor of love for many years as Rosie Barnes and Walter Rodriguez Mamani painstakingly made their way through the legal mire of renovating a colonial manse. The result is simply gorgeous, not least owing to the plethora of one-of-a-kind items that you simply won't find elsewhere, due to locals from all over Peru and Bolvia bringing their heirlooms to sell over the years before the store finally opened. ✉ *Calle Ruinas 105* ☎ *984/623–555.*

Center for Traditional Textiles of Cusco

TEXTILES/SEWING | Sweaters, ponchos, scarves, and wall hangings are sold at fair-trade prices at this nonprofit organization dedicated to the survival of traditional weaving. Weavers from local villages work in the shop, and the on-site museum has informative exhibits about weaving techniques and the customs behind traditional costume. There are additional branches in MAP and Museo Inka. ✉ *Av. El Sol 603* ☎ *084/228–117* 🌐 *www.textilescusco.org.*

Centro Artesanal Cusco

TEXTILES/SEWING | The municipal government operates the Centro Artesanal Cusco, containing 340 stands of artisan vendors. This is often your best bet for buying those souvenirs that you've seen everywhere but not gotten around to purchasing. Prices are typically negotiable (and often cheaper than you will find in Pisac), and the more you buy at one stall, the better discount you are likely to get. ✉ *Tullumayo and El Sol.*

El Palacio de Las Lanas

TEXTILES/SEWING | If you'd rather knit your own sweater than buy one, there are many places where you can buy yarn. Take a walk over toward the San Pedro market, where you will find a number of yarn stores, such as this one, where you can buy packets of the famous baby alpaca yarn. ✉ *Thupac Amaru 155* ☎ *084/228–741, 974/286–272.*

Ethnic Peru

TEXTILES/SEWING | For fine alpaca coats, sweaters, scarves, and shawls, check out this shop; there are two other central locations at Santa Catalina Ancha and Limacpampa Chico. ✉ *Portal Mantas 114, Plaza de Armas* ☎ *084/232–775* 🌐 *www.ethnicperu.com.*

Alpaca or Acrylic?

Vendors and hole-in-the-wall shopkeepers will beckon you in to look at their wares: "One of a kind," they proudly proclaim. "Baby alpaca, handwoven by my grandmother on her deathbed. It's yours for S/70."

Price should be the first giveaway. A real baby-alpaca sweater would sell for more than S/200. So maintain your skepticism even if the label boldly says "100% baby alpaca." False labels are common on acrylic-blend clothing throughout the Cusco area. Which brings us to our next clue: a good-quality label should show the maker's or seller's name and address. You're more likely to find high-quality goods at an upscale shop, of which there are several around town. Such a business is just not going to gamble its reputation on inferior products.

Texture is the classic piece of evidence. Baby-alpaca products use hairs, 16–18 microns in diameter, taken from the animal's first clipping. Subsequent shearings from a more mature alpaca yield hairs with a 20-micron diameter, still quite soft, but never matching the legendary tenderness of baby alpaca. (For that reason, women tend toward baby-alpaca products; men navigate toward regular alpaca.) A blend with llama or sheep's wool is slightly rougher to the touch and, for some people, itchier to the skin. And if the garment is too silky, it's likely a synthetic blend. (The occasional 100% polyester product is passed off as alpaca to unsuspecting buyers.)

Although "one of a kind" denotes uniqueness—and again, be aware that much of what is claimed to be handmade here really comes from a factory—the experts say there is nothing wrong with factory-made alpaca products. A garment really woven by someone's grandmother lacks a certain degree of quality control, and you may find later that the dyes run or the seams come undone.

—By Jeffrey Van Fleet

★ KUNA

TEXTILES/SEWING | Long-established and ubermodern KUNA has alpaca garments and is one of the only authorized distributors of high-quality vicuña scarves and sweaters. It's run by Peruvian design company Alpaca 111, which has eight other shops in Cusco. including at the Plaza Regocijo, the Monasterio hotel, the Marriott hotel, the Palacio del Inca hotel, and the airport. ✉ *Portal de Panes 127, Plaza de Armas* ☎ *084/243–191* 🌐 *www.kunastores.com.*

La Casa de la Llama

TEXTILES/SEWING | Alpaca gets the camelid's share of attention for use in making fine garments, but this store sells a fine selection of expensive clothing made from the softer hairs sheared from its namesake animal's chest and neck. It's difficult to tell the difference in texture between llama and adult alpaca, at least in this shop. There are some nice gifts for little ones here as well. ✉ *Palacio 121* ☎ *084/240–813.*

Sol Alpaca

TEXTILES/SEWING | Offering fine garments made from alpaca and vicuña fibers, this store is part of the Michell Group, which has more than 75 years of know-how in processing alpaca and is the leading alpaca producer and exporter in the world. There are also stores on Calle Espaderos, Portal de Mantas, Santa Catalina Ancha, and in the Plaza Nazarenas. ✉ *Santa Teresa 317, Plaza Regocijo* ☎ *084/232–687* 🌐 *www.solalpaca.com.*

San Blas

For spectacular views over Cusco's terracotta rooftops, head to San Blas. This is where the Incas brought the choicest artists and artisans, culled from recent conquests, to bolster their own knowledge base. The neighborhood has maintained its bohemian roots for centuries and remains one of the city's most picturesque districts with whitewashed adobe homes and bright-blue doors. The area and its surrounds is one of the trendier parts of Cusco, with several of the city's choicest restaurants and cafés opening their doors here. The Cuesta de San Blas (San Blas Hill), one of the main entrances into the area, is sprinkled with galleries that sell paintings in the Escuela Cusqueña style of the 16th through 18th centuries and carved traditional masks. Many of the stone streets are built as stairs or slopes (not for cars) and have religious motifs carved into them.

Sights

Museo Hilario Mendívil

MUSEUM | The former home of San Blas's most famous son, the 20th-century Peruvian religious artist Hilario Mendívil (1929–77), makes a good stop if you have an interest in Cusqeñan art and iconography. Legend has it that Mendívil saw llamas parading in the Corpus Christi procession as a child and later infused this image into his religious art, depicting all his figures with long, llama-like necks. **■ TIP→ In the small gallery are the maguey-wood and rice-plaster sculptures of the Virgin with the elongated necks that were the artist's trademark.** There's also a shop selling Mendívil-style work. ✉ *Plazoleta San Blas 634, San Blas* ☎ *084/240–527* 🎟 *Free.*

Templo y Plazoleta de San Blas

PLAZA | The little square in San Blas has a simple adobe church with one of the jewels of colonial art in the Americas—the pulpit of San Blas, an intricately carved, 17th-century, cedar pulpit that is arguably Latin America's most ornate. Tradition holds that the work was hewn from a single tree trunk, but experts now believe it was assembled from 1,200 individually carved pieces. Figures of Martin Luther, John Calvin, and Henry VIII—all opponents of Catholicism—as well as those representing the seven deadly sins are condemned for eternity to hold up the pulpit's base. The work is dominated by the triumphant figure of Christ. At his feet rests a human skull, not carved, but the real thing. It's thought to belong to Juan Tomás Tuyrutupac, the creator of the pulpit. ✉ *Plazoleta de San Blas, San Blas* ☎ *084/254–057* 🎟 *S/15; S/30 combined entrance with Catedral and Museo de Arte Religioso.*

Restaurants

Green Point

$ | **VEGETARIAN** | Although there are plenty of vegetarian options elsewhere, here vegetarians and vegans can order anything with a clear, animal-loving conscience. You can even have your coffee with nut milk. **Known for:** extensive vegan menu; inexpensive prix-fixe lunch; vegan products to go. Ⓢ *Average main: S/30* ✉ *Calle Carmen Bajo 235, San Blas* ☎ *084/431–146* 🌐 *www.greenpointrestaurants.com* 💳 *No credit cards.*

Jack's Cafe

$ | **CAFÉ** | Scrumptious breakfasts can be had all day at this bright, busy, American-style café with Aussie roots, where you can order granola and yogurt, large fluffy pancakes, or a grand "brekkie" with bacon and eggs. Also on the menu are gourmet sandwiches, fresh salads, and a variety of other satisfying dishes. **Known for:** lines out the door; big portions; comfort food. Ⓢ *Average main:*

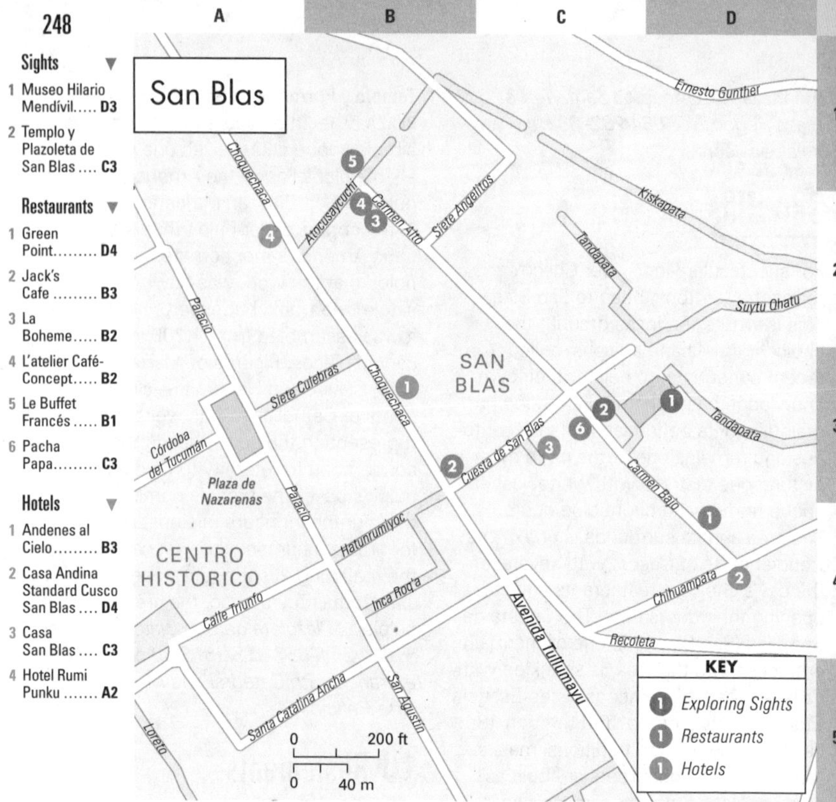

S/25 ✉ *Choquechaca 509, San Blas* ☎ *084/254–606* 🌐 *jackscafecusco.com* 💳 *No credit cards.*

La Boheme

$ | **FRENCH** | For a quick bite, it's hard to go wrong with real French crepes; with both savory and sweet to choose from, they're the perfect meal or pick-me-up any time of day. The prix-fixe lunch is a delicious deal and there's a great tea selection for an afternoon break. **Known for:** authentic crepes; prix-fixe lunch; tea selection. $ *Average main: S/20* ✉ *Carmen Alto 283, San Blas* ☎ *084/235–694* 🌐 *www.labohemecusco.com* ⏲ *Closed Mon.*

L'atelier Café-Concept

$ | **CAFÉ** | Slip into this sweet little café, which invites you to linger, especially if you manage to snag a balcony table. The coffee is as good as it should be in a French-owned place, and the handmade jewelry—some of which features Peruvian materials such as antique coins—the soft and stylish textiles, and the vintage clothing on sale and sprinkled throughout are downright dangerous. **Known for:** great coffee; chill atmosphere; vintage clothing and handmade jewelry. $ *Average main: S/10* ✉ *Calle Atoqsaycuchi 605-A, San Blas* ☎ *084/248–333* ⏲ *Closed Mon.* 💳 *No credit cards.*

Le Buffet Francés

$ | **FRENCH** | Although not a buffet in the American sense of all-you-can-eat, this French-owned café tests your restraint with the best pastries in town, as well as reasonably priced sandwiches on homemade bread, quiches, cheese and meat plates, salads, French wine, and, every Friday night, a special French dish of the week. Prix-fixe lunch menus are also available. **Known for:** delicious pastries;

fresh homemade food; great coffee. *Average main: S/18 ✉ Calle Atoqsaycuchi 616, San Blas ☎ 979/715–854 ⏲ Closed Sun.*

★ Pacha Papa

$$ | PERUVIAN | FAMILY | The menu at this restaurant, which is modeled after a typical open-air *quinta*, with wooden tables scattered around a large patio, gets its influences from all over Peru, and the waiters are happy to explain what makes each traditional dish special. For a special treat, go for the underground-oven-baked *pachamanca*, in which different types of meats are slow roasted together with potatoes and aromatic herbs. **Known for:** traditional Peruvian food; great place to try guinea pig; authentic atmosphere. *Average main: S/43 ✉ Plazoleta San Blas 120 ☎ 084/241–318 🌐 www.cuscorestaurants.com.*

Hotels

Andenes al Cielo

$ | HOTEL | A boutique hotel housed in a colonial mansion, Andenes is located just a few blocks from the Plaza de Armas but offers a quiet respite from the crowds there. **Pros:** bargain cost for a central location; comfortable rooms; lovely setting. **Cons:** not as luxurious as some of the other Cusco choices; street-facing rooms can have some noise; some rooms only have windows on the courtyard. *Rooms from: S/210 ✉ Calle Choquechaca 176, San Blas ☎ 084/222–237 🌐 www.andenesalcielo.com 15 rooms Free breakfast.*

Casa Andina Standard Cusco San Blas

$$ | HOTEL | Part of a national chain, all the Casa Andina hotels exude professionalism and are a great value, but each hotel differs in style—the San Blas branch, in a colonial house perched up on the hillside, offers great views over the city's terracotta rooftops. **Pros:** good value for top-end lodgings; excellent location with spectacular views over Cusco; professional atmosphere and pleasant service. **Cons:** can be a hard walk uphill to get here; some rooms have sub-par views over the neighboring houses; not a luxury accommodation. *Rooms from: S/330 ✉ Chihuampata 278, San Blas ☎ 084/263–694, 01/391–6500 Lima reservations 🌐 www.casa-andina.com 37 rooms Free breakfast.*

Casa San Blas

$$ | HOTEL | FAMILY | This small hotel with a large staff prides itself on exceptional service, and the rooms are quite comfortable, with colonial-style furniture and hardwood floors, but with more modern amenities than this restored 250-year-old house would imply. **Pros:** fabulous views; warm welcome from staff; fantastic location. **Cons:** it's a steep uphill walk to get here; rooms by lobby can be noisy; no central heating. *Rooms from: S/327 ✉ Tocuyeros 556, San Blas ☎ 084/237–900, 984/033-770 WhatsApp 🌐 www.casasanblas.com 18 rooms Free breakfast.*

Hotel Rumi Punku

$$ | HOTEL | A massive stone door—that's what *rumi punku* means in Quechua—opens onto a rambling complex of balconies, patios, gardens, courtyards, terraces, fireplace, and bits of Inca wall scattered here and there linking a series of pleasantly furnished rooms that have hardwood floors and comfy beds covered with plush blankets. **Pros:** great views from the upstairs sauna (USD$15 extra); charming rambling layout; great value for the money. **Cons:** located a bit uphill; some rooms are on the small side; older hotel can be a bit noisy. *Rooms from: S/330 ✉ Choquechaca 339 ☎ 084/221–102 🌐 www.rumipunku.com 41 rooms Free breakfast.*

Shopping

CERAMICS

★ Galería Mérida

CERAMICS/GLASSWARE | In San Blas, the Galería Mérida sells the much-imitated ceramics of Edilberto Mérida. His characters are so expressive you can practically hear them as you browse through the gallery, which doubles as a museum where you can learn more about this award-winning Peruvian artist and his work. ✉ *Carmen Alto 133, San Blas* ☎ *084/221–714* ⏲ *Closed Sun.*

CRAFTS AND GIFTS

★ Galería Mendívil

CRAFTS | Religious art, including elaborately costumed statues of the Virgin Mary, is sold at the shop at the Galería Mendívil. The popular Museo Hilario Mendívil is located across the plaza. ✉ *Plazoleta San Blas 615–619* ☎ *084/240–527, 084/274–6622.*

Hilo

CLOTHING | Like to find fun and unique clothing wherever you travel? This is the store for you. Not remotely Peruvian, Hilo is a boutique shop where you'll find all original pieces unlike anything you've ever seen. Irish-born Eibhlin Cassidy is more artist than mere dressmaker, and if you have the time, she's more than happy to design something especially for you. ✉ *Carmen Alto 260, San Blas* ☎ *084/254–536* 🌐 *www.hilocusco.com.*

SPAS

Healing House

SPA/BEAUTY | After a day of touring, climbing up and down hundreds of steps, you may be ready for a massage. Healing House is the place to go for a professional treatment with European- and American-trained therapists. This nonprofit also offers yoga classes, a variety of other therapies, as well as seminars, and it provides low-cost or free treatments and workshops to locals with limited resources. Limited rooms are available to rent in shared housing for those wanting a more spiritual place to stay. ✉ *560 Qanchipata, San Blas* ☎ *943/729–368* 🌐 *www.healinghousecusco.com.*

Sacsayhuamán

2 km (1 mile) east of Cusco.

This is the second-most important Inca site in the Cusco area after Qorikancha, and a primary reason for going on the standard Cusco City Tour, which also includes Qenqo, Puka Pukara, and Tambomachay.

GETTING HERE AND AROUND

Sacsayhuamán sits a stone's throw from Cusco and is easily visited in a half-day organized tour. A so-called mystical tour typically takes in the Templo de la Luna (which you can no longer enter) and other surrounding sites. If your lungs and legs are up to it, the self-guided 30-minute ascent from Cusco to Sacsayhuamán offers an eye-catching introduction to colonial Cusco. The walk starts from the Plaza de Armas and winds uphill along the pedestrian-only Resbalosa Street. Make your way past San Cristóbal Church, hang a left at the outstretched arms of the white statue of Christ, and you're almost there.

Sights

★ Sacsayhuamán

ARCHAEOLOGICAL SITE | Towering high above Cusco, the ruins of Sacsayhuamán are a constant reminder of the city's Inca roots. You may have to stretch your imagination to visualize how it was during Inca times—much of the site was used as a convenient source of building material by the conquering Spanish, but plenty remains to be marveled at. Huge stone blocks beg the question of how they were carved and maneuvered into position, and the masterful masonry is awe-inspiring. If you're not moved by

Did You Know?

The Inca built Cusco in the shape of a puma. If you're in Cusco, try to figure out what part of the puma body you're standing in.

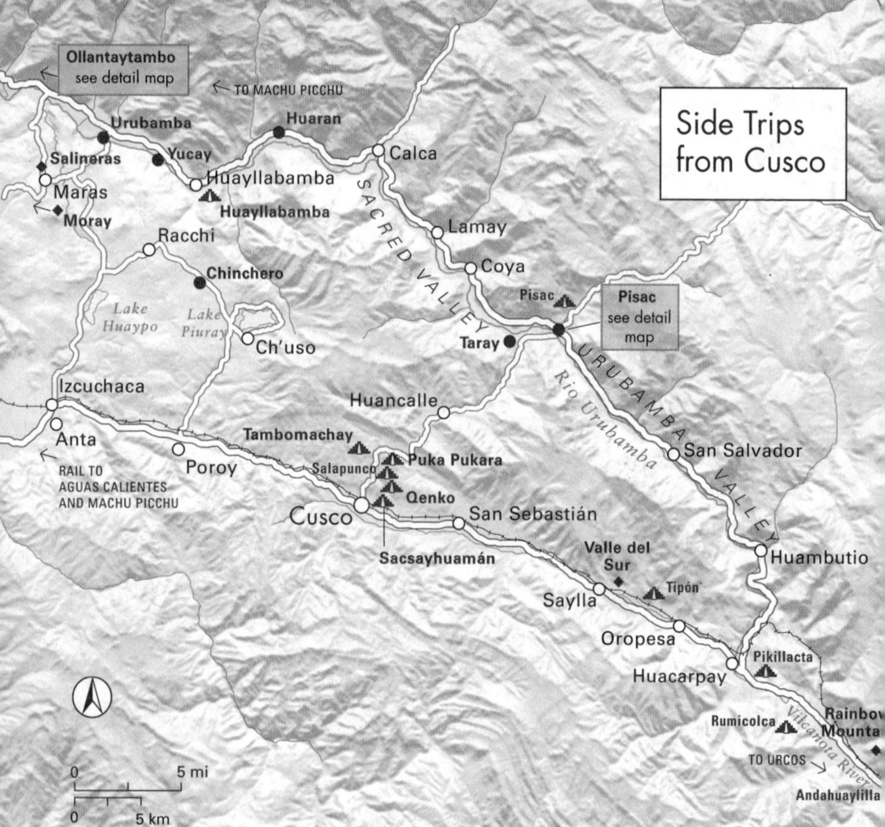

stonework, the spectacular views over the city are just as impressive.

If the Incas designed Cusco in the shape of a puma, then Sacsayhuamán represents its ferocious head. Perhaps the most important Inca monument after Machu Picchu, Sacsayhuamán is thought to have been a religious complex during Inca times. That being said, from its strategic position high above Cusco, it was also excellently placed to defend the city, and its zigzag walls and cross-fire parapets allowed defenders to rain destruction on attackers from two sides.

Construction of the site began in the 1440s, during the reign of the Inca Pachacutec. It's thought that 20,000 workers were needed for Sacsayhuamán's construction, cutting the astonishingly massive limestone, diorite, and andesite blocks—the largest gets varying estimates of anywhere between 125 and 350 tons—rolling them to the site, and assembling them in traditional Inca style to achieve a perfect fit without mortar. The Inca Manco Cápac II, installed as puppet ruler after the conquest, retook the fortress and led a mutiny against Juan Pizarro and the Spanish in 1536. Fighting raged for 10 months in a valiant but unsuccessful bid by the Inca to reclaim their empire. History records that thousands of corpses from both sides littered the grounds and were devoured by condors at the end of the battle.

Today only the outer walls remain of the original fortress city, but even with one-fifth of the original complex left, the site is impressive. Sacsayhuamán's three original towers, used for provisions, no longer stand, though the foundations of two are still visible. The so-called Inca's

Throne, the Suchuna, remains, presumably used by the emperor for reviewing troops. Today, those parade grounds, the Explanada, are the ending point for the June 24 Inti Raymi Festival of the Sun, commemorating the winter solstice and Cusco's most famous celebration.

■ **TIP→ A large map at both entrances shows the layout of Sacsayhuamán, but once you enter, signage and explanations are minimal.** You may find guides waiting outside the entrances who can give you a two-hour tour (negotiate the price ahead of time). Most are competent and knowledgeable, but depending on their perspective, you'll get a strictly historic, strictly mystical, strictly architectural, or all-of-the-above type tour, and almost all guides work the standard joke into their spiel that the name of the site is pronounced "sexy woman." It's theoretically possible to sneak into Sacsayhuamán after hours, but lighting is poor, surfaces are uneven, and robberies have occurred at night. ✉ *Cusco* ✣ *2 km (1 mile) north of Cusco* 🎫 *Boleto Turístico.*

Qenko

4 km (2½ miles) northeast of Cusco.

A stop on the Cusco City Tour, this ceremonial site predicted the season's harvest.

Sights

Qenko

RELIGIOUS SITE | It may be a fairly serene location these days, but Qenko, which means "zigzag," was once the site of one of the Incas' most intriguing and potentially macabre rituals. Named after the zigzagging channels carved into the surface, Qenko is a large rock thought to have been the site of an annual pre-planting ritual in which priests standing on the top poured llama blood into a ceremonial pipe, allowing it to make its way down the channel. If the blood flowed left, it boded poor fertility for the coming season. If the liquid continued the full length of the pipe, it spelled a bountiful harvest. ■ **TIP→ Today you won't see any blood, but the carved channels still exist, and you can climb to the top to see how they zigzag their way down.** Other symbolic carvings mix it up on the rock face, too—the eagle-eyed might spot a puma, condor, and a llama. ✉ *Km 4, Hwy. to Pisac, Cusco* 🎫 *Boleto Turístico.*

Did You Know? 

Quechua is not a written language. Therefore, there is no written history of the Inca before the time of the Spanish conquest. For this reason, much of what is believed about the local history is speculation. Don't be surprised if you hear different guides offering different versions of the past. Take it all with a grain of salt, and feel free to make up your own theories!

Puka Pukara

10 km (6 miles) northeast of Cusco.

A stop on the Cusco City Tour, this pink-stone Inca site offers great views of the valley below.

Sights

Puka Pukara

ARCHAEOLOGICAL SITE | Little is known of the archaeological ruins of Puka Pukara, a pink-stone site guarding the road to the Sacred Valley. Some archaeologists believe the complex was a fort—its name means "red fort"—but others claim it served as a hunting lodge and storage place used by the Inca nobility. Current theory holds that this center, likely built during the reign of the Inca

Pachacutec, served all those functions. Whatever it was, it was put in the right place. Near Tambomachay, this enigmatic spot provides spectacular views over the Sacred Valley. Pull up a rock, and ponder the mystery yourself. ✉ *Km 10, Hwy. to Pisac, Cusco* 🎫 *Boleto Turístico.*

Tambomachay

11 km (6½ miles) north of Cusco.

Inca-built fountains tap the natural spring at this site on the Cusco City Tour.

Sights

Tambomachay

RELIGIOUS SITE | Ancient fountains preside over this tranquil and secluded spot, which is commonly known as "El Baño del Inca," or Inca's Bath. The name actually means "cavern lodge," and the site is a three-tiered huaca built of elaborate stonework over a natural spring, which is thought to have been used for ritual showers. Interpretations differ, but the site was likely a place where water, considered a source of life, was worshipped (or perhaps it was just a nice place to take a bath). The huaca is almost certain to have been the scene of sacred ablutions and purifying ceremonies for Inca rulers and royal women. ✉ *Km 11, Hwy. to Pisac, Cusco* 🎫 *Boleto Turístico.*

Valle del Sur

26 km (16 miles) southeast of Cusco.

The Río Urubamba runs northwest and southeast from Cusco. The northwest sector of the river basin is the romantically named Sacred Valley of the Inca, but along the highway that runs southeast of Cusco to Sicuani, the region that locals call the Valle del Sur is just as interesting. The area abounds with opportunities for off-the-beaten-path exploration. Detour to the tiny town of Oropesa and get to know a self-proclaimed capital of brick-oven bread making, a tradition that has sustained local families for more than 90 years. Or you can side-trip to more pre-Inca and Inca sites. Apart from Andahuayillas, you'll have the ruins almost to yourself. Only admission to Tipón and Pikillacta is included in the Boleto Turístico. A common tour offers an excursion to all three sites.

Sights

Andahuaylillas

RELIGIOUS SITE | The main attraction of the small town of Andahuaylillas, 8 km (5 miles) southeast of Pikillacta, is a small 17th-century adobe-towered church built by the Jesuits on the central plaza over the remains of an Inca temple. The contrast between the simple exterior and the rich, expressive, colonial baroque art inside is notable: fine examples of the Escuela Cusqueña decorate the upper interior walls. ■ **TIP→ It's the ceiling that is the church's special claim to fame, leading it to be referred to as the Sistine Chapel of America.** ✉ *Km 40, Hwy. to Urcos, Cusco* 🎫 *S/15.*

Pikillacta

ARCHAEOLOGICAL SITE | For a reminder that civilizations existed in this region before the Incas, head to Pikillacta, a vast city of 700 buildings from the pre-Inca Wari culture, which flourished between AD 600 and 1000. Over a 2-km (1.25-mile) site you'll see what remains of what was once a vast walled city with enclosing walls reaching up to 7 meters (23 feet) in height and many two-story buildings, which were entered via ladders to doorways on the second floor. Little is known about the Wari culture, whose empire once stretched from near Cajamarca to the border of Tiahuanaco near Lake Titicaca. It's clear, however, that they had a genius for farming in a harsh environment and, like the Incas,

Alternatives to the Inca Trail

The popularity of the Inca Trail and the scarcity of available spots have led to the opening of several alternative hikes of varying length and difficulty.

The four- to seven-day **Salkantay** trek (typically five days) is named for the 6,270-meter (20,500-foot) peak of the same name. It begins at Mollepata, four hours by road from Cusco, and is a strenuous hike that goes through a 4,800-meter (15,700-foot) pass. The seven-day version of the Salkantay excursion joins the Inca Trail at Huayllabamba, and for this one you need an Inca Trail permit.

The **Ausangate** trek takes its name from the Nevado Ausangate, 6,372 meters (20,900 feet) in elevation, and requires a day of travel each way from Cusco in addition to the standard five to six days on the trail. Nearly the entire excursion takes you on terrain more than 4,000 meters (13,100 feet) high.

Multiday hikes through the **Lares Valley**, north of Urubamba and Ollantaytambo, offer a little bit of everything for anyone who enjoys the outdoors. A series of ancient trails once used by the Inca wind their way through native forests and past lakes fed by runoff from the snowcapped mountains nearby. Excursions also offer a cultural dimension, with stops at several traditional Quechua villages along the way. The Lares trek compares in difficulty to the Inca Trail.

The lesser-known but remarkably rewarding trek to **Choquequirao** (Cradle of Gold) takes in stunning Andean scenery as you make your way to ruins that have been heralded as Machu Picchu's "Sacred Sister." The site, another long-lost Inca city still under excavation and not yet engulfed by mass tourism, sits at 3,100 meters (10,180 feet). The four-day trek entails a series of steep ascents and descents. If you have more time, you can continue trekking on to Machu Picchu from here.

The **Chinchero–Huayllabamba** trek has two selling points: it can be accomplished in one day—about six hours—and is downhill much of the way, although portions get steep. The hike begins in Chinchero, north of Cusco, and follows an Inca trail that offers splendid views as you descend into the Sacred Valley toward the small village of Huayllabamba.

Although the **Rainbow Mountains** near Ausangate have been getting widely sold as a destination, it should be noted that doing this in a single day as it is often marketed is rather long, uncomfortable, and crowded. It's best to do this as a two-day trip from Cusco, including one night of camping.

built sophisticated urban centers such as Pikillacta (which means the "place of the flea"). At the thatch-roofed excavation sites, uncovered walls show the city's stones were once covered with plaster and whitewashed. A small museum at the entrance houses a smattering of artifacts collected during site excavation, along with a complete dinosaur skeleton. Across the road lies a beautiful lagoon, Lago de Lucre. ✉ *Km 32, Hwy. to Urcos, Cusco* 🎫 *Boleto Turístico.*

Rumicolca

MILITARY SITE | At Rumicolca, an enormous, 12-meter-high (39-foot-high) gate dating from the Wari period stands a healthy walk uphill from the highway. The

Inca enhanced the original construction of their predecessors, fortifying it with andesite stone and using the gate as a border checkpoint and customs post. ✉ *Km 32, Hwy. to Urcos, Cusco* 🎫 *Free.*

Tipón

ARCHAEOLOGICAL SITE | Everyone has heard that the Incas were good engineers, but for a real look at just how good they were at land and water management, head to Tipón. Twenty km (12 miles) or so south of Cusco, Tipón is a series of terraces, hidden from the valley below, crisscrossed by stone aqueducts and carved irrigation channels that edge up a narrow pass in the mountains. A spring fed the site and continually replenished a 900-cubic-meter (3,180-cubic-foot) reservoir that supplied water to crops growing on the terraces. **■ TIP→ So superb was the technology that several of the terraces are still in use today and still supplied by the same watering system developed centuries ago.** The ruins of a stone temple of undetermined function guard the system, and higher up the mountain are terraces yet to be completely excavated. The rough dirt track that leads to the complex is not in the best of shape and requires some effort to navigate. If you visit without your own car, either walk up (about two hours each way), or take one of the taxis waiting at the turnoff from the main road. ✉ *Cusco* ✣ *4 km (2½ miles) north of Km 23, Hwy. to Urcos* 🎫 *Boleto Turístico.*

Rainbow Mountain

139 km (86 miles) southeast of Cusco.

About a three-hour drive from Cusco, plus a 6-mile hike, this Instagram-famous mountain, also known as Vinicunca, is most comfortably experienced on a full-day trip from Cusco.

TOURS Rainbow Mountain Tours. ✉ *Plazoleta de San Blas 100B, Cusco* 🌐 *www.rainbowmountaintravels.com.*

Did You Know?

Those ceramic bulls often seen on rooftops, especially in the Sacred Valley, are for good luck. The custom began in Pucará (a town between Cusco and Puno), and the beasts are believed to protect the home and family, bringing good luck, health, and wealth. There is usually a cross between the pair, and there may be other elements as well, such as a condor, sacred in the Andes.

★ **Rainbow Mountain** (*Vinicunca*)

MOUNTAIN—SIGHT | With almost as many names as colors, Rainbow Mountain, aka Vinicunca, aka Montaña de Siete Colores (Mountain of Seven Colors) is a fairly recent addition to Peru's top-attraction list. Until a few years ago, the multicolored mountain was just another snow-capped peak. When the ice and snow that covered the mountain started to melt (this might be the one time in your life that you will want to say "thank you, global warming"), the water mixed with minerals in the ground like iron sulfide, chlorite, and goethite to create the striking stripes of color. Rainbow Mountain is about three hours from Cusco by car, and requires a strenuous, high-altitude hike, so you will need to plan your visit with time to acclimatize first. Do yourself a favor and book a tour. This is a full day's adventure and hiking in high altitude can really knock you out; you'll appreciate the chance to nap on the drive back to your hotel. **■ TIP→ Many photos of this mountain are heavily Photoshopped so do not be disappointed if the mountain is not quite as vivid as you have been led to expect. Also, dull weather conditions can dampen the effect, so try to plan around good weather, if you have flexibility in your schedule.** ✉ *Cordillera de Vilcanota.*

A B C D

1 2 3 4 5

Pisac

Sights ▼

1 Pisac Market...... **B1**

2 Pisac Ruins........ **D1**

Restaurants ▼

1 Horno Puma-chayoq...... **D1**

2 Mullu Café......... **B2**

3 Panaderia... **C1**

4 Ulrike's Café......... **B1**

Hotels ▼

1 Hotel Royal Inka Pisac........ **D1**

2 Paz y Luz.... **D5**

3 Pisac Inn.... **B2**

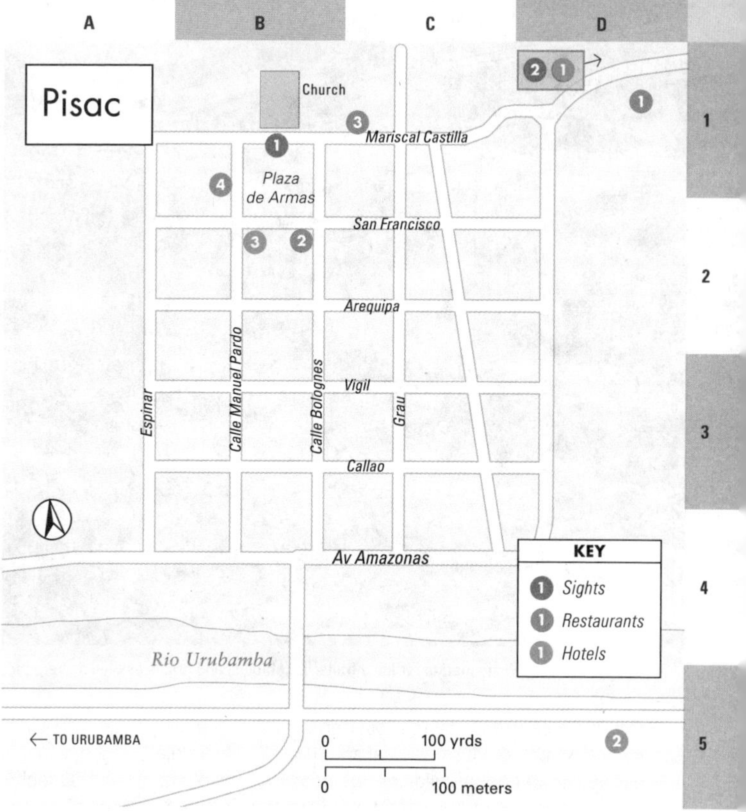

Church

Mariscal Castilla

Plaza de Armas

San Francisco

Arequipa

Vigil

Callao

Espinar

Calle Manuel Pardo

Calle Bolognes

Grau

Av Amazonas

Rio Urubamba

← TO URUBAMBA

0 100 yrds

0 100 meters

KEY

Sights

Restaurants

Hotels

Taray

23 km (14 miles) northeast of Cusco.

The road from Cusco leads directly to the town of Taray. The Pisac Market beckons a few kilometers down the road, but Taray makes a worthwhile pre-Pisac shopping stop.

Sights

Awana Kancha

STORE/MALL | **FAMILY** | Loosely translated as "palace of weaving," Awana Kancha provides an opportunity to see products made from South America's four camelids (alpaca, llama, vicuña, and guanaco) from start to finish: the animal, the shearing, the textile weaving and dyeing, and the finished products, which you can purchase in the showroom. This is a good place to shop for high-quality textiles that you can trust. It makes a great stop for the whole family, as kids can feed the camelids that are on-site. ✉ *Km 23, Carretera a Pisac* 🌐 *www.awanakancha.com* 🎫 *Free.*

Pisac

9 km (5 miles) northeast of Taray.

The colorful colonial town of Pisac, replete with Quechua-language Masses in a simple stone church, a well-known market, and fortress ruins, comes into view as you wind your way down the highway from Cusco. (You're dropping about 600 meters [1,970 feet] in elevation when you come out here from the big city.) Pisac, home to about 4,000 people, anchors the eastern end of the Sacred Valley. An orderly grid of streets

Head to the daily Pisac market for local fruits, vegetables, and grains as well as ceramics and textiles.

forms the center of town, most hemmed in by a hodgepodge of colonial and modern stucco or adobe buildings, and just wide enough for one car at a time. (Walking is easier and far more enjoyable.) The level of congestion (and fun) increases dramatically each Tuesday, Thursday, and especially Sunday, when one of Peru's most celebrated markets comes into its own, but much more spectacular are the ruins above. Admission to the ruins is included in both the Boleto Turístico and Boleto Parcial.

Sights

Pisac Market

MARKET | The market is held every day but is even larger on Tuesday, Thursday, and Sunday, when the ever-present ceramics, jewelry, and textiles on the central plaza share the stage with fruits, vegetables, and grains spilling over onto the side streets. Sellers set up shop about 9 am on market days and start packing up at about 5 pm. The market is not so different from many others you'll see around Peru, only larger. Go on Sunday if your schedule permits; you'll have a chance to take in the 11 am Quechua Mass at the Iglesia San Pedro Apóstolo and watch the elaborate costumed procession led by the mayor, who carries his *varayoc*, a ceremonial staff, out of the church afterward. Note that the market is not all it used to be: prices have escalated along with its popularity, and you now typically buy from middlemen, not the actual weaver. ✉ *Plaza de Armas.*

Pisac Ruins

ARCHAEOLOGICAL SITE | From the market area, drive or take a taxi for S/15–S/20 one-way up the winding road to the Inca ruins of Pisac. Archaeologists originally thought the ruins were a fortress to defend against fierce Antis (jungle peoples), though there's little evidence that battles were fought here. Now it seems that Pisac was a bit of everything: citadel, religious site, observatory, residence, and, possibly, a refuge in times of siege. The complex also has a temple to the sun and an astronomical observatory, from which priests calculated the growing season each year, but this part of the site was closed in 2015 for safety reasons, and there is no set date to reopen. Narrow trails wind tortuously between and through solid rock. You may find yourself practically alone on the series of paths in the mountains that lead you among the ruins, through caves, and past the largest known Inca cemetery (the Inca buried their dead in tombs high on the cliffs). Just as spectacular as the site are the views from it. ✉ *Pisac* 🎫 *Boleto Turístico.*

Restaurants

Horno Pumachayoq

$ | PERUVIAN | The empanadas are fantastic, but that's not the only reason to stop by at this classic empanada place. The real hook is a "cuy castle," a sort of Barbie mansion for guinea pigs. **Known for:** traditional oven; guinea pig castle; empanadas. *[$] Average main: S/3 ✉ Av. Federico Zamballoa s/n ☎ 84/203–120 ⏲ No dinner.*

Mullu Café

$$ | PERUVIAN | Rustic but stylish, Mullu Café has a cosmopolitan flair and specializes in Andean-fusion fare, with some especially good Asian-influenced plates. The food and drinks, along with the upbeat atmosphere, can't be topped. **Known for:** balcony overlooking Plaza de Armas; cocktails; Asian dishes. *[$] Average main: S/35 ✉ Plaza de Armas 352 ☎ 084/203–073.*

Panadería

$ | BAKERY | The unnamed bakery just off the Plaza Constitución is a Pisac institution. Empanadas (some vegetarian) and homemade breads are delivered from the clay oven and into your hands. **Known for:** fresh, hot empanadas; Andean bread; popular local spot. *[$] Average main: S/3 ✉ Mariscal Castilla 372 ▭ No credit cards ⏲ No dinner.*

Ulrike's Café

$ | CAFÉ | German transplant Ulrike Simic and company dish up food all day long, making this the perfect refueling stop during a day of market shopping and sightseeing. Breakfast gets under way before the market does, at 8 am. They've got good à la carte soups and pizzas, too, and yummy brownies, muffins, cheesecake, and chocolate-chip cookies for dessert. **Known for:** familiar comfort food; coffee and yummy desserts; rooftop view. *[$] Average main: S/24 ✉ Calle Pardo 613 ☎ 084/203–195 ▭ No credit cards.*

Hotels

Hotel Royal Inka Pisac

$$ | HOTEL | Just outside town, this branch of Peru's Royal Inka hotel chain and the closest lodging to the Pisac ruins, has rooms that vary in terms of design and views, with some having balconies affording vistas of the gorgeous surrounding landscape. **Pros:** lots of activities; clean and reasonably comfortable; pool on premises. **Cons:** outside town; rooms could use a retouch; extra fee for facilities. *[$] Rooms from: S/270 ✉ Km 1.5, Carretera a Pisac Ruinas ☎ 084/203–064, 866/554–6028 in U.S. 🌐 www.ximahotels.com 🛏 80 rooms 🍽 Free breakfast.*

Paz y Luz

$$ | HOTEL | FAMILY | Bright airy rooms, skylighted bathrooms, and mountain views characterize this growing hotel just outside of town, and the entire complex conjures feelings implied in its name: peace and light. **Pros:** excellent for families and big groups, especially conference cadres; beautiful, relaxing grounds; on-site spa with massage services available. **Cons:** not the most centrally located; spa therapists not always available; groups can take away from intimate feel. *[$] Rooms from: S/255 ✉ Pisac ✥ 1 km (½ mile) past bridge, on right ☎ 910/598–781 🌐 www.pazyluzperu.com 🛏 27 rooms 🍽 Free breakfast.*

Pisac Inn

$ | **HOTEL** | **FAMILY** | This cozy place with an unbeatable location right on the main square offers a home away from home—one in which common areas have murals crafted by the Peruvian-American owners, rooms are hung with Andean tapestries, and comfortable beds are made up with good clean linens. **Pros:** convenient location; serene space; good on-site restaurant. **Cons:** basic room amenities; in the middle of town; rooms and beds are small. *Rooms from: S/237 Plaza de Armas 084/203–062 www.pisacinn.com 11 rooms Free breakfast.*

Huaran

On your way from Pisac to Urubamba, and before you get to Huayllabamba, you will pass through Huaran. Even if you're not staying at the absolutely lovely Green House or Green House Villas, it's worth a stop for lunch at the Viva Perú Café.

Restaurants

★ Viva Perú Café

$ | **CAFÉ** | Enjoy absolutely fabulous sandwiches, salads, homemade ice cream and other desserts, craft beer, and much more at this cozy and comfortable café. The outdoor garden area is perfect for enjoying a sunny day under the gaze of the gorgeous Pitusiray Mountain. **Known for:** delicious lunch fare; great desserts; comfortable and relaxed atmosphere. *Average main: S/22 Km 60.2, Carretera Pisac–Ollantaytambo, Huaran 958/983-883 Closed Sun. No credit cards.*

Hotels

★ The Green House

$$ | **HOTEL** | This small hotel offers a quiet getaway in a gorgeous rural setting—indeed, it's the perfect place to experience nature without having to rough it, as the rooms are tastefully appointed and ultracomfortable. **Pros:** quiet and friendly; beautiful grounds; nestled under mountains. **Cons:** remote location; friendly dogs on-site are not for everyone; fills up fast. *Rooms from: S/405 Km 60.2, Carretera Pisac–Ollantaytambo, Huaran 941/299–944 www.thegreenhouseperu.com 4 rooms Free breakfast.*

Green House Villas

$$ | **RENTAL** | Each of the three villas has a fully equipped kitchen, a dining room, a fireplace, two bedrooms, and two baths, allowing for an independent stay in paradise. **Pros:** stunning location; beautiful villas and private space; housekeeping and breakfast included. **Cons:** off the beaten path; no restaurant on-site; two-night minimum stay. *Rooms from: S/420 Km 60.2, Carretera Pisac–Ollantaytambo, Huaran 989/486–047 for reservations or service, 989/989–486–047 alternate phone www.thegreenhousevillas.com 3 villas No meals.*

Acclimatizing in the Sacred Valley

An increasingly popular strategy for acclimatizing is to touch down in Cusco and head directly to the Sacred Valley. The patchwork of pastures rolls loosely alongside rocky red cliffs, and life sways lazily to the sibilant croon of the Urubamba River, a balmy and breath-catching 2,000 meters (6,562 feet) below the clamoring cobblestone streets of Cusco. Most Sacred Valley hotels will provide transportation to and from the airport in Cusco on request, but be sure to ask about price. It may be cheaper to arrange your own taxi.

Huayllabamba

On your way from Pisac to Yucay/ Urubamba, you will arrive at this small town. There's not much reason to stop unless you happen to be staying at the Aranwa or Inkaterra's Hacienda, but that alone might be reason enough.

Hotels

Aranwa Sacred Valley Hotel and Wellness
$$$ | **HOTEL** | The riverside location in the beautiful Sacred Valley is enough to make your stress melt away; add to that an extensive wellness center with treatments featuring local ingredients and therapies, hydrotherapy pools, a fitness center, and more, and your trip to Peru may become a wellness retreat. **Pros:** excellent service; beautiful property; extensive wellness treatments. **Cons:** located in a remote area; feels a bit like a compound; nothing else around translates to higher prices for meals and incidentals. *Rooms from: S/600 Antigua Hacienda Yaravilca 084/581–900 www.aranwahotels.com 115 rooms Free breakfast.*

Inkaterra Hacienda Urubamba
$$$$ | **HOTEL** | Whether you stay in the main house or your own private casita, all the guest quarters at this sprawling, 40-hectare (100-acre), sustainable estate—built to resemble the haciendas of old—have beautiful wood appointments and allow for peaceful dreams thanks to the finest beds and bedding and the dramatic views of the Sacred Valley and surrounding mountains. **Pros:** stunning views and setting; lunch or dinner also included; excellent service. **Cons:** remote location; not good for families; paths can be difficult. *Rooms from: S/1326 Km 63, Cusco-Urubamba-Pisac-Calca Hwy. 084/600–700 hotel reception, 800/442–5042 reservations from North America www.inkaterra.com/inkaterra/inkaterra-hacienda-urubamba/the-experience/ 36 rooms Free Breakfast.*

Boleto Turístico

Four Sacred Valley sites (Pisac, Chinchero, Moray, and Ollantaytambo) fall under Cusco's Boleto Turístico scheme, which is the only way to gain admission to them. Both the 10-day ticket and the abbreviated, two-day (S/70) ticket are valid for all four sites. Note, though, that Moray is not included in standard Sacred Valley tours.

Yucay

46 km (28 miles) northwest of Pisac.

Just a bit outside the much larger Urubamba, Yucay proper is only a few streets wide, with a collection of attractive colonial-era adobe-and-stucco buildings and a pair of good-choice lodgings on opposite sides of a grassy plaza in the center of town.

Hotels

La Casona de Yucay
$$ | **HOTEL** | This 1810 home of Manuel de Orihuela, once host to South American liberator Simón Bolívar, features bright, airy, and comfortable rooms arranged in blocks around four courtyards, lush with flowered gardens. **Pros:** historic setting; beautiful landscapes; central location for exploring the Sacred Valley. **Cons:** not much else in Yucay itself; rooms on the street side can be noisy; courtyard-style setup means no privacy if curtains are open. *Rooms from: S/390 Av. San Martín 104, Plaza Manco II 084/201–116 www.hotelcasonayucay.com 54 rooms Free breakfast.*

Sonesta Posada del Inca Yucay

$$ | **HOTEL** | This 300-year-old former monastery offers modern amenities while retaining its charm in such details as tile floors, wood ceilings, hand-carved headboards, and balconies that overlook the gardens or the terraced hillsides. **Pros:** good restaurant; historic setting; lovely surrounding landscape. **Cons:** there's not much else in Yucay; rooms could use an upgrade; some rooms are a bit noisy. *Rooms from: S/300 ✉ Plaza Manco II 123 ☎ 084/201–107, 084/201–107, 800/766–3782 in North America 🌐 www.sonesta.com/SacredValley 88 rooms 🍴 Breakfast.*

Urubamba

2 km (1 mile) northwest of Yucay; 29 km (17 miles) northwest of Chinchero.

Spanish naturalist Antonio de León Pinedo rhapsodized that Urubamba must have been the biblical Garden of Eden, but you'll be forgiven if your first glance at the place causes you to doubt that lofty claim: the highway leading into and bypassing the city, the Sacred Valley's administrative, economic, and geographic center, shows you miles of gas stations and convenience stores. But get off the highway and get lost in the countryside, awash in flowers and pisonay trees, and enjoy the spectacular views of the nearby mountains, and you might agree with León Pinedo after all. Urubamba holds little of historic interest, but the gorgeous scenery, a growing selection of top-notch hotels, and easy access to Machu Picchu rail service make the town an appealing base. Hikers will find that a multitude of small ruins can be visited in a day's outing.

Restaurants

★ El Huacatay

$$ | **PERUVIAN** | One of the best restaurants in the Cusco region was serving Peruvian fusion before it became trendy, perfecting the art of combining flavors in a way that each one can be savored. You'll need some time to decide between all the enticing options on the menu; the cuts of meat are amazingly tender, and there are some interesting vegetarian choices as well, not to mention an array of fabulous appetizers that might tempt you to just order a medley. **Known for:** alpaca carpaccio; lovely intimate atmosphere; excellent cocktails (frozen coca sour!) and wines. *Average main: S/42 ✉ Jr. Arica 620 ☎ 084/201–790 🌐 www.elhuacatay.com ⏲ Closed Sun.*

Kaia Shenai

$ | **CAFÉ** | **FAMILY** | If you're looking for something healthy, with plenty of choices for vegetarians, Kaia is the best bet in Urubamba for lunch or an early dinner (it closes at 6). With fresh salads, soups, sandwiches, wraps, and all sorts of snacks to choose from, you'll easily satisfy your post-hike hunger. **Known for:** healthy choices; vegetarian options; family friendliness. *Average main: S/18 ✉ Mariscal Castilla 563 ☎ 084/509–754 No credit cards.*

Kampu

$$ | **ASIAN** | On a side street behind the Plaza de Armas, Kampu is a delicious surprise, offering spicy curries, some Italian dishes (including the best gnocchi in Peru), Asian-fusion plates, and a pepper steak that will melt in your mouth. Be sure to check out the special-of-the-day chalkboard as you walk into this chill but lively locale. **Known for:** curries; relaxed atmosphere; cooking class with advanced reservation. *Average main: S/38 ✉ Jr. Sagrario 342 ☎ 974/955–977 ⏲ Closed Thurs.*

Hotels

Hotel Libertador Tambo del Inka

$$$$ | **HOTEL** | The sprawling complex, the first hotel in Peru to achieve LEED certification, sits on the edge of Urubamba's river with environmentally friendly rooms featuring hardwood floors and great mountain views. **Pros:** secluded with riverfront views; green hotel; convenient to train. **Cons:** huge modern resort; not for those seeking intimate atmosphere; high-quality service but a bit stiff. *Rooms from: S/1260 Av. Ferrocarril s/n 888/236–2437 for reservations from North America, 084/581–777 for hotel www.marriott.com 128 rooms Free breakfast.*

Hotel San Agustín (Monasterio de la Recoleta)

$$ | **HOTEL** | Set in a 16th-century Franciscan monastery amid the beautiful countryside of the Sacred Valley, this branch of a Peruvian chain features a cavernous dining room; guest rooms with hardwood floors, white walls, and Cusqueña paintings; and a bell tower with great views of the valley. **Pros:** unique historic setting; beautiful countryside; service oriented. **Cons:** slightly outside town; some rooms are cold; Wi-Fi can be spotty. *Rooms from: S/300 Jr. Recoleta s/n 084/201–666 www.hotelessanagustin.com.pe 32 rooms Free breakfast.*

Posada Las Casitas del Arco Iris

$$ | **HOTEL** | On a stay at this incredibly tranquil retreat in the gorgeous Urubamba countryside, you'll have even more peace of mind knowing that your soles help fund health care and education for underprivileged children. **Pros:** gorgeous landscape; reasonable prices; charitable organization. **Cons:** remote location; restaurant choices are limited; not as full service as other luxury hotels. *Rooms from: S/255 Querocancha 084/201–475 www.lascasitasdelarcoiris.com 11 rooms Free breakfast.*

★ Rio Sagrado

$$$$ | **HOTEL** | **FAMILY** | Sprawled across acres of greenery alongside the river, this retreat offers the utmost in tranquility and luxurious comfort, with riverfront views and light-filled rooms featuring cheery alpaca blankets and embroidered throw pillows, as well as natural materials that complement the surrounding landscape. **Pros:** gorgeous tranquil location; luxurious rooms; first-rate service with a friendly smile. **Cons:** a bit outside town; no televisions in rooms; rooms can be a bit cold. *Rooms from: S/1116 Km 75.8, Carratera Cusco–Urubamba 084/201–631 www.belmond.com 23 rooms Free breakfast.*

★ Sol y Luna Lodge & Spa

$$$$ | **HOTEL** | **FAMILY** | This Relais & Chateaux property oozes luxury with its private bungalows surrounded by gorgeous flower gardens and featuring amenities such as feather duvets and sunken bathtubs. **Pros:** tranquil setting; Peruvian art sprinkled throughout; charitable association attached to hotel. **Cons:** a few miles outside town; no television; excursions and restaurant on the expensive side. *Rooms from: S/1212 Fundo Huincho 2 km west of Urubamba 084/608–930 www.hotelsolyluna.com 43 bungalows Free Breakfast.*

Shopping

★ Cerámica Seminario

MUSEUM | Husband-and-wife team Pablo Seminario and Marilú Behar spent years developing their art into what is now known as the Seminario Style—taking the valley's distinctive red clay and turning it into ceramic works using modern adaptations of ancient indigenous techniques and designs. Their works are world-famous, with pieces seen as far off as Chicago's Field Museum. More than a shop or art gallery, here you have the ability to view the workshop where the magic happens and even speak with the artist directly. The store features

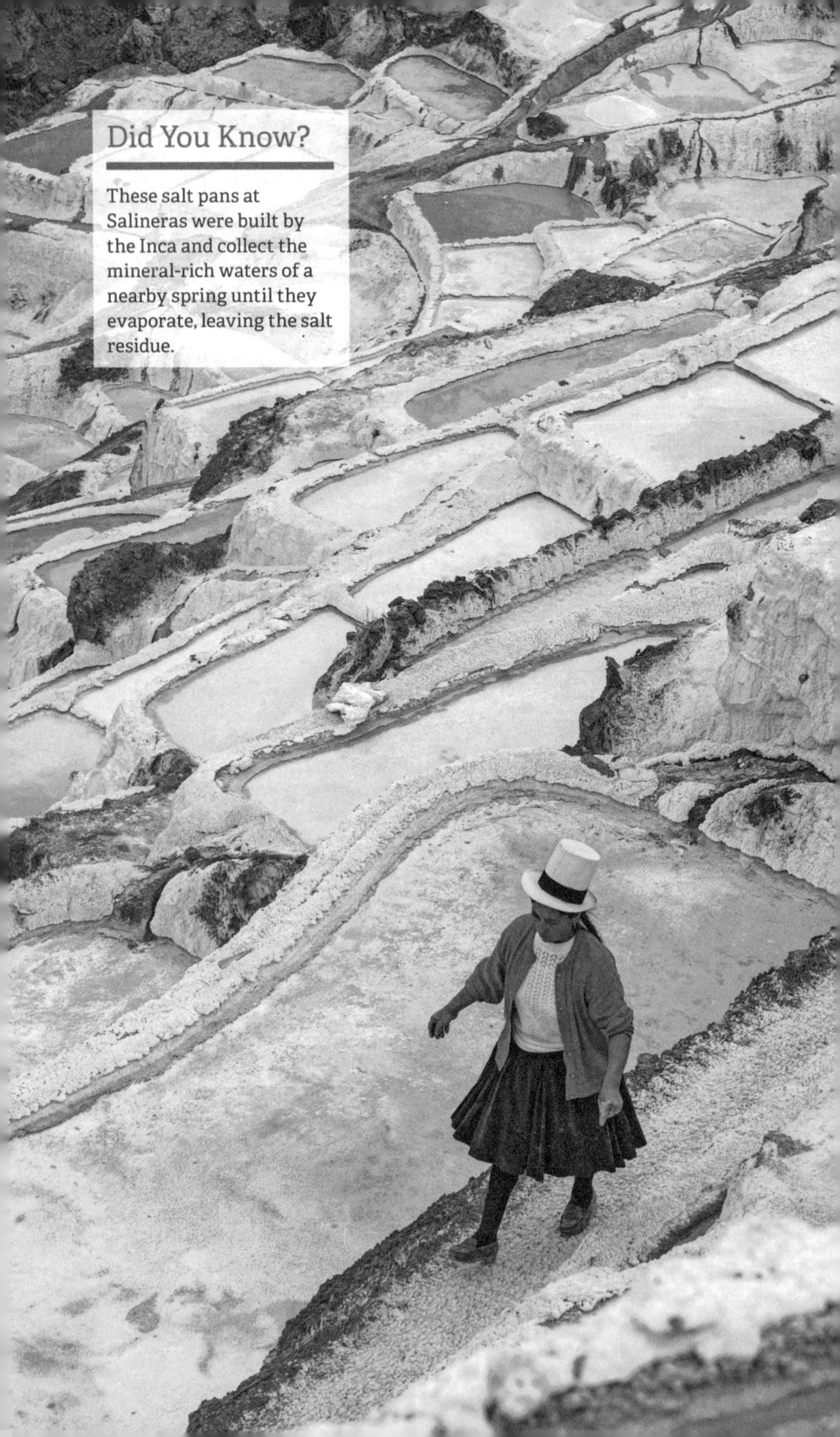

Did You Know?

These salt pans at Salineras were built by the Inca and collect the mineral-rich waters of a nearby spring until they evaporate, leaving the salt residue.

decorative and utilitarian pieces, as well as others that are pure art, all of which make fabulous Peruvian gifts for yourself or others. ■ **TIP→ Purchases can be shipped to any location.** ✉ *Berriozabal 111* ☎ *084/201–086* 🌐 *www.ceramicaseminario.com.*

Chinchero

28 km (17 miles) northwest of Cusco.

Indigenous lore says that Chinchero, one of the valley's major Inca cities, was the birthplace of the rainbow, and frequent sightings during the rainy season might convince you of the legend's truth. Chinchero is one of the few sites in the Sacred Valley that's higher (3,800 meters, or 12,500 feet) than Cusco.

Today, tourists and locals frequent the colorful Sunday artisan market on the central plaza, an affair that gets rave reviews as being more authentic and less touristed than the larger market in neighboring Pisac. A corresponding Chinchero produce market for locals takes place at the entrance to town. The market is there on other days, but on Sunday there are artisans who travel from the high mountain villages to sell their wares.

Amble about the collection of winding streets and adobe houses, but be sure to eventually make your way toward one of the weaving cooperatives, where a gaggle of local women will entertain you into understanding the art of making those lovely alpaca sweaters you eyed in the market.

Sights

Centro de Producción Artesanías Andina
TEXTILES/SEWING | This is one of the more organized places to learn about Chinchero's weaving tradition and techniques. Guests are welcomed with a cup of coca tea and then whisked through a series of hands-on explanations of the washing, dyeing, and weaving processes. There is also a good selection of hand-woven sweaters and tapestries for sale from the weavers themselves. ✉ *Calle Albergue 5.*

Chinchero Market
MARKET | Locals come from miles away to sell their produce at the Sunday Chinchero Market, making it a truly authentic market experience; come early, though, because it's all over by noon. The artisanal markets in Chinchero, which are open daily, are some of the best places to find textiles. Within the large market building are smaller owner-operated stands where local weavers sell their own and others' creations. There are also demonstrations of local dyeing and weaving techniques. ✉ *Chinchero* ✣ *Road to church.*

Church
RELIGIOUS SITE | A 1607 colonial church in the central plaza above the market was built on top of the limestone remains of an Inca palace, thought to be the country estate of the Inca Tupac Yupanqui, the son of Pachacutec. It's worth a visit if only to see the murals on the walls and ceiling. ✉ *Chinchero* 🎫 *Boleto Turístico* ⏲ *Open for Mass on Sun.*

Moray and Salineras

48 km (29 miles) northwest of Cusco.

Head to Salineras for a look at an ingenious way to harvest salt without mines or the ocean and to Moray for early, inventive farming and irrigation technology.

GETTING HERE AND AROUND

Moray and Salineras are difficult to reach without a tour and almost impossible during the rainy season. No public transportation serves Moray or Salineras. A taxi can be hired from Maras, the closest village, or from Cusco. Alternatively, it's a two-hour hike from Maras to either site.

Sights

Moray

ARCHAEOLOGICAL SITE | Scientists still marvel at the agricultural technology the Inca used at Moray. Taking advantage of four natural depressions in the ground and angles of sunlight, indigenous engineers fashioned concentric circular irrigation terraces, 150 meters (500 feet) from top to bottom. This design resulted in a temperature difference of 15°C (60°F) from top to bottom, creating a series of engineered microclimates perfect for adapting, experimenting, mixing, matching, and cultivating foods, especially varieties of maize, the staple of the Inca Empire and normally impossible to grow at this altitude. Though the technology is attributed to the Inca, the lower portions of the complex are thought to date from the pre-Inca Wari culture. Entrance to Moray is included in the Boleto Turístico. ✉ *Maras* 🎫 *Boleto Turístico.*

★ **Salineras** (*Maras Salt Flats*)

NATURE SITE | The famed terraced Inca salt pans of Salineras, which take advantage of a natural phenomenon, are still in use: The Inca dug shallow pools into a sloped hillside. The pools filled with water, and upon evaporation, salt crystallized and could be harvested. On-site shops offer many varieties of the salt mixed with different herbs for use at home—some for culinary seasoning, others for therapeutic soaks. This stunning site is somehow still somewhat of a secret, and is definitely worth a day-trip from Cusco. ✉ *Maras* 🎫 *S/10.*

Restaurants

★ **MIL Centro**

$$$$ | **PERUVIAN** | World-renowned chef Virgilio Martinez of Central fame has done it again with this tasting menu–style restaurant that allows you to devour Andean culture in a very personal way. Locally grown products that have been used in the Andes mountains for millennia are crafted into gourmet dishes that should be on any gastronomic tour of Peru. **Known for:** complete gastronomic experience; relationship with local farmers; stunning location. [$] *Average main: S/633* ✉ *Maras* ✣ *500 meters (550 yards) from the archaeological complex of Moray* ☎ *926/948–088* 🌐 *www.milcentro.pe* ⏲ *No dinner.*

Wi-Fi in Olly

Wi-Fi is nearly everywhere in town. Many hotels offer computer terminals and a place to check your email or look up tour information. There are also some cafés along and near the Plaza de Armas.

Ollantaytambo

19 km (11 miles) west of Urubamba.

Poll visitors for their favorite Sacred Valley community, and the answer will likely be Ollantaytambo—endearingly nicknamed Olly or Ollanta—which lies at the valley's northwestern entrance. Ollantaytambo's traditional air has not been stifled by the invasion of tourists. As you walk around, you'll see walls, doors, and water-drainage systems dating from Inca times and still in use today. You can even step into a working Inca-era home, learn about the ancient way of life, and see the guinea pigs, still a delicacy today, running around the kitchen floor. Ask around for the local *mercado,* just off the Plaza de Armas, close to the pickup point for colectivos and taxis. This busy marketplace quietly evades tourism's grasp and offers a behind-the-scenes peek at life beyond the ruins. The juice stations on the second floor, toward the back, might just be the town's best-kept secret.

■ **TIP→ Ollantaytambo makes a superb**

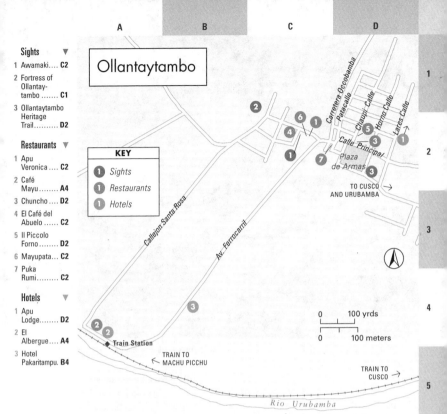

Ollantaytambo

Sights

1 Awamaki.... **C2**

2 Fortress of Ollantaytambo....... **C1**

3 Ollantaytambo Heritage Trail.......... **D2**

Restaurants

1 Apu Veronica.... **C2**

2 Café Mayu........ **A4**

3 Chuncho.... **D2**

4 El Café del Abuelo...... **C2**

5 Il Piccolo Forno........ **D2**

6 Mayupata... **C2**

7 Puka Rumi......... **C2**

Hotels

1 Apu Lodge........ **D2**

2 El Albergue.... **A4**

3 Hotel Pakaritampu. **B4**

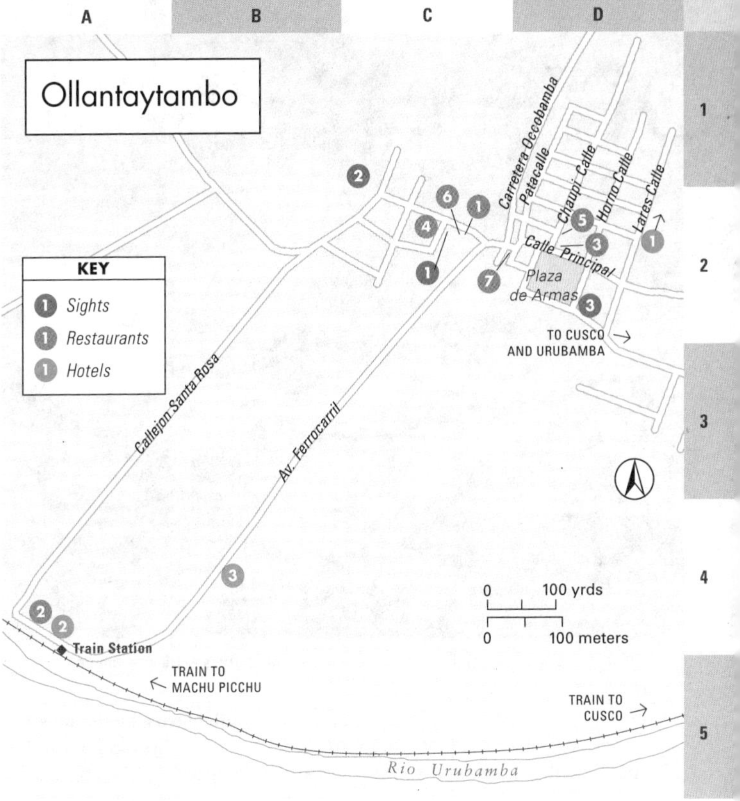

KEY

Sights

Restaurants

Hotels

base for exploring the Sacred Valley and has convenient rail connections to Machu Picchu.

Ollantaytambo is also the kickoff point for the Inca Trail. You'll start here at nearby Km 82 if you wish to hike to the Lost City, and lodging here will give you a bit more time to sleep in before hiking. Walk up to discover the Fortress of Ollantaytambo, one of the most fantastic ruins in the Sacred Valley.

Sights

Awamaki

TEXTILES/SEWING | If you've made it to the Sacred Valley, you've likely seen your share of woven garments. But it's worth swinging by this fair-trade shop just down the road from the Plaza de Armas on the way to the ruins. All the extremely high-quality goods are produced as part of the Awamaki weaving project, which supports a cooperative of Quechua women from the Patacancha Valley. The organization also has a variety of cultural tours and other offerings, including homestays and weaving courses, all of which you can find out about at the shop. ✉ *Calle Principal s/n* ☎ *084/436-744 Peru headquarters, 206/678-7881 U.S. office* 🌐 *www.awamaki.org.*

★ Fortress of Ollantaytambo

ARCHAEOLOGICAL SITE | Walk above town to a formidable stone structure, where massive terraces climb to a temple area honoring the sun god. Although the elaborate, walled complex was the valley's main defense against the Antis (jungle people) from the neighboring rain forests, with the sun temple, used for astronomical observation, as well

Before heading to Machu Picchu, check out the Inca fortress at Ollantaytambo.

as the Baños de la Ñusta (ceremonial princess baths), archaeologists believe that Ollantaytambo existed for more than defensive purposes, as was typical with Inca constructions. Construction, which began during the reign of Pachacutec but was never completed, incorporates rose-colored granite that was not mined in this part of the valley. The structure was the site of the greatest Inca victory over the Spanish during the wars of conquest. Manco Inca fled here in 1537 with a contingent of troops after the disastrous loss at Sacsayhuamán and routed Spanish forces under Hernando Pizarro. The victory was short-lived: Pizarro regrouped and took the fortress. If you come on your own, take the time to walk up above and through a wooden door at the back to see an Intihuatana ("hitching post of the Sun"). ⊠ *Plaza Mañay Raquy* *Boleto Turístico.*

Ollantaytambo Heritage Trail
TRAIL | The Old Town's distinctive appearance can be attributed to Inca organizational skills. They based their communities on the unit of the *cancha*, a walled city block, each with one entrance leading to an interior courtyard, surrounded by a collection of houses. The system is most obvious in the center of town around the main plaza. You'll find the most welcoming of these self-contained communities at Calle del Medio. A tourist information office on the Plaza de Armas can help direct you. ⊠ *Ollantaytambo.*

Restaurants

★ Apu Veronica
$ | **PERUVIAN** | The family that owns this small restaurant pours passion into their business and their excellent food, which is made using local ingredients that are carefully sourced in ways that lend poorer communities a helping hand. To ensure

that everyone who walks in gains a little more understanding of indigenous culture, the specialty here is meat prepared on stones that are full of nutritious, flavor-enhancing minerals. **Known for:** meats cooked on stone; traditional Peruvian atmosphere; great service. $ *Average main: S/30* ✉ *Calle Ventiderio s/n, 2nd fl.* ☎ *915/222–637.*

Café Mayu

$ | **CAFÉ** | It's best to hunker down for a day or two in Ollantaytambo, but if you've only got time for a pit stop, Café Mayu is conveniently located at the train station. This tiny spot serves big-city-style coffee, quick bites like empanadas, and to-go sandwiches that are perfect for your ride to Machu Picchu. **Known for:** great coffee; delicious baked goods; food to go. $ *Average main: S/10* ✉ *Train station* ☎ *084/204–014* ▭ *No credit cards.*

★ Chuncho

$$ | **PERUVIAN** | A labor of love from someone born and raised in Ollantaytambo has resulted in a must-visit restaurant experience—one in which you will savor traditional ancestral foods made with the freshest of local ingredients and prepared to appeal to the foreign palate. The all-wood décor makes for a warm and rustic yet chic atmosphere, with Peruvian accents sprinkled throughout. **Known for:** farm-to-table ingredients; the "Chuncho banquet" tasting menu; fabulous cocktails. $ *Average main: S/40* ✉ *Plaza de Armas at Chaupi Calle* ☎ *979/797–638* 🌐 *www.elalbergue.com.*

El Café del Abuelo

$ | **CAFÉ** | Want a time out but not super hungry? Head to this well-designed café-bar for a coffee drink or an alcoholic beverage, depending on the time of day and your mood—the vibe is great, as are the libations, plus they have a number of light food offerings including soups, sandwiches, pizza, and desserts. **Known for:** coffee drinks; pisco and other alcoholic beverages; quick bites. $ *Average main: S/15* ✉ *Calle La Convención 110* ☎ *980/732–111* ▭ *No credit cards.*

Il Piccolo Forno

$ | **CAFÉ** | This little café is the place to go for pizza, lasagna, breads, desserts, and, of course, coffee. There are some vegetarian and gluten-free options, and they also feature a small selection of organic products. **Known for:** pizza; baked goods; great Wi-Fi. $ *Average main: S/21* ✉ *Chaupi K'ikllu (Calle del Medio) 120* ☎ *944/060–933* ▭ *No credit cards.*

Mayupata

$ | **PERUVIAN** | Spacious and airy, furnished with large wooden tables and chairs, this restaurant has the unmistakable air of a tourist-friendly Andean establishment. The menu ranges from traditional Peruvian grilled meats and fish to slightly edgier dishes like Andean ravioli (filled with alpaca). **Known for:** Peruvian grilled meats; pizza and other visitor-friendly staples; view of the archaeological site. $ *Average main: S/30* ✉ *Jr. Concepcíon s/n* ☎ *084/610–258* ▭ *No credit cards.*

Puka Rumi

$ | **MEXICAN** | Where it lacks the polish and charm of other places in town, Puka Rumi gains ground with its colossal burritos and chicken fajitas—served with a tabletop's worth of sides, including a heaping bowl of homemade guacamole. The menu isn't strictly Mexican, despite what they claim; as with the patrons, you'll find an international mix, and the owner is known for only choosing the best-quality meats at the market. **Known for:** burritos and fajitas; high-quality meats; proximity to the site. $ *Average main: S/28* ✉ *Calle Ventiderio s/n* ☎ *084/214–828* ▭ *No credit cards.*

Hotels

Apu Lodge

$ | **HOTEL** | **FAMILY** | Taking its name from the spirit of the mountains, this lodge has clean, bright, and artfully furnished rooms with comfortable beds; it's also surrounded by gardens and commands a delightful view of the Ollantaytambo ruins from its private grassy perch, making it well worth the five-minute meander up cobbled Inca streets from the center of town.Free breakfast commences early over a communal table and is a great spot to pick other people's brains on things to see and do. **Pros:** gorgeous location; kid friendly; good place for tour advice. **Cons:** a few blocks from the center of town with no car access; first-floor rooms can be noisy; limited amenities. *Rooms from: S/225* ✉ *Lari Calle* ☎ *084/436–816* 🌐 *www.apulodge.com* *9 rooms* *Free breakfast.*

★ El Albergue

$$ | **HOTEL** | **FAMILY** | Right at the train station, the town's first and undoubtedly finest hotel is absolutely lovely, with spacious rooms featuring dark-wood accents, historic black-and-white photos of the region, and a tranquil garden area. **Pros:** convenient to train; great value for ubercomfort; children can use the family playground. **Cons:** books up fast; rooms on the train side can be noisy; no televisions in the rooms. *Rooms from: S/297* ✉ *Estación de Ferrocarril* ☎ *084/204–014* 🌐 *www.elalbergue.com* *16 rooms* *Free breakfast.*

Hotel Pakaritampu

$$$ | **HOTEL** | One of Ollantaytambo's better lodgings, with a Quechua name that translates as "house of dawn," offers rooms decorated in rich, earthy colors that complement the surrounding landscape, which includes lovely, flower- and hummingbird-filled grounds and an on-site orchard that supplies the fruit for your breakfast. **Pros:** gorgeous setting and grounds; good restaurant; close to train station. **Cons:** beds are on the hard side; rooms are basic; still need transport to station with luggage. *Rooms from: S/667* ✉ *Av. Ferrocarril s/n* ☎ *084/204–020* 🌐 *www.pakaritampu.com* *38 rooms* *Free breakfast.*

Chapter 7

MACHU PICCHU AND THE INCA TRAIL

7

Updated by
Maureen Santucci

Sights	Restaurants	Hotels	Shopping	Nightlife
★★★★★	★★★☆☆	★★☆☆☆	★☆☆☆☆	★☆☆☆☆

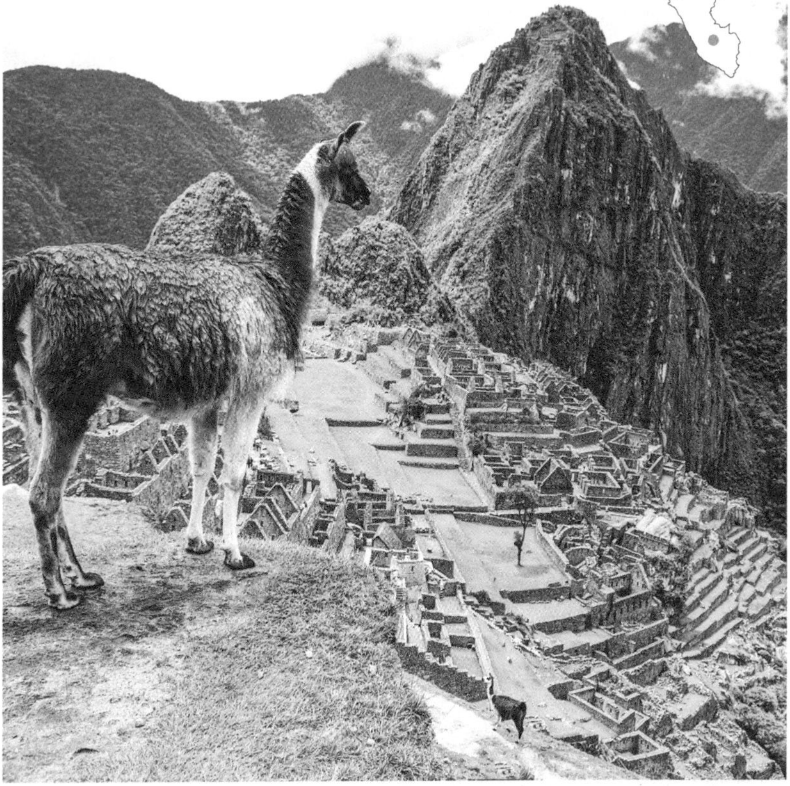

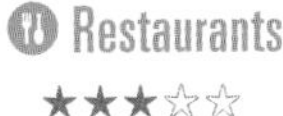

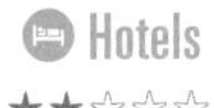

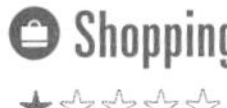

WELCOME TO MACHU PICCHU AND THE INCA TRAIL

TOP REASONS TO GO

★ **Discover Ancient Kingdoms:** Hiram Bingham "discovered" Machu Picchu in 1911. Your first glimpse of the fabled city will be your own discovery, and every bit as exciting.

★ **The Inca Trail:** The four-day hike of the Inca Trail from near Ollantaytambo to Machu Picchu is Peru's best-known outdoor expedition. Spaces fill up quickly, but never fear: tour operators continue to open up new alternative treks.

★ **Amazing Inca Technology:** It was the 15th century, yet the Inca made the stones fit perfectly without mortar. The sun illuminates the windows at the solstice, and the crops grow in an inhospitable climate. And they did it all without bulldozers, tractors, or computers.

★ **Mystery:** Mystics, shamans, spiritualists, astrologers, and UFO spotters, professionals and wannabes, flock to this serene region to contemplate history's secrets.

★ **Majestic Scenery:** The area's stunning mountain landscapes surround you.

The famed ruins of Machu Picchu, accessible only via rail or foot, lie farther down the Río Urubamba, in the cloud forest on the Andean slopes above the jungle. Cusco, the region's largest city, is about 112 km (70 miles) southeast.

1 **Machu Picchu.** These two words that are synonymous with Peru evoke images of centuries-old Inca emperors and rituals. Yet no one knows for certain what purpose this mountaintop citadel served or why it was abandoned. Machu Picchu is an easy day-trip from Cusco, but an overnight in Aguas Calientes or Ollantaytambo gives you more time to explore and devise your own theories.

2 **The Inca Trail.** A 43-km (26-mile) sector of the original Inca route between Cusco and Machu Picchu has become one of the world's signature treks. No question: you need to be in good shape, and the four-day excursion can be rough going at times, but it's guaranteed to generate bragging rights and immense satisfaction upon completion.

3 **Aguas Calientes.** Tucked amid cloud forest below the ruins lies the pleasant town of Aguas Calientes, officially called Machupicchu Pueblo. (No one uses the official name to avoid confusing the town with the ruins.) This is where the trains from Cusco and the Sacred Valley arrive, and you catch the bus to Machu Picchu. It's a nice enough place to refuel and spend the night.

CORDILLERA URUBAMBA
Aguas Calientes
WAKAYWILLKA (VERONICA)
Huayna Picchu
1
ACHU PICCHU
3
The Inca Trail
2
Rio Urubamba
Ollantaytambo
CORDILLERA VILCABAMBA
Huarocondo
TO CUSCO
Zurite
0
5 mi
0
5 km

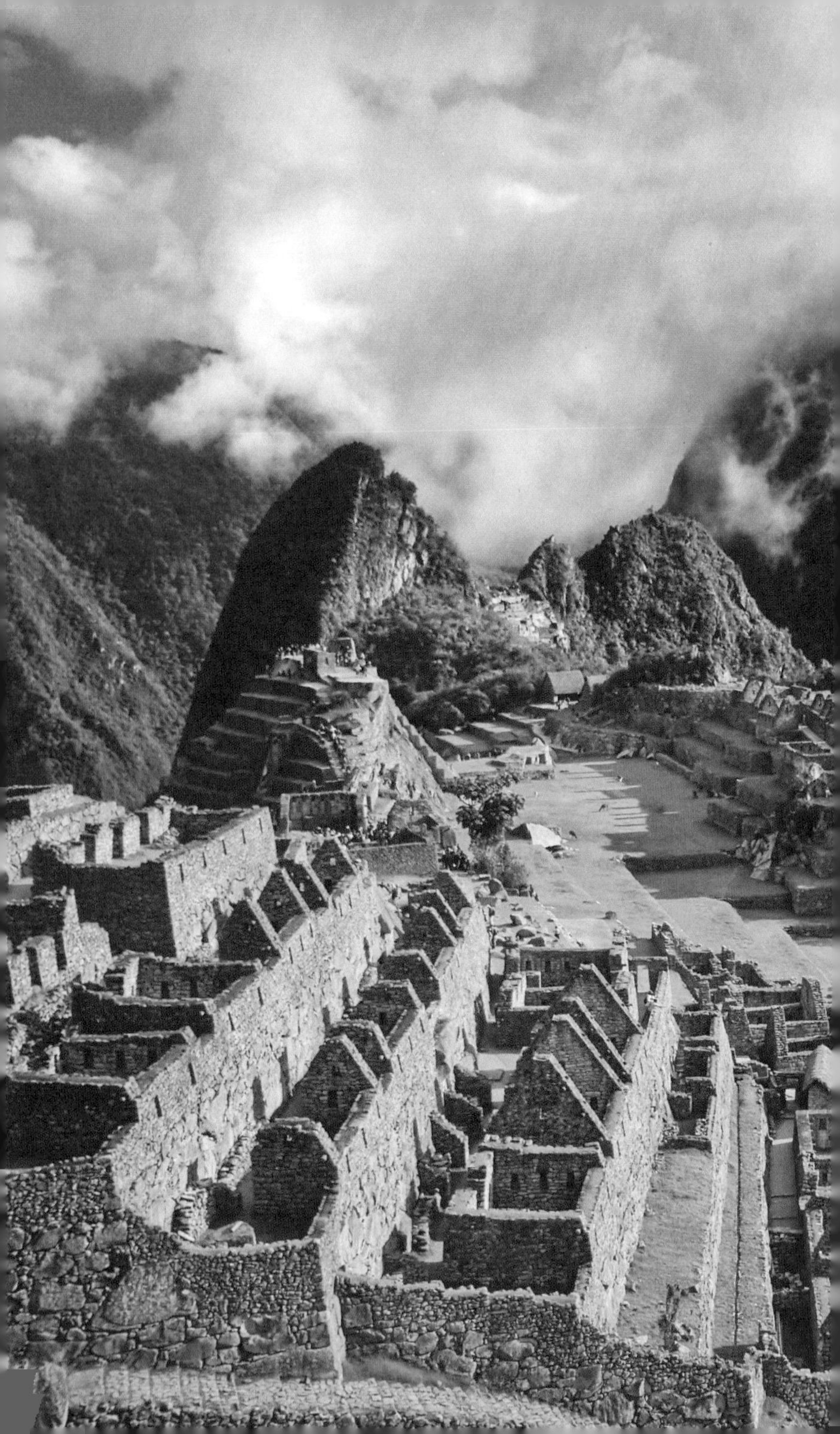

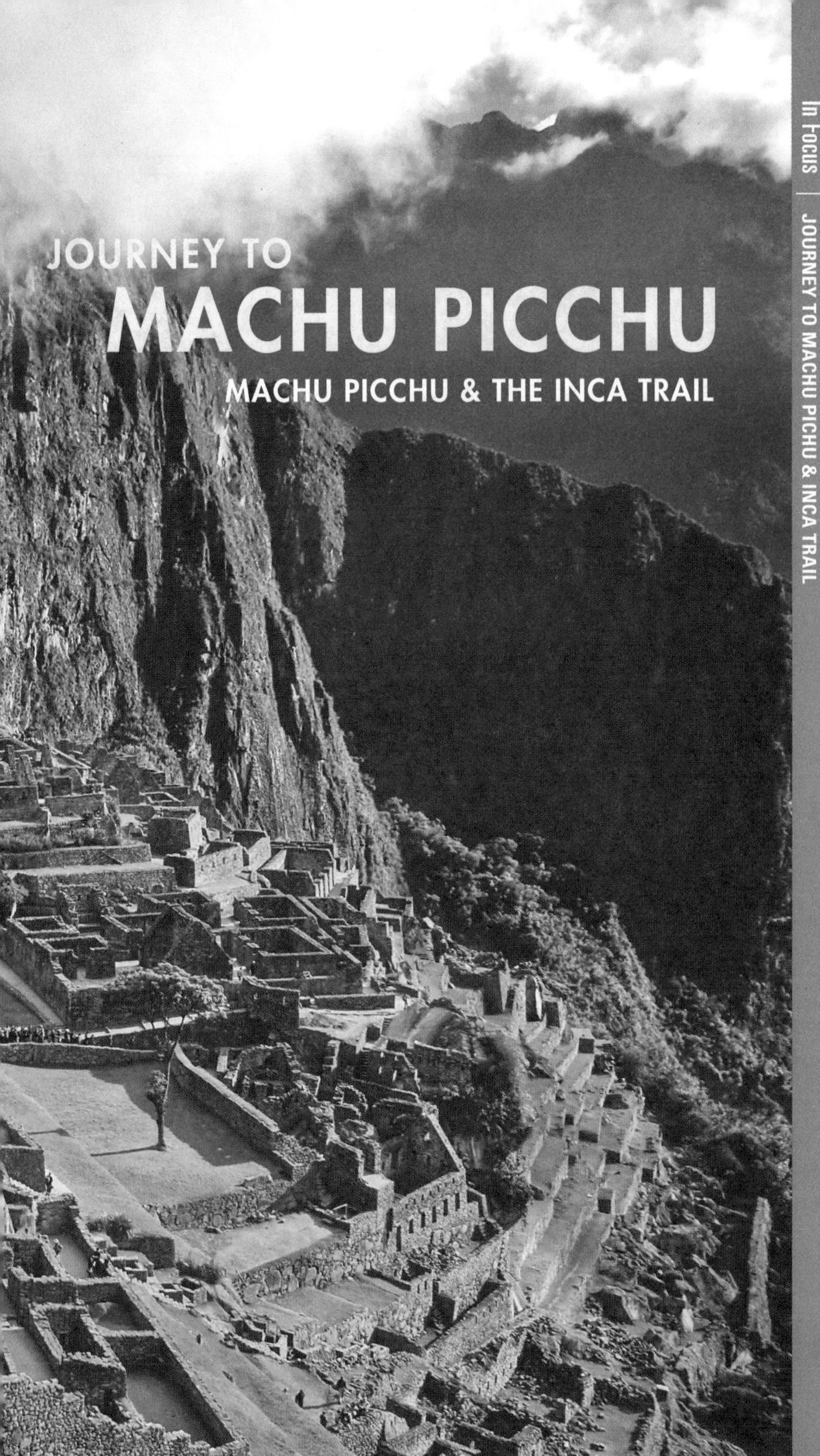

JOURNEY TO MACHU PICCHU

MACHU PICCHU & THE INCA TRAIL

MACHU PICCHU & THE INCA TRAIL

The exquisite architecture of the massive Inca stone structures, the formidable backdrop of steep sugarloaf hills, and the Urubamba River winding far below have made Machu Picchu the iconic symbol of Peru. It's a mystical city, the most famous archaeological site in South America, and one of the world's must-see destinations.

The world did not become aware of Machu Picchu's existence until 1911 when Yale University historian Hiram Bingham (1875–1956) announced that he had "discovered" the site. "Rediscovery" is a more accurate term; area residents knew of Machu Picchu's existence all along. This "Lost City of the Inca" was missed by the ravaging conquistadors and survived untouched until the beginning of the 20th century.

You'll be acutely aware that the world has since discovered Machu Picchu if you visit during the June–mid-September high season. Machu Picchu absorbs the huge numbers of visitors, though, and even in the highest of the high season, its beauty is so spectacular that it rarely disappoints.

DISCOVERY

American explorer and historian Hiram Bingham, with the aid of local guides, came across the Lost City in 1911. Though the name appeared on maps as early as 1860, previous attempts to find the site failed. Bingham erred in recognizing what he had uncovered. The historian assumed he had stumbled upon Vilcabamba, the last real stronghold of the Inca. (The actual ruins of Vilcabamba lie deep in the rainforest, and were uncovered in the 1960s.)

Bingham, who later served as governor of and senator from Connecticut, transported—some say stole—many of Machu Picchu's artifacts to Yale in 1912. Although they were intended to be on a short term loan, the artifacts did not begin to make their way back to Peru until 2011. They are now housed in the Museo Machu Picchu Casa Concha in Cusco.

In 1915, Bingham announced his discovery of the Inca Trail. As with Machu Picchu, his "discovery" was a little disingenuous. Locals knew about the trail, and that it had served as a supply route between Cusco and Machu Picchu during Inca times. Parts of it were used during the colonial and early republican eras as well.

Though archaeological adventuring is viewed differently now, Bingham's slog to find Machu Picchu and the Inca Trail was no easy feat. Look up from Aguas Calientes, and you still won't know it's there.

HISTORY

Ever since Bingham came across Machu Picchu, its history has been debated. It was likely a small city of some 200 homes and 1,000 residents, with agricultural terraces to supply the population's needs and a strategic position that overlooked—but could not be seen from—the valley floor.

New theories suggest that the city was a transit station for products, such as coca and hearts of palm that were grown in the lowlands and sent to Cusco. Exactly when Machu Picchu was built is not known, but one theory suggests that it was a country estate of an Inca ruler named Pachacutec, which means its golden age was in the mid-15th century.

Historians have discredited the romantic theory of Machu Picchu as a refuge of the chosen Inca women after the Spanish conquest; analysis shows a 50/50 split of male and female remains.

The site's belated discovery may indicate that the Inca deserted Machu Picchu before the Spanish conquest. The reason for the city's presumed abandonment is as mysterious as its original function. Some archaeologists suggest that the water supply simply ran out. Some guess that disease ravaged the city. Others surmise it was the death of Pachacutec, after which his estate was no longer needed.

"INDIANA" BINGHAM

Hiram Bingham at Machu Picchu, 1912.

A globe-trotting archaeological explorer, which was an especially romantic figure in early 20th century America, Hiram Bingham was a model for the Indiana Jones character in the film *Raiders of the Lost Ark*.

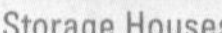

Storage Houses

Guardhouse

EXPLORING THE SITE

Everyone must go through the main entrance to have their ticket stamped. You have to show your passport to enter Machu Picchu—if you want it stamped, be sure to stop by the table on the left as you exit the site. From there you work your way up through the agricultural areas and to the urban sectors.

There are almost no signs inside to explain what you're seeing; booklets and maps are for sale at the entrance. You must purchase a timed ticket. Admission begins at 6am and continues hourly until 3pm, the final timeslot. According to regulations, you must be accompanied by a licensed guide, and while this is not necessarily enforced, you might not want to take a chance on the day. You will have just four hours in the site from entrance to exit. If you purchase an entry to hike Huayna Picchu or Machu Picchu Mountain, you may stay in the site for 6 hours.

The English-language names to the structures within the city were assigned by Bingham. Call it inertia, but those labels have stuck, even though the late Yale historian's nomenclature was mostly offbase.

The Storage Houses are the first structures you encounter after coming through the main entrance. The Inca carved terraces into the hillsides to grow produce and minimize erosion. Corn was the likely crop cultivated.

The Guardhouse and Funeral Rock are a 20-minute walk up to the left of the entrance, and they provide the quintessential Machu Picchu vista. Nothing beats the view in person, especially with a misty sunrise. Bodies of nobles likely lay in state here, where they would have been eviscerated, dried, and prepared for mummification.

The Temple of the Sun is a marvel of perfect Inca stone assembly. On June 21 (winter solstice in the southern hemisphere; sometimes June 20 or June 22), sunlight shines through a small, trapezoid-shape window and onto the middle of a large, flat granite stone presumed to be an Inca calendar. Looking out the window, astronomers saw the constellation Pleiades, revered as a symbol of crop fertility. Bingham dubbed the small cave below the Royal Tomb, though no human remains were found at the time of his discovery.

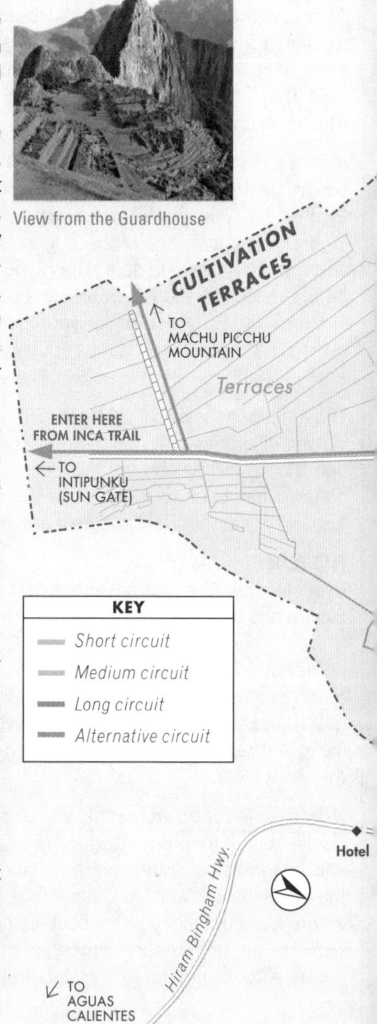

View from the Guardhouse

Main Gate

Temple of the Sun

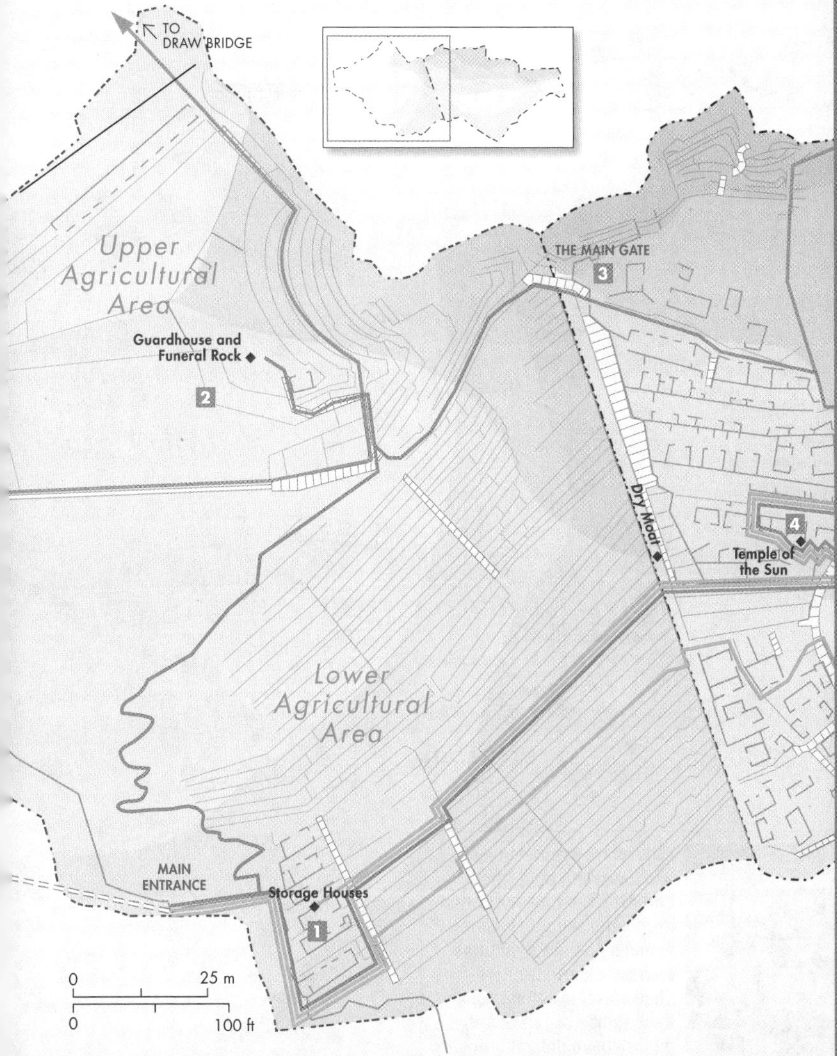

Principal Temple

Three Windows

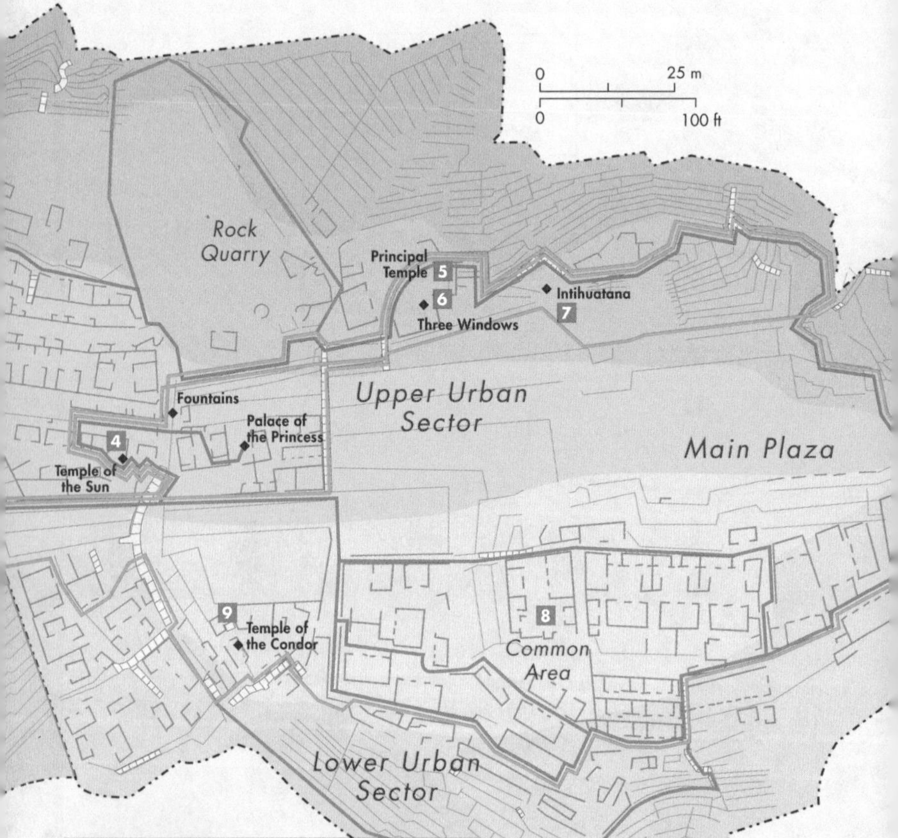

0 25 m
0 100 ft

Rock Quarry
Principal Temple 5
6 Three Windows
Intihuatana 7
Upper Urban Sector
Main Plaza
Fountains
Palace of the Princess
4 Temple of the Sun
9 Temple of the Condor
8 Common Area
Lower Urban Sector

Why no nice rectangular windows with right-angle corners? The Inca knew that irregularly shaped windows would help their structures withstand earth tremors. They must have done something right—regular earthquakes have not yet brought down the house.

Intihuatana

Common Area

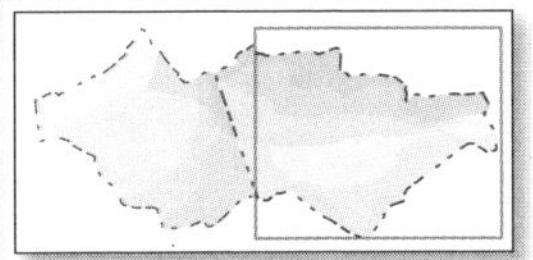

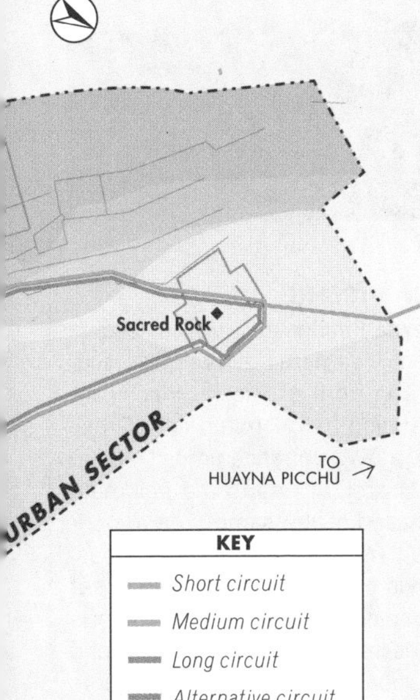

Temple of the Condor.

Fountains. A series of 16 small fountains are linked to the Inca worship of water.

The Palace of the Princess, a likely misnomer, is a two-story building that adjoins the temple.

The Principal Temple is so dubbed because its masonry is among Machu Picchu's best. The three-walled structure is a masterpiece of mortarless stone construction. A rock in front of the temple acts as a compass—test it out by placing your smartphone with compass app showing on top of it.

Three Windows. A stone staircase leads to the three-walled structure. The entire east wall is hewn from a single rock with trapezoidal windows cut into it.

Intihuatana. A hillock leads to the "Hitching Post of the Sun." Every important Inca center had one of these vertical stone columns (called gnomons). Their function likely had to do with astronomical observation and agricultural planning. The Spanish destroyed most of them, seeing the posts as objects of pagan worship. Machu Picchu's is one of the few to survive—partially at least. Its top was accidentally knocked off in 2001 during the filming of a Cusqueña beer commercial.

The Sacred Rock takes the shape in miniature of the mountain range visible behind it.

The Common Area covers a large grassy plaza with less elaborately constructed buildings and huts.

The Temple of the Condor is so named because the positioning of the stones resembles a giant condor, the symbol of heaven in the Inca cosmos. The structure's many small chambers led Bingham to dub it a "prison," a concept that did not likely exist in Inca society.

EXPLORING BEYOND THE LOST CITY

Inca Bridge

Several trails lead from the site to surrounding ruins.

INTIPUNKU (SUN GATE)

You can take a 45-minute walk on a gentle arc leading uphill to the southeast of the main complex. **Intipunku**, the Sun Gate, is a small structure in a nearby pass. This ancient checkpoint is where you'll find that classic view that Inca Trail hikers emerge upon. Some minor ancient outbuildings along the path occasionally host grazing llamas. A two- or three-hour hike beyond the Intipunku along the Inca Trail brings you to the ruins of **Huiñay Huayna**, a terrace complex that climbs a steep mountain slope and includes a set of ritual baths.

INCA BRIDGE

Built rock by rock up a hair-raising stone escarpment, The **Inca Bridge** is yet another example of Inca engineering ingenuity. From the cemetery at Machu Picchu, it's a 30-minute walk along a narrow path.

HUAYNA PICCHU

The **Huayna Picchu** trail, which follows an ancient Inca path, leads up the sugarloaf hill in front of Machu Picchu for an exhilarating trek. Limited to 400 visitors daily at two entrance times (7–8 am and 10–11 am), tickets to the trail must be purchased at the same time as your entrance to Machu Picchu. The arduous, vertiginous hike up a steep, narrow set of Inca-carved stairs to the summit and back takes between 2 and 3 hours round trip and there are some Inca structures at the top. Bring insect repellent; the gnats can be ferocious.

MACHU PICCHU MOUNTAIN

Hiking up Machu Picchu mountain is another possibility. Tickets must be purchased at the same time as the entrance to the site itself. Entrance is allowed between 7 am and 8 am and between 9 and 10 am. This hike is longer than Huayna Picchu but less steep; there are no structures on this route.

Huiñay Huayna

Aguas Calientes
Huayna Picchu
Km 112
The Sacred Rock
Temple of the Sun
Inca Bridge
MACHU PICCHU COMPLEX
Entrance Station
Parking
Intipunku
Inca Trail
Choquesuysuy
Huiñay Huayna

Walking the Inca trail through the Sacred Valley.

Inca Trail

Patallaqta

INCA TRAIL

One of the world's signature outdoor excursions, the Inca Trail (*Camino Inca*) is a 43-km (26-mile) sector of the stone path that once extended from Cusco to Machu Picchu. Nothing matches the sensation of walking over the ridge that leads to the Lost City of the Incas just as the sun casts its first yellow glow over the ancient stone buildings.

Though the journey by train is the easiest way to get to Machu Picchu, most travelers who arrive via the Inca Trail wouldn't have done it any other way. There are limits on the number of trail users, but you'll still see a lot of fellow trekkers along the way. The four-day trek takes you past ancient structures and through stunning scenery, starting in the thin air of the highlands and ending in cloud forests. The orchids, hummingbirds, and spectacular mountains aren't bad either.

The impressive Puyupatamarca ruins.

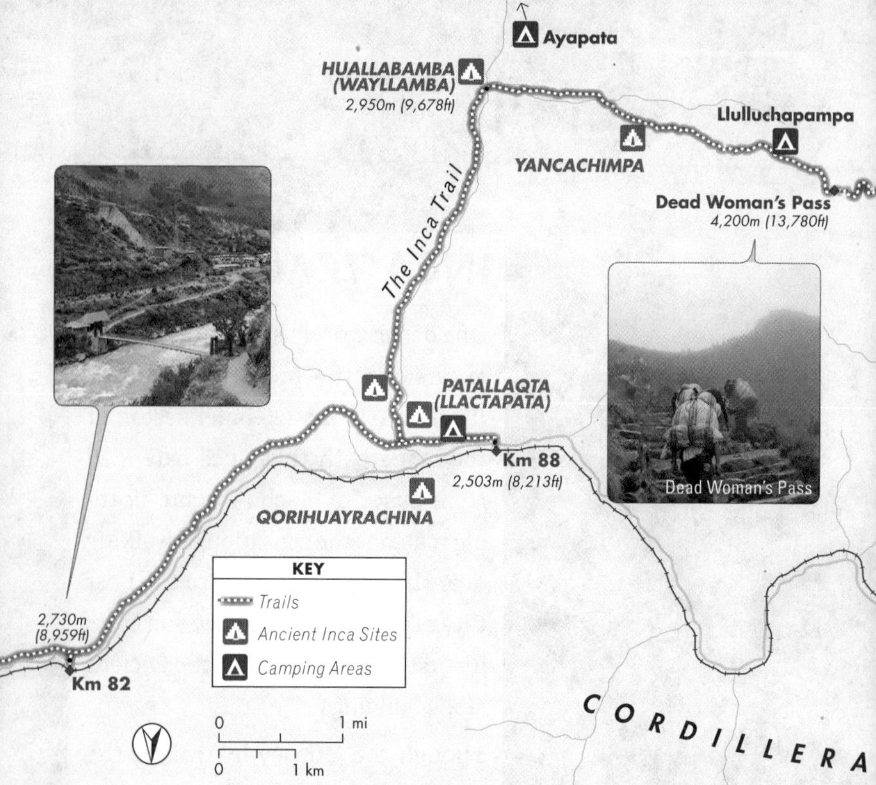

INCA TRAIL DAY BY DAY

The majority of agencies begin the traditional Inca Trail trek at **Km 82** after a two-to three-hour bus ride from Cusco.

DAY 1

Compared to what lies ahead, the first day's hike is a reasonably easy 11 km (6.8 miles). You'll encounter fantastic inca structures almost immediately. An easy ascent takes you to the first of those, **Patallaqta** (also called Llactapata). The name means "town on a hillside" in Quechua, and it is thought to have been a village in Inca times. Bingham and company camped here on their first excursion to Machu Picchu. You will see different types of architecture there, both pre-Inca and Inca.

At the end of the day, you arrive at **Huayllabamba** (also called Wayllamba), the only inhabited village on the trail and your first overnight. If the plan is to stay at Aguas Calientes the third night, you'll likely press on to the campsite at Ayapata.

DAY 2

It's another 10-km (6.2 mile) hike, but with a gain of 1,200 m (3,940 ft) in elevation. The day is most memorable for the spectacular views and muscle aches after ascending **Dead Woman's Pass** (also known as Warmiwañusca) at 4,200 m (13,780 ft). The pass is named for the silhouette created by its mountain ridges—they resemble a woman's head, nose, chin, and chest.

A tricky descent takes you to **Pacaymayu**, the second night's campsite, and you can pat yourself on the back for completing the hardest section of the Inca Trail. If cutting out the third night, you'll likely go on to Chaquicocha.

DAY 3

Downhill! You'll cover the most ground today (16 km, 9.9 miles) descending down 1,500 meters to the subtropical cloud forest where the

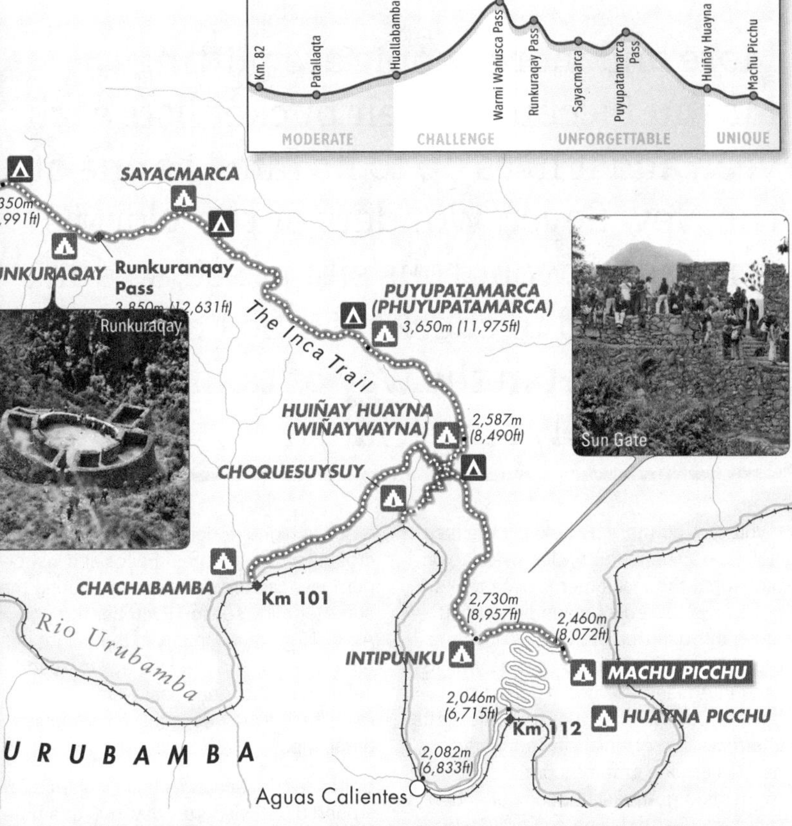

Amazon basin begins. There's some of the most stunning mountain scenery you'll see during the four days. The structure at **Runkuraqay** was a circular Inca storage depot for products transported between Machu Picchu and Cusco.

You also pass by **Sayacmarca**, possibly a way station for priests traversing the trail.

Most excursions arrive by mid-afternoon at **Huiñay Huayna** (also known as Wiñaywayna), the third night's stopping point, at what may now seem a low and balmy 2,712 m (8,900 ft). If heading on, you will have lunch here and keep going through the Sun Gate and down to Aguas Calientes to spend the night in a hotel.

There is time to see **Puyupatamarca** (also known as Phuyupatamarca) a beautifully restored site with ceremonial baths, and perhaps the best Inca Structures on the hike. At this point you catch your first glimpse of Machu Picchu peak, but from the back side.

DAY 4

This is it. Day 4 means the grand finale, arrival at **Machu Picchu**, the reason for the trail in the first place.

You'll be roused from your sleeping bag well before dawn to hike your last 6 km (3.7 miles)to arrive at the sanctuary in time to catch the sunrise. You'll be amazed at the number of fellow travelers who forget about their aching muscles and sprint this last stretch.

The trail takes you past the **Intipunku**, the Sun Gate. Bask in your first sight of this ancient wonder and your accomplishment, but you'll need to circle around and enter Machu Picchu officially through the entrance gate.

More and more people are putting Machu Picchu on their bucket lists each year, and it lives up to its fame as one of the New Seven Wonders of the World. It is indeed a wondrous site to see, so don't let the need to check off a box on your to-do list get in the way of taking the time to really appreciate it.

If you can, go there by trekking the Inca Trail—sleeping in the Andes, walking on paths that the Incas themselves took to get to this sacred site, and entering at dawn through the Sun Gate is absolutely breathtaking. Take some time as well to relax in Aguas Calientes before rushing back to Cusco. It may not have the same charm as that colonial city, but being nestled among green mountains, not to mention getting a hot shower and massage in after hiking around Machu Picchu, is definitely the icing on the cake.

Planning

When to Go

All the high-season/low-season trade-offs are here. Winter (June through August) means drier weather and easier traveling, but it's prime vacation time for those in the Northern Hemisphere. Don't forget that three major observances—Inti Raymi (June 24), Peru's Independence Day (July 28), and Santa Rosa de Lima (August 30)—fall during this time, and translate into exceptionally heavy concentrations of Peruvian travelers. (Also consider that Sundays are free for *cusqueños*.) The result is higher lodging prices and larger crowds at these times. Prices and visitor numbers can drop dramatically during the summer rainy season (October through April). Note that January is the height of rainy season, and the Inca Trail is closed in February. For near-ideal weather and manageable crowds, consider a spring or fall trip.

Entrance to Machu Picchu is limited to around 6,000 visitors a day, 600 at a time for 10 entry periods. In low season, this won't present a problem, but if you are traveling during the winter months (North American summer), be sure to purchase your entrance tickets ahead of time to ensure you get the time slot you want. If your heart is set on hiking Huayna Picchu, the mountain that is in front of Machu Picchu and affords great views of the citadel below, you should purchase tickets in advance regardless of the season. If you are not using an agency, you can purchase tickets yourself online at 🌐 *www.machupicchu.gob.pe.*

You often hear rumors that Machu Picchu will be closed to tourism in order to preserve it. Although this is highly unlikely to happen, there are ongoing discussions and proposals being considered to help protect it. Limiting the number of daily visitors is a good start, as is timed entry, but additional measures include enforcing existing regulations that require all tourists to be accompanied by licensed guides and restricting the amount of time that you can spend in the citadel. Be sure to check the current status of regulations with a tour operator when making your plans.

Although many travelers day-trip to Machu Picchu, an overnight in Aguas Calientes (the town below the site) lets you experience the ruins long after the day-trippers have left and before the first train and tour groups arrive in the morning. An alternative is to take an evening train back to the Sacred Valley and overnight there. **■ TIP→ When booking your return train, it's best not to do so for the same day you are flying out of Cusco, just to be safe.**

Getting Here and Around

There are two ways to get to Machu Picchu: by foot via a guided trek along the Inca Trail or by train to Aguas Calientes and then an official Consettur tourist bus to the famed ruins. The 20-minute bus ride offers hair-raising turns and stunning views of the Vilcanota Valley below. Rather than take the bus, you can also walk up to the ruins from Aguas Calientes, but it takes an hour and is uphill the whole way. You cannot drive yourself here. Trains to Aguas Calientes leave from Cusco's San Pedro station; the nearby Poroy station, which is 20 minutes from the Plaza de Armas; or Ollantaytambo in the Sacred Valley, almost two hours northwest of Cusco. The train from the San Pedro station is not recommended, as you will spend around 30 minutes in switchbacks to get out of the city. The bimodal service from the city of Cusco takes you by bus to Ollantaytambo. Taking a private taxi to Ollantaytambo and the train from there is faster and more pleasant.

BUS TRAVEL

If you don't plan on walking up to Machu Picchu (about an hour up the road from Aguas Calientes), you will have to catch a bus, easily identifiable by the Consettur name on the front. Consettur buses depart from the intersection of Imperio de los Incas Avenue and the Aguas Calientes River. Tickets cost US$12 one-way or US$24 round-trip and can be purchased in advance from the Consettur office just up the street from the departure point with your passport. Although there are no assigned seats, tickets are issued with your name and ID on them. Buses leave every 10 minutes starting at 5:30 am. The park is open from 6 am to 5:30 pm. Since park entrances are purchased for a specific hour, the buses board according to the entry tickets. Even for a 6 am entrance, showing up for the bus at 5:30 am is fine. If you're heading back to Cusco, take the bus back down at least an hour before your train departs. Note that the line for the bus back down can get quite long around lunch time, as many people have afternoon trains back to Cusco. **■ TIP→ Make your bus reservation online at the Consettur website www.consettur.com and either pay with a credit card or print out the reservation to make purchase in Aguas Calientes faster and easier.**

TAXI TRAVEL

You can take a *colectivo* taxi or van from Cusco to Ollantaytambo. They depart daily from Pavitos street near the intersection with Avenida Grau. The trip to Ollantaytambo takes 1½ to 2 hours and you'll need to arrive 30 minutes before your train departs.

TRAIN TRAVEL

Most Machu Picchu tour packages include rail tickets as well as bus transport between Aguas Calientes and Machu Picchu, admission to the ruins, and lodging if you plan to stay overnight. If you plan to go without a tour, it's an

The Skinny on Machu Picchu

Day-Tripping vs. Overnight

You can visit Machu Picchu on a day-trip, but it's best to stay overnight at a hotel in Aguas Calientes. A day-trip allows you about six hours at Machu Picchu, coinciding with the most crowded times (and the times when the guards tend to be more rigid about moving you through the site quickly). If you plan to stay overnight, you have more time to wander the ruins after most tourists have gone or can plan to visit twice (with two tickets) to really allow time to soak in the site. If you can, opt to spend two nights, one before visiting Machu Picchu, so you can be on the first bus up to the ruins in the morning, and one after your visit to allow you time to recuperate especially if you hike Huayna Picchu.

Buying a Ticket

Purchase Machu Picchu tickets at the very least a month in advance. If you have your heart set on hiking Huayna Picchu, purchase tickets at least two to three months in advance. If you are planning to visit on a day-trip, it's a good idea to get your trains squared away first as popular train times sell out fast. Also, you'll want to know your time of arrival in order to plan your entrance time. If you arrive without an admission ticket, you must purchase one in Aguas Calientes at the **Centro Cultural Machu Picchu** (✉ *Av. Pachacutec 103* ☎ *084/211–196*). Purchase must be made in cash (S/152, no credit cards) with your passport and in person. There is no ticket booth at the ruins' entrance. If you are with a tour, the tickets are most likely taken care of for you. The ticket is valid only for the date it is purchased.

If you want to go in both the morning and the afternoon of the same day, something that allows you to exit, have lunch, use the bathroom, and go back into the site, you will need two separate timed tickets. The ruins are open from 6 am to 5:30 pm (but last entry is at 3).

Practicalities

It gets warm, and the ruins have little shade, so sunscreen, a hat, and water are musts. Officially, no food or drinks are permitted, but you can get away with a non-single-use bottle of water and snacks. There's a snack bar a few feet from where the buses deposit you at the gate, and the Belmond Sanctuary Lodge Machu Picchu has a US$40 lunch buffet open to the public if you want to eat before or after your visit. Large packs must be left at the entrance. ■ **TIP→ You have to show your passport to enter—if you want it stamped with an image of the ruins, stop by the stand just past the exit.**

Bathrooms cost S/1, and toilet paper is provided. There are no bathrooms inside the ruins, and you may not exit and reenter to use them.

The Inca Trail, Abridged

Most Cusco tour operators market a two-day, one-night Inca Trail excursion. An Inca Trail permit is required, and you must go with a licensed operator; book well in advance. The excursion begins at Km 104, a stop on the Cusco/Sacred Valley–Machu Picchu trains. All of the hiking happens on the first day, and you get to enter Machu Picchu through the Sun Gate and spend the night at a hotel in Aguas Calientes. The second day is a visit to the ruins.

easy train ride from Ollantaytambo in the Sacred Valley to Machu Picchu (the train stops in Aguas Calientes, the town below the ruins). Most visitors board the train in Ollantaytambo, as trains leave more frequently from this station making it the best option. It is possible to take the train from Cusco's Poroy station (which is a 20-minute taxi ride away from the Plaza de Armas) to Machu Picchu, but it is more convenient to take a taxi to Ollantaytambo and board a train there; taxis are quicker than the train, and there are more train times available at Ollantaytambo. Two train operators serve Machu Picchu, PeruRail and Inca Rail.

PERURAIL

PeruRail is the longest-standing train operator and offers services from Cusco, Poroy, Urubamba, Ollantaytambo, and Aguas Calientes. It operates three trains of different classes and offering different services. The least expensive train is the *Expedition*. The cars have comfortable seats and tables, with sky windows for a full peek at the Sacred Valley. The next step up is the *Vistadome*, whose cars have sky domes for great views, snacks and beverages included in the price, and a return trip that includes a fashion show and folklore dancing. The luxury *Hiram Bingham* train provides a class of service unto itself (with prices to match). It leaves from Cusco's Poroy station, a 20-minute taxi ride from the Plaza de Armas, and will make a stop in Ollantaytambo if booked from there. The *Vistadome* and the *Expedition* trains depart from Cusco, Poroy, and Ollantaytambo. There is also one *Vistadome* per day traveling to and from Urubamba, which also stops in Ollantaytambo.

Train ticket prices vary by season and time of day. A ticket on the *Expedition* costs between US$104 and US$158 round-trip from Ollantaytambo; a round-trip on the *Vistadome* from Ollantaytambo costs between US$154 and US$190. A round-trip ticket on the *Hiram Bingham* train costs US$946. One-way-only rates are higher.

PeruRail's service is generally punctual. Schedules and rates are always subject to change, and there may be fewer trains per day to choose from during the December-to-March low season. A full train schedule is available on the company's website, and timetable fliers can be picked up from the one of its offices in Cusco.

In theory, same-day tickets can be purchased, but waiting that late is risky. Procure tickets in advance from PeruRail's sales office in the Plaza de Armas in Cusco; it is open every day, including weekends and holidays, from 8 am to 9 pm. The office on Avenida El Sol has extended hours, daily from 7 am to 10 pm. You can also purchase tickets online or by phone. Note that trains that include stops in Urubamba tend to fill up quickly.

INCA RAIL

Inca Rail also has trains departing from Cusco, Poroy, Ollantaytambo, and Aguas Calientes, as well as bi-modal service from Cusco throughout the year.

There are three types of tickets offered on Inca Rail: Voyager, which costs between US$108 and US$140 round-trip; the 360°, which costs between US$154 and US$163 round-trip and includes a box lunch, fresh juices, and herbal teas; and First Class, which costs US$474 round-trip and includes a pisco sour and three-course meal, a cocktail-making class, and fresh juices and teas. Coming with a group? Ask about chartering the company's Private Machu Picchu Train, which includes welcome champagne, pisco sours, a three-course gourmet meal, a special selection of wines and fresh juices, personalized cooking classes, an observatory lounge, and a private bus to the citadel.

You can purchase tickets in Cusco at the Inca Rail office in the Plaza de Armas, or by phone. It is also possible to purchase online with a credit card.

TRAIN CONTACTS Inca Rail. ✉ *Ticket Office, Portal de Panes 105, Plaza de Armas* ☎ *084/581–860 office* 🌐 *www.incarail.com.* **PeruRail.** ✉ *Ticket Office, Portal de Carnes 214, Plaza de Armas* ☎ *084/581–414 reservations* 🌐 *www.perurail.com.*

Restaurants

The town of Aguas Calientes near Machu Picchu has numerous restaurants, each offering its own (often not authentic) take on traveler-tested and approved plates like pizza, Mexican, and Chinese, as well as typical Andean food. Andean fusion, a gourmet play on traditional Peruvian fare, is available at better restaurants, as is the case throughout Peru. The busiest hours are between 1 and 3 and then again when dinner begins around 7 and tour groups tend to be gathering. Nevertheless, most places are open all afternoon if you wish to eat in between those times. Things typically start winding down around 9.

Hotels

There is only one hotel at Machu Picchu itself and that is the Belmond Sanctuary Lodge Machu Picchu. It will cost you to stay there, as it's an exclusive property owned by the Belmond Company, the same outfit that operates PeruRail, but it's also the only place you can sit in a Jacuzzi and look at the Inca city long after the crowds have left. In Aguas Calientes, you'll find many hostels and cheaper hotels lining the railroad tracks—that's not as down-at-the-heels as it first sounds: many rooms have great waterfront views. Aguas Calientes' budget lodgings are utilitarian places to lay your head, with a bed, a table, a bathroom, and little else. A handful of hotels offer surprising luxury for such an isolated location. Their rates can be shockingly luxurious, too.

All hotels collect guests just outside the front gate of the station. Lodgings keep surprisingly early checkout times. (Hotels free up the rooms for midmorning Cusco–Ollantaytambo–Machu Picchu trains.) Unless you are staying in one of the more expensive hotels, expect to vacate by 9 am, though this is less strictly enforced in the off-season. All hotels will hold your luggage if you're not leaving town until later in the day.

Many hotels keep the same official rates year-round but unofficially discount rates during the off-season, which can be anywhere from mid-November through March. It also pays to check the hotel website, if it has one, for current promotions. *Hotel reviews have been shortened. For full information, visit Fodors.com.*

WHAT IT COSTS in Nuevo Soles

$	$$	$$$	$$$$
RESTAURANTS			
under S/35	S/35–S/50	S/51–S/65	over S/65
HOTELS			
under S/250	S/250–S/500	S/501–S/800	over S/800

Aguas Calientes

But for the grace of Machu Picchu discoverer Hiram Bingham, Aguas Calientes would be just another remote, forgotten crossroads. But Bingham's discovery in 1911, and the tourist boom decades later, forever changed the community. At just 2,050 meters (6,724 feet) above sea level, Aguas Calientes will seem downright balmy if you've just arrived from Cusco. There are but three major streets—the pedestrian only Avenida Pachacutec, which leads uphill from the Plaza de Armas to the hot springs; the Avenida Imperio de los Incas, which isn't a street at all but rather the railroad tracks where you'll find many services; and the Avenida Hermanos Ayar, where you'll find the only vehicular traffic, limited to the buses that ferry tourists to the ruins. You'll have little sense of Aguas Calientes if you do the standard day-trip from Cusco. But the cloud-forest town pulses to a very lively tourist beat with hotels, restaurants, thermal baths, and a surprising amount of activity, even after the last afternoon train has returned to Cusco. It also provides a great opportunity to wander around the high jungle, particularly welcome if you aren't going to make it to the Amazon. Although you won't see wildlife other than several species of hummingbirds, the flora (especially the many varieties of orchids) is worth taking a wander to see. You can find information about the easy and relatively flat walk to Mandor Waterfalls or the more intense hike up Putucusi Mountain at the local iPeru office. If possible, stay two nights in town so you can be on the first bus to Machu Picchu, take as long as you like touring the ruins, and then relax and enjoy a hot shower after a long day exploring.

■ TIP→ Aguas Calientes (literally "hot waters") takes its name from the thermal springs that sit above town; however, we don't recommend paying a visit. The baths are not as hot as you might like nor are they up to a high level of cleanliness. Rather than take home a souvenir you'd rather not, consider visiting El MaPi Hotel's spa which is open to nonguests.

GETTING HERE AND AROUND

Trains to Aguas Calientes depart daily from Cusco's San Pedro station, Poroy about 20 minutes out of the city, and from Ollantaytambo and Urubamba in the Sacred Valley. In spite of its steep side streets, the city is small and easily explored by ambling about on foot. *See Planning above for train travel to Machu Picchu/Aguas Calientes.*

Sights

Mercado Artesanal (*Craft Market*)
MARKET | A warren of vendors' stalls lines the couple of blocks between the train station and the bus stop for shuttle transport up to the ruins. You can find some souvenirs here that you may not see in Cusco. The prices for crafts such as textiles, bags, and magnets may or may not be cheaper (this largely depends on your negotiating skill and patience), but it's a great way to spend time before your train leaves. ✉ *Aguas Calientes* ✣ *Near train station.*

Museo de Sitio Manuel Chávez Ballón
MUSEUM | The museum, dedicated to the history, culture, and rediscovery of Machu Picchu, sits on the way up to the ruins about 2 km (1 mile) from the edge of town at the entrance to the national park. Walking is the best way to get here. Plan on about a 30-minute hike. You'll get a bit more insight at the Casa Concha Museum in Cusco, where the repatriated artifacts returned from Yale University are being exhibited, but there are some interesting pieces on display here, some recovered as recently as 2004. Admission also includes entrance to a small but interesting botanical garden at the same site. ✉ *Puente de Ruinas, 2 km (1 mile) from Aguas Calientes* 🎫 *S/22.*

Restaurants

★ Chullpi Machupicchu Restaurante
$$$ | **PERUVIAN** | The kitchen at this rustic-chic restaurant, which is along the tracks heading out of town, turns out high-quality gourmet versions of Peruvian classics such as *ají de gallina* (creamed chicken) with quail eggs and *causa* (a potato dish) with salmon tartare. The beautifully presented plates are on the small side, so it's best to order at least two courses, or try the tasting menu of 6, 10, or 15 courses. **Known for:** gourmet food; creative presentation; locally sourced ingredients. 💲 *Average main: S/52* ✉ *Av. Imperio de los Incas 140* ☎ *084/211–350.*

Prepping for the Inca Trail

You Must Use a Guide

You must use a licensed tour operator, one accredited by SERNANP, the organization that oversees the trail and limits the number of hikers to 500 per day: 300 permits are allotted for guides and porters and 200 for tourists. (The two-day Inca Trail permits are separate.) There are some 260 licensed operators in Cusco.

When to Go

May through September is the best time to make the four-day trek; rain is more likely in April and October and a certainty the rest of the year. The trail fills up during the dry high season. Make reservations months in advance if you want to hike then—weeks in advance the rest of the year. The trek is doable during the rainy season, but it can become slippery and muddy by November. The trail closes for maintenance each February.

Getting Ready

Tour operators in Cusco will tell you the Inca Trail is of "moderate" difficulty, but it can be rough going, especially the first couple of days. You must be in decent shape, even if you choose to hire porters to carry your pack, which must be done at time of booking. The trail is often narrow and hair-raising and can be challenging for those with a fear of heights, although most will be fine. Be wary of altitude sickness. Give yourself two or three days in Cusco or the Sacred Valley to acclimatize.

While You're Hiking

Food: All operators have their own chefs that run ahead of you with the porters, set up camp, and create culinary feasts for breakfast, lunch, and dinner. This will probably be some of the best camp food you'll ever have.

Campsites: There are seven well-spaced, designated campsites along the trail.

Coca Leaves: Coca leaves are a mild stimulant as well as an appetite and pain suppressant. You'll only need about one bag of your own (around S/2) for the trail. Take about 15 leaves, and pick off and discard the stems. Stack the leaves on top of each other, and roll them into a tight little bundle. Place the bundle between your gum and cheek on one side, allowing the leaves to soften up so that the juice comes out—you're not actually meant to chew them. It's quite a bitter taste, but you'll feel better. All tour operators will also serve coca tea during snack breaks.

Bathrooms: Toilets could be a lot worse. You can sit down (if you want to) and flush in most of them, and there are usually working sinks. You must bring your own toilet paper. Campsites all have toilets, but the trail itself does not. Many tour operators now travel with toilet tents.

Luggage: Pack as lightly as possible in a duffel bag. If you hire porters, current regulations limit the porter's load to 18 kg (39.6 pounds) including his own gear. Agencies will typically offer a "half-porter" with a limit of 7 kg (15.4 pounds) for your personal gear. Leave the rest of your belongings with your hotel.

Packing List for the Inca Trail

You've booked your Inca Trail trek and are ready to pack your duffel bag. But what should you bring? Here is a list of essentials.

Duffel Bag Packing List

- Large, resealable plastic bag to keep your things dry
- Waterproof hiking boots with ankle support (broken in)
- Sleeping bag (can be rented), liner, and pad (often provided by agency—ask what type)
- 2 hiking pants (ideally convertible to shorts)
- 2–3 breathable short-sleeve and 2–3 long-sleeve T-shirts
- 1 medium and 1 thick fleece
- Protective sun hat or baseball cap
- 1 lightweight, packable down coat
- 1 set of warm comfortable clothes to change into at campsite or your sleepwear
- 1 set of thermals to sleep in
- 1 pair of warm sleeping socks
- 3–4 pairs of hiking socks
- 3 pairs of hiking liners (prevents blistering)
- Warm gloves and wool hat
- Comfortable sneakers or shoes (to change into at the end of the day—hiking sandals with socks work great as they can back up your trekking shoes as well)
- Flip-flops (to use the cold shower on the last day)
- Toiletries, including prescription medicines, pain relievers, face and body wet wipes, feminine products, toothbrush, and toothpaste
- 1 set of clothes to change into if you stay in Aguas Calientes after trek (you can get laundry done fast)

Gear for Day Pack

You will want a small day pack with back support to carry with you as you hike.

- Wear 1 set of layered clothing
- 1–2 water bottles or water bladder
- Hiking poles (can be rented or cheap wooden ones purchased; metal poles must have rubber tips)
- Hat and sunglasses
- Sunscreen and lip balm with sun protection
- Waterproof jacket and pants and backpack cover
- Bug repellent
- Toilet paper, tissues, and hand sanitizer
- Moleskin and Band-Aids for blisters
- Headlamp
- Camera
- Snacks (your operator will also provide snacks)
- Medicine (altitude sickness, antidiarrhea, etc.) and first-aid kit
- Small towel
- Cash for tipping porters and staff

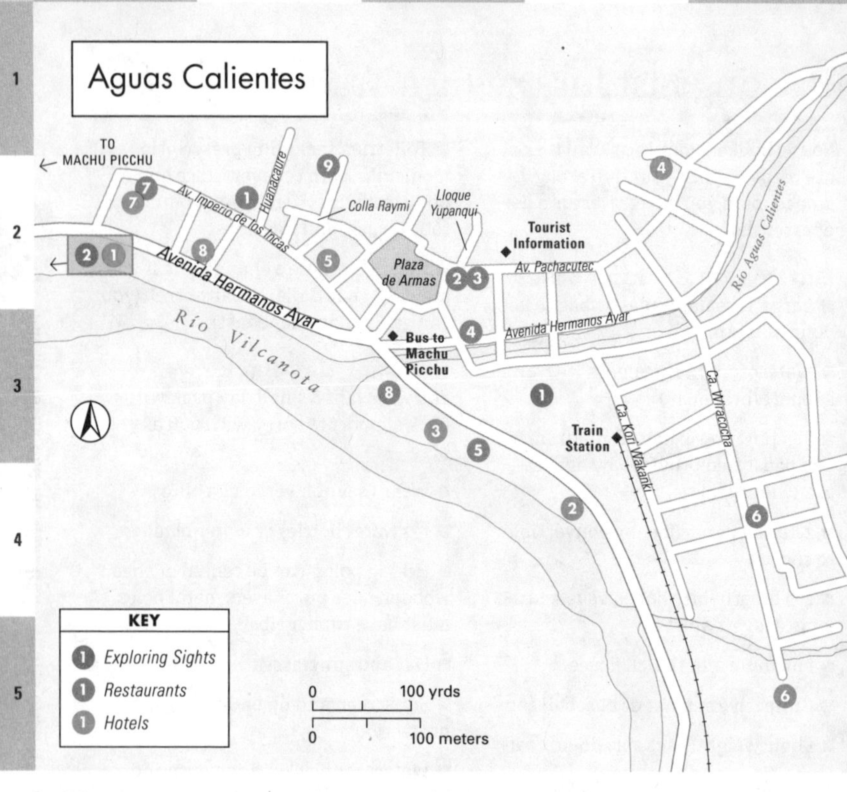

Sights

1 Mercado Artesanal..... **D3**

2 Museo de Sitio Manuel Chávez Ballón........... **A2**

Restaurants

1 Chullpi Machupicchu Restaurante **B2**

2 Incontri del Pueblo Viejo.............**C2**

3 Indio Feliz................**C2**

4 La Boulangerie de Paris..................**C3**

5 Mapacho Craft Beer Restaurant...............**C3**

6 Palate Pizza & Burger Bar............... **E4**

7 Qunuq Restaurant...... **A2**

8 Toto's House.............**C3**

9 Tree House Restaurant............... **B2**

Hotels

1 Belmond Sanctuary Lodge Machu Picchu **A2**

2 Casa Andina Classic Machu Picchu **D4**

3 Casa del Sol Boutique Hotel...........**C3**

4 El MaPi.................. **D2**

5 Hatun Inti Boutique..... **B2**

6 Inkaterra Machu Picchu Pueblo Hotel............. **E5**

7 Sumaq Hotel............ **A2**

8 Tierra Viva Cusco Machu Picchu Hotel ... **B2**

Incontri del Pueblo Viejo

$$ | **ITALIAN** | With an owner-chef who hails directly from Italy, you can be sure to find authentic Mediterranean fare here, as well as house-made pasta and Peruvian cuisine. The large, open space has comfortable seating with a cozy fireplace, and the fair prices, especially on the Italian wines, make this a great value. **Known for:** gourmet Italian food and wine; thin-crust pizza; tiramisu. *Average main: S/42 ✉ Pachacutec s/n ☎ 084/211–193.*

★ Indio Feliz

$$ | **FRENCH** | **FAMILY** | An engaging French-Peruvian couple manage one of the town's best restaurants, whose eclectic decor—think maritime kitsch—is worth a visit on its own. Quiche Lorraine, ginger chicken, and spicy *trucha a la macho* (trout in hot pepper and wine sauce) are favorites on the Peruvian-French fusion à la carte menu, but the reasonably priced (S/77), prix-fixe, three-course menu is the way to go, offering all the same options plus heavenly homemade bread. **Known for:** enormous portions where quality meets quantity; eclectic atmosphere; fast and excellent service. *Average main: S/39 ✉ Lloque Yupanqui s/n ☎ 084/211–090 🌐 www.indiofeliz.com.*

La Boulangerie de Paris

$ | **CAFÉ** | Paris's loss is Aguas Calientes' gain with the authentic French pastries served here, as well as coffee, sandwiches on house artisanal bread, quiche, and more. Eat in or take some of the delicious choices to go—the excellent boxed-lunch options are perfect for enjoying in Machu Picchu, and the restaurant opens at 5 am so you can pick them up on the way to the bus. **Known for:** oustanding pastries; great coffee; quick food to go. *Average main: S/10 ✉ Jr. Sinchi Roca ☎ 084/211–398 No credit cards No dinner.*

★ Mapacho Craft Beer Restaurant

$$ | **PERUVIAN** | Go for the awesome craft beer, but stay for the delicious food. Everything—from faster pub fare to full meals such as *lomo saltado* (beef stir-fry), grilled chicken, and osso buco—is served by a friendly, professional staff in a casual setting along the river. **Known for:** revolving varieties of craft beer; excellent customer service; something for everyone. *Average main: S/40 ✉ Calle Imperio de los Incas 614 ☎ 984/759–634.*

Palate Pizza & Burger Bar

$ | **AMERICAN** | Although this casual café is part of the Supertramp backpacker hostel, the food is first-rate, with burgers, pizzas, and salads that are perfect for satiating an appetite forged by hoofing around Machu Picchu. Unlike at many of the places lining the main streets in town, this restaurant's pizza and burgers are worthy of being included in its name, and both are available with a variety of tasty toppings such as blue cheese and *jamon serrano* (dry-cured Spanish ham). **Known for:** simple but good food; low-key atmosphere; lively rooftop bar. *Average main: S/24 ✉ Supertramp Eco Hostel, Calle Chaska Tika 203 ☎ 084/435–830 🌐 supertramphostel.com/palate-bistro.*

★ Qunuq Restaurant

$$$$ | **PERUVIAN** | The restaurant in the Sumaq Hotel is a must-experience for foodies thanks not only to culinary offerings that can easily hold their own against anything Lima's finest restaurants can dish out but also to a first-class setting and the utmost in professional yet warm service. European dishes like ravioli are given an Andean slant by stuffing them with ají de gallina, and traditional Peruvian fare is infused with international flavor. **Known for:** fabulous gourmet tasting menus; excellent service; outstanding river-trout ceviche. *Average main: S/71 ✉ Sumaq Hotel, Av. Hermanos Ayar Mz. 1, L-3 ☎ 084/211–059 🌐 machupicchuhotels-sumaq.com.*

Alternate Route to Aguas Calientes

No time to trek or go to the Amazon? If time permits, another option is to take a bus or shared car from Cusco to Santa Maria and from there a taxi to Santa Teresa. (This can also be arranged via private car through an agency). You can overnight here at the EcoQuechua Lodge (*www.ecoquechua.com*), a fantastic opportunity to spend some real quality time in the cloud jungle. This clean and comfortable eco-lodge offers a little bit of paradise, and a stay includes a gourmet dinner. The staff can also arrange treks, zipline outings, coffee tours, Machu Picchu adventures, and more. From here, a 20-minute taxi ride can take you to the *planta hidroeléctrica* (hydroelectric plant), from which you can hike an easy, flat, two- to three-hour trail into Aguas Calientes. If you are intrigued by a multiday trek but don't want to make the time or energy commitment, do the hike into Aguas and book your Machu Picchu entrance to include Huayna Picchu. This way, you will get a good amount of walking in without having to camp.

The Santa Teresa excursion also makes a nice addition for after your Machu Picchu trip, and you can hop on a PeruRail train (usually US$32 but can vary) from Aguas Calientes to the hydroelectric plant if you have had enough of walking. Note, however, that this excursion is not recommended during rainy season, as the roads to Santa Maria and Santa Teresa have sheer drop-offs and can become dangerous.

Toto's House

$$ | **PERUVIAN** | **FAMILY** | This well-established tourist favorite has long tables set up in the center of its cavernous dining room to accommodate the tour groups that come for the huge buffet lunch. In the evening, grilled dishes like *trucha andina* (Andean trout), beef, or alpaca—served amid the entertainment of a folkloric music show—are better bets than the buffet items. **Known for:** popular buffet lunch, especially for big groups; traditional Peruvian dishes; riverside location. $ *Average main: S/50 ✉ Av. Imperio de los Incas 600 ☎ 084/211–020.*

Tree House Restaurant

$$ | **INTERNATIONAL** | Perched high above the streets of Aguas Calientes, this small, wood-paneled restaurant serves some of the best international cuisine in town. Fresh, local ingredients are the backbone for such dishes like quinoa salad with goat cheese, gnocchi with lamb ragout, and Thai brochettes. **Known for:** romantic setting; fresh local ingredients in gourmet dishes; best choice in town for vegans. $ *Average main: S/45 ✉ Calle Huanacaure 180 ☎ 084/435–849 www.thetreehouse-peru.com/indexEN.html.*

Hotels

Belmond Sanctuary Lodge Machu Picchu

$$$$ | **HOTEL** | This upscale hotel at the entrance to Machu Picchu puts you closest to the ruins, a position for which you do pay dearly, but nowhere else can you sit in a hot tub, sip pisco sours or tea, and watch the sunset over the site after the last of the tourists depart each afternoon. **Pros:** prime location at ruins' entrance with views of Machu Picchu and no need to wait on line for bus; personalized service; all-inclusive. **Cons:** double the price of other luxury options in Aguas Calientes; small rooms and bathrooms; no additional Machu Picchu benefits. $ *Rooms from: S/4775 ✉ Entrance to Machu Picchu ☎ 084/211–094*

One of the pros of spending a night at the Belmond Sanctuary Lodge Machu Picchu: you can see the ruins and mountains from the property.

hotel, 01/610–8300 in Lima, 800/237–1236 in North America ⊕ www.belmond.com/sanctuary-lodge-machu-picchu ⇨ 31 rooms 🍴 All meals.

Casa Andina Classic Machu Picchu

$$ | HOTEL | FAMILY | Although the feel may be a bit more business than boutique, this is unquestionably the best bet for those wanting a comfortable, modern room and excellent service without a hefty price tag. **Pros:** comfortable modern rooms; friendly and attentive staff; adjoining rooms available. **Cons:** standard-category rooms are interior rooms; traditional rooms are near the train tracks; minimal design and few frills. [$] *Rooms from: S/393 ✉ Prolongacion Imperio de Los Incas E-34 ☎ 511/391–6500 ⊕ www.casa-andina.com ⇨ 53 rooms 🍴 Free breakfast.*

Casa del Sol Boutique Hotel

$$$$ | HOTEL | The decor and the setting by the river are what make this hotel special—wood floors, beams, and window frames give rooms an elegant yet warm atmosphere; textile art adorns the walls; and stone-and-marble bathrooms blend perfectly with the natural environment outside. **Pros:** beautiful design and lush comfort; less expensive than other luxury options; suites have balconies with Jacuzzis. **Cons:** train noise from tracks just outside the hotel—ask for a riverside room; less exclusive service than the other top options; only three suites with Jacuzzis. [$] *Rooms from: S/850 ✉ Av. Imperio de los Incas 608 ☎ 084/211–128 ⊕ www.hotelescasadelsol.com ⇨ 28 rooms 🍴 Free breakfast.*

El MaPi

$$$ | HOTEL | Designed to save travelers some dollars and cents without skimping on comfort and class, El MaPi delivers what it promises: simple but stylish rooms, top-tier service, and the same amenities you might expect from one of the more luxurious joints in town. **Pros:** great service for a good value; a la carte dinner included; spa with sauna and Jacuzzi open to nonhotel guests. **Cons:** not for those seeking a boutique hotel; some rooms are a bit cramped;

many rooms don't have a view. *Rooms from: S/580* *Av. Pachachutec 109* *511/610–0400* *www.inkaterra.com* *130 rooms* *Free breakfast.*

Hatun Inti Boutique

$$$ | **HOTEL** | Polished wood floors, white walls, and tasteful furnishings give this hotel an elegantly rustic and homey feel—it's ideal if you want something more upscale that feels like a boutique but don't want over-the-top prices. **Pros:** prime riverside location; lovely boutique feel with fireplaces in rooms; good value for the money. **Cons:** rooms on train side can be noisy; don't confuse this with sister property Hatun Inti Classic when booking online; small property. *Rooms from: S/598* *Av. Imperio de los Incas 606* *084/234–312* *grupointi.com* *14 rooms* *Free breakfast.*

★ **Inkaterra Machu Picchu Pueblo Hotel**

$$$$ | **RESORT** | **FAMILY** | A five-minute walk from the center of town takes you to this stunning eco-lodge, part of the Relais & Châteaux collection of hotels, made up of rustic-yet-elegant bungalows with exposed beams and cathedral ceilings, set in a minitropical cloud forest. **Pros:** natural setting with many activities, some included in the price; excellent restaurant with breakfast and dinner included; children under 12 stay free. **Cons:** expensive; time is needed to take advantage of the services; jungle location makes rooms a bit dark. *Rooms from: S/1806* *Av. Imperio de los Incas s/n* *084/211–032, 01/610–0400 in Lima, 800/442–5042 in North America* *www.inkaterra.com* *83 casitas* *Some meals.*

★ **Sumaq Hotel**

$$$$ | **HOTEL** | This upscale and luxurious hotel sits at the edge of town alongside the Vilcanota River and offers all the amenities plus outstanding service with a smile. **Pros:** gourmet restaurant with breakfast and lunch or dinner included; cooking class and tea time included, plus story hour for kids; fantastic friendly service. **Cons:** luxury costs; some rooms overlook the train tracks; a one-night stay may not allow time to appreciate all amenities. *Rooms from: S/1155* *Av. Hermanos Ayar Mz.1 L-3* *084/211–059, 866/847–7366 in North America* *machupicchuhotels-sumaq.com* *62 rooms* *Free breakfast.*

Tierra Viva Cusco Machu Picchu Hotel

$$ | **HOTEL** | Tierra Viva has a reputation for creating hotels that offer a great balance between quality and price, and this one, standing above the river at the edge of town, is no exception. **Pros:** excellent quality for the price; great location; supports local artisans. **Cons:** not as high design or comfortable as luxury options; rooms without a river view are not recommended; late checkout usually not available. *Rooms from: S/373* *Av. Hermanos Ayar 401* *084/211–201* *www.tierravivahoteles.com* *42 rooms* *Free breakfast.*

Spas

Otto's Spa

SPA/BEAUTY | In a place where many of the massage therapists have little or no training, Otto and his staff are real gems—professional and talented. A massage is the perfect way to end a day of hiking around Machu Picchu, especially if you climb Huayna Picchu or hike the Inca Trail. At about S/100 for an hour massage plus foot bath and shower, this is truly a bargain. Call for an appointment if the spa is not open; walk-ins are welcome. *Av. Imperio de los Incas 602* *984/382–567.*

Chapter 8

THE AMAZON BASIN

Updated by
Maureen Santucci

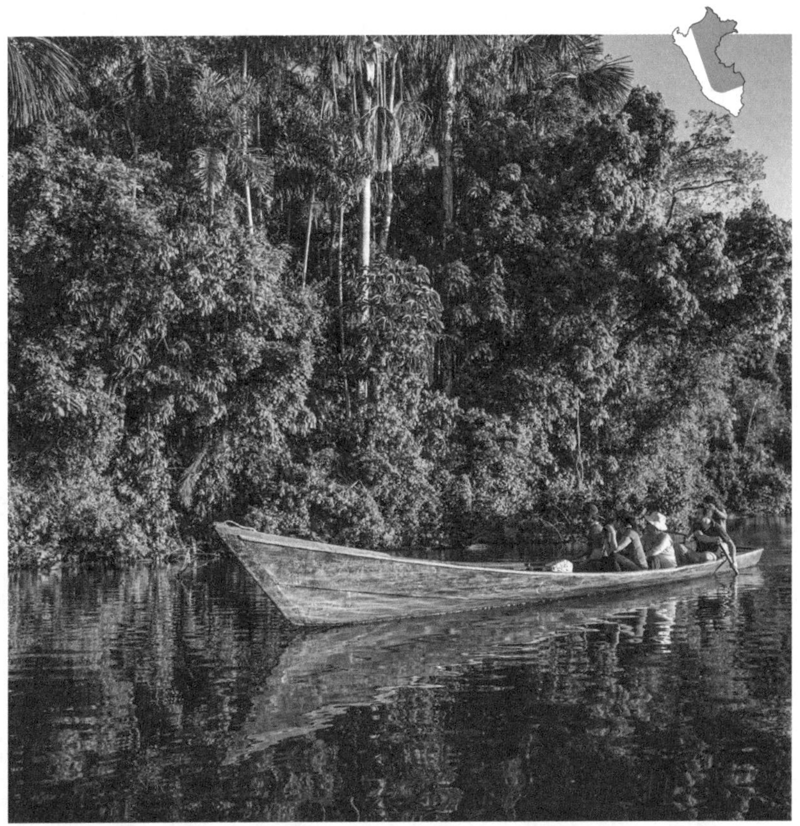

Sights	Restaurants	Hotels	Shopping	Nightlife
★★★★★	★★★☆☆	★★★★★	★★★☆☆	★☆☆☆☆

WELCOME TO THE AMAZON BASIN

TOP REASONS TO GO

★ **The River:** The Amazon River is a natural choice for adventures, but it is best explored on an organized tour.

★ **Wild Things:** Peru's Amazon Basin has more than 50,000 plant, 1,700 bird, 400 mammal, and 300 reptile species. Bring your binoculars.

★ **Sport Fishing:** Anglers can test their skills on dozens of river fish, including the feisty peacock bass.

★ **Nature Lodges:** Staying at a jungle lodge is almost obligatory when visiting the Amazon Basin if you really want to experience the rainforest.

★ **Cruising:** An Amazon River cruise to Pacaya Samiria National Reserve is the most comfortable, though expensive, way to explore this vast wilderness.

The logistics of travel and isolation make it difficult to visit both the northern and southern Amazon regions—separated by 600 km (370 miles) at their nearest point—during one trip to Peru. The city of Iquitos is the jumping-off point for the northern Amazon; Puerto Maldonado for the southern Amazon tributaries, the Madre de Dios and Tambopata Rivers. Some 1,200 km (740 miles) and connecting flights back in Lima separate the two cities. The Manu Biosphere Reserve, on the upper Madre de Dios River, can be reached by land and river from either Cusco or Puerto Maldonado. Both the northern and southern regions are dotted with excellent jungle lodges and can also be experienced on a cruise.

1 Puerto Maldonado. The jumping-off point for visiting the Tambopata National Reserve and surrounding rainforest.

2 Tambopata National Reserve and Bahuaja-Sonene National Park. This incredible reserve is easy to get to and more affordable than most similar experiences. Nature lodges protect significant expanses of rainforest in this national reserve, while providing guests with almost constant exposure to the impressive diversity of wildlife on display here.

3 Manu Biosphere Reserve. While a trip to this reserve is a rustic adventure, this is one of the most biodiverse places on earth. Its puna grasslands, cloud forests, and seemingly endless rainforest make it one of the best places in the Amazon Basin to see wildlife.

4 Iquitos. A colorful, dilapidated port town on the Río Amazonas.

5 The Peruvian Amazon. The best way to visit this incredible area is on a prearranged tour with one of the many jungle lodges or on a luxurious river cruise with highly trained naturalist guides who can take you to indigenous villages and on nature walks, birding tours, and nighttime outings.

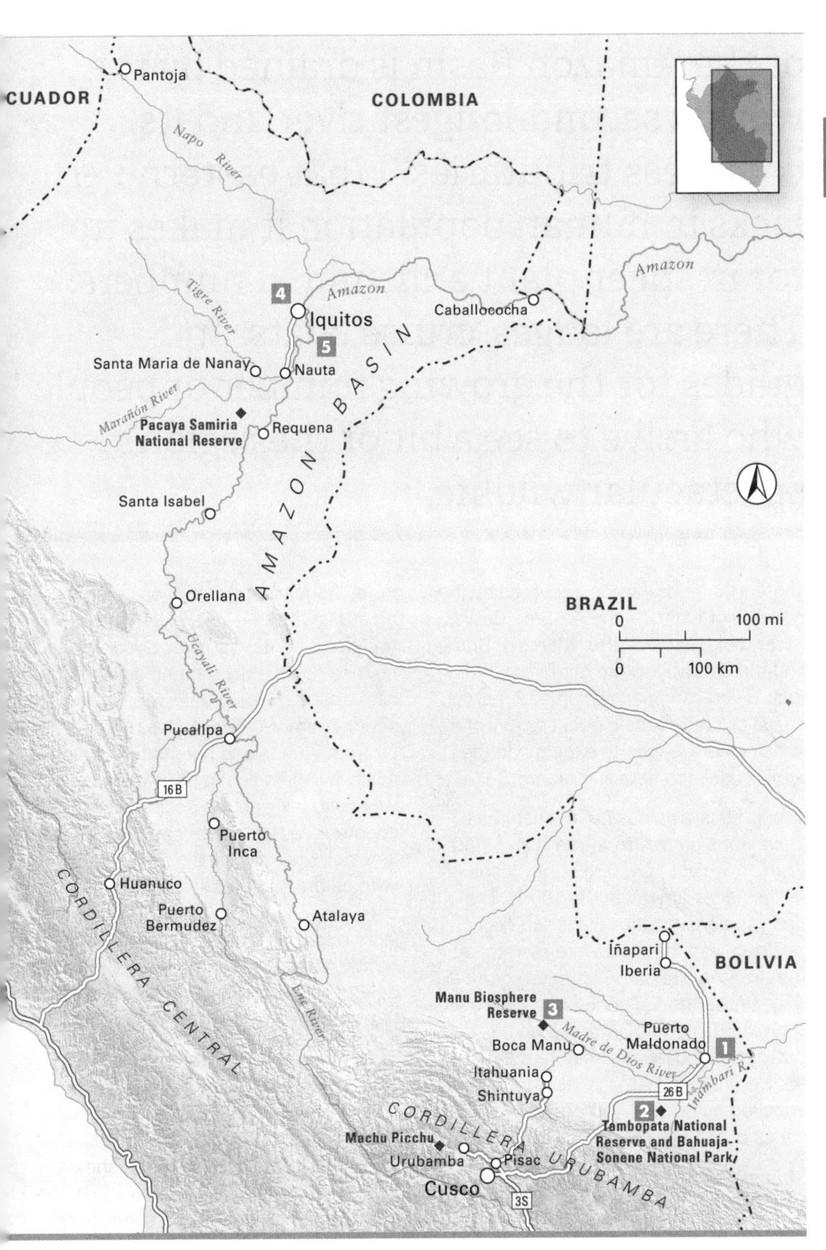

CUADOR
COLOMBIA
Pantoja
Napo River
Tigre River
Amazon
Iquitos
Caballococha
Amazon
4
5
Santa Maria de Nanay
Nauta
Marañón River
Pacaya Samiria National Reserve
Requena
AMAZON BASIN
Santa Isabel
Orellana
BRAZIL
0
100 mi
0
100 km
Ucayali River
Pucallpa
16B
Puerto Inca
Huanuco
Puerto Bermudez
Atalaya
CORDILLERA CENTRAL
Iñapari
Iberia
BOLIVIA
Manu Biosphere Reserve
3
Ene River
Puerto Maldonado
1
Boca Manu
Madre de Dios River
Inambari R.
Itahuania
Shintuya
26B
2
Tambopata National Reserve and Bahuaja-Sonene National Park
CORDILLERA URUBAMBA
Machu Picchu
Urubamba
Pisac
Cusco
3S

Peru's least-developed region occupies some two-thirds of the country, an area the size of California. The *selva* (jungle) of the Amazon Basin is drained by the world's second-longest river and its countless tributaries. What eastern Peru lacks in human population it makes up for in sheer plant and animal numbers. There are lodges, cruise boats, and guides for the growing number of people who arrive to see a bit of the region's spectacular wildlife.

The northern Amazon is anchored by the port city of Iquitos—the Amazon Basin's second-biggest city after Manaus, Brazil, and the gateway to the rainforest. From Iquitos you can head out on an Amazon cruise or take a smaller boat to any of a dozen jungle lodges to experience the region's diverse flora and fauna.

Though this area has been inhabited by indigenous groups for more than 5,000 years, it wasn't "civilized" until Jesuit missionaries arrived in the 1500s. The Spanish conquistador Francisco de Orellana was the first white man to see the Amazon. He came upon the great river, which the indigenous people called Tunguragua (King of Waters), on his trip down the Río Napo in search of El Dorado. He dubbed it Amazonas after he was attacked by female warriors along the banks of the river.

Most of the indigenous tribes—many small tribes are found in the region, the Boras, Yaguas, and Orejones being the most numerous—have given up their traditional hunter-gatherer existence and now live in small communities along the backwaters of the great river. You will not see the remote tribes unless you travel far from Iquitos and deep into the jungle, a harrowing and dangerous undertaking. What you will see are people who have adopted Western dress and other amenities but who still live in relative harmony with nature and preserve traditions that date back thousands of years. A common sight might be a fisherman paddling calmly on an Amazon tributary in his dugout canoe, angling to reel in one of its many edible fish.

Both Madre de Dios and the Peruvian Amazon are impressive, and while they share much of the same flora and fauna, each region has its own attractions. The Amazon River is notable for its sheer size, and has species that you won't find in Madre de Dios, such as two types of freshwater dolphin and the giant water lily. Because it has fewer inhabitants, Madre de Dios has more wildlife, including rare creatures like the giant river otter and large flocks of macaws that gather at its *collpas* (clay licks). Whichever region you visit, it will be a true adventure. Be prepared to spend some extra soles to get here. Roads, where they exist, are rough-and-tumble, so the preferred mode of transport is by boat. A dry-season visit is recommended—but, of course, "dry" is a euphemism in the rainforest. You'll most likely jet into Iquitos or Puerto Maldonado, respectively the northern and southern gateways to the Amazon, and climb into a boat to reach one of the region's famed nature lodges.

MAJOR REGIONS

Madre de Dios. Do the math: 20,000 plant, 1,200 butterfly, 1,000 bird, 200 mammal, and 100 reptile species (and many more yet to be identified). The southern sector of Peru's Amazon Basin, most readily approached via Cusco, is famous among birders, but any traveler will be impressed by the dawn spectacle of macaws and parrots gathered at one of the region's famed collpas. Ornithologists speculate that the birds ingest clay periodically to neutralize toxins in the seeds and fruit they eat. Madre de Dios also offers a chance to see large mammals, such as capybaras (the world's largest rodent), monkeys, and giant otters. If the zoological gods smile upon you, you may even encounter a tapir or a jaguar. Animal and plant life abounds, but this is the least populated of Peru's departments: a scant 76,000 people reside in an area slightly smaller than South Carolina, and almost two-thirds of them are in Puerto Maldonado.

While the discovery of gold in the 1970s drew new waves of fortune seekers to the region, tourism and conservation have triggered the newest generation of explorers in the species-rich southern Amazon. Two areas of Madre de Dios are of special interest. One is around the city of Puerto Maldonado, including the Tambopata National Reserve and the adjoining Bahuaja-Sonene National Park. Easily accessible, they offer lodges amid primary rainforest and excellent wildlife. Tambopata also serves sustainable agriculture purposes: some 1,500 families in the department collect Brazil nuts from the reserve and surrounding forest, an economic incentive to keep the rainforest intact rather than cut it down. The Manu Biosphere Reserve, directly north of Cusco, though more difficult to reach, provides unparalleled opportunity for observing wildlife in one of the largest virgin rainforests in the New World.

Iquitos and Nearby. Founded by Jesuit priests in the 1500s, Iquitos was once called the "Pearl of the Amazon." It isn't quite that lustrous today, but it's still a pleasant, friendly town that provides access to the Amazon River, rainforest wildlife, and various indigenous cultures. Although most travelers fly here specifically for an excursion into the surrounding rainforest, Iquitos has sites nearby that can be visited in a few hours or a day and deserves at least a night. The city itself may grow on you as you become accustomed to the humid climate and relaxed, easy ways of its citizens. Its *malecón* (riverwalk) is a popular place for an evening stroll, and you can enjoy a meal of fresh fish while floating on the river it came from.

Planning

When to Go

As you might expect, it rains plenty in the Amazon Basin, though that precipitation is somewhat seasonal. Although there's no true dry season in the Iquitos area, it rains less from June to October, when the river's level drops considerably. For Amazon cruises out of Iquitos, high-water season is best (December–June); tributaries become shallow during the dry months, making it hard to get to oxbow lakes.

The southern Amazon Basin has a pronounced dry season between May and October; and while most lodges are open year-round, some Manu lodges close between December and April. Tambopata sees a well-defined wet season/dry season; Manu's rainfall is more evenly dispersed throughout the year. Plan well in advance for trips in July and August, the peak tourist season, when some jungle lodges often take in large groups and cruise boats can be full. During the dry season, especially July and August, sudden *friajes* (cold fronts) bring rain and cold weather to Madre de Dios, so be prepared for the worst. Temperatures can drop from 32°C (90°F) to 10°C (50°F) overnight. No matter when you travel, bring a rain jacket or poncho.

Getting Here

AIR

LATAM flies to Iquitos four times daily from Lima. Peruvian Airlines has three flights daily, and Star Peru flies twice a day. Iquitos's Aeropuerto Internacional Francisco Secada Vignetta is 8 km (5 miles) from the city center. A taxi to the airport should cost around S/15. LATAM has five direct daily flights from Lima and two from Cusco to Aeropuerto Padre Aldamiz, 5 km (3 miles) from the center of Puerto Maldonado. Book early, especially if you're traveling from Cusco, or you may have to go through Lima which is a much longer journey.

BOAT

Boats are the most common form of transportation in the Amazon Basin and the only way to get to most of the nature lodges, with the exception of those in the cloud forests of Manu. If you stay at any of this region's nature lodges, you will be met at the airport in Puerto Maldonado or Iquitos and transported to a riverbank spot where you board a boat that takes you to your lodge. Once there, most excursions will also be by boat. If you opt for an Amazon cruise, you'll spend most of your time on the water.

BUS

The only areas that can be reached by road are Puerto Maldonado and the buffer zone of Manu National Park. The winding road to Puerto Maldonado from Cusco is a 10-hour bus ride that only a backpacker on a very tight budget would take. Several tour companies offer slower, but incredible, overland trips from Cusco to Manu, including seven hours over rugged terrain via Paucartambo. The road plunges spectacularly from the *páramo* (highlands) into the cloud forest, eventually reaching the Alto Madre de Dios River in Atalaya, where travelers board boats to Manu lodges.

Health and Safety

MALARIA

There is no vaccine for malaria, but prescription drugs help minimize your likelihood of contracting this mosquito-borne illness. Strains of malaria are resistant to the traditional regimen of chloroquine. There are three recommended alternatives: a weekly dose of mefloquine; a daily dose of doxycycline; or a daily dose of Malarone (*atovaquone/proguanil*). Any regimen must start before arrival and continue beyond departure. Talk to your physician well in advance of your trip. Wear long sleeves and pants, and use a mosquito repellent containing DEET whenever you enter the jungle.

YELLOW FEVER

The Peruvian Embassy recommends getting a yellow fever vaccine at least 10 days before visiting the Amazon. Though recent cases of yellow fever have occurred only near Iquitos, southern Amazon lodges in Manu and Tambopata tend to be sticklers about seeing your yellow fever vaccination certificate. Carry it with you.

Hotels

Puerto Maldonado and Iquitos have plenty of small hotels. Iquitos also has a few nicer hotels geared to business travelers. Beyond those urban centers lie the region's jungle lodges, which are reachable only by boat and vary in degree of rusticity and remoteness. They range from tented camps, where rooms consist of a bed inside a screened enclosure under a roof, to upscale eco-lodges with swimming pools and Wi-Fi. Most have limited electricity, however, and only one offers air-conditioning. Showers are often refreshingly cool.

All nature lodges offer fully escorted tours, with packages from one to eight nights including guided wildlife-viewing excursions. They all provide mosquito nets and three meals. Most lodges quote rates per person, based on double occupancy, that include meals and transportation plus most tours, and many take so long to reach that the minimum stay is two nights. *The price ranges given for lodges in this chapter reflect the cost of one night's stay for two people, meals included.* All lodges accept soles and U.S. dollars for drinks and souvenirs. *Hotel reviews have been shortened. For full information, visit Fodors.com.*

WHAT IT COSTS in Nuevo Soles

	$	$$	$$$	$$$$
RESTAURANTS				
	under S/35	S/35–S/50	S/51–S/65	over S/65
HOTELS				
	under S/250	S/250–S/500	S/501–S/800	over S/800

Restaurants

You can dine out at restaurants only in Iquitos and Puerto Maldonado, the Amazon Basin's two main cities, and even they have limited choices. Your sole dining option is your lodge if you stay in the jungle. The food, usually made of local ingredients, can be quite tasty.

Tours

Although it's possible to see a bit of the jungle on a day tour from Puerto Maldonado or Iquitos, exploring the Amazon Basin on your own isn't recommended because the areas that you could reach tend to have degraded forest and few animals. If you want to see rainforest wildlife, book a tour with a company that owns one or more lodges located in remote, wild areas.

Amazon Conservation Association

ECOTOURISM | This respected conservation organization (with offices based in the U.S.) protects vast expanses of tropical wilderness and has three biological research stations in pristine, private reserves near the Manu Biosphere Reserve or Tambopata National Reserve that few people visit. In recent years, the organization has built bungalows and begun operating tours that visit one or more research stations on 5- to 10-day trips that begin in either Cusco or Puerto Maldonado. Those tours offer excellent bird-watching and other wildlife encounters, and the profits support conservation. ✉ *1012 14th Street NW, Washington* ☎ *202/871–3777* 🌐 *birding.amazonconservation.org* 🎫 *From $507.*

★ InkaNatura Travel

ECOTOURISM | InkaNatura Travel runs 1- to 11-night nature tours to the Manu Biosphere Reserve or the Tambopata National Reserve with overnight stays at any of six nature lodges. These lodges are in some of the most pristine areas that travelers can visit in Peru, so the company's tours offer some of the best exposure to the wildlife of the Amazon Basin available anywhere. It has tours to both Manu and Tambopata out of Puerto Maldonado. ☎ *971/427–346* 🌐 *www.inka-natura.com* 🎫 *From $363 per person.*

Puerto Maldonado

500 km (310 miles) east of Cusco.

The inland port city of Puerto Maldonado lies at the confluence of the Madre de Dios and Tambopata rivers. The capital of the department of Madre de Dios, it is a rough-and-tumble town with 60,000 people and nary a four-wheeled vehicle in sight; rather, it has hundreds of motorized two- and three-wheeled motorbikes jockeying for position on its few paved streets.

The city is named for two explorers who ventured into the region 300 years apart: Spanish conquistador Juan Álvarez de Maldonado passed through in 1566; Peruvian explorer Faustino Maldonado explored the still-wild area in the 1860s, . never completing his expedition (he drowned in the Madeira River). Rubber barons founded this youngster of Peruvian cities in 1912, and its history has been a boom-or-bust roller-coaster ride ever since. The collapse of the rubber industry in the 1930s gave way to decades of dormancy that were ended by the discovery of gold in the 1970s and the opening of an airport 10 years later. High prices for gold and steady improvements to the road there—part of a "highway" connecting Peru with Brazil—have brought an influx of settlers in recent years, which has been a scourge for the region's forests and indigenous peoples.

Nevertheless, Puerto Maldonado bills itself as the "Biodiversity Capital of the World," because it is the jumping-off point for visiting the Tambopata National Reserve and surrounding rainforest. ■ **TIP→ Few travelers spend any time in the city, heading from the airport directly to docks, where they board boats to their respective jungle lodges.** Still, Puerto Maldonado has one decent hotel and can be used as a base for day-trips. And this is the only place to use an ATM or visit a pharmacy.

GETTING HERE AND AROUND

AIRPORT Aeropuerto Internacional Padre Aldamiz. ✉ *Ca. Faucett Km 7* ☎ *082/502–029.*

HEALTH AND SAFETY

Hospital Santa Rosa. ✉ *Jr. Cajamarca 171* ☎ *982/601–077, 974/944–702 alternate number* 🌐 *www.hospitalsantarosa.gob.pe.*

Sights

Collpa de la Cachuela

LOCAL INTEREST | A 20-minute boat trip up the Madre de Dios River from Puerto Maldonado takes you to this small collpa on the riverbank. Each day, more than 100 parrots, parakeets, and chestnut-fronted macaws gather here from 5:30 am to 8 am to eat the mineral-rich clay. ✉ *Puerto Maldonado* ✥ *10 km (6 miles) up Madre Dios River from town.*

Mariposario Tambopata

GARDEN | **FAMILY** | Tambopata's Butterfly Farm has a large screened-in area full of jungle plants where dozens of colorful butterflies float above the leaves and flowers and caterpillars hide amidst the foliage. There is information about the biology of these delicate creatures and a chamber full of cocoons, chrysalises, and recently hatched butterflies. The Mariposario is close to the airport and has a small restaurant that is a tranquil spot for a drink or snack. ✉ *Av. Elmer Faucett* ✥ *Km 7, 150 meters before Padre Aldamiz Airport* ☎ *082/792–157* 🌐 *peru-butterfly.com* 🎫 *S/18.*

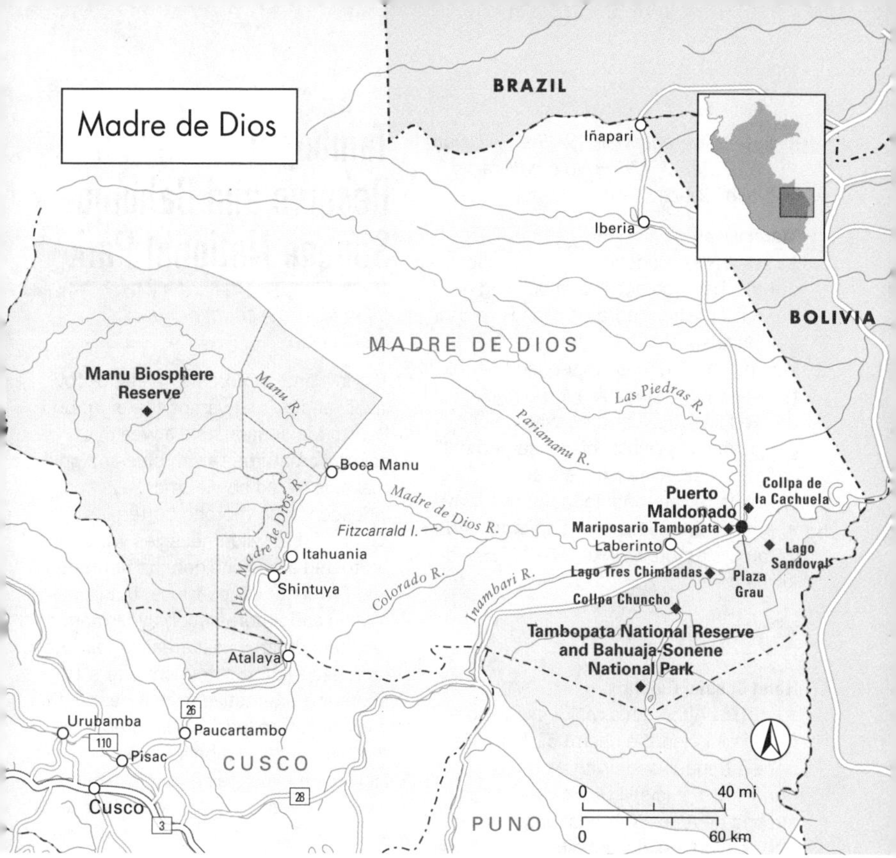

Plaza Grau

PLAZA | This grassy plaza one block northeast of the Plaza de Armas is dedicated to Miguel Grau, a Peruvian naval officer in the 19th century. But the attraction isn't the bust of him erected there: rather it's the sweeping view of the Rio Madre de Dios and the rainforest that lines its banks. ✉ *Jr. Bellinghurst at Jr. Arequipa.*

Restaurants

Burgos's Restaurant

$ | **PERUVIAN** | This funky, thatch-roofed restaurant with river views in the back has one of Puerto Maldonado's best kitchens, offering up a wide variety of local favorites such as *pollo con salsa de castañas* (chicken in a Brazil-nut sauce), *pescado en hoja* (fish fillet cooked in a leaf), or *lomo* (grilled tenderloin) with *tacacho* (fried plantain balls) and *ensalada de palmito* (heart of palm salad). The environment is appropriately Amazonian, with indigenous art on the walls. **Known for:** Amazonian specialties; grilled beef; Tambopata River views. $ *Average main: S/30* ✉ *Av. 26 de Diciembre 195* ☎ *082/573–653, 981/935–422* 🌐 *burgos-restaurant.com.*

Gustitos del Cura

$ | **PERUVIAN** | **FAMILY** | Conveniently located on the Plaza de Armas, this popular restaurant is a good spot for a light meal, dessert, or a fresh fruit drink. The menu includes a selection of sandwiches and salads, tamales, and entrees like chicken cordon bleu, but most people come for the homemade pastries and ice creamflavored with *castañas* (Brazil nuts) and local rainforest fruits such as *aguaje* and *camu camu*. **Known for:** homemade ice cream; light meals; tropical fruit juices. $ *Average main: S/19 ✉ Jr. Loreto 258 ☎ 082/572–175 ▭ No credit cards ⊙ Closed Wed.*

Maracuyeah
$ | **PERUVIAN** | It doesn't look like much, but this bamboo-and-wood building on the bank of the Madre de Dios River is a popular spot with locals, especially at sunset. The menu is limited, and people tend to share dishes like *lomo fino* (tenderloin strips sautéed with onions, garlic, and a splash of pisco) served with cassava fries. **Known for:** sunset viewing; typical Peruvian food; loud music. $ *Average main: S/22 ✉ Puerto Capitanía, 142 26 de Diciembre ☎ 993/358–757 ▭ No credit cards.*

Hotels

Hotel Cabaña Quinta
$ | **HOTEL** | Although a major expansion has diminished the charm of this hotel, once a tranquil spot with wooden bungalows, it is still Puerto Maldonado's second-best accommodation. **Pros:** central location; quiet; free airport transfers. **Cons:** basic rooms; walls are thin; some rooms are small. $ *Rooms from: S/200 ✉ Jr. Moquegua 422 ☎ 082/571–045 ⊕ www.hotelcabanaquinta.com 65 rooms Free breakfast.*

Wasaí Maldonado Lodge
$$ | **HOTEL** | Nestled in the rainforest one block from the main square, the Wasaí Maldonado offers the town's best accommodation. **Pros:** jungle setting with river views; good restaurant; free airport transfers. **Cons:** older bungalows can be musty; basic rooms; loud music nearby on weekends. $ *Rooms from: S/280 ✉ Jr. Billinghurst at Jr. Arequipa ☎ 01/436–8792, 997/516–355 ⊕ wasai.com 28 rooms Free breakfast.*

Tambopata National Reserve and Bahuaja-Sonene National Park

5 km (3 miles) south of Puerto Maldonado.

The lowland rainforests, rivers, oxbow lakes, and palm swamps that surround Puerto Maldonado hold a wealth of colorful creatures—from blue-and-gold macaws to red howler monkeys and iridescent blue morpho butterflies. Much of that wilderness lies within protected areas, indigenous territories, and Brazil-nut concessions, but illegal mining and deforestation by farmers and ranchers destroy vast areas of rainforest here each year. Ecotourism offers an economic alternative to that destruction, and the nature lodges scattered around the Tambopata National Reserve protect significant expanses of rainforest in private reserves, which provide their guests with almost constant exposure to the wonders of tropical nature.

GETTING HERE

Tambopata jungle lodges are possibly the easiest places in the world to experience the Amazon rainforest. They are much more accessible—and affordable—than those in the Manu Biosphere Reserve, Madre de Dios's other ecotourism area. And Tambopata is no poor man's Manu either—its numbers and diversity of wildlife are very impressive. An hour flight from Cusco takes you to Puerto Maldonado, the Tambopata jumping-off point. The closest lodges are less than an hour by boat down the Madre de Dios River, but the best lodges for wildlife-watching take anywhere from two to four hours to reach. Some of the lodges offer two-night packages, but a three-night stay is really the least you should spend in this area, and if you really want to see animals, you should book a five-day trip.

Continued on page 315

THE PERUVIAN AMAZON

by Doug Wechsler

Green-winged Macaw (Ara chloroptera) foraging high in rain forest canopy.

An observant naturalist living in the Peruvian Amazon can expect to see something new and exciting every day in his or her life. To the casual traveler much of this life remains hidden at first but reveals itself with careful observation.

Western Amazonia may be the most biologically diverse region on earth. The areas around Puerto Maldonado and Iquitos are two of the best locales to observe this riot of life.

In the Tambopata Reserve, for example, 620 species of birds and more than 1,200 species of butterflies have been sighted within a few miles of one eco-lodge. To put that into perspective, only about 700 species of birds and 700 species of butterflies breed in all of North America. Within the huge Manu National Park, which includes part of the eastern slope of the Andes, about 1⁄10 of the world's bird species can be sighted. A single tree can harbor the same number of ant species as found in the entire British Isles. A single hectare (2.4 acres) of forest might hold nearly 300 species of trees.

This huge diversity owes itself to ideal temperatures and constant moisture for growth of plants and animals and to a mixture of stability and change over the past several million years. The complex structure of the forest leads to many microhabitats for plants and animals. The diversity of plants and animals is overwhelming and the opportunity for new observations is limitless.

STARS OF THE AMAZON

Pink River Dolphin: The long-snouted pink river dolphin enters shallow waters, flooded forest, and even large lakes. Unlike the gray dolphin of river channels, this species rarely jumps out of the water.

Eats: Fish. **Weighs:** 350 lbs. **Myth:** Often blamed for pregnancies when father is unknown.

Red-and-Green Macaw: The loud, raucous shrieks first call attention to red-and-green macaws, the largest members of the parrot family in the Amazon. Clay licks near a number of jungle lodges in Madre de Dios are great places to observe these spectacular birds.

Eats: Seeds of trees and vines. **Weighs:** 3 lbs.
Length: 3 ft. **Odd habit:** Consumes clay from steep banks.

Hoatzin: The clumsy-flying, chicken-sized Hoatzin sports a long frizzled crest and bare blue skin around the eye, suggesting something out of the Jurassic. Its digestive system features a fermentation chamber and is more bovine than avian.

Eats: Leaves, especially arum. **Weighs:** 1.8 lbs.
Unusual feature: Nestlings can climb with claws on their wings. **Favorite Hangout:** Trees and shrubs in swampy vegetation near lakes.

Squirrel Monkey: The small, active squirrel monkeys live in groups of 20 to 100 or more. These common monkeys can be distinguished by a black muzzle and white mask.

Eats: Large insects and fruit. **Weighs:** 2 lbs.
Favorite Hangout: Lower and mid-levels of vine-tangled forest especially near rivers and lakes. **Associates:** Brown capuchin monkeys often hang out with the troop.

Red Howler Monkey: A loud, long, deep, roaring chorus from these large, sedentary, red-haired monkeys announces the coming of dawn, an airplane, or a rainstorm. The swollen throat houses an incredible vocal apparatus.

Eats: Leaves and fruits. **Weighs:** 8 to 23 lbs.
Favorite Hangout: Tree tops and mid-levels of forest.
Unfortunate trait: They will urinate and defecate on you if you walk beneath them.

Three-toed Sloth: This slow-moving, upside down ball of fur is easiest to spot in tree crowns with open growth like cecropias. The dark mask and three large claws on the hands distinguish it from the larger two-toed sloth.

Eats: Leaves. **Weighs:** 5 to 11 lbs. **Favorite Hangout:** Tree tops and mid-levels of forest. **Unusual habit:** Sloths climb to the ground once a week to move their bowels.

Cecropia Tree: The huge, multi-lobed leaves, open growth form, and thin light-colored trunks make cecropias among the most distinctive Amazonian trees. Cecropias are the first trees to shoot up when a forest is cut or a new river island is formed. Their long finger-like fruits are irresistible to birds.

Height: Up to 50 ft. or more. **Bark:** Has bamboo-like rings.
Attracts: Toucans, tanagers, bats, monkeys, sloths.
Relationships: The hollow stems house stinging ants that protect the tree—beware.

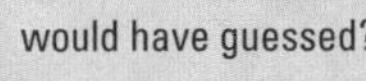

Horned Screamer: A bare, white quill arches from the crown of this ungainly, dark, turkey-sized bird. Its long toes enable it to walk on floating vegetation. Occasionally it soars among vultures.

Eats: Water plants. **Weighs:** up to 7 lbs.
Favorite Hangout: Shores of lagoons and lakes.
Relatives: Screamers are related to ducks and geese—who would have guessed?

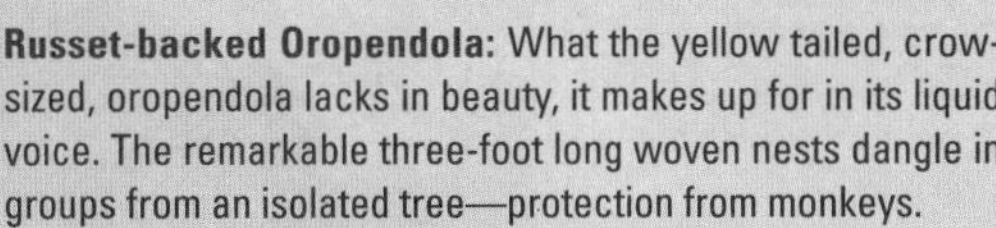

Russet-backed Oropendola: What the yellow tailed, crow-sized, oropendola lacks in beauty, it makes up for in its liquid voice. The remarkable three-foot long woven nests dangle in groups from an isolated tree—protection from monkeys.

Eats: Insects and fruit. **Favorite Hangout:** Forest near clearings and rivers. **Look for:** Flocks of hundreds going to and from roosting islands in the river at dusk and dawn.

Giant Amazon Water Lily: This water lily has leaves up to 7 ft. across and 6–12 inch white or pink flowers that bloom at night. The edges of the leaves bend upward. Leaf stems grow with the rising flood.

Length: Stems up to 20 ft. **Eaten by:** Fish eat the seeds.
Favorite Hangout: River backwaters, oxbow lakes.
Sex changes: Female parts flower the first night, then the flower turns pink and the male parts open.

TIPS:

Don't expect all those species to come out and say hello! The Amazon's great biodiversity is made possible by the jungle's sheltering, almost secretive nature. Here are tips to help train your eye to see through nature's camouflage.

1. Listen for movement. Crashing branches are the first clue of monkeys, and rustling leaves betray secretive lizards and snakes.

2. Going upstream on the river means your boat will stay steady close to shore—where all the wildlife is.

3. Look for birds in large mixed-species flocks; stay with the flock while the many birds slowly reveal themselves.

4. Concentrate your observation in the early morning and late afternoon, and take a midday siesta to save energy for night-time exploration.

5. Wear clothes that blend in with the environment. Exception: hummingbird lovers should wear shirts with bright red floral prints.

6. Train your eye to pick out anomalies—what might, at first, seem like an out-of-place ball of debris in the tree could be a sloth.

7. At night, use a bright headlamp or hold a flashlight next to your head to spot eye-shine from mammals, nocturnal birds, frogs, boas, moths, and spiders.

8. Crush leaves and use your nose when getting to know tropical plants.

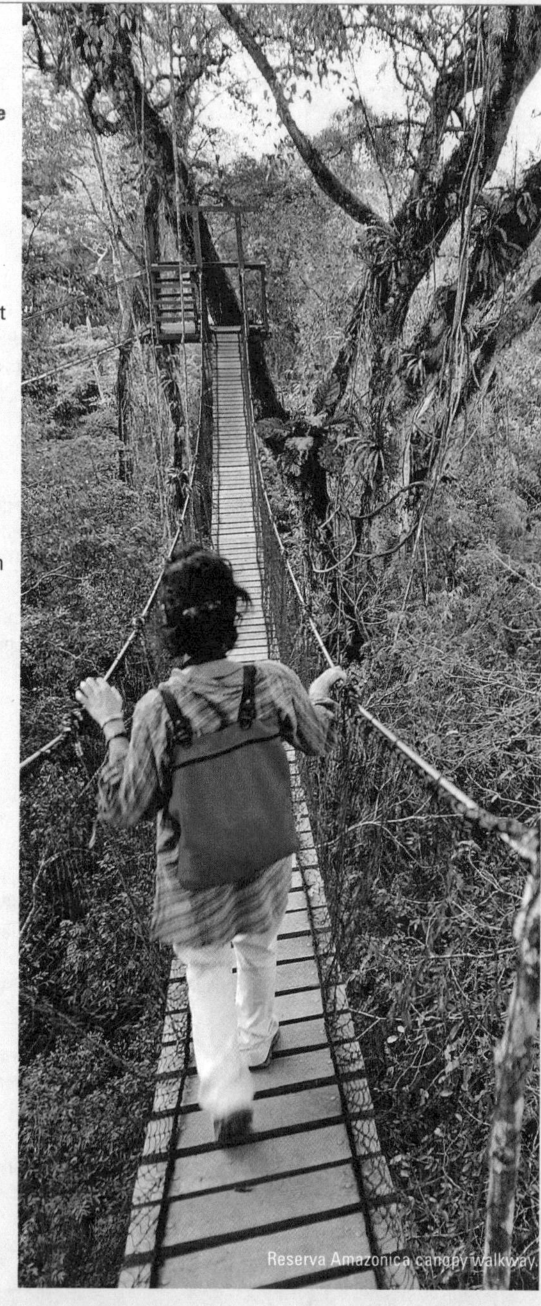

Reserva Amazonica canopy walkway.

TOURS

Amazon Conservation Association

ECOTOURISM | This respected conservation organization protects vast expanses of wilderness in the Peruvian Amazon and has three biological research stations near the Manu Biosphere Reserve and Tambopata National Reserve. In recent years, the association has built bungalows for tourists and begun operating bird-watching tours that visit one or more research stations on 5- to 10-day trips. These tours offer opportunities to see all kinds of wildlife, and the profits support conservation. ☎ *202/871–3777 in U.S.* 🌐 *birding.amazonconservation.org* 🎟 *From USD$507.*

Rainforest Expeditions

ECOTOURISM | The Tambopata experts, Rainforest Expeditions runs three- to seven-day nature tours to lodges near or in the Tambopata National Reserve, with accommodations at one or more of the company's three lodges: the Posada Amazonas, Refugio Amazonas, and Tambopata Research Center. ✉ *Av. Aeropuerto, Km 6, La Joya, Puerto Maldonado* ☎ *01/719–6422* 🌐 *www.perunature.com* 🎟 *From USD$439.*

Wasaí Lodges and Expeditions

ECOTOURISM | With an eco-lodge and a camp on the Tambopata River and a hotel in Puerto Maldonado, Wasaí is able to offer tours that visit this area's two most spectacular spots: the Copa Chuncho and Lago Sandoval. ✉ *Jr. Billinghurst s/n, Puerto Maldonado* ☎ *01/436–8792* 🌐 *wasai.com* 🎟 *From USD$295.*

Sights

★ Tambopata National Reserve and Bahuaja-Sonene National Park

NATURE PRESERVE | A vast expanse of protected wilderness stretches eastward from Puerto Maldonado to Bolivia and southward all the way into the Andean foothills. Its forests, rivers, palm swamps, and oxbow lakes are home to hundreds of bird and butterfly species, monkeys, tarantulas, turtles, and countless other jungle critters. This amazing natural diversity can be experienced from any of a dozen nature lodges scattered along the Madre de Dios River, the Tambopata River, which flows into the Madre de Dios at Puerto Maldonado, or the more distant Heath River.

Together, the contiguous Tambopata National Reserve and Bahuaja-Sonene National Park protect 3.8 million acres: an area the size of Connecticut. Several indigenous Ese'Eja communites border the park; "Bahuaja" and "Sonene" are the Ese'Eja names for the Tambopata and Heath Rivers, respectively. The Río Heath forms Peru's southeastern boundary with neighboring Bolivia, and the former Pampas de Río Heath Reserve, along the border, is now incorporated into Bahuaja-Sonene. It includes a looks-out-of-place "pampas" ecosystem that resembles an African savannah more than the lush Amazon forest that borders it.

Peru collaborates on conservation with Bolivia, whose adjoining Madidi National Park forms a vast, cross-border protected area that covers 7.2 million acres. Only environmentally friendly activities are permitted in Tambopata. In addition to participating in tourism, local communities collect castañas from the forest floor, and aguaje palm fruit in the swampland.

Elevations here range from 500 meters (1,640 feet) to a lofty 3,000 meters (9,840 feet), providing fertile habitat for an astounding diversity of animals and plants. The area holds a world record in the number of butterfly species (1,234). **■ TIP→ These protected areas contains Peru's largest collpas, or clay licks, which are visited by more than a dozen parrot, parakeet, and macaw species each morning. They congregate at dawn to eat the mineral-rich clay in the steep riverbank.** ✉ *Puerto Maldonado* ☎ *082/571–247.*

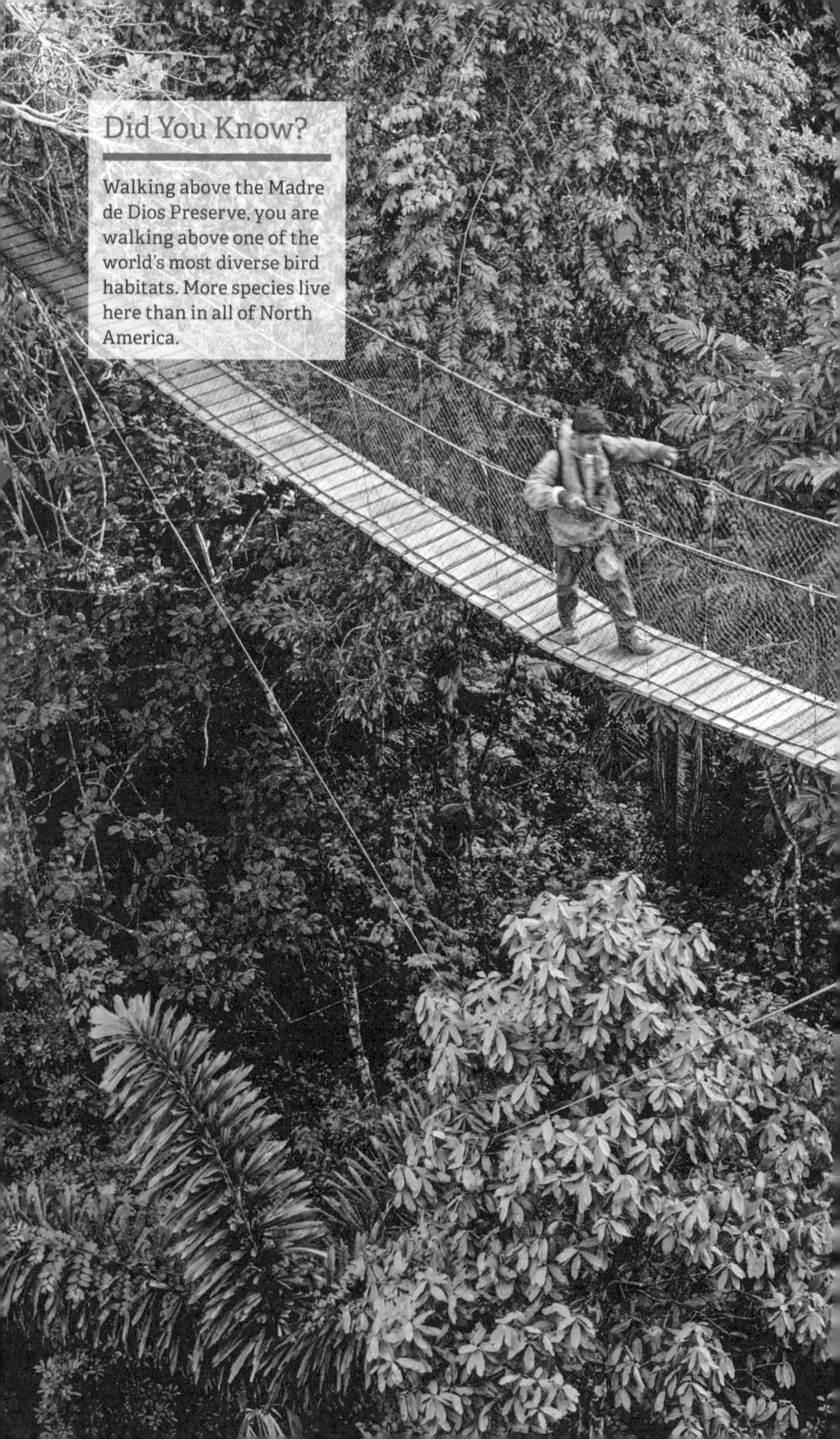

Did You Know?

Walking above the Madre de Dios Preserve, you are walking above one of the world's most diverse bird habitats. More species live here than in all of North America.

Collpa Chuncho

LOCAL INTEREST | The largest collpa in this region is located in Bahauja-Sonene National Park, behind an island on the Tambopata River. On any given morning, hundreds of birds congregate here to eat the clay. The action starts at the break of dawn, when flocks of parakeets begin to arrive. They are followed by several parrot species and five macaw species, which first gather in the treetops and wait for a moment when it seems safe to descend to the clay lick. When they do, it is an amazing sight. Collpa Chuncho can only be visited on excursions from various lodges on the Tambopata River. You'll also see other wildlife along the river on the trip here. ✉ *Puerto Maldonado* ✥ *Tambopata River, 122 km (76 miles) southwest of town.*

★ Lago Sandoval

BODY OF WATER | Changes in the course of Amazon tributaries have created countless oxbow lakes, which are formed when the riverbed shifts and the abandoned bend fills with water. Lago Sandoval, created by the Madre de Dios River, lies just inside the Tambopata National Reserve, a short trip from Puerto Maldonado. It is a lovely sight, hemmed with lush jungle and a wall of aguaje palms on one end. It is also an ideal spot for wildlife-watching. Herons, egrets, kingfishers, and other waterfowl hunt along its edges; several species of monkeys forage in the lakeside foliage; and chestnut-fronted macaws fly squawking overhead. A family of elusive giant otters lives in Lake Sandoval, making it one of the few places you can hope to see that endangered species. The lake is a 30-minute boat ride east from Puerto Maldonado. Once you disembark, there's a flat-but-muddy 3-km (1.8-mile) hike to a dock in the aguaje palm swamp from where you'll be rowed to the actual lake. Unfortunately, Sandoval is very popular, so you'll see plenty of tourists on the trail and lake. **■ TIP→ Fewer people visit the lake in the afternoon, but it is best experienced by spending a night or two at the Sandoval Lake Lodge.** ✉ *Puerto Maldonado* ✥ *14 km (9 miles) east of Puerto Maldonado.*

Lago Tres Chimbadas

BODY OF WATER | This oxbow lake, a short hike from the Tambopata River, is a great place to see wildlife, including the endangered giant river otter. It is also home to side-necked turtles, hoatzins, sun grebes, jacanas, and dozens of other bird species. Its dark waters hold black caimans (reptiles that resemble small alligators) and a plethora of piranha, so try to resist any urge you have to go for a swim. Most people visit Tres Chimbadas on an early-morning excursion from the nearby Posada Amazonas. ✉ *Puerto Maldonado* ✥ *42 km (26 miles) southeast of town.*

Hotels

Eco-lodges in this area are reached by a combination of bus and boat and range from the jungle luxury of Inkaterra's Reserva Amazónica to the rustic Tambopata Research Center, deep inside the Tambopata National Reserve. Rates for all lodges include transportation, bilingual nature guides, three meals per day, and varied excursions. The Corto Maltes, Hacienda Concepción, and Reserva Amazónica are the region's most accessible lodges. They lie less than an hour down the Madre de Dios River from Puerto Maldonado, whereas the Sandoval Lake Lodge requires an additional 90-minute hike. The next closest is Posada Amazonas, which is two hours from Puerto Maldonado up the Tambopata River. The rest require boat trips ranging from three to five hours. Whichever lodge you choose, you will be met at the Puerto Maldonado Airport and transported to and from the lodge by bus and boat.

Jungle Days

The knock at the door comes early. "*¡Buenos días!* Good morning!" It's 5 am, and your guide is rousing you for the dawn excursion to the nearby *collpa de guacamayos*. He doesn't want you to miss the riotous, colorful spectacle of hundreds of parrots and macaws descending to the vertical clay lick to ingest mineral-rich earth. Roll over and go back to sleep? Blasphemy! You're in the Amazon.

A stay at any of the remote Iquitos or Madre de Dios lodges is not for the faint of heart. You'll need to gear up for a different type of vacation experience. Relaxing and luxuriating it will not be, although some facilities are quite comfortable. Your days will be packed with activities: bird- and wildlife-watching, boat trips, rainforest hikes, visits to indigenous communities, kayaking, and so on. You'll be with guides from the minute you're picked up in Iquitos, Puerto Maldonado, or Cusco. Most lodges hire top-notch guides who know their areas well, and you'll be forever amazed at their ability to spot that camouflaged howler monkey from a hundred paces.

The lodge should provide mosquito netting, sheets or blankets, and some type of lantern for your room. (Don't expect electricity.) But check the lodge's website, or with your tour operator, for a list of what to bring and what the lodge provides. Your required inventory will vary proportionally by just how much you have to rough it. Pack sunscreen, sunglasses, insect repellent containing DEET, a hat, hiking boots, sandals, light shoes, a waterproof bag, and a flashlight. Also, a light, loose-fitting, long-sleeve shirt and equally loose-fitting long trousers and socks are musts for the evening when the mosquitoes come out. Carry your yellow fever vaccination certificate and prescription for malaria prevention, plus an extra supply of any medicine you might be taking. Bring along antidiarrheal medication, too. You'll need a small day-pack for the numerous guided hikes. Also bring binoculars and a camera, as well as plastic bags to protect your belongings from the rain and humidity. Everything is usually included in the package price, though soft drinks, beer, wine, and cocktails carry a hefty markup.

Few things are more enjoyable at a jungle lodge than dinner at the end of the day. You'll eat family-style around a common table, discussing the day's sightings, comparing notes well into the evening, knowing full well there will be another 5 am knock the next day.

—By Jeffrey Van Fleet

Corto Maltes Amazonia

$$$$ | RESORT | FAMILY | A short boat ride down the Madre de Dios River from Puerto Maldonado, this lodge provides an affordable introduction to the rainforest and easy access to beautiful Lago Sandoval. **Pros:** great value; spacious, private bungalows; swimming pool. **Cons:** less of a jungle experience than the more remote lodges; may see fewer animals this close to town; rooms are basic. *Rooms from: S/1104* ✉ *Madre de Dios River, Puerto Maldonado* ✣ *10 km (6 miles) east of Puerto Maldonado* ☎ *082/573–831* 🌐 *www.cortomaltes-amazonia.com* *27 bungalows* 🍽 *All meals.*

Hacienda Concepción

$$$$ | **RESORT** | A good option for travelers who want to experience the rainforest in comfort or are short on time, this lodge is in a 2,000-acre private nature reserve with a small lake and plenty of wildlife. **Pros:** easy to reach; comfortable, screened rooms; near Lago Sandoval. **Cons:** less wildlife than more remote lodges; can hear neighbors from bungalows; first-floor lodge rooms lack privacy. *Rooms from: S/1108* ✉ *Puerto Maldonado* ✣ *20-min boat trip east of Puerto Maldonado* ☎ *800/442–5042 toll-free in U.S. and Canada, 808/101–2224 toll-free in U.K., 01/610–0400 in Peru* 🌐 *www.inkaterra.com* *6 rooms, 19 bungalows* 🍴 *All meals.*

★ **Heath River Wildlife Center**

$$$$ | **RESORT** | The spacious screened bungalows at this InkaNatura-owned lodge are among the most comfortable accommodations in Madre de Dios, and they're in a remote area where you often see such rare animals as tapirs or jaguars. **Pros:** lots of wildlife; macaw clay lick nearby; comfortable bungalows. **Cons:** long boat ride; basic rooms; limited electricity. *Rooms from: S/1986* ✉ *Puerto Maldonado* ✣ *123 km (76 miles), or 5 hrs by boat, east of Puerto Maldonado* ☎ *888/870–7378 in U.S. and Canada, 01/203–5000 in Peru* 🌐 *www.inkanatura.com* *10 bungalows* 🍴 *All meals.*

Los Amigos Biological Station

$$$$ | **RESORT** | Though farther from the Tambopata National Reserve than the other lodges, this off-the-beaten-path biological station lies within a 1,119-acre private reserve that holds most of the same wildlife, including giant river otters, 11 primate species, and more than 550 bird species. **Pros:** abundant wildlife; few tourists; profits support conservation. **Cons:** 5-hour boat ride; basic meals with no bar; lowest price as listed does not include tours. *Rooms from: S/990* ✉ *Puerto Maldonado* ✣ *5-hr boat ride west of Puerto Maldonado* ☎ *202/871–3777 in U.S.* 🌐 *birding.amazonconservation.org* *6 bungalows* 🍴 *All meals.*

★ **Posada Amazonas**

$$$$ | **RESORT** | Guest rooms are in long buildings with high, thatched roofs, and wide, screenless windows; mosquito nets protect sleepers, and kerosene lanterns provide light at night, though the bar/restaurant and superior rooms have electricity. **Pros:** abundant wildlife; great excursions; lodge benefits local community. **Cons:** noise from neighboring guest rooms; no screens to keep mosquitoes out; not as far into the jungle as some other lodges. *Rooms from: S/1317* ✉ *Puerto Maldonado* ✣ *2-hr bus and boat trip on Tambopata River south of Puerto Maldonado* ☎ *877/231–9251 in U.S., 01/719–6422* 🌐 *www.perunature.com* *30 rooms* 🍴 *All meals.*

Refugio Amazonas

$$$$ | **RESORT** | **FAMILY** | One of three lodges on the Tambopata River run by Rainforest Expeditions, the *refugio* lies within a 500-acre protected forest that is contiguous with the Tambopata National Reserve, so it has plenty of wildlife. **Pros:** surrounded by wilderness; family-friendly, with trail geared toward children; sustainable tourism including eco-friendly toiletries in all rooms. **Cons:** no window screens; noise somewhat audible from other rooms; longer boat ride than to Posada. *Rooms from: S/1863* ✉ *Puerto Maldonado* ✣ *Tambopata River, 3½ hrs by bus and boat south of Puerto Maldonado* ☎ *877/231–9251 in U.S., 01/719–6422 in Peru* 🌐 *www.perunature.com* *33 rooms* 🍴 *All meals.*

Reserva Amazónica

$$$$ | **RESORT** | With a massive thatched restaurant and airy bungalows overlooking the Madre de Dios River, Reserva Amazónica is this region's fanciest lodge. **Pros:** easy to reach; excellent food, service, and guides; comfortable, tasteful bungalows. **Cons:** bungalows close enough to hear neighbors; less wildlife

than other lodges; noise from boat motors. $ *Rooms from: S/1422* ✉ *Puerto Maldonado* ✣ *30-min boat trip east of Puerto Maldonado* ☎ *800/442–5042 in U.S. and Canada, 01/610–0400 in Peru* 🌐 *www.inkaterra.com* 🛏 *35 bungalows* 🍴 *All meals.*

Sandoval Lake Lodge
$$$$ | RESORT | Despite its relative proximity to Puerto Maldonado, this lodge sits deep in the rainforest, overlooking lovely Lago Sandoval, inside the Tambopata National Reserve, so there is plenty of wildlife. **Pros:** gorgeous location; abundant wildlife; decent rooms. **Cons:** the boat-2-mile-hike-canoe access isn't for everyone; walls between rooms do not go to ceiling; no Wi-Fi. $ *Rooms from: S/1089* ✉ *Puerto Maldonado* ✣ *14 km (9 miles) east of Puerto Maldonado* ☎ *888/870–7378 in U.S. and Canada, 01/203–5000 in Peru* 🌐 *www.inkanatura.com* 🛏 *25 rooms* 🍴 *All meals.*

★ **Tambopata Research Center**
$$$$ | RESORT | In the heart of the Tambopata National Reserve, this remote, rustic lodge is one of the best places in Peru to experience the wildlife and diversity of the Amazon rainforest. **Pros:** abundant wildlife; excellent guides; sustainable tourism. **Cons:** long boat rides; one wall of room is open to jungle; sound travels between rooms. $ *Rooms from: S/2199* ✉ *Puerto Maldonado* ✣ *Tambopata River, 7 hrs by bus and boat south of Puerto Maldonado* ☎ *877/231–9251 in U.S., 01/719–6422 in Peru* 🌐 *www.perunature.com* 🛏 *26 rooms* 🍴 *All meals.*

Wasaí Tambopata Lodge
$$$$ | RESORT | Nestled between the Tambopata River and a 7,400-acre private nature reserve traversed by miles of trails, this eco-friendly lodge offers access to lots of wildlife, especially on early-morning trips to the nearby Collpa Chuncho clay lick to see hundreds of macaws and parrots. **Pros:** gorgeous forest; great excursions; sustainable tourism. **Cons:** basic rooms; long trip to get there; no hot water. $ *Rooms from: S/1020* ✉ *Puerto Maldonado* ✣ *Tambopata River, 100 km (62 miles) southwest of Puerto Maldonado* ☎ *01/436–8792* 🌐 *wasai.com* 🛏 *19 bungalows* 🍴 *All meals.*

Manu Biosphere Reserve

90 km (55 miles) north of Cusco.

Manu is a remote and wild area with spectacular scenery that ranges from lush cloud forest to pristine rainforest dominated by massive tropical trees. It is one of the best places in the Amazon Basin to see wildlife, home to a dozen species of monkeys and more than 1,000 bird species. But visiting this area is expensive. It also entails many hours by road plus many more in a small wooden boat on the Madre de Dios River, and nearly all the accommodations are rustic. A trip to Manu is truly an adventure, and it can involve a little discomfort, but the payoff is the opportunity to explore enchanting, pristine areas that few people have seen and that are home to a mind-boggling diversity of plants and animals.

GETTING HERE AND AROUND

A Manu excursion is no quick trip. Overland travel from Cusco, which includes at least one overnight in the cloud forest. requires a five-day minimum stay. It is also possible to fly to Puerto Maldonado and travel by land and up the Madre de Dios River to the Manu Wildlife Center, which can be done on a four-day tour. The most spectacular trip is to enter by land and river from Cusco—passing amazing Andean cloud-forest and rainforest scenery along the way—and depart by river and land, either to Puerto Maldonado, where you catch a flight to Lima, or by driving five hours to Cusco.

TOURS

Manu Expeditions

ECOTOURISM | These Cusco-based specialists in bird-watching and nature tours offer decades of experience on excursions deep into the Manu Biosphere Reserve. Trips last four to seven days and include overnights at several remote nature lodges. ☎ *084/224–135* ⊕ *www.manuexpeditions.com* *From $1450.*

Pantiacolla

ECOTOURISM | Pantiacolla organizes ecotours to Manu with overnights at one or more of the company's three lodges: the Posada San Pedro, Pantiacolla Lodge, and Sachavaca Campsite. Tours range from two nights in the cloud forest to a nine-day expedition into Manu's reserved zone. Pantiacolla's lodges are more rustic than the competition's, but the guides are excellent, and the tours are less expensive. ☎ *084/238–323* ⊕ *pantiacolla.com* *From $470.*

Sights

★ Manu Biosphere Reserve

NATURE PRESERVE | Scientists consider the Manu Biosphere Reserve to be one of the most biodiverse places on earth, and much of its vast wilderness has barely been studied, since it is still home to uncontacted indigenous groups. Straddling the boundary of the Madre de Dios and Cusco provinces, the reserve is Peru's second-largest protected area, encompassing more than 4½ million acres of pristine tropical forests. Its extraordinary biological diversity is in part due to its precipitous terrain, which ranges in altitude from 3,450 meters (12,000 feet) down to 300 meters (less than 1,000 feet). This geographical diversity results in varied ecosystems—from high-altitude puna grasslands to luxuriant cloud forest and seemingly endless rainforest—which, in turn, shelter a stunning range of flora and fauna. To top it off, a near-total absence of humans means that the animals here are less skittish and more easily observed.

Whereas Manu's highland cloud forest is home to dozens of hummingbird species, the spectacular cock-of-the-rock, and the Andean bear (aka spectacled bear), the reserve's lower parts hold most of its more than 200 mammal species, including 13 species of monkeys, which scrutinize visitors with the same curiosity they elicit. White caimans sun themselves on sandy riverbanks, while the larger black caimans lurk in the oxbow lakes. With luck, you may see a tapir, giant river otter, or one of the region's elusive jaguars. You are bound to see a sampling of the avian life that has made Manu world-famous. The area counts more than 1,000 bird species, one-ninth of those known to science. They include several species of macaws, toucans, jacamars, cocoi herons, harpy eagles, razor-billed currasows, blue-headed parrots, and horned screamers. ■ **TIP→ Manu is also home to hundreds of colorful butterfly species and an array of ants, beetles, and spiders, as well as millions of mosquitoes, so be sure to take an ample supply of insect repellent.**

A UNESCO World Heritage Site, the Biosphere Reserve is divided into three distinct zones. The smallest, and most accessible, is what's known as the "cultural zone," home to several indigenous groups and the majority of the jungle lodges. Access is permitted to all—even independent travelers, in theory—though it would be extremely difficult to visit it on your own. About three times the size of the cultural zone, Manu's "reserved zone" contains various nature lodges, which can only be visited on a guided tour with one of a dozen agencies authorized to take people into the area. The western 80% of Manu is designated a national park and is closed to all but authorized researchers and the indigenous peoples who reside there.

Hotels

Accommodations in Manu are scattered along the area's various life zones: from the cloud forest of the eastern Andes—reached by land from Cusco—to the montane and lowland rainforests that line the Madre de Dios and Manu Rivers, which are reached by a combination of bus and boat travel. Lodges here tend to be more rustic and more expensive than lodges near Puerto Maldonado or Iquitos. This is because of the logistical challenges of transporting guests to, and maintaining facilities in, this remote and rainy region. Keep in mind that lodge rates include all meals; a bilingual, naturalist guide; and days of transportation in buses and wooden boats with outboard motors, which consume barrels of gasoline.

Campsite Sachavaca

$$$$ | **RESORT** | This bare-bones camp operated by the tour company Pantiacolla is near Cocha Salvador, an oxbow lake in Manu's Reserved Zone, which is home to an amazing array of wildlife. **Pros:** deep in the rainforest; abundant wildlife; eco-friendly. **Cons:** very rustic; shared bathrooms; candles for lighting. *Rooms from: S/1550 ✉ Cocha Salvador, Manu Biosphere Reserve ✣ 70 km (44 miles) northwest of Boca Manu ☎ 084/238–323 🌐 www.pantiacolla.com 8 rooms 🍽 All meals.*

Cock of the Rock Lodge

$$$$ | **RESORT** | At the edge of the cloud forest in the Manu Cultural Zone, affording an amazing view of the lush Kosñipata River valley, InkaNatura's property takes its name from Peru's red-and-black national bird, which can usually be seen nearby, along with dozens of other avian species, among them 35 types of hummingbirds. **Pros:** great bird-watching; gorgeous setting; pleasant climate. **Cons:** expensive; a seven-hour drive from Cusco; no electricity in rooms. *Rooms from: S/2820 ✉ Cusco ✣ 163 km (101 miles) northeast of Cusco ☎ 888/870–7378 in U.S., 800/234–8659 in U.K., 01/203–5000 in Peru 🌐 www.inkanatura.com 12 bungalows 🍽 All meals.*

Manu Park Wildlife Center

$$$$ | **RESORT** | Located deep in the wilderness of the Manu Biosphere Reserve, this InkaNatura property has elevated bungalows, each with screened walls, two single beds, mosquito nets, and a private bathroom with cold-water shower. **Pros:** amazing wildlife; a true adventure; good food. **Cons:** remote; rustic; expensive. *Rooms from: S/3452 ✉ Manu Reserved Zone, Puerto Maldonado ✣ 145 km (90 miles) from northwest of Manu Wildlife Center; 400 km (249 miles) northwest of Puerto Maldonado ☎ 888/870–7378 in U.S., 01/203–5000 in Peru 🌐 www.inkanatura.com 7 rooms 🍽 All meals.*

★ Manu Wildlife Center

$$$$ | **RESORT** | Though outside the Manu Biosphere Reserve, the Manu Wildlife Center is still a great place to see animals, since it is close to macaw and tapir collpas and has 48 km (30 miles) of rainforest trails. **Pros:** plenty of wildlife; knowledgeable guides; decent rooms. **Cons:** remote; expensive; no electricity in cabins. *Rooms from: S/3452 ✉ Puerto Maldonado ✣ 255 km (158 miles), or 7 hrs, west of Puerto Maldonado ☎ 888/870–7378 in U.S., 01/203–5000 in Peru 🌐 www.inkanatura.com 22 bungalows 🍽 All meals.*

Pantiacolla Lodge

$$$$ | **RESORT** | Named for the mountain range that towers above, the Pantiacolla Lodge sits in a 2,223-acre, private, Manu Cultural Zone nature reserve that has 600 bird species and an array of mammals. **Pros:** great bird-watching; lots of mammals; beautiful spot. **Cons:** quite rustic; little privacy in bungalows (2 of 11 rooms share bath); candles for lighting. *Rooms from: S/1225 ✉ Cusco ✣ 290 km (180 miles) northeast of Cusco ☎ 084/238–323 🌐 www.pantiacolla.com 11 rooms 🍽 All meals.*

Posada San Pedro Lodge
$$$$ | **RESORT** | Nestled in the cloud forest of the Manu Biosphere Reserve Cultural Zone, midway between Cusco and the Pantiacolla Lodge, this small lodge offers earthy accommodations amid extraordinary scenery and bird life. **Pros:** great bird-watching; gorgeous scenery; tours include visit to nearby lake. **Cons:** rustic; little privacy in rooms; shared bathhouse. *Rooms from: S/1225* ✉ *Cusco* ✣ *164 km (102 miles) northeast of Cusco* ☎ *084/238–323* 🌐 *www.pantiacolla.com* *8 rooms* 🍴 *All meals.*

Romero Rainforest Lodge
$$$$ | **RESORT** | Offering comfortable accommodations inside the Manu Reserved Zone, several hours by boat up the Manu River, the Romero Rainforest Lodge provides access to impressive natural attractions (including two oxbow lakes). **Pros:** decent rooms for a jungle lodge; stellar wildlife; run by a conservation organization. **Cons:** remote; closed in February; no room amenities. *Rooms from: S/1630* ✉ *Manu Biosphere Reserve, Puerto Maldonado* ✣ *20 km (12 miles) northwest of Boca Manu, 350 km (217 miles) northwest of Puerto Maldonado* ☎ *207/193–8759* 🌐 *crees-manu.org* *8 bungalows* 🍴 *All meals.*

Wayqecha Cloud Forest Birding Lodge
$$$$ | **RESORT** | Perched above the cloud forest tree line with a sweeping view of Manu's mountainous area, this eco-lodge and biological station provides access to a 1,450-acre reserve adjacent to Manu that protects rare bird and orchid species. **Pros:** gorgeous area; home to rare bird species; profits support conservation. **Cons:** cold at night; limited Internet; lights out at 9pm. *Rooms from: S/900* ✉ *Carretera a Manu s/n* ✣ *3½ hr drive from Cusco via Paucartambo* ☎ *202/871–3777 in U.S.* 🌐 *birding.amazonconservation.org* *6 rooms* 🍴 *All meals.*

Iquitos

1,150 km (713 miles) northeast of Lima.

A sultry port town on the Río Amazonas, Iquitos is quite probably the world's largest city that cannot be reached by road. It has nearly 500,000 inhabitants and is the capital of the vast Loreto department. It is a colorful, dilapidated town where motorcycles and three-wheeled mototaxis buzz down narrow streets shaded by massive tropical trees, tiny houses built atop wooden rafts float in the nearby river, and indigenous women hawk their handicrafts in the plazas.Many of the people who live in Iquitos are members of Amazonian indigenous tribes, and although most have adopted Western dress, you'll find bushmeat and jungle herbs for sale at the local market, and you can learn about the Amazon's native cultures at the Museo de Culturas Indígenas. You can also watch the locals pass in dugout canoes as you sample an Amazon fish fillet at the floating restaurant of Al Frio y al Fuego. Or savor the tropical surroundings while sipping a cool drink on the malecón and contemplating the rainforest foliage that lines the estuary. Speaking of drinks, bars and clubs tend to cater to a younger and less-discerning crowd. You're best off finding a riverside restaurant for your evening libation.

The area around Iquitos was first inhabited by small, independent Amazonian tribes. In the 1500s, Jesuit missionaries began venturing into the area, trying to Christianize the local population, but the city wasn't officially founded until 1757.

Iquitos saw unprecedented growth and opulence during the rubber boom but became an Amazonian backwater overnight when the boom went bust. The economy slouched along, barely sustaining itself with logging and exotic-animal exports. Then, in the early 1970s, petroleum was discovered. The black gold, along with ecotourism and logging, have since become the backbone of the region's economy, though drug running also provides significant income.

The city's historic center stretches along a lagoon formed by the Río Itaya, near the confluence of the Río Nanay and the Río Amazonas. Most of its historic buildings, hotels, restaurants, and banks are within blocks of the Plaza de Armas, the main square, and the nearby Malecón Maldonado riverwalk. On the plaza, keep an eye out for the Casa de Fierro, a building forged in Europe, disputedly by Gustave Eiffel.

GETTING HERE AND AROUND

LATAM has daily direct flights to Iquitos, while those of StarPeru stop at Pucallpa or Tarapoto, adding an hour to the trip, so LATAM is the way to go. The best way to travel around the Iquitos area is by boat: hundreds of vessels come and go each day, from tiny dugout canoes bound for jungle enclaves to seagoing ships that travel all the way through Brazil to the Atlantic Ocean.

Various companies run cruises out of the town of Nauta, a 90-minute drive south of Iquitos, providing comfortable—albeit expensive—access to the province's protected areas and indigenous villages. Nature lodges transport guests in swift launches with outboard engines and canvas tops to protect you from the sun and rain.

Some hotels pick guests up at the airport, but there are always taxis available if yours doesn't. The most common mode of transportation around town is the mototaxi, a three-wheeled motorcycle with a canvas top. Service costs S/3 in town, whereas a trip to the outskirts costs around S/10 to S/15. It should cost S/6 to reach Port Bellavista Nanay, where you can hire a boat to the butterfly farm. Most hotels offer free taxi service from the airport but, if yours does not, have them send a trusted driver to get you. If you need one from the hotel, ask hotel staffers to call one for you. This will help you avoid having to negotiate fares.

TAXI

Taxi Flores. ☎ *065/232–014.*

BORDER CROSSINGS

Various companies offer speedboat service to the Brazilian and Colombian borders. It's a 9- to 10-hour boat ride to the border town of Santa Rosa, across the river from Leticia (Colombia) and Tabatinga (Brazil). The one-way trip costs only US$80. Each company runs twice a week, so boats depart every day; all the ticket offices are on the 300 block of Calle Raymondi, three blocks north of the Plaza de Armas. Just go there and buy a ticket from the company that departs on the day you want to travel.

American citizens don't need a visa to enter Colombia, but they do need one for Brazil, which is best organized from a consulate at home.

Brazilian Consulate
INFO CENTER | ✉ *Sgto. Lores 363* ☎ *065/235–151.*

TOURS

Dawn on the Amazon. ✉ *Malecón Maldonado 185* ☎ *065/223–730* 🌐 *www.dawnontheamazon.com.*

VISITOR INFORMATION

Tourist Information Office. ✉ *Napo 161* ☎ *065/236–144.*

Sights

Centro de Rescate Amazónico
ZOO | **FAMILY** | At this animal-rescue center, a short trip south of town, you can get a close look at one of the region's rarest, and most threatened, species: the manatee. Despite being protected by Peruvian law, manatees continue to be hunted for their meat. The center, a collaboration of the Dallas World Aquarium and Zoo and two Peruvian institutions, raises orphaned manatees and nurses injured ones back to health for eventual release in the wild. It also serves as an environmental education center to raise awareness of the gentle creature's plight. ✉ *Km 4.6,*

Sights

1 Centro de Rescate Amazónico.............. A7
2 Malecón Tarapacá D4
3 Museo de Barcos Históricos................ D2
4 Museo de Culturas Indígenas................ D4
5 Pilpintuwasi Butterfly Farm........... D1
6 Port Bellavista Nanay.................... D1

Restaurants

1 Al Frío y al Fuego........ D1
2 Dawn on the Amazon Café............ D3
3 Espresso Café............ C4
4 Fitzcarraldo.............. D3
5 Karma Café.............. D3
6 Le Bateau Ivre D4

Hotels

1 Casa Morey D2
2 Doubletree by Hilton Hotel Iquitos..... D3
3 Época C5
4 Victoria Regia Hotel....................... C5

Carretera Iquitos-Nauta ☎ *991/476–519* 🌐 *centroderescateamazonico.com* 🎫 *S/20* ⏲ *Closed after 3 pm daily.*

Malecón Tarapacá (*Malecón Maldonado*)
PROMENADE | This pleasant waterfront walk between Brasil and Pevas is a good place for an evening stroll. During high-water season, the Itaya River reaches the cement, but during the dry months (May–November), it recedes into the distance. You'll find some lovely rubber-boom-era architecture here, such as the Hotel Palacio, now a police station. There are also a few bars and restaurants on the malecón's northern end, near the Plaza de Armas. Its southern end gets less traffic, and muggings have been reported there at night, so stick to the three northernmost blocks after 6 pm. ✉ *Iquitos.*

Museo de Barcos Históricos
MUSEUM | FAMILY | The Ayapua, a 33-meter (108-foot) boat built in Hamburg, Germany, in 1906, navigated the Brazilian Amazon for much of the rubber boom and was brought to Iquitos by the nonprofit Fundamazonia in 2005 to be renovated and turned into a museum. It is now moored next to Plaza Ramón Castilla, on the Itaya River, and contains displays about the rubber boom and historic photos of the region from that era. The bridge has been refurbished, and there is a small bar where you can have a beer or soft drink. ✉ *Plaza Ramón Castilla* 🎫 *S/15.*

★ Museo de Culturas Indígenas
MUSEUM | This small museum housed in a pale-blue building on the Malecón Tarapacá has an impressive collection of colorful headdresses made from the feathers of jungle birds and an array of other traditional handiwork by the main Amazonian tribes. If you're interested in indigenous cultures, you won't want to miss it. The displays include a wealth of information about the lives of the Amazon Basin's native peoples and an array of artifacts collected in Peru, Brazil, Colombia, and the Guianas over the course of decades. Items range from the quotidian (clothing, paddles, woven bags) to the ceremonial (musical instruments, headdresses, necklaces with the teeth of jungle animals). Among the more striking items are the jewelry, embroidered cloths and *cushmas* (tunics), painted ceramic wares, blow guns, spears, bows and arrows, and ceremonial headdresses. ✉ *Malecón Tarapacá 332* ☎ *065/235–809* 🎫 *S/15.*

Pilpintuwasi Butterfly Farm
NATURE PRESERVE | FAMILY | A 20-minute boat ride from the port of Bellavista Nanay and a short (15-minute) walk or a tuk-tuk ride in dry season will bring you to Pilpintuwasi Butterfly Farm, which raises some 42 butterfly species and serves as home for wild animals that have been confiscated from hunters and wildlife traffickers. It has macaws, a jaguar, a manatee, monkeys (some free roaming), and other animals. During wet season, the boat may take you the whole way. A private boat to and from Padre Cocha should cost 60 soles, depending on the type of motor. ⚠ **Some boat operators may try to take you to a smaller butterfly farm, so insist on Pilpintuwasi; ask for Gudrun.** ✉ *Padre Cocha, Nanay River* ✣ *20-min boat trip from Bellavista Nanay* ☎ *935/443–248* 🌐 *www.amazonanimalorphanage.org* 🎫 *S/30 without transportation* ⏲ *Closed Mon.*

Port Bellavista Nanay
MARKET | About 3 km (1½ miles) north of downtown Iquitos, at the end of Avenida La Marina, is this muddy beehive of activity with a large open-air market where vendors sell everything from jungle fruits to grilled *suri* (palm grubs). Boats of all shapes and sizes populate the riverbank, and seedy bars are perched over the water on wooden posts. You can hire a boat to take you to the Pilpintuwasi Butterfly Farm. ✉ *Iquitos.*

Restaurants

★ Al Frío y al Fuego

$$$ | **PERUVIAN** | Step through the unassuming doorway on Avenida La Marina, descend the long stairway to the dock, and a boat will ferry you to this floating, thatch-roofed restaurant on the Itaya River. The setting is gorgeous, and they prepare excellent versions of traditional dishes such as *patarashca* (a fish fillet topped with herbs and garlic and roasted in a *bijao* leaf) and doncella (Amazon catfish) fillet à la *loretana* (in a mild chili sauce), as well as ample other intriguing favorites. **Known for:** views of Itaya River traffic; excellent Amazonian dishes; swimming pool. *Average main: S/62 Av. La Marina 134-B 965/607–474 alfrioyalfuego.com No dinner Sun.*

Dawn on the Amazon Café

$ | **AMERICAN** | **FAMILY** | A great place for breakfast, lunch, or dinner, the menu here is so vast that even the pickiest eaters will find something to tempt their tummies. Selections include lighter fare such as soups and salads, as well as heartier mains that include Peruvian favorites, American-style comfort food, international dishes, and plenty of vegetarian/vegan options. **Known for:** good portions; varied menu; friendly, mostly English-speaking service. *Average main: S/26 Malecón Maldonado 185 065/234–921 www.dawnontheamazoncafe.com.*

Espresso Café

$ | **PERUVIAN** | Housed in one of the grand rubber-era mansions, this café-bar-restaurant concept brings a much-lacking touch of elegance to the city, complete with an art gallery. Dishes include regional and Peruvian standards, as well as some original creations that fuse local ingredients from the jungle into tasty new experiences for your palate. **Known for:** creative fusion dishes; attractive ambience; social commitment. *Average main: S/28 Jr. Prospero 418 065/241–576, 992/832–381 cell/WhatsApp espresso-cafe.com.pe Closed Mon.*

Fitzcarraldo

$$ | **PERUVIAN** | Conveniently located on the Malecón Maldonado, this restaurant specializes in traditional regional specialties such as *cecina con tacacho* (a smoked pork steak with fried plantain balls) and *pescado a la loretana* (fish fillet in a mild chili sauce). The restaurant occupies a historic building and has an air-conditioned room, an airy front dining room with ceiling fans, and sidewalk tables on the malecón. **Known for:** traditional Amazonian dishes; sidewalk tables with river views; varied menu. *Average main: S/39 Malecón Maldonado at Napo 065/507–545 www.restaurante-fitzcarraldo.com.*

Karma Café

$$ | **ECLECTIC** | A tasty mix of international dishes—together with Wi-Fi, comfy couches and armchairs, local paintings on the walls, and a convenient location between the Plaza de Armas and the malecón—make this a popular traveler hangout. The eclectic selection includes plenty of vegetarian options and an array of salads and sandwiches, as well as fruit smoothies and vegetable extracts; just be prepared for slow service. **Known for:** eclectic menu; fruit smoothies; chill-out vibe. *Average main: S/37 Calle Napo 138 065/222–663 No credit cards Closed Mon.*

Le Bateau Ivre

$$ | **BISTRO** | This tastefully restored rubber-boom-era mansion is well worth a visit—if not for a meal, at least for a drink or much-needed espresso—with sidewalk tables on the malecón and plenty more inside. The French-inspired menu features both basic bistro fare (think escargots, fish sautéed in butter, or chicken cordon bleu) and international favorites like hamburgers and pastas, as well as lighter salads and sandwiches. **Known for:** traditional French cuisine; sidewalk-café dining; imported beers and wine. *Average main: S/38 Malecón Tarapacá 268 065/242–918.*

Hotels

★ Casa Morey

$$ | **B&B/INN** | Built by rubber baron Luis Morey in 1913, this restored mansion offers the most historic setting in Iquitos with high ceilings, colorful tile floors, and antique prints and photos that evoke the turn of the century when Iquitos was one of the world's main rubber suppliers. **Pros:** lovely building; spacious rooms; some river views. **Cons:** street noise in plaza-fronting rooms; furniture a bit sparse for the size of the rooms; reception not fluent in English. *Rooms from: S/261 ✉ Calle Loreto 200, on Plaza Ramón Castilla ☎ 065/231–913 🌐 www.casamorey.com 14 suites Free breakfast.*

Doubletree by Hilton Hotel Iquitos

$$ | **HOTEL** | This well-equipped, contemporary hotel is in the heart of Iquitos, on the Plaza de Armas, and features carpeted guest rooms with giant windows, flat-screen TVs, and other modern conveniences. **Pros:** great location; comfortable rooms; modern amenities. **Cons:** less amenities than in a typical Hilton; street noise in front-facing rooms; service can be hit or miss. *Rooms from: S/375 ✉ Napo 258 ☎ 855/605–0318 toll-free from North America 🌐 www.hilton.com 65 rooms Free breakfast.*

Época

$ | **B&B/INN** | Occupying a renovated, turn-of-the-century home at the southern end of the malecón, Época offers comfortable, friendly lodging with a bit of historic atmosphere. **Pros:** historic atmosphere; peaceful; friendly. **Cons:** guest rooms less charming than common rooms; some rooms have no external windows; not luxury accommodations. *Rooms from: S/195 ✉ Ramirez Hurtado 616 ☎ 065/224–172 🌐 www.epoca.com.pe 11 rooms Free breakfast.*

Victoria Regia Hotel

$$ | **HOTEL** | Named for giant lily pads found in the region's lakes, this simple, modern hotel is popular with business travelers and a short walk from the main square. **Pros:** nice rooms; pool; relatively quiet. **Cons:** relatively small rooms; rooms in the back of the hotel are a bit dark; basic amenities. *Rooms from: S/255 ✉ Ricardo Palma 252 ☎ 065/231–983 🌐 www.terraverde.pe 61 rooms Free breakfast.*

Shopping

Street vendors display their wares on the Malecón Maldonado at night and around the corner, on the first block of Nauta, by day. Look for pottery; hand-painted cloth from Pucallpa; and jungle items such as preserved piranhas, seed necklaces, fish and animal teeth, blowguns, spears, and balsa-wood parrots.

Casa del Artesano Amazónico

CRAFTS | Handicrafts from several of the province's indigenous cultures can be found in the souvenir stands at the Casa del Artesano Amazónico. *✉ Malecón Maldonado 167.*

Centro Artesanal Turístico Anaconda

GIFTS/SOUVENIRS | This collection of handicraft stalls on a wooden platform perched over a seasonal swamp is worth wandering through even if you don't want to buy anything. It's down the stairs from the Malecón Maldonado, at the end of Jirón Napo. *✉ Malecón Maldonado s/n, down stairway.*

The Peruvian Amazon

The Amazon Basin is the world's most diverse ecosystem. The numbers of cataloged plant and animal species are astronomical, and scientists regularly discover new ones. There are more than 25,000 classified species of plants in the Peruvian Amazon (and 80,000 in

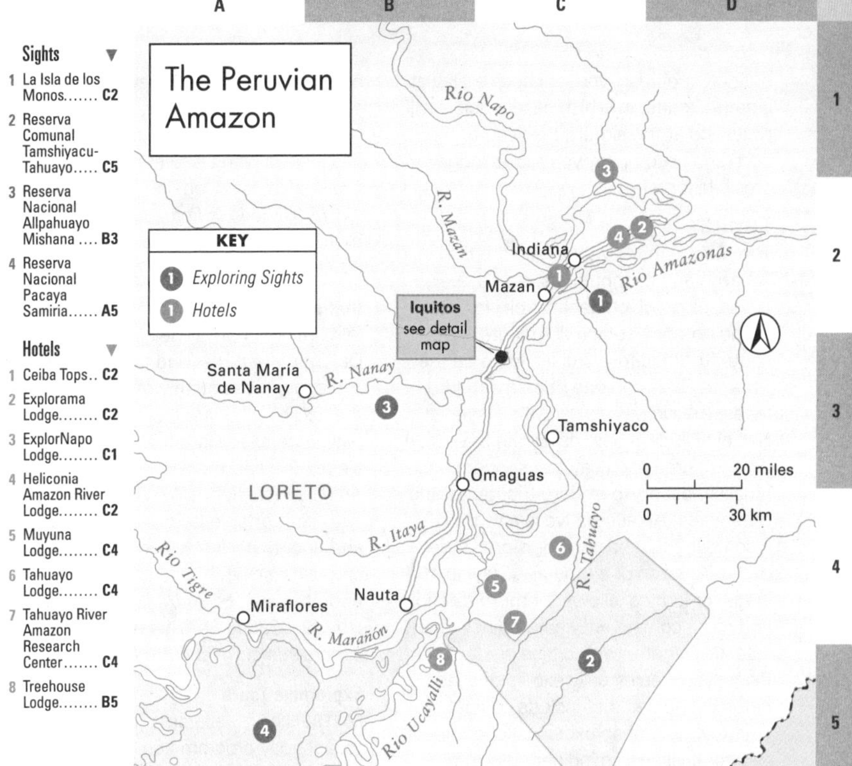

the entire Amazon Basin), including the 2-meter-wide (6-foot-wide) Victoria Regia water lilies. Scientists have cataloged more than 4,000 species of butterfly and more than 2,000 of fish—a more diverse aquatic life than that of the Atlantic Ocean. Scientists estimate that the world's tropical forests, while comprising only 6% of the Earth's landmass, may hold up to 75% of the planet's plant and animal species. This land is also the largest natural pharmacy in the world: one-fourth of all modern medicines have botanical origins in tropical forests.

You'll see monkeys, and perhaps a sloth, but most mammals are nocturnal and difficult to spot. ■ TIP→ **You're likely to see an array of birds, butterflies, and monkeys, as well as bufeos (freshwater dolphins) along the Amazon and its tributaries.**

It's interesting and worthwhile to visit a small indigenous village, and take advantage of the opportunity to buy some handicrafts.

The best way to visit the area is on a prearranged tour with one of the many jungle lodges or cruise boats. All have highly trained naturalist guides. Among the activities offered are nature walks, birding tours, nighttime canoe outings, fishing trips, and stops at indigenous villages.

GETTING HERE

With the exception of Reserva Nacional Allpahuayo Mishana, which is a 40-minute drive from town, you'll reach the Amazon's sites by water. You basically have two options: travel to a nature lodge in one of that company's boats, or take a cruise. The cruises are more expensive, but quite comfortable, and they allow you to explore different areas on daily excursions in small boats. Otherwise, you can book a stay at a nature lodge, in which case a guide will meet you at the airport, take you to the port, and accompany you to the lodge in a small, fast boat.

TOURS

The most popular way to explore the Amazon and its tributaries is on a river cruise, all of which depart from Iquitos or the port of Nauta, a 90-minute drive south from Iquitos. Cruises head up the Amazon River and one of its main tributaries, the Ucayali, toward the Reserva Nacional Pacaya Samiria. Boats travel to a different area each day: passengers board smaller vessels to explore tributaries and other sites. An alternative is a tour with a company that has one or more lodges on the Amazon or a tributary. Staying at a lodge, or lodges, allows for more freedom and more contact with nature (including insects). Whether you cruise or stay at a lodge, you'll enjoy daily excursions led by naturalist guides that include navigating a narrow river or an oxbow lake, a forest hike, or a visit to an indigenous village.

★ Amazonia Expeditions

ECOTOURISM | Amazonia Expeditions runs eight-day trips into the megadiverse Reserva Comunal Tamshiyacu-Tahuayo, with stays at the company's two rustic lodges on the Tahuayo River. The company's naturalist guides are first rate, and part of the profits support conservation, scientific research, and improvement of life in the reserve's remote communities. *800/262–9669 in U.S. perujungle.com From USD$895 per person.*

★ Aqua Expeditions

BOAT TOURS | Aqua Expeditions runs high-end nature cruises along the upper Amazon between Nauta and the Pacaya Samiria Reserve on a sleek, eco-friendly riverboat. Ships have 16 luxurious suites with a number of amenities, including floor-to-ceiling windows for a panoramic view, and an incredible gourmet dining experience filled with indigenous ingredients and designed by one of Peru's top chefs. Passengers board small boats each day for expert-guided trips up Amazon tributaries and other excursions to find sloths, giant water lilies, and pink dolphins, and to fish for piranha. Cruises last for three, four, or seven nights. *01/434–5544 in Peru, 866/603–3687 U.S. and Canada www.aquaexpeditions.com From USD$2820.*

Delfin

BOAT TOURS | Part of Relais & Châteaux, Delfin offers three- and four-night Amazon eco-cruises on any of three boats: the luxurious *Delfin I,* which takes eight passengers; the larger *Delfin II,* which sleeps 28; and the more economical *Delfin III,* which sleeps 43. All feature suites with comfortable beds, a seating area, and floor-to-ceiling windows. A private cruise for seven nights is also available upon request. *844/433–5346 in U.S., 01/719–0999 in Peru www.delfinamazoncruises.com From USD$3000.*

Explorama Tours

ECOTOURISM | Explorama Tours runs three- to eight-day programs down the Amazon River that combine stays at their rustic Explorama and ExplorNapo nature lodges as well as at the more comfortable Ceiba Tops Lodge, with varied outdoor adventures every day. *065/252–530, 800/707–5275 in U.S. and Canada www.explorama.com From USD$415.*

Sights

La Isla de los Monos

NATURE PRESERVE | **FAMILY** | A popular spot for explorers of all ages, Isla de los Monos (Monkey Island) is home to more than 40 monkeys of eight species. The 250-hectare (618-acre) island is a private reserve, where monkeys that were once held in captivity or were confiscated from animal traffickers now live in a natural environment. In addition to the monkeys, there are sloths, parrots, macaws, and a small botanical garden. Since most of the animals are former pets, you can get very close to them; maybe even closer than you might want. The easiest way to visit the island is on a tour. ✉ *Iquitos* ✣ *30 km (18 miles) northeast of Iquitos* ☎ *065/235–887, 965/841–808* 🌐 *laisladelosmonos.org* 🎫 *S/30.*

Reserva Comunal Tamshiyacu-Tahuayo

NATURE PRESERVE | Covering approximately 4,144 square km (1,600 square miles), the Tamshiyacu-Tahuayo Communal Reserve is larger than the state of Rhode Island. It comprises an array of ecosystems that includes seasonally flooded forests, terra firma forests, aguaje palm swamps, and oxbow lakes. It holds a wealth of biological diversity, including almost 600 bird species: cocoi herons, wire-tailed manakins, and blue-and-gold macaws among them. It is also home to 15 primate species, including the rare saki and uakari monkeys. The government manages the reserve in coordination with local people. (They still hunt and fish here but have reduced their impact on its wildlife.) Local eco-lodges provide employment and support education and healthcare in those communities, which has strengthened their interest in protecting the environment. ✉ *Iquitos* ✣ *100 km (60 miles) south of Iquitos* ☎ *No phone.*

Reserva Nacional Allpahuayo Mishana

NATURE PRESERVE | Around Iquitos are large tracts of protected rainforest, of which Allpahuayo Mishana is the easiest to get to, since it is just 27 km (16 miles) southwest of Iquitos via the road to Nauta, making it possible to visit on a day-trip. It isn't a great place to see large animals, but it is a good destination for bird-watchers. Scientists have identified 475 bird species in the reserve, including such avian rarities as the pompadour cotinga and Zimmer's antbird. It is also home to several monkey species. ✉ *Km 27, Carretera Iquitos-Nauta, Iquitos.*

Reserva Nacional Pacaya Samiria

NATURE PRESERVE | This hard-to-reach park comprises a vast expanse of wilderness between the Marañón and Ucayali Rivers, which flow together to form the Amazon. The reserve is Peru's largest, encompassing more than 20,000 square km (7,722 square miles)—which makes it about the size of El Salvador. The landscape is diverse, comprising a patchwork of seasonally flooded forests, oxbow lakes, black-water rivers, aguaje palm swamps, and vast expanses of lowland rainforest. The diversity extends to the animal inhabitants, which include pink river dolphins, black caimans, more than a dozen kinds of monkeys, and more than 500 bird species. As with many South American reserves, there are people living in Pacaya Samiria, around 40,000 according to recent estimates. The park can be reached only by boat, and some cruises visit its northern sector, which is relatively close to the town of Nauta. ✉ *Confluence of Marañón and Ucayali Rivers* 🎫 *S/30 per day, usually included with tour.*

 Hotels

Rates for the rainforest lodges near Iquitos are high, but they all include transportation, meals, guides, and two or more excursions per day. Transportation to the lodges is usually in fast boats and can take 90 minutes to three hours.

★ Ceiba Tops

$$$$ | **RESORT** | One of the region's few eco-lodges features comfortable, air-conditioned rooms—with tile floors and private, hot-water baths—as well as amenities that include a pool, bar, laundry services, and a hammock house. **Pros:** great river view; interconnecting rooms for families; Wi-Fi in main lodge. **Cons:** only 40 km (25 miles) from Iquitos; more expensive than rustic lodges; dinner is late for small children. $ *Rooms from: S/1200* ✉ *Iquitos* ✣ *Amazon River, 40 km (25 miles) east of Iquitos* ☎ *800/707–5275 in U.S., 065/252–533* 🌐 *www.explorama.com* 🛏 *78 rooms* 🍽 *All meals.*

Explorama Lodge
$$$$ | **RESORT** | At Explorama's original lodge, rooms are screened in and have private baths with running cold water and electric fans. **Pros:** deep in the jungle; good guides; Wi-Fi in main lodge. **Cons:** no hot water; not much privacy in rooms; less wildlife than at some lodges. *Rooms from: S/1050 ✉ Iquitos ✣ 80 km (50 miles) east of Iquitos ☎ 065/252–530, 800/707–5275 in U.S. 🌐 www.explorama.com 40 rooms All meals.*

ExplorNapo Lodge
$$$$ | **RESORT** | Located 100 miles from Iquitos on the Napo River, this Explorama lodge is wonderfully remote and near the world's second-longest canopy walkway, which consists of bridges that connect 14 platformed trees. **Pros:** surrounded by primary forest reserve; canopy walkway; Wi-Fi in the main lodge. **Cons:** very rustic; walls between rooms do not go up to the ceiling; no outlets or bathrooms in guest quarters. *Rooms from: S/1350 ✉ Iquitos ✣ On Napo River, 160 km (100 miles) east of Iquitos ☎ 65/252–530, 800/707–5275 in U.S. 🌐 www.explorama.com 30 rooms All meals.*

Heliconia Amazon River Lodge
$$$$ | **RESORT** | Perched along the Amazon, a 90-minute boat ride from Iquitos, the Heliconia has a blue-tile swimming pool as well as comfortable rooms with screened windows and private (hot-water) bathrooms. **Pros:** comfortable rooms; Amazon River views; good value. **Cons:** less wildlife than at some lodges; no Internet; no electicity (so no fans) during the day. *Rooms from: S/1278 ✉ Yanamono ✣ 104 km (62 miles) east of Iquitos ☎ 01/442–4515 🌐 www.amazonriverexpeditions.com 21 rooms All meals.*

★ **Muyuna Lodge**
$$$$ | **RESORT** | Poised at the edge of a seasonally flooded forest on the tranquil Yanayacu River, this solar-powered eco-lodge is surrounded by exuberant tropical forest teeming with wildlife. **Pros:** abundant wildlife; knowledgeable guides; good value. **Cons:** three-hour boat ride from Iquitos; solar-powered showers can be cold if no sun; accommodations are not luxurious. *Rooms from: S/1360 ✉ San Juan de Yanayacu, Iquitos ✣ 140 km (87 miles) southwest of Iquitos ☎ 995/918–964 🌐 www.muyuna.com 17 cabins All meals.*

Tahuayo Lodge
$$$$ | **RESORT** | This rustic eco-lodge owned by Amazonia Expeditions is an excellent base for experiencing the rainforest. **Pros:** plentiful wildlife; personalized tours; solar-powered lighting. **Cons:** sound travels between cabins; cold showers and not all rooms have private baths; very basic amenities. *Rooms from: S/1790 ✉ Iquitos ✣ Río Tahuayo, 130 km (80 miles) south of Iquitos ☎ 065/242–792, 800/262–9669 toll-free in U.S. 🌐 perujungle.com 19 rooms All meals.*

Tahuayo River Amazon Research Center
$$$$ | **RESORT** | Inside the Reserva Comunal Tamshiyacu-Tahuayo, this rustic lodge provides almost constant exposure to nature. **Pros:** abundant wildlife; great food and excursions; knowledgeable guides. **Cons:** on the rustic side; no en-suite bathrooms; cold showers. *Rooms from: S/1554 ✉ Iquitos ✣ Río Tahuayo, 145 km (90 miles) south of Iquitos ☎ 800/262–9669 toll-free in U.S. 🌐 www.perujungle.com 12 rooms All meals.*

Treehouse Lodge
$$$$ | **RESORT** | Bungalows at this unique jungle lodge are perched high in the branches of tropical trees, providing an unforgettable bird's-eye view of the rainforest and a 24-hour jungle soundtrack. **Pros:** idyllic treetop setting; good food; bungalows are well-equipped and comfortable. **Cons:** less wildlife than at other lodges; bungalows near river get boat noise; cold showers. *Rooms from: S/2085 ✉ Yarapa River, Iquitos ✣ 152 km (94 miles) southwest of Iquitos ☎ 801/797–2777 in U.S. 🌐 treehouselodge.com 12 treehouses All meals.*

Chapter 9

THE CENTRAL HIGHLANDS

Updated by
Mike Gasparovic

Sights ★★★★★ Restaurants ★★★★☆ Hotels ★★★☆☆ Shopping ★★★★★ Nightlife ★☆☆☆☆

WELCOME TO THE CENTRAL HIGHLANDS

TOP REASONS TO GO

★ **Handicrafts:** Ayacucho has *retablos* (carved portable boxes with scenes of religious and historical events). Quinua has ceramic workshops. The Mantaro Valley has *mates burilados* (ornately decorated gourds), silver filigree, and alpaca textiles.

★ **Highland Cuisine:** Enjoy the sublime delights of freshly caught trout, *pachamanca* (herb-roasted meats, potatoes, and vegetables cooked in an earthen oven), and *papa a la huancaína* (potatoes covered in a spicy cheese sauce).

★ **Market Day:** Head to the Mantaro Valley, where there's a market every day.

★ **World's Second-Highest Train:** It's no longer number one, but you can still chug your way from Lima to 4,782 meters (15,685 feet) above sea level before dropping down to the valleys surrounding Huancayo.

★ **Jungle Heat:** Head to Chanchamayo, near Tarma, to escape the dry highland air and enjoy the soothing warmth of the high jungle.

A mere hour's journey east of Lima puts you in the foothills of the Andes, a windy, barren landscape where llamas and alpacas graze on vast, puddle-filled fields. Under the blinding highland sun, roads and rails twist around the peaks and pass through ramshackle mountain towns before sliding down through cloud forests and thick jungle en route to Tingo María and Pucallpa. Southeast of Tarma, passing through Huancayo and on to Ayacucho, massive green mountains and the endless *altiplano* (high plains) protect hidden Inca ruins and uncanny stone forests.

1 **Huánuco.** Just outside this Andean hamlet lies Kotosh, whose 4,000-year-old Temple of the Crossed Hands is one of the earliest shrines in the Americas.

2 **Valle Yanahuanca.** Inca way stations, Huari temples, and stone roads from the massive Capac Ñan superhighway are among this valley's scattering of ruins.

3 **Tarma.** Poised on the cusp of the jungle, this friendly town is a jumping-off point for visiting the cascade-filled rainforests at Chanchamayo, as well as one of South America's deepest cave systems.

4 **Jauja.** Gleaming white churches and rugged, lake-filled vistas characterize this, Peru's first capital.

5 **Concepción.** The highlands' most beautiful convent makes this teensy village a must-see on the road to Huancayo.

6 **Huancayo.** This mining boomtown has Andean eats—along with exotic markets, lively nightlife, and the second-highest train system on the planet.

7 **Huancavelica.** Once the source of mercury for Spain's mines in South America, today this quiet, church-filled village is a base for exploring pristine mountain panoramas.

8 **Quinua.** This tiny hamlet is the site of the battle that ended 300 years of Spanish dominion in the Americas.

9 **Ayacucho.** In the 1980s, Ayacucho was the epicenter for the Shining Path; today the sierra's crown jewel is undergoing a cultural rebirth, fueled by stunning handicraft altarpieces and an exuberant Holy Week.

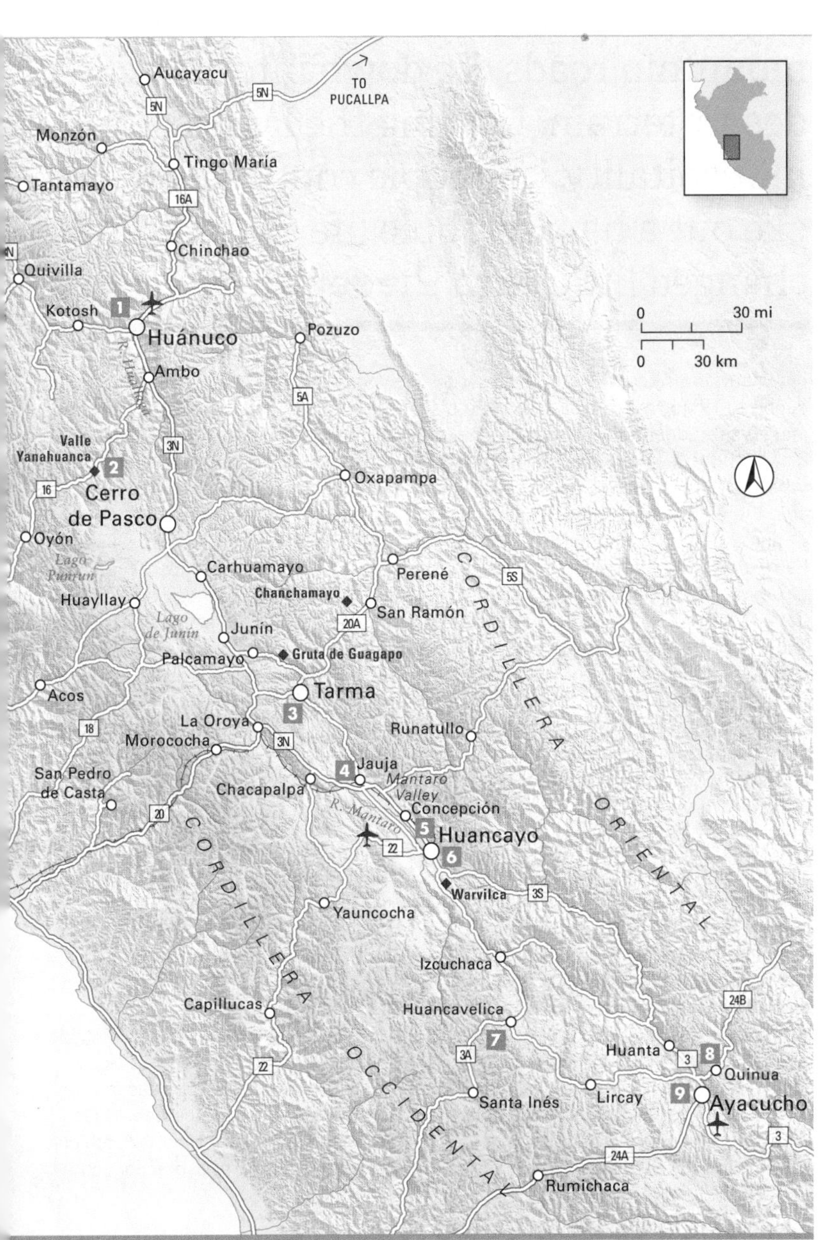

Aucayacu
5N
TO PUCALLPA
Monzón
Tingo María
Tantamayo
16A
Chinchao
Quivilla
Kotosh
1
Huánuco
R. Huallaga
Pozuzo
Ambo
5A
0 30 mi
0 30 km
Valle Yanahuanca
2
3N
16
Cerro de Pasco
Oxapampa
Oyón
Lago Punrun
Carhuamayo
Perené
CORDILLERA ORIENTAL
5S
Huayllay
Chanchamayo
San Ramón
Lago de Junín
Junín
20A
Palcamayo
Gruta de Guagapo
Acos
Tarma
3
18
La Oroya
Runatullo
Morococha
San Pedro de Casta
4
Jauja
Mantaro Valley
Chacapalpa
Concepción
R. Mantaro
20
5
Huancayo
6
22
CORDILLERA OCCIDENTAL
Warvilca
3S
Yauncocha
Izcuchaca
24B
Capillucas
Huancavelica
7
3A
Huanta
8
Quinua
22
Santa Inés
Lircay
9
Ayacucho
24A
Rumichaca

The Central Highlands are where the Andes crash into the Amazon rainforest, and winding, cloud-covered mountain roads dip down into stark desert terrain. Defying the land's inhospitality, its people continue to eke out a hardscrabble life that has changed little with the centuries.

For years, the Andean sierra, from Ayacucho to Tingo María, was one of Peru's least-visited destinations. Geographically remote, with poor or nonexistent infrastructure in many stretches, it was also the epicenter of terrorist violence during the Sendero Luminoso (Shining Path) era of the 1980s, when thousands of peasants lost their lives in one of Latin America's bloodiest convulsions. Today, however, with Peru's internal conflict safely in the past, and improved transportation in virtually every district, increasing numbers of tourists are discovering the stark beauty and genial hospitality of what locals call *el Perú profundo* (deepest Peru).

No one knows when the first bands of settlers arrived on the *puna* (highland plains) or how long they stayed. ■ **TIP→ Archaeologists have unearthed what they believe to be the oldest cave site in Peru at Pikimachay, near Ayacucho, as well as one of the oldest temples in the Americas at Kotosh.** Other archaeological sites at Tantamayo and Garu show that indigenous cultures were thriving here long before the Inca or Spanish empires ever set foot on local soil.

When the Inca overran the region in the late 1400s, they incorporated the already stable northern settlement of Huánuco into their empire, making it an important stop on the route from the capital at Cusco to the northern hub of Cajamarca. To this day, Inca ruins can be seen scattered along the pampas. Then came the Spanish, who founded a colonial city at Huánuco in 1539, and turned nearby Cerro de Pasco's buried gold, silver, copper, and coal into the focus of the mining industry west of the Amazon Basin. They ruled until 1824, when Simón de Bolívar's troops secured Peru's autonomy by defeating the Spanish on the Pampa de Quinua near Ayacucho.

The Central Highlands have seen some of the fiercest clashes in Peruvian history. Apart from the wars between the Inca and the Huanca in the 16th century, and the battles for independence in the 19th, the Shining Path movement, led by ex-philosophy professor Abimael Guzmán Reynoso, quickly earned the distinction of being Latin America's most bloodthirsty guerrilla organization as it terrorized the local peasantry in the 1980s. Between this sinister Maoist death cult and the military's brutal reaction, some

70,000 people died before police finally captured Guzmán in a Lima dance studio in 1992. Shining Path is now a shadow of its former self, and apart from narcotrafficking and the occasional protest from coca growers and unions, the region is generally calm.

Most Central Highlands residents still depend on the crops they grow and the animals they breed—including guinea pigs and alpaca. Local festivals coincide with the rhythms of the harvest, and traditional recipes and artisanship predate the Incas by hundreds of years. Visitors to the region are invariably beguiled by local hospitality, even as they marvel at the thundering rivers, frozen peaks, and icy waterfalls that make up the sublime landscape around them.

MAJOR REGIONS

Central Altiplano. The most important city in Peru's Central Highlands is a place of no interest to tourists whatsoever. Founded by the Spanish in 1630, Cerro de Pasco was, for centuries, one of the crown's richest mining towns, pumping out silver and then copper in an unremitting flow that made it Peru's number-two city, even into the 20th century. Today, Cerro de Pasco is shunned by visitors, as much for the vast open pit that's slowly gobbling up the downtown—and poisoning many locals—as for the bleak, tundra-like climate that reflects its 4,330-meter (14,210-foot) elevation. Environmental problems apart, the town remains a key player in Peru's all-important mining industry.

It's outside Cerro de Pasco that the area's interest to visitors begins. To the north, the city of Huánuco provides a base for exploring ancient ruins in the surrounding valleys (including the mysterious Kotosh), as well as for trips to Tingo María, a warm tropical outpost on the fringes of the Amazon. Meanwhile, farther south, the immense Reserva Nacional de Junín is the Central Highlands at their most starkly beautiful, with *vizcachas* scurrying through the brush and Chilean flamingos winging their way upward from mirroring mountain tarns. The lake's icy winds give way to milder air just down the road at Tarma, where citrus fields and waterfalls beckon from over the ridge in the *ceja de la selva* ("jungle's eyebrow").

Central Sierra. Traveling onward from Tarma's orchards, you leave the warm cradle of its Andean valley and head back into the crisp air at altitudes exceeding 3,500 meters (11,482 feet). The road to Huancayo runs along a high plain buffeted by wind and pocked by herds of highland cattle, with the Río Mantaro etching a crystalline gash in the otherwise uniform landscape. Flowing out of the massive Lago de Junín, the river has long sustained civilization in the Central Sierra, irrigating corn, artichoke, and potato fields throughout the region.

The southbound road also affords a trip through Peru's tangled history and politics. Huanca and Inca ruins still dot the fields around Jauja, the former capital of the Peruvian Viceroyalty, even as greener hills cradle the tiny pueblo of Concepción, home to one of highland Peru's most stunning convents. The trip back in time ends as you approach Huancayo, a modern town enjoying the fruits of a decades-long mineral boom. But don't be put off by its hustle and bustle: Huancayo still pays its respects to tradition, serving up the region's best cuisine and most exquisite handicrafts, all in the shadows of its soaring colonial churches.

Central Valley. The road from Huancayo to Huancavelica and on to Ayacucho shoots over high green plains before spilling into the folds of the Andes and again picking up the Río Mantaro along a winding, two-lane highway. In the rainy season, landslides, or *huaycos,* often block the road, making this trip a difficult one. Breathtaking scenery and vertigo-inducing climbs reward travelers who push onward.

Despite its seeming proximity on a map, Ayacucho lies at least 10 hours from Huancayo, as the road alternately cuts through high-altitude plains and winds in coils alongside steep crevasses. ■ **TIP→ As you go, look for spots of black, brown, and white—wild vicuñas and alpacas that roam this cold, rocky range.** Here it's important to acclimate to the oxygen-poor air: several passes reach heights of well over 4,000 meters (13,123 feet), making *soroche* (altitude sickness) a serious issue. The mountain pass at Abra Huayraccasa, near Huancavelica, is one of the highest in Peru.

Those who withstand the (literally) breathtaking heights will be welcomed by two of Peru's loveliest, most unspoiled cites. Huancavelica, for centuries the source of the mercury that fueled Spain's New World mining operations, is a town of quaint churches and placid mountain lakes. Meanwhile, farther south, Ayacucho has a fair bid to be the sierra's crown jewel, a city of gifted artisans and fiercely independent spirit, where republican troops in 1824 achieved a crushing victory that finally broke Spain's hold over its colonies. Today *ayacuchano* pride is evident on every corner, as the locals enjoy a cultural and economic resurgence after years of terrorist oppression.

Planning

When to Go

The region's best weather falls in the dry season—May through October—when the skies are clear, and daytime temperatures are moderate (nights can be frigid). The rainy season is November through April, when many roads are inaccessible.

Getting Here and Around

AIR

LATAM Perú (🌐 *www.latam.com*) flies from Lima to Ayacucho and Jauja. Star Perú (🌐 *www.starperu.com*) flies from Lima to Andahuaylas and Huánuco. Airlines often cancel flights because of unpredictable weather, so always confirm your flight, even outside the rainy season.

BUS

Lima is the country's travel hub. Cruz del Sur, Tepsa, and Excluciva, among others, run overnight services (10 hours) from Lima to Ayacucho. Likewise, Cruz del Sur, Oltsura, and Movil Bus have many daily buses between Huancayo and Lima (7 hours). Alternatively, you can reach Huancayo from Ayacucho (12 hours) by overnight service on Expreso Internacional Molina—but prepare for a very rough road. If you're looking to go from Lima to Huancavelica, Expreso Antezana and Megabus have daily buses, while GM International has overnight service (7 hours) between Huánuco and Lima. *Colectivos* (shared taxis) travel between the Central Highlands cities and can be much quicker (though slightly more expensive) than bus travel. The location of the *paraderos* (taxi stops) changes, so ask your hotel receptionist for directions.

CAR

The Central Highlands have some of the country's most scenic driving routes, and paved roads link Lima and Huánuco to the north and Huancayo to the south. It's five hours from the capital to the crossroads at La Oroya, from which a gorgeous Andean panorama stretches in three directions: north toward Huánuco, east toward Tarma, and south to Huancayo. Most sights around Huancayo in the Valle del Mantaro are accessible by car. You should travel the rugged road from Huancayo to Ayacucho in a four-wheel-drive vehicle, and be sure to bring emergency supplies for the 12-hour trip. Except for the highway, there are mostly dirt roads in this region, so be prepared. There is no place to rent a car in this region.

TRAIN

The train journey from the capital is the most memorable travel option, but service is limited, with bimonthly trips running only from May to November. On the route from Lima to Huancayo, the 12-hour, 335-km (207-mile) railway cuts through the Andes, across mountain slopes, and above deep crevasses where thin waterfalls plunge into icy streams far below.

Health and Safety

Altitude sickness, or soroche, is a common risk in the Andes, though it's not a major concern unless you're hiking or climbing. Hydrate with water and coca tea, avoid alcohol, and move slowly until you have acclimated.

Safety and security have improved dramatically since Shining Path's heyday in the 1980s, and the Central Highlands benefit from a strong military presence. Occasional conflicts do shake the area, though, with illegal coca growers and militant unions often blocking roads, particularly in the area from Huánuco to Pucallpa. This has little effect on tourism, although a regional strike can throw off a tight itinerary.

Petty crime is rarer in the highlands than in Lima. By staying alert and taking standard precautions, you shouldn't have any trouble. Carry identification on you at all times. Call 105 for an ambulance, the fire department, or the police.

Restaurants

Dining out in the Central Highlands is a casual experience. Restaurants are mostly small, family-run eateries serving regional fare. Breakfast is usually bread with jam or butter and juice, but they can include anything from eggs to soups. Lunch, the day's largest meal, combines soup, salad, and a rice-and-meat dish. You'll find snacks everywhere, from nuts and fruit to ice cream and pastries. Dinner is after 7 and tends to be light. Don't worry about dressing up or making reservations. Tipping isn't customary, but waiters appreciate the extra change. All parts of the animal and almost every edible species are considered. Guinea pig husbandry is a centuries-old tradition, so *cuy* served grilled or fried is a menu staple. Highland potatoes, *choclo* (large-grained corn), fresh cheese, and rich stews spiced with *aji* (chili pepper) round out the highland culinary experience.

The cuisine of the Central Highlands, which focuses on local ingredients and techniques, reflects its isolation. Huancayo's local specialty is papa a la huancaína , served cold with a sliced egg and an olive. Pachamanca is wrapped in local herbs, then slow-cooked on hot stones in an earthen oven. Huánuco's favorites include *picante de cuy* (guinea pig in hot-pepper sauce), pachamanca, fried trout, *humitas* (a local tamale made of ground corn and stuffed with cheese or raisins), and *caldo de cabeza* (sheep's-head soup). Ayacucho is famous for its filling, flavorful *puca picante* (a nutty pork-and-potato stew), served with rice and topped with parsley. During Semana Santa (Holy Week), the city's favorite drink is the warm *ponche*, flavored with milk, cinnamon, cloves, sesame, peanuts, walnuts, and sugar.

Hotels

Accommodations in the Central Highlands lean toward the basic. Not all properties have hot water or private baths, and almost none have (or require) air-conditioning. If you don't need pampering, and don't expect top-quality service, you'll travel easily—and cheaply. The majority of hotels have clean, modest rooms with simple

Andean motifs. Bathrooms usually have showers only, and you should confirm that the hot water does function before paying for a room. Most better hotels have a restaurant or at least a dining room with some type of food service. If you want a homestay experience, ask your hotel or a local travel company, who can often hook you up with hosts in the area.

Rooms are usually available, but if you'll be traveling during the region's popular Semana Santa or Fiestas Patrias (July 28), book tours and hotels early. Also book early around the anniversary of the Battle of Ayacucho in mid-December. *Hotel reviews have been shortened. For full information, visit Fodors.com.*

WHAT IT COSTS in Nuevo Soles			
$	$$	$$$	$$$$
RESTAURANTS			
under S/35	S/35–S/50	S/51–S/65	Over S/65
HOTELS			
under S/250	S/250–S/500	S/501–S/800	Over S/800

Tours

A&R Tours

GUIDED TOURS | Ayacucho is surrounded by archaeological ruins and natural wonders, all of which can be viewed on a package tour. A&R Tours has city excursions and routes to Huari, Quinua, Valle Huanta, and Vilcashuamán. ✉ *Jr. 9 de Diciembre 130, Ayacucho* ☎ *066/311–300* 🌐 *www.viajesartours.com* 🎫 *From S/60.*

Dargui Tours

GUIDED TOURS | This outfitter offers multiday tours of the region, with a focus on the archaeological ruins around Huancayo. ✉ *Jr. Ancash 367, Plaza de la Constitución, Huancayo* ☎ *01/422–7137* 🌐 *www.darguitours.com* 🎫 *From S/55.*

Incas del Perú

GUIDED TOURS | Around Huancayo, you can hike, bike, and explore local villages with the amazing Incas del Perú, which also has a Spanish-language school, book exchange, and folk-art collection. The company will also arrange volunteering and hiking throughout the Mantaro Valley and high jungle, as well as music, cooking, weaving, and gourd-carving workshops. ✉ *Jr. José Gálvez 400, Huancayo* ☎ *064/393–298* 🌐 *www.incasdelperu.org* 🎫 *From S/50.*

Max Adventures

ADVENTURE TOURS | For standard day tours around Tarma, including adventure activities like rappelling and mountain biking, call Max Adventures. It also offers multiday trips to the Reserva Nacional de Junín and high jungle around Chanchamayo, including Oxapampa and Villarica. ✉ *Jr. 2 de Mayo 682, Tarma* ☎ *994/973–286* 🌐 *maxaventuraperu.com* 🎫 *From S/50.*

Perla Tours

GUIDED TOURS | Veteran outfitter Perla Tours specializes in day-trips around Tarma, with stops like the Gruta de Huagapo cave, as well as longer trips into the central jungle. ✉ *Jr. Moquegua 615, Tarma* ☎ *998/080–812* 🌐 *perlatours.com.pe* 🎫 *From S/45.*

Huánuco

390 km (242 miles) northeast of Lima; 105 km (65 miles) north of Cerro de Pasco.

At first glance, Huánuco looks like any other Spanish settlement: a picturesque collection of colonial buildings and churches surrounded by rocky, forested mountains and cut through by the Huallaga River. History, however, runs far deeper here. Evidence of some of Peru's earliest human settlements, and some of the oldest ruins in the country, were found nearby at Lauricocha and Kotosh.

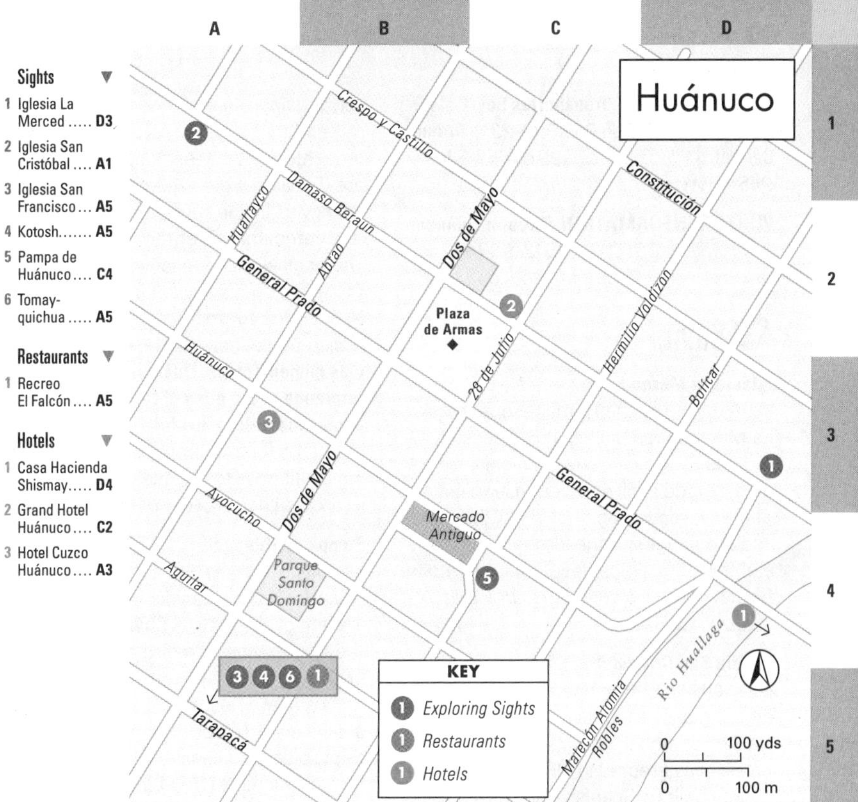

Pre-Inca ruins have turned up throughout these mountains, notably at Tantamayo and Garu. Huánuco was an Inca stronghold and a convenient stopover on their route from Cusco north to Cajamarca. Thousands of Inca relics litter the surrounding pampas.

Huánuco's cool, 1,894-meter (6,212-foot) elevation makes for pleasant winter days and crisp nights, but in the rainy summer, a thick mountain fog blankets the town. The Spanish-style architecture reflects the town's 1539 founding, and later buildings tell the story of Huánuco's importance as a cultural hub. Still, the original Peruvian traditions run deep, particularly during the annual Huánuco anniversary celebrations. Mountain hikes, swims in natural pools, and dips in nearby hot springs add to the area's natural appeal.

GETTING HERE AND AROUND

Most of Huánuco can be seen on foot or via short, cheap cab rides. A guide is recommended for exploring beyond the city. The area is a major coca-growing region, and farmers are leery of unfamiliar characters hanging about. Tours from several agencies on the Plaza de Armas will bring you to the major sites within a few hours of the city for less than S/50. David Figueroa Fernandini Airport (HUU) is 8 km (5 miles) from Huánuco and has daily flights to Lima.

AIRPORT David Figueroa Fernandini Airport. ✉ *Carretera al Aeropuerto* ☎ *062/513–066* 🌐 *www.corpac.gob.pe/Main.asp?T=4222.*

BUS Expreso Acosta León de Huánuco. ✉ *Malecón Alomia Robles 821* ☎ *062/282–121.* **Transmar.** ✉ *Av. 28 de Julio 1065* ☎ *995/737–261* 🌐 *www.*

transmar.com.pe. **Transportes Rey.** ✉ *Jr. 28 de Julio 1215* ☎ *062/503–231.* **Turismo Central.** ✉ *Jr. Tarapacá 598* ☎ *062/624–945* 🌐 *www.turismocentral.com.pe.*

VISITOR INFORMATION Dircetur Huánuco. ✉ *Jr. Bolívar 381* ☎ *064/512–980* 🌐 *www.facebook.com/dircetur.huanuco.*

Sights

Iglesia La Merced

RELIGIOUS SITE | The Romanesque Iglesia La Merced was built in 1566, possibly by the friar Diego de Porras. Colonial treasures include a silver tabernacle, paintings of the Cusco School (Escuela Cusqueña), and the images of the Virgen Purísima and the Corazón de Jesús that were gifts from King Phillip II. ✉ *Jr. Huánuco at Jr. Valdizán* 🎫 *Free.*

Iglesia San Cristóbal

RELIGIOUS SITE | Fronting a landscape of steep, grassy mountain slopes, the Iglesia San Cristóbal, with its three-tiered bell tower, was erected in 1542, the first local church built by Spanish settlers. Inside is a valuable collection of colonial-era paintings and baroque wood sculptures of San Agustín, the Virgen de la Asunción, and the Virgen Dolorosa. ✉ *Jr. San Cristóbal at Jr. Beraún* 🎫 *Free.*

Iglesia San Francisco

RELIGIOUS SITE | The 16th-century Iglesia San Francisco, the city's second-oldest church, has Cusco School paintings and a few colonial-era antiques. Peek inside to see the spectacular gilt wall and arches behind the altar. ✉ *Jr. San Martín at Jr. Beraún* 🎫 *Free.*

Kotosh

ARCHAEOLOGICAL SITE | Considered one of South America's oldest temples, the 4,000-year-old Kotosh is famous for the Templo de las Manos Cruzadas (Temple of the Crossed Hands). Some of the oldest Peruvian pottery relics were discovered below one of the niches surrounding the main room of the temple, and the partially restored ruins are thought to have been constructed by a pre-Chavín culture whose origins are still unknown. Inside the temple you'll see re-created images of the crossed hands. The original mud set is dated 2000 BC and is on display in Lima's Museo Nacional de Antropología, Arqueología, e Historia del Perú. ■ **TIP→ The site was named Kotosh, Quechua for "pile," in reference to the piles of rocks found strewn across the fields.** Taxi fare is S/20 for the round-trip journey from Huánuco, including a half-hour to sightsee. ✉ *Huánuco* ✣ *5 km (3 miles) west of Huánuco* 🎫 *S/5.*

Pampa de Huánuco

ARCHAEOLOGICAL SITE | Also known as Huánuco Viejo, this was formerly the ancient capital city of Chinchaysuyo, the northern portion of the Inca Empire. These highland pampas contain Inca ruins and are near the town of La Unión, a S/30 taxi ride from Huánuco. Note the trapezoidal double-jamb doorways, an Inca hallmark. ■ **TIP→ During the last week of July, the Fiesta del Sol (Sun Festival) takes place at the ruins.** ✉ *Huánuco* ✣ *137 km (85 miles) northwest of Huánuco near town of La Unión* 🎫 *Free.*

Tomayquichua

TOWN | This small village was reportedly the birthplace of Micaela Villegas, a famous indigenous actress in the 18th century and the mistress of Viceroy Manuel de Amat y Juniet, Peru's most prominent colonial official during the Enlightenment. Also known as La Perricholi, the spunky *peruanita* was the basis of Prosper Mérimée's comic novella *Le Carrosse du Saint-Sacrement* before becoming an important character—along with the viceroy—in Thornton Wilder's *The Bridge of San Luis Rey.* A festival in July with parades, music, and dancing celebrates her vitality. Beautiful mountain views are the main attraction of the 2,000-meter-high

(6,500-foot- high) area. Sixteenth-century San Miguel Arcángel, one of the first churches built in the Huánuco area, is nearby in the village of Huacar. ✉ *Huánuco ⊕ 15 km (9 miles) south of Huánuco.*

Restaurants

Restaurants in Huánuco are simple and small, mostly offering local cuisine with a smattering of Chinese and continental selections. Little eateries cluster around the plaza and markets. **■ TIP→ Most large hotels have a small restaurant.**

Recreo El Falcón
$ | **PERUVIAN** | Perched on the banks of the Huallaga River, this family-style restaurant offers the best of Huánuco cooking, including specialties like *gallina con locro* (chicken soup), pachamanca, and fresh river trout. Come at lunch, and lounge on the open-air terrace while you enjoy the view and live music. **Known for:** regional home cooking; generous portions; pleasant riverside setting. *$ Average main: S/22 ✉ 2 de Mayo 190 ☎ 962/002–093 ⊕ www.facebook.com/RecreoFalcon ⊙ No dinner.*

Hotels

Hotels in Huánuco are basic, with shared, cold-water bathrooms at most budget places. Spend a little more, and you'll get more comfort, including a private bath, hot water, and a better mattress. But don't expect the Ritz.

★ Casa Hacienda Shismay
$ | **B&B/INN** | For lovers of beautiful landscapes and peaceful scenery, Casa Hacienda Shismay, founded in 1851, is a slice of paradise in the highlands of Peru. **Pros:** incredible value; national historic monument; spectacular scenery. **Cons:** 45 minutes from Huánuco; no public transportation; might be too rustic for some. *$ Rooms from: S/140 ✉ Shismay ☎ 062/631–174 ⊕ www.shismay.com 4 rooms Free breakfast.*

Grand Hotel Huánuco
$$ | **HOTEL** | This colonial-style building, built in 1943, is chic, swanky, and completely out of place in simple Huánuco, which explains the business travelers wandering its wide halls. **Pros:** on the plaza; good restaurant; pool, sauna, and gym. **Cons:** rooms overlooking the plaza are noisy; paper-thin walls in some areas; breakfast is ho-hum. *$ Rooms from: S/250 ✉ Jr. Dámaso Beraún 775 ☎ 062/512–410 ⊕ grandhotelhuanuco.com 35 rooms Free breakfast.*

Hotel Cuzco Huánuco
$ | **HOTEL** | This local favorite has a boutiquey feel, with its ample spaces and contemporary photography on the walls. **Pros:** great price; modern renovations; pool. **Cons:** basic rooms; bad ventilation in some rooms; street outside is busy. *$ Rooms from: S/60 ✉ Jr. Huánuco 616 ☎ 062/517–653 ⊕ www.hotelcuzcohuanuco.com 60 rooms Free breakfast.*

Tingo María

129 km (80 miles) north of Huánuco.

Not many travelers visit this settlement at the border between mountains and jungle, as it has gotten a bad rap for being in the midst of the country's coca-growing core. It's a shame, though, to miss Tingo María's vibrancy and beauty, evident in its colorful, bustling markets and frenzied festivals. A strong military presence keeps out drug smugglers from the Río Huallaga valley to the north.

With a backdrop of mountains shaped like La Belle Durmiente (Sleeping Beauty), Tingo María is a haven of 55,000 residents who make their living tending the surrounding coffee, rubber, and sugarcane farms. Banana and tea plantations also wind their way up the slopes, and, less than 15 km (9 miles) farther out, there are hidden lakes, waterfalls, and caves to explore. Most travelers come

Quechua of the Andes

The Quechua are some of the original inhabitants of the Andes. Their traditions and beliefs have survived Inca domination, Spanish conquests, and the gradual incursion of modern technology. Throughout the Central Highlands, many locals speak Quechua as their first language and wear traditional costumes woven on backstrap looms. A good number make their living by farming maize and coca in the valleys or potatoes and quinoa in the higher altitudes, while other families herd llamas and alpacas on the cold, windy puna.

Quechua Attire

Walk through the narrow, cobbled streets of any village, and you'll spot Quechua men by the large patterned and fringed ponchos draped over their shoulders; many sport matching tasseled cloths beneath broad-brimmed felt hats with conelike peaks. Knee-length pants are held up with a wide, woven belt that often has local motifs, such as condors or coca leaves. Despite the cold, men usually wear rubber sandals, often fashioned from old tires.

Quechua women's attire is equally bright, with knit sweaters and a flouncing, patterned skirt over several petticoats (added for both warmth and puff). Instead of a poncho, women wear an *aguayo*, a length of sarong-like fabric that can be tied into a sling for carrying a baby or market goods or wrapped around their shoulders for warmth. Hats for the women differ from village to village; some wear black-felt caps with a neon fringe and elaborate patterns of sequins and beads, whereas others wear a plain, brown-felt derby. Women also wear rubber sandals for walking and working in the fields but often go barefoot at home.

Quechua Homes

As you travel through the Andes, look for gatherings of stone or adobe-brick homes with thatched roofs. These *wasis*, or typical Quechua houses, are basic inside and out. Food is cooked either in an adobe oven next to the dwelling or over an open fire inside. Mud platforms with llama wool or sheepskin blankets make do for beds; occasionally a family will have the luxury of a wooden bed frame and grass mattress. All members of the family work in the fields as soon as they are able. Members of the *ayllu* (extended family) are expected to contribute to major projects like harvesting the fields or building a new home.

The Morochuco Quechua

The Morochuco are a unique group of formerly nomadic Quechua who live near Ayacucho on the Pampas de Cangallo. They have light skin and blue eyes, and, unlike other Quechua, many Morochuco men wear beards. The Morochuco are first-rate horseback riders—women and children included—who take advantage of their swiftness and agility to round up bulls on the highland pampas. Renowned for their fearlessness and strength, the Morochuco fought for Peru's independence on horseback with Simón de Bolívar. Women ride in long skirts and petticoats, whereas men don thick wool tights and dark ponchos. Both men and women wear *chullos*, wool hats with earflaps, beneath a felt hat tied under the chin with a red sash.

here to visit Parque Nacional Tingo María, in the midst of the Pumaringri Mountains. Many highland and rainforest species live here, including parrots, primates, and bats. **■ TIP→ This is also the home of the rare, nocturnal guacharo (oilbird), a black-and-brown, owl-like bird with a hooked beak and a 1-meter (3-foot) wingspan.** You can also explore the famed Cueva de las Lechuzas (Owl Cave), on the skirts of the Bella Durmiente, an enormous limestone cave that shelters an important colony of guacharos (also known as *santanas*). If you do visit the region, be prepared: the warmth and humidity of the Andean foothills hit you as you descend from the Huánuco highlands.

GETTING HERE AND AROUND

Tingo María is about three hours north of Huánuco on a paved road. You'll pass through several military checkpoints along the way, which are precautions to prevent drug trafficking and intermittent guerrilla activity. **■ TIP→ Summer and autumn rains often cause landslides, and the road is frequently under repair.** Given the military presence and road conditions, rural travel at night is not recommended. Léon de Huánuco provides bus service twice daily to Huánuco, the nearest metropolis of any size, with connections from there to Lima. Tingo María has an airport just west of town, but as of this writing there are no flights available.

BUSES León de Huanuco. ✉ *Av. Enrique Pimentel 164* ☎ *062/562–030.*

Restaurants

El Encanto de la Selvaina

$$ | PERUVIAN | Located just off the main plaza, this bustling local favorite will have you feeling the jungle vibe in no time. Try the *mojadito amazónico*—jungle fried rice with a sweet-and-sour sauce—with a pitcher of one of the exotic fruit juices to wash it down. **Known for:** heaping platters of jungle favorites; good tacacho con cecina (mashed plantains with prok rind); lots of vegetarian options. *$ Average main: S/35* ✉ *Av. Alameda Perú 288* ☎ *062/562–848* 🌐 *el-encantodelaselva.com.*

Hotels

Villa Jennifer Farm and Lodge

$ | B&B/INN | Most international travelers stay at this excellent Danish-Peruvian-run lodge, a nine-room bird-watchers' haven on 10 hectares (25 acres) not far from the national park. **Pros:** two pools; excellent wildlife-watching opportunities; solid on-site restaurant. **Cons:** rooms are basic; remote location; service can be a bit chaotic. *$ Rooms from: S/130* ✉ *Km 3.4, Castillo Grande* ☎ *062/794–714* 🌐 *www.facebook.com/villajenniferlodge* *10 rooms* *Free breakfast.*

Valle Yanahuanca

112 km (70 miles) southwest of Huánuco; 80 km (50 miles) north of Huancayo; 65 km (40 miles) northwest of Cerro de Pasco.

One of the longest-surviving stretches of Inca road, otherwise known as the Capaq Ñan, passes through the massive rocky outcrops and deep meadows of the Valle Yanahuanca. Forested hills threaded by shallow, pebbled rivers lead 4 km (2½ miles) from the village of Yanahuanca to the village of Huarautambo, where pre-Inca ruins dot the rugged terrain. Continue along the 150-km (93-mile) Inca track, and you'll pass La Unión, San Marcos, Huari, Llamellín, and San Luis.

Reserva Nacional de Junín

238 km (148 miles) south of Yanahuanca; 165 km (102 miles) north of Huancayo.

This out-of-the-way, high-altitude reserve is an important natural and historical site. It sees few tourists, though within you'll find the country's second-largest lake, rare flora and fauna, and a significant 19th-century battle site.

GETTING HERE AND AROUND

Most travelers visit the Reserva Nacional de Junín on a day trip from Tarma. All agencies in town run tours here.

Sights

Reserva Nacional de Junín

NATURE PRESERVE | This reserve is at the center of the Peruvian puna, a high-altitude cross-section of the Andes, which, at 3,900 to 4,500 meters (12,792 to 14,760 feet), is one of the highest regions in the world inhabited by humans. Its boundaries begin about 10 km (6 miles) north of town along the shores of Lago de Junín, which, at 14 km (9 miles) wide and 30 km (19 miles) long, is Peru's second-largest lake after Titicaca. Most visitors arrive via day tours from Tarma, but anyone traveling overland from Huánuco via Cerro de Pasco will pass through the reserve.

Flat, rolling fields cut by clear, shallow streams characterize this cold, wet region between the highest Andes peaks and the eastern rainforest. Only heavy grasses, hearty alpine flowers, and tough, tangled berry bushes survive in this harsh climate, although farmers have cultivated the warmer, lower valleys, turning them into an agricultural oasis of orchards and plantations. The mountains are threaded with cave networks long used as natural shelters by humans, who hunted the llamas, alpacas, and vicuñas that graze on the plains. The dry season is June through September, with the rains pouring in between December and March.

The reserve is also the site of the **Santuario Histórico Chacamarca** (Chacamarca Historical Sanctuary), an important battleground where republican forces triumphed over the Spanish in August 1824. A monument marks the victory spot. The sanctuary is within walking distance of Junín, and several trails lead around the lake and across the pampas. **■ TIP→ Bird fans stop here to spot Andean geese, flamingos, and other wildlife on day trips from Tarma.** ✉ *Carretera between Cerro de Pasco and Tarma.*

Tarma

274 km (170 miles) east of Lima; 65 km (40 miles) southeast of Junín.

The hidden mountain town known as "The Pearl of the Andes" has grown into a city of 40,000 whose traditions and sights reflect its ancient Peruvian roots. Long before the Spanish arrived, indigenous peoples built homes and temples in the hills that framed the town, the ruins of which local farmers continue to uncover as they turn the rich soil into flower and potato fields, coffee plantations, and orchards. The town's look is Spanish, though, with a small Plaza de Armas and several colonial-style churches and mansions.

At an elevation of 3,050 meters (10,004 feet), Tarma has a cool and breezy climate, with crisp nights all year. **■ TIP→ Take advantage of these nights, as candlelight processions are a major part of the town's many festivals—notably the Fiesta San Sebastián in January, Semana Santa in March or April, Semana de Tarma in July, and Fiesta El Señor de Los Milagros in October.** Tarma is definitely not a tourist town, but rather a place to visit for authentic Peruvian traditions and easy access to the jungle to the east.

Quechua Lesson

Here's a small sampling of Quechua words. It won't make you fluent, but people appreciate the effort when you learn a few of words of their language.

Words:

House—wasi
Mother—mama
Father—papa, tayta
Son—wawa
Daughter—wawa
Yes—arí
No—mana
Please—allichu
Hello—rimaykullayki, napaykullayki

Phrases:

What is your name?—Imataq sutiyki?
My name is ... —Nuqap ... sutiymi
Good-bye—rikunakusun
Good morning—windía
How are you?—Ima hinalla?
Thank you—añay

Numbers:

Zero—ch'usaq
One—huq, huk
Two—iskay
Three—kinsa, kimsa
Four—tawa
Five—pishqa, pisqa, pichqa
Six—soqta, suqta
Seven—qanchis
Eight—pusaq, pusac
Nine—isqun
Ten—thunka

Tarma's **Oficina de Turismo,** on the Plaza de Armas, can help you find qualified local guides for sights in the region.

GETTING HERE AND AROUND

Transportes Chanchamayo and Transportes Junín offer daily bus service, each two or three times a day, between Tarma and Lima. Transportes Chanchamayo also offers continuing service to Huancayo or La Merced. Colectivos to all Central Highlands cities can be found at corners throughout the city; just ask.

BUS Transportes Chanchamayo. ✉ *Jr. Callao 1002* ☎ *064/321–882.* **Transportes Junín.** ✉ *Jr. Amazonas 667* ☎ *064/321–234* 🌐 *transportes-junin.webnode.es.*

Sights

Chanchamayo

NATURE PRESERVE | Tarma sits at more than 3,000 meters (10,000 feet), but it's just a stone's throw from the ceja de selva , where many of Peru's citrus plantations lie. For around S/60, you can organize a day trip from town to visit Chanchamayo's magnificent waterfalls, butterfly-filled forests, and local indigenous groups. These tours take you to the major attractions in the area and typically include a refreshing dip in the 30-meter (98-foot) Tirol Falls, a jungle lunch of *cecina* (cured pork) or doncella (river fish), a visit to the local Ashaninka tribe at Pampa Michi, and a tasting of local coffees and other artisanal products. If you can't otherwise make it to the Amazon during your time in Peru, this is an inexpensive way to experience the pleasures of jungle living (as well as a welcome escape from the cool highland air). Peru Latino Tarma offers daily tours. It's also possible to take a bus directly to La Merced, the main town in Chanchamayo. There are simple hotels and restaurants surrounding the small plaza, and from there you can undertake excursions that go deeper into the central jungle to the fascinating German-Austrian colony of Oxapampa or the coffee plantations near Villarica. ✉ *La Merced* ✣ *50 km (20 miles) from Tarma.*

Gruta de Huagapo

CAVE | Head northwest of Tarma 28 km (17 miles) to Palcamayo, then continue 4 km (2½ miles) west to explore the Gruta de Huagapo limestone cave system, a National Speleological Area. Guides live in the village near the entrance and can give you a basic short tour, but you'll need full spelunking equipment for deep cavern explorations. Numerous tour operators in Tarma offer day-trips to the caves and the surrounding villages. It is also possible to arrive at the caves independently by taking a colectivo at the corner of Jr. 2 de Mayo and Jr. Puno. ✉ *Palcamayo.*

Restaurants

Restaurant Chavín de Grima

$ | **PERUVIAN** | This popular, country-style restaurant has simple local décor and lively lunchtime crowds. It serves tamales and sweet coffee for breakfast and *comida típica,* including hearty stews, rice dishes, grilled meat, and fish for lunch and dinner. **Known for:** convivial atmosphere; hearty fare; belly-filling portions. *Average main: S/25* ✉ *Jr. José Galvez 1197* ☎ *964/647–446* 🌐 *www.facebook.com/RESTAURANTCHAVIN.*

Hotels

★ **Hacienda La Florida**

$ | **B&B/INN** | Experience life at a Spanish hacienda at this charming bed-and-breakfast just a 10-minute drive from Tarma. **Pros:** children can feed the on-site farm animals; hiking trails lead from property; lovely mountain views. **Cons:** simple accommodations; car ride from town; some amenities are lacking. *Rooms from: S/245* ✉ *Tarma* ✣ *6 km (4 miles) north of Tarma* ☎ *064/341–041 in Tarma* 🌐 *www.haciendalaflorida.com* *5 rooms* *Free breakfast.*

LP Hotel Tarma

$ | **HOTEL** | By far the most luxurious hotel in town, this frequently updated, colonial-style mansion surrounded by gardens offers warmth as well as grandeur. **Pros:** historical charm; package deals; lots of amenities. **Cons:** filled during the week with business travelers; mediocre restaurant; no food available at night. *Rooms from: S/180* ✉ *Av. Ramón Castilla 512* ☎ *064/321–411* 🌐 *www.losportaleshoteles.com.pe/hotel-tarma* *45 rooms* *Free breakfast.*

Jauja

266 km (165 miles) east of Lima; 60 km (37 miles) south of Tarma.

Jauja has the distinction of having been Peru's original capital, as declared by Francisco Pizarro when he swept through the region; he changed his mind in 1535 and transferred the title to Lima. ■ **TIP→ Jauja still has many of the ornate 16th-century homes and churches that mark its place in the country's history.** The Wednesday and Sunday markets display Andean traditions at their most colorful, showing the other side of life in this mountain town. Although there are several moderately priced hotels, many travelers come here on a day-trip from Huancayo. Those who stay usually visit Laguna de Paca, 4 km (2½ miles) from town, which has a few small lakeside restaurants and rowboat rentals.

Concepción

25 km (16 miles) southeast of Jauja; 22 km (14 miles) northwest of Huancayo.

Visitors rarely linger in the small mountain town of Concepción, and neither should you. Aside from being a battle site during the War of the Pacific, where a force of more than 1,000 Peruvian soldiers vastly outmatched 77 Chileans, the village has one impressive convent with a historic library.

Convento de Santa Rosa de Ocopa

RELIGIOUS SITE | Originally a Franciscan mission whose role was to bring Christianity to the Amazon peoples, the 1725 building now has a reconstructed 1905 church and a massive library with more than 25,000 books—some from the 15th century. The natural-history museum displays a selection of regional archaeological finds, including traditional costumes and local crafts picked up by the priests during their travels. A restaurant serves excellent, if simple, Andean food, and several spare but comfortable accommodations are available in the former monks' quarters. Take a S/25 taxi ride for a round trip to the convent from Concepción's Plaza de Armas. Admission includes a guided tour. ✉ *Concepcíon* ✥ *6 km (4 miles) outside Concepcíon* 🎫 *S/5* ⏲ *Closed Tues.*

Currency Tip 

It's best to bring nuevo soles in bills smaller than 50 to the smaller towns of this region, as traveler's checks, credit cards, and U.S. dollars usually aren't accepted. Travel agencies or larger hotels might change money if you're in a pinch.

Huancayo

22 km (14 miles) southeast of Concepción; 48 km (30 miles) southeast of Jauja.

It's not hard to see how the modern city of Huancayo, with close to 520,000 residents, was once the capital of pre-Inca Huanca (Wanka) culture. Set in the middle of the Andes and straddling the verdant Río Mantaro valley, the city has been a source of artistic inspiration from the days of the earliest settlers and has thrived as the region's center for culture and wheat farming. A major agricultural hub, Huancayo was linked by rail with the capital in 1908, making it a terminus for what was once the world's highest train line. It's now in second place: the Qingzang Railway (aka Qinghai–Tibet Railway) in China is now the first highest. Although it's a large town, its mom-and-pop stores, quaint restaurants, blossoming plazas, and broad colonial buildings give it a comfortable, compact feel.

Huancayo was historically a stronghold for the toughest Peruvian indigenous peoples, including the Huanca, who outfought both the Inca and the Spanish. Little wonder that Peru finally gained its independence in this region, near Quinua, in 1824. **■ TIP→ The Spanish left their mark in the town's hacienda-style homes and businesses, most with arching windows and fronted by brick courtyards with carefully manicured gardens.** For an overview of the city, head northeast 4 km (2½ miles) on Avenida Giráldez, 2 km (1 mile) past Cerro de la Libertad Park, to the eroded sandstone towers in the hillsides at Torre Torre.

The drive from Lima to Huancayo is breathtaking, with the road rising to more than 4,700 meters (15,416 feet) before sliding down to the valley's 3,272-meter (10,731-foot) elevation. As you enter the city, four-lane Calle Real is jammed with traffic and crammed with storefronts, but look more closely, and you'll see the elegant churches and colorful markets tucked into its side streets, hallmarks of the provincial life that makes the city so charming. Women with long black braids beneath black-felt hats still dress in multitiered skirts and blouses with *mantas* (bright, square, striped cloths) draped over their shoulders. Note the intricate weavings—particularly the belts with the famous train worked into the pattern.

GETTING HERE AND AROUND

Tiny Francisco Carle Airport (JAU) is 45 km (27 miles) north of Huancayo near Jauja. LATAM Perú offers regular flights from Lima. Although Huancayo is big, most of the areas of interest to travelers are within walking distance of the Plaza de la Constitución. The exceptions are the crafts villages in the Mantaro Valley. *Combi* vans circle the city streets looking for passengers for the 20- to 40-minute

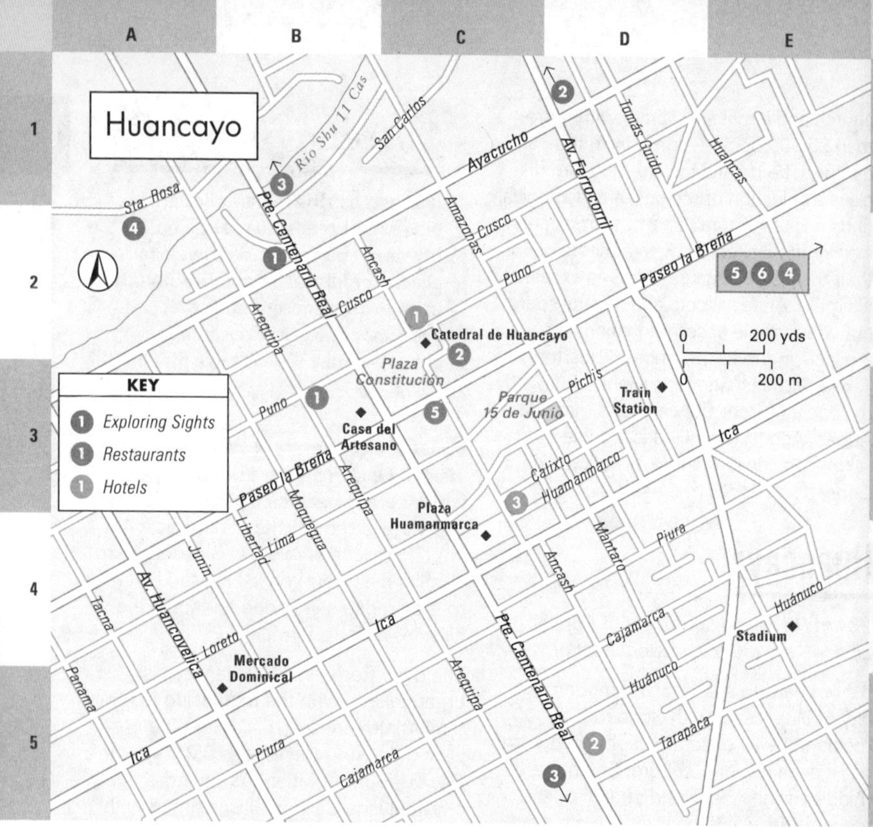

Sights

1 Capilla de la Merced **B2**

2 Ferrocarril Central Andino **D1**

3 Huarihuilca **C5**

4 Museo Salesiano **A2**

5 Parque de la Identidad Huanca........ **E2**

6 Parque del Cerro de la Libertad............. **E2**

Restaurants

1 Antojitos **B3**

2 Detrás de la Catedral.... **C2**

3 Huancahuasi **B1**

4 La Cabaña **E2**

5 Restaurante Olímpico ... **C3**

Hotels

1 Hostal El Márquez **C2**

2 Hotel Presidente **D5**

3 Hotel Turismo Huancayo................. **C3**

ides to each town, or you can take a :omprehensive valley tour from any)f the travel agencies in Huancayo for ;/50–S/60. Taxis are another option, as hey're quite economical.

AIR Francisco Carle Airport. *(JAU) ☎ 064/362–109.*

BUS Cruz del Sur. ✉ *Av. Ferrocarril 151 ☎ 064/221–767 🌐 www.cruzdelsur.com.* *pe.* **ETUCSA.** ✉ *Jr. Puno 220 ☎ 064/226–524.* **Expreso Molina.** ✉ *Jr. Angaraes 334 ☎ 064/224–501 🌐 www.facebook.* *com/1992molinaunionhyo.* **Ormeño.** ✉ *Av. Mariscal Castilla 1379 ☎ 964/346–056, 01/472–5679 in Lima 🌐 www.grupo-or-meno.com.pe.*

Sights

Capilla de la Merced

HISTORIC SITE | In front of the Río Shulcas, he Capilla de la Merced is a nation-al monument marking where Peru's Constitutional Congress met in 1830 and he constitution was signed in 1839. In addition to information about this historic gathering, the Chapel of Mercy also exhibits Cusco School paintings. ✉ *Cl. Real at Jr. Ayacucho* 🎫 *Free* 🕒 *Closed weekends.*

★ Ferrocarril Central Andino

TRANSPORTATION SITE (AIRPORT/BUS/FERRY/TRAIN) | The Central Highlands' Ferro-carril Central Andino once laid claim o being the world's highest rail route. With the 2006 opening of China's Qinghai–Tibet Railway, the Peru route was knocked down to second place. No matter, though: this is one of the country's most scenic areas, and tracks cut through the mountains and plains all the way from Lima to Huancayo. The line these days is a shadow of what it once was, and trains ply the route only a few times a year. Tickets are easy to come by, but you will have to plan around he infrequent departures if you want the journey to be a centerpiece of your visit to Peru. The railway's website lists departure dates, with Lima–Huancayo service operating just a handful of days between April and November. Trains depart the capital's Desamparados train station for the 12-hour journey to Huancayo, twisting along the 335-km (207-mile) route through the Andes at an average elevation of 4,782 meters (15,685 feet). The engine chugs its way up a slim thread of rails that hugs the slopes, traveling over 59 bridges, around endless hairpin curves, and through 66 tunnels—including the 1,175-meter-long (3,854-foot-long) Galera Tunnel, which, at an altitude of 4,758 meters (15,606 feet), is the climax of the journey. Snacks, lunch, and soft drinks are included in the price. You can request oxygen if you get short of breath over the high passes, and *mate de coca* flows freely at all hours. The decades-old *clásico* cars are okay in a pinch, but the newer *turístico* cars are much more comfortable, with reclining seats and access to the observation and bar car. ✉ *Huancayo Station, Av. Ferrocarril* ☎ *01/226–6363 ticket office in Lima* 🌐 *www.ferrocarrilcentral.com.pe* 🎫 *S/500 one-way, S/700 round-trip.*

Huarihuilca

ARCHAEOLOGICAL SITE | This ruined temple was built by the pre-Inca Huanca culture between 800 and 1200 AD. It consists of stone walls enclosing cells where captives were held prior to being sacri-ficed, as well as underground conduits to bring water to the region. You can still see the sacred spring that flows through the channels; legend says that this spring gave rise to the foreparents of the Huan-ca people. Several mummies have been discovered at the site. The closest village is Huari, which has a little museum on the main square with ceramic figures, pottery, and a few bones and skulls. ✉ *Huancayo* ⊕ *6 km (3½ miles) from Huancayo, near Huari* 🎫 *S/3.*

Museo Salesiano

MUSEUM | Look for the well-preserved rainforest creatures and butterflies from the northern jungles among this museum's more than 10,000 objects. Local fossils and archaeological relics are also on display. ✉ *Jr. Santa Rosa 299, in Colegio Salesiano* ☎ *064/247–763* 🎫 *S/5* ⏲ *Closed Sun.*

Parque de la Identidad Huanca (*Huanca Identity Park*)

CITY PARK | **FAMILY** | The focus of the beautiful Parque de la Identidad Huanca is the pre-Inca Huanca culture, which once occupied the area but left few clues to its lifestyle. A 5-km (3-mile) drive from Huancayo, the park has pebbled paths and small bridges that meander through blossoming gardens and past a rock castle just right for children to tackle. An enormous sculpture at the park's center honors the local artisans who produce the city's mates burilados. ✉ *San Antonio.*

Parque del Cerro de la Libertad

CITY PARK | **FAMILY** | An all-in-one amusement site 1 km (½ mile) northeast of the city, the Parque del Cerro de la Libertad lets you picnic in the grass, watch the kids at the playground, swim in the public pool, dine at a restaurant, or stroll through the zoo. ■ **TIP→ Folkloric dancers and musicians perform at the Liberty Hill Park amphitheater on weekends.** A 15-minute walk from the park brings you to the site of Torre Torre, a cluster of 10- to 30-meter (30- to 98-foot) rock towers formed by wind and rain erosion. ✉ *Av. Giráldez.*

Restaurants

The local specialty is papa a la huancaína, potatoes in a nutty cheese sauce served cold with an olive and slice of hard-boiled egg. Budget restaurants with set lunch menus are on Jiron Arequipa south of Antojitos pizzeria, as well as along Avenida Giráldez. You can pick up a quick morning meal at the Mercado Modelo after 7, and juice stands, with fresh fruit brought in daily from the high jungle, are on every street.

Antojitos

$ | **PERUVIAN** | Grilled meats, wood-smoked pizzas, and hearty sandwiches draw a diverse crowd of travelers and locals alike to this dimly lit, wood-paneled restaurant. The daily lunch special is filling and varied, and the locale is an excellent venue for lazy midday people-watching. **Known for:** wood-fired pizzas; live music; bargain-priced lunches. $ *Average main: S/25* ✉ *Jr. Puno 599* ☎ *064/237–950.*

Detrás de la Catedral

$ | **PERUVIAN** | Rustic wood tables and soft candlelight set the mood for a meal of roasted lamb, grilled trout, pasta, and other *platos típicos* in this cozy restaurant, just steps from the cathedral. Service can be slow, so be prepared to linger or take advantage of the free Wi-Fi. **Known for:** regional Peruvian cooking; intimate atmosphere; yummy trout dishes. $ *Average main: S/25* ✉ *Jr. Ancash 335* ☎ *064/212–969* 🌐 *www.facebook.com/detrasdelacatedral.*

★ **Huancahuasi**

$$ | **PERUVIAN** | A festival-hall atmosphere and mind-blowing updates of Peruvian classic dishes make this Huancayo institution one of the sierra's best restaurants. The versions of papa a la huancaína and *alpaca saltado* (stir-fried alpaca with onions and tomatoes) are like nothing you've had before, and the brightly costumed waiters take joy in introducing the region's cuisine to visitors. **Known for:** exquisite regional cooking; vibrant fiesta-like atmosphere; friendly waitstaff. $ *Average main: S/40* ✉ *Av. Mariscal Castilla 2222* ☎ *064/244–826* 🌐 *www.huancahuasi.com.*

The hills around Tarma are covered in a pretty patchwork of farmland.

★ La Cabaña

$ | PERUVIAN | Over-the-top decorations and labyrinthine rooms give this restaurant charm, but the food has made it a favorite. Wash down wood-fired pizzas and grilled meats with a pitcher of *calientitos* (hot spiced rum punch). **Known for:** convivial atmosphere; artisanal pizzas; friendly owner. *Average main: S/25* *Av. José Gálvez 400* *064/222–395* *www.pizzerialacabana.org* *No lunch.*

Restaurant Olímpico

$ | PERUVIAN | This throwback restaurant, open for more than 60 years, still serves cheap, hearty Andean specials to a downtown crowd. It's the kind of place you come to with your grandparents for a leisurely Sunday lunch; tables are consistently packed, but the food is worth the wait. **Known for:** classic Peruvian cooking; social atmosphere; hearty soups. *Average main: S/30* *Av. Giráldez 199* *064/588–705* *restauranteolimpico.com/huancayo.*

Hotels

Hostal El Márquez

$$ | HOTEL | Rooms at the El Márquez are relatively modern, if a bit bland; some have flat-screen TVs, heaters, and cathedral views, while others don't, so choose carefully, and negotiate hard. **Pros:** centrally located; good café on the premises; suites with Jacuzzi tubs. **Cons:** bland décor; the hot water isn't always hot; the front gate is closed early at night. *Rooms from: S/250* *Jr. Puno 294* *064/219–026* *www.elmarquezhuancayo.com* *29 rooms* *Free breakfast.*

Hotel Presidente

$ | HOTEL | The most popular lodging among visiting *limeños* has the comforts of a modern hotel: rooms have Andean fabrics and accents, TVs, Wi-Fi, phones, and private baths with hot water. **Pros:** good amenities; train packages; 24-hour restaurant. **Cons:** mostly business clientele; thin walls; service can be surly.

Shopping at the Source

The wide Mantaro Valley stretches northwest of Huancayo, embracing not only the Río Mantaro but also a vast area of highland lakes and plains. Trails run along the jagged mountainsides to archaeological sites and crafts villages. By road, the first places you'll reach are Cochas Chico and Cochas Grande, gourd-carving centers 11 km (7 miles) north of Huancayo, with some of the most talented mate burilado artists in the country. From there, the road northwest leads 10 km (6 miles) to Hualhuas, a weaving village where you can watch blankets and sweaters being crafted from alpaca and lamb's wool dyed with local plants. About 5 km (3 miles) farther north is San Jerónimo de Tunán, where the Wednesday market specializes in gold and silver filigree. Finally, cross the Río Mantaro, and head 10 km (6 miles) west to Aco, a village of potters and ceramics artists.

Group tours from Huancayo cover the valley, but the roads are good enough that you can drive on your own, though if you fly solo you won't have the advantage of a guide or a translator. Minibuses from Avenida Giráldez also reach these villages.

Rooms from: S/225 ✉ Cl. Real 1138 ☎ 064/231–275 🌐 huancayo.hotelpresidente.com.pe 95 rooms Free breakfast.

Hotel Turismo Huancayo

$$ | **HOTEL** | The hacienda-style exterior of this elegant hotel gives it a worldly charm that sets it above the newer options. **Pros:** excellent service; sparkling rooms with modern conveniences; convenient location. **Cons:** street and plaza in front often see protests; quality of rooms varies; hotel can be noisy. *Rooms from: S/260 ✉ Jr. Ancash 729 ☎ 064/231–072 🌐 turismo.hotelpresidente.com.pe 95 rooms Free breakfast.*

Nightlife

Huancayo's nightlife is surprisingly spunky. Many restaurants turn into *peñas* with dancing, live music, and folkloric performances from Friday to Sunday between 7 pm and midnight (though some may start and end earlier). If you arrive around or after the time the show begins, expect to pay a cover of about S/7–S/15.

Rock and Pop

DANCE CLUBS | One of the more popular discos in Huancayo, this two-story behemoth features live rock and salsa bands and reasonably priced drinks. *✉ Jr. Puno 152 ☞ Closed Sun.–Wed.*

729 Café-Bar

BARS/PUBS | *Cocteles del autor* and old-fashioned, round-the-hearth furnishings make this bar a favorite on cold Andean nights. Sit back in one of the easy chairs, and listen to the DJ spin Latin pop hits, or order a *piqueo* (snack tray) from the excellent kitchen. *✉ Jr. Ancash 729 ☎ 064/231–072 🌐 www.facebook.com/729cafebar.*

Shopping

Huancayo and the towns of the surrounding Valle del Mantaro are major crafts centers. The region is famous for its mates burilados (large, intricately carved and painted gourds depicting scenes of local life and historic events), many of which are made 11 km (7 miles) outside town in the villages of Cochas Grande and Cochas Chico. Silver filigree and utensils are the specialties of San Jerónimo de Tunán, and exquisite knitwear, woolen sweaters, scarves, wall hangings, and hats are produced in San Agustín de Cajas and Hualhuas. You will find better prices outside town, especially when buying from the artisans directly.

FOOD

Mercado Mayorista

OUTDOOR/FLEA/GREEN MARKETS | Stretching around the blocks near the train station is the daily produce market. You'll need several hours to wander through the stalls of local crafts and foodstuffs, where you'll find traditional medicines and spices among such local delicacies as gourds, guinea pigs, fish, and frogs. ✉ *Av. Ferrocarril.*

HANDICRAFTS

Casa del Artesano

CRAFTS | You'll find top-quality, locally made goods near the Plaza de la Constitución at Casa del Artesano, where independent artists sit in their tiny shops working on their respective crafts. ✉ *Cl. Real 475* ☎ *064/213–657* 🌐 *www.casadelartesano.org.*

Sunday Market

OUTDOOR/FLEA/GREEN MARKETS | The city's main shopping venue is the Sunday *mercado,* which is spread down one of the city's main thoroughfares and its side streets for about a kilometer. It is one of the largest weekly markets in the country, yet it sees few tourists. In particular, look for mates burilados, mantas, straw baskets, and retablos (miniature scenes framed in painted wooden boxes). ✉ *Av. Huancavelica.*

Huancavelica

147 km (91 miles) south of Huancayo.

Spread out high in the Andes, Huancavelica was founded in the 16th century by Spanish conquistadors, who discovered deep veins of mercury threading its rocky hillsides. The poisonous metal was vital in the extraction of silver from the mines in Peru and Bolivia, including the staggeringly rich Cerro Rico in Potosí. Although harvesting it was difficult at 3,680 meters (12,979 feet), the Spanish were nonetheless able to turn Huancavelica into a key commercial town that today has settled into a population of around 50,000.

Huancavelica is partitioned by the river of the same name that divides the commercial district in the south from the residential area in the north. Happily, the road between it and Huancayo has been completely revamped in recent years, with smoothly paved surfaces and better overall safety—though it still closes occasionally in the rainy season due to landslides.

Owing to the improved transportation, Huancavelica's traditional culture and relaxed atmosphere are now more accessible to the adventurous traveler. Here you'll see local women sporting *chukus* (spangled, flowered hats) in the markets and shops, while the narrow, cobbled streets are still lined with elegant, colonial-style mansions and 16th-century churches. On weekends, residents from all over the region crowd the sprawling Sunday market, where you can buy everything from hand-knitted scarves to seemingly endless varieties of potatoes.

Most local crafts and clothing are made in the villages on the outskirts of Huancavelica, and visiting the artisans' shops provides a fascinating glimpse into the local economy. Other nearby attractions include the *miradores* (lookouts) from Qoripaqcha, a short stroll up the hill from San Cristóbal, as well as the thermal baths on the hillside across from town.

GETTING HERE AND AROUND

Huancavelica is notoriously difficult to access. Few roads lead there, and many of the surrounding villages can be reached only on foot. As if that weren't enough, buses are tiny, routes are unpredictable, and departure points for colectivos from Huancayo and Ayacucho change constantly, so asking the locals about where to go once you're on the ground is a must. The town, however, is quite compact, meaning a few short streets in the center contain nearly everything of interest. A good, albeit steep, sightseeing path starts from behind the rail station and affords pleasant views of the city and surrounding mountains. The altitude is a common problem for visitors here, so take it slow.

VISITOR INFORMATION Instituto Nacional de Cultura . ✉ *Jr. Antonio Raimondi 193* ☎ *067/453–420* 🌐 *www.facebook.com/MinisterioCulturaHvca.* **Oficina de Información Turística Municipal.** ✉ *Av. Manchego Muñoz 299* ☎ *067/452–870* 🌐 *munihuancavelica.gob.pe.*

Feria Dominical
MARKET | The Sunday market (*feria dominical*) attracts artists and shoppers from all the nearby mountain towns. It's a good place to browse for local crafts—although you'll get better quality (and sometimes better prices) in the villages. ✉ *Jr. Garma at Jr. Barranca.*

Iglesia de San Francisco
RELIGIOUS SITE | Begun in 1673, the Iglesia de San Francisco took nearly a century to complete. The dual white towers and red stone doorway—carved with regional motifs—make the church one of the most attractive buildings in town. ✉ *Plaza Bolognesi, Jr. García los Godos at Jr. Torre Tagle* 🎫 *Free.*

★ Mines of Santa Bárbara
MINE | This ghostly abandoned mine dates from 1563, when the discovery of mercury in the hills south of Huancavelica turned the region into a key cog in Spain's precious-metals machine. It closed in 1786, after one of the mine shafts collapsed, killing 200 workers. If you make the two-hour trek from town, you can see what remains of the former mining village, complete with church and school. The mine itself, however, is sealed off due to the poisonous gases still present inside. You can also pay a taxi driver S/60 to take you and wait as you explore. The mine is tentatively slated to become a UNESCO World Heritage Site, so to get the jump on the crowds, go now. ✉ *Huancavelica* 🎫 *Free.*

Piscina de Aguas Termales de San Cristóbal
HOT SPRINGS | Locals believe that these hot-spring mineral baths, found in the tree-covered slopes north of town, have healing powers. Hundreds of pilgrims come from the surrounding villages during holy days. ✉ *Av. 28 de Abril, San Cristóbal* ☎ *067/753–222* 🎫 *S/5 private room, S/2 public area.*

Plaza de Armas
PLAZA | Huancavelica's main gathering place showcases wonderful colonial architecture. Across from the plaza is the restored 17th-century cathedral, which contains a silver-plated altar. ✉ *Plaza de Armas.*

Nesul Coffee
$ | **PERUVIAN** | With its simple platos típicos and selection of warm beverages, this café-restaurant is one of the most consistent options in Huancavelica. Don't expect gourmet cooking: just solid versions of old standbys like pastas and lomo saltado , plus good dessert coffees. **Known for:** belly-warming drinks; good, simple food; tasty desserts and quick bites. 💲 *Average main: S/25* ✉ *Jr. Virrey Toledo 210* ☎ *965/076–018.*

Gran Hostal la Portada
$ | **HOTEL** | This standard guesthouse provides travelers with a clean bed, hot shower, and friendly service at a bargain price. **Pros:** great location; piping-hot water; rooms on the top floor have nice views of the surrounding mountains. **Cons:** building lacks charm; Wi-Fi is

weak; many rooms face an uninspiring courtyard. *Rooms from: S/50* ✉ *Jr. Virrey Toledo 252* ☎ *067/451–050* 🌐 *www.facebook.com/hostallaportada.huancavelica* *No credit cards* *20 rooms* *No meals.*

Hotel Presidente Huancavelica

$ | **HOTEL** | On the plaza, Huancavelica's top hotel is in an attractive, Spanish-colonial building with bland but sizable rooms that have phones, Wi-Fi, and hot showers. **Pros:** historical building; prime plaza setting; comfortable, spacious rooms. **Cons:** mixed amenities; pretty basic for the best hotel in town; poor soundproofing in some rooms. *Rooms from: S/210* ✉ *Plaza de Armas s/n* ☎ *067/452–760* 🌐 *huancavelica.hotelpresidente.com.pe* *45 rooms* *Free breakfast.*

Quinua

37 km (23 miles) northeast of Ayachuco.

The Battle of Ayacucho, the decisive confrontation with Spanish forces during South America's Wars of Independence, took place on the Pampas de Quinua grasslands 37 km (23 miles) northeast of the city, near the village of Quinua, on December 9, 1824. Today, a white obelisk rises 44 meters (144 feet) above the pampas to commemorate Peru's victory over Spain, as well as the role of local troops in bringing that victory about.

TIP→ Quinua is one of the crafts centers of Peru. It's best known for its ceramics, and you'll find various examples on the windowsills and rooftops of the adobe houses. Miniature churches, delicately painted with ears of corn or flowers, are seen as symbols of good luck. The ubiquitous ceramic bulls were once used in festivities associated with cattle-branding ceremonies. Tours from Ayacucho bring you into the workshops of the many artisans in the village, among the better-quality of which are Cerámica Artística Sánchez, Rumi Wasi, and Galería Artesanal Límaco; all are on Jirón Sucre off the main plaza. Tours of Huari, Vilcashuamán, and Vischongo often include Quinua, but you can also get here by bus from Ayacucho.

Sights

Museo de Quinua

MUSEUM | Immerse yourself in Latin American revolutionary history through exhibits in the compact Museo de Quinua, which has on display relics from the Battle of Ayacucho. Next door, be sure to visit the room where the Spanish signed the final peace accords recognizing Latin America's independence. Come the first week in December to celebrate the town's role in Peru's democracy, when you'll see extravagant local performances, parties, parades, and crafts fairs. There's also a little local market on Sunday. ✉ *Plaza de Armas* *S/2.*

Restaurants

★ **QuinuaQ**

$ | **PERUVIAN** | This lovely hillside restaurant is a perfect lunchtime pit stop after seeing the battlefield and before heading back to Ayacucho. The owners work with a Dutch nonprofit to provide training for disadvantaged local kids, and the food—including a heavenly *asado negro con puré* (beef roast over mashed potatoes)—rivals that of any (okay, almost any) top Lima chef. **Known for:** stunning mountain views; programs for disadvantaged youth; best food in Ayacucho. *Average main: S/25* ✉ *Rasuhuilca s/n* *From Quinua's Plaza de Armas, go north on Rasuhuilca for five blocks. Turn left, then right, then follow the signs down the dirt road.* ☎ *946/393–258* 🌐 *www.quinuaq.com* *Closed Tues. No dinner.*

Ayacucho

114 km (71 miles) south of Huancavelica; 364 km (226 miles) northeast of Pisco.

Tucked into the folds of the Andes, 2,760 meters (9,055 feet) up on the slopes, Ayacucho is a colorful, colonial-style town. Though its looks are Spanish—think glowing white-alabaster mansions with elegant columns and arches—at heart it's an indigenous enclave inhabited by people who still speak Quechua as a first language and don traditional costume for their daily routine. Locals greet visitors with warmth and amazement, and the city's 180,000 people revere artists with an energy matched only by that expended during religious celebrations like Carnaval and Semana Santa. Religion is a serious pursuit in this city of churches, where more than 30 sanctuaries beckon worshippers at all hours.

Human settlement in Peru began in the valleys around Ayacucho about 20,000 years ago. Dating from this era are the oldest human remains in the country—and perhaps in the Americas—found in a cave network at Piquimachay, 24 km (15 miles) west of the city. Over the centuries, the region was home to many pre-Hispanic cultures, including the Huari (Wari), who set up their capital of Huari 22 km (14 miles) from Ayacucho some 1,300 years ago. When the Inca arrived in the 15th century, they ruled the lands from their provincial capital at Vilcashuamán.

In the 1530s, the Spanish came and conquered the reigning Inca, and Francisco Pizarro founded Ayacucho in 1540. First named Huamanga ("land of falcons") for the local avian species, Ayacucho grew from a small village into a bustling city known for its many colonial-style churches. Nearly 300 years later, it was one of the centers of Peru's bid for independence from the Spanish, when a Peruvian army led by Antonio José de Sucre defeated the last peninsular forces at the nearby Pampa de Quinua on December 9, 1824. The Iglesia Santo Domingo in Ayacucho sounded the first bells of Peru's independence, trumpeting the city's role in achieving the country's freedom.

It took a century more before the city built its first road links west to the coast, and the road to Lima went unpaved through the 1960s. Ayacucho might have opened to tourism then but for the influence of Abimael Guzmán Reynoso, a philosophy teacher at the San Cristóbal University of Huamanga. His charismatic preaching touted a Maoist-style revolution in response to the age-old problems of rural poverty among the country's indigenous peoples. Guzmán founded Sendero Luminoso (Shining Path) in the late 1960s, and spurred it to militant action in March of 1982, when bombs and gunfire first shook Ayacucho's cobbled streets. The fighting between the Shining Path and the government killed thousands of ayacuchanos, and by the mid-1980s, the city was cut off from the rest of Peru. Then, in 1992, police arrested Guzmán in a hideout above a Lima dance studio, and the Shining Path fell apart. Although Ayacucho is now peaceful, tourism has been slow to establish itself outside of Semana Santa, and the city receives only about 1,000 visitors a month. Those who do come enjoy the benefits of hassle-free strolls down the well-built pedestrian promenades.

Ayacucho's isolation from the modern world means that to visit is to step back to colonial days. Elegant white *huamanga* buildings glow in the sunlight, with bright flowers spilling out of boxes fronting high, narrow wooden balconies. Beyond the slim, straight roads and terracotta roofs, cultivated fields climb the Andes foothills up to the snow line. Electricity, running water, and phones are occasionally unreliable, but infrastructure is generally modern, and deep

Sendero Luminoso (Shining Path)

Inspired by the Maoism of China's Cultural Revolution, Sendero Luminoso (Shining Path) first formed in the late 1960s under philosophy professor Abimael Guzmán Reynoso and his "Gonzalo Thought." After Peru's military coup in 1968 and ambitious land reform in 1969, the country's political left became fractured, driving Sendero to forsake politics and launch its "revolutionary war" in 1980 after 12 years of military rule. In setting fire to ballot boxes—the symbols of institutional democracy—in a town outside Ayacucho, Sendero launched the opening salvo of its campaign of terror.

Sendero's Maoism quickly took on the trappings of a death cult. Guzmán and his disciples saw in Ayacucho's deep poverty and discontent the preconditions needed to destroy the country's existing political structure and replace it with a peasant dictatorship. By means of a core group of fanatical, highly disciplined operatives, they assassinated political figures and bombed police posts, spreading panic and chaos throughout the country. Over time, their methods grew increasingly macabre: dead dogs hung from lampposts, electrical towers bombed to induce blackouts, blazing hammer-and-sickle emblems on the hillsides. Sendero also began committing atrocities against the very communities it claimed to be helping. Throughout the Highlands, Sendero used "people's trials" to purge anyone connected with the capitalist economy, including trade unionists, civic leaders, and the managers of farming collectives. What was once a "shining" path quickly became a witches' sabbath of blood and horror.

Sendero's emergence was violent, but the government's response was no less brutal. Peru's leaders sent in the military to quell what they viewed as a localized uprising, and the military in turn exacerbated the unrest by violating human rights and committing indiscriminate massacres of peasant populations. The anger of centuries of discrimination and disenfranchisement welled up and unleashed a torrent of bloodshed that Peruvians are still coming to terms with today. In 2003, the country's Truth and Reconciliation Commission released a report estimating that nearly 70,000 people had died or disappeared during the conflict. The commission attributes more than half of these victims to Sendero, and at least one third to government security forces.

The Dancer Upstairs, a film directed by John Malkovich, is a fascinating look at the search for, and capture of, Sendero leader Guzmán in 1992. With his arrest by a crack team of Lima police officers, Sendero began a rapid decline—though it remains nominally active to this day, driven more by narcotrafficking profits than radical ideology. In 2012, *senderistas* kidnapped 36 employees of a major gas company near the VRAE (Apurímac and Ene River valley), the country's main coca-growing region. The military freed the employees, but in the process lost three of its own. Profits from the drug trade will likely sustain low-level Sendero activities into the near future.

—*By Michael Goodwin*

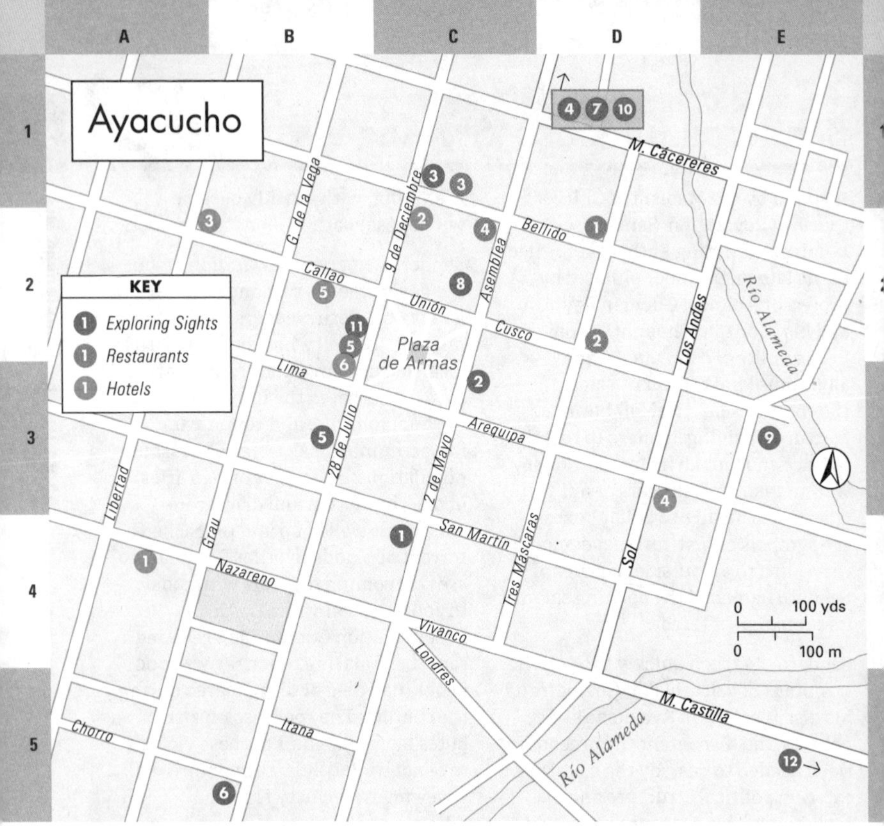

Sights

1 Casa Museo Joaquín López Antay.... **C4**
2 Casa Ruiz de Ochoa..................... **C3**
3 Catedral.................. **C1**
4 Iglesia Santo Domingo.......... **D1**
5 La Compañía de Jesús..................... **B3**
6 Museo Cáceres......... **B5**
7 Museo de Arqueología y Antropología Hipólito Unánue................... **D1**
8 Museo de la Memoria.................. **C2**
9 Palacio del Marqués de Mozobamba.............. **E3**
10 Prefectura.............. **D1**
11 Ruinas Huari............. **B2**
12 Vilcashuamán and Intihuatana............... **E5**

Restaurants

1 Carbon y Vino........... **D2**
2 Casa Grill................ **D2**
3 La Casona................ **C1**
4 Pizzería Italiana.......... **C2**
5 ViaVia Café.............. **B2**

Hotels

1 Hotel La Crillonesa **A4**
2 Hotel Plaza Ayacucho... **C2**
3 Hotel San Francisco de Paula **A2**
4 Hotel Santa María...... **D3**
5 Hotel Santa Rosa **B2**
6 ViaVia Hotel **B3**

poverty in the region has diminished significantly. Visitors are frequently delighted to see banks and businesses housed in 16th-century *casonas* (colonial mansions), even as women in traditional Quechua shawls draped over white blouses, their black hair braided neatly, stroll through markets packed with produce and crafts stalls.

GETTING HERE AND AROUND

Most of the city can be explored on foot, as most tourist amenities, hotels, restaurants, and the bulk of the churches and colonial buildings are within a few blocks of the Plaza de Armas. Getting to out-of-the-way workshops in Santa Ana and La Libertad requires a quick cab ride. Basic city tours (S/25) offered at every agency depart daily and will save you a good deal of hassle.

Ayacucho's Alfredo Mendívil Duarte Airport (AYP) is 4 km (2½ miles) from the city. Fom the Plaza de Armas, you can take a taxi (about S/6) or catch a bus or colectivo, which will deliver you about a half block from the airport. Also, Ayacucho has no central bus station, so for tickets, you have to go to each operator's office individually.

AIRPORT Alfredo Mendívil Duarte Airport. ✉ *Av. del Ejército 950* ☎ *066/312–418.*

BUS Civa. ✉ *Jr. Manco Capac 355* ☎ *01/418–1111* 🌐 *www.civa.com.pe.* **Cruz del Sur.** ✉ *Av. Mariscal Cáceres 1264* ☎ *01/311–5050 in Lima* 🌐 *www.cruzdelsur.com.pe.* **Internacional Palomino.** ✉ *Av. Manco Capac 216* ☎ *01/202–0600* 🌐 *www.grupopalomino.com.pe.* **Ormeño.** ✉ *Jr. Libertad 257* ☎ *064/812–495* 🌐 *www.grupo-ormeno.com.pe.*

VISITOR INFORMATION La Dirección General de Comercio Exterior y Turismo. ✉ *Jr. Asamblea 481* ☎ *066/780–931* 🌐 *www.dirceturayp.com.*

Sights

Casa Museo Joaquín López Antay

MUSEUM | Joaquín López Antay was Ayacucho's most renowned maker of retablos; this lovely museum pays homage to his work. Biographical displays, explications of the retablo- making process, and on-site classes make this a must-visit for art lovers. You can also buy finished works in the museum shop. ✉ *Jr. Cuzco 424* ☎ *956/695-466* 🌐 *www.facebook.com/cmjoaquinlopezantay* *S/4* *Closed Sun.*

Casa Ruiz de Ochoa

BUILDING | Across from the Iglesia Merced, one block from the Plaza de Armas, you'll see the colonial-style Casa Ruiz de Ochoa. The intricate, 18th-century doorway mixes European and indigenous techniques in a style known as Mestizo. Climb up to the second floor for a bird's-eye view of the cobbled patio. ✉ *Jr. Dos de Mayo 210* ☎ *066/314–612* *Free.*

Catedral

RELIGIOUS SITE | The twin bell towers of Ayacucho's catedral, built in 1612 under Bishop Don Cristóbal de Castilla y Zamora, crown the Plaza de Armas. Step inside to view the cathedral's carved altars with gold-leaf designs, a silver tabernacle, and an ornate wooden pulpit, all built in a style mixing baroque and Renaissance elements. Look for the plaque inside the entrance that quotes from Pope John Paul II's speech during his visit in 1985. ✉ *Plaza de Armas* *Free.*

Iglesia Santo Domingo

RELIGIOUS SITE | The 1548 Iglesia Santo Domingo is now a national monument. The first bells ringing out Peru's independence from the Spanish after the Battle of Ayacucho were sounded here. The church's facade features Churrigueresque architectural elements, a style of baroque Spanish architecture popular in the 16th century, while the interior is coated in *pan de oro* (gold leaf). ✉ *Jr. 9 de Diciembre at Jr. Bellido* *Free.*

La Compañía de Jesús

RELIGIOUS SITE | You can't miss the striking red trim on the baroque-style exterior of this 17th-century Jesuit church. The towers were added a century after the main building, which has religious art and a gilt altar. ✉ *Jr. 28 de Julio 128* 🎫 *Free.*

Museo Cáceres

MUSEUM | Located in the Casona Vivanco, a 17th-century mansion, the Museo Cáceres was once the home of Andrés Cáceres, an Ayacucho resident and former Peruvian president best known for his successful guerrilla leadership during the 1879–83 War of the Pacific against Chile. This is one of the city's best-preserved historic buildings, which today houses a mix of military memorabilia and ancient local artifacts, including stone carvings and ceramics. Note the gallery of colonial-style paintings. The **Museo de Arte Religioso Colonial** can also be found within these storied walls, and exhibits antique objects from the city's early days. ✉ *Casona Vivanco, Jr. 28 de Julio 508* ☎ 🌐 *www.facebook.com/pg/MuseoAndresA.Caceres* 🎫 *S/2* 🕒 *Closed Sun.*

Museo de Arqueología y Antropología Hipólito Unánue

MUSEUM | Regional finds from the Moche, Nazca, Ica, Inca, Chanka, Chavín, Chimu, and Huari cultures are on display here, at the Centro Cultural Simón Bolívar. Highlights of the archaeology and anthropology museum include ceremonial costumes, textiles, everyday implements, and even artwork from some of the area's earliest inhabitants. The museum is locally referred to as Museo INC. ✉ *Centro Cultural Simón Bolívar, Av. Independencia 502* ☎ *066/312–056* 🌐 *museos.cultura.pe/museos/museo-hist%c3%b3rico-regional-hip%c3%b3lito-unanue* 🎫 *S/4* 🕒 *Closed Mon.*

Museo de la Memoria

MUSEUM | Designed and run by a women's nonprofit in Ayacucho, this small but moving museum recounts the atrocities of the Sendero Luminoso era from the perspective of the local peasantry. The walls feature folk-art depictions of the violence, as well as photographs of the conflict's victims. The exhibit detailing the tortures and mass graves at the nearby Los Cabitos military base is chilling. ✉ *Prolongación Av. Libertad, cuadra 14* ☎ *066/317–170* 🌐 *anfasep.org.pe/museo-de-la-memoria* 🎫 *S/3* 🕒 *Closed Sun.*

Palacio del Marqués de Mozobamba

HOUSE | Built in 1550 and now part of the cultural center for San Cristobal de Huamanga University, the Palacio del Marqués de Mozobamba is one of the oldest mansions in Peru. The colonial-era, baroque-style architecture includes *portales* (stone arches) in front and a monkey-shaped stone fountain in the courtyard. ■ **TIP→ On the left side as you enter, you'll see the remains of Inca stone walls discovered during restorations in 2003.** ✉ *Portal Unión 37, Plaza de Armas* 🎫 *Free.*

Prefectura

HOUSE | Also known as the Boza and Solís House, the Prefectura is tucked into a two-story, 1748 *casona histórica* (historic mansion). Local independence-era heroine María Prado de Bellido was held prisoner in the Prefectura's patio room until her execution by firing squad in 1822. The balcony opens out onto a lovely view of the Plaza de Armas. ✉ *Portal Constitución 15* 🎫 *Free* 🕒 *Closed Sun.*

★ Ruinas Huari

ARCHAEOLOGICAL SITE | Recent excavations at this massive archaeological site have uncovered multilevel underground galleries, burial chambers, circular plazas, arched portals, and other architectural wonders. Together they make this capital city of the Huari culture one of the most impressive non-Inca ruins in the Peruvian sierra. The Huari flourished from around 700 to 1100 AD, and wandering the quiet alleys of this 2,023-hectare (5,000-acre) complex gives you a sense of how its 60,000 residents lived, worshipped, and died. Especially noteworthy are the temples and communal tombs. There's a small museum on

Did You Know?

Indigenous cultures from the Ayacucho region have been perfecting their textile skills for some 3,000 years.

site with mummies and ceramics, as well as a lounge to rest in after roaming the cactus-covered grounds. The best way to visit is to take a tour from a travel agency in town for S/30, as taxis and colectivos to the site are sporadic and hard to figure out. ✉ *Quinua Hwy.* ⊕ *22 km (14 miles) northeast of Ayacucho* ☎ *066/312–056* 🎫 *S/3* ⏲ *Museum closed Mon.*

★ Vilcashuamán and Intihuatana

ARCHAEOLOGICAL SITE | Four long hours south of Ayacucho on winding, unpaved roads is the former Inca provincial capital of Vilcashuamán, set where the north–south Inca highway crossed the east–west trade road from Cusco to the Pacific. You can still see the Templo del Sol y de la Luna and a five-tiered platform, known as the Ushnu, crowned by an Inca throne and surrounded by stepped fields once farmed by Inca peasants. An hour's walk from Vilcashuamán (or a half-hour's walk south past the main road from Ayacucho) is the Intihuatana, where Inca ruins include a palace and tower beside a lagoon. Former Inca baths, a Sun temple, and a sacrificial altar can also be seen on the grounds. Check out the unusual, 13-angled boulder, one of the odd building rocks that are an Inca hallmark. Ayacucho travel agencies can organize tours of both sites (S/65), or you can catch a bus or colectivo for S/15–S/20. ■ **TIP→ Ask around to confirm where these public transport options are leaving from, as pickup points change frequently.** ✉ *Km 118, Vilcashuamán Hwy.* 🎫 *S/5.*

Restaurants

Outside of a few international restaurants catering to visitors, Ayacucho stands by its Andean specialties. The city is famous for its filling, flavorful puca picante, served with rice and topped with a parsley sprig. ■ **TIP→ The city's favorite drink is the hot, creamy, pisco-spiked ponche (flavored with milk, cinnamon, cloves, sesame, peanuts, walnuts, and sugar).** The best time to sample this popular concoction is during Semana Santa. In the first week of November, ayacuchanos are busy baking sweet breads shaped like *caballos* (horses) and *guaguas* (babies) to place in baskets for the spirits at the family grave sites. You'll find inexpensive restaurants where you can grab a cheap *almuerzo* (lunch) along Jirón San Martín. Many restaurants are closed Sunday morning.

Carbon y Vino

$ | **PERUVIAN** | Grilled meats and local fare like puca picante are the stars at this popular lunchtime spot, housed in a pretty old mansion with both front and back patios. During the week, the three-course fixed-price lunch is a steal at S/10. **Known for:** grilled entrées; great fixed-price lunches; tasty plates with cuy. 💲 *Average main: S/20* ✉ *Jr. Bellido 593* ☎ *948/275–353* 🌐 *www.facebook.com/carbonyvinoayacucho* ⏲ *No dinner* 💳 *No credit cards.*

★ Casa Grill

$$ | **STEAKHOUSE** | Dining in this charmingly refitted family home is like dining at Grandpa's house—if Grandpa were an internationally trained grill expert who served only the most exquisite cuts of meat. That's because the steaks, fire-cooked pork, and whole salmon at the sumptuous *parrilla* (grill) are the best in Ayacucho, with delicious sauces to boot. **Known for:** best grilled meat in the Central Sierra; warm hospitality; generous portions. 💲 *Average main: S/35* ✉ *Jr. Tres Máscaras 390* ☎ *966/137–090* 🌐 *www.facebook.com/Casagrillrestobar* ⏲ *Closed Mon.–Wed.* 💳 *No credit cards.*

La Casona

$ | **PERUVIAN** | Dining in this Spanish-style home is like attending an intimate party in a fine hacienda. The sun bathes the leafy courtyard during lunch, while the clientele tucks into the best of ayacuchano cooking, including heaping plates of puca picante and fried trout. **Known**

for: bargain lunch special; hearty local stews; relaxed, tree-shaded atmosphere. *Average main: S/20 Jr. Bellido 463 066/312–733 www.facebook.com/LaCasonaRestaurantTuristico.*

Pizzería Italiana

$ | **ITALIAN** | On cold Andean nights, this wood-oven pizzeria will have you hugging yourself in the glow of its crackling fires. There's no décor to speak of, just delicious, belly-warming pizzas and pastas in a cheerful communal setting of wooden benches and stone walls. **Known for:** friendly owners; best pizzas in town; surprisingly good pastas. *Average main: S/20 Jr. Bellido 492 066/317–574.*

ViaVia Café

$ | **PERUVIAN** | Perched above the Plaza de Armas, this wood-paneled restaurant offers an ample menu that includes both highlands specialties and backpacker favorites. Enjoy a relaxed breakfast in the morning or an artisanal ice cream in the afternoon while taking in the view of the cathedral from the expansive terrace. **Known for:** great views; dessert; international flair. *Average main: S/25 Portal Constitución 4, Plaza de Armas 066/312–834 viavia-ayacucho.negocio.site.*

Hotels

★ Hotel La Crillonesa

$ | **B&B/INN** | With a lovely rooftop terrace offering panoramic views of the city and clean, comfy rooms, this budget inn is one of the best values in the Peruvian sierra. **Pros:** spectacular views from the terrace; great value; wonderful staff. **Cons:** adjoining street is noisy; some rooms are rather small; bells from the nearby church start their tolling early. *Rooms from: S/40 Cl. Nazareno 165 066/312–350 hotelcrillonesa.com 36 rooms No meals.*

Hotel Plaza Ayacucho

$ | **HOTEL** | The city's most expensive hotel, in a gracious colonial building partly overlooking the Plaza de Armas, has spacious gardens and opulent sitting areas that belie the modest rooms with worn carpet and nicked modern furnishings. **Pros:** some rooms overlook Plaza de Armas; the place to stay for Semana Santa; perfect location. **Cons:** stuffy atmosphere; some rooms need a makeover; can be noisy if there's a fiesta outside. *Rooms from: S/200 Jr. 9 de Diciembre 184 066/312–202, 066/312–314 www.dmhoteles.pe 69 rooms Free breakfast.*

Hotel San Francisco de Paula

$ | **HOTEL** | At this rambling Spanish mansion, folk art, textiles, and local crafts lend charm to a building that dates back centuries. **Pros:** nice views of city and hills; regional art everywhere; rooftop restaurant. **Cons:** plain rooms; poor lighting; no elevator. *Rooms from: S/130 Jr. Callao 290 066/312–353 www.hotelsanfranciscodepaula.com 41 rooms Free breakfast.*

Hotel Santa María

$ | **HOTEL** | Just three blocks from the Plaza de Armas, the Santa María is a quiet, tastefully appointed hotel with brightly colored textiles and minimalist furnishings. **Pros:** colorful decor; helpful staff; good value for the price. **Cons:** rooms are a bit gloomy; Wi-Fi can be spotty; breakfast is rudimentary. *Rooms from: S/180 Jr. Arequipa 320 066/314–988 santamariahotelayacucho.com 22 rooms Free breakfast.*

Hotel Santa Rosa

$ | **HOTEL** | The rooms in this pleasant little hotel, located one block from the Plaza de Armas, have a mix of antiques, handmade fabrics, and contemporary furnishings, plus modern amenities like TV and Wi-Fi. **Pros:** beautiful courtyard; good restaurant; local charm with a modern feel. **Cons:** room sizes vary; restaurant is closed at night; some beds need upgrading. *Rooms from: S/170* *Jr. Lima 166* *066/312–083* *www.facebook.com/hotelsantarosaayacucho* *40 rooms* *Free breakfast.*

ViaVia Hotel

$ | **HOTEL** | This hotel and its eponymous café sit in a restored colonial building on the plaza and offer some of the city's best, most eclectic lodging. **Pros:** excellent location; views of the plaza; cheery communal atmosphere. **Cons:** some rooms are noisy; amenities need updating; in some rooms, bathroom is separated from the main area only by a partition. *Rooms from: S/200* *Portal Constitución 4, Plaza de Armas* *066/312–834* *viavia-ayacucho.negocio.site* *20 rooms* *Free breakfast.*

Nightlife

Taberna Magía Negra

BARS/PUBS | Admire the local art on the walls and dozens of upside-down black umbrellas on the ceiling while grabbing a drink or pizza at the "black magic" pub. This is a good spot for craft-beer lovers. *Jr. Bellido 349* *066/287–644.*

Shopping

Ayacucho is home to many of Peru's best artists, who you can often visit at work in their neighborhood shops or galleries. Look for retablos, the multitiered, three-dimensional displays of plaster characters in scenes of the city's famed religious processions and historic battles. The busy Mercado Domingo (Sunday Market) in Huanta, an hour north, is fun to visit.

HANDICRAFTS

★ Casa del Retablo

ART GALLERIES | If you think Ayacucho's retablos are incredible, just wait until you see the precision that goes into their making. Maestro Silvestre Ataucusi Flores invites you into his workshop, after which you can do a little mask-painting yourself, or browse among his stunning depictions of Carnavals, musical instruments, and bullfights. A 15-minute taxi ride from the Plaza de Armas gets you here. *Los Artesanos Mz. F, Lote 1* *999/025–495* *casadelretablo.mystrikingly.com.*

Mercado Artesanal Shosaku Nagase

CRAFTS | The widest selection of handicrafts in Ayacucho, from retablos *retablos* to sweaters, can be found at Mercado Artesanal Shosaku Nagase, about a kilometer north of the city center near the big sports complex. *Plazoleta El Arco, Av. Maravillas 101* *975/714–234.*

Santa Ana

TEXTILES/SEWING | The Santa Ana neighborhood is dotted with some of Peru's finest workshops. These local artists and their galleries are clustered around the Plazoleta Santa Ana, and most are happy to share their knowledge and even their life stories with visitors. In particular, look for complex *tejidos* (textiles), which have elaborate, and often pre-Hispanic, motifs that can take more than half a year to design and weave. Many artists painstakingly research their designs, pulling abstract elements from Huari ceremonial ponchos. These creations, made of natural fibers and dyes, can cost US$400 or more for high-quality work. Standouts include the textile workshops of Alejandro Gallardo (Plaza Santa Ana 105) and Edwin Sulca Lagos (Plaza Santa Ana 82), who also makes carpets. And don't miss the beautiful alabaster (huamanga) carvings of José Gálvez. *Plaza Santa Ana.*

Chapter 10

10

THE NORTH COAST AND NORTHERN HIGHLANDS

Updated by
Mike Gasparovic

Sights
★★★★★

Restaurants
★★★★☆

Hotels
★★★★☆

Shopping
★★★☆☆

Nightlife
★★☆☆☆

WELCOME TO THE NORTH COAST AND NORTHERN HIGHLANDS

TOP REASONS TO GO

★ **The Ancient World:** Along the coast, Moche pyramids and undulating Chimú parapets date as far back as the time of Christ. In the highlands are Wari sites, as well as Kuélap, a stunning complex built by the Chachapoyans a thousand years before Machu Picchu.

★ **Superb Eating:** The North Coast offers one of Peru's richest regional cuisines. Abundant shellfish and extensive pre-Columbian influences make for some of the country's most delectable dishes.

★ **Outdoor Adventure:** The Northern Highlands provide plenty of trekking, climbing, and rafting, especially around Huaraz, home of the highest mountains outside the Himalayas.

★ **Colonial Architecture:** Trujillo, on the coast, and Cajamarca, in the highlands, are the two top spots for colonial architecture.

★ **Beaches:** The extreme North Coast offers year-round sun, white-sand beaches, and a relaxed, tropical atmosphere.

1 **Barranca.** A sleepy coastal town and site of a massive Chimú fortress.

2 **Casma.** This hamlet's pre-Columbian ruins include some of the oldest carvings in Peru.

3 **Playa Tortugas.** Fishing boats, a deep semicircular bay, and ramshackle *cebicherías.*

4 **Trujillo.** Find gorgeous colonial architecture and some of South America's best food.

5 **Huanchaco.** Loud and vibrant, this beachside village offers great seafood and sunsets.

6 **Magdalena de Cao.** The *huacas* (sacred sites) at this coastal town are some of the South American archaeological circuit's hottest properties.

7 **Sipán.** The site of the 20th century's biggest archaeological finds.

8 **Chiclayo.** Come for the awesome food and the mind-blowing archaeological sites.

9 **Lambayeque.** Home to Peru's finest archaeological museum.

10 **Ferreñafe.** A well-curated gallery is the top draw here.

11 **Piura.** A popular stop en route to the *balnearios* (beach villages) farther north.

12 **Máncora.** This seaside resort has world-class surfing and some of Peru's poshest hotels.

13 **Punta Sal.** More *tranquilo* than Máncora, this beach town is one of Peru's top vacation spots.

14 **Tumbes.** The point for the border crossing into Ecuador.

15 **Huaraz.** The perfect base for trekking and mountain-climbing expeditions.

16 **Chavín de Huántar.** A 3,000-year-old complex with a malevolently grinning idol.

17 **Yungay.** This tragic town was the site of one of Peru's great cataclysms.

18 **Lagunas de Llanganuco.** Luminous pools of pure turquoise.

19 **Caraz.** A non-touristy access point for some of the area's stunning mountain scenery.

20 **Cajamarca.** One of the prettiest, least-visited spots in Peru.

21 **Chachapoyas.** Perched between the Andes and the Amazon, this is a perfect base for exploring Kuélap.

22 **Kuélap.** Peru's untouristed "Machu Picchu 2.0."

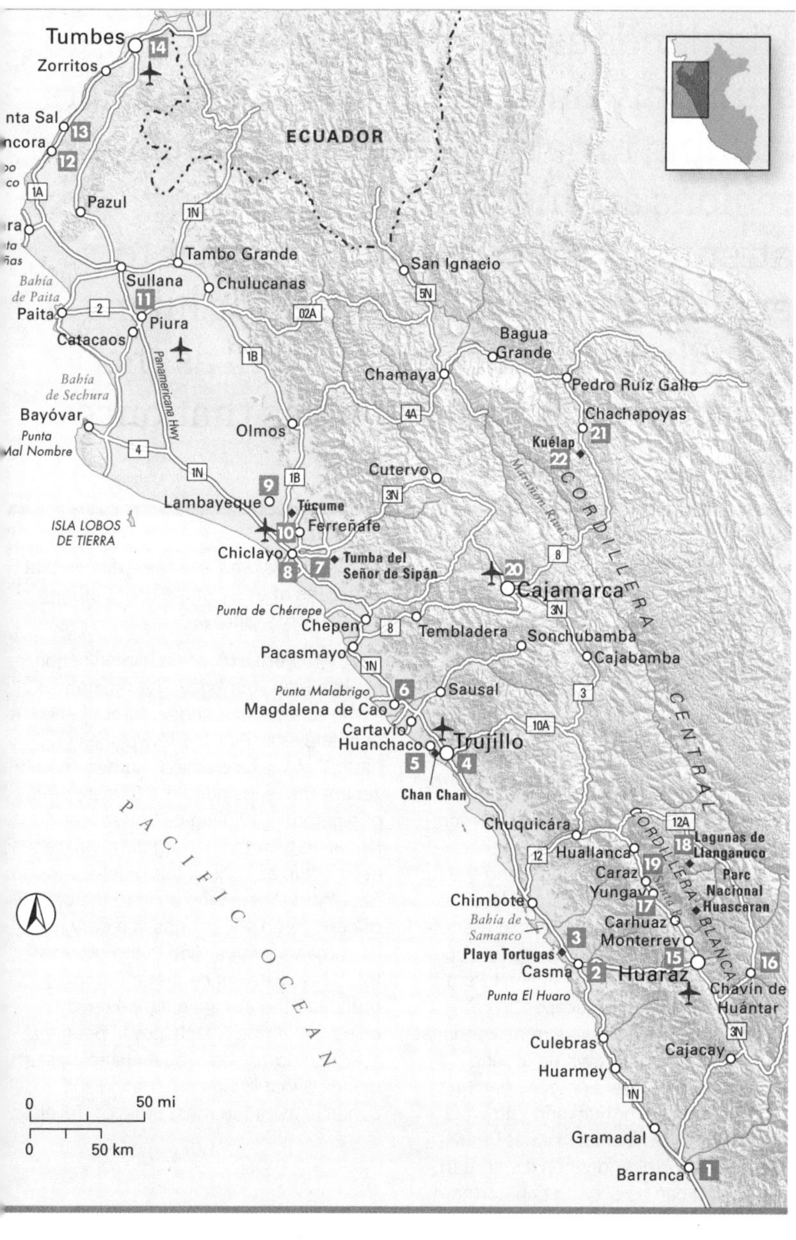
Tumbes
Zorritos
ECUADOR
Pazul
Tambo Grande
Sullana
Chulucanas
San Ignacio
Bahía de Paita
Paita
Piura
Catacaos
Panamericana Hwy
Bagua Grande
Chamaya
Pedro Ruíz Gallo
Bahía de Sechura
Bayóvar
Punta Mal Nombre
Olmos
Chachapoyas
Kuélap
Cutervo
Lambayeque
Túcume
ISLA LOBOS DE TIERRA
Ferreñafe
Marañon River
CORDILLERA
Chiclayo
Tumba del Señor de Sipán
Cajamarca
Punta de Chérrepe
Chepen
Tembladera
Sonchubamba
Pacasmayo
Cajabamba
Punta Malabrigo
Sausal
Magdalena de Cao
CENTRAL
Cartavio
Huanchaco
Trujillo
Chan Chan
PACIFIC OCEAN
Chuquicára
Huallanca
Lagunas de Llanganuco
Caraz
Yungay
Parc Nacional Huascaran
CORDILLERA BLANCA
Santa R.
Chimbote
Bahía de Samanco
Carhuaz
Monterrey
Playa Tortugas
Casma
Huaraz
Punta El Huaro
Chavín de Huántar
Culebras
Cajacay
Huarmey
Gramadal
Barranca
0 50 mi
0 50 km

Glaciers swathed in mist, virgin tracts of forest, endless stretches of lunar desert: Peru's North Coast and Northern Highlands are as diverse as they are stunning. Once passed over by travelers rushing to get to Cusco, these enchanted regions are increasingly attracting attention from adventurers eager to explore their opportunities for hiking, trekking, and surfing—as well as the mysterious ancient cultures that once flourished here.

Nature takes pride of place in northern Peru. Here you'll find 6,000-meter (19,700-foot) peaks streaked with snow in the Cordillera Blanca, as well as sands guarding hidden tombs along the coast. To the east, ancient cloud forests back up onto the jungles of the Amazon, while in the valleys of the northern sierra, emerald hills stand luminous in the blue haze.

All this means northern Peru is a prime place for outdoor activities. Whether you're on muleback, edging along the turquoise lakes of the Callejón de Huaylas, or a surf god riding the swells at Máncora, you'll find yourself fumbling for superlatives as you pit yourself against Peru's northern land- and seascapes. What's more, in recent years an extensive tourist infrastructure has grown up around these pastimes. Renting gear, finding a mountain lodge, or hunkering down at a coastal resort is a snap in what Peruvians call *el norte*. And when it's time to refuel, you can do so with rich northern *secos* (stews) and *cebiches*, dishes that Peruvians of every stripe count among the country's glories.

Northern Peru excites your imagination no less than your body. The region was home to a bewildering number of ancient peoples, as one of the few places on earth that was a cradle of human civilization. These included the Chavín, who originated a terrifying cult of a fanged jaguar-deity in the underground passages at Huántar, as well as the Moche, a race of brilliant artists who drained the blood of conquered adversaries in a gory ritual of human sacrifice. Add in the greatest tomb discovery since that of Tutankhamun, and the stunning, little-known cloud city of the Chachapoyas people at Kuélap, and you have an archaeologist's paradise that brings out the Indiana Jones in even the most timid of travelers.

MAJOR REGIONS

The North Coast. Desert, desert, and more desert: this is the face Peru's northern coast presents to the uninitiated. Venture into that sandy barrenness, however, and you'll discover a region that's incredibly fertile in culture, from 2,000-year-old pyramids to ultramodern beach resorts, all fed by a culinary tradition many consider to be the country's best.

If you're at all archaeologically minded, northern Peru will have you mesmerized upon arrival. That's because it's one of only six places on the planet where civilization arose, and its deserts are littered with ruins to prove it. The complex cultures that developed here—the Moche, Chimú, and Huari, among others—were not only superb artists. They also practiced terrifying rituals of human sacrifice and shamanism that are abundantly on display at the pyramids and tombs in Trujillo and Chiclayo. Meanwhile, the so-called *norte chico* region north of Lima is the site of the oldest cities in the Americas.

Peru's North Coast is more than just history. After your Tomb Raider–style adventures, relax and cool off on the region's stunning beaches, where blazing white sands, first-class resorts, and rides in reed-woven canoes are all standard. As you watch the sun sink over the Pacific, enjoy some of the world's best seafood, in a regional cuisine that extends back to pre-Hispanic times.

Huaraz and the Cordillera Blanca. The Cordillera Blanca is one of the world's great mountain ranges. The soaring, glaciated peaks strut more than 6,000 meters (19,700 feet) above sea level; only Asia's mountain ranges are higher. Glaciers also carve their lonely way into the green of the Río Santa valley, forming streams, giant gorges, and gray-green alpine lagoons. Meanwhile, on the western side of the valley is the Cordillera Negra. Less impressive than the Cordillera Blanca, its steep mountains have no permanent glaciers and are verdantly, ruggedly scenic. A drive along the paved stretch of road through the valley offers heart-stopping views of both ranges. You'll also find an abundance of flora and fauna in the narrow gorges that snake down from the high mountains. Deer, *vizcacha* (rodents resembling rabbits, without the long ears), vicuñas, pumas, bears, and condors are among the area's inhabitants. And don't overlook the 10-meter-tall (32-foot) *Puya raimondii*, the world's largest bromeliad, whose spiked flower recalls that of a century plant.

The valley between the Cordillera Blanca and the Cordillera Negra is often called the Callejón de Huaylas, after the town of Huaylas at its northern end. **■ TIP→ This area is possibly the most important climbing and trekking destination in South America.** From here, arrange to go white-water rafting, head out on a 10-day trek through the wilderness, or stay closer to home—one-day excursions can take you to the 3,000-year-old ruins at Chavín de Huántar, as well as to local hot springs, a nearby glacier, and an alpine lagoon. Climbers come during the dry season to test their iron on the more than 40 peaks in the area that exceed 6,000 meters (19,700 feet). The 6,768-meter (22,200-foot) summit of Huascarán is the highest in Peru and is clearly visible from Huaraz on sunny days. To the south of Huaraz, the remote and beautiful Cordillera Huayhuash offers numerous trekking and climbing excursions as well. Some say it's even more impressive than the Cordillera Blanca.

The Northern Highlands. The green valleys and mountaintops that make up the Northern Highlands are some of the area's prime attractions, as is the abundance of history in the region. Lamentably, however, few non-Peruvian travelers venture here, since it's hard to reach and far from the more popular destinations of Cusco, Puno, and Machu Picchu.

Intrepid souls who do go will find themselves amply rewarded. ■ **TIP→ The pre-Inca fortress of Kuélap, near Chachapoyas, is one of the region's best-preserved ruins.** Moreover, the region's largest town, Cajamarca, is a gem of colonial architecture and was the site of one of history's quickest and wiliest military victories, the capture and defeat of the Inca Atahualpa by the Spanish in 1532. The resulting clash of cultures set the course of Latin American history for the next 500 years. In and around Cajamarca you'll also find a handful of Inca and pre-Inca sites, as well as chances for horseback riding and hiking in the gently rolling hills.

Planning

When to Go

The weather along the North Coast is usually pleasant, although a strong sun causes temperatures to climb from November to May. The Northern Highlands weather is more capricious—rainy season is November to early May, and it's drier from mid-May to mid-September. September and October have fairly good weather, but occasional storms can frighten off would-be mountaineers.

Planning Your Time

EXPLORING ANCIENT CIVILIZATIONS

If seeing the important archaeological sites and museums is your main priority, start your journey in Trujillo with the important Moche pyramids of the Huaca de la Luna and Huaca del Sol, as well as Chan Chan, built by the Chimú people (though be sure to take at least a day to walk around and enjoy the spectacular colonial architecture). From here, head north to Chiclayo and peer into the Tomb of Sipán, check out the pyramids at Túcume, and explore world-class historical museums. If you can extend your trip beyond a week, preferably another four to five days, take the bus from Chiclayo to Chachapoyas and visit Kuélap, which rivals Machu Picchu in magnificence and was built more than a thousand years before.

EXPLORING THE OUTDOORS

If you want to see the spectacular mountains of the Northern Highlands, head up (and up and up) to the mountain town of Huaraz. Drink lots of water, and allow a day or so to acclimatize to the altitude, taking in the local sights and hot springs. From there, make a three-day trek around the Cordillera Blanca. If you can extend your trip past a week, head to Trujillo to enjoy the architecture and ruins.

REST AND RELAXATION

If you want to take a week to relax, fly from Lima to Piura, walk around the city, eat in one of the excellent restaurants, and sleep in one of the first-rate hotels. After a leisurely breakfast at your hotel (almost always included in the price of your room), head to Máncora or Punta Sal for a few days. Regardless of where you stay, you'll be able to lie back on the beach or poolside, and—if you're inspired to get out of your beach chair—go on a fishing trip, learn to surf, or try the even more adventurous kitesurfing.

Getting Here and Around

AIR

The easiest way to get around is by plane. You'll definitely want to fly to destinations like Piura, Tumbes, and Cajamarca. LATAM (⊕ *www.lan.com*), Star Perú (⊕ *www.avianca.com*), and Viva Air Perú (⊕ *www.peruvian.pe*) fly to several cities in the region.

BUS

Bus service throughout the region is generally quite good. Oltursa (☎ *01/708–5000* ⊕ *www.oltursa.pe*) runs all the way up the coast. Other reputable companies for the coastal communities include Cruz del Sur (☎ *01/311–5050 in Lima* 🌐 *www.cruzdelsur.com.pe*), CIVA (☎ *01/418–1111 in Lima* 🌐 *www.civa.com.pe*), and Transportes Chiclayo (☎ *074/607–032 in Chiclayo* 🌐 *www.transporteschiclayo.com*). For the highlands, Móvil (🌐 *www.movilbus.pe*) is a good choice. Whenever possible, pay for a *bus-cama* or *semi-cama,* which gets you an enormous seat that fully reclines and attendant service that includes at least one meal and a movie. Some buses, such as CIVA's Excluciva buses, have Wi-Fi.

CAR

Driving can be a challenge—locals rarely obey rules of the road—but a car is one of the best ways to explore the region. The Pan-American Highway serves the coast. From there, take Highway 109 to Huaraz and Highway 8 to Cajamarca. Small, reputable, rental-car agencies can be found in Trujillo, Chiclayo, Piura, and Huaraz. Think twice before driving to archaeological sites; some are hard to find, and it's easy to get lost on the unmarked roads. Consider hiring a driver or taking a tour. Roads in the Northern Highlands are always in some degree of disrepair.

TAXI

Taxi rides in town centers should cost around S/5 to S/10; rates go up at night. A longer ride to the suburbs or town environs costs S/8 to S/25. Negotiate the price before you head off. Taxis hire out their services for specific places, with costs of S/20 and up, depending on the distance, or around S/300 for the entire day.

Health and Safety

Use purified water for drinking and brushing your teeth. If you're out trekking, bring an extra bottle with you. Also, eat foods that have been thoroughly cooked or boiled. If vegetables or fruit are raw, be sure they're peeled. In the highlands, especially Huaraz, relax and take the time to acclimatize for a few days, drinking lots of water to avoid dehydration and altitude sickness.

In the big cities on the coast, be on your guard and take simple precautions, such as asking the concierge at the hotel to get you a taxi and carrying only the cash you need. In small coastal towns or in the highlands, things are more secure, but be aware of your belongings at all times.

Restaurants

The North Coast has excellent seafood, whereas simpler, but equally delicious, meat-and-rice dishes are more common in the highlands. Some of the fancier restaurants in Trujillo and Chiclayo expect you to dress up for dinner, but most spots along the coast are quite casual. Depending on the restaurant, the bill may include a 10% service charge; if not, a 10% tip is appropriate. Throughout the region, *almuerzo* (lunch) is the most important meal of the day and is usually eaten between 12 and 3 pm. *Cena* (dinner) is normally a lighter meal, but always check with restaurants before going out at night: many only serve lunch.

Hotels

Cities along the North Coast, especially Trujillo and Chiclayo, have a wide range of lodgings, including large business hotels and converted colonial mansions. The latter, usually called *casonas,* offer personalized service not found in the larger hotels. In smaller towns, such as Yungay and Caraz, there are no luxury lodgings, but you'll have no problem finding a clean and comfortable room. The highlands have excellent lodges with horse stables and hot springs; you can also find family-run inns with basic rooms. Assume that hotels do not have air-conditioning unless otherwise indicated.

Finding a hotel room throughout the coastal and highlands areas ought to be painless throughout the year, although coastal resorts like Máncora and Punta Sal are often jammed in summer and during holiday weeks. Sports enthusiasts head to Huaraz and Cajamarca in summer, so make reservations early. Plan at least two months in advance if you want to travel during Easter week, *fiestas patrias* (Peruvian Independence Day, the week of July 28), or Christmas, when Peruvians take their holidays. *Hotel reviews have been shortened. For full information, visit Fodors.com.*

WHAT IT COSTS in Nuevo Soles			
$	$$	$$$	$$$$
RESTAURANTS			
under S/35	S/35–S/50	S/51–S/65	over S/65
HOTELS			
under S/250	S/250–S/500	S/501–S/800	over S/800

Tours

Mayte Tours offer excellent tours to the ruins around Trujillo. Clara Bravo and Michael White are great guides for Trujillo, and they also lead trips farther afield. Moche Tours is one of Chiclayo's best tour companies for trips to the tomb of El Señor de Sipán.

There are many tour companies in Huaraz; locally owned Eco Ice Tours is among the best, arranging customized trekking and mountain-climbing expeditions. Clarín Tours is said to be one of Cajamarca's best.

In Chachapoyas, contact Vilaya Tours. The company arranges tours to Kuélap, as well as to the remote ruins of Gran Vilaya, which requires a 31-km (19-mile) hike, and to the Pueblo de Los Muertos, which requires a 23-km (14-mile) hike.

Canechi Tours
EXCURSIONS | Aside from beach trips to Mancora and Punta Sal, Canechi arranges day trips around Piura and private transportation around the region. ✉ *Av. Luis Montero 490, Piura* ☎ *073/344–602* 🌐 *www.facebook.com/CANECHI.TOURS.SAC* 🎫 *From S/50.*

Clara Bravo and Michael White
GUIDED TOURS | Peruvian-born Clara and British-born Michael are two of Trujillo's most reputable guides and are highly recommended. They lead tours to all of the region's major archaeological attractions and take tourists on extended circuits. ✉ *Jr. Cahuide 495, Trujillo* ☎ *949/662–710* 🌐 *trujilloperu.xanga.com* 🎫 *From S/25.*

Clarín Tours
GUIDED TOURS | With offices in Lima and Cajamarca, Clarín Tours specializes in multiday package deals that include transportation, hotels, and tours in northern Peru, particularly in Cajamarca. ✉ *Jr. Del Batán 165, Cajamarca* ☎ *979/955–479* 🌐 *www.clarintours.com* 🎫 *From S/180.*

Eco Ice Tours
ECOTOURISM | This excellent Peruvian-owned company has a full range of adventure and ecotours of the Central Sierra. Choose from day hikes, trekking, or mountaineering—or design your own. ✉ *Augustín Mejía 100, Huaraz* ☎ *958/032–249* 🌐 *www.ecoice-peru.com.*

Go2Andes
ADVENTURE TOURS | This hiking and trekking operator runs well-prepared trips into the Cordillera Huayhuash and Cordillera Blanca, including technical climbs to Alpamayo and other peaks. ✉ *Psje. Pacífico 204, Nueva Florida, Huaraz* ☎ *043/428–941* 🌐 *go2andes.com* 🎫 *From S/70.*

Mayte Tours
SPECIAL-INTEREST | Specializing in organized tours to difficult-to-reach destinations, such as Cerros de Amotape and Santuario Los Manglares, Mayte will also

set up secure transportation to Guayaquil and other parts of Ecuador. ✉ *Jr. Bolognesi 196, Tumbes* ☎ *072/523–219* 🌐 *maytetours.com* 🎫 *From S/80.*

Moche Tours

GUIDED TOURS | This is Chiclayo's largest operator, with trips to most archaeological and cultural attractions in the region, including standard day trips and excursions to less-visited destinations like Ferreñafe for the Museo Nacional de Sicán and the Chaparrí bear reserve. ✉ *Cl. 7 de Enero 638, Chiclayo* ☎ *074/232–184* 🌐 *www.mochetourschiclayo.com.pe* 🎫 *From S/65.*

North Shore Expeditions

BOAT TOURS | Whale-watching (from June to October) and deep-sea sport-fishing trips off the Pacific coast are available through this operator. ✉ *Km 1,186, Panamericana Norte, Tumbes* ☎ *962/397–255* 🌐 *www.northshore.pe* 🎫 *From S/200.*

Vilaya Tours

GUIDED TOURS | With 20 years' experience, Chachapoyas's most reputable operator runs private and customized tours to Kuélap, the sarcophagi of Karajia, the Gocta waterfall, and the Mummy Museum of Leymebamba. ✉ *Jr. La Merced 1096, Chachapoyas* ☎ *941/708–798* 🌐 *www.facebook.com/vilaya.tours.chachapoyas* 🎫 *From S/50.*

Barranca

200 km (124 miles) northwest of Lima on the Pan-American Hwy.

A nondescript town with little to visit except a large Chimú temple nearby and one iconic restaurant, this is a stop for those who either are determined to see every archaeological site in Peru or who do not have time to go to Trujillo or Chiclayo but would like to see some northern ruins.

GETTING HERE AND AROUND

To get to Barranca, head north from Lima on the Panamericana (Pan-American Highway) through the bleak, empty coastal desert and past several dusty villages.

Sights

Paramonga

ARCHAEOLOGICAL SITE | With its seven defensive walls, the gigantic pyramid at Paramonga is worth a look. Nicknamed "the fortress" for its citadel-like ramparts, it may have only been a ritual center for the Chimú people back in the 13th century. In any case, it was already in ruins when the Spanish arrived in Peru in 1532. A small museum has interesting displays on Chimú culture. The archaeological site sits just off the Pan-American Highway, about 3 km (2 miles) north of the turnoff for Huaraz. For a few soles you can take a taxi to the ruins from the nearby town of Barranca. ✉ *Pan-American Hwy.* 🎫 *S/10.*

Restaurants

Restaurante Tato

$ | **SEAFOOD** | Overlooking the beach, Tato's is something of a cult restaurant—a rustic eatery known for seafood, from cebiches to fried calamari. The most famous dish on the menu is the *tacu tacu relleno de mariscos* (refried rice and beans stuffed with shellfish). **Known for:** hearty portions; fresh seafood; beach views. $ *Average main: S/30* ✉ *Av. Chorrillos 383* ☎ *01/235–2562* 🌐 *www.restauranttato.com* ⊗ *No dinner.*

Hotels

Hotel Chavín

$ | **HOTEL** | **FAMILY** | The best deal in Barranca, this full-service hotel—in a plain, concrete, six-story building—has wood-floored rooms (ask for one in the rear if noise is a concern) and a decent restaurant serving criollo food.

Pros: extensive facilities for a low price; poolside bar; good Peruvian restaurant on the premises. **Cons:** on a busy main road; outdated decor; on-site karaoke can be noisy. $ *Rooms from: S/190* ✉ *Jr. Gálvez 222* ☎ *01/235–2253* 🌐 *www.hotelchavin.com.pe* 🛏 *72 rooms* 🍴 *No meals.*

Casma

182 km (113 miles) north of Barranca.

Once known as the "City of Eternal Sun," Casma, like Lima, is now subject to cloudy winters and sunny summers. With its leafy Plaza de Armas and a number of pleasant parks, however, it makes the best base for visiting the nearby ruins. If you're not into the archaeology thing, you might want to omit Casma from your itinerary.

GETTING HERE AND AROUND

Casma lies about six hours north of Lima and just over two hours from Barranca. Cruz del Sur buses stop here on their Lima–Trujillo routes. Once in town, mototaxis are the best way to get around.

Sights

Pañamarca

ARCHAEOLOGICAL SITE | Several ruins can be found near the town of Casma, but the heavily weathered Mochica city of Pañamarca is the one to see after Sechín. Located 10 km (6 miles) from the Pan-American Highway on the road leading to Nepeña, Pañamarca has some interesting murals. If they're not visible right away, ask a guard to show you, as they are often closed off. The site was later occupied by the Incas. **■ TIP→ A taxi will take you to the ruins for about S/20 an hour; negotiate the price before you leave.** ✉ *Casma* 🎫 *S/6, includes admission to Sechín.*

Sechín

ARCHAEOLOGICAL SITE | The origins of Sechín, one of the country's oldest archaeological sites, remain a mystery. It's not clear what culture built this coastal temple around 1600 BC, but the bas-relief carvings ringing the main sanctuary, some up to 4 meters (13 feet) high, graphically depict triumphant warriors and their conquered, often beheaded enemies. Some researchers have even speculated that this was a center for anatomical study, due to the sheer number of detached body parts engraved on the rocks. The site was first excavated in 1937 by the archaeologist J.C. Tello. It has since suffered from looters and natural disasters. Archaeologists are still excavating here, so access to the central plaza is not permitted. **■ TIP→ A trail leading up a neighboring hill provides good views of the temple complex and the surrounding valley.** A small museum has a good collection of Chavín ceramics and a mummy that was found near Trujillo. To get to the ruins, head southeast from Casma along the Pan-American Highway for about 3 km (2 miles), turning east onto a paved road leading to Huaraz. The ruins sit about 2 km (1¼ miles) past the turnoff. ✉ *Casma* 🎫 *S/6, includes admission to Pañamarca.*

Restaurants

El Tío Sam

$ | SEAFOOD | The best restaurant in Casma, this local favorite serves just about every type of seafood imaginable. The *arroz chaufa con mariscos* (shellfish with Chinese-style fried rice) is especially good, but if you're not in the mood for seafood, try the *cebiche de pato*. This isn't traditional cebiche, but cooked duck, served with rice, yucca, and beans. **Known for:** home-style seafood dishes; hearty meat plates; rustic atmosphere. $ *Average main: S/25* ✉ *Av. Huarmey 138* ☎ *043/580–659* ⏲ *Closed weekends.*

El Farol

$ | **HOTEL** | You'll find a respite from the dusty streets at this pleasant hotel surrounded by gardens. **Pros:** quiet, safe complex is surrounded by walls; good, reasonably priced restaurant; rooms are well above average for Casma. **Cons:** service requires patience; decor could use some sprucing up; some common areas look old. *Rooms from: S/120* *Av. Túpac Amarú 450* *043/411–064* *www.facebook.com/ElFarolCasma* *28 rooms* *No meals.*

Playa Tortugas

20 km (12 miles) north of Casma.

Between the towns of Casma and Chimbote, this idyllic, perfectly round bay is the area's best beach escape. Facilities are quite simple and are limited to just a few small hotels and restaurants.

GETTING HERE AND AROUND

Playa Tortugas is most easily reached by taxi from Casma. Expect to pay S/20 for the 15-minute drive.

Playa Tortugas

BEACH—SIGHT | An easy drive from the Sechín area, this small beach is a low-key base for exploring the nearby ruins. A ghost town in winter, it is much more pleasant, in terms of both weather and people, in summertime. The stony beach, in a perfectly round cove surrounded by brown hills, offers limited hotel and restaurant options, but with its fleet of fishing boats and pleasant lapping waves, it's a relaxing destination. **Facilities:** food and drink; toilets. **Best for:** sunset; swimming. *Malecón Grau, Playa Tortuga.*

Restaurants

Restaurante Tarawasi

$$ | **PERUVIAN** | This homey seafood joint has a lounge that looks like your grandma's living room, with lots of local crafts hanging from the walls. Portions are huge, and prices reasonable: try the *arroz con mariscos* (seafood with rice), and enjoy the views of the bay as you linger afterward. **Known for:** all types of seafood; owners also rent rooms; nice vistas of the ocean. *Average main: S/35* *Malecón Grau, Playa Tortuga* *977/256–859* *www.facebook.com/Tarawasi-275588715865449* *No dinner* *No credit cards.*

Pororoca Hotel

$$ | **HOTEL** | Clean and comfortable, with an attentive staff, this just-the-basics lodging gets the job done. **Pros:** suites have kitchenettes; good oceanside view; indoor pool is odd, but nice. **Cons:** some noise from the neighbors; decor is basic; Wi-Fi can be spotty. *Rooms from: S/260* *Caleta Sur, Manzana F, Lote 10, Playa Tortuga* *998/282–317* *www.facebook.com/pororocatortugas/* *8 rooms* *No meals.*

Trujillo

174 km (108 miles) north of Playa Tortugas; 561 km (350 miles) northwest of Lima on the Pan-American Hwy.

Well-preserved colonial architecture, rich local cuisine, and spectacular archaeological sites make Trujillo a must-see tourist destination. Inhabited for centuries by the Moche and Chimú peoples, who practiced human sacrifice and left some of the greatest structures and artworks in pre-Colombian Peru, the town was later conquered by the Spanish and filled with graceful colonial architecture. Today, Trujillo is renowned for its spicy northern

Which Culture Was That Again?

It's a common question after a few days of exploring the extensive archaeological sites in the north. So many different civilizations were emerging, overlapping, and converging in coastal Peru, it can be difficult to keep track of them all.

Chavín: One of the earliest major cultures in the region was the cat-worshipping Chavín (900-200 BC). Described as the "mother culture of the Andes" by the great Peruvian archaeologist Julio Tello, this civilization stretched through much of Peru's Northern Highlands, as well as along the northern and central coasts. Artifacts dating from 850 BC tell us that the Chavín people were excellent artisans, and their pottery, with its squat stirrup vessels, can be seen in the museums of Trujillo and Lima.

Moche: About 200 years after the Chavín culture's demise, a highly advanced civilization called the Moche emerged. It was their carefully planned irrigation systems, still in use today, that turned the northern desert into productive agricultural land. Their fine ceramics and large pyramids, still standing near present-day Trujillo and Chiclayo, give us insight into their architectural advances and daily lives. A consistent theme of their art is the ritual combat between captives, followed by elaborate bloodletting ceremonies. Despite voracious *huaqueros*, or looters, the tomb of the Lord of Sipán was still largely intact when it was unearthed in 1987, revealing precious insights into this complex culture.

Chimú to Inca: The Chimú came on the scene around AD 850. They continued to conquer and expand until around 1470, when they, like most others in the area, were assimilated by the huge Inca Empire. The awe-inspiring city of Chan Chan, built by the Chimú, sits near present-day Trujillo. Meanwhile, although the Inca center of power lay farther south, in the Cusco–Machu Picchu area, its cultural influence stretched far beyond Peru's northern borders. When Francisco Pizarro, the Spanish pig-farmer-turned-conquistador, first landed near present-day Tumbes in 1532, his greed was inflamed by glimpes of the riches of this largest of New World empires.

cuisine and warm hospitality, which are abundantly on display in its excellent hotels and restaurants. You'll see why this City of Eternal Spring, officially founded in 1534, competes with Arequipa for the title of Peru's second city. The only problem is trying to find time to visit all the sights—literally, since many places close from 1 to 4 for lunch.

GETTING HERE AND AROUND

LATAM Perú flies from Lima to Trujillo's Aeropuerto Carlos Martínez de Pinillos (TRU), 5 km (3 miles) north of the city on the road to Huanchaco.

Almost everything is within walking distance in the center of the city, and for everything else there are reasonably priced taxis. If you don't have a car, ask your hotel to arrange for a taxi for the day or to tour a specific place. For the archaeological sights, another option is to join a day tour from a travel agency.

VISITOR INFORMATION iPerú. ✉ *Jr. Independencia 467* ☎ *044/294–561* 🌐 *peru.info.*

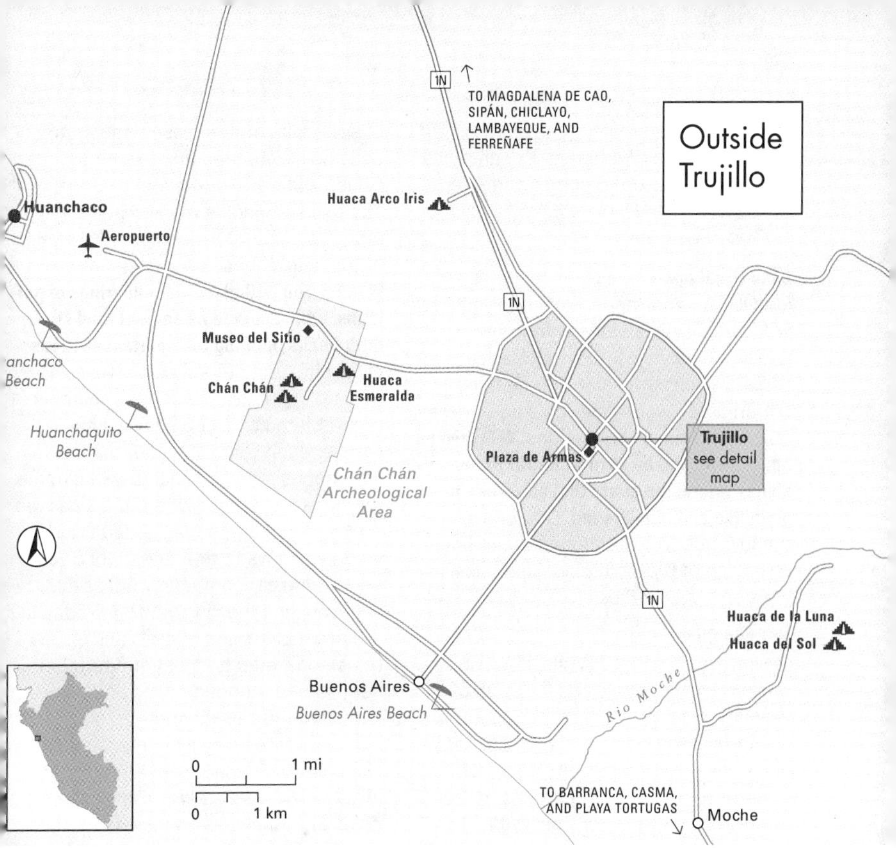

Outside Trujillo

TO MAGDALENA DE CAO, SIPÁN, CHICLAYO, LAMBAYEQUE, AND FERREÑAFE
1N
Huaca Arco Iris
Huanchaco
Aeropuerto
Museo del Sitio
Chán Chán
Huaca Esmeralda
anchaco Beach
Huanchaquito Beach
Chán Chán Archeological Area
Plaza de Armas
Trujillo see detail map
Huaca de la Luna
Huaca del Sol
Río Moche
Buenos Aires
Buenos Aires Beach
0 1 mi
0 1 km
TO BARRANCA, CASMA, AND PLAYA TORTUGAS
Moche

Sights

More than any other city in Peru, Trujillo maintains much of its colonial charm, especially inside Avenida España, which encircles the heart of the city. This thoroughfare replaced a wall 9 meters (30 feet) high erected in 1687 to deter pirates. Two pieces of the wall stand at the corner of Estete and España.

Casa de la Emancipación
HOUSE | This branch of Banco Continental is unlike any bank you've ever been in. Go through the central courtyard and up to the small art gallery on the right. Enjoy the current exhibition—anything from modern to traditional works of art—and see a scale model of Trujillo when it was a walled city. **■ TIP→ Continue to the back, taking in the chandeliers, the large gold mirrors, and the small fountain, and imagine how, in this house, Peruvian republicans plotted the country's independence from Spain, which was declared on December 29, 1820.** The house later became the country's first capitol building and meeting place for its first legislature. Fun fact: much of the furniture is original. ✉ *Pizarro 610* ☎ *044/246–061* 🌐 *fundacionbbva.pe/casonas-y-museos/casa-de-la-emancipacion* 🎫 *Free* 🕒 *Closed Sun.*

Casa del Mayorazgo de Facalá
HOUSE | The open courtyard, from 1709, is surrounded by beautiful cedar columns, greenery … and bankers: as with many colonial mansions in Peru, this one is now owned by a bank. Scotiabank, however, welcomes tourists and clients into the house to see its wonderfully restored beauty. Notice the classic brown stucco-covered adobe walls and Moorish-style carved-wood ceiling. The

security guards are happy to answer questions about the house. The entrance is on the corner of Bolognesi and Pizarro. ✉ *Jr. Pizarro 314* ☎ *044/249–994* 🎫 *Free* ⏲ *Closed weekends.*

Casa Urquiaga

HOUSE | The enormous, elaborately carved wooden door is a stunning entrance to this beautifully restored neoclassical mansion from the early 19th century. Simón de Bolívar reportedly stayed here during his military campaigns. ■ **TIP→ The house is owned by Peru's Central Bank; simply inform the guard that you'd like to go inside and look around.** Don't miss the lovely rococo furniture and the fine collection of pre-Columbian ceramics. ✉ *Pizarro 446* 🎫 *Free.*

★ Chan Chan

ARCHAEOLOGICAL SITE | With its strange, honeycomb-like walls and labyrinth of wavelike parapets, this sprawling ancient capital is the largest adobe city in the world. Its surreal geometry once held boulevards, aqueducts, gardens, palaces, and some 10,000 dwellings. Within its precincts were nine royal compounds, one of which, the royal palace of Tschudi, has been partially restored and opened to the public. Although the city began with the Moche civilization, the Chimú people took control of the region 300 years later and expanded the city to its current size. Less known than the Incas, who conquered them in 1470, the Chimú were nonetheless the second-largest empire in South America, with territory stretching along 1,000 km (620 miles) of the Pacific, from Lima to Tumbes.

Before entering this UNESCO World Heritage Site, check out the extensive photographic display of the ruins at the time of their discovery and restoration. Then begin at the Tschudi complex's Plaza Principal, a monstrous square where ceremonies and festivals were held. The throne of the king is thought to have been in front where the ramp is found. The reconstructed walls have depictions of sea otters at their base. From here, head deep into the ruins toward the royal palace and tomb of the lord of Chimú. The main corridor is marked by fishnet representations, marking the importance of the sea to these ancient people. ■ **TIP→ You will also find renderings of pelicans, which served as ancient road signs, their beaks pointing to important sections of the city.** Just before you arrive at the Recinto Funerario, the funeral chamber of the Chimú lord, you pass a small natural reservoir called a *huachaque*. Forty-four secondary chambers surround the funeral chamber where the king was buried. In his day, it was understood that when you pass to the netherworld you could bring all your worldly necessities with you, and the king was interred with live concubines and officials and a slew of personal effects, most of which have been looted. Although wind and rain have damaged the city, its size—20 square km (8 square miles)—still impresses. ✉ *Ctra. Huanchaco, 5 km (3 miles) northwest of Trujillo* ☎ *044/206–304* 🌐 *chanchan.gob.pe* 🎫 *S/11, includes admission to Huaca Arco Iris, Huaca Esmeralda, and Museo del Sitio; ticket valid for 48 hrs.*

Chan Chan's Museo del Sitio

MUSEUM | Begin your archaeological exploration at this small but thorough museum, which has displays of ceramics and textiles from the Chimú Empire. The entrance fee to the museum includes Chan Chan, Huaca Arco Iris, and Huaca Esmeralda, so hold on to your ticket (you may also go directly to the ruins and purchase the same ticket there, for the same price). From Trujillo, take a taxi or join a tour from an agency. Each location is a significant distance from the next. Guides are available at the entrance of each site for S/10 or more (S/25 for Chan Chan) and are strongly recommended, both for the information they can provide and also for safety reasons (a few robberies have occurred in the more remote sectors of the archaeological sites). At the museum, and all sites, there are

The Chan Chan ruins, just outside of Trujillo, are the largest adobe city in the world.

clean restrooms and a cluster of souvenir stalls and snack shops, but no place to buy a full meal. ✉ *Ctra. Huanchaco, 5 km (3 miles) northwest of Trujillo* ☎ *044/206–304* 🌐 *museamos.cultura.pe/museos/museo-de-sitio-de-chan-chan* 🎫 *S/11, includes admission to Chan Chan, Huaca Arco Iris, and Huaca Esmeralda; ticket valid for 48 hrs* 🕒 *Closed Mon.*

Huaca Arco Iris

ARCHAEOLOGICAL SITE | Filled with intriguing symbolic carvings, the restored Huaca Arco Iris, or Rainbow Pyramid, stands out against its urban backdrop. Named for its unusual rainbow ornamentation (the area rarely sees rain), it's also known as the Huaca El Dragón, or Pyramid of the Dragon, because of the central role dragons play in the friezes. This structure, built by the early Chimú, also has a repeating figure of a mythical creature that looks like a giant serpent. On the walls, mostly reconstructions, you will see what many archaeologists believe are priests wielding the knives used in human sacrifices. Half-moon shapes at the bottom of most of the friezes indicate that the Chimú probably worshipped the moon at this temple. You can climb the ramps up to the top of the platform and see the storage bins within. ✉ *La Esperanza* 🎫 *S/11, includes admission to Chan Chan, Huaca Esmeralda, and Museo del Sitio; ticket valid for 48 hrs.*

★ Huaca de la Luna and Huaca del Sol

ARCHAEOLOGICAL SITE | Stark and strange beneath the ash-gray hill that towers over them, these astonishing Moche pyramids were the scenes of bloody human sacrifices. Their exteriors may have eroded, but inside archaeologists have uncovered sinister octopus-shaped reliefs of the great Moche god Ai-Apaec, as well as evidence of a cataclysmic El Niño sequence that effectively destroyed Moche civilization.

The Huacas of the Sun and Moon are located some 10 km (6 miles) outside Trujillo, near the Río Moche. The former is the bigger of the two, but it's not open to the public due to its decayed state. (Built up of 130 million adobe bricks in eight continually expanding stages, its treasures were literally cleaned out of it in 1610, when the Spanish diverted the Río Moche to wash the imperial gold and silver from its innards.) The Huaca of the Moon is awesome in its own right, with numerous exterior and interior walls blazoned with bizarre mythological reliefs. These include spider-like creatures, warriors, and the scowling face of Ai-Apaec, the ferocious god to whom captives were sacrificed at the pyramid's base. These sacrifices probably occurred to propitiate the gods of the weather, but alas, it didn't work. A series of violent El Niño events around the year 600 brought drought and sandstorms, eventually ending the Moche civilization.

When you visit the Huaca de la Luna, you'll start from the top, near the sacrificial altars, and work your way down through the inner galleries to the murals at the base. This was where archaeologists discovered bones of the Moches' victims in recent decades. ■ **TIP→ Be sure to allot time for the excellent museum, which includes exhibits of Moche artwork and informative discussions of the culture's history and religion.** ✉ *Av. Santa Rosa, off Panamericana Norte* ☎ *044/600–457* 🌐 *huacasdemoche.pe* 🎫 *S/10; S/5 for museum.*

Huaca Esmeralda

ARCHAEOLOGICAL SITE | As with the other Chimú pyramids, the most interesting aspects of these ruins are the carved friezes, unrestored and in their original state. The images include fish, seabirds, waves, and fishing nets, all central to the life of the Chimú. Like other Chimú pyramids on the northern coast, the ancient temple mound of Huaca Esmeralda, or the Emerald Pyramid, is believed to have served as a religious ceremonial center. ⚠ **The pyramid is in an area that's dangerous for unaccompanied tourists, so go with a guide.** ✉ *Huanchaco Hwy., 2 km (1¼ miles) west of Trujillo* 🎫 *S/11, includes admission to Chan Chan, Huaca Arco Iris, and Museo del Sitio; ticket valid for 48 hrs.*

Monasterio El Carmen

RELIGIOUS SITE | Still used as a nunnery, this handsome edifice, built in 1725, is regarded as the city's finest example of colonial art. It has five elaborate altars and some fine floral frescos. Next door is a museum, the Pinacoteca Carmelita, with religious works from the 17th and 18th centuries and an interesting exhibition on restoration techniques. Be warned: visiting hours are sporadic. ✉ *Av. Colón at Av. Bolívar* ☎ *044/233–091* 🎫 *Free.*

Museo Arqueológico Municipal de Moche

MUSEUM | This small but well-curated museum is the new home to the Cassinelli collection, one of the most impressive assemblages of Moche and other artifacts in Peru. Mummies, pottery that imitates bird calls, and a bewildering array of stirrup vessels are among the highlights. The museum is on the third floor of the Municipal Building of the village of Moche, just a short cab ride from downtown Trujillo. ✉ *Cl. Bolognesi 359* ✣ *Inside the Moche Municipalidad* ☎ *044/465–471* 🎫 *S/5* ⏲ *Closed Sat.*

Museo de Arqueología, Antropología e Historia UNT

MUSEUM | Originally built in the 17th century, this museum displays pottery and other artifacts recovered from the archaeological sites surrounding Trujillo. There are excellent reproductions of the colorful murals found at the Huaca de la Luna, the pyramids southeast of the city, as well as a lovely courtyard. ✉ *Jr. Junín 682* ☎ *044/474–850* 🎫 *S/5* ⏲ *Closed Sun.*

Museo del Juguete

MUSEUM | **FAMILY** | Puppets, puzzles, toys, games—what could be more fun than a toy museum? This private museum houses a large collection of toys from all over the world and shows the transformation of toys through the centuries. ■ **TIP→ The toys from pre-Columbian Peru are especially interesting, affording a rare glimpse into the daily lives of ancient people.** You can't play with the toys, so it may not be appropriate for very young children. ✉ *Jr. Independencia 705* ☎ *044/208–181* 🌐 *museodeljuguete.negocio.site* 🎫 *S/5* ⏰ *Closed Tues.*

Palacio Iturregui

CASTLE/PALACE | One look at the elaborate courtyard, with its two levels of white columns, enormous tiles, and three-tiered chandeliers, and you'll know why this is called a palace rather than a house. From the intricate white-painted metalwork to the gorgeous Italian marble furnishings, every detail of what was once considered the most exquisite house in South America has been carefully restored and maintained. Remodeled from an earlier mansion in 1842, it's now the home of the private Club Central de Trujillo. Unfortunately, the club only allows visitors limited access, and permission to enter seems to depend principally on the guard's mood for the day. If you do go, prepare to be impressed. ✉ *Pizarro 688* ☎ *044/234–212.*

Plaza de Armas

PLAZA | Brightly colored, well-maintained buildings and green grass with walkways and benches make this one of the most charming central plazas in Peru. Fronted by the 17th-century cathedral and surrounded by the colonial-era mansions that are Trujillo's architectural glory, this is not, despite claims by locals, Peru's largest main plaza, but it is one of the nicest. ✉ *Trujillo.*

Restaurants

Trujillo serves up delicious fresh seafood and a variety of excellent meat dishes. Try the cebiche made with fish or shellfish; *causa,* a casserole made of mashed potatoes and layers of fillings; tasty *cabrito al horno* (roast kid) or *seco de cabrito* (stewed kid); or *shámbar,* a bean stew tinged with mint.

Al Dente

$ | **ITALIAN** | With this simple but classy Italian trattoria , artisanal pizza comes to Trujillo. The pies are, indeed, tempting—with thin, flaky crusts and generous toppings—but don't let them distract you from the excellent pastas, which are homemade and inventive. **Known for:** cozy ambience; three-pepper steak; some of the best pizza in Peru. *$ Average main: S/30* ✉ *Jr. Independencia 589* ☎ *044/303–432* 🌐 *www.facebook.com/aldenteperu.*

El Celler de Cler

$$ | **STEAKHOUSE** | With its wooden balconies overlooking the street and its rustic-chic interior, this steak house gets high marks for ambience as well as flavor. Vegetarians have a few pastas to choose from, but the main reason to go are the rib eyes and filets mignons. **Known for:** meat, meat, and more meat; solid wine list; intimate but classy digs. *$ Average main: S/50* ✉ *Jr. Independencia 588* ☎ *044/317–191* 🌐 *www.facebook.com/elcellerdeclerrestaurant* ⏰ *No lunch.*

El Mochica

$$ | **PERUVIAN** | Half a century's worth of tradition has gone into this Trujillo standby. Bustling at lunch- and dinnertime, it's a fun place to eat that specializes in regional cuisine—and does it well. **Known for:** fresh takes on seafood classics; elegant setting close to the plaza; leisurely service. *$ Average main: S/35* ✉ *Bolívar 462* ☎ *044/370–1524* 🌐 *elmochica.com.*

★ La Toscana

$$$$ | **ITALIAN** | Dining at this closed-door, reservations-only private house is like partaking of a sumptuous family meal in an Italian villa. There are no menus, no sign outside—instead, the owner, Sheyla, comes to your table; asks what you'd like to eat; and then heads to her kitchen to whip up fresh, organic dishes such as melon-and-prosciutto salad, wood-fired

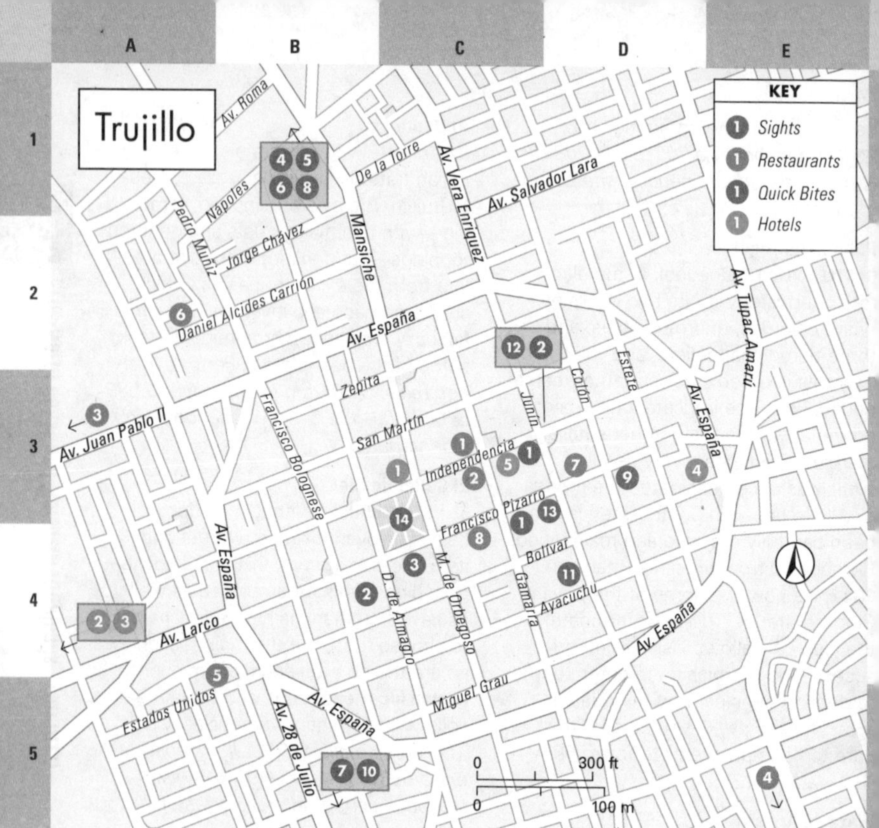

Sights

1 Casa de la Emancipación........... C3

2 Casa del Mayorazgo de Facalá.................. B4

3 Casa Urquiaga........... C4

4 Chan Chan............... B1

5 Chan Chan's Museo del Sitio....................... B1

6 Huaca Arco Iris......... B1

7 Huaca de la Luna and Huaca del Sol........... B5

8 Huaca Esmeralda....... B1

9 Monasterio El Carmen................ D3

10 Museo Arqueológico Municipal de Moche... B5

11 Museo de Arqueología, Antropología e Historia UNT............. D4

12 Museo del Juguete..... D3

13 Palacio Iturregui........ D3

14 Plaza de Armas.......... C3

Restaurants

1 Al Dente.................. C3

2 El Celler de Cler.......... C3

3 El Mochica A3

4 La Toscana E5

5 Restaurant Romano Rincón Criollo B4

6 Restaurante Doña Peta A2

7 Romano.................. D3

8 Taberna Calixto C4

Quick Bites

1 Casona Deza Café....... C3

2 Museo Café Bar D3

Hotels

1 Costa del Sol Trujillo Centro C3

2 Costa del Sol Wyndham Trujillo A4

3 El Gran Marqués........ A4

4 Gran Bolívar............. D3

5 Hotel Colonial C3

pizzas, and fusilli with mushroom ragù. **Known for:** personalized attention; unique, private-home setting for a maximum of eight guests; high-quality ingredients imported from Europe. *Average main: S/80 Manzana W Lt. 3-B Semi-Rustica, Urbanizacion El Bosque 949/650–496 www.la-toscana-trattoria.com No lunch. Closed Sun.*

Restaurante Doña Peta

$ | PERUVIAN | Seco de cabrito is the star of the menu at this wildly popular institution among Trujillo locals, and no wonder: the version here is among the best you'll find. Colorfully woven decorations and *marinera* music add to the atmosphere. **Known for:** stick-to-your-ribs goat stews; festive atmosphere; duck with tacu-tacu. *Average main: S/30 Alcides Carrion 354 949/328–282 No dinner.*

★ Restaurant Romano Rincón Criollo

$$ | PERUVIAN | There's a reason why this criollo eatery is consistently mobbed by hungry locals at lunchtime: its innovative cooking is some of the best in northern Peru. From shellfish and goat to duck and causas (stuffed mashed-potato-sandwiches), the menu just goes on and on. **Known for:** unusual cebiches; encyclopedic menu; massive portions. *Average main: S/50 Cl. Estados Unidos 162 044/244–207 www.restaurantromano.com No dinner.*

Romano

$ | ECLECTIC | Although this Trujillo establishment has grown a bit shopworn since it opened in 1951, it still offers good food and friendly service. For dinner, enjoy seafood and pasta dishes, followed by excellent homemade desserts. **Known for:** criollo cooking; excellent desserts; local tradition. *Average main: S/25 Jr. Pizarro 747 044/252–251.*

★ Taberna Calixto

$ | PERUVIAN | Sandwiches are among the lesser-known glories of Peruvian cuisine, but if folks continue to throng this sunny patio café like they do now, it's only a matter of time before word gets out. Burgers here are among Peru's best, but even tastier is the sandwich *de lechón al cilindro,* made from pork slow-roasted inside a barrel. **Known for:** outdoor seating; scrumptious sandwiches, especially with pork; salads and vegetarian small plates. *Average main: S/15 Jr. Pizarro 552 933/557–989 www.facebook.com/taberncalixto.*

Festivals

Considered the cultural capital of Peru, Trujillo is known for its festivities, including an international ballet festival, a contemporary art biennial, and a horse show. Consider coming to town for the Festival Internacional de la Primavera (International Spring Festival), held every year in late September or early October (check local listings for the exact dates). Trujillo is also busy during the last week of January, when it holds a spectacular dance competition called the National Fiesta de La Marinera, which showcases the country's virtuosic, flirtatious national dance.

Coffee and Quick Bites

Casona Deza Café (*Casona de los Leones*)

$ | CAFÉ | This beautiful café sits inside the Casa Ganoza Chopitea, which was constructed around 1735 and is one of the best-preserved colonial mansions in Trujillo. The interior has original woodwork and frescoes, and the exterior features a balcony and a unique polychrome facade featuring a male and a female lion (which is why it is sometimes referred to as Casona de los Leones). **Known for:** colonial atmosphere; cheap snacks; patio seating. *Average main: S/15 Independencia 630 044/474–756 www.facebook.com/CasonaDeza.*

North Coast Menu

Peru's coast is characterized by heaps of fresh seafood, which, when served cold, is a refreshing meal on a hot day. The highlander diet consists of root vegetables, like yucca and potato, and a variety of meats, with all parts of the animal being eaten. Both regions have spicy and nonspicy dishes, so ask before you order.

Arroz con pato: Tender duck is paired with rice that's colored green with cilantro in this iconic dish that originated in Chiclayo.

Cabrito con tacu-tacu: This dish of goat kid with refried rice and beans is classic Peruvian comfort food. It's rich in flavor but has little spice.

Cangrejo reventado: This is a fresh, spicy dish of boiled crab, eggs, and onions. The crab is usually served in the shell with a side of yucca.

Cebiche de conchas negras: Cebiche (raw seafood with lemon or lime juice and chili peppers) made of black conch, believed to be an aphrodisiac, is an iconic dish in the region, though it's not for everyone. The taste of the conch is quite strong, and seasonal bans should be respected to help with conservation.

Cuy: Guinea pig is one of the more popular dishes in Peru. It's tasty and similar to rabbit, but it's usually served whole, so you need to decide whether you can deal with seeing a big-eared, buck-toothed critter on your plate before ordering it.

Parrilladas: At restaurants serving *parrilladas* (barbecues) you can choose from every imaginable cut of beef, including *anticuchos* (beef hearts) and *ubre* (cow udder).

Shámbar: Particular to Trujillo, this wheat-and-bean stew is a nice, semispicy meat alternative that is served only on Monday.

Museo Café Bar

CAFES—NIGHTLIFE | Feel like you're part of the colonial history while enjoying a delicious cocktail at this swanky bar and lounge beside the Museo del Juguete. With its wood floors, dark-wood bar, floor-to-ceiling glass cabinets, and cushioned leather seats, it's a relaxed café in the afternoon and a hopping bar with live jazz in the early evening. ✉ *Jr. Independencia 701* ☎ *986/290–528* 🌐 *www.facebook.com/museocafebartrujilloperu.*

Hotels

Costa del Sol Trujillo Centro

$$ | **HOTEL** | **FAMILY** | Situated right on the Plaza de Armas, this elegant *posada* in a converted colonial mansion is at the top of the pecking order for Trujillo hotels. **Pros:** top-notch service; perfect location on the main square; superior range of amenities. **Cons:** rooms vary in size and lighting; adjoining plaza can be noisy at times; restaurant is not on a level with Trujillo's top hotel. 💲 *Rooms from: S/300* ✉ *Jr. Independencia 485* ☎ *044/232–741* 🌐 *www.costadelsolperu.com/trujillo-centro* 🛏 *73 rooms* 🍽 *Free breakfast.*

Costa del Sol Wyndham Trujillo

$ | **RESORT** | **FAMILY** | If you want to stay outside the city, this modern hotel is ideal. **Pros:** quiet, attractive setting; spacious grounds; two pools. **Cons:** can be isolating without a car; decor is a bit bland; on-site restaurant is a chain. 💲 *Rooms from: S/225* ✉ *Los Cocoteros 500* ☎ *044/484–150* 🌐 *www.costadelsolperu.com/trujillo* 🛏 *120 rooms* 🍽 *Free breakfast.*

Trujillo Time

Many of the museums are closed at lunchtime from about 1 to 4 or 4:30. It can be quite hot around midday, so it's best to plan on indoor activities. It's easy to hail a taxi in Trujillo, and the in-town fare of about S/4 is quite reasonable. As always when traveling, be on your guard if you visit the market area—access your cash discreetly, and keep your valuables close.

El Gran Marqués

$$ | **HOTEL** | This upscale, full-service hotel and spa is just a short cab ride from the city center and has solid, comfortable rooms overlooking a pool surrounded by lush gardens. **Pros:** efficient service; two pools; sleek modern decor. **Cons:** caters to business travelers and can be impersonal; Wi-Fi can be slow; not a walkable distance from city center. *Rooms from: S/270* ✉ *Díaz de Cienfuegos 145, Urb. La Merced* ☎ *044/481–710* 🌐 *www.elgranmarques.com* *50 rooms* *Free breakfast.*

Gran Bolívar

$ | **HOTEL** | Behind the historic facade of this centrally located building hides a modern hotel with spacious rooms that overlook a sun-filled courtyard. **Pros:** colonial architecture with a lovely central courtyard; good staff; central location. **Cons:** some rooms have lots of light, but others have very little; tacky decorations; some bathrooms are small. *Rooms from: S/155* ✉ *Jr. Bolívar 957* ☎ *044/262–200* 🌐 *www.perunorte.com/granbolivar* *35 rooms* *Free breakfast.*

★ Hotel Colonial

$ | **HOTEL** | Charming décor and location are the top draws at this cozy downtown inn. **Pros:** rooftop patio has splendid views of the city; ambience is unbeatable for the price; plentiful public areas for lounging. **Cons:** amenities in the rooms can be basic; rooms vary widely in size; on-site restaurant is uninspiring. *Rooms from: S/140* ✉ *Jr. Independencia 618* ☎ *044/258–261* 🌐 *www.hotelcolonial.com.pe* *75 rooms* *No meals.*

Nightlife

El Boticario

BARS/PUBS | A speakeasy vibe and cocktails *d'auteur* are what draw locals to this basement bar, located a short cab ride from downtown. For ambience, think brick walls, dim lighting, and a design concept based on an old-fashioned apothecary's shop. Perfect for an intimate, low-key evening. ✉ *Av. Larco 992, Basement* ☎ *044/287–632* ☞ *Closed Sun.*

El Trasgu

BARS/PUBS | Named after a Spanish gnome who's considered the embodiment of mischief, this friendly, Irish-style pub features live music, cheap *piqueos* (snacks for sharing), and bar hands who are generous with the hooch. It's good for happy hour or for dancing on weekends. ✉ *Cl. Las Hortensias 588* ☎ *991/783–001* ☞ *Closed Sun.*

Shopping

Along Avenida España, especially where it intersects with Junín, stalls display locally made leather goods, particularly shoes, bags, and coats. Be wary of pickpockets during the day, and avoid it altogether after sunset.

Huanchaco

12 km (7 miles) northwest of Trujillo.

Less than half an hour away from the city, Huanchaco is a little beach community where surfers, tourists, affluent *trujillianos,* families, and couples easily mix. With excellent restaurants, comfortable hotels, and never-ending sunshine, this is a nice place to unwind for a couple of days or to live it up at one of the many annual fiestas. The Festival del Mar is held every other year during May, the Fiesta de San Pedro occurs every June 29, and multiple surfing and dance competitions happen throughout the year.

■ **TIP→ Head to the beach in the late afternoon to watch fishermen return for the day, gliding along in their caballitos de totora, traditional fishing boats that have been used for thousands of years.** These small boats, made from totora reeds, can be seen in Moche ceramics and other pre-Columbian handiwork. The boat's name, *caballito,* means "little horse"; fishermen appear to be on horseback as they straddle the boats. Offer them a few soles, and they'll be glad to give you a ride.

GETTING HERE AND AROUND

Huanchaco sits well enough within the Trujillo orbit that taxiing it is the best way to get out here. The drive takes about 15 minutes, and the fare runs about S/12. Buses also run between the two points from all parts of the city for about S/3.

ESSENTIALS

ATMs are plentiful here, including a GlobalNet ATM beside the Municipalidad. You can exchange cash at any bank back in Trujillo.

Beaches

The beaches around Huanchaco are popular, though the water can be rather cold.

Playa Huankarote

BEACH—SIGHT | This wide, rocky beach south of the pier is less popular for swimming, but there's good surfing. **Amenities:** none. **Best for:** solitude, surfing. *Huanchaco* ⊕ *South of municipal pier.*

Playa Malecón

BEACH—SIGHT | North of the pier, this is the town's most popular beach, and it is filled with rows upon rows of restaurants. Local craftspeople sell their goods along the waterfront walk, and fishermen line up their caballitos de totora, the reed fishing rafts that are used more as a photo op or to rent to tourists than for actual fishing. **Amenities:** food and drink. **Best for:** sunset; surfing; swimming; walking. *Huanchaco* ⊕ *North of municipal pier.*

Sights

El Santuario de Huanchaco

RELIGIOUS SITE | Although people come to Huanchaco for the beach, one of Peru's oldest churches, El Santuario de Huanchaco, on a hill overlooking the village, is a nice side trip. The sanctuary was built on a Chimú ruin around 1540. In the second half of the 16th century, a small box containing the image of Nuestra Señora del Socorro (Our Lady of Mercy) floated in on the tide and was discovered by locals. The image, which is kept in the sanctuary, has been an object of local veneration ever since. *Andrés Rázuri and Unión* *Free.*

Restaurants

Big Ben

$$ | **SEAFOOD** | Skip the first floor and head upstairs to the terrace for great views of the beach at Huanchaco's largest and most popular restaurant. Enjoy Huanchaquero specialties, including *cangrejo reventado* (baked crab stuffed with egg) and *cebiche de mococho* (algae cebiche). **Known for:** unusual seafood dishes; sweeping beach views; casual vibe. *Average main: S/35* *Av. Victor Larco 1184* *044/461–378* *www.bigbenhuanchaco.pe/home* *No dinner.*

Chocolate Café

$ | **CAFÉ** | This cute coffeehouse serves as a nice break from seafood if you find yourself spending too much time indulging in Huanchaco's cebicherías. The Dutch-and-Peruvian-owned café sources its coffee and other organic ingredients from local and regional producers. **Known for:** gourmet desserts; European atmosphere; good organic coffee. *Average main: S/15* *Av. La Rivera 752*

Get Off the Beaten Path

The small fishing port of Puerto Pizarro, 14 km (9 miles) north of Tumbes on the way to the Ecuadorean border, sits near the point where the Río Tumbes and the Pacific Ocean meet and not far from the Santuario Nacional Manglares de Tumbes. The mix of fresh- and saltwater is ideal for mangroves, not to mention the aquatic creatures that thrive among their roots. Tour operators in Tumbes and Mancora sell half- or full-day tours starting from the port, but it is just as easy to come here and arrange a trip directly. Prices are based on the time and the number of stops, which include bird and wildlife watching in the mangroves, a small reptile zoo, and tiny islands with pleasant beaches and informal beach-shack restaurants.

044/626–973 www.facebook.com/Chocolatecafehuanchaco No dinner.

Mi Casa Thai Food

$ | **THAI** | Thai food is all but unknown in Peru, making this rooftop restaurant a tiny miracle. Inevitably, the cooks have had to substitute local ingredients for a few Thai veggies and spices, but just being able to find red and yellow curries on one's plate—with lots of much-missed leafy greens—is a welcome break from carb-heavy Peruvian fare. **Known for:** cozy rooftop setting; small but well-prepared menu; great pad Thai. *Average main: S/30 Jr. Miguel Grau 426 981/044–356 No lunch. Closed weekends.*

Hotels

Hotel Bracamonte

$ | **HOTEL** | **FAMILY** | This pleasant hotel, across the boulevard from Playa Huanchaco, is popular with Peruvian families, especially in summer, giving it a good "neighborhood" feel. **Pros:** if you have kids, this is the place to be; pool is perfect for relaxing; attractive landscaping. **Cons:** if you don't have kids, this is not the place for you; rooms can be smallish; decor can be basic. *Rooms from: S/187 Jr. Los Olivos 160 044/461–162 www.hotelbracamonte.com.pe 34 rooms No meals.*

Las Palmeras

$ | **HOTEL** | Across from the tranquil Playa Los Tumbos, a beach on the northern end of the waterfront, Las Palmeras is a welcoming hotel (once you get past the gated entrance) with ocean views. **Pros:** pristine and comfortable rooms with terraces and views; very quiet and relaxing; gated grounds for security. **Cons:** prices vary based on which floor the room is on; decor is tacky; Wi-Fi can be unreliable. *Rooms from: S/130 Av. Victor Larco 1624 044/461–199 21 rooms Free breakfast.*

Nightlife

InstaBar

BARS/PUBS | Huanchaco's version of the beachside tiki bar features humorous decor (think *caballitos de totora* instead of canoes and "Polynesian" heads that resemble Sideshow Bob from *The Simpsons*), but the drinks are delicious, and you can dance while the sun goes down. There's also a menu of seafood snacks. *Av. La Ribera, Playa El Elio On the beach south of the Municipalidad de Huanchaco 938/378–884 www.facebook.com/InstabarHCO.*

Sabes?

BARS/PUBS | Worth checking out, especially on the weekend, this laid-back spot at the northern end of the main drag has good music and drinks, as well as decent pizza. ✉ *Av. Victor Larco 1220* ☎ *044/462–526* 🌐 *sabesbar.com.*

Magdalena de Cao

47 km (29 miles) northwest of Huanchaco.

Chances are, if you are coming to this small, remote village in the Chicama Valley, it's to see the El Brujo archaeological complex, which is quickly growing in popularity.

GETTING HERE AND AROUND

As the site is about 1½ hours from Trujillo by road, and public transportation is sporadic, you'll either want to rent a car or join a tour from Trujillo.

Sights

★ El Brujo

ARCHAEOLOGICAL SITE | This intriguing complex is currently one of the hot properties on the Peruvian archaeological circuit. Plopped down in a barren dune about 6 km (4 miles) from Magdalena, it consists of three distinct huacas, or holy sites: Huaca Cao, Huaca Prieta, and Huaca Cortada. Huaca Cao is the star: in 2006, it was the site of the electrifying discovery of the Lady of Cao, a 1,600-year-old mummy whose tattoos marked her as a Moche priestess or ruler. The finding was immediately compared with that of King Tut's tomb in Egypt, as it completely turned notions of power in pre-Columbian Peru upside down. Equally impressive is the huaca's pyramid itself, where the multicolored friezes of warriors and human sacrifices give a powerful idea of the Moches' artistic skill. The excellent on-site museum is among the most informative of its kind. The other two huacas are still undergoing excavation, but the entrance fee covers all three. The site is well worth the trip from Trujillo. ✉ *Magdalena de Cao* ☎ *939/326–240* 🌐 *www.elbrujo.pe/en* 🎟 *S/10.*

Sipán

165 km (102 miles) north of Magdalena de Cao; 35 km (21 miles) east of Chiclayo.

This tiny village, with a population of about 1,700, doesn't offer much, but nearby is one of the country's major archaeological sites. Arrange for a taxi or tour to take you to the Tomb of the Lord of Sipán.

Sights

Tumba del Señor de Sipán (*Tomb of the Lord of Sipán*)

ARCHAEOLOGICAL SITE | The road to this archaeological site, which was excavated by renowned archaeologist Walter Alva in 1987 and which is not far from the town of Sipán, winds past sugar plantations and through a fertile valley. You'll soon reach a fissured hill—all that remains of a temple called the Huaca Rajada. ■ **TIP→ The three major tombs found here date from about AD 290 and earlier and form one of the most complete archaeological finds in the Western Hemisphere.** The tombs have been attributed to the Moche culture, known for its ornamental pottery and fine metalwork. The most extravagant funerary objects were found in the tomb, which is now filled with replicas placed exactly where the originals—currently on permanent display in the Museo Tumbas Reales de Sipán in Lambayeque—were discovered. The Lord of Sipán did not make the journey to the next world alone—he was buried with at least seven people: a warrior (whose feet were amputated to ensure that he didn't run away), three young women, two assistants, and a child. The tomb also contained a dog and two llamas. Hundreds of ceramic pots contained snacks for the long trip. Archaeological work here is ongoing, but you can see some of the excavated objects in the on-site museum. ✉ *Sipán* ☎ *978/977–622* 🎫 *S/10, S/20 for a guide (strongly recommended).*

Chiclayo

204 km (127 miles) north of Trujillo.

A lively commercial center, Chiclayo is prosperous and easygoing. Although it doesn't have much colonial architecture or special outward beauty, it's surrounded by numerous pre-Columbian sites. ■ TIP→ **The Moche and Chimú people had major cities in the area, as did the Lambayeque, who flourished here from about 700 to 1370.** Archaeology buffs flocked to the area after the 1987 discovery nearby of the unlooted Tomb of the Lord of Sipán. Chiclayo is a comfortable base from which to visit that tomb, as well as other archaeological sites.

GETTING HERE AND AROUND

LATAM Perú, Viva Air Perú, and Star Perú connect Lima with Chiclayo's Aeropuerto José Quiñones González (CIX) just outside the city.

For the most part, you'll need to take a taxi around Chiclayo. Within the city limits, each ride should cost about S/5; ask for help at your hotel to negotiate anything beyond the city. Look at the map before hailing a taxi, though, because some attractions are within walking distance.

VISITOR INFORMATION iPerú. ✉ *Cl. San Jose 823* ☎ *074/205–703* 🌐 *www.peru.travel/en/useful-data/iperu.*

Sights

Cathedral

RELIGIOUS SITE | The enormous Chiclayo cathedral, dating from 1869, is worth a look for its Neoclassical facade on the Plaza de Armas and its well-maintained central altar. ✉ *Plaza de Armas* 🎫 *Free.*

Paseo Las Musas

PROMENADE | For some fresh air and great people-watching, head to this pedestrian walking path. It borders a stream and has classical statues depicting scenes from mythology. ✉ *La Florida and Falques.*

Restaurants

Much like Trujillo, Chiclayo and Lambayeque offer seco de cabrito, causas, and *tortilla de raya* (skate omelet). The area is more famous for King Kong, a large, crispy pastry that was invented around the time that the original movie premiered. It features *manjar blanco,* a sweet filling made of sugar, condensed milk, and cinnamon boiled down until it's thick and chewy.

★ Fiesta Gourmet

$$ | **PERUVIAN** | This exquisite eatery is one of Peru's not-to-be-missed culinary experiences. In 1983, the Solis family began serving modern interpretations of *comida norteña* (northern Peruvian cuisine) out of their home. **Known for:** northern Peruvian cooking raised to an art form; classic surroundings; attentive service. 💲 *Average main: S/50* ✉ *Salaverry 1820* ☎ *074/201–970* 🌐 *www.restaurantfiestagourmet.com* 🕓 *No dinner Sun.*

Hebrón

$ | **PERUVIAN** | **FAMILY** | A friendly staff serves a wide range of Peruvian and international specialties from 7 am to midnight daily at this centrally located eatery. *Pollo a la brasa*, sandwiches, grilled meats, *arroz con pato* (duck

Side Trip: Túcume

Archaeology aficionados looking to see some ancient sites in their crude state will enjoy this pyramid complex, located 35 km (22 miles) north of Chiclayo. Grand but largely unexcavated, it's the site of Huaca Larga, one of the largest adobe pyramids in South America, as well as dozens of smaller structures spread across a dry desert. Most are badly deteriorated. A small museum, **Museo de Sitio,** offers tours with English-speaking guides to learn about the history of the complex

The rugged desert landscape, sprinkled with hardy little *algarrobo* (mesquite) trees, is probably very similar to what it looked like when—so the legend goes—a lord called Naymlap arrived in the Lambayeque Valley and with his dozen sons founded the Lambayeque dynasty. It was this line of Sicán rulers who built the pyramids seen today. ■ **TIP→ Keep an eye out for burrowing owls as you make your way from the entrance toward the pyramids.**

Adjacent to the archaeological site is a lovely hotel designed from adobe and algarrobo wood, **Los Horcones de Tucume** (☎ *951/831–705* 🌐 *www.loshorconesdetucume.com*), whose architect-owner seamlessly incorporated pre-Columbian designs into the walled complex. There are 12 airy guest rooms with private terraces and a small pool at the hotel. The staff can arrange various horseback-riding trips through algarrobo forests and meetings with local *curanderos*, or shamans.

with rice): it's all there. There's also an excellent breakfast menu, free Wi-Fi, big corner windows for people-watching, and a playground, Hebrónlandia, in the back. **Known for:** kid-friendly environment; grilled chicken; breakfast. $ *Average main: S/20* ✉ *Av. Balta 605* ☎ *074/222–709* 🌐 *www.facebook.com/HebronRestaurant.*

La Parra

$ | **PERUVIAN** | Despite the bland decor, this restaurant serves delicious grilled meats, and specializes in parrilladas, with an extensive menu that includes every imaginable part of the cow. The anticuchos and ubre are well-prepared house specials. **Known for:** sizzling mixed grills; relaxed, casual vibe; service can be slow. $ *Average main: S/20* ✉ *Manuel María Izaga 752* ☎ *074/227–471.*

Pizzeria Venecia

$ | **PIZZA** | **FAMILY** | This hugely popular Italian restaurant serves decent pizza on a wooden block fresh from the oven. The list of toppings is extensive, and there are some pasta choices as well. **Known for:** unusual pizza toppings; raucous, hearty vibe; leisurely service. $ *Average main: S/20* ✉ *Av. Balta 413* ☎ *074/233–384* 🌐 *www.pizzeriavenecia.com.pe* ⏲ *No lunch.*

Sabores Peruanos

$$ | **PERUVIAN** | **FAMILY** | Locals in the know come to this rustic, bamboo-accented eatery for some of the best seafood in town, including marvellous cebiches and *sudados* (fish stews). There are also a few fusion-style entrees, including risottos, and a long list of mixed appetizers for those who like to sample. **Known for:** a variety of seafood specialties; seco de cabrito; massive portions. $ *Average main: S/36* ✉ *Av. Los Incas 136* ☎ *979/779–741* ⏲ *No dinner. Closed Mon.*

Hotels

Casa Andina Select Chiclayo

$ | **HOTEL** | A sleek modern lodging with well-trained staff, spacious rooms, and a good range of amenities, this Casa Andina is as popular with executives in town for a meeting as it is with travelers here to see the ancient ruins. **Pros:** central location; first-rate accommodations and amenities; well-trained staff. **Cons:** occasionally large business groups overtake the hotel; decor lacks character; surrounding area can be noisy. *Rooms from: S/245* *Av. Federico Villareal 115* *074/234–911* *www.casa-andina.com* *145 rooms* *Free breakfast.*

Costa del Sol Wyndham Chiclayo

$ | **HOTEL** | This modern tower just a few blocks from Chiclayo's main plaza attracts business travelers and tourists on a budget who come for the many amenities. **Pros:** central location; great service; pool and gym. **Cons:** can be noisy outside; decor is plain; hotel restaurant is a chain. *Rooms from: S/240* *Av. Balta 399* *074/227–272* *www.costadelsolperu.com* *82 rooms* *Free breakfast.*

Intiotel

$ | **HOTEL** | With refurbished décor and noise-proof glass for street-side rooms, this hotel is one of the best deals in Chiclayo. **Pros:** good rooms at a low price; well-equipped gym; friendly staff. **Cons:** dimly lighted hallways; mediocre hotel restaurant; noisy location. *Rooms from: S/130* *Av. Luis Gonzales 622* *979/341–022* *www.intiotel.com* *65 rooms* *Free breakfast.*

Las Musas Hotel & Casino

$ | **HOTEL** | People stay here for the view of the Paseo Las Musas, the statue-lined promenade overlooked by each of the hotel's rooms. **Pros:** location and views; on-site casino; decent restaurant. **Cons:** rooms are uninspiring; casino can be noisy; Wi-Fi can be slow. *Rooms from: S/155* *Los Faiques 101, Santa Victoria* *074/231–548* *www.lasmusashotel.com.pe* *46 rooms* *Free breakfast.*

Winmeier Hotel & Casino

$ | **HOTEL** | This full-scale casino resort features a whole host of amenities, including a poolside bar and outdoor fireplace for cool nights, two restaurants and a karaoke bar, efficient staff, and excellent accommodations. **Pros:** first-rate service and amenities; central location; pool is nice (if occasionally crowded). **Cons:** run-of-the-mill interior design; decor could use some updating; can be noisy on weekends. *Rooms from: S/170* *Av. Francisco Bolognesi 756* *074/228–172* *www.winmeier.com/en/hotel* *94 rooms* *Free breakfast.*

Nightlife

★ Cafe 900

BARS/PUBS | This bi-level restaurant and bar opens at 8 am for breakfast and doesn't close until late. Decorated with old guitars and various knickknacks and furnished with leather couches, it's one of the few options in Chiclayo with charm. Tapas and sandwiches dominate the long menu, and there are 20 or so different desserts. The superb cocktail list features new looks at Peruvian favorites, like the *chilcano de hierba luisa* (made with lemongrass, pisco, lime, bitters, and ginger ale). There's occasionally live jazz and folk music. *Calle Izaga 900* *074/209–268* *www.cafe900.com* *Closed Sun.*

Ozone Disco

DANCE CLUBS | The line for this ever-popular disco starts to form around 11, as locals in their early twenties to early fifties gear up for the (excessively) loud salsa and reggaeton and good cocktails. The first-floor bar and dance floor cost S/10 to enter. *Av. José L. Ortiz 490* *946/070–059* *www.facebook.com/OzoneDisco.*

Shopping

Mercado Central

FOOD/CANDY | The indoor market on Avenida Balta is no longer Chiclayo's main market. Once famed for its ceramics, weavings, and charms made by local *curanderos* (folk healers), it's now known mainly for selling fresh food and for having a nice little "food court" in the back. ✉ *Av. Balta and Vicente de la Vega.*

Mercado Modelo

OUTDOOR/FLEA/GREEN MARKETS | Beginning at the intersection of Avenida Balta and Avenida Arica, this vast and popular market has fresh meat, vegetables, and fruit from local farms, as well as clothing, DVDs and CDs, handbags, and more. You can also ask at any of the stalls to point you to the southwest corner, where there is an extensive *mercado de brujos (witchdoctor's market).* As elsewhere in Peru, this is a place where dozens of herbalists, curanderos, and shamans offer their folk remedies, many of them made of dried animals like armadillos and llama fetuses. Wander around and enjoy, but don't lose your companions in the crowd, and keep a close guard on your belongings. ✉ *Av. Balta and Av. Arica.*

Activities

Pimentel

BEACHES | The closest beach to Chiclayo is in this small port town, 14 km (8½ miles) west of the city. Access via taxi should cost about S/25 each way, or bus fare is just a few soles. Although the beach isn't very attractive, and the century-old curved pier is now closed to the public, there are many other enjoyable sights along the beach, including a small fleet of caballitos de totora and a lively boardwalk lined with restaurants. Walk along and observe the old colonial beach houses, the naval officers in white outside the maritime station, and an excessive number of young Peruvian couples walking hand in hand. **Amenities:** food and drink. **Best for:** surfing, sunset, swimming. ✉ *Malecón Seoane, Pimentel.*

Lambayeque

12 km (7 miles) north of Chiclayo.

This small town has some well-preserved colonial-era buildings, but the reason to come is for the outstanding museums. Their exhibits provide details about the Moche civilization and original artifacts from the tomb in Sipán.

GETTING HERE AND AROUND

The town is small enough to walk around from place to place, or you can take an inexpensive taxi (S/3 within town) to the different museums. To get here from Chiclayo, you can easily hire a taxi or rent a car.

Sights

Museo Arqueológico Nacional Brüning

MUSEUM | While not as exciting as the Sipán museum next door, this archaeological museum opens a window onto daily life as it transpired among different pre-Inca civilizations. Excellent interpretive displays show how the Moche, Lambayeque, and other pre-Inca cultures such as the Cupisnique, Chavín, Chimú, and Sicán fished, harvested, and kept their homes. There's also a wonderful photography exhibit detailing the archaeologist Hans Heinrich Brüning and his experiences in Peru beginning in the late 1800s. Descriptions are in Spanish, so an English-speaking guide is recommended. ✉ *Huamachuco and Atahualpa* ☎ *074/282–110* 🌐 *www.naylamp.gob.pe* 🎫 *S/10, S/20 for a guide.*

★ Museo Nacional Tumbas Reales de Sipán
MUSEUM | This striking pyramidal complex, which ranks among the country's best museums, displays the artifacts from the Tomb of the Lord of Sipán, one of the greatest archaeological finds of the 20th century. The discovery showed the world how advanced the Moche and other pre-Inca civilizations in Peru once were, and these stunning exhibits detail what and where every piece of jewelry, item of clothing, or ceramic vase was found. As you descend through the different floors, you'll see spectacular turquoise-and-gold earrings, bizarre hairless dogs buried with the Señor, and life-size mockups of Sipán warriors. This museum is very highly recommended. **TIP→ English-speaking guides are available to help with the Spanish-only descriptions and confusing order of exhibits.** *Av. Juan Pablo Vizcardo and Guzmán* *074/283–977* *www.naylamp.gob.pe* *S/10, S/30 for a guide* *Closed Mon.*

Hotels

★ Hosteria San Roque
$ | **HOTEL** | The most atmospheric place to base yourself while exploring the Chiclayo area's archaeological attractions is not in the city itself but rather in this 18th-century casona in Lambayeque. **Pros:** authentic colonial-era style; romantic manor house; pleasant pool. **Cons:** nothing nearby to do in the evenings; dim lighting in some rooms; some rooms bigger than others. *Rooms from: S/200* *2 de Mayo 437* *074/282–860* *www.hosteriasanroque.com* *20 rooms* *Free breakfast.*

Ferreñafe

18 km (11 miles) northeast of Chiclayo.

It's produced more winners of the Miss Peru contest than any other town, but Ferreñafe has other charms as well. The Iglesia Santa Lucia, begun in 1552, is a good example of baroque architecture. Nevertheless, most visitors come for its excellent Sicán museum.

GETTING HERE AND AROUND

Minibuses ply the streets of Chiclayo and Lambayeque for the short ride to Ferreñafe, and many tours will stop here on the way to Túcume. Taxis can also be hired. The Sicán museum is on the northern end of town.

Sights

Museo Nacional Sicán
MUSEUM | Offering insight into the culture of the Sicán people, this interesting museum also has unique exhibits on such topics as the El Niño effect and where the pre-Inca civilizations fit into world history. Visual timelines hammer home just how far back Peruvian history goes. The displays introducing the Sicán (also known as the Lambayeque) touch on everything from common eating utensils to ceremonial burial urns, with models of what their homes might have looked like and a central room full of amazing headdresses and masks. The replicas of the tombs are especially cool. *Av. Batán Grande, Cuadra 9* *074/286–469* *www.naylamp.gob.pe* *S/8* *Closed Mon.*

Piura

216 km (134 miles) north of Chiclayo.

The sunny climate, friendly people, and good food make Piura a delightful stop on your way north. Since most of the major flight and bus routes to the North Coast beaches travel through Piura, stopping here is not just easy, it's often required.

As a central commercial hub and the country's fifth-largest city (population 380,000), it's hard to believe how relaxed and friendly Piura is to tourists. Historically, however, it's a community used to transition. Founded in 1532 by Francisco Pizarro before he headed inland to conquer the Inca, the

Side Trip: Chaparrí Reserve

Getting to the Chaparri Reserve on your own can be difficult—it's 75 km (47 miles) northeast of Chiclayo, a little more than an hour's journey—but if you can get a group together or join a tour to this community-owned, dry-forest nature preserve, it might just be one of your most memorable experiences in Peru. The 34,412-hectare (85,000-acre) reserve was created to help safeguard rare native species such as the white-winged guan, the Andean condor, and the guanaco (a type of camelid similar in appearance to a llama). Perhaps its most important work is protecting the spectacled bear, for which it has a rescue center that works to reintroduce rehabilitated animals into this last refuge for populations of the species.

While you can visit the reserve anytime from 7 am to 5 pm, you'll up your chances of seeing wildlife if you stay overnight in the 12-room **Chaparri Ecolodge** (☎ *084/255–718* 🌐 *www.chaparrilodge.com*) in the heart of the park. Stays include three daily meals and a guide to the reserve. **■ TIP→ Advance booking for day visits and overnight stays is highly recommended, as space is limited and all visitors must be accompanied by a guide.** 🌐 *www.chaparri.org*

community changed locations three times before settling on the modern-day setting along the banks of the Río Piura.

GETTING HERE AND AROUND

LATAM Perú and Viva Air Perú fly between Lima and the Aeropuerto de Piura (PIU), 2 km (1 mile) east of the city. The best way to get around Piura is on foot, as most amenities and attractions are within a short walk of the plaza. Inexpensive and safe taxis are available from the street if you have heavy bags or are ready for a siesta.

VISITOR INFORMATION iPerú. ✉ *Av. Ayacucho 459* ☎ *073/320–249* 🌐 *www.peru.travel.*

Sights

Catedral de Piura

RELIGIOUS SITE | On the city's main square, the cathedral, built in 1588, is one of the country's oldest churches and is worth a visit. Inside you'll find an altarpiece dedicated to the Virgen de Fátima dating back more than 350 years. ✉ *Plaza de Armas* 🎫 *Free.*

Museo Vicus

MUSEUM | This archaeological museum, sometimes called the Museo Municipal, was extensively renovated during the first decade of this century. It houses the city's collection of pre-Columbian ceramics and gold artifacts, primarily from the Vicus culture, as well as changing art exhibits. ✉ *Av. Sullana and Av. Huánuco* ☎ *073/322–307* 🌐 *museamos.cultura.pe/museos/sala-de-oro-del-museo-municipal-vic* 🎫 *S/4* 🕒 *Closed Sun. and Mon.*

Restaurants

Bottega Capuccino

$ | PERUVIAN | This attractive restaurant has an extensive international menu offering traditional rice and meat dishes, as well European-inspired salads, sandwiches, and entrées mixing local and imported ingredients. Whether you choose the Thai salad or *lomo saltado* (stir-fried beef and potatoes), expect to savor your meal. **Known for:** alternatives to Peruvian cuisine; yummy desserts; café fare. $ *Average main: S/25* ✉ *Cl. San Miguel 298* ☎ *074/301–111* 🌐 *bottegacapuccino.com.*

★ **Picanteria La Santitos**
$ | **PERUVIAN** | Ask anyone in Piura the best place in town to go for typical dishes, and they'll tell you to come here. Two dining rooms—one air-conditioned, one not—with cracked white walls and waitresses in flowing peasant dresses form the backdrop for regional dishes like tamales *verdes* (green tamales) and *seco de chavelo* (fried green bananas and pork). **Known for:** offbeat regional food; countrified atmosphere; consistently high quality. *Average main: S/25 La Libertad 1001 074/309–475 www.lasantitos.com No dinner.*

Hotels

Costa del Sol Wyndham Piura
$$ | **HOTEL** | This excellent hotel, part of the Costa del Sol chain, has modern rooms and facilities, a high-end bar, and attentive service. **Pros:** catering to business travelers means better all-around service; nice pool area; soundproofed windows. **Cons:** the modern architecture lacks charm; some rooms have little natural light; on-site restaurant is an uninspiring chain. *Rooms from: S/260 Av. Loreto 649 073/302–864 www.wyndhamhotels.com/wyndham/piura-peru 95 rooms Free breakfast.*

LP Los Portales Hotel Piura
$ | **HOTEL** | A venerable hotel on the tree-shaded Plaza de Armas, the LP (Los Portales) has charming colonial architecture paired with plenty of modern amenities. **Pros:** beautiful colonial architecture; up-to-date technology, including LCD TV and Wi-Fi; valet parking. **Cons:** some rooms are better than others; breakfast buffet is limited; some bathrooms could be improved. *Rooms from: S/220 Libertad 875 01/611–9001 www.losportaleshoteles.com.pe/hotel-piura 87 rooms Free breakfast.*

Shopping

Catacaos
CERAMICS/GLASSWARE | The tiny pueblo of Catacaos, 12 km (7 miles) southwest of Piura, is famous for its textiles, gold and silver figurines and jewelry, and excellent pottery. The small market, filled with street stalls and shops, is open daily until 6 pm. Look around as much as you like, but to get the best price, only closely examine what you really want to buy. The town also has excellent *picanterías* in which to sample northern cuisine. To get to Catacaos, take the Pan-American Highway. A taxi should cost around S/30 round-trip.

Máncora

181 km (113 miles) north of Piura.

This laid-back beach destination, famous for its sunshine and white-sand shores, has excellent waves for surfing and great opportunities for fishing and adventure sports. Although the relaxed but dusty town has tourist offices, restaurants, and small shops, the real attraction is the line of hotels about 2 km (1 mile) south along Las Pocitas, a lovely string of beaches with rocky outcrops that hold tiny pools of seawater at low tide.

GETTING HERE AND AROUND

Comfortable Excluciva and Cruz del Sur buses ply the long 14-hour route between Lima and Máncora. If you wish to fly, LATAM Perú connects Lima with the Aeropuerto de Tumbes (TCP), about 1½ hours away, while LATAM Perú and Viva Air Perú fly to Piura, about 2½ hours away. Taxis at the airport charge about S/160 for the trip between Máncora and Tumbes and S/250 between Máncora and Piura. Once you arrive at Máncora, mototaxis are the best way to get around.

Restaurants

★ La Sirena D'Juan

$$ | **PERUVIAN** | Chef Juan Seminario rides his motorcycle to local markets every day to find the fish and produce that make this narrow restaurant the rival of many top eateries in Lima. This means Mediterranean and Asian elements find their way into dishes such as a Nikkei-style *tiradito* (sashimi-style fish with a spicy sauce) and house-made pastas. **Known for:** Asian-fusion cuisine; top-notch ingredients; delicious cocktails. *Average main: S/40 Av. Piura 316 073/258–173 www.facebook.com/laSirenaDeJuan Closed Tues.*

★ DCO Suites, Lounge & Spa

$$$ | **HOTEL** | With sleek, design-forward bungalows open to the sea breezes, DCO has a trendy, South Beach–type vibe. **Pros:** hip vibe and design; spa on-site; attracts a beautiful crowd. **Cons:** expensive; a long walk from town; staff is not always communicative. *Rooms from: S/610 Las Pocitas, 3 km south of Máncora 073/258–171 www.hoteldco.com 7 rooms Free breakfast.*

Hotelier Arte y Cocina

$ | **HOTEL** | **FAMILY** | Sandwiched between the fishing pier and the start of Las Pocitas beach, just south of Máncora, this small hotel is owned by the son of famed Peruvian TV chef Teresa Ocampo, whose recipes are used in the excellent beachfront restaurant, Donde Teresa. **Pros:** quiet and remote yet close to town; great restaurant; large rooms with good amenities. **Cons:** restaurant has sporadic hours; pool is small; beach is not as attractive as other stretches in Máncora. *Rooms from: S/240 Acceso Máncora, off Panamericana Norte, Las Pocitas 073/258–702 8 rooms Free breakfast.*

Hold On!

As a rule, taxis are abundant, cheap, and mechanically safe throughout Peru. Enter the mototaxi, a three-wheeled motorcycle, attached to a double seat, covered by an awning. No metal, no glass, nothing between you, the road, and the other vehicles. Regular car taxis are your best (read: safest) bet. The good news? Mototaxis often are slower and go only short distances, so, for those places—especially Máncora and Punta Sal—where they're the main form of transport, hold on, and enjoy the ride!

KiChic

$$$$ | **RESORT** | This tiny, Zen-like property on Las Pocitas beach, near other top boutique hotels, is perhaps the first to really do the New Age concept right in Máncora. **Pros:** unique emphasis on wellness; well planned; great rooms and facilities. **Cons:** concept not for everyone; accepts adult couples only; quite expensive. *Rooms from: S/860 Acceso Máncora, off Panamericana Norte, Las Pocitas 922/104–569 www.kichic.com 9 rooms Free breakfast.*

Los Corales

$$ | **HOTEL** | Directly on the beach south of the town, with very reasonable rates, this little lodging is one of the best deals in Máncora. **Pros:** same beachside location and service as other hotels for less; on-site restaurant; helpful staff. **Cons:** one of the oldest properties in town; pool is small; no room service. *Rooms from: S/369 Acceso Máncora, off Panamericano Norte 073/258–309 www.loscorales.pe 15 rooms Free breakfast.*

It doesn't take long to fall in love with under-the-radar Máncora, a strip of sandy beaches on the country's northern Pacific coast.

Selina Máncora Hotel

$ | HOTEL | At this dramatic hotel—just south of town and designed by Jordi Puig, who also did the MV Aqua luxury riverboats in the Amazon—among the first things you'll notice are the three-story, open-sided white box, which contains the bar and the front desk, and the stairs leading down to the longest infinity pool on the North Coast of Peru. **Pros:** close to town; beautiful pool; flexible lodging options. **Cons:** the beach in front can get dirty; not the best choice for those seeking privacy; service can be chaotic. *Rooms from: S/200* *Acceso Máncora, off Panamericano Norte* *073/258–614* *www.selina.com/es/peru/mancora* *12 rooms* *Free breakfast.*

Activities

Escuela de Buceos Spondylus

DIVING/SNORKELING | This PADI-licensed dive school runs immersion courses for beginners, and you can get your license for open-water diving, rescue diving, and underwater photography. Dive trips go to Los Organos, Punta Sal, and Cabo Blanco. *Av. Piura 216* *073/496–932* *spondylusdc.com* *From S/300.*

Punta Sal

25 km (15 miles) north of Máncora; 85 km (53 miles) southwest of Tumbes.

Sit on the beach, go for a swim, relax in the afternoon sun—what more could you want from a beach resort? It's no mystery why Punta Sal has become a popular vacation spot in recent years. Situated a few kilometers north of the Pan-American Highway, it's an area full of hotels and resorts, with plenty of tourists and vacationing *limeños* flocking for the blond-sand beach and comfortable ocean breezes. It's also quieter than Máncora, with fewer facilities, so plan on spending most of your time at or near your hotel.

Hotels

Punta Sal Suites & Bungalows Resort
$$ | RESORT | FAMILY | Offering a variety of bungalows, rooms, and beach areas, this upscale, all-inclusive resort is the place to go for luxury and relaxation. **Pros:** wonderful ocean views; wide range of activities and sports; super-friendly staff. **Cons:** regular rooms are nothing special; few places to buy food or other necessities nearby; no air-conditioning. *Rooms from: S/500 ✉ Km 173, Sullana–Tumbes Hwy. ☎ 072/596–700 ⊕ www.puntasal.com.pe 27 rooms All-inclusive.*

Tumbes

183 km (114 miles) north of Piura; 70 km (43 miles) north of Punta Sal.

About an hour's drive north of the beach resorts of Máncora and Punta Sal is Tumbes, the last city on the Peruvian side of the Peru–Ecuador border. Tumbes played a major role in Peruvian history: it was here that Francisco Pizarro first glimpsed the riches of the vast Inca Empire in 1528, prompting his return with his conquistadors in 1532. After Peru became independent, tensions with neighboring Ecuador were high—it wasn't until 1941 that Tumbes became part of Peru after a military skirmish—but things are now *tranquilo,* as Peruvians say. Still, hot, muggy Tumbes is unlike anywhere else in the country. The coastal desert that follows the Pan-American Highway all the way from Chile here peters out; in its place is a landscape that is decidedly more tropical, with mangrove forests and banana plantations. For most visitors, Tumbes is just a transit point to or from Ecuador or a quick stop before an early flight. The city has few attractions or comfortable places to spend the night. But for those with the urge to explore, there are several excellent national parks and plenty of inexpensive shellfish—as well as an atmosphere you won't find anywhere else in Peru.

If you find yourself crossing the border at Aguas Verdes, be extra aware of your belongings. Like many border towns, it has its fair share of counterfeit money, illegal goods, and scams to bilk money out of foreigners.

GETTING HERE AND AROUND

Tumbes is the stopping point for most bus lines, including Cruz del Sur, that travel the Pan-American Highway for the 18- to 19-hour trip to Lima. To get to Ecuador, there are direct buses run by CIFA (*www.cifainternacional.com*) to Guayaquil and Machala, where you can transfer to Cuenca. For most, the airport will be their point of entry. LATAM offers several flights per week from Lima to the Aeropuerto de Tumbes (TCP), just a few kilometers north of the city.

Hotels

Casa Andina Select Zorritos Tumbes
$$ | RESORT | National chain Casa Andina's first foray into the beach-resort game has proven to be a smart one—this resort in Zorritos, south of Tumbes, is one of the north's most convenient beach getaways. **Pros:** lovely views throughout the complex; great pool; spacious suites. **Cons:** resort is in an isolated area; service can be slow; local beach is not as pretty as others in the area. *Rooms from: S/421 ✉ Km 1232, Panamericana Norte, Bocapán, Zorritos ☎ 072/596–800 ⊕ www.casa-andina.com 57 rooms Free breakfast.*

Wyndham Costa del Sol Tumbes
$ | HOTEL | In the heart of downtown, this hotel makes for a comfortable option in Tumbes, which has a dearth of nice places to stay. **Pros:** large, inviting pool area; superior cleanliness and comfort; sport and fitness amenities. **Cons:** Wi-Fi can be spotty; decor is bland; on-site restaurant is a chain. *Rooms from: S/200 ✉ Jr. San Martín 275 ☎ 072/523–991 ⊕ www.costadelsolperu.com 54 rooms Free breakfast.*

Continued on page 40

THE CORDILLERA BLANCA

by Oliver Wigmore

The lofty ice-clad peaks of Cordillera Blanca soar above 6,000 meters (20,000 feet) and stretch for over 100 kilometers (62 miles) north to south across the Andes. These mountains, worshipped by Andean peoples for thousands of years, are now the idols of global adventure tourism.

Explore ancient ruins, ascend icy summits at the crack of dawn, hike isolated alpine valleys, be absorbed by the endless azure blue of glacial lakes, or put your feet up at a mountain lodge.

The formation of the present Andean mountain chain began as the Nazca plate collided with and was forced beneath the South American plate, driving the ocean floor up to produce the world's longest exposed mountain range. This resulted in the formation of the Pacific coastal desert, the highland puna, and the verdant Amazon basin. Since then the Andes have been the bridging point between these diverse environmental and ecological zones. The Cordilleras Blanca, Negra and Huayhuash, and the Callejón de Huaylas Valley were formed 4 to 8 million years ago, producing spectacular peaks and many distinct ecological niches.

The May to September dry season brings the most stable weather—and the big crowds. Increasingly people are battling the rain and snow for the isolation that comes with the off-season.

Peruvians cross a log bridge in the Jancapampa Valley, as the Cordillera Blanca looms before them.

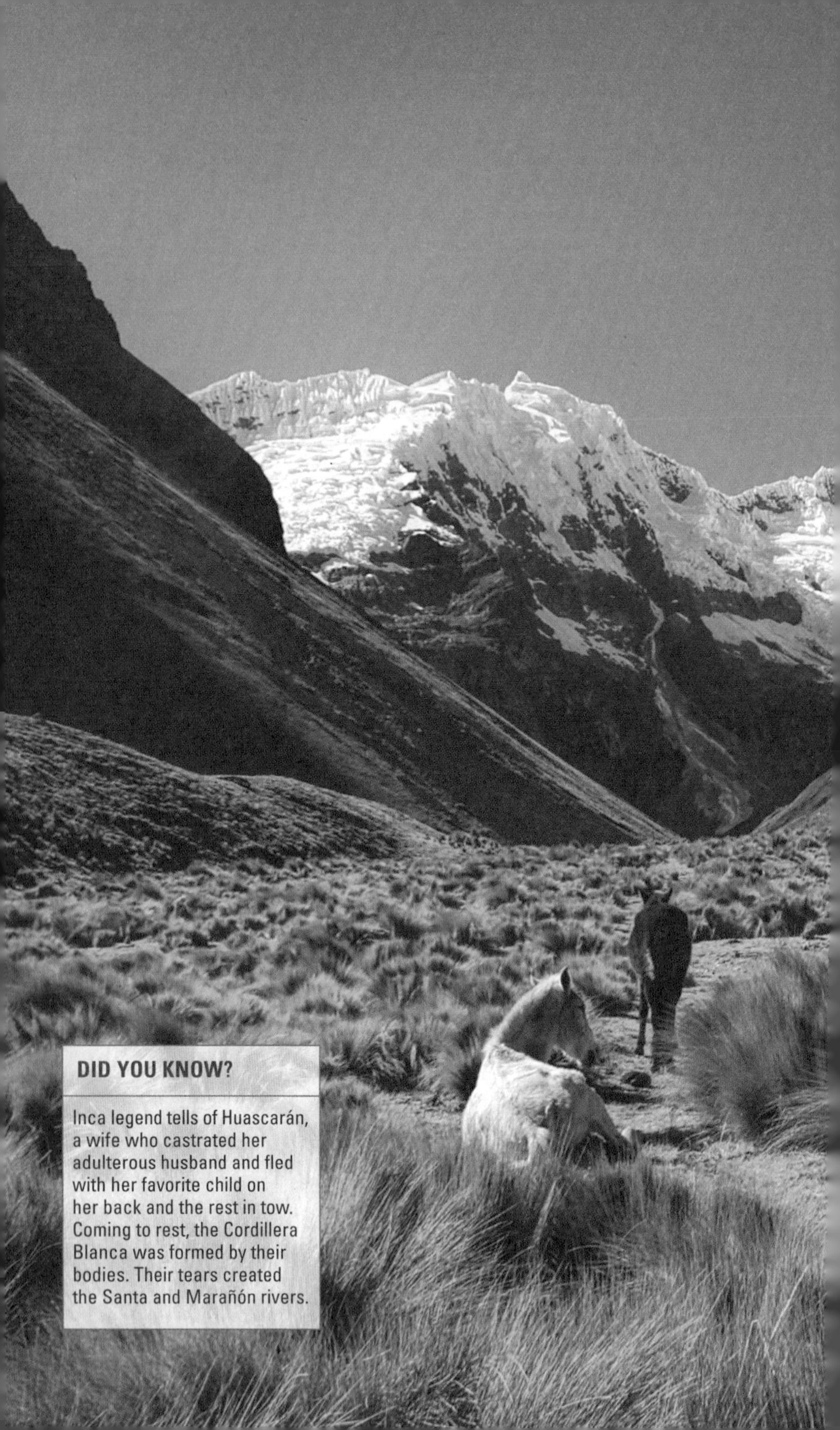

DID YOU KNOW?

Inca legend tells of Huascarán, a wife who castrated her adulterous husband and fled with her favorite child on her back and the rest in tow. Coming to rest, the Cordillera Blanca was formed by their bodies. Their tears created the Santa and Marañón rivers.

CORDILLERA BLANCA

Taulliraju Mount, Cordillera Blanca, Huascarán National Park, Peru.

The Cordillera Blanca encompasses the mighty Huascarán, Peru's highest peak at 6,767 m (22,204 ft), and Alpamayo 5,947 m (19,511 ft), once proclaimed the most beautiful mountain in the world by UNESCO. Most of the Cordillera Blanca is within the Huascarán National Park, for which an entry ticket is required. Valid for one day or one month, these can be purchased at the entry gates or from the park headquarters in Huaraz.

Thanks to the newly paved road, the glacial lakes are now a popular day trip from Huaraz. Their beauty is still worth the trip.

HIGH POINTS

1. The Santa Cruz Trek: You ascend the Santa Cruz valley, crossing the Punta Union pass at 4,760 m (15,617 ft) beneath the breathtaking peaks, then descend to the spectacular azure blue of the Llanganuco Lakes. One of Peru's most popular alpine treks, it's often overcrowded, with litter and waste becoming a serious problem. For pristine isolation, look elsewhere.

2. Pastoruri Glacier: While you could once ice-climb and ski on this tropical galcier, today a visit allows you to witness the impacts of climate change firsthand. Popular day tours from Huaraz often combine the trip here with a visit to see the impressive Puya raimondii trees.

3. Chavín de Huántar: On the eastern side of the cordillera is Chavín de Huántar, where in around 900 BC the first pan-Andean culture developed. The Chavín culture eventually held sway over much of central Peru. The site can be visited on a long day trip from Huaraz.

4. Olleros to Chavín Trek: A short three-day trek across the Cordillera terminates at Chavín de Huántar. Guiding companies in Huaraz offer this trek with llama hauling your gear.

5. Quilcayhuanca and Cojup Valley Loop: This trek is becoming popular due to its relative isolation and pristine condition. It explores two spectacular high alpine valleys, crosses the 5,000 m (16,404 ft) Pico Choco Pass, passing beautiful glacial lakes, one of which caused the 1941 destruction of Huaraz city in a flood of mud, rocks, and ice.

6. Laguna 69: Spectacular glaciers encircle the lake and give it deep turquoise color. It can be seen on a long day hike from Huaraz. However, spending the night allows you to explore, and you will likely have the lake to yourself once the day trippers leave. This is an ideal acclimation trek.

7. Alpamayo Basecamp: An arduous week-long trek takes you on a northern route through the Cordillera, passing the spectacular north face of Nevado Alpamayo (5947 m/19,511 ft).

8. Huascarán: Peru's highest peak is one of the Cordillera's more challenging summits.

Climbing: Relatively easy three to five day guided summit climbs of Ishinka (5,550 m/18,208 ft), Pisco (5,752 m/18,871 ft) and Vallunaraju (5,684 m/18,648 ft) are arranged at any of the guiding outfitters in Huaraz. Prices and equipment vary—get a list of what's included. Many smaller companies operate purely as booking agencies for the larger companies.

1 The Santa Cruz Trek
7 Alpamayo 5,947m (19,511ft)
Huaicayan
0 3 mi
0 3 km
Cashapampa
Pirámide
Artesonraju
Huaripampa
Caraz
Pisco 5,752m (18,871ft)
Laguna 69 6
Chacraraju
Yanama
Huandoy
Caraz
CORDILLERA BLANCA
(HUASCARAN NATIONAL PARK)
Chopicalqui
Contrahierbas
Río Santa
Huascarán 8 6,768m (22,204ft)
Pueblo Libre
Yungay
Chacas
Utla
Pompey
Musho
Huaypan
Hualcan
Ulta
Mancos
Copa
Shilla
Huaicán
Copa
CORDILLERA NEGRA
Bayoraju
Vicos
Paqcharaju
Copa Chico
Carhuaz
Ranrahirca
Marcará
Akilpo
Vicos
Kekepatipa
Pashpa
Toellaraju
Anta
Joncopampa
Palcaraju
Ishinka 5,550m (18,208ft)
Taricá
Collón
Pucaranra
Jangas
Ranrapaica
Vallunaraju 5,684m (18,648ft)
Pico Choco
COJUP VALLEY
Churup
Monterrey
Wilkawain
Quilcayhuanca and Cojup Valley Loop 5
Pitec
QUILCAYHUANCA VALLEY
Huaraz
Huahulac
Macashca
Río Santa
Chavín de Huántar 3
Pastoruri Glacier 2
Olleros 4
Agocancha

A llama—member of the camelid family and provider of wool for Andean weavers—ChavÍn, Cordillera Blanca.

GOOD TO KNOW

CLIMBING HISTORY

The first climbers in the region were probably pre-Colombian priests, attempting difficult summits to perform sacred rituals atop icy peaks. This climbing tradition was continued by the Spanish conquistadors who wanted to exploit the rich sulphur deposits atop many of Peru's volcanic cones, and to show their dominance over Mother Nature. Modern climbing in the region took off in 1932 when a German-Austrian expedition completed many of the highest summits, including Huascarán Sur. Since then the peaks of the Cordillera Blanca and Peru have attracted climbers from around the world for rapid-summit sport climbs and solo summits. Extended duration expeditions and large support crews are less common here than in the Himalayas.

SAFETY TIPS

This area is a high alpine environment and weather patterns are unpredictable. Be prepared for all weather possibilities. It's not uncommon to experience snow storms and baking sun over the course of a single day, and at night temperatures plummet. Sunburn, dehydration, exhaustion, and frostbite are all potential problems, but by far the major issue is soroche (altitude sickness). It's extremely important to pace yourself and allow enough time for acclimatisation before attempting any long-distance high-altitude treks or climbs.

(above) Cullicocha; (below) Sheperds hut, Huaraz.

ENVIRONMENTAL CHANGE

The warming climate is producing alarming rates of retreat in glacial water reserves of the Cordillera Blanca. The heavily populated Pacific coast relies almost exclusively on seasonal runoff from the eastern Andes for water supplies and hydroelectricity. The feasibility of transporting water across the Andes from the saturated Amazon basin is now being debated.

MAPS

For serious navigation, get the Alpenvereins-karte (German Alpine Club) topographic map sheets, which cover the Cordillera Blanca over two maps (north and south). They are sold by Casa de Guías and the gift store below Café Andino. Many local expedition outfitters sell an "officially illegal" copy with a little persuasion.

Huaraz

400 km (248 miles) north of Lima.

Peru's number-one trekking and adventure-sports destination, Huaraz is a perfect starting point for those wishing to explore the vast wilderness of the Cordillera Blanca. Unfortunately, the town has been repeatedly leveled by natural disasters. In the latter part of the 20th century, three large earthquakes destroyed much of the city center, claiming more than 20,000 lives.

Despite the setbacks and death toll, Huaraz rallied, and today it's a pleasant town filled with good-natured people. As one of the most popular tourist destinations in northern Peru, it also has a great international scene, and although sights in the city itself are few and far between, the lively restaurants and hotels are some of the best in the region. ■ **TIP→ Many businesses close between September and May, when the town practically shuts down without its hordes of climbers and trekkers.** It can be hard to find an outfitter at this time; call ahead if you plan a rainy-season visit.

GETTING HERE AND AROUND

Most travelers come to Huaraz on an eight-hour bus ride from Lima. In the past, there were occasional flights to the area's small airport in Anta, 32 km (20 miles) north of town, but for now, these flights appear to have been suspended indefinitely. Getting around Huaraz is easy, as it is small enough to walk almost anywhere. Or, if you've just arrived and are feeling a little breathless from the altitude, take a taxi for S/5. To get the most out of the nearby treks and sights, hire a guide for safety.

VISITOR INFORMATION iPerú. ✉ *Psje. Atusparia* ☎ *043/428–812* 🌐 *www.peru.info.*

Sights

Jirón José Olaya

HISTORIC SITE | To see Huaraz's colonial remnants, head to Jirón José Olaya, a pedestrian-only street that's one of the few places left untouched by the 1970 earthquake. The handsome, white-and-green facades stand east of the town center, on the right-hand side of Raimondi and a block behind Confraternidad Inter Este. The best time to visit is on Sunday, when there's a weekly *feria de comida típica,* a regional street festival with local food and craft stalls. ✉ *Huaraz.*

Mercado Central

MARKET | For a down-to-earth look at Andean culture, head to this market, where you'll see fruits and vegetables grown only in the highlands, as well as *cuyes* (guinea pigs), chickens, ducks, and rabbits, all available for purchase alive or freshly slaughtered. ✉ *Entrance at Jr. de la Cruz Romero and Av. Cayetano Requena.*

Mirador de Rataquenua

VIEWPOINT | The lookout point has an excellent view of Huaraz, the Río Santa, and the surrounding mountains. It's a 45-minute walk up, and the directions are complicated, so it's best to hire a guide or, better yet, take a taxi. ✉ *Av. Confraternidad Inter Sur and Av. Confraternidad Inter Este.*

Museo Arqueológico de Ancash

MUSEUM | What draws visitors to this small museum is the park out back, which has a delightful assortment of pre-Hispanic statues from the Chavín and Recuay cultures. The musicians, warriors, and gods here will keep you company as you reflect on the mummies and ceramics you've examined in the museum's inner rooms. ■ **TIP→ Upstairs, numerous skulls bear the scars (or rather holes) from trepanation, the removal of bone from the skull.** There are also textiles, metalwork, and a room dedicated to ancient Andean beliefs about the afterlife. ✉ *Av. Luzuriaga 762* ☎ *043/421–551* 🌐 *museamos.cultura.pe/museos* 🎫 *S/5* 🕐 *Closed Mon.*

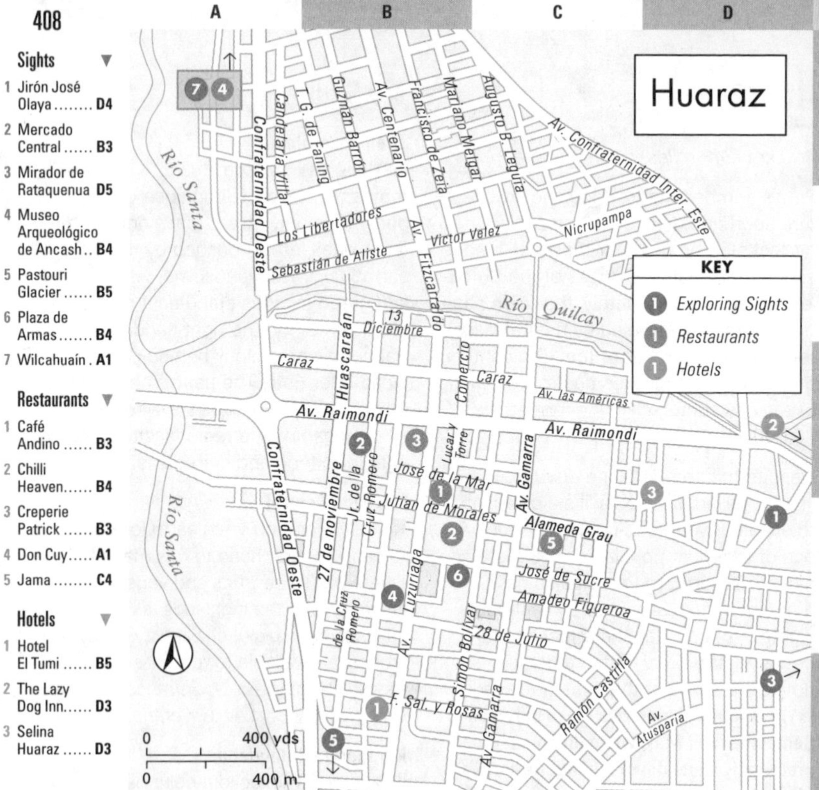

Pastouri Glacier

NATURE SITE | A popular day-trip from Huaraz is a visit to the Pastoruri Glacier, where you can hike around the 8-square-km (3-square-mile) berg. The rapidly shrinking ice field, which could disappear within the next few years, has become a symbol of global climate change. ■ **TIP→ On this trip you'll ascend to well above 4,000 meters (13,000 feet), so make sure you're used to the high altitude.** Wear warm clothing, sunscreen, and sunglasses, as the sun is intense. Drink lots of water to avoid altitude sickness. The easiest and safest way to get here is with a tour company from Huaraz. The tour costs about S/30 to S/40 and takes eight hours. You can also hire diminutive horses to take you up to the glacier from the parking lot for about S/15. It's not the most spectacular glacier in the world, but if you've never seen one up close, it's worth the trip. The glacier is 70 km (43 miles) south of Huaraz, off the main highway at the town of Recuay—a journey of about three hours. ✉ *Huaraz* 🎫 *S/5.*

Plaza de Armas

PLAZA | This pretty square is the key spot for people-watching in Huaraz. The cathedral looks splendid when lit up at night, and *tiendas artesenales* (artisanal kiosks) border the central fountain. ✉ *Av. Luzuriaga and Jr. José de Sucre.*

Wilcahuaín

ARCHAEOLOGICAL SITE | Some 8 km (5 miles) north of Huaraz, this small archaeological site contains a Wari temple, dating from AD 1100, that resembles the larger temple at Chavín de Huántar. Each story of the crumbling three-tiered temple has seven rooms. There's are also a small museum, basic bathroom facilities, and a limited restaurant. Trained and knowledgeable local students will be your guide for a small tip (suggested minimum: S/10). ✉ *Huaraz* ✣ *Bus service available from corner of Jr. 13 de Diciembre and Jr. Cajamarca* 🌐 *munidi.gob.pe/turismo* 🎫 *S/5* ⏲ *Closed Mon.*

Restaurants

★ Café Andino

$ | CAFÉ | Equal parts funky and friendly, this café offers light snacks, hot and cold beverages, free Wi-Fi, and a seemingly endless supply of newspapers and books in English. Warm up by the fireplace on a cold night, or sit on the outdoor terrace with your laptop and sip a fresh-pressed cup of tea. **Known for:** good views; cozy, home-away-from-home vibe; best breakfasts in town. [$] *Average main: S/25* ✉ *Jr. Lucar y Torre 530, 3rd fl.* ☎ *043/421–203* 🌐 *www.cafeandino.com* 💳 *No credit cards.*

Chilli Heaven

$ | ECLECTIC | An eclectic mix of Indian curries, Mexican burritos, and Thai favorites makes this cozy dining room a magnet for tourists seeking international edibles. The spicy concoctions are belly warming; a big beer selection helps put out the flames. **Known for:** fajitas; vindaloos; warm hospitality. [$] *Average main: S/25* ✉ *Parque Ginebra* ☎ *043/425–532* 🌐 *www.facebook.com/chilliheaven.*

Creperie Patrick

$$ | FRENCH | With a breezy terrace upstairs and a cozy bistro downstairs, this French eatery covers a lot of bases. There are couscous and fondue, as well as hard-to-find local dishes such as grilled alpaca. **Known for:** European fare; crepes with fruit and ice cream; Old World atmosphere. [$] *Average main: S/40* ✉ *Av. Luzuriaga 422* ☎ *043/426–037* 🌐 *www.facebook.com/CreperiePatrick* ⏲ *No lunch.*

★ Don Cuy

$ | PERUVIAN | To experience the Andean delicacies that *huarasinos* eat on special occasions, take a 10-minute taxi ride outside downtown to this excellent *restaurante campestre* (country restaurant beneath a trellised arbor). Here you'll find *pachamanca* (meats and vegetables cooked over coals in a pit), pork cooked in a cylindrical box, and yes, cuy, or guinea pig (it's actually scrumptious). **Known for:** grilled meats; Andean delicacies; great service. [$] *Average main: S/25* ✉ *Av. Centenario 2621* ☎ *043/232–472* 🌐 *www.facebook.com/DONCUYPERU* ⏲ *No dinner.*

★ Jama

$ | PERUVIAN | With this intimate, five-table bistro, Peruvian *cocina del autor* comes to Huaraz. Young chef Junior Reymundo doesn't just provide exquisite takes on Peruvian classics: he tells stories. **Known for:** innovative, ever-changing menu; personal attention from one of Peru's top chefs; haute cuisine for ridiculously low prices. [$] *Average main: S/30* ✉ *Psje. Guzman Arenas* ☎ *964/307–503* 🌐 *jama-restaurante.negocio.site.*

Hotels

Hotel El Tumi

$ | HOTEL | FAMILY | The great location and amenities make this comfy inn a perennial favorite among travelers. **Pros:** great location; comfortable beds; good spa and restaurant. **Cons:** some rooms are a bit small; decor is a bit antiquated; bathrooms need an upgrade. [$] *Rooms from: S/125* ✉ *Jr. San Martín 1121* ☎ *043/421–784* 🌐 *www.hoteleseltumi.com.pe* 🛏 *82 rooms.*

The Lazy Dog Inn

$$ | B&B/INN | The Canadian owners who built this eco-friendly adobe lodge are heavily involved with community and environmental activities in Huaraz and the Cordillera Blanca, so if it's a laid-back mountain experience you're after, drop in here rather than stay in town. **Pros:** cabins can sleep four to five people; secluded and close to nature; some rooms have fireplaces. **Cons:** main-floor guest room has shared bathroom; 12 km (7 miles) from town; Wi-Fi can be spotty. *$ Rooms from: S/320 ✉ Km 3.3, Cachipampa Alto ☎ 043/978–9330 🌐 www.thelazydoginn.com 5 rooms 🍴 Some meals.*

Selina Huaraz

$ | HOTEL | FAMILY | This brightly colored hostel-meets-hotel is perched on a hillside and has community rooms for backpackers and hikers on a budget, as well as rooms and suites, some with great views of the Cordillera Blanca, to appeal to upscale travelers. **Pros:** good place to meet other travelers; variety of useful common areas; bright, sunny decor. **Cons:** a bit of a hike from Huaraz's city center; not a good option for those seeking privacy; some rooms are small. *$ Rooms from: S/160 ✉ Jr. Italia 1124 ☎ 043/425–856 🌐 www.selina.com/en/peru/huaraz 31 rooms 🍴 No meals.*

Nightlife

To warm yourself up at night, enjoy one of the city's many laid-back bars and dance clubs. Be on the lookout for locally brewed craft beer Sierra Andina.

Cafe Bar 13 Buhos

BARS/PUBS | Homey furnishings and a super-chill vibe make this three-story lounge a cozy nightspot after an all-day trek. The menu includes an in-house brew (called Lucho's) and inexpensive pub grub like *piqueos* and burgers. Pool tables and a DJ add to the relaxed, house-party feel. *✉ Parque Ginebra ☎ 043/784–423 🌐 www.facebook.com/trecebuhos.*

Tambo

DANCE CLUBS | The ever-popular Tambo has low ceilings and curvy walls, and there's a large dance floor where you can groove to salsa and Latin pop until the wee hours of the morning. *✉ Jr. José de la Mar 776 ☎ 043/425–859 🌐 www.facebook.com/Tambodiscoteca.*

Shopping

Crafts booths on either side of the Plaza de Armas have tables piled high with locally woven textiles.

Montañas Mágicas

SPORTING GOODS | This outdoors shop stocks many popular brands of gear. *✉ Parque Ginebra ☎ 949/680–107 🌐 www.facebook.com/montmagicas.*

Activities

BIKING

If you're an experienced mountain biker, you'll be thrilled at what the area offers along horse trails or gravel roads passing through the Cordilleras Blanca and Negra.

Chakinani Peru Mountain Bike Adventures

BICYCLING | This shop rents specialized mountain bikes and has experienced guides to take you to the good single-track spots. *✉ Jr. Lucar and Torre 530, 2nd fl. ☎ 043/424–259 🌐 www.chakinaniperu.com From S/100.*

CLIMBING AND TREKKING

If dreams of bagging a 6,000-meter (19,700-foot) peak or trekking through the wilderness haunt your nights, Huaraz is the place for you. The town sits at a lofty 3,090 meters (10,138 feet), and the surrounding mountains are even higher. Allowing time to acclimatize is a lifesaving necessity. Drinking lots of water and pacing yourself will help avoid high-altitude pulmonary edema (commonly known as altitude sickness, or *soroche* in Peru). **■ TIP→ The climbing and trekking season runs from May through September—the driest months.** You can trek during the off-season, but trudging every day through heavy rain isn't fun. Climbing during the off-season can also be downright dangerous, as crevasses get covered by new snow. Even if you're an experienced hiker, you shouldn't venture into the backcountry without a guide.

Guided treks in the region vary by the number of days and the service. You can opt for one-, two-, and three-day hikes or an expedition of 10 to 20 days. Most guided treks provide donkeys to carry your equipment, plus an emergency horse. There are so many outfitters in the area that looking for a qualified company can be overwhelming. Visit a few places, talk with the guides, and make sure you're getting what you really want. Many of the climbs are quite technical and can be dangerous. Deaths do occur on occasion, so it is essential to hire guides with experience.

Casa de Guías

CLIMBING/MOUNTAINEERING | An association of certified freelance guides, Casa de Guías offers excellent advice and personalized trips, including mountaineering and trekking as well as rock- and ice-climbing courses. ✉ *Parque Ginebra 28-G* ☎ *043/421–811* 🌐 *www.agmp.pe* *Prices vary* ⏲ *Closed Sun.*

WHITE-WATER RAFTING

There's good rafting on the Río Santa, a glacial river with heart-pumping, Class III and IV rapids. The most-often-run stretch of river is between Jangas and Caraz. The river can be run year-round but is at its best during the wettest months of the rainy season, between December and April. Be prepared with the right equipment: the river is cold enough to cause serious hypothermia.

★ Huascaran Adventure Travel Agency

WHITE-WATER RAFTING | Offering local guides familiar with this beautiful region's many adventure opportunities, Huascaran Adventure Travel Agency can cater to any group size, degree of difficulty, and adventure. For rafting, the guides can take you out to play on the rapids of the Santa River, while enjoying the wilderness of the Cordillera Blanca and Cordillera Negra. ✉ *Jr. Pedro Campos 711* ✥ *In front of Sport Soledad* ☎ *51/43-422–523* 🌐 *www.huascaran-peru.com/rafting.php.*

Chavín de Huántar

98 km (61 miles) southeast of Huaraz.

This small, unassuming village thrives on tourists coming to visit the ruins of the same name that are found at one end of town. Few stay overnight, although those who do will find a few small shops, restaurants, and basic hostels near the Plaza de Armas.

GETTING HERE AND AROUND

If you have a car—and an excellent map and good sense of direction—you can head out and explore the windy, confusing roads around town. For all others, taking an inexpensive taxi will ensure that you get where you need to go. The overwhelming majority of visitors come on day-trips from Huaraz.

★ Chavín de Huántar

ARCHAEOLOGICAL SITE | Indiana Jones would feel right at home in these fascinating ruins, which feature an underground labyrinth of stone corridors and a terrifying idol at their center. The idol, known as the Lanzón, is a 4-meter (13-foot) daggerlike slab with a jaguar's face and serpentine hair, and it was the Holy of Holies for the Chavín people, who were the mother civilization for the Andes. Pilgrims from all over South America would come here to worship, eventually spreading the cult of the so-called Fanged Deity throughout the continent. To make things even crazier, during ceremonies here, Chavín priests and their acolytes would ingest the psychedelic San Pedro cactus, thus facilitating their transformation into the smiling, ferocious god.

Visiting the Chavín archaeological complex, which dates from 1500 BC, is a favorite day-trip from Huaraz. The UNESCO World Heritage Site sits on the southern edge of the tiny village of the same name and comprises two separate wings of the main temple, a large U-shaped main plaza, a second plaza surrounded with mysterious carvings, and an on-site museum that houses the grinning stone heads that once looked out from the temple's outer wall. On the drive southeast from the city, you get good views of two Andean peaks, Pucaraju (5,322 meters/17,460 feet) and Yanamarey (5,237 meters/17,180 feet), as well as of the alpine Laguna de Querococha. The eight-hour tour costs about S/50 per person, not including the entrance fee to the ruins. If you'd prefer to get here on your own, regular buses run between Huaraz and Chavín, and you can hire a guide at the entrance to the site. ✉ *Chavín* ☎ *043/454–011* 🌐 *museamos.cultura.pe/museos/museo-nacional-chav%c3%adn* 🎟 *S/10* 🕑 *Museum closed Mon.*

Yungay

59 km (37 miles) north of Huaraz.

On May 31, 1970, an earthquake measuring 7.7 on the Richter scale shook loose some 15 million cubic meters of rock and ice that cascaded down the west wall of Huascarán Norte. In the quiet village of Yungay, some 14 km (8½ miles) away, people were going about their normal activities. Some were waiting for a soccer game to be broadcast on the radio; others were watching the Verolina Circus set up in the stadium. Then the debris slammed into town at a speed of more than 322 km (200 miles) per hour. Almost all of Yungay's 20,000 inhabitants were buried alive. The quake ultimately claimed nearly 70,000 lives throughout Peru.

The government never rebuilt Yungay, but left it as a memorial to those who had died. It's now a town-size burial ground, and people visit daily. **■ TIP→ Walking through the ruined town, you'll see upturned buses, the few remaining walls of the cathedral, and, oddly, a couple of palm trees that managed to survive the disaster.** There's a large white cross at the old cemetery on the hill south of town. It was here that 92 people who were tending the graves of friends and relatives were on high-enough ground to survive. You pay a nominal S/5 to enter the site.

New Yungay was built just beyond the *aluvión* path—behind a protective knoll. It's a modern town with little of interest, though it serves as a starting point for those visiting the spectacular Lagunas de Llanganuco.

GETTING HERE AND AROUND

Buses between Huaraz and Caraz all stop here. Let the driver know you want to get off at Yungay Viejo or Camposanto if you want to go directly to the memorial site.

Lagunas de Llanganuco

These two gorgeous mountain lakes, sitting near the base of Mt. Huascarán and within the national park, are the destination of one of the most common day-trips from Huaraz. They can be visited year-round.

GETTING HERE AND AROUND

Most visitors arrive here on a day-trip from Huaraz or to start a longer trekking excursion, though you can also come by taxi from Yungay. Be prepared to negotiate a wait time, as you won't otherwise find transportation back.

★ Lagunas de Llanganuco

BODY OF WATER | Make sure your camera memory card is empty when you go to see these spectacular glaciers, gorges, lakes, and mountains. Driving through a giant gorge formed millions of years

Cordillera Huayhuash Treks

Although much smaller than the Cordillera Blanca, the main chain of the Cordillera Huayhuash is known for its isolation and pristine environment. For years, the area remained essentially off-limits to foreign tourism, as it was a major stronghold for the Shining Path insurrection that terrorized much of Peru's Central Highlands throughout the 1980s. Today this isolation is what makes the region so special. Treks here are measured in weeks, not days, with road access and tourist infrastructure almost nonexistent. The opportunities to spot rare Andean wildlife are much greater here and the chances of meeting tour groups next to zero.

Cordillera Huayhuash Circuit: This taxing trek, the major draw here, can take up to two weeks, passing through some of the region's most spectacular mountain scenery. Access to this trail was traditionally via Chiquián, but the road has been extended to Llamac. Tours and supplies are best organized in Huaraz, although Chiquián does provide some limited facilities, and porters and mules can be arranged here.

Siula Grande (6,344 meters, 20,814 feet): See the mountain made famous by Joe Simpson in his gripping tale of survival in *Touching the Void.*

Yerupaja (6,617 meters, 21,709 feet): The second-highest mountain in Peru.

ago by a retreating glacier, you arrive at Lagunas de Llanganuco. The crystalline waters shine a luminescent turquoise in the sunlight; in the shade they're a forbidding inky black. **TIP→ Waterfalls of glacial melt snake their way down the gorge's flanks, falling lightly into the lake.** There are many *quenual* trees (also known as the paper-bark tree) surrounding the lakes. Up above, you'll see treeless alpine meadows and the hanging glaciers of the surrounding mountains. At the lower lake, called Lago Chinancocha, you can hire a rowboat (S/5 per person) to take you to the center. A few trailside signs teach you about local flora and fauna. The easiest way to get here is with an arranged tour from Huaraz (about S/40 plus entrance fee), though if you are going on the Santa Cruz trek you will probably start here. The tours stop here and at many other spots on the Callejón de Huaylas, finishing in Caraz. *S/5*

★ Laguna 69 (*Lake 69*)

BODY OF WATER | Regularly featured on "most beautiful lakes in the world" lists and Instagram bucket lists, this small but stunning turquoise glacial lake near the city of Huaraz and within Parque Nacional Huascarán merits all the hype for its natural beauty and for the spectacular and scenic hike leading to the lake. ⚠ **Treat your visit to Laguna 69 like a high-altitude hike, not a photo op, and be prepared.** The trek to Laguna 69 will take your breath away, figuratively and literally, as the lake sits 4,600 meters (15,092 feet) above sea level. Remind yourself that this altitude is just 2,000 feet below base camp at Mount Everest, and then train, pack, and plan time to acclimatize accordingly. It's possible to get to Laguna 69 and do the hike solo, but it is cheaper (and safer) to take a tour. If you are an experienced high-altitude hiker, you can beat the crowds by staying at a campsite by Llanganuco lake near the hike's trailhead to start your morning hike as early as you wish. ✉ *Parque Nacional Huascarán, Huaraz* 🌐 *www.sernanp.gob.pe/huascaran* 🎫 *Park admission: S/10 day pass, S/65 multiday pass.*

★ **Parque Nacional Huascarán** (*Huascarán National Park*)

NATIONAL/STATE PARK | The Lagunas de Llanganuco are one of the gateways to the Parque Nacional Huascarán, which covers 3,400 square km (1,300 square miles) and was created in 1975 to protect flora and fauna in the Cordillera Blanca. ■ **TIP→ This incredible mountain range has a total of 663 glaciers and includes some of the highest peaks in the Peruvian Andes.** Huascarán, which soars to 6,768 meters (22,200 feet), is the highest in Peru. The smaller Alpamayo, 5,947 meters (19,511 feet), is said by many to be the most beautiful mountain in the world. Its majestic flanks inspire awe and wonder in those lucky enough to get a glimpse. Not far away, the monstrous Chopicalqui and Chacraraju rise above 6,000 meters (19,700 feet).

Within the park's boundaries you'll also find more than 750 plant types. There's a tragic scarcity of wildlife in the park—many animals have been decimated by hunting and the loss of natural habitats. Among the 12 species of birds and 10 species of mammals, you're most likely to see wild ducks and condors. With a great deal of time and an equal amount of luck you may also see foxes, deer, pumas, and vizcachas.

The giant national park attracts a plethora of nature lovers, including campers, hikers, and mountain climbers. Myriad treks weave through the region, varying from fairly easy one-day hikes to 20-day marathons. Within the park, you can head out on the popular **Llanganuco–Santa Cruz Loop,** a three- to five-day trek through mountain valleys, past crystalline lakes, and over a 4,750-meter-high (15,584-foot-high) pass. Other popular hikes include the one-day Lake Churup Trek, the two-day Quilcayhuanca–Cayesh trek, and the two-day Ishinca Trek. Check with guide agencies in Huaraz for maps, trail information, and insider advice before heading out. ■ **TIP→ If possible, plan on visiting Laguna 69, one of the park's loveliest lakes; it's frequently included in hikes and day-trips from Huaraz.**

Although experienced hikers who know how to survive in harsh mountain conditions may decide to head out on their own, it's always safer to arrange for a guide in Huaraz. You can opt to have donkeys or llamas carry the heavy stuff, leaving you with just a day pack. The most common ailments on these treks are sore feet and altitude sickness. Wear comfortable hiking shoes that have already been broken in, and take the proper precautions to avoid feeling the height (drink lots of water, avoid prolonged exposure to the sun, and allow yourself time to acclimatize before you head out). The best time to go trekking is during the dry season, which runs May through September. July and August are the driest months, though dry season doesn't mean a lack of rain or even snow, so dress appropriately.

Some hikers decide to enter the park at night to avoid paying the hefty S/65 for a multiday pass (from 2 to 30 days), but the money from these fees goes to protect the Andean habitat; consider this before you slip in during the dead of night (nighttime safety is a concern, too). You can purchase a pass at the Huaraz office of Parque Nacional Huascarán, at the corner of Rosas and Federico Sal, as well as at Llanganuco. ■ **TIP→ Be sure to carry a copy of your passport with you.** ✉ *Huaraz office of Parque Nacional Huascarán, Rosas 555 and Federico Sal, Huaraz* ☎ *043/422–086* 🌐 *www.sernanp.gob.pe/huascaran* 🎫 *S/10 day pass, S/65 multiday pass.*

Hotels

Llanganuco Mountain Lodge

$$ | **B&B/INN** | This quiet, remote lodge with spectacular views is right on the edge of the Huascarán National Park, wedged between Llanganuco and Rajururi gorges and adjacent to Keushu lake—a great place to get away from it all. **Pros:** close to nature; abundant hiking opportunities; on the lakeshore. **Cons:** cash only and no withdrawal facilities; no choice at dinner; devices must be charged in the hotel bar as there are no plugs in the rooms. *Rooms from: S/400 ✉ Yungay ☎ 976/592–524 🌐 llanganucolodge.com ▭ No credit cards ⇆ 4 rooms 🍽 All-inclusive.*

Caraz

67 km (42 miles) north of Huaraz.

One of the few towns in the area with a cluster of colonial-era architecture, Caraz is at the northern tip of the valley; only a partly paved road continues north. North of Caraz on the dramatic road to Chimbote is the Cañon del Pato, the true northern terminus of the Callejón de Huaylas. Caraz is an increasingly popular alternative base for trekkers and climbers. While in town be sure to try the ultrasweet manjar blanco, Peru's version of dulce de leche. It's available in numerous *dulcerías*, such as that of Villa Luisa.

GETTING HERE AND AROUND

There are frequent buses here from Huaraz, most stopping in Carhuaz and Yungay first. In the other direction your options are fewer.

Sights

Lake Parón

BODY OF WATER | The largest lake in Huascarán National Park glows with the same miraculous turquoise hue as its sister lagoons farther south—but with very few visitors to spoil the solitude. The placid waters are surrounded by peaks that climb 20,000 feet into the clouds. Lake Parón is more easily accessed from Caraz, and many hikers take the opportunity to explore Mt. Artesonraju to the north. ✉ *Caraz.*

Hotels

Chamanna

$ | **B&B/INN** | This cluster of *cabañas* (cabins) among beautifully landscaped gardens, with views of mountain streams and towering peaks, is an attractive lodging option. **Pros:** location provides peace and quiet; beautiful vistas; good restaurant. **Cons:** hiring taxis and traveling means less time to enjoy the great outdoors; some shared bathrooms; a bit far from the town center. *Rooms from: S/150 ✉ Av. Nueva Victoria 185 ☎ 043/595–343 🌐 www.chamanna.com ⇆ 10 cabins 🍽 No meals.*

Cajamarca

855 km (531 miles) northeast of Lima; 295 km (183 miles) northeast of Trujillo.

Peaceful Cajamarca is one of the most undervisited places in Peru. As the town where the conquistador Pizarro captured and later executed the Inca ruler Atahualpa, it's the crucible of South American history, with abundant ruins testifying to the clash of civilizations that unleashed all of Latin America's subsequent tumult. But even if history isn't your forte, you'll be enchanted by the gently sloping hills, waterfalls, and friendly dairy farms that dot the landscape around this sleeper of an Andean city.

For Cajamarca, 1532 was the crucial date. That year, while the Inca ruler was relaxing at the thermal springs just outside town, 168 Spaniards, led by Francisco Pizarro, entered the main square and requested an audience. Thinking to enslave the visiting strangers and steal their horses, Atahualpa agreed, but when he arrived in the plaza with his retinue, he was quickly captured by Pizarro himself and made to witness the slaughter of some 6,000 of his followers. Imprisoned in a stone room, he tried to ransom his life with heaps of gold and silver, but the treacherous Spanish garotted him anyway in 1533.

Visitors to Cajamarca today can see reminders of this tragic history, both in the city's picturesque Plaza de Armas and in the surrounding hills, which feature some choice pre-Hispanic ruins. The town's colonial churches and houses are so well preserved that they were declared a Historic and Cultural Patrimony Site by the Organization of American States in 1986. But for many, the region's chief beauty lies in the lush green sierra outside the city limits. There, cheap day-trips allow you to sample the organic dairy products for which the area is famous, as well as shady forests, cataracts, and, at one farm, some of the smartest cows in South America.

GETTING HERE AND AROUND

LATAM Perú, Viva Air Perú, and Star Perú fly several times per week between Lima and the Aeropuerto de Cajamarca (CJA), 3 km (2 miles) east of town. Most places are within walking distance, but taxis are abundant if you feel a little breathless from the altitude or want to go somewhere outside the city center. If you like your taxi driver, arrange a pickup for another day. For major exploration outside the city, the best option is to join a day tour; they are inexpensive and include transportation. Cajamarca is 2,650 meters (8,694 feet) above sea level. Although not high by Andean standards, the elevation can still affect some visitors. Take your time, wear sunscreen, and drink plenty of water to avoid altitude sickness.

Sights

Baños del Inca

HOT SPRINGS | About 6 km (4 miles) east of Cajamarca are these pleasant hot springs, which flow into public pools and private baths of varying levels of quality, as well as some spa facilities such as a sauna with its attendant massage tables. Each service has a separate price, though everything is quite inexpensive. The central bath, the Pozo del Inca, is where Atahualpa was relaxing when he received news of the conquistadors' arrival in 1532. It's an intact pool with a system of aqueducts built by the Incas and still in use today. Be sure to check out the volcanic pools in the center of the complex, but don't touch! The temperatures can reach 70°C (160°F). **■ TIP→ Don't forget to bring your swimsuit and a towel!** ✉ *Av. Manco Cápac* ☎ *076/348–563* 🎫 *S/6.*

Catedral de Cajamarca

RELIGIOUS SITE | Originally known as the Iglesia de Españoles (Spanish Church, because only Spanish colonialists were allowed to attend services), this cathedral on the Plaza de Armas was built in the 17th and 18th centuries. It has an ornate baroque facade that was sculpted from volcanic rock. Like many of the town's churches, the cathedral has no belfry; the Spanish crown levied taxes on completed churches, so the settlers left the churches unfinished, freeing them from the tight grip of the tax collector. ✉ *Jr. Del Batán and Amalia Puga* 🎫 *Free.*

Cerro Santa Apolonia

VIEWPOINT | At the end of Calle 2 de Mayo, steps lead to this hilltop *mirador,* or scenic lookout, where a bird's-eye view of the city awaits. At the top are many carved bricks dating from pre-Columbian times. **■ TIP→ One of the rocks has the shape of a throne and has been dubbed the Seat of the Inca.** According to local legend, it was here that Inca rulers would sit to review their troops. You'll also find pretty gardens and a maze of winding paths. You can either walk or go by taxi (round trip S/6). ✉ *Calle 2 de Mayo* 🎫 *Free.*

El Conjunto de Belén

MUSEUM | Built in the 17th century, this large complex, originally a hospital, now houses the city's most interesting museums and a colonial church. At the **Museo Arqueológico de Cajamarca,** the town's archaeological museum, are exhibits of Cajamarcan ceramics and weavings. The pre-Inca Cajamarcans were especially famous for their excellent patterned textiles, which were often dyed vivid shades of blue. The **Museo Etnográfico** has a few displays of everyday bric-a-brac—there's even an old saddle and a dilapidated coffee grinder—dating from precolonial times. The **Iglesia de Belén** is a charming church with a polychrome pulpit and cupola. ✉ *Jr. Belén and Jr. Junín* ☎ *076/362–601* 🌐 *museos.cultura.pe* 🎫 *S/5* ⏲ *Closed Mon.*

★ **El Cuarto del Rescate**

HISTORIC SITE | This ransom chamber is the only Inca building still standing in Cajamarca. After Pizarro and his men captured Atahualpa, the Inca king offered to fill the chamber once with gold and twice with silver. The ransom was met, up to a marking on the stone wall, but the war-hardened Spaniards killed Atahualpa anyway. Today, visitors aren't allowed in the room itself, but if you look closely, you can still make out the marks the Inca left in an attempt to buy off his captors. ✉ *Jr. Amalia Puga 750* ☎ 🎫 *S/5.*

Iglesia de San Francisco

RELIGIOUS SITE | Built in the 17th and 18th centuries, the Church of San Francisco sits proudly on the Plaza de Armas in front of the main cathedral. The church's two bell towers were begun in republican times and finished in 1951. The church was called the Iglesia de Indios (Church of the Indians), as indigenous peoples were not allowed to attend services at the main cathedral; many consider it to be more beautiful than the whites-only cathedral. ■ **TIP→ Inside you'll find catacombs and a small museum of religious art.** To the right of the church, the Capilla de la Virgen de Dolores is one of Cajamarca's most beautiful chapels. A large statue of Cajamarca's patron saint, La Virgen de Dolores, makes this a popular pilgrimage destination for local penitents. ✉ *Cajamarca* ✥ *East side of Plaza de Armas* 🎫 *Church free, museum S/5.*

La Collpa Farm

FARM/RANCH | Cajamarca is famous for its dairy products, and you can experience this industry up close at this charming farm 11 km (7 miles) outside town. In addition to sampling the farm's cheeses and sweet manjar blanco, you can also visit an artificial lake and check out Peru's biggest all-clay church. The highlight is the "calling of the cows," in which Rosa, Betsy, and Flor answer to their names as they line up to return to their pens. It's the perfect experience for kids of all ages. ✉ *Cajamarca* 🎫 *S/5.*

Plaza de Armas

PLAZA | This main square occupies the same location where Pizarro had his dramatic encounter with Atahualpa, and though all traces of Inca influence are long since gone, it's impressive to stand on the spot where Latin American history began. Today, the fountain, benches, and street vendors make the square a nice place to hang out. ✉ *Cajamarca.*

Ventanillas de Otuzco (*Otuzco Windows*)

ARCHAEOLOGICAL SITE | One of the oldest cemeteries in Peru, the Ventanillas de Otuzco date back more than 3,500 years. The ancient necropolis, 8 km (5 miles) northeast of Cajamarca, comprises several large burial niches carved into a cliff. From afar, the niches look like windows: hence the area's name. On closer inspection, you see that many of the burial niches have carved decorations. Sadly, the site is gradually being eroded by wind and rain, though measures are being taken to slow the degradation. If

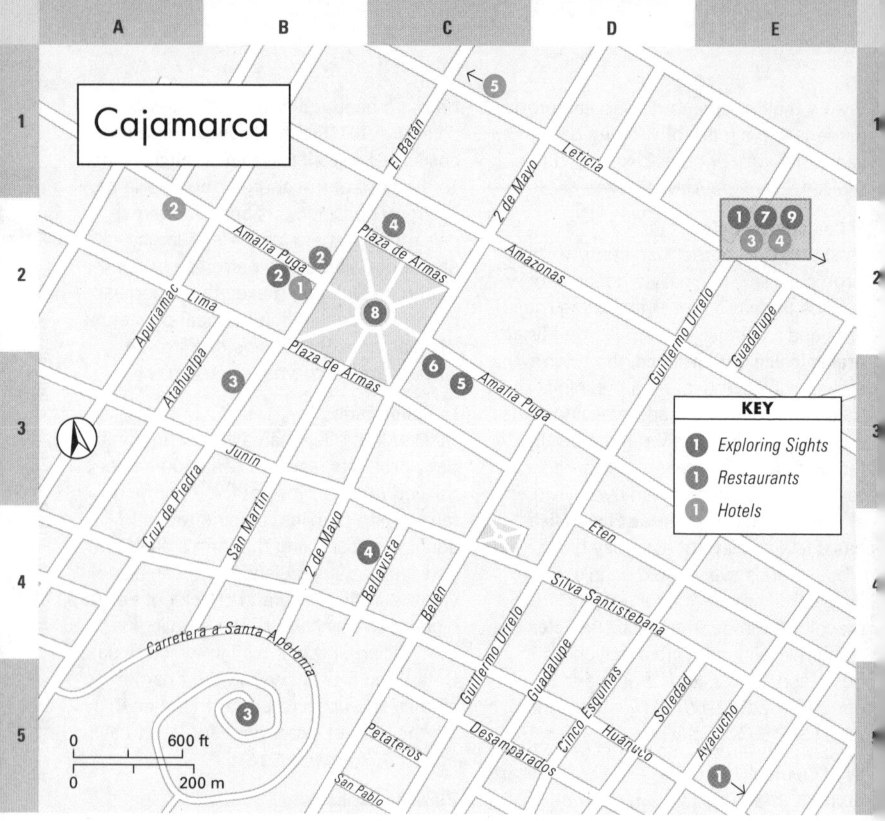

Sights

1 Baños del Inca **E2**

2 Catedral de Cajamarca **B2**

3 Cerro Santa Apolonia **B5**

4 El Conjunto de Belén **C4**

5 El Cuarto del Rescate ... **C3**

6 Iglesia de San Francisco **C3**

7 La Collpa Farm **E2**

8 Plaza de Armas **C2**

9 Ventanillas de Otuzco ... **E2**

Restaurants

1 La Chanita **E5**

2 Paprika **B2**

3 Pez Loco **B3**

4 Salas **C2**

Hotels

1 Costa del Sol Wyndham Cajamarca **B2**

2 EL Portal del Marqués **A2**

3 Hotel El Ingenio **E2**

4 Hotel Laguna Seca **E2**

5 La Posada del Puruay ... **C1**

you're inspired by this cemetery, you can go about 30 km (18 miles) from Combayo, in the same direction, and visit the better-preserved Ventanillas de Combayo. A three-hour guided tour to Ventanillas de Otuzco costs around S/35. If you prefer to go by yourself, *combis* (small buses) take 30 minutes to arrive from the Plaza de Armas. ✉ *Cajamarca* 🎫 *S/5.*

Cumbe Mayo

This pre-Inca site, 23 km (14 miles) southwest of Cajamarca, is surrounded by a large rock outcropping, where you'll find various petroglyphs left by the ancient Cajamarcans. There are also petroglyph-adorned caves, as well as a thousand-year-old network of Andean aqueducts. The site was designed to direct the ample water from the mountains into the drier area of Cajamarca, where there was a large reservoir. Amazingly, more than 8 km (5 miles) of the ancient aqueduct are intact today. Guided tours cost around S/35 and take four hours.

Restaurants

La Chanita

$ | **PERUVIAN** | In one corner of the Mercado Central, amid stalls selling *charqui* (dehydrated meat) and rainbow-colored displays of quinoa, you'll find a lunchtime crowd of people lining up for *cebiche frito,* a locally famous fried version of cebiche. The fish here comes battered and topped with a spicy mayo, along with *leche de tigre* and all the usual cebiche fixings. **Known for:** imaginative take on a Peruvian classic; bustling market setting; opportunity to dine with real Cajamarcans. $ *Average main: S/7* ✉ *Mercado Central, Jr. Apurimac and Jr. Amazonas* ⏲ *No dinner.*

Paprika

$$ | **PERUVIAN** | Situated in the Wyndham Costa del Sol Hotel, this graceful, white-tablecloth affair serves up better-than-average versions of Peruvian and international classics. The menu rotates, but the quality of the pastas, seafood, and desserts is reliably consistent. **Known for:** breakfast buffet; broad views of main square; variety of tasty piqueos. $ *Average main: S/40* ✉ *Costa del Sol Wyndham Hotel Cajamarca, Jr. Cruz de Piedra 707* ☎ *076/362–472* 🌐 *www.costadelsolperu.com.*

Pez Loco

$ | **SEAFOOD** | Surf and turf, Peruvian style, is the focus at this down-to-earth joint that's half cebichería , half *parrilla.* No bells and whistles here, just top-quality steaks, cebiches (try the *mixto*), and seafood classics like arroz con mariscos. The prices are a steal for food this good. **Known for:** grilled entrées; seafood far from the coast; hearty portions. $ *Average main: S/30* ✉ *Jr. Cruz de Piedra 631* ☎ *076/361–806.*

Salas

$ | **PERUVIAN** | On the Plaza de Armas, this is the place to get no-frills, typical food from the region. The menu includes authentic regional specialties such as cuy, *perico* (a lake fish), and Spanish-style tortillas. **Known for:** cheap daily specials; lively, social atmosphere; local color and tradition. $ *Average main: S/25* ✉ *Plaza de Armas, Av. Puga 637* ☎ *076/362–867.*

Hotels

Costa del Sol Wyndham Cajamarca

$$ | **HOTEL** | Set right on Cajamarca's main plaza, this hotel may seem modern, but it's actually converted from a historic mansion of a notable local family, and its restaurant has what might be the best view of the city. **Pros:** spa on-site; superb location with good city views; good value. **Cons:** the plaza can be noisy in the evenings; undistinguished decor; some rooms can get stuffy. $ *Rooms from: S/260* ✉ *Jr. Cruz de Piedra 707* ☎ *076/362–472* 🌐 *www.*

costadelsolperu.com/cajamarca 71 *rooms* *Free breakfast.*

El Portal del Marqués

$ | **B&B/INN** | **FAMILY** | Within Cajamarca's historic district, this lovely casona surrounds two sunny courtyards, overlooked by rooms furnished in a modern style, with bold color schemes and striking artwork. **Pros:** in the heart of Cajamarca city; charming colonial ambience; nicely appointed rooms. **Cons:** the city can be noisy; Wi-Fi is spotty; windowless rooms can get stuffy. *Rooms from: S/168* *Jr. del Comercio 644* *076/368–464* *www.portaldelmarques.com* 43 *rooms* *Free breakfast.*

Hotel El Ingenio

$ | **HOTEL** | Like many other hotels in the area, this one is in a renovated hacienda with extensive grounds, but it is the best bargain in Cajamarca and only a 10-minute walk from the plaza. **Pros:** quality service at a very reasonable price; beautiful, well-tended grounds; friendly staff. **Cons:** some rooms are better than others; decor needs updating; Wi-Fi is weak. *Rooms from: S/168* *Av. Los Cipreses 545* *076/368–733* *www.facebook.com/pages/category/Hotel-Resort/Hotel-El-Ingenio-Cajamarca-407067649419190* *39 rooms* *Free breakfast.*

★ **Hotel Laguna Seca**

$$ | **HOTEL** | **FAMILY** | "Pampering" is the operant concept at this refurbished hacienda, which has well-manicured garden areas throughout its extensive grounds, as well as a Jacuzzi in every room and public baths fed by thermal hot springs. Try a massage or other spa treatment, or tour the grounds on horseback. **Pros:** nice on-site spa; in-room hot-spring water; plenty of activities for kids. **Cons:** outside the city limits; room decor isn't quite on a par with the beauty of the grounds; lighting is dim in some areas. *Rooms from: S/400* *Av. Manco Cápac 1098, Baños del Inca* *076/584–300* *www.lagunaseca.com.pe* *42 rooms* *Free breakfast.*

La Posada del Puruay

$ | **B&B/INN** | **FAMILY** | This country hacienda is far from the noise of Cajamarca and has extensive gardens, a trout hatchery, and green hills for horseback riding and hiking. **Pros:** historical atmosphere; excellent staff; roaring fire on cold Andean nights. **Cons:** might be too intimate if you don't enjoy socializing with other guests; some rooms get cold in the evening; restaurant menu is limited. *Rooms from: S/200* *Km 4.5, Ctra. Porcón* *076/367–028* *www.posadapuruay.com.pe* *13 rooms* *Free breakfast.*

Nightlife

Arlekin Discotec

BARS/PUBS | Locals flock to this laid-back restaurant-bar to toss back *chelas* (beers) and listen to live music. The decor is inviting, the atmosphere mega-friendly. *Jr. Junin 1243* *976/355–609.*

Taita

DANCE CLUBS | This cavernous disco bar is one of the stalwarts of Cajamarca's dance scene. The stone walls add to the sonic mayhem. *Plazuela Belen, Calle Santisteban.*

Usha Usha

BARS/PUBS | Friendly locals, charming hosts, and sing-alongs with the local musicians that drop in make this watering hole a Cajamarca favorite. The owner, Don Jaime, shares stories and songs to promote local Cajamarca culture. *Amalia Puga 142* *910/762–290.*

Activities

There are a number of hikes in the area around Cajamarca, from trails along the rivers of the region, to treks leading past Inca and pre-Inca ruins. Most follow the **Capac Ñan**, or Royal Inca Road, that ran from Cusco all the way north to Quito. One of the most popular walks is to the pre-Inca necropolis of **Combayo.** To get to the trailhead, drive 20 km (12 miles) north of the Baños del Inca. The hike takes around four or five hours. The **Ruta del Tambo Inca** takes you to an old Inca *tambo,* or resting point. It's difficult to find this trailhead, and roads sometimes get washed out during the rainy season, so ask in town to confirm the following: Drive 46 km (29 miles) from Cajamarca on the road to Hualgayoc. Near Las Lagunas, turn onto a dirt road and follow it to the milk depository at Ingatambo. The trail begins here. The 16-km (10-mile) trip takes about eight hours. The best time to go trekking is during the dry season, which runs from May through September.

Clarín Tours

TOUR—SPORTS | With offices in Lima and Cajamarca, Clarín Tours specializes in multiday package deals that include transportation, hotels, and tours in northern Peru, particularly in Cajamarca. ✉ *Jr. Del Batán 165* ☎ *979/955–479* 🌐 *www.clarintours.com* 🎫 *From S/160.*

Chachapoyas

435 km (271 miles) east of Chiclayo.

Located in the *ceja de la selva* (jungle's eyebrow, i.e., where the Andes backs up onto the Amazon), Chachapoyas is the capital of Peru's Amazonas region. ■ **TIP→ The town is a good jumping-off point for exploring some of Peru's most fascinating and least-visited pre-Inca ruins.** The giant fortress at Kuélap, the Gocta waterfall, the Karajía sarcophagi, and the ruins of Purunllacta and Gran Vilaya are nearby. Despite the Amazonas moniker, there's nothing jungle-like about the area around Chachapoyas. The surrounding greenery constitutes what most people would call a highland cloud forest. Farther east, in the region of Loreto (won by Peru in the 1941 border dispute with Ecuador), you'll find true jungle.

Drinking the Aguardientes

Aguardientes (homemade liqueurs) are common throughout the region. They're made in sundry flavors, including *mora* (blackberry), *maracuyá* (passion fruit), *café* (coffee), and *leche* (milk). In some jungle towns, such as Chachapoyas and Pucallpa, people sell bottles of these strong concoctions and are more than willing to offer tourists a sample.

Chachapoyas is a sleepy little town of 32,000. It has a well-preserved colonial center and one small archaeological museum outside town. Difficult to reach because of the poor roads through the mountains, it is most easily accessed from Chiclayo.

GETTING HERE AND AROUND

There are several daily buses between Chachapoyas and Chiclayo, with some originating in Lima. There are also buses from Cajamarca several times per week, as well as from Tarapoto, though they are occasionally canceled because of road conditions. In town, everything is close and within walking distance. There are plenty of taxis, but you'll have little need for one.

Sights

★ **Gocta Waterfall**

BODY OF WATER | Surprisingly, Gocta, a 771-meter (2,529-foot) waterfall, believed to be the fourth tallest in South America, wasn't brought to the attention of the Peruvian government until 2006. The falls, about 50 km (31 miles) outside town, are strongest during the rainy season, from November to April, though during the dry season, the sun will likely be out, and you will be able to swim at their base. Occasionally, on the 2½-hour hike from Cocachimba (you can hire guides there if you are not coming on a tour from Chachapoyas), you may be able to spot toucans or the endemic yellow-tailed woolly monkey. The best way to appreciate the falls is by staying at the charming, 16-room Gocta Lodge, especially if you prefer the light of the morning or afternoon. ✉ *Chachapoyas.*

Iglesia Santa Ana

RELIGIOUS SITE | The town's oldest church was one of Peru's first "Indian churches," where indigenous people were forced to attend services. It was built in the 17th century and is on a small square of the same name. ✉ *Av. Santa Ana.*

Pozo de Yanayacu

HOT SPRINGS | This small, rocky natural hot spring a few blocks west of the Plaza de Armas isn't much but is nice to look at. It's said the spring magically appeared during a visit from Saint Toribio de Mogrovejo. ✉ *Jr. Salamanca.*

SIDE TRIPS FROM CHACHAPOYAS

★ Karajía

ARCHAEOLOGICAL SITE | Discovered in 1985, the six coffins that make up this uncanny funeral site 48 km (30 miles) northwest of Chachapoyas overlook a ruined village and are thought to contain the mummies of shamans and great warriors. The Chachapoyas people built the tombs into a sheer cliffside sometime around the year 1460, and today the eerie funeral masks—together with the bones scattered around the site—provide a haunting reminder of the great chieftains that once held sway over the surrounding country. The Karajía sarcophagi, or "ancient wise men" as the locals call them, originally included eight coffins, but two have collapsed due to earthquakes. This has allowed archaeologists to study the contents of the wood-and-clay structures, which were found to house a single individual in the fetal position, along with all the ceramics and other belongings the deceased carried with him into the afterlife. Visitors today can't get close to the sarcophagi due to their remote location, but the view of them watching over the ravine below is awe-inspiring. ✉ *Chachapoyas.*

Museo Leymebamba

MUSEUM | One of the most striking museums in all of Peru, the Museo Leymebamba, which opened in 2000, is situated in a small village 60 km (37 miles) south of Chachapoyas. Inside are more than 200 mummies, some dating back over 500 years, that were discovered high on a limestone cliff above the Laguna de los Condores in 1997, together with other artifacts from the Chachapoyas culture. Day-trips are available from downtown Chachapoyas; otherwise you can take a Cajamarca-bound bus (via Celendin) and ask to be let off at Leymebamba. ✉ *Av. Austria s/n, Leymebamba* ☎ *971/104–909* 🌐 *museoleymebamba.org* 🎫 *S/15.*

Purunllacta

ARCHAEOLOGICAL SITE | About 35 km (22 miles) southeast of Chachapoyas are the ruins of Purunllacta, a good place for hiking. With pre-Inca agricultural terraces, dwellings, ceremonial platforms, and roads extending for more than 420 hectares (1,038 acres), but few tourists, this can be a peaceful spot, though somewhat mystifying as you have no explanation of what you're seeing. To get here, drive to the town of Cheto, and ask for directions. From the town, it's a one-hour walk uphill to the site. Few people even know about this area, so don't be frustrated if you have to ask more than one person. ✉ *Chachapoyas* 🎫 *Free.*

Restaurants

Café Fusiones

$ | **CAFÉ** | A great hangout and meeting spot for travelers, this eclectic café with cheery yellow walls and wood-beamed ceilings works with local farming co-ops and has a commitment to organic principles and fair trade. The menu is small, but the quality is good. **Known for:** yummy desserts; vegetarian and vegan options; ideal café atmosphere. *Average main: S/15 Jr. Ayacucho 952 990/285–862 cafefusiones.com.*

El Batán del Tayta

$$ | **PERUVIAN** | Chachapoyas's trendiest eatery tends to elicit sharply polarized reactions: for those in the "love it" camp, local chef David Sancón's innovative take on Amazonian cuisine is a foodie's dream, with imaginative presentations (think guinea pig on a clothesline and ant-studded cocktails), hip jungle decor, and a level of culinary imagination unavailable elsewhere in Chachapoyas. For those in the "hate it" faction, it's all style and no substance. **Known for:** imaginative jungle decor; bold fusion takes on Amazonian cuisine; a culinary philosophy where presentation is as important as flavor. *Average main: S/40 Jr. La Merced 604 982/777–219 www.facebook.com/ElBatanDelTayta.*

La Tushpa

$ | **STEAKHOUSE** | A good choice for carnivores, La Tushpa features juicy grilled steaks with homemade chimichurri and other sauces. There are also pizzas and other items from the on-site bakery. **Known for:** grilled meats; very friendly service; gut-busting portions. *Average main: S/30 Jr. Ortiz Arrieta 753 041/777–198 No dinner.*

Mistura Urco

$ | **PERUVIAN** | This jungle-themed *restaurante popular* specializes in seafood, but its versions of Amazonian specialties and the usual Peruvian standbys are more than creditable. If you're really hungry, try one of the unusual combos, many featuring cebiche, which will have you as sated as an anaconda after feeding time. **Known for:** unusual combo plates; fresh seafood; colorful murals and relaxed atmosphere. *Average main: S/30 Jr. Puno 325 978/121–875 No dinner.*

Ceramic Stop

About 10 km (6 miles) north of Chachapoyas is the tiny pueblo of **Huancas**, where the citizens are well known for their pottery; this is a good place to buy artisanal goods and locally made ceramics. There are also two miradores, or scenic lookouts, with soul-stirring views of the Sonche and Huanca Urco canyons.

Hotels

Gocta Andes Lodge

$$ | **B&B/INN** | **FAMILY** | At this remote lodge near Gocta Waterfall, each room looks out over the cascades, and the lush surrounding hills comprise one of the most verdant settings in all of Peru. **Pros:** balconies with unbeatable views; staff are happy to arrange tours via car or on horseback; far from civilization. **Cons:** menu system is confusing; some amenities are oddly missing; walk to waterfalls is a little challenging for some. *Rooms from: S/375 Caserio de Cocachimba 042/526–694 goctalodge.com 16 rooms.*

La Casa de los Balcones

$ | **HOTEL** | Comfy beds, central location, brightly decorated rooms: if you're looking for an economical base camp while exploring Chachapoyas, this friendly inn fits the bill. **Pros:** quiet location near the Plaza de Armas; good showers; staff makes you feel like family. **Cons:** Wi-Fi is slow; sound carries from room to room; breakfast is bland. *Rooms from: S/120 Jr. Triunfo 828 982/180–794 www.facebook.com/Lacasadelosbalcones 18 rooms Free breakfast.*

La Casona Chachapoyas

$ | **B&B/INN** | This colorful old house, which dates from the 1800s, is the finest in Chachapoyas, with a bougainvillea-filled courtyard and pleasant terraces.

Pros: amazing old house with modern touches; cozy sitting area with fireplace; good breakfast. **Cons:** some rooms are better than others; limited amenities; floors creak at night. *Rooms from: S/200* ✉ *Jr. Chincha Alta 569* ☎ *041/477–353* 🌐 *lacasonadechachapoyasperu.com* *14 rooms* *Free breakfast.*

Nightlife

Licores La Reina

BARS/PUBS | A large selection of aguardientes in flavors that range from leche to mora is available at this friendly local bar. Also on tap: mixed drinks typical of the Peruvian jungle and live music on weekends. ✉ *Jr. Ayacucho 544* ☎ *973/834–664* 🌐 *www.facebook.com/LaReinaChachapoyas1.*

Kuélap

72 km (45 miles) south of Chachapoyas.

This phenomenal archaeological site, about two hours from Chachapoyas, is increasingly one of Peru's main attractions. It's much more remote than Machu Picchu and sees far fewer visitors, which makes it all the more magical. There are no facilities at the site, so bring everything you need.

GETTING HERE AND AROUND

A trip to Kuélap is an all-day affair, and it's best to visit with a tour group from Chachapoyas. The excursion costs around S/100 per person. Chachapoyas Expedition (Jirón Ortiz Arrieta 530) is highly recommended and has the widest selection of tours in the region. In the past, you had to hike (four hours) or take a taxi (two hours) to travel the 4 kilometers (2½ miles) from the village of Tingo to the ruins, but now a cable-car system operated by Peru's government allows you to cover the same distance in 20 minutes.

Sights

★ Kuélap

ARCHAEOLOGICAL SITE | Consistently compared to Machu Picchu by visitors, this extraordinary site high in the cloud forests of Chachapoyas was a walled city sufficient unto itself, housing farmers, shamans, and administrators, as well as the "warriors of the cloud" that made up the Chachapoyans' military class. Wandering the circular ruins, with their 12-meter-high (39-foot-high) stone walls and enigmatic carvings of faces and snakes, you catch a haunting glimpse of a fierce people that resisted the Inca Empire to the bitter end.

Kuélap sits at a dizzying 3,100 meters (10,170 feet), high above the Río Utcubamba. Consisting of more than 400 small, rounded buildings, it contains lookout towers, huts with grass roofs (now reconstructed), turrets, and rhomboid friezes typical of the region. The most interesting of the rounded buildings has been dubbed El Tintero (The Inkpot), and features a large underground chamber with a huge pit. Archaeologists hypothesize that the Chachapoyans kept pumas in this pit, dropping human sacrifices into its depths during religious rituals. The ruins are in surprisingly good condition considering the antiquity (1,000 or so years) of the site: the Incas appear to have left it alone when they overran the Chachapoyas people in 1472.

✉ *Ctra. Kuélap, Chachapoyas* *S/20, cable car S/20.*

Index

D

E

F

G

H

Photo Credits

Front Cover: Getty Images/EyeEm [Description: Rear View Of Woman Standing On Mountain Against Blue Sky, Peru]. **Back cover, from left to right:** pawopa3336/iStockphoto, Marie-Jeanne Sol/Shutterstock, DC_Colombia/iStockphoto. **Spine:** drmonochrome/Dreamstime. **Interior, from left to right:** Donyanedomam/Dreamstime.com (1). 579079324-shutterstock.com (2). agap / Shutterstock (5). **Chapter 1: Experience Peru:** Angelo Cavalli / eStock Photo (6-7). sorincolac/iStockphoto (8). Pakhnyushchy/Shutterstock (9). Mikadun/Shutterstock (9). saiko3p/iStockphoto (10). Mark Green/Shutterstock (10). Blinovita/Dreamstime.com (10). colacat/Shutterstock (11). Christian Vinces/Shutterstock (11). Apers/Dreamstime (12). Christian Vinces/Shutterstock (12). Cristinnastoian/Dreamstime (12). Ludmila Ruzickova/Shutterstock (13). Edgar Daniel Yanchapaxi/Shutterstock (14). Amy Corti/Shutterstock (14). Yasushitanikado/Dreamstime (14). Christianvinces/Dreamstime (14). Yasemin Olgunoz Berber/shutterstock.com (15). May_Lana/Shuttestock (15). Christian Vinces/shutterstock (15). Walkabout Photo Guides/ Shutterstock (15). Astrid & Gastón (16). NiarKrad/Shutterstock (16). J Duggan/Shutterstock (16). THONGCHAI.S/Shutterstock (17). vitmark/ Shutterstock (17). Amaz Restaurant (22). José Cáceres/Maido (22). Astrid & Gastón (22). Mark Green/Shutterstock (23). Central Restaurante (23). Fotos593/shutterstock (24). a35mmporhora/Shutterstock (24). Kateryna Mostova/shutterstock (24). LarisaBlinova/iStockphoto (24). Courtesy of The Vegan Peruvian Kitchen (25). Milton Rodriguez/Shutterstock (26). Mark Green/shutterstock (26). Carlos Ibarra/PROMPERÚ (26). Ksenia Ragozina/shutterstock (26). Municipality of Pachacamac (27). Guillermo Figueroa/PROMPERÚ (27). Estivillml/Dreamstime (27). Sandro Sandoval/Shutterstock (27). Karol Moraes/shutterstock (28). aioacquesta/Shutterstock (29). Tony Morrison/South American Pictures (35). INTERFOTO/age fotostock (36). Tony Morrison/South American Pictures (36). J Marshall/Tribaleye Images/Alamy (36). Kathy Jarvis/ South American Pictures (37). Beren Patterson/Alamy (37). TB Photo Communications, Inc./Alamy (37). Danita Delimont/Alamy (38). José Fuste Raga/age fotostock (38). Tony Morrison/South American Pictures (38). Mireille Vautier/Alamy (39). Tim Jarrell (39). Visual Arts Library (London)/Alamy (40). public domain (40). Classic Vision/age fotostock (41). North Wind Picture Archives/Alamy (41). ZUMA Wire Service / Alamy (42). Mike Yamashita/Woodfin Camp/Aurora Photos (42). **Chapter 3:** Lima: Rest77/Dreamstime (65). Photochris/Dreamstime (76). Charles Wollertz / Alamy Stock Photo (92). alexander s. heitkamp/Shutterstock (97). Luke Peters / Alamy (98). Tim Hill / Alamy (98). Mo Al-Nuaimy/Flickr, [CC BY 2.0] (99). Emilio Ereza / age fotostock (99). Too Labra (100). Corey Wise / Alamy (100). Mary Evans Picture Library / Alamy (100). Too Labra (100). Michele Molinari / Alamy (101). Emilio Ereza/agefotostock (101). Jeffrey Jackson / Alamy (101). Jose Fuste Raga (103). **Chapter 4:** Nazca and the Southern Coast: Tom Hanslien Photography / Alamy Stock Photo (117). Donyanedomam/Dreamstime (130). JTB Photo Communications, Inc. / Alamy (143). Philip Scalia / Alamy (145). BennettPhoto / Alamy (146). Dan Bannister/Shutterstock (147). South American Pictures/Tony Morrison (147). **Chapter 5:** The Southern Andes and Lake Titicaca: saiko3p/Shutterstock (151). Stephanie van Deventer/Shutterstock (164). Milton Rodriguez/Shutterstock (166). Jon Arnold Images Ltd / Alamy (171). saiko3p (181). David Ranson/Shutterstock (197). Jarno Gonzalez Zarraonandia/Shutterstock (198-199). JTB Photo Communications, Inc. / Alamy (200). GARDEL Bertrand/agefotostock (201). Danita Delimont / Alamy (201). Ildipapp/Dreamstime (202). Ian Nellist / Alamy (202). DC_Colombia (207). **Chapter 6:** Cusco and the Sacred Valley: Christian ouellet (215). Mark Titterton / Alamy (232). SuperStock (238-239). Kevin Schafer / Alamy (251). Tomwyness/Dreamstime (258). David Noton Photography / Alamy (264). Donyanedomam/Dreamstime (268). **Chapter 7:** Machu Picchu and the Inca Trail: Mirmoor/Dreamstime (271). agap / Shutterstock (274-275). Chris Howey / Shutterstock (276). The Granger Collection, New York / The Granger Collection (277). Tim Jarrell (Top left & right, 278). Adam Taplin (Bottom, 278). Tim Jarrell (279). Fabricio Guzmán (279). Robert Harding Picture Library Ltd / Alamy (280). Rachael Bowes / Alamy (280). Christine McNamara (280). Jordan Klein/wikipedia.org (281). Tim Jarrell (281). Nick Jewell/Flickr, [CC BY 2.0] (281). Dislentev/Dreamstime (282). James Brunker / Alamy (283). Pep Roig/agefotostock (284-285, background). Jason Scott Duggan/Shutterstock (284). Adam Taplin (285-287). Julie Baudin (299). **Chapter 8:** The Amazon Basin: Christian Vinces/Shutterstock (301). Mark Jones/agefotostock (311). Mark Bowler Amazon-Images / Alamy (312). Mark Jones/agefotostock (312). Kevin Schafer/VIREO (312). Andoni Canela/agefotostock (312). infocusphotos.com / Alamy (312). Robert E. Barber / Alamy (313). Public Domain (313). S. Holt/VIREO (313). Mathew Tekulsky/VIREO (313). Andoni Canela/agefotostock (313). Andoni Canela/agefotostock (314). Hemis / Alamy (316). **Chapter 9:** The Central Highlands: Christian Vinces/Shutterstock (333). Jkraft5/Dreamstime (353). Joam Boam / Alamy (363). **Chapter 10:** The North Coast and Northern Highlands: Ludmila Ruzickova/Shutterstock (367). Jess Kraft/Shutterstock (381). Milton Rodriguez/Shutterstock (399). Galen Rowell/Mountain Light / Alamy (401). Michalknitl/Dreamstime (402-403). Tolo Balaguer/agefotostock (404). J Marshall - Tribaleye Images / Alamy (405). alun richardson / Alamy (406). Galen Rowell/Mountain Light / Alamy (406). **About Our Writers:** All photos are courtesy of the writers.

*Every effort has been made to trace the copyright holders, and we apologize in advance for any accidental errors. We would be happy to apply the corrections in the following edition of this publication.

NTIAL PERU

Horowitz, *General*

Stallings, *Editorial Director*, ta O'Halloran, Amanda or *Editors*; Kayla Becker, chael Roth, *Editors*

alaney, *Director of Design* n; Jessica Gonzalez, *Graphic* iana Tabares, *Design &* tern

nnifer DePrima, *Editorial* Manager; Elyse Rozelle, *Senior* Editor; Monica White, *Production*

cca Baer, *Senior Map Editor*; Mark oon Street Cartography), David *Cartographers*

Photography: Viviane Teles, *Senior Photo Editor;* Namrata Aggarwal, Ashok Kumar, Carl Yu, *Photo Editors;* Rebecca Rimmer, *Photo Intern*

Business and Operations: Chuck Hoover, *Chief Marketing Officer*; Robert Ames, *Group General Manager*; Devin Duckworth, *Director of Print Publishing*; Victor Bernal, *Business Analyst*

Public Relations and Marketing: Joe Ewaskiw, *Senior Director Communications and Public Relations*

Fodors.com: Jeremy Tarr, *Editorial Director;* Rachael Levitt, *Managing Editor*

Technology: Jon Atkinson, *Director of Technology;* Rudresh Teotia, *Lead Developer*, Jacob Ashpis, *Content Operations Manager*

rs: Marco Ferrarese, Michael Gasparovic, Maureen Santucci

tor: Jacinta O'Halloran

Production Editor: Jennifer DePrima

2nd Edition

ISBN 978-1-64097-314-5

ISSN 2476–0978

All details in this book are based on information supplied to us at press time. Always confirm information when it matters, especially if you're making a detour to visit a specific place. Fodor's expressly disclaims any liability, loss, or risk, personal or otherwise, that is incurred as a consequence of the use of any of the contents of this book.

SPECIAL SALES
This book is available at special discounts for bulk purchases for sales promotions or premiums. For more information, e-mail SpecialMarkets@fodors.com.

PRINTED IN CANADA

10 9 8 7 6 5 4 3 2 1

About Our Writers

Travel writer, journalist, and author **Marco Ferrarese** is usually based in Malaysia, from where he covers the least trodden corners of South and Southeast Asia for some of the world's best publications. After a decade of trying, he finally found the perfect way to make use of his near-native Spanish working in Southern Peru and the Bolivian side of Lake Titicaca for this edition of Fodor's Essential Peru. When COVID-19 broke out in Latin America, Marco was on assignment for this volume and spent a month locked down at high altitude near the remote Colca Canyon. This is where he experienced real Peruvian hospitality and, in an odd turn of fate, the tragic death of his parents Maurizio and Tundra back in his native Lombardy, Italy. Marco's work on his book is lovingly dedicated to their memory. *"Nunca os olvidaré, mama y papa, y nos vamos a ver en Cielo."*

Mike Gasparovic is a writer and translator based in Lima, Peru. He has traveled extensively throughout the Spanish-speaking world, and writes about its history and culture for numerous online publications, including his blog, Latin America Confidential (🌐 *latinamericaconfidential.com*). For this edition, he updated the sections on Lima, Nazca and the Southern Coast, The Central Highlands, the North Coast and Northern Highlands, and Peru Today.

Freelance tr
Maureen San
Peru in Janua
after two mor
same year, mo
November. Now a U.S.-Pe
citizen, she spent almost e
living in Cusco and the Sac
allowing her to indulge her
trekking, as well as positio
perfectly to update those ch
well as the ones on Machu
the Inca Trail. She is now bas
US but continues to play tou
friends, and is keeping in touc
her extensive local network be
visits. In addition to working w
Fodor's, Maureen regularly wri
articles for online publications o
traveling in South America in ge
and Peru in particular, and has pe
an article on Machu Picchu for Briti
magazine *Explore History.*